Sixth Edition

Blue Book of Modern Black Powder Arms™

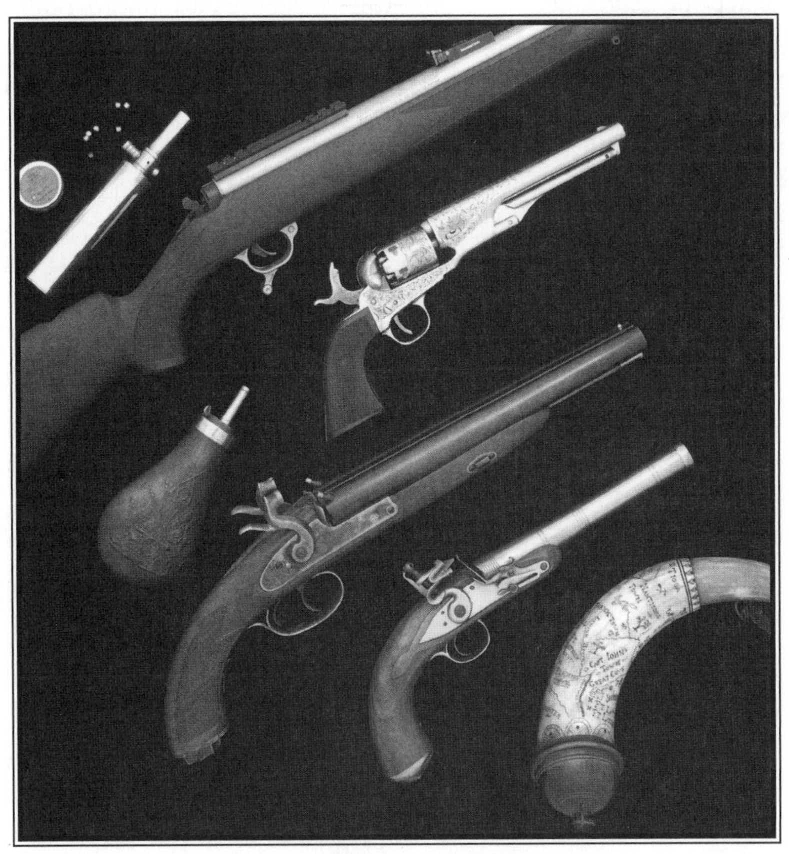

by John B. Allen

$24.95
Publisher's Softcover
Suggested List Price

$39.95
Publisher's Hardcover
Suggested List Price

Blue Book of
Modern Black Powder Arms™
Sixth Edition

Publisher's Note:
This book is the result of nonstop and continuous research obtained by attending and/or participating in trade shows, gun shows, auctions, and also communicating with contributing editors, gun dealers, collectors, company historians, and other knowledgeable industry professionals worldwide each year. This book represents an analysis of prices for which collectible black powder reproductions and replicas and modern muzzleloaders have actually been selling during that period at an average retail level. Although every reasonable effort has been made to compile an accurate and reliable guide, gun prices may vary significantly (especially auction prices) depending on such factors as the locality of the sale, the number of sales we were able to consider, and economic conditions. Accordingly, no representation can be made that the reproductions, replicas, and modern muzzleloaders listed might be bought or sold at prices indicated, nor shall the author or publisher be responsible for any error made in compiling and recording such prices and related information.

Blue Book Publications, Inc.
8009 34th Avenue South, Suite 175
Minneapolis, MN 55425 U.S.A.

Orders Only: 800-877-4867, ext. 3 (domestic only)
Phone No.: 952-854-5229
Fax No.: 952-853-1486
General Email: bluebook@bluebookinc.com
Web site: www.bluebookinc.com

Published and printed in the United States of America

ISBN 10: 1-886768-89-7
ISBN 13: 978-1-886768-89-5

Electronic Access ID Code: JLA0209

Distributed in part to the book trade by Ingram Book Company and Baker & Taylor.

Distributed throughout Europe by *Deutsches Waffen Journal*
Rudolf-Diesel-Strasse 46
Blaufelden, D-74572 Germany
Fax No.: 011-497-7953-9787-882
Website: www.dwj.de

CONTENTS

GENERAL INFORMATION

While many of you have probably dealt with Blue Book Publications, Inc. for years, it may be helpful for you to know a little bit more about our operation, including information on how to contact us regarding our various titles, software programs, and other informational services.

Blue Book Publications, Inc.
8009 34th Avenue South, Suite 175
Minneapolis, MN 55425 USA
Phone No.: 952-854-5229 • Orders Only (domestic and Canada): 800-877-4867
Fax No.: 952-853-1486 (available 24 hours a day)
Web site: www.bluebookinc.com
General Email: support@bluebookinc.com - we check our email at 9am, 12pm, and 4pm M - F (excluding major U.S. holidays). Please refer to individual email addresses listed below with phone extension numbers.

To find out the latest information on our products, including availability and pricing, and consumer related services, and up-to-date industry information (blogs, trade show recaps with photos/captions, upcoming events, feature articles, etc.), please check our web site, as it is updated on a regular basis. Surf us - you'll have fun!

Since our phone system is equipped with voice mail, you may also wish to know extension numbers which have been provided below:

Extension 10 - Beth Schreiber	beths@bluebookinc.com
Extension 11 - Katie Sandin	katies@bluebookinc.com
Extension 12 - John Andraschko	johnand@bluebookinc.com
Extension 13 - S.P. Fjestad	stevef@bluebookinc.com
Extension 15 - Clint Schmidt	clints@bluebookinc.com
Extension 16 - John Allen	johna@bluebookinc.com
Extension 17 - Zachary R. Fjestad	zachf@bluebookinc.com
Extension 18 - Tom Stock	toms@bluebookinc.com
Extension 19 - Cassandra Faulkner	cassandraf@bluebookinc.com
Extension 22 - Kelsey Fjestad	kelseyf@bluebookinc.com
Extension 27 - Shipping	

Office hours are: 8:30am - 5:00pm CST, Monday - Friday.

Additionally, an after-hours message service is available for ordering. All orders are processed within 24 hours of receiving them, assuming payment and order information is correct. Depending on the product, we typically ship either Fed Ex Ground, Media Mail, or Priority Mail. Expedited shipping services are also available domestically for an additional charge. Please contact us directly for an expedited shipping quotation.

All correspondence regarding technical information/values on black powder reproductions and replicas is answered in a FIFO (first in, first out) system. That means that letters, faxes, and email are answered in the order in which they are received, even though some people think that their emails take preference over everything else.

Online subscriptions and individual downloading services for the *Blue Book of Gun Values, Blue Book of Modern Black Powder Arms, Ammo Encyclopedia, American Gunsmiths, Blue Book of Airguns, Blue Book of Pool Cues, Blue Book of Electric Guitars, Blue Book of Acoustic Guitars,* and the *Blue Book of Guitar Amplifiers* are also available.

As this edition goes to press, the following titles/products are currently available, unless otherwise specified:

Black Powder Revolver Reproductions & Replicas by Dennis Adler (highly recommended)
Blue Book of Gun Values, 30th Edition by S.P. Fjestad
Blue Book of Guns Inventory Software Program CD-ROM (ISP) (inventory software program which includes updated databases from 30th Edition *Blue Book of Gun Values,* 6th Edition *Blue Book of Modern Black Powder Arms* and 7th Edition *Blue Book of Airguns*)
7th Edition *Blue Book of Airguns* by Dr. Robert Beeman & John Allen
3rd Edition *The Book of Colt Firearms* by R.L. Wilson
Blue Book Pocket Guide for Colt Dates of Manufacture by R.L. Wilson
American Gunsmiths, 2nd Edition by Frank Sellers
Ammo Encyclopedia by Michael Bussard, edited by John B. Allen & Dave Kosowski
Parker Gun Identification & Serialization, compiled by Charlie Price and edited by S.P. Fjestad
Gianfranco Pedersoli – Master Engraver by Dag Sundseth, edited by S.P. Fjestad & Elena Micheli-Lamboy
Firmo & Francesca Fracassi – Master Engravers by Elena Micheli-Lamboy & Steven Lamboy
Blue Book of Electric Guitars, 11th Edition, by Zachary R. Fjestad, edited by S.P. Fjestad
Blue Book of Acoustic Guitars, 11th Edition, by Zachary R. Fjestad, edited by S.P. Fjestad

Blue Book of Guitar Amplifiers, 3rd Edition, by Zachary R. Fjestad, edited by S.P. Fjestad
Blue Book of Guitars CD-ROM
Blue Book of Guitar Amplifiers CD-ROM
The Gibson Flying V by Larry Meiners & Zachary R. Fjestad
Gibson Amplifiers: 1933-2008 by Wallace Marx Jr.
Blue Book of Pool Cues, 3rd Edition, by Brad Simpson
The Nethercutt Collection - The Cars of San Sylmar by Dennis Adler

If you would like to get more information about any of the above publications/products, simply check our web site: www.bluebookinc.com.

We would like to thank all of you for your business in the past – you are the reason we are successful. Our goal remains the same – to give you the best products, the most accurate and up-to-date information for the money, and the highest level of customer service available in today's marketplace. If something's right, tell the world over time. If something's wrong, please tell us immediately – we'll make it right.

MEET THE STAFF

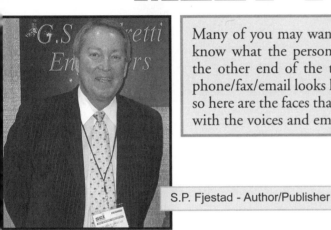

Many of you may want to know what the person on the other end of the telephone/fax/email looks like, so here are the faces that go with the voices and emails.

S.P. Fjestad - Author/Publisher

John B. Allen
Author & Associate Editor Arms Division

Cassandra Faulkner
Executive Editor

Dave Kosowski
Copy Editor

Tom Stock
CFO

Clint Schmidt
Art Director

John Andraschko
Technology Director

Beth Schreiber
Operations Manager

Katie Sandin
Operations

Kelsey Fjestad
Operations/Proofing

Zachary R. Fjestad
Author/Editor Guitar & Amp Division

ACKNOWLEDGEMENTS

Dennis Russell
Jerry Bowe
Kevin Cherry & Gurney Brown - Cherry's Fine Guns
Cav. Guiseppe, Alberto & Alesandro Pietta - F.A.P. Pietta
Stefano & Pierangelo Pedersoli - Davide Pedersoli & C
Paolo & Luciano Amadi - Euroarms Italia
Suzanne Webb & Giacomo Merlino - Uberti Srl
Rino & Susanne Chiappa - Armi Chiappa
Jim Bruno & Kevin Renwick - Traditions
Charles & Hunter Kirkland - Dixie Gun Works
Sue Hawkins & Tammy Loy - Taylor's
Mike Harvey - Cimarron
Val Forgett III - Navy Arms
Kathy Hoyt & Beverly Haynes - Colt Historical Archives

Dennis Adler
Dave Kosowski
Phil Spangenberger
Neil Sanders - Thompson/Center
Randy Johnson - Ultimate Firearms Inc.
Joe Latona
Al Raychard of MDM, Ltd.
John Stimson, Jr.
Jim Supica - Nat'l Firearms Museum
Eric Bye & Denise Goodpaster - *Muzzle Blasts*
Mike Kizzire - Grandview Media
Anthony Imperato
Paul Warden - America Remembers

ABOUT THE COVER

ON THE FRONT COVER:

Pictured is an eclectic yet historic mixture of fine replica black powder arms illustrating the evolution of flintlock and percussion lock designs. At the bottom, a Pedersoli Queen Anne Pistol c.1700s, based on the original British flintlock pistols that came into use during the reign of Queen Anne (1702 to 1714). This Deluxe version, serial number PD15607, has a polished brass smoothbore barrel chambered in .50 caliber. Showing the percussion lock at its double best, a Pedersoli Howdah smoothbore pistol chambered in 20x20; a fine engraved 3rd. Generation Colt Blackpowder Arms 1861 Navy, serial number 45742; and at top a modern day in-line Thompson/Center Omega .50 caliber rifle, serial number S49594. Also shown are a handcrafted contemporary powder horn made by Steve Shroyer; a 2nd. Generation Colt pewter powder flask; and a modern Deluxe tubular brass powder flask manufactured by Pedersoli. (Front Cover Photo by Dennis Adler, pistols and revolvers from the photographer's collection, T/C Omega courtesy Mark McNeely and Chuck Ahearn/Allegheny Trade Co., Duncansville, PA.)

ON THE BACK COVER:

Percussion pistols and revolvers came in all sizes, and here are three that really make the point. At bottom a steel frame Pietta .31 caliber Remington Pocket Model, serial number H004702; a Pedersoli Liegi Screw Barrel Derringer with cannon-style barrel in .36 caliber; in stark contrast a massive Pietta LeMat 9-shot .44 caliber revolver (with grape shot barrel underneath) done in polished steel with Deluxe factory engraving, serial number L14149; and at top a modern inline .50 caliber. Pedersoli muzzleloading rifle known as the Denali, with break open action and Mossy Oak camo coverage.

(Photography by Dennis Adler)

FOREWORD

John B. Allen (l), author of the *Blue Book of Modern Black Powder Arms*, Michael Bussard, author of the new *Ammo Encyclopedia*, black-hatted Doug Turnbull of Turnbull Restorations, S.P. Fjestad, author/publisher, and Howard Coleman, Hollywood entertainment consultant.

Welcome to the expanded 6th edition *Blue Book of Modern Black Power Arms*. No other single source gives you as much information and up-to-date values of almost all reproductions and replicas manufactured since 1959. Also included are all the high tech modern muzzleloaders, which have been directly responsible for the resurgence for both black powder shooting and hunting.

Clint Eastwood originally made black powder replicas famous, but so have Robert Duvall, Tom Selleck, Tommy Lee Jones, Ed Harris, Kim Darby, Viggo Mortensen, Kevin Costner, Russell Crowe, Rachel Griffiths, Val Kilmer, and countless other actors of both the silver screen and television. The fact is, without modern black powder reproductions and replicas, many movies and television favorites wouldn't be as historically accurate as they could have been, since they would have had to use original guns, which are both costly and in many cases, rare and not available.

Not to mention that reenactments might never have been started, as the actors simply wouldn't have had enough authentic guns to make their acting realistic and life-like. The pioneering efforts of black powder reproductions and replica manufacture can be directly traced to the gunmaking ingenuity of the Val Trompia Valley in northern Italy during the late 1950s. These innovators probably never realized what affect they would have on future generations of both shooters and hunters, and that their ingenuity and efforts would eventually become an industry onto itself.

The second rebirth of black powder arms came through the efforts of combined high tech innovations which have resulted in today's new crop of in-line muzzleloaders. As a result of using a .209 primer for powder detonation, a wide variety of action types are now available, making them a lot closer to their firearms counterparts for shooting and operating. Hunting with modern muzzleloaders has already morphed into its own unique field, and because of this, hunting can now be categorized into three segments – modern muzzleloaders (this may include flintlocks), bowhunting, and traditional hunting with firearms, which include handguns, rifles and shotguns. Today, thanks to this new technology, design, and a willingness for both hunters and shooters to embrace this newest crop of high tech modern muzzleloaders, modern black powder arms have never been more popular.

Because of the variety of changes and innovations in today's black powder industry, the secondary marketplace has also changed. Many used in-line rifles are more desirable (and expensive) than most traditional .50 cal. muzzleloaders due to their "shootability" factor. Technology has revolutionized this industry to the point where a new $250 in-line muzzleloader will shoot much better than most of the expensive rifles which sold for over $500 a decade ago. Both muzzleloader hunters and shooters are the real winners of this advanced technology. Simplified shooting has also added to the number of people who no longer have to worry about the tedious clean-up and messiness required on older percussion and flintlock rifles.

Colt 2nd and 3rd Generation pistols are certainly the most collectible replicas and reproductions in this publication. With many 1st Generation guns now being auctioned off well into the six figures, many collectors have decided that filling in their collections with 2nd and/or 3rd Generation pistols is more realistic and obtainable. Many newer Colt black powder collectors also find these 2nd and 3rd Generation guns a lot more affordable and easier to locate. Accordingly, the values of all the Colt 2nd and 3rd Generation revolvers have been completely updated, and you may be surprised at how much some of these guns have gone up since the 5th Edition was published. It should come as no surprise that because of original, poor condition 1st Generation Walkers starting out at approx. $300,000 these days, today's collectors and shooters are willing to shell out over $1,000 for a mint 2nd or 3rd Generation Colt Walker.

Once again, black powder ignition types, modern black powder proofmarks, and a new listing for recommended revolver loads have also been included. The Trademark Index has also been extensively revised, and will provide you with the most up-to-date listings of manufacturers and importers available.

Thanks again for all your help & support on this publication. Upcoming editions will continue to provide you with accurate and reliable information on this ever-changing field of black powder reproductions and inline muzzleloaders.

Sincerely,

S.P. Fjestad
Editor & Publisher
Blue Book Publications, Inc.

INTRODUCTION

First things first, THANK YOU for purchasing this *Sixth Edition Blue Book of Modern Black Powder Arms.* This edition has been expanded and improved to be the only book covering modern black powder arms manufactured after 1954, with complete descriptions and the most up-to-date information and values available. The A-Z chapters covering manufacturers, importers, distributors and custom makers (new for this edition) have grown over forty pages. Also, expanded model descriptions and over two hundred new images help to make this book an identification and value guide unmatched in the industry.

If this is your first copy of our *Blue Book of Modern Black Powder Arms,* it is important to read through and familiarize yourself with most everything between the front and back covers in order to get the most out this book. You don't have to memorize it, but knowing where to look when a question comes up won't hurt. The Table of Contents is a good place to start; this can lead you to the parts of our identification and value guide that can answer questions at a glance. The editorial up front "Identifying Black Powder Ignition Types", "Modern Black Powder Proofmarks – Unraveling the Mystery of Icons" and "Black Powder Revolvers Laid Out By Caliber With Flasks, Wads, Balls" by Dennis Adler are packed full of information that can be priceless when trying to identify the manufacturer or the model of the next addition to your collection. How To Use This Book, Serialization, Glossary, Abbreviations, and Trademark Index are all sections that can answer questions at a glance if you take the time to review them.

As a value guide and with the values based on the percentage of original finish, it is important to know how to determine condition. This is covered on our website www.bluebookinc.com in the Firearms section under Photo Percentage Grading System. There are high resolution images with complete descriptions to help you determine the condition of an arm you are interested in. One of the things you will notice in this book is the grading line with values being listed for conditions 100%, 98%, 90%, and 80%. This is because in most cases the value of a common modern black powder arm will bottom out in about 80% condition (values for arms below 80% will approximate the 80% value). This is true for most any shooter and some of the collectable trade marks. The exceptions to this will be those limited/special edition arms that have such a limited production number or are so greatly embellished that they rarely see the light of day. In these cases you will find N/A (Not Applicable) for values in the condition ranges that are rarely encountered in the secondary market. If you have any questions regarding how to evaluate the condition of a black powder arm of interest, it is recommended you look at the newly updated and expanded Photo Percentage Grading System available online at www.bluebookinc.com for a complete explanation.

Don't forget this is a work in progress, as with the *Blue Book of Gun Values* (currently in its 30th Edition) expansion is ongoing. If there is something specific you are looking for additional information on, lets us know, your input is always welcome.

Sincerely,

John B. Allen
Blue Book Publications, Inc.

HOW TO USE

The prices listed in this edition of the *Blue Book of Modern Black Powder Arms* are based on the national average retail prices a consumer can expect to pay. This is not a blackpowder wholesale pricing guide (there is no such thing). More importantly, do not expect to walk into a gun/pawn shop or trade/gun show and think that the proprietor/dealer should pay you the retail price listed within this text for your gun. Resale offers on most models could be anywhere from near retail to 50% less than the values listed. These prices paid will be depending upon locality, desirability, dealer inventory, and potential profitability. In other words, if you want to receive 100% of the price (retail value), then you have to do 100% of the work (become the retailer, which also includes assuming 100% of the risk).

Percentages of original finish, (condition factors with corresponding prices/values, if applicable) are listed between 80% and 100%.

Please refer to "Identifying Popular Modern Black Powder Revolvers" to learn more about the various blackpowder models. Also, you may want to check the Glossary and the Abbreviations for more detailed information about both nomenclature and blackpowder terminology.

A Trademark Index listing the current blackpowder manufacturers, importers, and distributors is provided. This includes the most recent emails, websites, and other pertinent contact information for these individuals and organizations. The Index is a handy way to find the make/model you are looking for in a hurry. To find a model in this text, first look under the name of the manufacturer, trademark, brand name, and in some cases, the importer (please consult the Index if necessary). Next, find the correct category name(s), typically Pistols, Revolvers, Rifles and Shotguns.

Once you find the correct model or sub-model under its respective subheading, determine the specimen's percentage of original condition, and find the corresponding percentage column showing the price of a currently manufactured model or the value on a discontinued model.

Since this publication consists of 288 pages, you may want to take advantage of our index as a speedy alternative to going through the pages, and our comprehensive Trademark Index for a complete listing of blackpowder manufacturers, importers, and distributors.

For the sake of simplicity, the following organizational framework has been adopted throughout this publication.

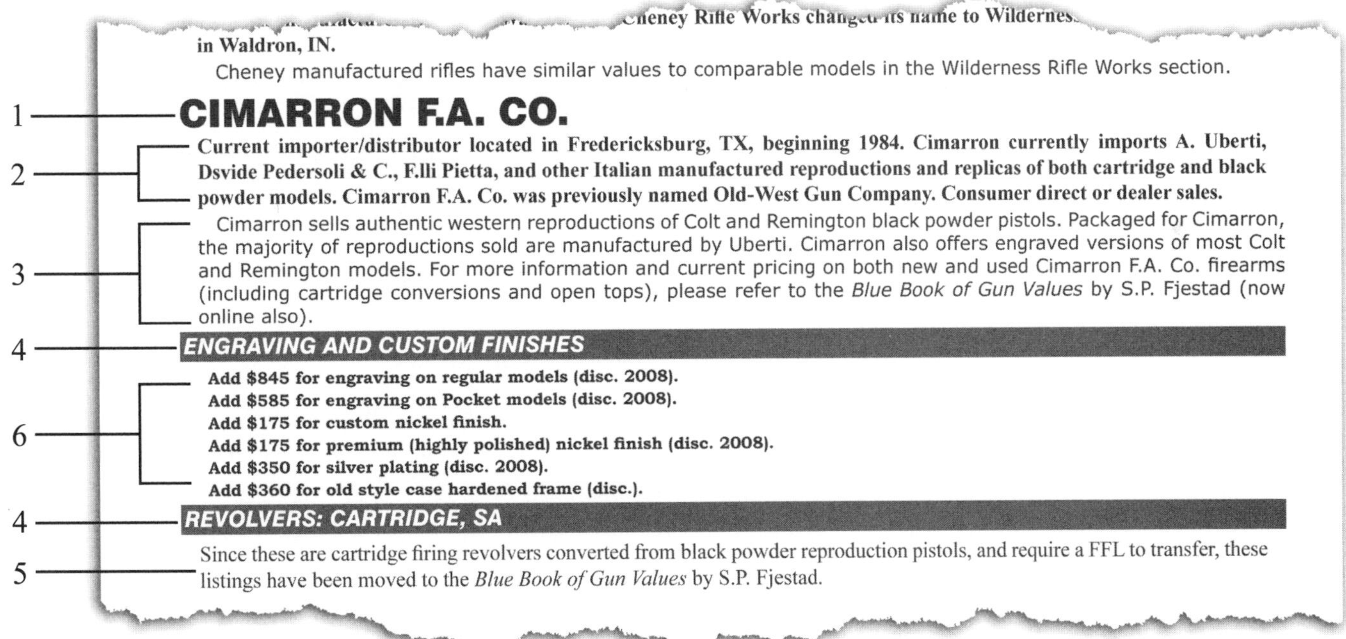

in Waldron, IN.

Cheney manufactured rifles have similar values to comparable models in the Wilderness Rifle Works section.

CIMARRON F.A. CO.

Current importer/distributor located in Fredericksburg, TX, beginning 1984. Cimarron currently imports A. Uberti, Dsvide Pedersoli & C., F.lli Pietta, and other Italian manufactured reproductions and replicas of both cartridge and black powder models. Cimarron F.A. Co. was previously named Old-West Gun Company. Consumer direct or dealer sales.

Cimarron sells authentic western reproductions of Colt and Remington black powder pistols. Packaged for Cimarron, the majority of reproductions sold are manufactured by Uberti. Cimarron also offers engraved versions of most Colt and Remington models. For more information and current pricing on both new and used Cimarron F.A. Co. firearms (including cartridge conversions and open tops), please refer to the *Blue Book of Gun Values* by S.P. Fjestad (now online also).

ENGRAVING AND CUSTOM FINISHES

Add $845 for engraving on regular models (disc. 2008).
Add $585 for engraving on Pocket models (disc. 2008).
Add $175 for custom nickel finish.
Add $175 for premium (highly polished) nickel finish (disc. 2008).
Add $350 for silver plating (disc. 2008).
Add $360 for old style case hardened frame (disc.).

REVOLVERS: CARTRIDGE, SA

Since these are cartridge firing revolvers converted from black powder reproduction pistols, and require a FFL to transfer, these listings have been moved to the *Blue Book of Gun Values* by S.P. Fjestad.

1. Manufacturer Name or Trademark - brand name, importer, or organization is listed alphabetically in uppercase bold face type.

2. Manufacturer Status - This information is listed directly beneath the trademark heading, providing current status and location along with importer information for foreign trademarks.

3. Manufacturer Description - These notes may appear next under individual heading descriptions and can be differentiated by the typeface. This will be specific information relating to the trademark or models.

4. Category Name - (normally, in alphabetical sequence) in upper case (inside a screened gray box), referring mostly to a blackpowder configuration.

5. Category Note - May following a category name to help explain the category, and/or provide limited information on models and values.

6. Category Price/Value Adjustment - The last potential piece of information that may appear below a category name (above a model name) is a category price/value adjustment. These may be included here only if the adjustment applies to all models in the category.

7. Model Name and Description - appear flush left, are bold faced, and all upper-case letters, either in chronological order (normally) or alphabetical order (sometimes, the previous model name and/or close sub variation will appear at the end in parentheses) and are listed under the individual category names. These are followed by the model descriptions and usually include descriptive information about the model.

16

15 **C** 56 *COLT BLACKPOWDER ARMS CO., cont.*

10

GRADING - PPGS™	100%	98%	90%	80%

7 **1862 POCKET POLICE** — .36 cal. perc., 5.5 inch round barrel with creeping-style loading lever, color case hardened frame, loading lever, plunger, and hammer, 5 shot semi-fluted cylinder, silver plated backstrap and square back trigger guard, 25 oz. Mfg. 1997-2002.

	$550	$375	$225	$175

Last MSR was $675.

1862 TRAPPER MODEL — .36 cal. perc., 3.5 in. round barrel, color case hardened frame, and hammer, silver plated backstrap and trigger guard, no loading lever but supplied with 4.65 in. brass ramrod. Disc. 2002

	$600	$425	$250	$200

14 **Last MSR was $675.**

REVOLVERS: PERCUSSION LIMITED/SPECIAL EDITION

1842 PATERSON — .36 cal. perc., No. 5 Holster Model with hinged loading lever, 5 shot, 7.5 inch octagon barrel, steel backstrap, period-style scrollwork with punch-dot background on both sides of barrel lug, frame, standing breech, loading lever rod tip, hammer, and backstrap. Mfg. 1998-2002.

	$3,000	$2,025	N/A	N/A

Last MSR was $4,500.

13 This model was available on a special order basis and took approximately four months to manufacture and hand engrave.

1847 WALKER 150TH AN...
and loading lever, 73 oz. ...
Limited production model.

3RD MODEL DRAGOON ...
...e hard...

...& Pietta.

MSR $255	$230	$205	$150	$125

1858 REMINGTON ARMY — .44 cal. perc., 8 in. octagon barrel, blue or old silver finish, color case hardened hammer, steel frame, backstrap, and trigger guard, 3 lbs. Mfg. by Uberti & Pietta.

8

courtesy Taylor's & Co., Inc.

MSR $295	$265	$235	$175	$145

9

Add $225 for "Old Silver" silver plated frame.

11 * ***1858 Remington Army (Short Model)*** — .44 cal. perc., 5.5 in. octagon barrel, steel frame, blue, white or color case hardened finish, brass backstrap, and trigger guard, 2.75-3 lbs. Mfg. by Uberti & Pietta.

MSR $305	$275	$245	$185	$155

12 **Add $45 for white finish.**
Add $82 for stainless steel.

8. Image - Next in this long line of information may (but not always) follow an image (with credit) of the model. A picture truly can say a thousand words.

9. Price/Value line - This information will either follow directly below the model name and description or, if there is an image, below the image. The information appears in descending order from left to right with the values corresponding to a condition factor shown in the Grading Line near the top of the page. 100% price on a currently manufactured gun also assumes not previously sold at retail. In some cases, N/As (Not Applicable) are listed and indicate that the condition is not frequently encountered so the value is not predictable. On a currently manufactured gun, the lower condition specimens will bottom out at a value, and a lesser condition gun value will approximate the lowest value listed. An MSR automatically indicates the gun is currently manufactured, and the MSR (Manufacturer's Suggested Retail) is shown left of the 100% column. Recently manufactured 100% specimens without boxes, warranties, etc., that are currently manufactured must be discounted slightly (5%-20%, depending on the desirability of make and model).

10. Grading Line - Grading lines will normally appear at or near the top of each page.

11. Sub-model Name - Variations within a model appear as sub-models, they are differentiated from model names because they are preceded by a bullet, indented, and are in upper and lower case type, and are usually followed by a short description of that sub-model. These sub-model descriptions have a smaller typeface than the model descriptions.

12. Model Price/Value Adjustments - Extra cost features/special value orders and other value added/subtracted features are placed directly under individual price lines or in some cases, category names. These individual lines appear bolder than other descriptive typeface. On many guns less than 15 years old, these add/subtract items will be the last factory MSRs (manufacturer's suggested retail price) for that option.

13. Model Note - Manufacturer and other notes/information appear in smaller type, and should be read since they contain both important and other critical, up-to-date information.

14. On many discontinued models/variations, a line may appear under the price line, indicating the last manufacturer's suggested retail price (MSR).

15. Alphabetical Designator/Page Number – Capital letter indicating which alphabetical section you are in and the page number you are on.

16. Manufacturer Heading/Continued Heading – These appear at the top of the page to indicate which manufacturer the models listed are manufactured by.

Identifying Black Powder Ignition Types

BY DENNIS ADLER

1.) Since the 1600s, there have been three principal ignition systems for black powder pistols and longarms. Pictured from left to right, the flintlock c.1620 to 1836, the percussion lock c. 1807 to 1868, and percussion cylinder c. 1836 to 1871. There was a continual overlap of these designs; flintlocks were still being used during the Civil War, and single shot and percussion revolvers well into the 1870s.

It began with a loud boom! The first black powder pistol was a hand cannon developed in the late 14th century, and the soldier firing one of these devices, essentially a barrel on a stick, was as likely to take his own life as that of his intended target. Historian Claude Blair notes that development of a true pistol, a one-handed gun, was inhibited by two factors:

1. Firearms were regarded essentially as infantry weapons to be used en masse. Various attempts to arm horsemen with firearms are recorded during the later Middle Ages, but these appear to have been intended to function as mounted infantry. There was therefore no known tactical reason for the development of the pistol.

2. No purely mechanical system of ignition existed.[1]

The invention of the matchlock in the early 15th century, essentially a barrel on a better stick, fitted with a burning rope or match for ignition of the powder, was just slightly less precarious of a device than the hand cannon. The matchlock remained in use for more than 100 years going through various design improvements, though none safer or more reliable. Then in the early 16th century, the wheel lock design appeared. This very complex, clockwork-like mechanism assured a safe and reliable ignition of the powder charge, and by the mid to late 1500s the first practical pistols were being developed in Europe.

The wheel lock reigned supreme in the world of firearms design for more than a century. Then in the 1600s, a new, more reliable and less costly ignition system was devised. The flintlock.

This is the first of the examples pictured (image 1 (left) and image 2), and is typical of all flintlock designs utilizing a cock (hammer) to hold the flint, a pan to retain a small amount of priming powder, and a steel (frizzen) which was hinged to close over the pan and provide a metal surface against which the flint was struck, simultaneously creating a spark and igniting the powder in the pan, which in turn flashed through a small hole in the side of the barrel, igniting the

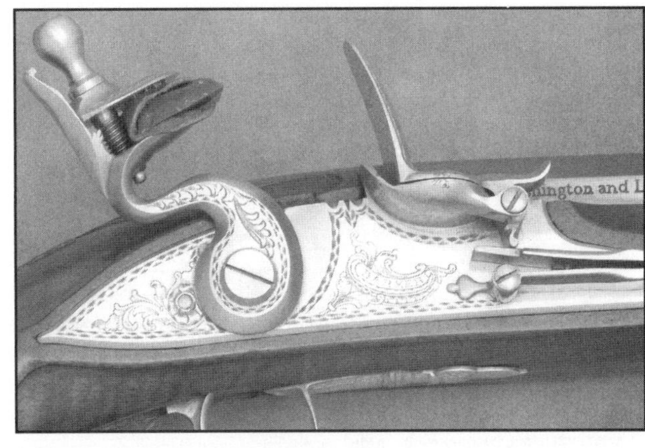

2.) This is a good example of a c.1776 American flintlock design. Note the style of the cock (hammer) and the jaws to retain the flint, the pan and steel, and feather spring for the steel and pan cover.

larger powder charge within, and discharging the firearm. This all happened in a split second, and with a good flint, it was a very reliable means of ignition. So much so, that the flintlock remained in popular use until the 1830s!

There are various tales about the development of the first percussion lock in the early 1800s, but none is more inspirational than the story of the Reverend Alexander Forsyth, minister of Belhelvie, Aberdeenshire, and an avid hunter, who, displeased with his flintlock, sat down and designed an improved means of ignition in 1805 that eliminated the momentary delay between the drop of the hammer and the ignition of the powder charge in the barrel. The good reverend reasoned that if the spark went directly into the main powder charge, rather than being ignited second handedly by the ignition of the powder in the priming pan, the gun would be more efficient, faster to load, and most important of all, would not require the ignition of the priming pan which often alerted his intended dinner before the shot was fired.

The part of the firearm pictured in image 3 is a typical percussion lock of the early 1800s. The guns themselves changed little from flintlock to percussion lock, and in many instances old flintlocks were refitted for the new ignition system. Gun makers simply continued to make the same models but with percussion locks.

As is shown in image 3, the cock (now officially the hammer) was used to strike the percussion cap seated on top of the nipple, which was threaded into the breech of the barrel. Thus when the fulminating mercury in the cap was ignited by the impact of the hammer, the flame went directly into the powder charge at the breech and boom... instantaneous ignition. With a good eye and a clean shot, Reverend Forsyth's dinner was in the bag.

The single shot percussion lock was the most short-lived of all firearms ignition systems [2] but the concept was carried forth beginning in 1837 into an entirely new type of firearm, the revolving cylinder pistol.

The idea of a revolving cylinder is nearly as old as the matchlock, but making it work was something altogether different. Flintlock revolvers with a manually rotated cylinder were produced as far back as the 1600s, and there were various multi-barreled pistols, such as

3.) The basic style of pistol did not change significantly with the advent of the percussion lock in the early 1800s. The cock (hammer) was now designed to strike the top of the nipple, which was threaded into the breech and fitted with a percussion cap (not shown). Lock designs were essentially the same, as were trigger guards and triggers. The percussion lock was a much more elegant design with fewer exposed components and a far superior seal against the elements.

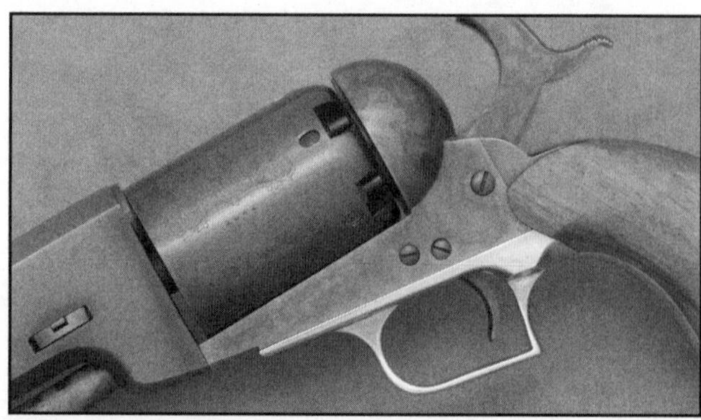

4.) With the advent of the Colt's patent revolver in 1836 and its subsequent development by Samuel Colt, the single shot percussion pistol was delegated to a lesser role as a small, hideout gun, such as those popularized by Henry Deringer. The revolver led the way to a new era in firearm's design and after 168 years, Sam Colt's basic design is still in use.

the early percussion Pepperbox, introduced by the Darling Brothers of Massachusetts in 1836, and the double action Pepperbox models developed by Ethan Allen. But these were all heavy, unwieldy designs. Then young Sam Colt came along and changed everything.

On February 25, 1836, twenty-one year old Samuel Colt received his third patent for the revolving cylinder pistol, (he had already received a British patent on October 22, 1835, as well as a French patent) and began final development of what would become the Paterson revolver introduced in the fall of 1837.

Though Colt's first revolvers were not a huge success, nor was the Patent Arms Mfg. Co. of Paterson, New Jersey (which went out of business in 1842), the Colt design reemerged in 1847 as the massive .44 caliber Walker revolver, the most powerful and successful handgun of its time, and the wellspring for 162 years of Colt's Patent Firearms Manufacturing Company production.

The third type of ignition illustrated then is the Walker pistol. The cylinder has six chambers, each nipple capped with a percussion cap, (not shown). A loaded chamber rotates into battery each time the hammer is cocked. Pull the trigger and up to 60 gr. of black powder backing a .44 caliber lead ball are unleashed with a thundering roar. The Texas Rangers of the 1840s and 1850s swore by them, as did many others in the U.S. military during the war with Mexico from 1846 to 1848.

The Walker revolver, designed by Sam Colt and Capt. Sam Walker, brought forth a revolution in firearms design. Followed by the Colt Baby Dragoon, First through Third Model Dragoons, the 1851 Navy and 1860 Army, among others, Colt's design was copied by countless arms manufacturers after his patent extension expired in 1858. The Colt design became the most popular ignition system of the black powder era. And even with the advent of the metallic cartridge in the late 1860s, the venerable Colt cap-and-ball revolvers remained popular among lawmen, gunslingers, and pioneers during the post Civil War era and settling of the American West.

Whether you pour your black powder down the barrel or into the chambers of a cylinder, use a flint or a percussion cap, the principals of black powder longarms and pistols changed very little from the late 17th century to the mid 19th century. It still ended in a loud boom! ■

[1] *Handguns of the World* by Edward C. Ezell, 1981 Barnes & Noble Books, New York.

[2] The single shot percussion pistol, principally the Henry Deringer designs, and various single shot percussion boot pistols, principally underhammer designs, remained in use well into the 1860s.

Modern Black Powder Proofmarks

Unraveling The Mystery Of Icons

BY DENNIS ADLER

When you purchase either a 2nd or 3rd Generation Colt Blackpowder Arms revolver, it bears the Colt patent stamping on the frame and the Colt address on the top of the barrel. There is also a serial number stamped on the bottom of the frame, again on the bottom of the barrel lug, trigger guard and buttstrap. The serialization indicates the year or period of manufacture, and this is as straightforward as model identification gets. Even though many of the Colt parts for the 2nd Generation, and all of the Colt parts for the 3rd Generation were cast in Italy, the guns were finished and assembled in the United States by Colt or the Colt Blackpowder Arms Company, and Colt pistols, regardless of the origin of their components, bear only Colt markings.

The same model gun, an 1860 Army for example, manufactured in Italy and sold by Uberti or F.LLI Pietta, is stamped with a variety of markings – Italian Proof House devices, manufacturer's symbols and an encoded date of manufacture. It is usually a combination of heraldry and letters, which need to be decoded. The same is true of flintlock and percussion lock pistols and long rifles manufactured by Uberti, F.LLI Pietta, ArmiSport, Davide Pedersoli, and Armi San Paolo SRL (Euroarms) which comprise the major Italian manufacturers currently in production.

The Italian proof houses in Gardone and Valtrompia have been around for a very long time but as far as reproduction black powder arms are concerned, the dating begins in 1954. Prior to 1954, the year of proof was indicated in full Arabic numerals.

Following is a chart displaying the year of proof symbols used from 1954 to 2009. These are traditionally found within a box next to the individual proof house symbols. From 1954 through 1970 Roman Numerals were used. Roman Numerals and Arabic Numerals were combined in 1971, 1972, and 1973, and Roman Numerals were used again in 1974. Since 1975 two capital letters have been used exclusively.

Symbol	Year of Proof	Symbol	Year of Proof	Symbol	Year of Proof
X	1954	XVIII	1962	XXVI	1970
XI	1955	XIX	1963	XX7	1971
XII	1956	XX	1964	XX8	1972
XIII	1957	XXI	1965	XX9	1973
XIV	1958	XXII	1966	XXX	1974
XV	1959	XXIII	1967	AA	1975
XVI	1960	XXIV	1968	AB	1976
XVII	1961	XXV	1969	AC	1977

Symbol	Year of Proof	Symbol	Year of Proof	Symbol	Year of Proof
AD	1978	AU	1989	BN	2000
AE	1979	AZ	1990	BP	2001
AF	1980	BA	1991	BS	2002
AH	1981	BB	1992	BT	2003
AI	1982	BC	1993	BU	2004
AL	1983	BD	1994	BZ	2005
AM	1984	BF	1995	CA	2006
AN	1985	BH	1996	CB	2007
AP	1986	BI	1997	CC	2008
AS	1987	BL	1998	CD	2009
AT	1988	BM	1999		

As to the placement of proof house symbols, it depends upon the model of gun, and the level of embellishment, the latter often dictating a discrete location on the underside of the barrel or frame on highly engraved examples.

There are two standardized proof house marks. The first is the provisional Gardone proof, consisting of a star surrounded by eight lands and grooves over a coat of arms featuring a hammer and anvil and crossed bayoneted rifles; the second is a star surrounded by eight lands and grooves over the capital letters PN. All firearms produced in Italy since 1950, regardless of type, receive the first stamping. The second, also instituted in 1950, is the first black powder proof for Gardone and Brescia, and is only used on black powder arms. Thus all black powder arms must bear both proof house symbols.

Finally, there is the manufacturer's mark. This is often confusing unless one is familiar with the manufacturers' insignia. Most use their logo, while some combine their name and logo, or use an abbreviation as their logo. Earlier guns generally bear only their manufacturers' mark, while more recent production has been seen using both an emblem and company name.

Davide Pedersoli, one of Italy's oldest manufacturers has had three logos since 1957. The earliest was a diamond inside a circle. This is rarely seen. This mark

These are the three standard stampings on every Italian-made black powder revolver, pistol, rifle and shotgun. From left to right: year of manufacture, Gardone V.T. black powder proof house stamping, and Gardone proof house stamping. The year of manufacture is?

The underside of this screw barrel deringer manufactured by Pedersoli shows only the dp logo. Both proof house marks are present and a boxed BL denoting the year of manufacture as 1998.

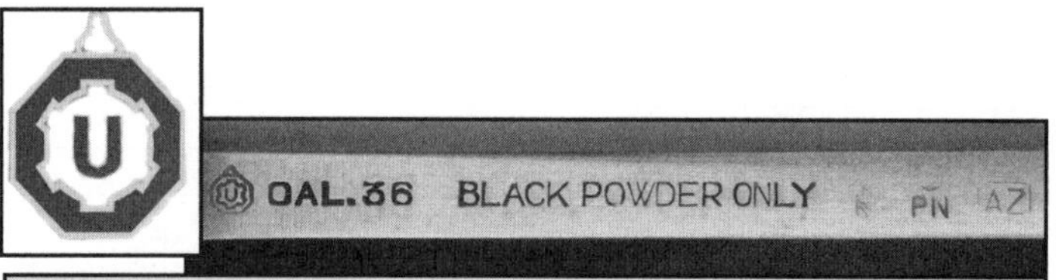

Aldo Uberti S.r.l. was founded in 1959 and has always used a capital U surrounded by an octagonal device, which is actually the muzzle of an 1851 Navy (their first gun) with six lands and grooves and the front sight. This photo of a Paterson barrel has a boxed AZ indicating a manufacturing date of 1990.

F.LLI Pietta always uses its diamond logo with the initials FAP. This is the barrel from a Le Mat revolver and it also bears the company name and country of origin. The proof house marks and manufacturing code are stamped elsewhere on the gun.

Here is an example of a manufacturer using two different styles. The standalone Palmetto palm tree logo on this screw barrel derringer, and the logo and company name on the barrel of this 1851 Navy.

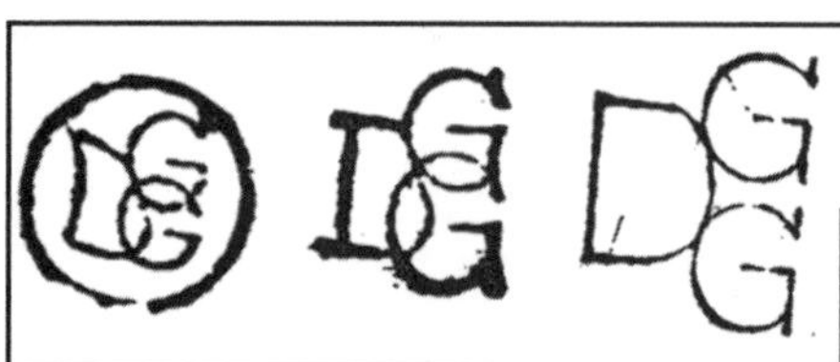

Arms originally manufactured by Armi San Paolo S.r.l. or Euroarms S.r.l., now the proprietary name, bear the DGG emblem representing the company's founders, Grassi, Doninelli, and Gazzola.

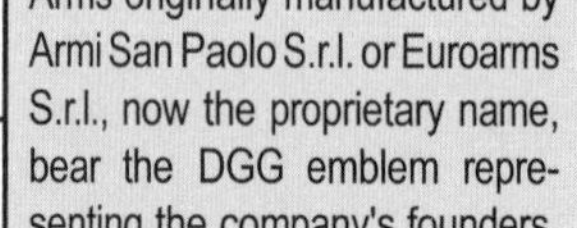

Armi Sport uses a circular device with the capital letters AC.

was followed by the image of an anvil with PEDERSOLI above it in capital letters and the initials DAP inside the anvil. This again is rarely seen, except on very early models. The company logo, a lowercase dp within an oval, has been used for more than 40 years. This logo is often followed by the DAVIDE PEDERSOLI or PEDERSOLI name in capital letters. In short, there is no mistaking a Pedersoli product!

The same is true of Aldo Uberti, S.r.l, which has used the same logo since its founding in 1959 – a capital U contained within an octagonal barrel device.

For Fratelli Pietta, another of Italy's leading manufacturers of black powder pistols and long arms, the initials FAP contained within a horizontal diamond identify F.LLI Pietta; often followed by F.LLI PIETTA in capital letters.

Palmetto, which manufactured a variety of black powder arms distributed primarily through Dixie Gun Works, used a very recognizable palm tree within a circle as their company logo.

Armi San Paolo S.r.l., established in 1970, uses the last names of the original founders Grassi, Doninelli, and Gazzola as a symbol, DGG, usually contained within a circle. Beginning December 31, 2001, Armi San Paolo officially became Euroarms Italia S.r.l. The same logo is used on all Euroarms models.

Armi Sport, which produces an exceptional line of single shot percussion pistols like the French Le Page, Sharps rifles, and the popular Spencer rifle for Taylor's & Co., uses an AC within a circle, (AC for Armi Chiappa founder Rino Chiappa's last name).

Armed with this information it is now possible to identify the maker and year of manufacture on any black powder rifle, shotgun, pistol, or revolver produced since 1950. ■

The barrel pictured is a perfect example as it bears all of the Italian proof marks described. This is from a Deluxe engraved Pedersoli Le Page pistol, and all of the stampings are on the underside of the barrel. From left to right (upside down) are the test house and black powder proof house stampings, followed by a boxed BM, denoting a manufacturing date of 1999, then the gun's serial number, a dp oval manufacturer's mark, as well as the PEDERSOLI name, pistol caliber and notification that the gun is for black powder only. This warning appears on the barrel or barrel lug of all black powder arms manufactured in Italy.

Black Powder Revolvers Laid Out By Caliber With Flasks, Wads, Balls

Guns and calibers. From the smallest to the largest pistols, our recommended loads are lighter than maximum for safety and accuracy. A big bang, more recoil, and lots of smoke looks impressive, but wears everything faster. We prefer a conservative load to reduce wear and tear on the pistol. Lighter loads can also provide more consistent accuracy. Between Goex FFFg and Pyrodex Pistol powder, and other black powder substitutes such as Goex Pinnacle, it becomes a matter of personal preference. The advantage of a substitute is a cleaner, less corrosive formula that allows more shooting before a gun becomes fouled.

Guns and Recommended Loads

All Colt and Remington, .31 cal: 12 gr. Goex FFFg, Wonder Wad, .315 ball. (Max load 13 gr.)

Colt Pocket Pistols, .36 cal: 18 gr. Goex FFFg, Wonder Wad, .375 ball. (Max load 20 gr.)

Colt 1851 Navy, 1861 Navy (similar copies) .36 cal: 22 gr. Goex FFFg, Wonder Wad, .375 ball. (Max load 25 gr.)

Colt 1860 Army, (Remington 1858 Army) .44 cal: 30 gr. Goex FFFg, Wonder Wad, .451 ball. (Max load 35 gr.)

Colt Dragoons (all but Walker Dragoon and Ruger Old Army) .44 cal: 40 gr. Goex FFFg, Wonder Wad, .451 ball. (Max load 50 gr.)

Walker .44 and Ruger Old Army: 40 gr. Goex FFFg, Wonder Wad, .455 ball. (Max load 60 gr.)

Pyrodex Data

.31 cal:	9 gr.	(Max load 10 gr.)
.36 cal Pocket:	15 gr.	(Max load 17 gr.)
.36 cal 1851/1861 Navy:	17 gr.	(Max load 20 gr.)
.44 cal. 1860 Army:	20 gr.	(Max load 28 gr.)
Dragoons:	35 gr.	(Max load 35 gr.)
Walker and Ruger Old Army:	40 gr.	(Max load 40 gr.)

Note: Although Pyrodex powder charges are actual weights not volume measures, the same spouts used for measuring Goex FFFg "by weight" can be used to measure Pyrodex "by volume." For example, in a Walker Colt the spout used to dispense 40 gr. of FFFg by weight, will deliver a correct measure of Pyrodex by volume.

Flasks and accessories courtesy of Taylor's & Co.

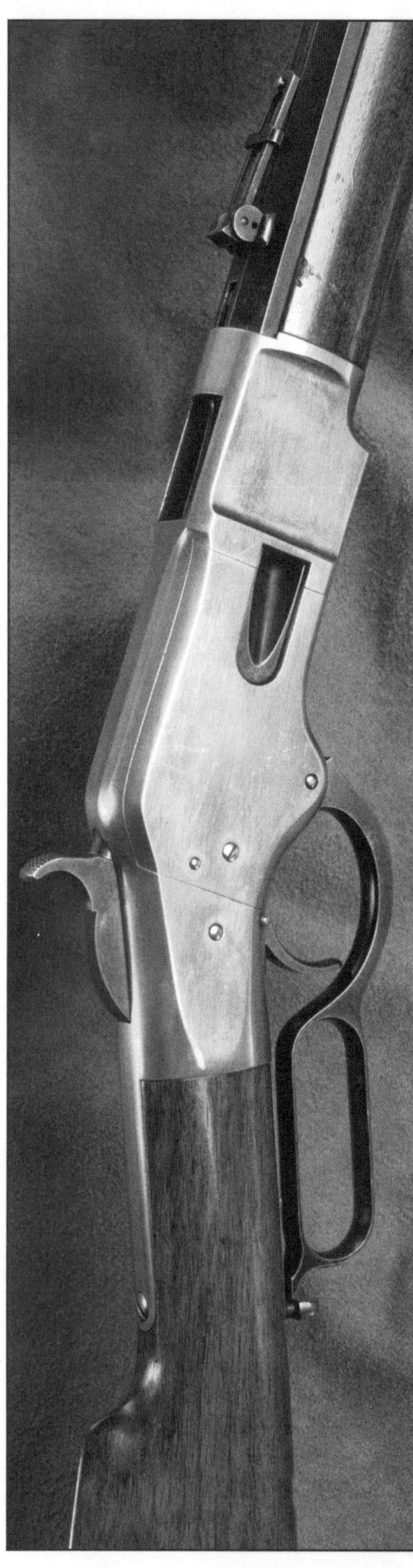

A SECTION

ALLEN FIREARMS

Previous importer located in Santa Fe, NM, importing Aldo Uberti & Co. reproductions and replicas until early in 1987.

After Allen Firearms closed, Old-West Gun Co., now Cimarron F.A. Co. located in Fredericksburg, TX, purchased the remaining inventory. Since all guns sold by Allen Firearms were manufactured by Uberti (they even used the same catalog), please refer to Uberti in the U section of this text.

For more information and current pricing on Allen Firearms' line of firearms, please refer to the *Blue Book of Gun Values* by S.P. Fjestad (now online also).

AMERICA REMEMBERS

Current organization established in 1993 and currently located in Ashland, VA. Previously located in Mechanicsville, VA, until 1999. America Remembers privately commissions historical, limited/special editions in conjunction with various manufacturers. Consumer direct sales.

America Remembers is a private, non-governmental organization dedicated to the remembrance of notable Americans and important historical American events. Along with its affiliates, the Armed Forces Commemorative Society®, American Heroes and Legends®, and the United States Society of Arms and Armour, the company produces special issue limited edition firearms. America Remembers purchased the antique arms division of the U.S. Historical Society on April 1, 1994. Older U.S.H.S. reproductions and replicas can be located in the U section of this text.

Please refer to *Colt Blackpowder Reproductions & Replicas - A Collector's & Shooter's Guide* for color pictures of the America Remembers pistols described below. America Remembers Colt Commemoratives can be found on pages 90, 99, 100, 102, 105, 110, and 111.

For more information and current pricing on America Remembers firearms, please refer to the *Blue Book of Gun Values* by S.P. Fjestad (now online also).

LIMITED/SPECIAL EDITIONS

Values listed below reflect America Remembers official issue prices, for sold-out issues prices appear as Last issue price. These do not necessarily represent secondary marketplace prices. No other values are listed since America Remembers limited/special editions do not appear that frequently in the secondary marketplace. This is because America Remembers typically sells to consumers directly, without involving normal gun dealers and distributors. Because of this consumer direct sales program, many gun dealers do not have a working knowledge about what America Remembers models are currently selling for. The publisher suggests that those people owning America Remembers limited/special editions contact America Remembers (see Trademark Index) for current information, including secondary marketplace liquidity.

REVOLVERS: PERCUSSION

While not specifically mentioned, the revolvers listed below all have various degrees of ornamentation and other embellishments (including some inscriptions).

AMERICAN EAGLE 1860 ARMY — .44 cal. perc., engraved cylinder, American Eagle highlighting the barrel, color case hardened frame, hammer and loading lever, 24Kt. gold plated backstrap, front sight and trigger guard, silver plated trigger. Edition limited to 500. Mfg. by Uberti.

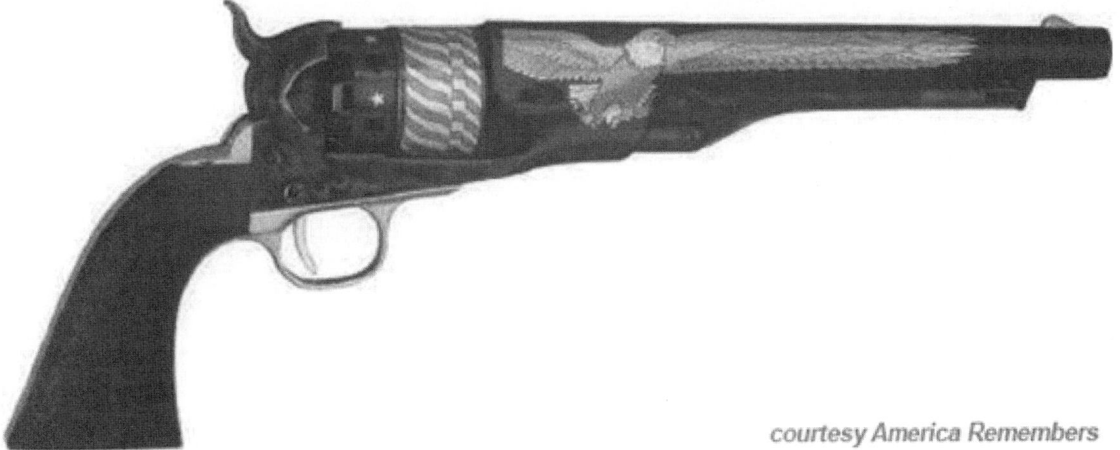

courtesy America Remembers

Current issue price is $1,695.

BUFFALO BILL'S WILD WEST TRIBUTE REVOLVER — .44 cal. perc., 8 in. octagon bbl., based on Remington 1858 New Model Army, blue frame, cylinder, and barrel with 24Kt. gold decorated artwork including "1883 - Buffalo Bill's Wild West - 1917" inscribed on both sides of the barrel and a recreation of Buffalo Bill's signature on backstrap, gold plated trigger, trigger guard, and sight, walnut grips. Edition limited to 300 beginning 2008. Mfg. by Uberti.

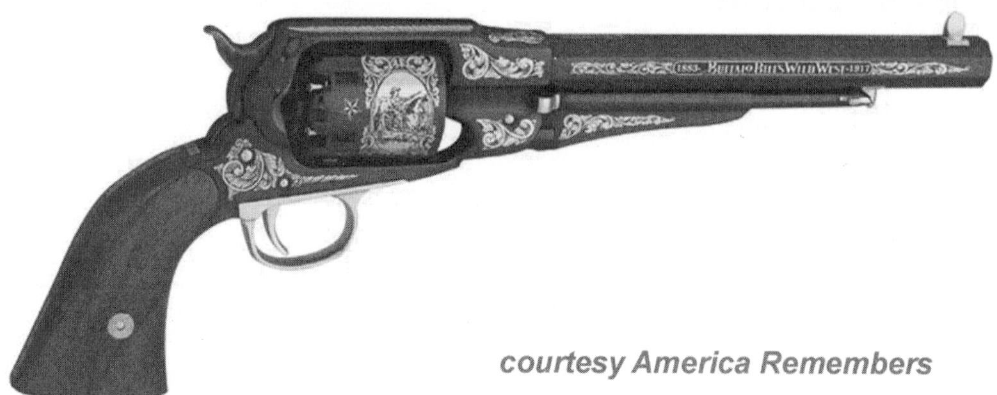

courtesy America Remembers

Current issue price is $1,995.

CALIFORNIA SESQUICENTENNIAL TRIBUTE WALKER REVOLVER — .44 cal. perc. Edition limited to 150 beginning 2000. Mfg. by Colt Blackpowder Arms Co.

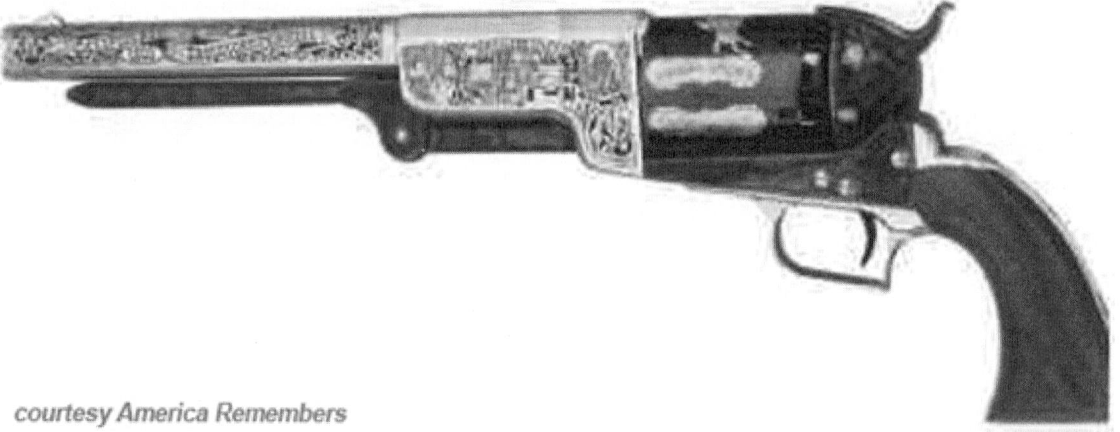
courtesy America Remembers

Current issue price is $2,195.

C.S.S. H.L. HUNLEY 1851 NAVY REVOLVER — .36 cal. perc. Edition limited to 750. Mfg. by Uberti.

courtesy America Remembers

Current issue price is $1,795.

GETTYSBURG 1863 REVOLVER — .44 cal. perc., 1860 Army commemorating the July 1863 battle. This model features a 24Kt. gold battle scene surrounding the rebated cylinder. The left side of the barrel bears the legend "GETTYSBURG PENNSYLVANIA JULY 1863." On the right side is an inscription from Lincoln's Gettysburg Address, "We here highly resolve that these dead shall not have died in vain." The backstrap, trigger guard and front sight blade are 24Kt. gold plated. A French fit solid walnut display case contains the revolver and both Union and Confederate belt buckles in solid brass, and a parchment paper replica of the Gettysburg Address. Edition limited to 1,863. Mfg. by Uberti.

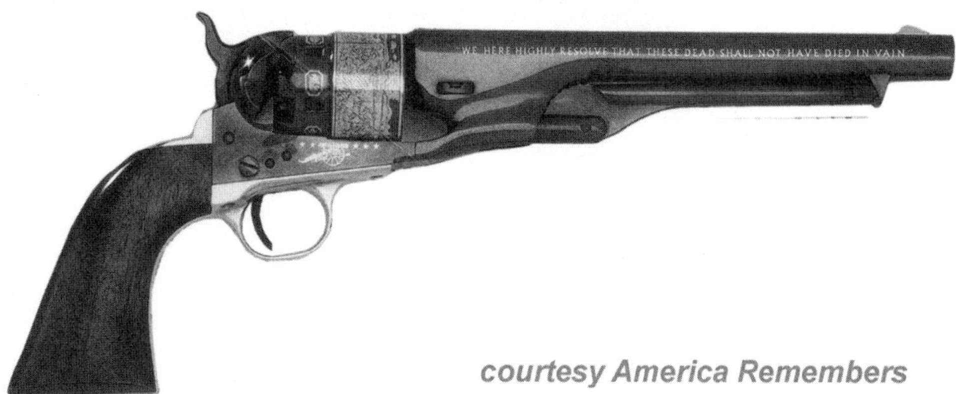

courtesy America Remembers

Current issue price is $1,395.

GOD BLESS DIXIE TRIBUTE — .44 cal. perc., blue frame, cylinder, and barrel with 24Kt. gold and silver decorated artwork, gold plate the trigger, hammer, backstrap, trigger guard, and sight, Rosewood grips. Edition limited to 250. New 2005. Mfg. by Colt Blackpowder Arms Co.

courtesy America Remembers

Current issue price is $1,995.

HISTORIC U.S. NAVY TRIBUTE 1851 NAVY — .36 cal. perc., cylinder engraved with naval battle scene in gold and nickel silver, decorated barrel lug, recoil shield, frame, and barrel, 24Kt. gold plated hammer, trigger guard, and backstrap. Edition limited to 500. Mfg. by Uberti.

courtesy America Remembers

Current issue price is $1,595.

LONE STAR TRIBUTE WALKER .44 — .44 cal. perc., deep black finish and 24Kt. gold embellishment with portraits of Houston, Austin, and Seguin on the left barrel lug, "Victory or Death" and the Alamo on the left frame, Bowie, Travis, and Crockett on the right barrel lug. Texas longhorns on the right frame, medallions on the cylinder and the legend "Come and Take it" on the backstrap. The top of the barrel lug has "Texas" written over it, bordered by "The Lone Star State" and "1845 The 28th State". Edition limited to 150. Mfg. by Uberti.

courtesy America Remembers

Current issue price is $1,795.

JOHNNY CASH TEXAS PATERSON — .36 cal. perc. Edition limited to 1,000. Mfg. by Uberti.

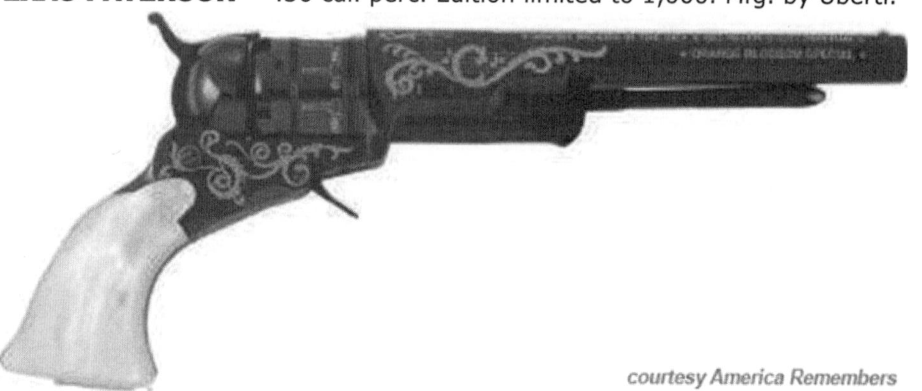
courtesy America Remembers

Last issue price was $1,500.

MUSEUM OF THE CONFEDERACY TRIBUTE REVOLVER — .44 cal. perc., w/20 ga. lower barrel, built on the LeMat nine shot revolver design with gold and silver artwork on barrels, frame, cylinder, hammer, and trigger. Edition limited to 500. New 2004.

courtesy America Remembers

Current issue price is $2,495.

PATERSON BELT MODEL REVOLVER — .36 cal. perc., antique blue finish, antique gray finish, or charcoal blue finish, Belt Model based on the Ehlers Fifth or New Model No. 2 revolver. The first in America Remembers' new Heritage Series, offering never before reproduced Colt models, the Paterson features the unique Ehlers-type backstrap and grip design, short 3.5 in. octagonal barrel and early Paterson-style loading lever. Designed by Dennis Adler, handcrafted by R.L. Millington from Uberti Paterson components. Hand finished and cased with accessories in a period style French fit, solid walnut presentation box built by Pennsylvania furniture maker Duncan Everhart. Each Paterson revolver has the appearance of an aged original pistol. Edition limited to 100. Offered 2001-2008.

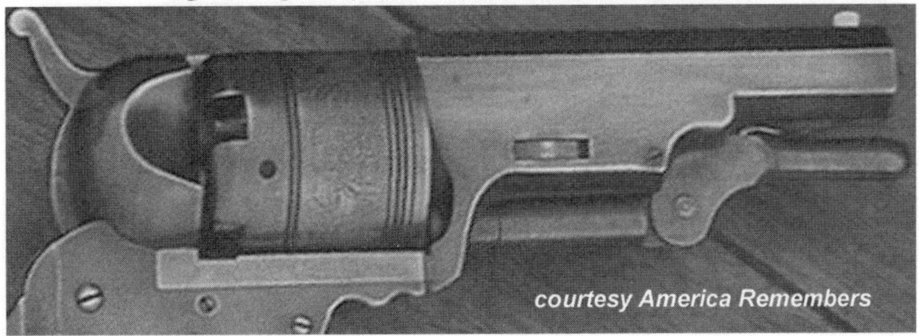
courtesy America Remembers

Add $200 for antique gray or charcoal blue finish.

Last issue price was $1,995.

PATERSON IMPROVED BELT MODEL NO. 2 REVOLVER — .36 cal. perc., high polish blue finish, and charcoal blue finish, Belt Model based on the Ehlers Improved Model No. 2 revolver. The second in America Remembers' new Heritage Series, offering never before reproduced Colt models, the Paterson features the unique Ehlers-type backstrap and grip design, 5 in. octagonal barrel and early Paterson-style loading lever. Hand finished and cased with accessories in a period style French fit, solid walnut presentation box. Edition limited to 100. Offered 2004-2008.

Last issue price was $4,295.

SAMUEL WALKER COLT REVOLVER — .44 cal. perc., deep black finish 3rd Generation Colt Blackpowder Arms Walker embellished with 18Kt. gold bust of Texas Rangers Samuel Walker on the left recoil shield and Walker's signature hand engraved in gold on the left barrel lug, barrel address "US 1847" on the right barrel lug and is hand finished with a case-colored frame and loading lever, high-polished blued barrel and backstrap accented by nitrite blue screws and wedge, Sam Colt signature hand engraved in gold script on backstrap. Edition limited to 100. New 2006. Mfg. by Colt Blackpowder Arms.

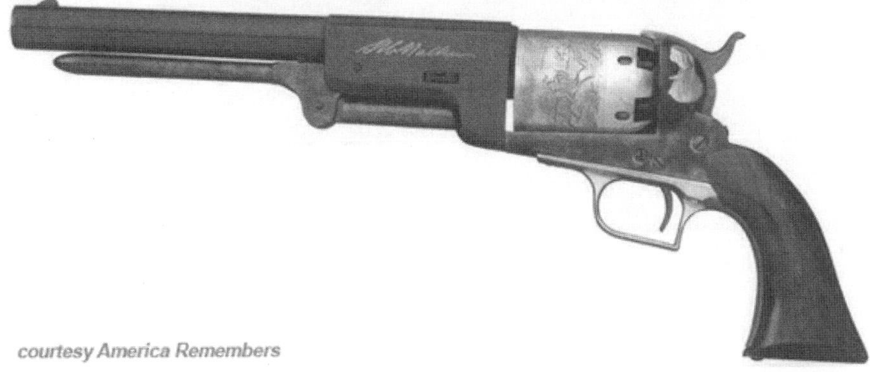
courtesy America Remembers

Current issue price is $3,495.

SPIRIT OF THE AMERICAN INDIAN TRIBUTE REVOLVER — .44 cal. perc., deep black finish 3rd Generation Colt Blackpowder Arms Walker color-case hardened frame and recoil shield, hammer, and loading lever, with all artwork featured in 24Kt. gold and nickel, 24Kt. gold portrait of Sitting Bull and Geronimo on the cylinder and right side frame features a majestic lone buffalo roaming the plains with Indian tepees spanning the distance, left side of the frame is a buffalo hunt with four bison and a pair of hunters on horseback. Edition limited to 300. New 2006. Mfg. by Colt Blackpowder Arms.

Current issue price is $2,195.

TEXAS RANGER DRAGOON — .44 cal. perc., Whitneyville Hartford Dragoon embellished with the portrait of Col. Jack Hayes on the left barrel lug, the barrel bears the legend "TEXAS RANGERS HALL OF FAME AND MUSEUM," silver plated cylinder, backstrap, trigger guard, and medallion inset on the left grip inscribed "Free as the breeze, Swift as a Mustang, Tough as a cactus". Cased with a gold plated 3rd Generation Colt Signature Series powder flask, blue bullet mold, combination tool and Eley Bros. cap tin. Edition limited to 1,000. Mfg. by Uberti. Disc. 2006.

courtesy America Remembers

Last issue price was $1,795.

TEXAS RANGER WALKER COLT REVOLVER — .44 cal. perc., deep black finish 3rd Generation Colt Blackpowder Arms Walker embellished with gold-plated barrel, backstrap and trigger guard, etched 24Kt. gold portraits of legendary Texas Rangers Samuel Walker and John Coffee Hays flank a group photograph dating from the late 1800s on the left barrel lug, portraits of Bill McDonald and William A. Wallace on the right barrel lug, and gold plated figures on the roll engraved cylinder. The gun is further embellished with Texas Rangers etched along the the length of the barrel and the Texas Ranger Hall of Fame and Museum logo on the backstrap along with classic 19th century scroll engraving. Edition limited to 300. Offered 2000-2008. Mfg. by Colt Blackpowder Arms.

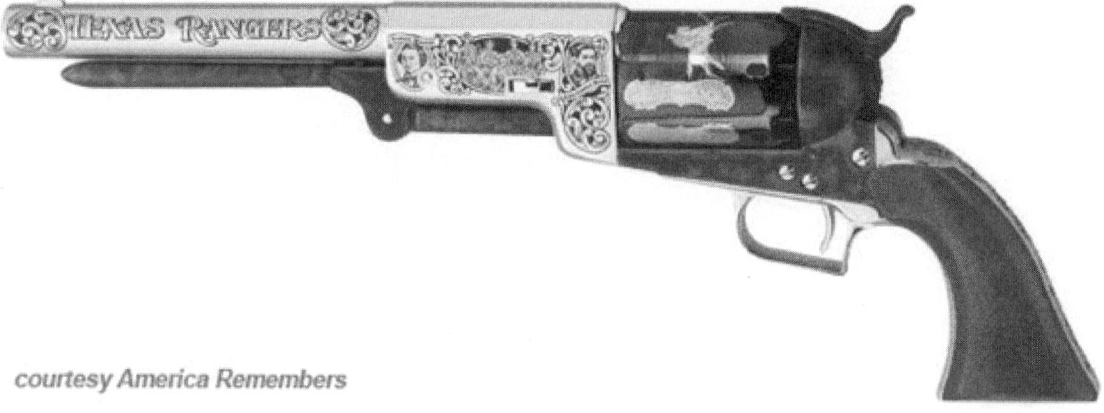

courtesy America Remembers

Last issue price was $2,195.

TEXAN TRIBUTE WALKER REVOLVER — .44 cal. perc., deep black finish Model 1847 Walker revolver embellished with gold-plated barrel, backstrap and trigger guard, etched on the cylinder in 24Kt. gold, the outline of the state of Texas with single star in the center and a Texas longhorn, left side of the frame features portraits of Sam Houston and American folk hero, Davy Crockett, right side of the frame features portraits of Samuel H. Walker and Stephen Austin, on the backstrap is a portrait of William Travis and "The Texan" Edition limited to 200 beginning 2008. Mfg. by Colt Blackpowder Arms.

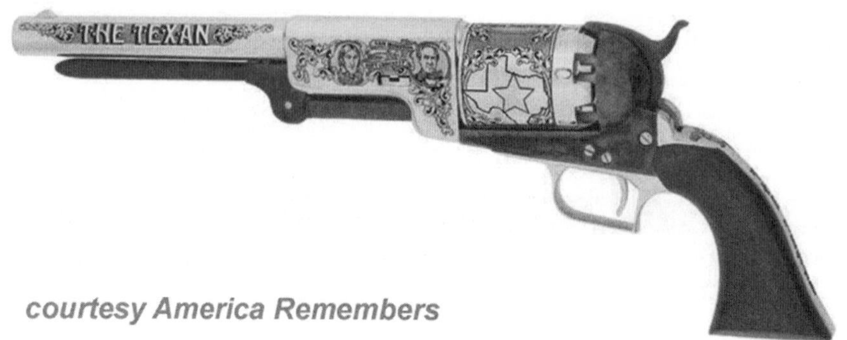

courtesy America Remembers

Current issue price is $2,295.

GRADING - PPGS™	100%	98%	90%	80%

WALKER SESQUICENTENNIAL TRIBUTE REVOLVER — .44 cal. perc., deep black finish, embellished with 24Kt. gold portraits of Sam Colt, Capt. Sam Walker, Eli Whitney, Jr., medallions on the cylinder, banner along barrel, 24Kt. gold-plated backstrap, hammer, trigger guard, ebony grips. Edition limited to 150. Mfg. by Uberti.

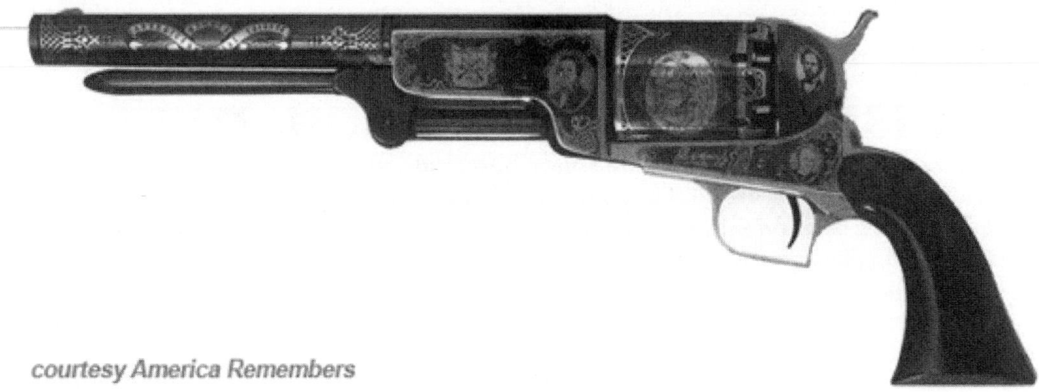

courtesy America Remembers

Current issue price is $1,695.

WHITNEYVILLE HARTFORD SESQUICENTENNIAL DRAGOON — .44 cal. perc., Colt blue finish, nickel silver embellishment with portraits of Sam Colt and Eli Whitney, Jr. on the barrel lugs, Sesquicentennial banner along barrel, action figures on cylinder finished in nickel silver against blue background, Hartford Conn. medallion inset into both grips, vine scroll engraving and eagle's head on backstrap, serial number XXX of 100 engraved on the bottom of the trigger guard. Color case hardened frame, hammer, and loading lever, silver backstrap and trigger guard. Designed by Dennis Adler and America Remembers, and cased in a two-drawer cabinet French fit for the gun, with a pull out drawer containing a signed leather bound and numbered edition of Dennis Adler's book, *Colt Blackpowder Reproductions & Replicas - A Collector's & Shooter's Guide*. Edition limited to 100. Mfg. by Colt Blackpowder Arms Co.

courtesy America Remembers

Last issue price was $1,895.

RIFLES: PERCUSSION

THOMPSON CENTER HISTORIC WHITETAIL MUZZLELOADER — .50 cal. perc. Edition limited to 300. Mfg. by Thompson Center Arms, Co.

Last issue price was $1,495.

MODEL 1853 CONFEDERATE ENFIELD — .58 cal. perc. Edition limited to 500. Mfg. by Armi Sport.

Last issue price was $1,900.

AMERICAN ARMS, INC.

Previous importer and manufacturer located in N. Kansas City, MO, until 2000.

American Arms imported a line of black powder revolvers manufactured by Pietta, and a line of lever action rifles by Uberti. Please refer to the individual manufacturer's listings for pricing. For more information and current pricing on American Arms, Inc. firearms, please refer to the *Blue Book of Gun Values* by S.P. Fjestad (now online also).

RIFLES: IN-LINE IGNITION

HAWKEYE — .50 or .54 cal. perc., 22 in. round blue or stainless steel barrel, dual safety, contemporary-styled design, stock has rubber recoil pad. Disc. 1993.

	100%	98%	90%	80%
	$375	$325	$265	$200

Last MSR was $275.

Add 45% for stainless steel.

AMERICAN FRONTIER FIREARMS MFG., INC.

Previous manufacturer located in Aguanga, CA, 1995-2000.

These were cartridge firing revolvers converted from reproduction Colt and Remington black powder pistols. The guns were hand-assembled and finished from parts specially cast in Italy for American Frontier Firearms. Last produced in 2000. Only available on secondary market. Since these are cartridge firing revolvers converted from black powder reproduction pistols and require an FFL to transfer, these listings have been moved to the *Blue Book of Gun Values* by S.P. Fjestad.

AMERICAN HISTORICAL FOUNDATION, THE

Current private organization which privately commissions historical commemoratives in conjunction with leading manufacturers and craftsmen around the world. The Foundation is currently located in Ashland, VA, previously located in Richmond, VA. During 2005, the assets of the Foundation were acquired by America Remembers, located in Ashland, VA. Consumer direct sales only, via phone, correspondence, or personal visit.

The Foundation's limited edition models are not all manufactured at one time. Rather, guns are fabricated as demand dictates to always keep availability below demand. Please refer to *Colt Blackpowder Reproductions & Replicas - A Collector's & Shooter's Guide* for color pictures of the American Historical Foundation pistols described below.

For more information on The American Historical Foundation firearms, please refer to the *Blue Book of Gun Values* by S.P. Fjestad (now online also).

LIMITED/SPECIAL EDITIONS

Values listed below reflect the Foundation's original or most recent issue prices. These do not necessarily represent secondary marketplace prices. No other values are listed since the Foundation's limited/special editions do not appear that frequently in the secondary marketplace. This is because the Foundation has always sold to consumers directly, without involving normal gun dealers and distributors. Foundation collectors include museums, veterans, and other interested parties who normally keep these items for a considerable time period. Because of this consumer direct sales program, many gun dealers do not have a working knowledge about what AHF models are currently selling for. The publisher suggests that those people owning the Foundation's Commemorative Issue models contact the Foundation (see Trademark Index) for current information, including secondary marketplace liquidity.

REVOLVERS: PERCUSSION

While not specifically mentioned, the revolvers listed below all have various degrees of ornamentation and other embellishments (including some inscriptions). Values listed below do not include original display cases (typically priced between $179 and $395).

BILLY YANK UNION MODEL 1860 ARMY — .44 cal. perc., barrel, cylinder, and frame engraved in Union themes and vine scroll motifs, plated in 24Kt. gold. Edition limited to 250.

Last issue price was $2,695.

THE BLUE AND THE GRAY DRAGOONS — .44 cal. perc., individually cased set offered as "The Blue" and "The Gray." "The Blue" is hand-engraved in the vine scroll motif with a gold inlaid US on the barrel lug, and "E PLURIBUS UNUM" engraved in the barrel. The backstrap and trigger guard are 24Kt. gold plated. Cased with powder flask, combination tool, and bullet mold. The Confederate counterpart, "The Gray" has an antique gray finish with duplicate engraving, except for a Confederate emblem on the barrel lug, and the words "DEO VINDICE" on the barrel. Both models were manufactured by Colt and priced separately.

Last issue price was $2,495.

A second series was also produced with a 24Kt. gold plated Union 3rd Model Dragoon fully engraved, and a silver plated Confederate 2nd Model Dragoon. This pair was issued to commemorate the 125th Anniversary of the Civil War. Priced separately.

COL. J. S. MOSBY MODEL 1860 ARMY — .44 cal. perc., barrel, lug, frame, loading lever, hammer, backstrap and trigger guard fully engraved in vine scroll motif, with Confederate flag engraved above the wedge, Colonel John Singleton Mosby engraved in script along the barrel, 24Kt. gold plated cylinder, hammer, and trigger. Remainder of gun finished in sterling silver. A striking commemorative pistol in a French fit case. Edition limited to 150. Mfg. by Colt.

Last issue price was $2,495.

COLT GOLDEN TRIBUTE MODEL 1847 WALKER — .44 cal. perc., barrel, frame, and barrel lug, loading lever, hammer, trigger guard and backstrap hand engraved in Gustave Young style, entire gun 24Kt. gold plated. In presentation case with spare cylinder, powder flask, bullet mold, and combination tool. Edition limited to 950. Mfg. by Uberti.

Original issue price was $2,195.

Last issue price was $2,495.

COLT GOLDEN TRIBUTE MODEL 1860 ARMY — .44 cal. perc., barrel, lug, frame, loading lever, hammer, backstrap and trigger guard engraved in vine scroll motif and plated in 24Kt. gold. Banner along the barrel inscribed "COLONEL SAMUEL COLT". Edition limited to 950. Mfg. by Colt.

Last issue price was $1,195.

COLT GOLDEN TRIBUTE MODEL 1862 POCKET POLICE — .36 cal. perc., barrel, lug, frame, hammer, backstrap and trigger guard engraved in vine scroll motif and plated in 24Kt. gold. Cased with gold plated bullet mold, powder flask, and combination tool. Edition limited to 950.

Original issue price was $1,895.

Last issue price was $1,795.

GEN. J.E.B. STUART LEMAT — .44 cal. perc. and grapeshot barrels, cylinder, barrels and frame etched in 24Kt. gold with Confederate emblems, scrollwork, crossed sabers, and "GEN. J.E.B. STUART" on the grapeshot barrel. Loading lever, trigger, grip screw, and lanyard ring plated in 24Kt. gold. Edition limited to 500. Mfg. by Navy Arms.

Original issue price was $2,895.

Current issue price is $3,395.

GEN. ROBERT E. LEE MODEL 1851 NAVY — .36 cal. perc., engraved tribute model commemorating the great Confederate military commander. Edition limited to 1,000. Mfg. by Uberti. Disc. 2008.

Original issue price was $2,195.

Last issue price was $3,495.

GEN. THOMAS J. "STONEWALL" JACKSON LEMAT — .44 cal. perc. and grapeshot barrels, cylinder, barrels and frame etched in 24Kt. gold with Confederate emblems, scrollwork, crossed sabers, and "GEN. STONEWALL JACKSON" engraved on the grapeshot barrel. Edition limited to 500. Disc. 2008.

Original issue price was $2,895.

Last issue price was $3,295.

JEFFERSON DAVIS 1851 NAVY WITH SHOULDER STOCK — .36 cal. perc., barrel, frame, barrel lug, loading lever, hammer, trigger guard, backstrap and all metal surfaces of shoulder stock superbly hand engraved in Gustave Young style. Copied from an original 1851 Navy presented to Jefferson Davis by Samuel Colt, when Davis was U.S. Secretary of War in 1858. Available with a full-length gray velvet lined presentation case allowing the gun to be displayed with the shoulder stock attached. The case also provides for a powder flask, bullet mold, combination tool, and two covered compartments for accessories. Edition limited to 250. Mfg. by Uberti.

Add $395 for display case.

Last issue price was $2,995.

JOHNNY REB CONFEDERATE 1851 NAVY — .36 cal. perc., barrel, cylinder, and frame engraved in Confederate themes and vine scroll motifs, plated in sterling silver. Edition limited to 250.

Last issue price was $2,695.

MODEL 1849 WELLS FARGO — .31 cal. perc., barrel, lug, frame, hammer, backstrap and trigger guard fully engraved in vine scroll motif and plated in 24Kt. gold. Excellent relief of the roll engraved cylinder scene. Edition limited to 950. Mfg. by Uberti.

Original issue price was $1,995.

Last issue price was $2,295.

NORTH AND SOUTH LIMITED EDITION DRAGOONS — .44 cal. perc., offered individually and as cased pair in both Collector and Deluxe edition configuration, "The North" is blue finished hand-engraved in the vine scroll motif with a gold inlaid US on the barrel lug, and "E PLURIBUS UNUM" engraved in the barrel. The backstrap and trigger guard are 24Kt. gold plated. Cased with powder flask, combination tool, and bullet mold. "The South" has a smooth French gray finish with duplicate engraving, except for a Confederate emblem on the barrel lug, and the words "DEO VINDICE" on the barrel. Collector edition limited to 250 each mfg. by Uberti and Deluxe edition limited to 50 each mfg. by Colt. Disc. 2008.

Add $1,795 for Collector cased pair (North and South).
Add $1,400 for Deluxe (North or South).
Add $4,595 for Deluxe cased pair (North and South).

Last issue price was $1,795.

TEXAS PATERSON — .36 cal. perc., 9 in. barrel, frame and barrel lug hand engraved in Gustave Young style, entire gun 24Kt. gold plated. In presentation case with spare cylinder, powder charger, circular capper, combination tool and cleaning rod. Edition limited to 950. Mfg. by Pedersoli.

Original issue price was $2,195.

Last issue price was $2,495.

GRADING - PPGS™	100%	98%	90%	80%

WILD BILL HICKOK MODEL 1851 NAVY — .36 cal. perc., hand engraved scrollwork on barrel lug, loading lever, frame, backstrap and trigger guard, silver plated and fitted with engraved ivory stocks; a tribute to the "Prince of Pistoleers." The 1851 Navy was also sold as a pair (Hickok always carried two) displayed in a French fit, glass-top case, with the "Deadman's Hand" (Aces and Eights), and two simulated badges from Hickok's career as a frontier lawman. Edition limited to 500. Guns were priced separately, as was the display case. Mfg. by Uberti.

Current issue price is $1,995.

SHOTGUNS: PERCUSSION

WESTERN OVERLAND STAGE LINE COACH GUN — 10 gauge perc., side-by-side hammer shotgun,13 in. barrel with "From the Atlantic to the Pacific States" etched and selectively plated with 24Kt. gold along the right barrel, 24 in. overall length, 4 lbs. 10 oz. Edition limited to 250. Disc. 2008. Mfg. by Pedersoli.

Last issue price was $2,595.

AMERICAN WESTERN ARMS, INC.

Previous trademark and importer located in Del Ray Beach, FL, previously located in El Paso, Texas. Manufacturing is located in Gardone, Italy, 2000-04. During late 2004, the remaining assets of this company were sold and a new company was established as AWA USA in Hialeah, FL. SAA revolver components were manufactured in the former Armi San Marco factory in Italy (now AWA International, Inc.), and assembled in the U.S. This plant was thoroughly updated during 2000 with all new tooling, stringent quality control, and now has bone-colored case hardening in house. Dealer sales.

American Western Arms, Co. purchased Armi San Marco and formed American Western Arms Italia to manufacture authentic Colt SAA models, and Richards-Mason-type cartridge conversions of the Colt 1851 Navy, 1860 Army, 1861 Navy, and 1872 Open Top. After a short production run, the cartridge conversion models were discontinued in order to increase production of the 1873 Colt Single Action Army.

Since these are cartridge firing revolvers converted from black powder reproduction pistols, and require an FFL to transfer, these listings were moved to the *Blue Book of Gun Values* by S.P. Fjestad. For more information and current pricing on American Western Arms, Inc. firearms, please refer to the *Blue Book of Gun Values* by S.P. Fjestad (now online also).

ARDESA S.A.

Current manufacturer located in Vizcaya, Spain. Currently imported by Traditions Performance Firearms located in Old Saybrook, CT.

Ardesa S.A. manufactures top quality reproductions of famous flintlock and percussion rifles and pistols. They also offer 209 primed in-line ignition rifles and a full line of accessories. Please refer to the Traditions Performance Firearms listing for current information on these models, including U.S. pricing and availability.

ARMI SAN MARCO

Previous manufacturer located in Gardone, Italy, acquired by American Western Arms, Inc. in 2000 and reorganized as American Western Arms, Italia. See American Western Arms Inc. listing. Previously imported by E.M.F., located in Santa Ana, CA, and sold through E.M.F., Traditions, Cabela's, and retail gun stores.

All Armi San Marco black powder cap and ball and cartridge conversion models were discontinued in 2000.

In 1993, the Hartford line was introduced by E.M.F. These models have steel frames with German silver plated backstrap and trigger guard, inspector's cartouche on grip, and trade for approximately $20-$40 higher than standard Armi San Marco versions.

PISTOLS: FLINTLOCK & PERCUSSION

1777 CHARLEVILLE PISTOL — .69 cal. flintlock, 7.5 in. white steel smooth bore barrel, brass furniture, belt hook, walnut stock, 2.75 lbs.

	100%	98%	90%	80%
	$225	**$195**	**$150**	**$125**

SINGLE SHOT PERCUSSION DERRINGER — .31 cal. perc., Colt-style, single shot, 2 in. round brass plated barrel, blue frame, walnut grips. Disc. 2000.

	100%	98%	90%	80%
	$90	**$75**	**$60**	**$50**

Last MSR was $95.

Add 50% for presentation case.

REVOLVERS: PERCUSSION

1847 WALKER MODEL — .44 cal. perc., 9 in. barrel, color case hardened frame, loading lever and hammer, brass trigger guard and steel backstrap, 4.5 lbs. Disc. 2000.

	100%	98%	90%	80%
	$315	**$275**	**$205**	**$175**

Last MSR was $320.

GRADING - PPGS™	100%	98%	90%	80%

1ST MODEL DRAGOON — .44 cal. perc., 8 in. barrel, color case hardened frame, loading lever and hammer, silver plated backstrap and trigger guard. Disc.

	$295	$260	$195	$160

2ND MODEL DRAGOON — similar to 1st Model Dragoon, except 7.5 in. barrel. Disc. 2000.

	$295	$260	$195	$160

Last MSR was $304.

3RD MODEL DRAGOON — .44 cal. perc., 7.5 in. barrel, Western Model has silver plated brass backstrap, Military Model has steel backstrap - cut for stock, Texas Model has brass backstrap. Disc. 2000.

	$295	$260	$195	$160

Last MSR was $312.

Add 10% for Western Model.

1849 WELLS FARGO — .31 cal. perc., 3 in., 4 in., 5 in. octagon barrel, 5 shot, color case hardened frame and hammer, no loading lever, brass trim, 1.5 lbs. Disc.

	$265	$240	$180	$150

1851 NAVY — .36 or .44 cal. perc., 7.5 in. octagon barrel, (roll) engraved cylinder, color case hardened frame and loading lever, silver plated brass backstrap and square back trigger guard. Sheriff's Model has 5 in. barrel, brass trigger guard and backstrap. Disc. 2000.

	$225	$200	$150	$125

Last MSR was $192.

Subtract 5% for brass back strap and trigger guard.
Subtract 5% for brass frame.
Add 50% for engraved steel frame.
Add 80% for shoulder stock.

1860 ARMY — .44 cal. perc., 8 in. round barrel, color case hardened frame, hammer and loading lever, Sheriff's Model has 5 in. barrel, 2.75 lbs. Disc. 2000.

	$250	$220	$165	$135

Last MSR was $216.

Add 5% for Sheriff's Model.
Add 25% for fluted cylinder model.
Add 50% for engraved steel.
Add 65% for stock.
Subtract 20% for brass frame.

1861 NAVY — .36 cal. perc., 7.5 in. round barrel, color case hardened frame, hammer and loading lever, silver-plated brass backstrap and trigger guard (very similar to 1860 Army, except cal. and shorter Navy grips). Disc. 2000.

	$225	$200	$150	$125

Last MSR was $248.

1862 POLICE POCKET — .36 cal. perc., 4.5, 5.5, or 6.5 in. barrel, color case hardened steel frame, hammer and loading lever or brass frame, cylinder semi-fluted or engraved, 1.6 lbs. Disc. 2000.

	$225	$200	$150	$125

Last MSR was $248.

Subtract 30% for brass frame model.

1858 REMINGTON ARMY — .44 cal. perc., 6 shot, 8 in. octagon barrel, brass frame, trigger guard and backstrap, walnut grips, 2.38 lbs. Disc. 2000.

	$225	$200	$150	$125

Last MSR was $176.

Add 100% for stainless steel target model.
Add 80% for engraving on brass frame.
Add 25% for steel frame.
Add 80% for 12 in. barrel Buffalo Target Model.

RIFLES: PERCUSSION

HAWKEN RIFLE — .45, .50, .54, or .58 cal. perc., color case hardened hammer and lock, brass patch box. Disc. 2000.

	$295	$260	$195	$165

Last MSR was $325.

GRADING - PPGS™	100%	98%	90%	80%

ST. LOUIS HAWKEN — .50, .54, or .58 cal. perc., color case hardened hammer and lock, 28 in. octagon barrel, brass trim, 7 lbs. 15 oz.

	$340	$295	$225	$190

Add 25% for curly maple stock.

ROCKY MOUNTAIN SHORT RIFLE — .50 cal. perc., 24 in. octagon barrel, brass furniture.

	$295	$260	$195	$165

ARMI SAN PAOLO S.r.l.

Previous trademark previously named Armi San Paolo beginning 1971 and originally located in San Paolo, Italy. Armi San Paolo S.r.l. currently located in Concesio, Italy, changed its name to Euroarms Italia S.r.l. in January 2002. Euroarms Italia S.r.l. (formerly Armi San Paolo) also owns Euroarms of America and is currently imported by Cabela's, located in Sydney, NE, Euroarms of America located in Winchester, VA, Dixie Gun Works, Inc. located in Union City, IN, and Navy Arms Co. located in Union City, NJ. Previously imported by Kendall International located in Paris, KY, and Muzzle Loaders, Inc. located in Burke, VA. Available through dealers and catalog houses. See the Euroarms Italia S.r.l. section for current model pricing.

The origin of Armi San Paolo can be traced back to 1957 when two young Americans asked Luciano Amadi to reproduce the original 1851 Colt Navy revolver. Val Forgett, Sr., a businessman in the firearms field, and William B. Edwards, the technical editor of *Guns* magazine, were in Europe as part of an American gun tour, and in search of a manufacturer for black powder reproductions and replicas. At that time, Luciano Amadi was employed at Beretta, and assisted a group of Indonesian military officers who resided in Gardone VT, Italy, for three years to follow up a commitment of 55,000 M1 Garands for their government. He was also one of the few people at the plant who could speak English at the time. During dinner with Forgett and Edwards while in Gardone, plans were made to go ahead with the project.

It took Mr. Amadi many months to import an original Colt 1851 Navy, and even more time to find an Italian manufacturer willing to accept this new manufacturing proposal. Vittorio Gregorelli, who owned a parts supply company making components for Beretta firearms in Brescia, was not licensed to manufacture guns at the time, and finally believed in the project when Mr. Amadi presented him with an initial order for 250 Colt 1851 Navy revolvers. A $500 check started the tooling process! During this same time period, Aldo Uberti, also a previous Beretta employee, began manufacturing black powder reproductions in Gardone, next to Brescia. Uberti records indicate that the first Uberti model was returned from the Italian proof house on Oct. 14th, 1959. By 1959, the black powder reproduction and replica industry was already off to a good start in Italy, and Gregorelli was followed by Davide Pedersoli, who started producing muzzle loading replicas in 1960-1961, when Amadi presented him with a Kentucky pistol to replicate.

In the early 1960s Giacomo Grassi, Giuseppe Doninelli, along with a person named Gazzola, were involved in a company manufacturing small caliber semi-auto pistols called Gradoga. In 1971, when Gradoga closed, Giacomo Grassi and Giuseppe Doninelli joined Luciano Amadi (who already had a small gun trading company) to form Armi San Paolo in a small town 25 Km south of Brescia called San Paolo. Armi San Paolo grew to employ approx. 60 people, and Euroarms of America Inc. was formed in Winchester, VA, to distribute all Armi San Paolo products. In 1987, the replica market shrank, and Armi San Paolo started the move from San Paolo, Italy to Concesio, Italy with the move being completed during 1990.

ARMI SPORT (ARMI CHIAPPA)

Current manufacturer established in 1958, and located in Brescia, Italy. Currently imported by Chiappa Firearms, Ltd. located in Dayton, OH. Currently distributed by Cimarron F.A. Co. located in Fredericksburg, TX, Collector's Armoury, Ltd. located in Lorton, VA, I.A.R. Inc. located in San Juan Capistrano, CA, KBI Inc. located in Harrisburg, PA, Maxsell Corp. located in Coconut Creek, FL, Taylor's & Co., Inc., located in Winchester, VA, Traditions Inc. located in Old Saybrook, CT, and Valor Corp. located in Sunrise, FL. Previously distributed until 2009 by E.M.F. Company Inc., located in Santa Ana, CA.

Armi Sport manufactures top quality reproductions of famous rifles/carbines. Please refer to the distributors' listings for current information on these models, including U.S. pricing and availability. For more information and current pricing on both new and used Armi Sport firearms, please refer to the *Blue Book of Gun Values* by S.P. Fjestad (now online also).

ARMSPORT, INC.

Previous importer located in Miami, FL. Previously available through dealers and distributors.

GRADING - PPGS™	100%	98%	90%	80%

CANNONS

BORDA MODEL — .50 cal., wick ignition, nickel plated. Disc. 1994.

	$230	$200	$150	$125

Last MSR was $195.

Add 40% for gold plating.

NAPOLEON MODEL — .45, .50, .69, or .75 cal., wick ignition, nickel plated. Disc. 1994.

	$500	$445	$335	$275

Last MSR was $525.

Add 25% for gold plating.
Add 35% for .75 cal.
Add 30% for .69 cal.

YORKTOWN MODEL — .50 cal., wick ignition, nickel plated. Disc. 1994.

	$230	$200	$150	$125

Last MSR was $195.

Add 50% for gold plating.

PISTOLS: FLINTLOCK & PERCUSSION

CORSAIR MODEL — .44 cal. perc. double barrel, blue finish, color case hardened hammer and lock, brass trim.

	$295	$260	$195	$165

DUELING MODEL — .45 cal. perc., blue finish, color case hardened hammer and lock, brass trim.

	$245	$215	$165	$130

KENTUCKY MODEL — .45 or .50 cal. perc. or flintlock, blue finish, color case hardened hammer and lock, brass trim.

	$210	$185	$135	$115

Add 5% for flintlock.

REVOLVERS: PERCUSSION

1847 WALKER — .44 cal. perc., color case hardened frame, hammer, and loading lever, brass trigger guard, steel backstrap, 6 shot, 4.5 lbs.

	$315	$275	$210	$175

Last MSR was $305.

1851 NAVY — .36 or .44 cal. perc., brass or color case hardened frame, brass trigger guard and backstrap, 6 shot.

	$225	$200	$150	$125

Last MSR was $160.

Add 40% for color case hardened steel with engraved cylinders.
Add 100% for engraved gold and nickel.

1858 REMINGTON ARMY — .44 cal. perc., blue frame, brass trigger guard, steel backstrap, 6 shot.

	$225	$200	$150	$125

Last MSR was $230.

Add $115 for stainless steel.
Add $90 for engraved gold and silver.
Add $25 for Target Model.
Subtract $25 for brass frame.
Subtract $30 for nickel plated brass.

1860 ARMY — .44 cal. perc., brass frame, trigger guard, and backstrap, color case hardened hammer and loading lever, 6 shot.

	$250	$220	$165	$140

Last MSR was $165.

Add 40% for color case hardened steel.
Add 110% for stainless steel.
Add 80% for engraved gold and silver.
Add 30% for steel Sheriff Model.

GRADING - PPGS™	100%	98%	90%	80%

REMINGTON BUFFALO TARGET — .44 cal. perc., 12 in. octagon barrel, brass frame and trigger guard, adj. sights, based on 1858 Army frame, 38 oz.

	$250	$220	$165	$140

Last MSR was $220.

Add $10 for nickel plated brass.

REMINGTON POCKET — .31 cal. perc., 5 shot, 4 in. octagon barrel, brass frame, 15 oz. Disc. 1994.

	$200	$180	$135	$115

Last MSR was $160.

RIFLES: FLINTLOCK & PERCUSSION

BRISTOL KID RIFLE — .32 or .36 cal. perc. Disc. 1984.

	$225	$195	$145	$115

Add $15 for standard version, $25 for deluxe.

HAWKEN RIFLE — .45, .50, .54, or .58 cal. perc. or flintlock, color case hardened hammer and lock, percussion cap holder in stock, chrome-lined barrels.

	$425	$375	$275	$225

Add $25 for flintlock.

HAWKENTUCKY RIFLE — .36 or .50 cal. perc. or flintlock, color case hardened hammer and lock, percussion cap holder in stock, chrome-lined barrels.

	$375	$335	$245	$210

Add $10 for flintlock.

KENTUCKY RIFLE — .36, .45, or .50, cal. perc. or flintlock, color case hardened hammer and lock, percussion cap holder in stock, chrome-lined barrels, brass trim.

	$350	$295	$225	$185

Add $10 for flintlock.
Add $55 for deluxe with engraved white steel hammer and lock.

SHARPS RIFLE/CARBINE — .45 or .54 cal. perc., 22 (carbine) or 28 in. barrel. Mfg. by Industria Armi Bresciane. New 1992.

	$585	$520	$390	$325

Last MSR was $750.

Add $25 for 28 in. octagon barrel.

TRYON BACK ACTION RIFLE — .50 or .54 cal. perc., 28 and 30 in. barrel. Mfg. 1992-94.

	$610	$540	$405	$335

Last MSR was $825.

Add $55 for silver finish.

TRYON TRAILBLAZER — .50 or .54 cal. perc., color case hardened hammer and lock, cap holder in stock.

	$450	$395	$295	$245

Add $45 for deluxe engraved.

SHOTGUNS: PERCUSSION

KENTUCKY RIFLE/SHOTGUN COMBO — .45 or .50 cal. perc., 20 ga., similar to Kentucky Rifle.

	$475	$420	$315	$260

SxS SHOTGUN — 12 or 10 ga. perc., blue finish, color case hardened hammer and lock.

	$425	$375	$275	$225

Add $20 for 10 ga.

ARMSPORT LLC

Current customizer located in Platteville, CO.

Gunsmith R.L. Millington specializes in authentic, hand-built conversions of Colt and Remington black powder pistols to metallic cartridge, custom engraving, refinishing, and antique refinishing. Antiquing and period-style engraving are available. Contact ArmSport LLC (see Trademark Index) directly for current pricing and availability. Since these are cartridge firing revolvers converted from black powder revolvers, and require an FFL to transfer, they are not covered in this book.

GRADING - PPGS™	100%	98%	90%	80%

ARTAX S.r.l.

Current manufacturer located in Cellatica, Italy. Please contact the company directly (see Trademark Index) for information on pricing and availability.

ARTAX S.r.l. manufactures reproduction matchlock, flintlock and percussion muzzle loading handguns and rifles.

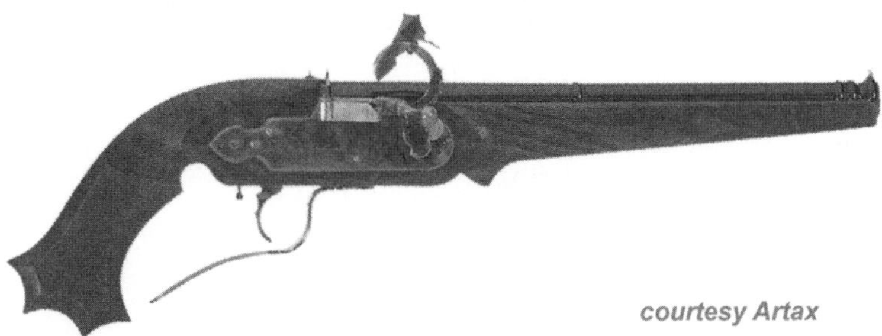

courtesy Artax

ASSOCIATION FOR THE PRESERVATION OF WESTERN ANTIQUITY

Previously distributed by William Benjamin Ltd. located in Ashville, NC.

REVOLVERS: PERCUSSION

1862 COLT NAVY — .36 cal. perc., standard construction, roll engraved cylinder with 24Kt. gold inlay, only 100 revolvers made, sold in custom cameo art presentation case depicting a miner panning for gold. Some sets also contained a seated Liberty silver dollar and a $20 Double Eagle gold piece. Disc. 1994.

	100%	98%	90%	80%
	$825	**$675**	**$530**	**$400**

Last MSR was $995.

The coins values should be based on current numismatic pricing.

AUSTIN & HALLECK GUN CRAFTERS

Previous manufacturer located in Provo, UT, Austin & Halleck announced the suspension of operations effective 10/01/06. Previously located in Weston, MO, until 2002. Consumer and dealer sales.

During 2006 and 2007, Austin & Halleck, Inc. liquidated remaining inventory. During early 2004, Austin & Halleck, Inc. was purchased by North American Arms, Inc. located in Provo, UT. Austin & Halleck, Inc. added (during late 2003) expanded service, support, and a full custom shop offering a variety of custom barrels, finishes, stocks, and accessories.

RIFLES: FLINTLOCKS & PERCUSSION

MOUNTAIN RIFLE FLINTLOCK — .50 cal. flintlock, 32 in. octagon barrel, double throw adj. set triggers, curly maple stock, slow rust brown furniture and barrel finish, fixed buck horn rear and silver blade w/brass base front sights, 1:66 in. twist for round ball or 1:28 in. twist for bullets, 49 in. OAL, 7.5 lbs. Disc. Nov. 2006.

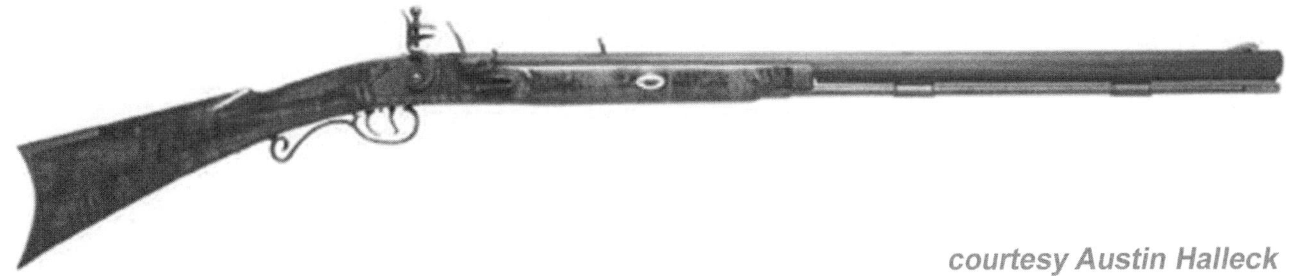

courtesy Austin Halleck

	100%	98%	90%	80%
	$575	**$495**	**$395**	**$295**

Last MSR was $589.

Add $180 for Hand Select (75% plus figure) grade stock.

GRADING - PPGS™	100%	98%	90%	80%

MOUNTAIN RIFLE PERCUSSION — .50 cal. perc., 32 in. octagon barrel, double throw adj. set triggers, curly maple stock, slow rust brown furniture and barrel finish, fixed buck horn rear and silver blade with brass base front sights, 1:66 in. twist for round ball or 1:28 in. twist for bullets, 49 in. OAL, 7.5 lbs. Disc. November 2006.

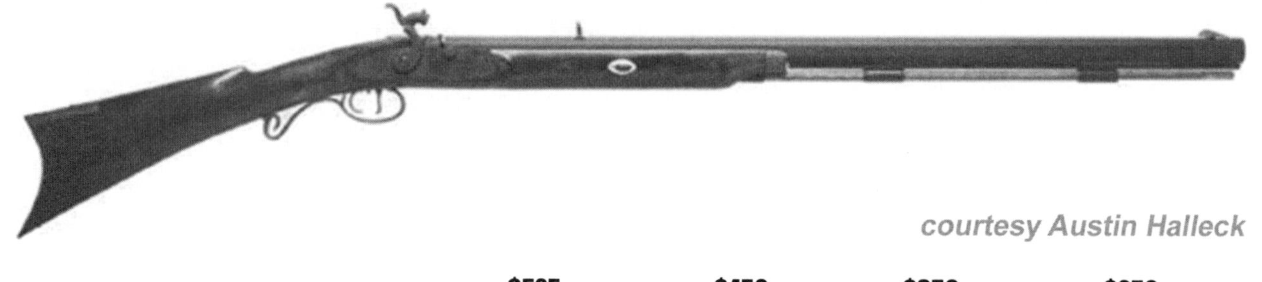
courtesy Austin Halleck

	$525	$450	$350	$250

Last MSR was $539.

Add $180 for Hand Select (75% plus figure) grade stock.

RIFLES: IN-LINE IGNITION

Beginning in 2004 all bolt action in-line rifles came with a Bold™ fully adjustable match grade trigger and the new universal hammer allowing the use of 209 primers, musket, or standard No. 11 percussion caps for ignition by simply changing the percussion nipple to a 209 primer adapter. Also beginning 2004 each Model 420 rifle was supplied with a complimentary composite hunting stock.

MODEL 320 LR BLU — .45 (new 2005) or .50 cal.,Universal Hammer 3-Way (new 2004) perc. ignition, 26 in. octagon to tapered round barrel, high polish blue finish, adj. rear and fixed front Tru-Glo fiber optic sights, drilled and tapped for scope mounting, Bold™ (new 2004) adj. match grade trigger w/trigger block safety, black, Realtree-Hardwoods High Definition Green (new 2004) or Brown, Realtree Max 4 (new 2004), Rocky Mountain camo (new 2004), Mossy Oak Breakup, or Mothwing (Woodland, Canyon, or Winter) Mimicry (new 2006) checkered synthetic stock, black 1 in. recoil pad, 1:28 in. twist, 47.5 in. OAL, 7.88 lbs. Disc. Nov. 2006.

courtesy Austin Halleck

	$385	$335	$255	$180

Last MSR was $419.

Add $40 for Realtree-Hardwood High Definition Green (new 2004) or Brown stock.
Add $40 for Realtree Max 4 stock (new 2004).
Add $40 for Mossy Oak Breakup stock (new 2003).
Add $40 for Rocky Mountain Camo stock (new 2004).
Add $40 for Mothwing (Woodland, Canyon, or Winter) Mimicry stock (new 2006).

MODEL 320 LR S/N — .45 (new 2005) or .50 cal. Universal Hammer 3-Way (new 2004) perc. ignition, similar to Model 320 LR BLU, except electroless nickel finish, 7.88 lbs. Disc. November 2006.

courtesy Austin Halleck

	$415	$355	$285	$205

Last MSR was $449.

Add $40 for Realtree-Hardwood High Definition Green (new 2004) or Brown stock.
Add $40 for Realtree Max 4 stock (new 2004).
Add $40 for Mossy Oak Breakup stock (new 2003).
Add $40 for Rocky Mountain Camo stock (new 2004).
Add $40 for Mothwing (Woodland, Canyon, or Winter) Mimicry stock (new 2006).

GRADING - PPGS™	100%	98%	90%	80%

MODEL 420 LR CLASSIC BLU — .45 (new 2005) or .50 cal. Universal Hammer 3-Way (new 2004) perc. ignition, 26 in. octagon to tapered round barrel, adj. rear and fixed front Tru-Glo fiber optic sights, drilled and tapped for scope mounting, Bold™ (new 2004) adj. match grade trigger w/trigger block safety, checkered fancy grade maple flat comb stock, 1 in. recoil pad, 1:28 in twist, 47.5 in. OAL, 7.88 lbs. Disc. November 2006.

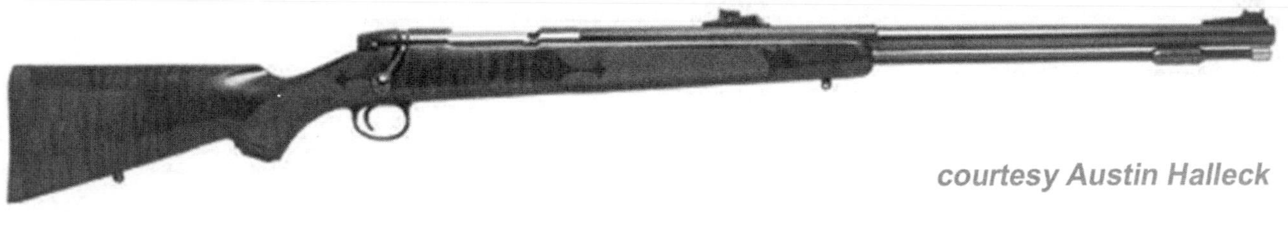

courtesy Austin Halleck

	$515	$465	$385	$305

Last MSR was $549.

Add $160 for Hand Select grade wood.
Add $450 for Exhibition grade wood.

Austin & Halleck, Inc. disc. publishing Exhibition grade wood prices beginning 2004.

MODEL 420 LR CLASSIC S/N — .45 (new 2005) or .50 cal. Universal Hammer 3-Way (new 2004) perc. ignition, similar to Model 420 LR Classic, except electroless nickel-plated finish, 7.88 lbs. Disc. November, 2006.

courtesy Austin Halleck

	$525	$485	$410	$320

Last MSR was $579.

Add $160 for Hand Select grade wood.
Add $450 for Exhibition grade wood.

Austin & Halleck, Inc. disc. publishing Exhibition grade wood prices beginning 2004.

MODEL 420 LR MONTE CARLO — .45 (new 2005) or .50 cal. Universal Hammer 3-Way (new 2004) perc. ignition, 26 in. octagon to tapered round barrel, adj. rear and fixed front Tru-Glo fiber optic sights, drilled and tapped for scope mounting, Bold™ (new 2004) adj. match grade trigger w/trigger block safety, checkered fancy grade maple Monte Carlo stock, 1 in. recoil pad, 1:28 in. twist, 47.5 in.OAL,7.88 lbs. Disc. November 2006.

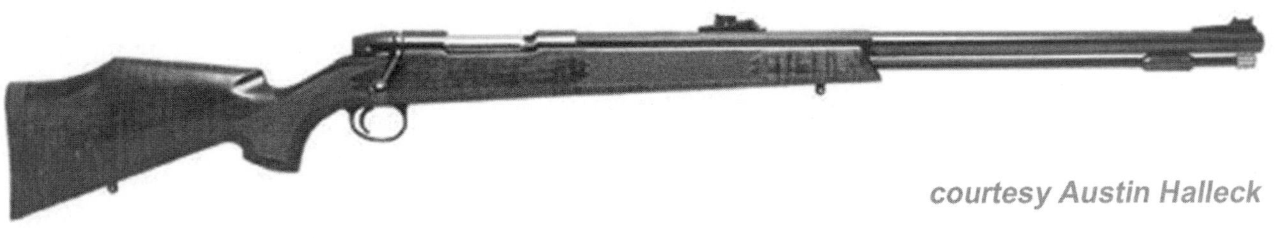

courtesy Austin Halleck

	$515	$465	$385	$305

Last MSR was $549.

Add $160 for Hand Select grade wood.
Add $450 for Exhibition grade wood.

Austin & Halleck, Inc. disc. publishing Exhibition grade wood prices beginning 2004.

GRADING - PPGS™	100%	98%	90%	80%

MODEL 420 LR MONTE CARLO S/N — .45 (new 2005) or .50 cal. Universal Hammer 3-Way (new 2004) perc. ignition, similar to Model 420 LR Monty Carlo, except electroless nickel-plated finish, 7.88 lbs. Disc. November 2006.

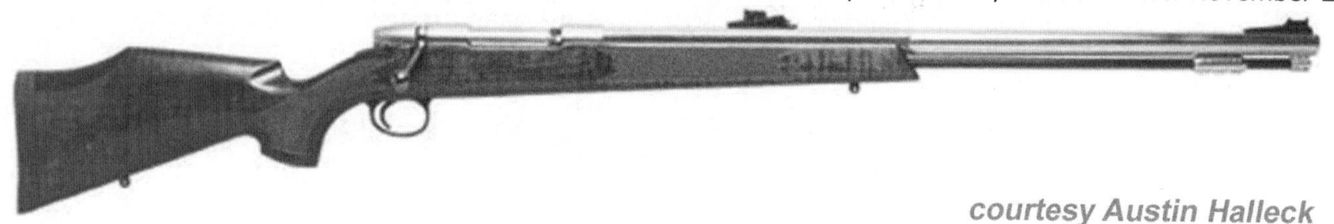

courtesy Austin Halleck

	$525	$485	$410	$320

Last MSR was $579.

Add $160 for Hand Select grade wood.
Add $450 for Exhibition grade wood.

Austin & Halleck, Inc. disc. publishing Exhibition grade wood prices beginning 2004.

MODEL 694 AMERICAN CLASSIC — .45 or .50 cal., lever action, Universal Hammer 3-Way perc. ignition, 22 in. round barrel, Black Ice Teflon finish, adj. rear and fixed front Tru-Glo fiber optic sights, A&H Bush Country trigger w/ trigger block safety, Boyd's walnut or maple satin finish stock, black 1 in. vented recoil pad, 1:24 in. twist, 39.5 in. OAL, 6.7 lbs. While advertised during 2006 with a MSR of $599, this model did not reach production.

SHOTGUNS: IN-LINE IGNITION

MODEL 520 MUZZLELOADING SHOTGUN — 12 gauge, inline perc. ignition, 26 in. round straight tapered cromemoly barrel with vented rib and screw in chokes, Black Ice Teflon finish, Tru-Glo fiber optic front sight, Bold™ (new 2004) adj. match grade trigger w/trigger block safety, Boyd's Classic satin luster finish stock w/GET (grip enhancement technology), black 1 in. recoil pad, 47.5 in. OAL, 6.5 lbs. Mfg. 2006.

	$515	$465	$385	$305

Last MSR was $549.

AWA USA INC.

Current importer established during late 2004 and located in Hialeah, FL.

AWA USA Inc. purchased the remaining assets of American Western Arms, Inc. in late 2004. Please contact the company directly for more information, including current model lineup and retail pricing (see Trademark Index). For more information and current pricing on AWA USA Inc. firearms, please refer to the *Blue Book of Gun Values* by S.P. Fjestad (available online also).

GRADING - PPGS™	100%	98%	90%	80%

B SECTION

BARTLETT, FRANK

Current contemporary longrifle artisan located in Gallatin, TN.

Frank Bartlett specializes in transitional designs between the German Jaeger and the American Kentucky longrifle. Rifles are typically engraved in script on the top flat, "F. Bartlett" framed on either side by two digits of the year manufactured (i.e. 19 F. Bartlett 87) and followed by the rifles number. Values will range from $2,500-$7,500.

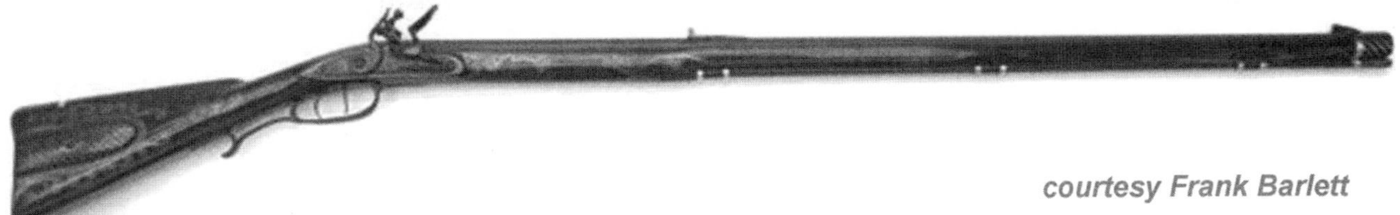

courtesy Frank Barlett

BENSON FIREARMS, LTD.

Previous importer/distributor of A. Uberti reproductions and replicas 1987-1989, located in Seattle, WA. All reproductions and replicas were manufactured in Gardone, Italy.

Benson Firearms imported A. Uberti models that were marked "Benson Firearms Seattle, WA." In 1989, Benson Firearms, Ltd. combined with Uberti USA, Inc. located in New Milford, CT.

All reproductions and replicas were manufactured to the same exact specifications as the original models. Crafted with an unmistakable fire blue finish. See similar models from A. Uberti for current Benson pricing.

BERETTA

Current manufacturer located in Brescia, Italy, 1526-present. Imported exclusively by Beretta U.S.A. Corp. since 1980. Beretta U.S.A. Corp. was formed in 1977 and is located in Accokeek, MD. 1970-1977 manufacture was imported exclusively by Garcia. Distributor and dealer direct sales.

Beretta is one of the world's oldest family owned industrial firms, having started business in 1526. In addition to Beretta owning Benelli & Franchi, the company also purchased Sako and Tikka Companies in late 1999, Aldo Uberti & Co. in 2000, and Burris Optics in 2002. For more information and current pricing on both new and used Beretta firearms, please refer to the *Blue Book of Gun Values* by S.P. Fjestad (now online also).

SHOTGUNS: PERCUSSION, O/U

TRICENTENNIAL COMMEMORATIVE MODEL M1000 — 12 ga. perc., 30 in. O/U barrels, hand-engraved locks, hammers, and trigger guard, blue, bright, or case-color finish with brown barrels, walnut straight grip stock and forearm, two barrel bands, sling swivels, metal buttplate, 47 in. OAL, 7 lbs. 300 mfg. 1980-1994.

	100%	98%	90%	80%
	$825	**$695**	**$575**	**$465**

Last MSR was $840.

BLACK HART LONG ARMS

Current custom long arm manufacturer located in Eastford, CT.

Ed Parry has honed the skills necessary to create handcrafted copies of long arms originally created in 1740-1840 by master Pennsylvanian gunsmiths, such as J.P Beck, John Bonewitz, Adam Ernest, Frederick Sell, and others with base rifle prices starting in the $2,500 range. Please contact Mr. Parry directly (see Trademark Index for contact information) for price and availability of arms.

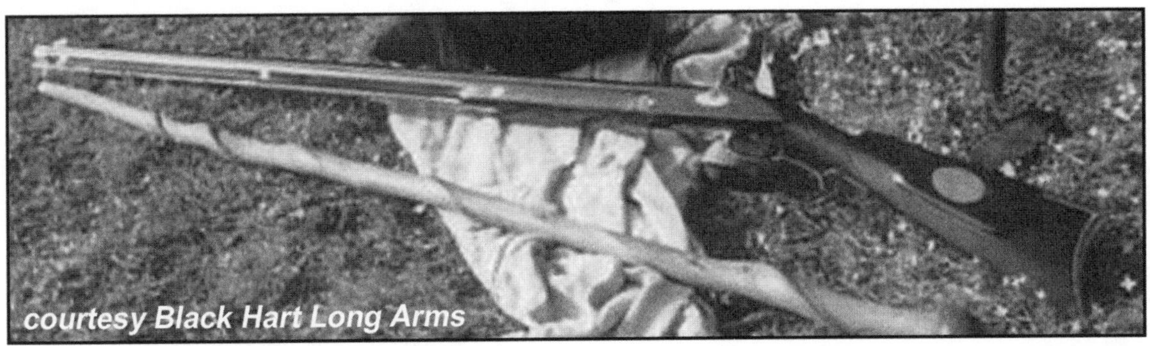

courtesy Black Hart Long Arms

GRADING - PPGS™	100%	98%	90%	80%

BONDINI

Previous manufacturer located in Italy. Previously imported by Helmut Hofman, Inc. located in Placitas, NH, House Of Muskets located in Pagosa Lakes, CO, and Austin-Sheridan, USA, located in Middlefield, CT.

PISTOLS: FLINTLOCK & PERCUSSION

ASHABELLA COOK UNDERHAMMER — .45 cal. perc., unique underhammer design uses trigger guard as mainspring.

	$250	$190	$135	$95

WM. PARKER PISTOL — .45 cal. flintlock or perc., 11 in. octagon brown barrel, silver-plated furniture, double set triggers.

	$325	$285	$205	$145

Add 10% for flintlock.

F. ROCHATTE — .45 cal. perc., round barrel, single set trigger, hand checkered stock.

	$280	$200	$145	$100

RIFLES: PERCUSSION

SANFTL SCHUETZEN RIFLE — .45 cal. perc., 31 in. octagon barrel, unique backward lock, both aperture and open iron sights, Schuetzen style buttplate and trigger guard, brass furniture.

	$850	$695	$550	$400

SHOTGUNS: PERCUSSION

GALLYON SHOTGUN — 12 ga., perc., blue barrel, single shot.

	$330	$255	$195	$155

Add $150 for extra 12 ga. barrel.

BRENNAN, JUDSON

Current contemporary longrifle master gunmaker located in Delta Junction, AK.

Mr. Brennan is a master artisan that still learns by studying fine guns, from the finest wheellock guns up to percussion target rifles. Favorites are flintlocks of the 1700's, fine Germans, Jagers, English and French guns of the period. Mr. Brennan defines himself as a "new school" gunmaker. Brennan flintlock rifles have sold in the high five figures. Please contact Mr. Brennan directly (see contact listing in Trademark Index) regarding availability.

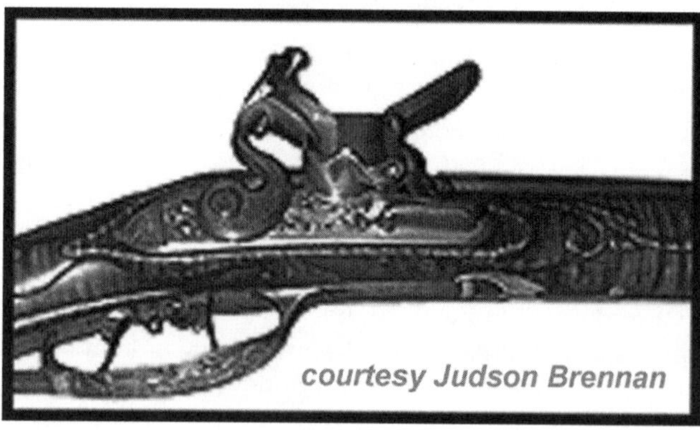

courtesy Judson Brennan

GRADING - PPGS™	100%	98%	90%	80%

BROOKS, JACK

Current contemporary longrifle master gunmaker located in Englewood, CO. Please contact Mr. Brooks directly (see contact listing in Trademark Index) regarding style of longrifle making expertise and availability.

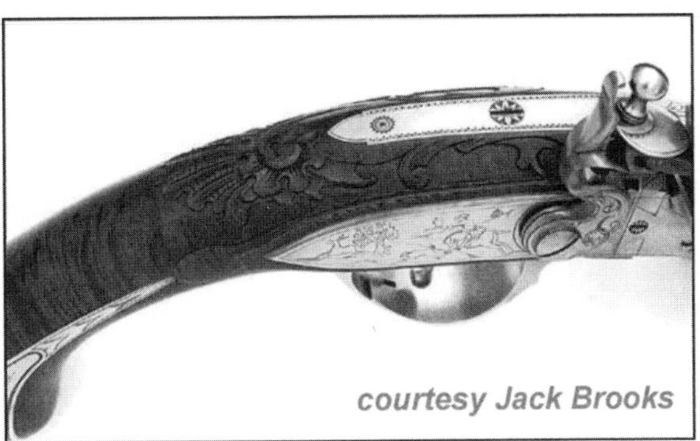
courtesy Jack Brooks

BROWNING

Current manufacturer/importer with headquarters located in Morgan, UT. Browning guns originally were manufactured in Ogden, UT, circa 1880. Browning firearms are manufactured by Fabrique Nationale in Herstal and Liege, Belgium. Since 1976, Browning has also contracted Miroku of Japan and A.T.I. in Salt Lake City, UT, to manufacture both long arms and handguns. In 1992, Browning (including F.N.) was acquired by GIAT of France. During late 1997, the French government received $82 million for the sale of F.N. Herstal from the Walloon business region surrounding Fabrique Nationale in Belgium.

For more information and current pricing on both new and used Browning firearms, please refer to the *Blue Book of Gun Values* by S.P. Fjestad (now online also).

RIFLES: PERCUSSION

JONATHAN BROWNING MOUNTAIN RIFLE — .45 or .54 cal. perc., similar to Jonathan Browning Mountain Rifle, without Centennial embellishments, not cased.

	100%	98%	90%	80%
	$750	$595	$265	$385

JONATHAN BROWNING CENTENNIAL MOUNTAIN RIFLE — .50 cal. perc., 30 in. octagon barrel, single set trigger, engraved lock plate, select walnut stock, cased with medallion and powder horn. 1,000 mfg. in 1978.

courtesy Browning

	100%	98%	90%	80%
	$1,150	$795	$645	$495

Last MSR was $650.

BRUMFIELD, GARY

Current semi-retired contemporary longrifle master gunsmith located in Williamsburg, VA.

Mr. Brumfield finished building his first flintlock rifle in about 1962. That first rifle was for a customer. His second rifle was relief carved in the style of the J. Hoak rifle pictured in *Thoughts on the Kentucky Rifle in its Golden Age [1960]* and had a shop made lock that was largely sawn from steel by hand. The stock architecture was inspired by 19th century eastern PA rifles and the patch box was based on "Kettering, Allison and Others" rifles from the Pittsburg/Ohio River area. Please contact Mr. Brumfield directly (see contact listing in Trademark Index) regarding availability.

NOTES

BRUMFIELD, GARY

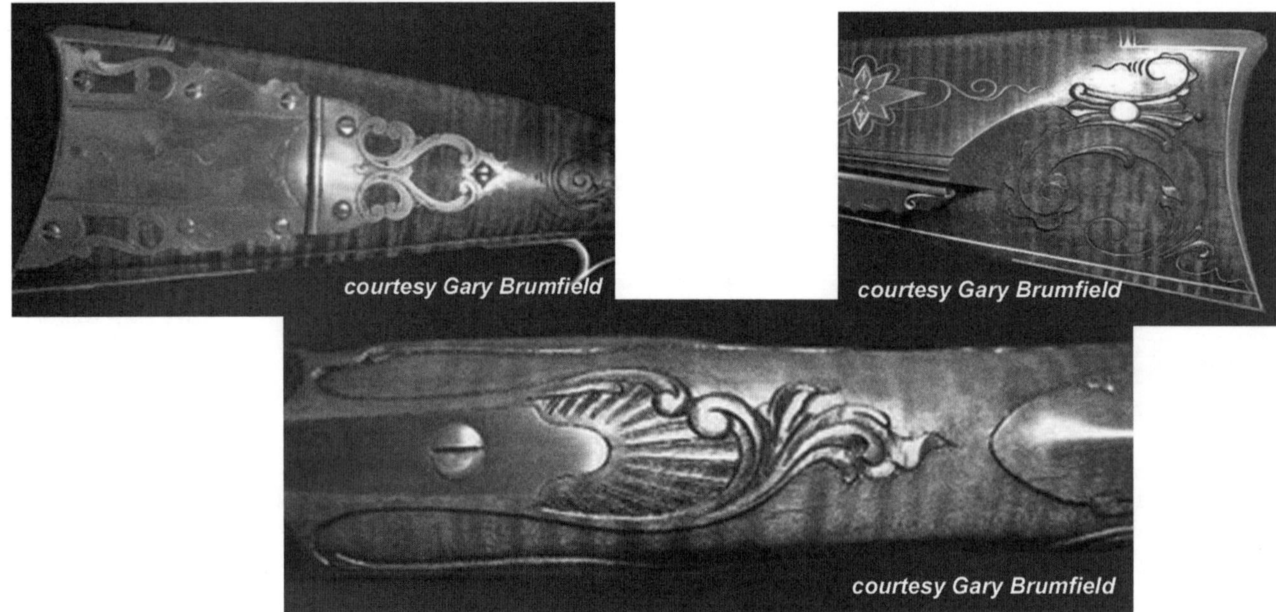
courtesy Gary Brumfield

courtesy Gary Brumfield

courtesy Gary Brumfield

GRADING - PPGS™	100%	98%	90%	80%

C SECTION

CABELA'S INC.

Current sporting goods retailer with catalog sales, headquarters located in Sydney, NE. Consumer direct (store or mail order) sales only.

Cabela's should be contacted directly (see Trademark Index) to receive a catalog on their extensive black powder model lineup. Cabela's continues to be a primary U.S. retailer for Pedersoli, Pietta, and A. Uberti black powder pistols, rifles and shotguns (please see individual sections for more information).

CASTEEL, KEITH

Contemporary longrifle master gunmaker located in Bruceton Mills, WV.

Mr. Casteel began building muzzle loading rifles in Oakland, Maryland circa 1969 and is known best for Jaeger and Transition style flintlocks with early high relief hunting scenes executed in the stock and metal. Average rifle values start in the $5,000 range. Please contact Mr. Casteel directly (see contact listing in Trademark Index) regarding availability.

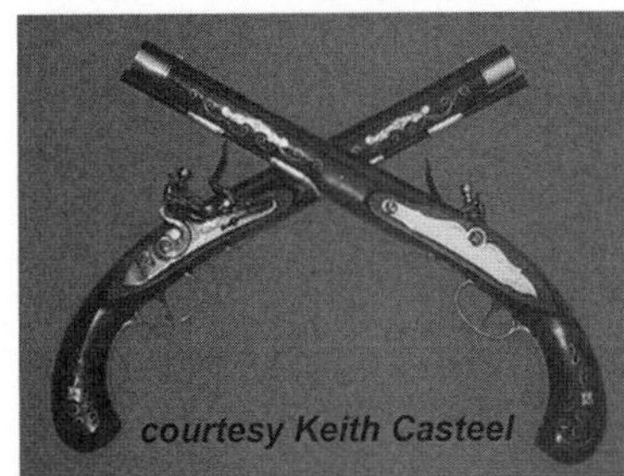
courtesy Keith Casteel

CHATTAHOOCHEE BPA

Previous manufacturer located in Cumming, GA. Chattahoochee BPA manufactured authentic reproduction of the Colt 1861 Special Rifle-Musket originally manufactured by Amoskeag and LG&Y. Consumer direct sales.

Chattahoochee reproduction rifles are approved by the North-South Skirmish Association.

RIFLES: PERCUSSION

COLT 1861 SPECIAL RIFLE/MUSKET — .58 cal. perc., 31.5 in. 2 band or 40 in. 3 band Infantry and Artillery barrel lengths, Armory bright polished steel finish with authentic markings, hand-finished walnut stock, Artillery, 8 lbs. 4 oz., Infantry, 9 lbs. 3 oz., all models come with "match grade" internal lock parts.

	100%	98%	90%	80%
	$640	**$560**	**$465**	**$315**

Last MSR was $695.

Add $650 for "A" style engraving (30% coverage) disc.

CHENEY RIFLE WORKS

Previous manufacturer located in Waldron, IN. Cheney Rifle Works changed its name to Wilderness Rifle Works, located in Waldron, IN.

Cheney manufactured rifles have similar values to comparable models in the Wilderness Rifle Works section.

CIMARRON F.A. CO.

Current importer/distributor located in Fredericksburg, TX, beginning 1984. Cimarron currently imports A. Uberti, Dsvide Pedersoli & C., F.lli Pietta, and other Italian manufactured reproductions and replicas of both cartridge and black powder models. Cimarron F.A. Co. was previously named Old-West Gun Company. Consumer direct or dealer sales.

Cimarron sells authentic western reproductions of Colt and Remington black powder pistols. Packaged for Cimarron, the majority of reproductions sold are manufactured by Uberti. Cimarron also offers engraved versions of most Colt and Remington models. For more information and current pricing on both new and used Cimarron F.A. Co. firearms (including cartridge conversions and open tops), please refer to the *Blue Book of Gun Values* by S.P. Fjestad (now online also).

ENGRAVING AND CUSTOM FINISHES

Add $845 for engraving on regular models (disc. 2008).
Add $585 for engraving on Pocket models (disc. 2008).
Add $175 for custom nickel finish.
Add $175 for premium (highly polished) nickel finish (disc. 2008).
Add $350 for silver plating (disc. 2008).
Add $360 for old style case hardened frame (disc.).

REVOLVERS: CARTRIDGE, SA

Since these are cartridge firing revolvers converted from black powder reproduction pistols, and require a FFL to transfer, these listings have been moved to the *Blue Book of Gun Values* by S.P. Fjestad.

GRADING - PPGS™	100%	98%	90%	80%

REVOLVERS: PERCUSSION

TEXAS PATERSON — .36 cal. perc., 7.5 in. oct. barrel, 5 shot, blue finish, standard hidden trigger design, loading lever, 11.5 OAL, 2.5 lbs. Disc. 2006.

	$400	$360	$325	$255

Last MSR was $400.

Add $40 for blue charcoal or white (disc.) finish.
Add $50 for antique Original finish.
Subtract $40 if w/o loading lever.

1847 WALKER — .44 cal. perc., 6 shot, 9 in. barrel, blue finish, color case hardened frame, hammer, and loading lever, brass trim, engraved cylinder, 15.75 in. OAL, 4.4 lbs.

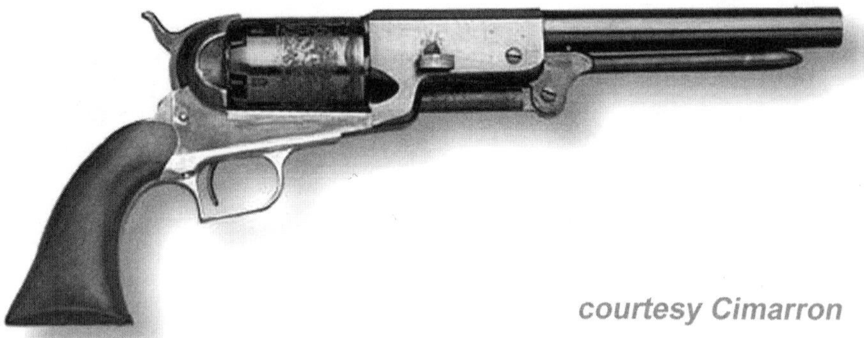
courtesy Cimarron

MSR $422	$385	$340	$255	$215

Add $40 for blue charcoal or white (disc.) finish.
Add $50 for antique Original finish.

1848 BABY DRAGOON — .31 cal. perc., 4 in. barrel, 5 shot, color case hardened frame, hammer, no loading lever, engraved cylinder, 1.4 lbs.

MSR $333	$295	$260	$195	$165

Add $25 for silver plated backstrap and trigger guard (disc. 2003).
Add $40 for charcoal or white (disc.) finish.
Add $50 for antique Original finish.

DRAGOON (WHITNEYVILLE-HARTFORD) — .44 cal. perc., 6 shot, brass grip strap, color case hardened frame, hammer, and loading lever, brass trim, 3.9 lbs.

MSR $422	$385	$340	$255	$215

Add $250 for shoulder stock (special order only, disc.).
Add $40 for blue charcoal or white (disc.) finish.
Add $50 for antique Original finish.
Add $25 for silver plated backstrap, or cut for stock (3rd Model Dragoon, disc.).

FIRST MODEL DRAGOON — .44 cal. perc., 6 shot cylinder w/oval bolt slots, 7.5 in. blue or antique original bbl., brass grip strap and square back trigger guard, color case hardened frame, hammer, and loading lever, 3.9 lbs.

MSR $400	$360	$320	$240	$200

Add $250 for shoulder stock (special order only, disc.).
Add $40 for blue charcoal or white (disc.) finish.
Add $50 for antique Original finish.
Add $25 for silver plated backstrap, or cut for stock (3rd Model Dragoon, disc.).

SECOND MODEL DRAGOON — .44 cal. perc., 6 shot cylinder w/square bolt slots, 7.5 in. blue or antique original bbl., brass grip strap and square back trigger guard, color case hardened frame, hammer, and loading lever, 3.9 lbs.

MSR $400	$360	$320	$240	$200

Add $250 for shoulder stock (special order only, disc.).
Add $40 for blue charcoal or white (disc.) finish.
Add $50 for antique Original finish.
Add $25 for silver plated backstrap, or cut for stock (3rd Model Dragoon, disc.).

GRADING - PPGS™	100%	98%	90%	80%

THIRD MODEL DRAGOON — .44 cal. perc., 6 shot cylinder w/square bolt slots, 7.5 in. blue or antique original bbl., steel grip strap and brass oval trigger guard, color case hardened frame cut for shoulder stock, hammer, and loading lever, 3.9 lbs.

MSR $400	$360	$320	$240	$200

Add $250 for shoulder stock (special order only, disc.).
Add $40 for blue charcoal or white (disc.) finish.
Add $50 for antique Original finish.
Add $25 for silver plated backstrap.
Add $8 if cut for stock.

1849 POCKET — .31 cal. perc., with loading lever, 4 in. barrel, 5 shot, color case hardened frame, hammer, and loading lever, brass trim, 1.5 lbs.

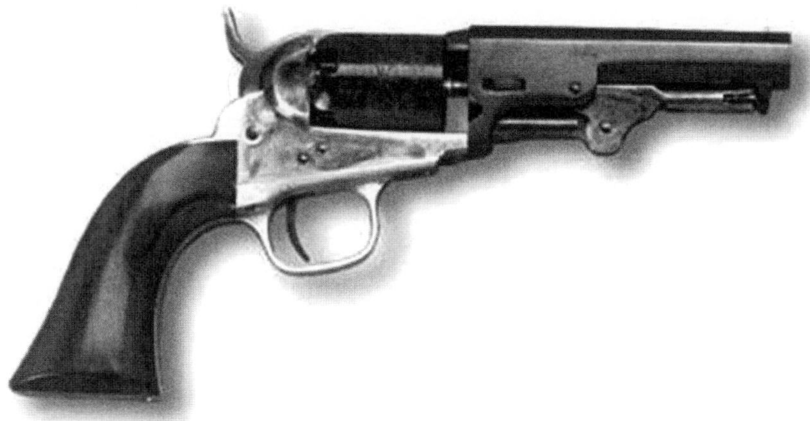

courtesy Cimarron F.A. Co.

MSR $333	$295	$260	$195	$165

Add $25 for silver plated backstrap and trigger guard.
Add $30 for charcoal or white (disc.) finish.
Add $50 for antique Original finish.

1849 WELLS FARGO POCKET — .31 cal. perc., 4 in. octagon barrel, 5 shot, color case hardened frame, hammer, no loading lever, brass trim, 1.5 lbs.

courtesy Cimarron F.A. Co.

MSR $333	$295	$260	$195	$165

Add $25 for silver plated backstrap and trigger guard.
Add $40 for blue charcoal or white (disc.) finish.
Add $50 for antique Original finish.

GRADING - PPGS™	100%	98%	90%	80%

1851 NAVY — .36 cal. perc., 7.5 in. octagon barrel, 6 shot, roll engraved cylinder, brass grip frame, round or square back trigger guard, 2.8 lbs.

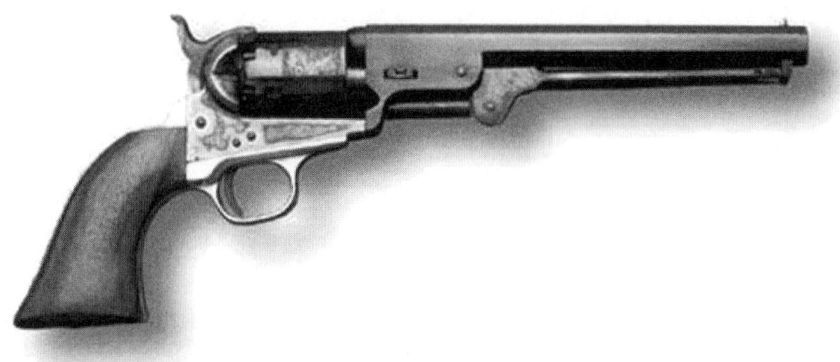

courtesy Cimarron F.A. Co.

MSR $314	$280	$250	$185	$155

Add $25 for silver plated backstrap and trigger guard (disc.).
Add $40 for blue charcoal or white (disc.) finish.
Add $50 for antique Original finish.

1851 NAVY LONDON MODEL — .36 cal. perc., 7.5 in. octagon barrel, 6 shot, roll engraved cylinder, steel grip frame, round or square trigger guard, 2.8 lbs.

MSR $347	$310	$275	$205	$175

Add $25 for silver plated backstrap and trigger guard (disc.).
Add $40 for blue charcoal or white (disc.) finish.
Add $50 for antique Original finish.

1858 REMINGTON — .44 cal. perc., 7.5 in. barrel, 6 shot, blue steel, brass trigger guard, 2.6 lbs.

	$245	$215	$160	$135

Last MSR was $260.

Add $40 for adj. sights.

1858 REMINGTON ARMY — .44 cal. perc., 6 shot, 5.5 (new 2005), 7.5 in. (disc. 2006), or 8 in. (new 2007) bbl., blue finish, brass trigger guard, 2.6 lbs.

MSR $333	$295	$260	$195	$165

Add $40 for charcoal finish.
Add $50 for antique Original finish.
Subtract $50 for new millenium finish (new 2004).

1858 REMINGTON NAVY — .36 cal. perc., 6 shot, 7.5 in. bbl., blue finish, brass trigger guard, 2.5 lbs. Disc. Reintroduced 2005.

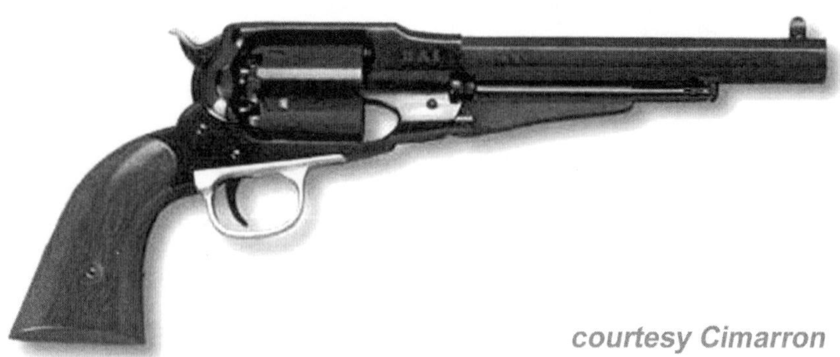

courtesy Cimarron

MSR $333	$295	$260	$195	$165

Add $40 for charcoal finish.
Add $50 for antique Original finish.

GRADING - PPGS™	100%	98%	90%	80%

1858 REMINGTON NEW NAVY — .36 cal. perc., 6.5 in. octagon barrel, 6 shot, blue frame, 2.5 lbs. Disc. 1994.

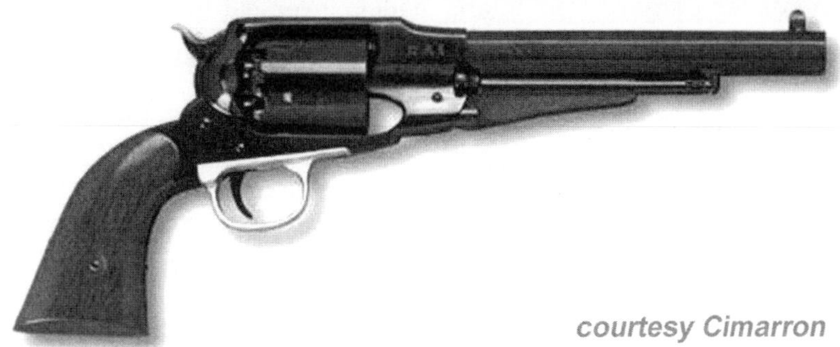

courtesy Cimarron

	$245	$215	$160	$135

Last MSR was $185.

Add $40 for adj. sights.

1858 REMINGTON ARMY STAINLESS — .44 cal. perc., 6 shot, 5.5 or 7.5 in. oct. bbl., blue finish, stainless steel. New. 2005.

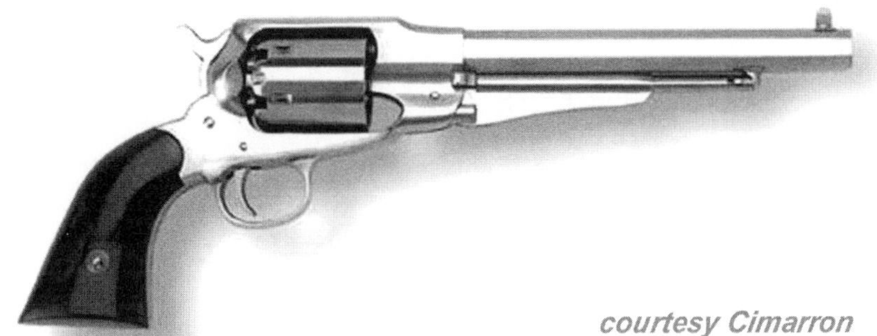

courtesy Cimarron

MSR $427	$385	$340	$255	$215

1858 REMINGTON STAINLESS — similar to 1858 Remington, has brass strap and trigger guard. Disc. 1994.

	$315	$245	$185	$145

Last MSR was $260.

Add $40 for adj. sights.

1860 ARMY CIVILIAN MODEL — .44 cal. perc. 8 in. barrel, 6 shot, loading lever, color case hardened frame, hammer, and loading lever, rebated cylinder, brass or steel backstrap and brass trigger guard, 2.6 lbs.

MSR $333	$295	$260	$195	$165

Add $25 for silver plated backstrap and trigger guard (disc. 2003).
Add $30 for charcoal or white (disc.) finish.
Add $50 for antique Original finish.

1860 ARMY MILITARY MODEL — .44 cal. perc., 8 in. barrel, 6 shot, loading lever, color case hardened frame, hammer, and loading lever, fluted or rebated cylinder, steel backstrap and trigger guard, cut for stock, 2.6 lbs.

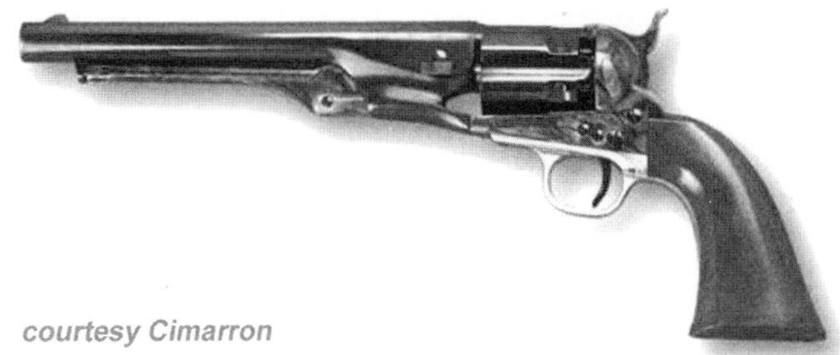

courtesy Cimarron

MSR $333	$295	$260	$195	$165

Add $25 for silver plated backstrap and trigger guard (disc.).
Add $40 for charcoal or white (disc.) finish.
Add $50 for antique Original finish.
Add $14 for fluted cylinder.

GRADING - PPGS™	100%	98%	90%	80%

1861 NAVY (CIVILIAN) — .36 cal. perc., 7.5 in. blue round bbl., fluted (disc.) or rebated cylinder, brass backstrap and trigger guard, color case hardened frame, hammer, and loading lever, cut for stock, 2.5 lbs.

MSR $320	$290	$255	$190	$160

Add $25 for silver plated backstrap and trigger guard (disc.).
Add $40 for charcoal or white (disc.) finish.
Add $50 for antique Original finish.

1861 NAVY (MILITARY) — .36 cal. perc., 7.5 in. round barrel, fluted (disc.) or rebated cylinder, steel backstrap and trigger guard, color case hardened frame, hammer, and loading lever, cut for stock, 2.5 lbs.

MSR $328	$300	$265	$200	$165

Add $25 for silver plated backstrap and trigger guard (disc.).
Add $40 for charcoal or white (disc.) finish.
Add $50 for antique Original finish.

1862 POCKET NAVY — .36 cal. perc., 5.5, or 6.5 in. blue bbl., color case hardened frame, hammer, and loading lever, rebated cylinder, 1.6 lbs.

MSR $340	$310	$275	$205	$170

Add $25 for silver plated backstrap and trigger guard (disc.).
Add $30 for charcoal or white (disc.) finish.
Add $50 for antique Original finish.

1862 POCKET POLICE — .36 cal. perc., 4.5 (new 2009), 5.5 or 6.5 in. blue bbl., color case hardened frame, hammer, and loading lever, cylinder, semi-fluted cylinder, 1.6 lbs.

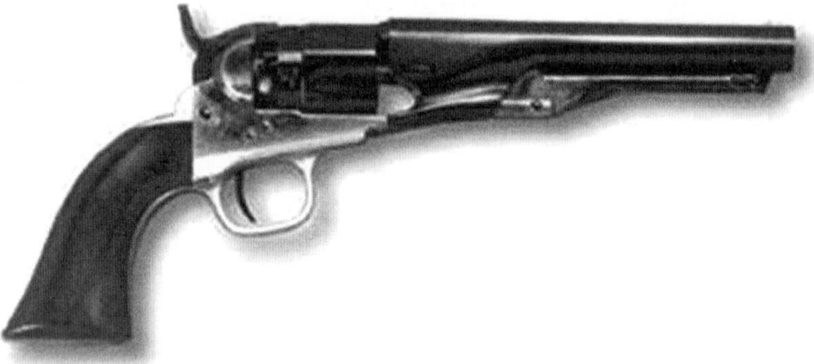

courtesy Cimarron F.A. Co.

MSR $347	$310	$275	$205	$175

Add $25 for silver plated backstrap and trigger guard (disc.).
Add $40 for charcoal or white (disc.) finish.
Add $50 for antique Original finish.

AUGUSTA CONFEDERATE — .36 cal. perc., 7.5 in. octagon barrel, color case hardened hammer and trigger, all brass frame, engraved cylinder, 2.5-2.75 lbs.

	$210	$165	$125	$85

Last MSR was $210.

GRISWOLD AND GUNNISON CONFEDERATE — .36 or .44 cal. perc., similar to Augusta Confederate Model, except has round barrel forward of lug, and plain, non-engraved cylinder. Disc. 1994.

	$210	$165	$125	$85

Last MSR was $150.

GRADING - PPGS™	100%	98%	90%	80%

LEECH AND RIGDON CONFEDERATE — .36 cal. perc., 7.5 in. blue oct. bbl, color case hardened frame, hammer and trigger, engraved cylinder, brass backstrap and trigger guard, 2.75 lbs.

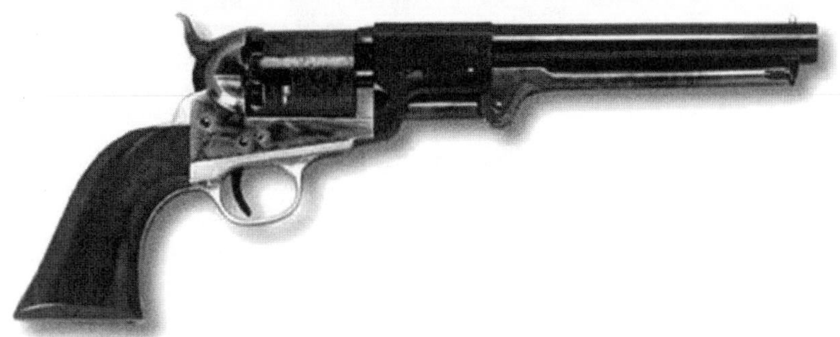

courtesy Cimarron F.A. Co.

MSR $328	$300	$265	$200	$165

Add $50 for antique Original finish.
Add $40 for charcoal finish.

TEXAS CONFEDERATE DRAGOON — .44 cal. perc., 7.5 in. round barrel, color case hardened frame, hammer, and loading lever, brass trim, "Tucker, Sherrard, and Co". 4 lbs. Disc. 1994.

	$265	$200	$145	$100

Last MSR was $210.

RIFLES: FLINTLOCK & PERCUSSION

1858 REMINGTON ARMY REVOLVING CARBINE — .44 cal. perc., 18 in. blue bbl., 6 shot, brass trigger guard and crescent butt plate, adj. rear and blade front sights, walnut stock, 4.6 lbs. New 2005.

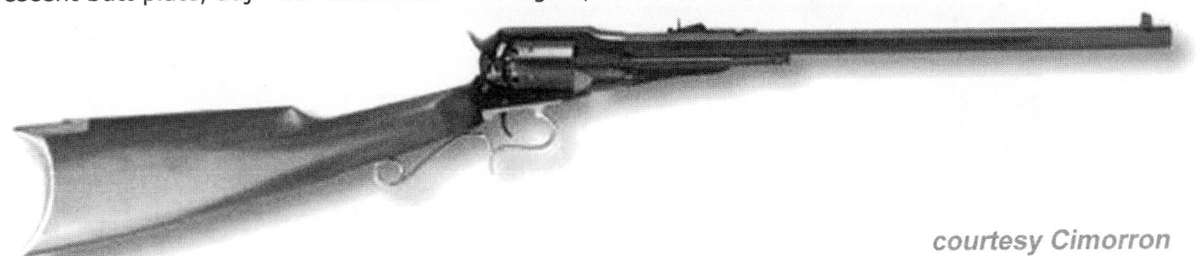

courtesy Cimorron

MSR $556	$500	$440	$330	$275

1866 REVOLVING CARBINE — .44 cal. perc., 18 in. barrel, 6 shot, blue steel, brass trigger guard, walnut stock, 4.6 lbs. Disc. 1994.

	$345	$275	$225	$170

Last MSR was $320.

HAWKEN SANTA FE — .54 cal. perc., single shot, 32 in. oct. barrel, damascened finish, double set triggers, walnut stock, 9.5 lbs. Disc. 1994.

	$385	$300	$235	$195

Last MSR was $350.

JEREDIAH SMITH SANTA FE HAWKENS — .50 or .54 cal. flintlock or perc., similar to above.

	$385	$300	$235	$195

Last MSR was $445.

Add $35 for Flintlock.

LEMAN TRADE RIFLE — .45, .50, .54, or .58 cal. perc. Disc. 1994.

	$250	$190	$135	$95

Last MSR was $250.

Add $15 for .54 or .58 cal.

GRADING - PPGS™	100%	98%	90%	80%

ST. LOUIS RIFLE — .45, .50, .54, or .58 cal. flintlock or perc., color case hardened hammer, lock, and trigger guard, octagon barrel. Disc. 1994.

	$345	$275	$225	$170

Last MSR was $280.

Add $15 for .54 or .58 cal. percussion.
Add $15 for flintlock.

COLLECTOR'S ARMOURY, LTD.

Current importer and distributor located in Lorton, VA. Consumer direct and dealer sales.

In 1968, Replica Models, Inc. was founded as a mail order company designed to provide collectors with a new and innovative product: Non-firing Replica Guns. Replica Models was the first to offer these quality replica guns in the United States. In 1972, a sister company, Unique Imports, Inc., was established to furnish military collectors with a wide range of original and high quality military collectibles. In 1980 Replica Models, Inc. and Unique Imports, Inc. merged to form Collector's Armoury. In 2008, Collector's Armoury, Ltd added accurate 19th centrury fully functional replica black powder arms to their product lines of historic reproductions from the Middle Ages through the 20th Century. Product lines now include anything from Medieval swords and armour to Old West Revolvers and modern replica firearms.

PISTOLS: PERCUSSION

KENTUCKY PISTOL — .45 cal. perc., 10 in. blue barrel, 1:21 in. twist, color case hardened hammer and lock, brass furniture, walnut bird's head grip stock, 15.75 in. OAL, 2.2 lbs. Mfg. by Chiappa/Armi Sport. New 2008.

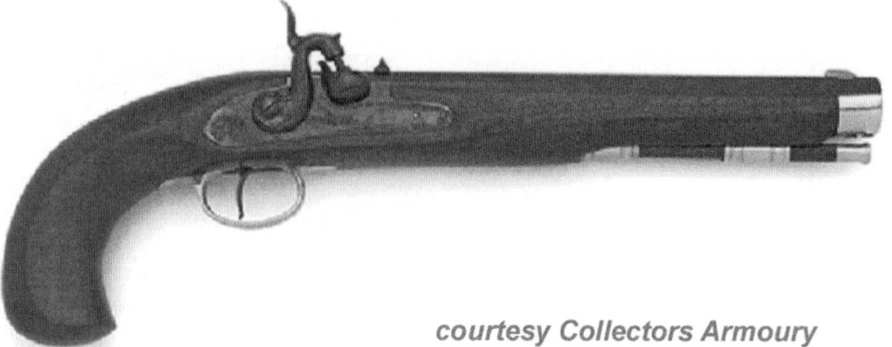

courtesy Collectors Armoury

MSR $259	$245	$225	$170	$125

KENTUCKY CONNECTICUT PARLOR PISTOL — .177/BB cal. perc., 10 in. blue barrel, 1:21 in. twist, color case hardened hammer and lock, brass furniture, walnut bird's head grip stock, 15.75 in. OAL, 2.2 lbs. Mfg. by Chiappa/Armi Sport. New 2008.

courtesy Collectors Armoury

MSR $259	$245	$225	$170	$125

This Kentucky style percussion pistol is modified to function without black powder. This pistol uses only a primer cap to fire a standard bb up to 10 meters. This pistol comes with a loading ramrod and brushes.

GRADING - PPGS™	100%	98%	90%	80%

LE PAGE DUELING PISTOL — .45 cal. perc., 10 in. barrel, 1:21 in. twist, silver plated butt-cap and trigger guard w /spur finger rest, double set triggers, highly polished lock and barrel, one-piece walnut stock, 16.50 in. OAL, 2.2 lbs. New 2008.

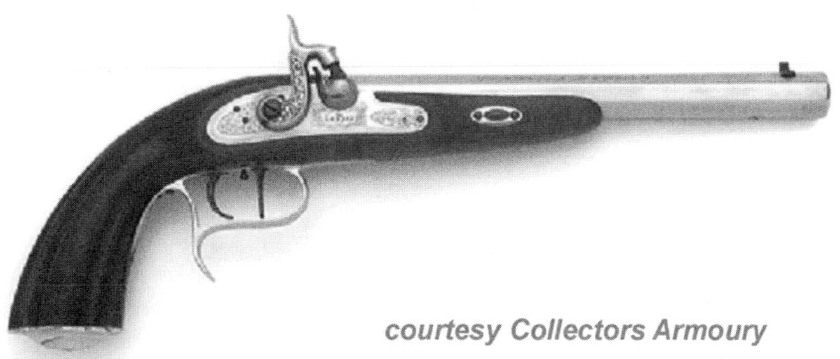

courtesy Collectors Armoury

MSR $349	$325	$285	$215	$165

REVOLVERS: PERCUSSION

1851 NAVY BRASS — .36 cal. perc., 7.5 in. octagon barrel, 1:30 in. twist, brass frame, color case hardened hammer and loading lever, brass backstrap and trigger guard, walnut stocks, 13 in. OAL, 2.5 lbs. Mfg. by Pietta 2008.

courtesy Collectors Armoury

MSR $249	$225	$200	$150	$125

1851 NAVY SHERIFF BRASS — .36 cal. perc., 5.5 in. octagon barrel, 1:30 in. twist, brass frame, color case hardened hammer and loading lever, brass backstrap and trigger guard, walnut stocks, 10.75 in. OAL, 2.25 lbs. Mfg. by Pietta 2008.

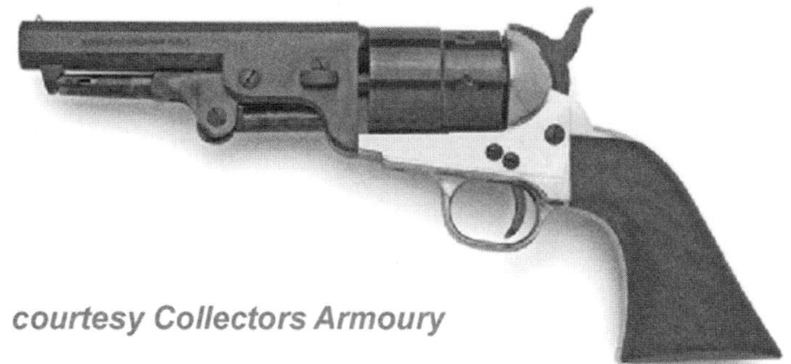

courtesy Collectors Armoury

MSR $249	$225	$200	$150	$125

1858 REMINGTON BRASS — .44 cal. perc., 8 in. octagon barrel, 1:30 in. twist, color case hardened hammer, walnut grip, brass frame, backstrap, and trigger guard, blue finish, 14.5 OAL, 2.75 lbs. Mfg. by Pietta 2008.

	$215	$190	$145	$120

Last MSR was $241.

GRADING - PPGS™	100%	98%	90%	80%

1860 ARMY — .44 cal. perc., 8 in. octagon barrel, 1:30 in. twist, brass frame, color case hardened hammer and loading lever, brass backstrap and trigger guard, walnut stocks, 13.5 in. OAL, 2.75 lbs. Mfg. by Pietta. New 2008.

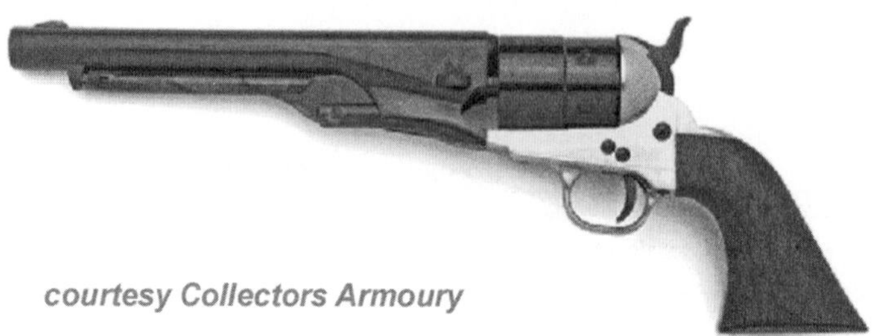

courtesy Collectors Armoury

MSR $249	$225	$200	$150	$125

RIFLES: PERCUSSION SINGLE SHOT

KENTUCKY RIFLE — .45 cal. perc., case hardened lock plate, 35 in. oct. blue barrel, 1:36 in. twist, brass blade front and steel open rear sight, one-piece walnut stock w/oil finish, brass buttplate, triggerguard, patchbox, side plate, thimbles and nosecap, 50 in. OAL, 6.6 lbs. Mfg. Chiappa/Armi Sport. New 2008.

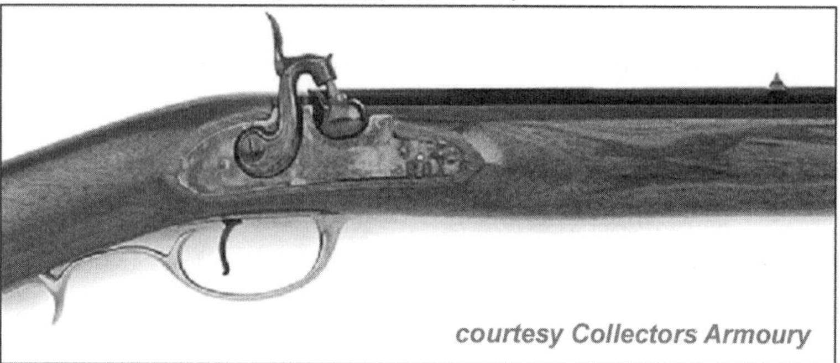

courtesy Collectors Armoury

MSR $450	$405	$360	$270	$225

MISSOURI RIVER HAWKEN — .50 cal. perc., case hardened lock plate, 30 in. oct. blue barrel, 1:24 in. twist, brass blade front and steel open rear sight, one-piece walnut stock w/oil finish, steel buttplate, triggerguard, and nosecap, 47 in. OAL, 9.75 lbs. Mfg. Pedersoli. New 2009.

courtesy Collectors Armoury

MSR $799	$725	$640	$480	$400

MODEL 1842 SPRINGFIELD RIFLE — .69 cal. perc., 42 in. round smooth bore white steel barrel, hammer, lock trigger guard and trigger, marked "SPRING-FIELD" in two lines behind the hammer, lock and tang dated 1847, barrel stamped with the correct style V.P. and eagle head proof marks on the breech, one-piece American walnut stock, 58 in. OAL, 10.5 lbs. Mfg. by Chiappa/Armi Sport. N-S.S.A. approved. New 2008.

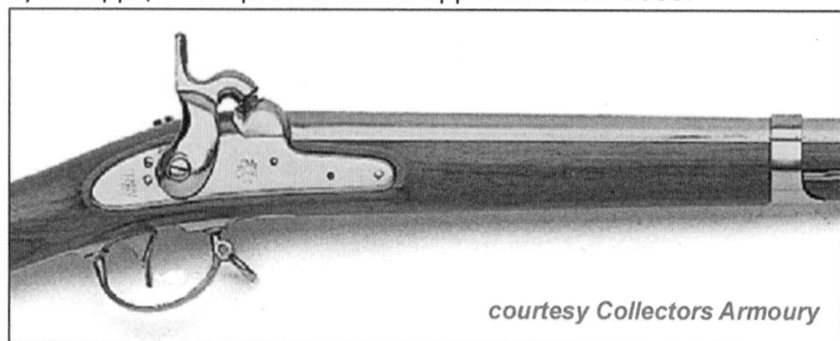

courtesy Collectors Armoury

MSR $715	$645	$575	$435	$365

GRADING - PPGS™	100%	98%	90%	80%

MODEL 1853 ENFIELD (3 BAND) — .58 cal. perc., 39 in. round blue barrel, 1:64.75 in. twist, color case hardened hammer and lock, one piece oil finished American walnut stock, brass furniture, blue barrel bands, 55 in. OAL, 8.8 lbs. Mfg. by Chiappa/Armi Sport. New 2008.

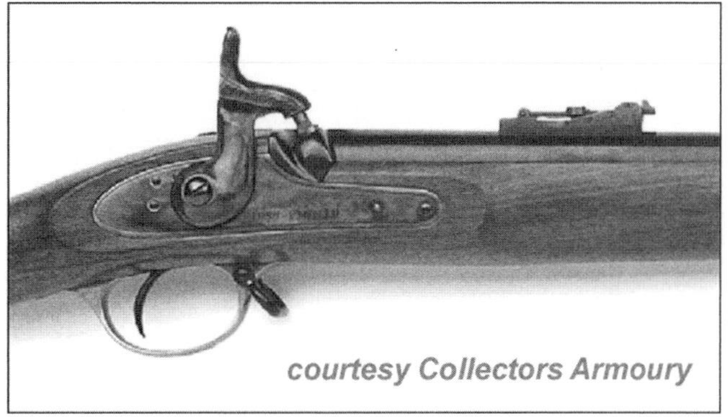
courtesy Collectors Armoury

MSR $620	$555	$495	$365	$300

MODEL 1859 SHARPS CAVALRY CARBINE — .54 cal. perc., 22 in. blue round barrel, 1:47.5 in. twist, adj. rear and fixed front sight, 1 metal band, color case hardened hammer and receiver, includes patchbox, 39 in. OAL, 9.75 lbs. Mfg. by Pedersoli. New 2009.

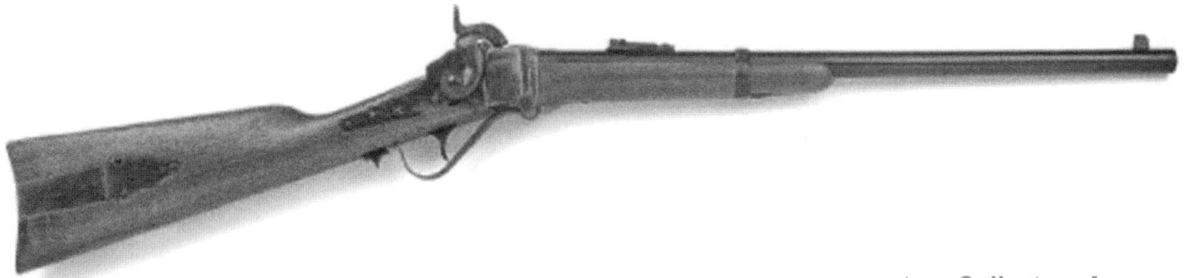
courtesy Collectors Armoury

MSR $699	$635	$560	$420	$350

MODEL 1861 SPRINGFIELD MUSKET — .58 cal. perc., lock is marked "1861 Springfield" w/eagle, 40 in. round barrel, white steel barrel, hammer, lock, trigger, and trim, one-piece walnut oil finished stock, 56 in. OAL, 10.1 lbs. NSSA approved. Mfg. by Chiappa/Armi Sport. New 2008.

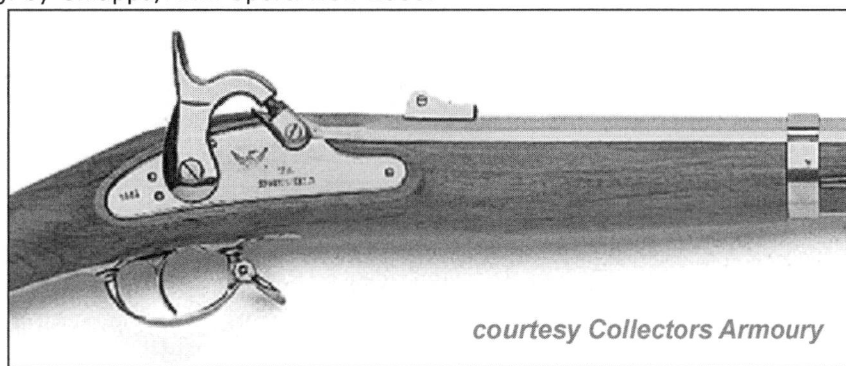
courtesy Collectors Armoury

MSR $675	$610	$540	$405	$335

GRADING - PPGS™	100%	98%	90%	80%

MODEL 1863 ZOUAVE RIFLED MUSKET — .58 cal. perc., 33 in. blue round barrel, 1:64.75 in. twist, color case hardened hammer, lock, and trigger, brass patchbox, trigger guard, and barrel bands, color case-hardened lock marked "US" with an eagle, one piece walnut stock, trigger guard, barrel bands and patchbox are finished in highly polished brass, 49 in. OAL, 7.9 lbs., Mfg. by Chiappa/Armi Sport. New 2008.

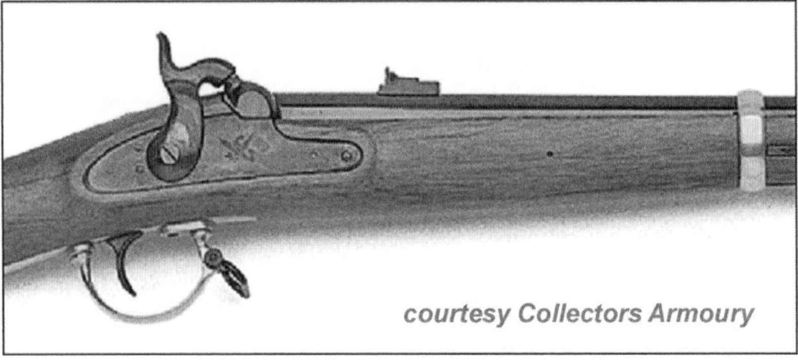
courtesy Collectors Armoury

MSR $599	$545	$480	$360	$295

COLT BLACKPOWDER ARMS CO.

Previous manufacturer and retailer of 3rd Generation Colt Black Powder pistols and muskets located in Brooklyn, NY 1994-2002.

The author and publisher wish to thank Mr. Dennis Russell for his valuable assistance updating the following information in this edition of the *Blue Book of Modern Black Powder Arms.*

All 3rd Generation Colt blackpowder models are also referred to as Signature Series Models.

A reprise of the original Colt Blackpowder line, along with historic models not offered in the 2nd Generation, and a new series of Commemoratives, each model (with the exception of the Heirloom Tiffany 1860 Army and 1842 Texas Paterson) bears the Sam Colt signature on the backstrap. These 3rd Generation models were manufactured under an authorized licensing agreement with Colt Firearms by Colt Blackpowder Arms Company - the same company (and many of the same craftsmen)responsible for the 2nd Generation Colt revolvers. Although parts for the Signature Series were cast in Italy, they were fully assembled and hand finished in the United States using the proprietary Colt formulas for bluing and color case hardening.

Colt Blackpowder Arms Company Signature Series revolvers are regarded as authentic Colt pistols. The 3rd Generation models have original Colt markings, including the barrel address and serial number stampings. There are no foreign proof marks on these authentic Colt models.

Please refer to *Colt Blackpowder Reproductions & Replicas* - A Collector's & Shooter's Guide by Dennis Adler for color pictures of the 3rd Generation Colt Blackpowder Arms Co. models listed below. 3rd Generation Colt blackpowder models can be found on pages 23-26, 28-37, and pages 77, 84, 85, 86, 87, and 94.

REVOLVERS: PERCUSSION

The revolvers listed below were originally packed and shipped inside a gray French fit style cardboard box that was hinged at the back. Additionally, the gray box was packed inside a protective white tab lock cardboard box. All descriptive information, including model number and serial number, is located on the end of the white box. Therefore, the presence of both of these boxes is extremely important to collectors of this revolver series.

Accessory sets were originally packed and shipped inside a gray French fit style cardboard box that was hinged at the back. Additionally, the gray box was packed inside a protective white tab lock cardboard box. All descriptive information, including model number is located on the end of the white box. Therefore, the presence of both of these boxes is extremely important to collectors.

Add $150 - $200 for Colt Presentation Case.

Add $150 - $175 for Colt Accessory Set including Powder Flask, Bullet Mold, Nipple Wrench, Cap Tin and both original white and gray cardboard boxes.

Deduct $25 from the value of the accessory set if the white accessory box is missing.

Deduct $25 from the value of the accessory set if the gray accessory box is missing.

Deduct $50 from the value of the accessory set if both the white and gray accessory boxes are missing.

Deduct $50 - $75 from the value of a revolver model below for a missing white cardboard box.

Deduct $50 - $75 from the value of a revolver model below for a missing gray cardboard box.

Deduct $100 - $150 from the value of a revolver model below if both white and gray cardboard boxes are missing.

TEXAS PATERSON — .36 cal. perc., No. 5 Holster Model with hinged loading lever, 5 shot, 7.5 inch octagon barrel, and steel backstrap. Standard model without engraving. Mfg. 2002 only.

	$1,750	$1,350	$800	$650

Last MSR was $1,200.

GRADING - PPGS™	100%	98%	90%	80%

1847 WALKER — .44 cal. perc., 9 in. barrel, color case hardened frame, hammer, and loading lever, 73 oz. Mfg. 1994-2002.

	$700	$500	$300	$250

Last MSR was $750.

1847 WALKER NICKEL — .44 cal. perc., 9 in. barrel, nickel finish, 73 oz. Mfg. 2002 only.

	$1,200	$850	$500	$400

Last MSR was $850.

BEWARE OF FAKES - ORIGINAL BOXES ARE A MUST FOR PROVENANCE!

WHITNEYVILLE HARTFORD DRAGOON — .44 cal. perc., 7.5 in. barrel, oval bolt cuts in cylinder, color case hardened 3 screw frame, loading lever, plunger, and hammer, silver plated grip strap and square back trigger guard, one-piece walnut grips. Mfg. 1996-2002.

	$700	$500	$300	$250

Last MSR was $750.

1ST MODEL DRAGOON — .44 cal. perc., 7.5 in. barrel, oval bolt cuts in cylinder, color case hardened frame, loading lever, plunger, and hammer, square back trigger guard, one-piece walnut grips. Mfg. 1998-2002.

courtesy Colt

	$600	$425	$250	$200

Last MSR was $750.

2ND MODEL DRAGOON — .44 cal. perc., 7.5 in. barrel, rectangular bolt cuts in cylinder, color case hardened frame, loading lever, plunger, and hammer, square back trigger guard, one-piece walnut grips. Mfg. 1998-2002.

	$600	$425	$250	$200

Last MSR was $750.

3RD MODEL DRAGOON — .44 cal. perc., 7.5 in. barrel, rectangular bolt cuts in cylinder, color case hardened frame, loading lever, plunger, and hammer, brass backstrap and round trigger guard, one-piece walnut grips. Mfg. 1996-2002.

courtesy Colt

	$600	$425	$250	$200

Last MSR was $750.

GRADING - PPGS™	100%	98%	90%	80%

* ***3RD Model Dragoon (Steel Backstrap)*** — .44 cal. perc., 7.5 in. barrel, rectangular bolt cuts in fluted cylinder, color case hardened frame, loading lever, plunger, and hammer, blue steel backstrap cut for optional shoulder stock, silver plated brass round trigger guard and one-piece walnut grips. Mfg. 1996-2002.

	$1,000	$750	$450	$350

1848 BABY DRAGOON — .31 cal. perc., 5-shot, 4 in. barrel, unfluted straight cylinder, color case hardened frame, short frame, no loading lever, silver plated backstrap and square back trigger guard, walnut grips, 1.5 lbs. Mfg. 1998-2002.

courtesy Colt

	$550	$375	$225	$175

Last MSR was $675.

1849 POCKET — .31 cal. perc., 5-shot, 4 in. barrel, unfluted straight cylinder, color case hardened frame, short frame, silver plated backstrap and round trigger guard, walnut grips, 1.5 lbs. Disc. 2002.

	$550	$375	$225	$175

Last MSR was $675.

1851 NAVY — .36 cal. perc., 7.5 in. octagon barrel, color case hardened frame, loading lever, plunger, and hammer, silver plated backstrap, square trigger guard, one-piece grip, 42 oz. Mfg. 1994-2002.

courtesy Colt

	$600	$425	$250	$200

Last MSR was $695.

* ***1851 Navy London Model*** — features original London barrel address. Mfg. 1997-2002.

	$650	$475	$275	$225

Last MSR was $695.

1860 ARMY — .44 cal. perc., 8 in. round blue barrel, color case hardened, frame, loading lever, plunger, and hammer, round brass trigger guard, walnut stock, 2.75 lbs. Five versions were manufactured - one with a roll engraved rebated cylinder, one with blue fluted cylinder, the Officer's Model with hand-crafted brilliant blue finish and traditional crossed sabers in 24Kt. gold above the wedge pin, cut for shoulder stock, the U.S. Cavalry Gold with 24Kt. gold plated cylinder engraved with crossed saber emblem, and U.S. 1860, and 1860 in nickel finish.

GRADING - PPGS™	100%	98%	90%	80%

* ***1860 Army w/Rebated Cylinder*** — Mfg. 1994-2002.

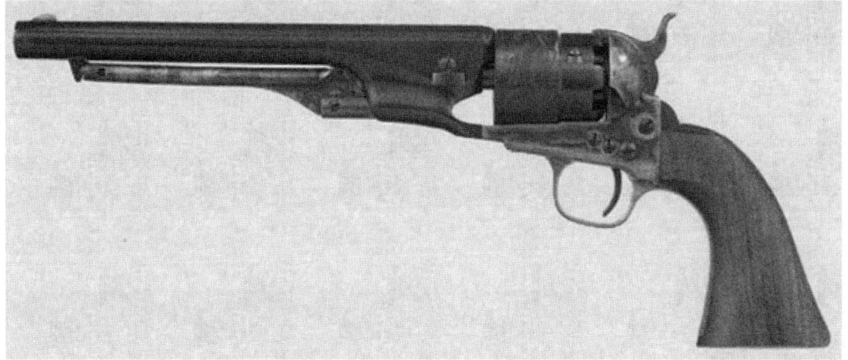

courtesy Colt

	$600	$425	$250	$200

Last MSR was $695.

* ***1860 Army w/Fluted Cylinder*** — Mfg. 1995-2002.

	$650	$475	$275	$225

Last MSR was $695.

* ***1860 Army Officer's Model*** — fluted cylinder, gold U.S. 1860 and crossed sabers on barrel, gold trigger guard. Mfg. 1995-2002.

	$650	$475	$275	$225

Last MSR was $750.

* ***1860 Army Gold U.S. Cavalry Model*** — gold rebated cylinder with U.S. 1860 and crossed sabers, two gold bands around muzzle, gold-plated backstrap and trigger guard. Mfg. 1996-2002.

	$700	$500	$300	$250

Last MSR was $800.

* ***1860 Army w/Nickel Finish*** — Mfg. 1997-2002.

	$750	$550	$325	$250

Last MSR was $750.

1861 NAVY — .36 cal. perc, 7.5 in. round barrel, color case hardened frame, loading lever, plunger, and hammer, steel backstrap and trigger guard, roll-engraved cylinder and barrel, one-piece walnut grips. 42 oz. Mfg. 1995-2002.

	$650	$475	$275	$225

Last MSR was $695.

1862 POCKET NAVY — .36 cal. perc., 5.5 in. octagon barrel, color case hardened frame, loading lever, plunger, and hammer, silver plated backstrap and round trigger guard, rebated roll engraved cylinder. 25 oz. Mfg. 1996-2002.

courtesy Colt

	$550	$375	$225	$175

Last MSR was $675.

GRADING - PPGS™	100%	98%	90%	80%

1862 POCKET POLICE — .36 cal. perc., 5.5 inch round barrel with creeping-style loading lever, color case hardened frame, loading lever, plunger, and hammer, 5 shot semi-fluted cylinder, silver plated backstrap and square back trigger guard, 25 oz. Mfg. 1997-2002.

	$550	$375	$225	$175

Last MSR was $675.

1862 TRAPPER MODEL — .36 cal. perc., 3.5 in. round barrel, color case hardened frame, and hammer, silver plated backstrap and trigger guard, no loading lever but supplied with 4.65 in. brass ramrod. Disc. 2002

	$600	$425	$250	$200

Last MSR was $675.

REVOLVERS: PERCUSSION LIMITED/SPECIAL EDITION

1842 PATERSON — .36 cal. perc., No. 5 Holster Model with hinged loading lever, 5 shot, 7.5 inch octagon barrel, steel backstrap, period-style scrollwork with punch-dot background on both sides of barrel lug, frame, standing breech, loading lever rod tip, hammer, and backstrap. Mfg. 1998-2002.

	$3,000	$2,025	N/A	N/A

Last MSR was $4,500.

This model was available on a special order basis and took approximately four months to manufacture and hand engrave.

1847 WALKER 150TH ANNIVERSARY EDITION — .44 cal. perc., 9 in. barrel, color case hardened frame, hammer, and loading lever, 73 oz. "A COMPANY No. 1" on barrel lug, frame and cylinder. Serial numbers begin with #221. Limited production model. Mfg. 1997-2002.

	$700	$400	N/A	N/A

Last MSR was $900.

3RD MODEL DRAGOON COCHISE COMMEMORATIVE — .44 cal. perc., 7.5 in. barrel, rectangular bolt cuts in cylinder, color case hardened frame, loading lever, plunger, and hammer, 24Kt. gold-plated backstrap and round trigger guard, 24Kt. gold inlays on barrel, lug, and frame, one-piece carved black horn grips. Mfg. 1997-2002.

	$900	$550	N/A	N/A

Last MSR was $1,295.

3RD MODEL DRAGOON MARINE COMMEMORATIVE — .44 cal. perc., 7.5 in. barrel, rectangular bolt cuts in cylinder, silver plated frame and barrel, 24Kt. gold plated cylinder, loading lever, plunger, wedge, trigger, hammer, backstrap, and square back trigger guard, one-piece walnut grips. Semper Fidelis engraved on backstrap. 950 mfg. 1997.

	$800	$475	N/A	N/A

Last MSR was $895.

1849 POCKET 150TH ANNIVERSARY GOLD RUSH EDITION — .31 cal. perc., 5-shot, 4 in. barrel, unfluted straight cylinder, color case hardened frame, short frame, 24Kt. gold plated backstrap and round trigger guard, walnut grips, gold-plated cylinder with engraved prospecting scenes, Gold Rush medallion inlaid in the walnut grips, engraved "150th ANNIVERSARY GOLD RUSH" along the face of the barrel, 1.5 lbs. Limited Edition. Mfg. 1999-2002.

	$650	$375	N/A	N/A

Last MSR was $895.

1851 NAVY 150TH ANNIVERSARY 1851-2001 COMMEMORATIVE — .36 cal. perc., 7.5 in. octagon barrel. The 1851 Navy commemorative has the seldom seen round trigger guard, and is hand engraved in a nautical theme with 70% coverage and genuine ivory grips showing a carved fouled anchor. The barrel and frame are Colt Royal Blue finish and all other parts are 24Kt. gold plated. Limited edition. Mfg. 2000-02.

	$3,250	$2,250	N/A	N/A

Last MSR was $5,000.

This model was available on a special order basis and took approximately four months for production and hand engraving.

1860 ARMY HEIRLOOM — .44 cal. perc., made to order Tiffany-style revolver, with creeping-style loading lever, 6 shot 24Kt. gold plated, roll engraved, rebated cylinder, 8-inch round barrel, 100% coverage with L.D. Nimschke style scrollwork, silver and 24Kt. gold plated, silver plated Tiffany-style grips. Mfg. 1998-2002.

	$3,500	$2,450	N/A	N/A

Last MSR was $6,000.

This model was available on a special order basis and took approximately four months for production and hand engraving.

GRADING - PPGS™	100%	98%	90%	80%

1861 NAVY GENERAL CUSTER EDITION — .36 cal. perc., 7.5 in. round barrel, antique silver finish, 70% coverage Nimschke-style vine scroll engraving, carved rosewood stock bearing the eagle and shield. Mfg. 1996-2002.

	$1,000	$625	N/A	N/A

Last MSR was $1,295.

RIFLES: PERCUSSION

1861 MUSKET — .58 cal. perc., 40 in. round barrel with 3 barrel bands, all metal parts bright finished white steel, one-piece oil finished walnut stock. Mfg. 1995-2002.

	$800	$600	$350	$275

Last MSR was $1,000.

Add $100 for Colt 1861 bayonet with scabbard.

* ***1861 Musket Artillery Model*** — 31.5 in. barrel with two barrel bands. Mfg. 1996-2002.

	$900	$675	$400	$325

Last MSR was $1,000.

Add $100 for Colt 1861 bayonet with scabbard.

* ***1861 Musket 1 of 1,000*** — this edition was serialized, and included a wood presentation box. Disc. 2001.

	$1,750	$1,275	$750	$600

Last MSR was $2,165.

COLT'S MANUFACTURING COMPANY, INC.

Current firearms manufacturer with headquarters located in West Hartford, CT.

The author and publisher wish to thank Mr. Dennis Russell for his valuable assistance updating the following information in this edition of the *Blue Book of Modern Black Powder Arms.*

Colt's Manufacturing Company, Inc. is the previous manufacturer of 2nd Generation Colt percussion revolvers located in Hartford, CT. Colt used subcontractors to supply rough castings for the manufacture of these black powder pistols. Throughout the production years 1971-1982, these rough castings were produced in Italy and the reproductions were completed in the United States. Initially, Val Forgett and Navy Arms provided these parts/components during 1971-73. Lou Imperato supplied these parts from 1974 to 1976. In both instances, these revolvers were assembled and finished in Colt's facilities in Connecticut. Finally, from 1978 to 1982, Colt subcontracted both parts procurement and final production to Lou Imperato and Iver Johnson Arms in Middlesex, NJ. Colt percussion revolvers produced by Iver Johnson had frames, center pins, nipples, and screws manufactured in the United States. In all instances, these revolvers were manufactured in accordance with Colt's strict specifications and quality control. Additionally, Colt performed final inspection for all models. All percussion models manufactured from 1971 through 1982, either by Colt or its subcontractor, are regarded as authentic Colt pistols and not Italian replicas.

The Colt Custom Shop also produced a limited number of special editions through the early 1990s from 2nd Generation production inventory.

Please refer to *Colt Blackpowder Reproductions & Replicas- A Collector's & Shooter's Guide* for additional color pictures of the 2nd Generation Colt Percussion Revolver makes and models listed below. Second Generation Colts can be found on pages 12 through 22, and pages 78, 82, and 83.

For more information and current pricing on both new and used Colt firearms, please refer to the *Blue Book of Gun Values* by S.P. Fjestad (now online also).

REVOLVERS: PERCUSSION, 2ND GENERATION

Colt 2nd Generation Percussion models are listed in Series order as produced by Colt Firearms.

Special note regarding all prices listed for NIB (New in Box) specimens.

Subtract approx. $100-$150 for revolvers under $2,000 if without original box or with damaged packaging.

Subtract approx. $200-$250 for revolvers over $2,000 if without original box or with damaged packaging.

On cased revolvers listed below, subtract 20% or more for missing or damaged accessories and/or damaged presentation case.

"C" SERIES

These Colt percussion revolvers were reintroduced in 1971 (1851 Navy) and 1974 (3rd Model Dragoon). Both models were discontinued in late 1976 (no reference is made to them in either the 1977 Colt Catalog or Colt Price List). The 1851 Navy and Third Model Dragoon were the only models to be produced in both the "C" Series and "F" Series configurations. While the fit and finish of both series is of the highest quality, the difference is unmistakable. The "C" Series has a beautiful bright "Royal Blue" finish while the "F" Series has a more durable dark "Colt Blue" finish. Another distinguishing feature is the serial number range (4201 to 25099 for the "C" Series 1851 Navy and 20901 to 25099 for the "C" Series Third Model Dragoon).

GRADING - PPGS™	100%	98%	90%	80%

3RD MODEL DRAGOON "C" SERIES — .44 cal. perc., 7.5 in. round barrel, hinged loading lever, six-shot cylinder with rectangular bolt cuts and roll engraved Texas Ranger and Indian scene, "C" Series Royal Blue barrel and cylinder, case hardened frame, loading lever, plunger and hammer, brass backstrap and round trigger guard, one-piece walnut stocks, 66 oz. This is the first series of second generation 3rd Model Dragoons produced. Serial number range 20901-25099. 3,899 mfg. 1974-78.

	$750	$550	$325	$250

Last MSR was $259.

* ***3rd Model Dragoon "C" Series Prototype*** — serial number range 20801-20825. 25 mfg.

	$1,500	$1,075	$625	$500

1851 NAVY "C" SERIES — .36 cal. perc., 7.5 in. octagon barrel, hinged loading lever and six shot cylinder with roll engraved naval battle scene, "C" Series Royal Blue barrel and cylinder, color case hardened frame, loading lever, plunger, and hammer, silver plated brass backstrap and square back trigger guard, one-piece walnut stocks, 42 oz. This is the first series of second generation 1851 Navy revolvers produced. Serial number range 4201-25099. Mfg. 1971-78.

	$675	$500	$300	$225

Last MSR was $200.

Note: The prices quoted above are for "C" Series 1851 Navy revolvers with wood grain cardboard box and styrofoam insert. "C" Series 1851 Navys with the early SAA style black flip top box in excellent condition command a $150 premium (serial number range 4201 to 5199). "C" Series 1851 Navys with the tan and brown flip top box in excellent condition command a $50.00 premium (serial number range 5200 to 13499).

1851 NAVY "C" SERIES (THE SHOOTER MODEL) — .36 cal. perc., 7.5 in. octagon barrel, hinged loading lever and six shot cylinder with roll engraved naval battle scene, "C" Series Royal Blue barrel and cylinder, color case hardened frame, loading lever, plunger, and hammer, brass backstrap and square back trigger guard, one-piece walnut stocks, 42 oz. 500 mfg. 1978 only.

	$750	$525	$325	$250

Last MSR was $200.

1851 NAVY "C" SERIES (ROUND TRIGGER GUARD) — .36 cal. perc., 7.5 in. octagon barrel, hinged loading lever and six shot cylinder with roll engraved naval battle scene, "C" Series Royal Blue barrel and cylinder, color case hardened frame, loading lever, plunger, and hammer, silver plated or solid brass backstrap and round trigger guard, one-piece walnut stocks. Round trigger guard revolvers were produced in very small quantities in several serial number ranges within the primary "C" Series 1851 Navy range (4201-25099). Approx. 100 mfg.

	$1,750	$1,275	$750	$600

Last MSR was $200.

"C" SERIES LIMITED/SPECIAL EDITIONS

3RD MODEL DRAGOON BICENTENNIAL COMMEMORATIVE — .44 cal. perc., 7.5 in. round barrel, hinged loading lever, six-shot cylinder with rectangular bolt cuts and roll engraved Texas Ranger and Indian scene, high polish blue barrel and cylinder, case hardened frame, loading lever, plunger, and hammer, silver plated brass backstrap and round trigger guard, one-piece walnut stocks with eagle medallion inlaid in left side. This revolver was originally part of a three gun set that also included Bicentennial versions of the Colt Single Action Army and Colt Python. Over the years, many of these sets have been broken up. Prices are for the Third Model Dragoon model alone. 1,776 mfg. 1976.

	$850	$525	N/A	N/A

3RD MODEL DRAGOON L. D. NIMSCHKE 1 OF 50 SPECIAL EDITION — .44 cal. perc., 7.5 in. round barrel, hinged loading lever, six-shot cylinder with rectangular bolt cuts and roll engraved Texas Ranger and Comanche Indian scene, silver plated barrel, frame, trigger guard, and backstrap, gold plated hammer, cylinder, wedge, trigger, and loading lever, high polish blue screws, one-piece ivory stocks with high relief American eagle hand carved on both sides. Includes an Arlo Werner hand-made presentation case that is covered in blue leather and tooled in gold. The French fit purple velvet lined interior is designed to hold a single revolver without accessories. American Master Engravers produced these revolvers exclusively for The Heritage Guild from "in-the-white" Third Model Dragoons supplied by Colt.

	$3,500	$2,450	N/A	N/A

Last MSR was $3,790.

GRADING - PPGS™	100%	98%	90%	80%

3RD MODEL DRAGOON (MN SERIES) — .44 cal. perc., 7.5 in. round barrel, hinged loading lever, six-shot cylinder with rectangular bolt cuts and roll engraved Texas Ranger and Indian scene, brass backstrap and round trigger guard, high polish blue barrel and cylinder, color case hardened frame, loading lever, plunger, and hammer, one-piece walnut stocks, 66 oz. Only 100 mfg., 75 as described above, 5 as described above but with one-piece ivory stocks, 20 with full bright nickel finish and one-piece ivory stocks.

* ***3rd Model Dragoon (MN Series) w/High Polish Blue/Walnut***

	100%	98%	90%	80%
	$1,200	$725	N/A	N/A

* ***3rd Model Dragoon (MN Series) w/High Polish Blue/Ivory***

	100%	98%	90%	80%
	$1,650	$1,050	N/A	N/A

* ***3rd Model Dragoon (MN Series) w/Full Bright Nickel/Ivory***

	100%	98%	90%	80%
	$2,100	$1,400	N/A	N/A

3RD MODEL DRAGOON STATEHOOD EDITION — .44 cal. perc., 7.5 in. round barrel, hinged loading lever, six-shot cylinder with rectangular bolt cuts and roll engraved Texas Ranger and Indian scene, high polish blue barrel and cylinder, case hardened frame, loading lever, plunger, and hammer, gold-plated brass backstrap and round trigger guard, two-piece ivory stocks. These revolvers were gold-inlaid and engraved, honoring the 50 states, Washington, D.C., and the USA. The serial numbers were the name of each state. Includes a special custom walnut presentation case with a French fit green velvet lined drawer designed to accommodate the Statehood Dragoon as well as a complete set of Colt Third Model Dragoon accessories that are numbered to the gun. 52 mfg.

	100%	98%	90%	80%
	$8,500	$6,200	N/A	N/A

Last MSR was $12,500.

3RD MODEL DRAGOON 150TH ANNIVERSARY ENGRAVING SAMPLER — .44 cal. perc., 7.5 in. round barrel, hinged loading lever, six-shot cylinder with rectangular bolt cuts and roll engraved Texas Ranger and Indian scene, high polish blue barrel and cylinder, brass backstrap and round trigger guard, color case hardened frame, loading lever, plunger, and hammer, one-piece ivory stocks, scrimshawed on the left side in script with: R. Henshaw 1831, L. Nimschke 1850-1900, C. Helfricht 1871-1921, & Contemporary. Models were "B" engraved with samples of each engraving style. 50 mfg., 25 in high polish blue, and 25 in bright nickel.

* ***3rd Model Dragoon 150th Ann. Eng. Sampler w/High Polish Blue Finish***

	100%	98%	90%	80%
	$2,750	$1,875	N/A	N/A

Last MSR was $1,560.

* ***3rd Model Dragoon 150th Ann. Eng. Sampler w/Full Bright Nickel Finish***

	100%	98%	90%	80%
	$3,000	$2,025	N/A	N/A

Last MSR was $1,764.

1851 NAVY/3RD MODEL DRAGOON BERMAN CASED SET 1 OF 50 SPECIAL EDITION — .36 (Navy) and .44 (Dragoon) cals. perc., this set includes two revolvers: a Colt Model 1851 Navy percussion revolver with 7.5 in. octagon barrel, hinged loading lever, six-shot cylinder with roll engraved naval battle scene, silver-plated brass backstrap and square back trigger guard, and a Colt Third Model Dragoon percussion revolver with 7.5 in. round barrel, hinged loading lever, six-shot cylinder with rectangular bolt cuts and roll engraved Texas Ranger and Indian scene, and polished brass round trigger guard and backstrap. Both revolvers feature a "C" Series "Royal Blue" barrel and cylinder with a case hardened frame, loading lever, plunger and hammer, each revolver is class "C" engraved, has gold inlaid frame border and barrel bands, and two-piece ivory grips with gold Colt medallions. This set includes an English fit presentation case with red velvet lined interior that is designed to accommodate two revolvers, a Colt 1851 Navy accessory set, and a Colt Third Model Dragoon accessory set. Produced 1978-79 for Jerry Berman & Sons in a series of 50 sets.

	100%	98%	90%	80%
	$8,500	$6,200	N/A	N/A

Last MSR was $10,500.

GRADING - PPGS™	100%	98%	90%	80%

1851 NAVY/3RD DRAGOON W/GOLD BARREL BAND AND "B" ENGRAVING — Two revolvers featuring class "B" engraving, gold barrel band at the muzzle, and gold rampant Colt flush inlaid on the left barrel lug. First revolver is a 1851 Navy .36 cal. percussion with 7.5 in. octagon barrel, hinged loading lever, six-shot cylinder with roll engraved naval battle scene, "C" Series Royal Blue barrel and cylinder, case hardened frame, loading lever, plunger and hammer, brass backstrap and square back trigger guard, one-piece walnut stocks. 42 oz. 50 Mfg. Second revolver is a 3rd Model Dragoon .44 cal. percussion with 7.5 in. round barrel, hinged loading lever, six shot cylinder with rectangular bolt cuts and roll engraved Texas Ranger and Indian scene, "C" Series Royal Blue barrel and cylinder, case hardened frame, loading lever, plunger and hammer, brass backstrap and round trigger guard, one-piece walnut stocks. 66 oz. 50 mfg.

* ***1851 Navy Single Revolver w/Gold Barrel Band and "B" Engraving*** — with enhancements as described above. Single 1851 Navy only (no presentation case or accessories). Issued from the same production quantity for the model listed above.

	$1,750	$1,125	N/A	N/A

Last MSR was $1,350.

* ***1851 Navy Cased Pair w/Gold Barrel Band and "B" Engraving*** — with enhancements as described above. Includes two 1851 Navy revolvers, two Colt 1851 Navy accessory sets and a two drawer dark walnut chest. Each drawer has an English fit dark blue velvet interior that is designed to house one revolver and a complete set of Colt accessories. Issued from the same production quantity for the model listed above.

	$4,250	$2,800	N/A	N/A

Last MSR was $4,895.

* ***3rd Model Dragoon Single Revolver w/Gold Barrel Band and "B" Engraving*** — with enhancements as described above. Single 3rd Model Dragoon only (no presentation case or accessories). Issued from the same production quantity for the model listed above.

	$1,750	$1,125	N/A	N/A

Last MSR was $1,350.

* ***3rd Model Dragoon Cased Pair w/Gold Barrel Band and "B" Engraving*** — with enhancements as described above. Includes two 3rd Model Dragoon revolvers, two Colt 3rd Model Dragoon accessory sets and a two drawer dark walnut chest. Each drawer has an English fit dark blue velvet interior that is designed to house one revolver and a complete set of Colt accessories. Issued from the same production quantity for the model listed above.

	$4,250	$2,800	N/A	N/A

Last MSR was $4,895.

* ***1851 Navy & 3rd Model Dragoon Cased Pair w/Gold Barrel Band and "B" Engraving*** — with enhancements as described above. Includes an 1851 Navy revolver with Colt 1851 Navy accessories, a 3rd Model Dragoon revolver with Colt 3rd Model Dragoon accessories, and a two drawer walnut chest similar to the one provided with the 1851 Navy Cased Pair and 3rd Model Dragoon Cased Pair listed above. These revolvers were issued from the same production quantities for the models listed above.

	$4,250	$2,800	N/A	N/A

Last MSR was $4,895.

* ***1851 Navy & 3rd Model Dragoon Cased Pair w/Gold Barrel Band, "B" Engraving and Ivory Grips*** — Includes one 1851 Navy revolver and one 3rd Model Dragoon revolver with the following exceptions to the enhancements as described above: The backstraps and trigger guards of each revolver are silver plated rather than plain brass. The grip is one-piece smooth ivory rather than one-piece walnut. This set also includes a Colt Custom Shop walnut presentation case with a French fit Tyrol red velvet interior. This case is designed to house the two revolvers only (no accessories). These revolvers were issued from the same production quantities for the models listed above. However, it is estimated that less than 10 sets of this type were produced.

	$4,500	$3,000	N/A	N/A

1851 NAVY CONQUISTADORES DEL CIELO SPECIAL EDITION — .36 cal. perc., 7.5 in. octagon barrel, hinged loading lever, six-shot cylinder with roll engraved naval battle scene, "C" Series Royal Blue barrel and cylinder, color case hardened frame, loading lever, plunger, and hammer, nickel-plated brass backstrap and square back trigger guard, one-piece walnut stocks. This set includes a custom walnut presentation case with French fit gold velvet lining and glass top. The case is designed to accommodate a single revolver, James Dixon & Sons bag type powder flask, "L" shaped nipple wrench/screw driver, two cavity brass bullet mold, cap tin, and a 1976 edition of the Conquistadores Del Cielo newsletter rolled into a scroll and secured with a leather strap. The 1851 Navy revolver is engraved with the original owner's name on the backstrap as well as special Conquistador roll markings on the barrel and barrel lug. 174 mfg.

	$3,500	$2,250	N/A	N/A

GRADING - PPGS™	100%	98%	90%	80%

1860 ARMY FLUTED CYLINDER — .44 cal. perc., 8 in. round barrel, creeping loading lever, six-shot full fluted cylinder without engraving, "F" Series Colt Blue barrel, cylinder, and backstrap, case hardened frame, loading lever, plunger, and hammer, brass trigger guard, one-piece walnut stocks. 2,670 mfg.

	$850	$575	$350	$275

Last MSR was $456.

1860 ARMY STAINLESS STEEL — .44 cal. perc., 8 in. round barrel, creeping loading lever, six-shot cylinder roll engraved with naval battle scene, brushed stainless steel barrel, cylinder, frame, loading lever, plunger, hammer, backstrap, and trigger guard, one-piece walnut stocks, 42 oz. 1,596 mfg. 1982 only.

	$900	$675	$400	$325

Last MSR was $485.

1861 NAVY — .36 cal. perc., 7.5 in. round barrel, creeping loading lever, six-shot cylinder roll engraved with naval battle scene, "F" Series Colt Blue barrel and cylinder, case hardened frame, loading lever, plunger, and hammer, silver plated brass backstrap and trigger guard, one-piece walnut stocks, 42 oz. 3,166 mfg. 1980-81.

	$800	$550	$325	$250

Last MSR was $420.

1861 NAVY STAINLESS STEEL — .36 cal. perc., 7.5 in. round barrel, creeping loading lever, six-shot cylinder roll engraved with naval battle scene, stainless steel barrel, cylinder, frame, loading lever, plunger, hammer, backstrap, and trigger guard, one-piece walnut stocks. 8 mfg. 1982 only.

	$7,500	$6,000	N/A	N/A

Last MSR was $473.

1862 POCKET NAVY — .36 cal. perc., 5.5 in. octagon barrel, hinged loading lever, five shot cylinder with roll engraved stagecoach scene, "F" Series Colt Blue barrel and cylinder, case hardened frame, loading lever, plunger, and hammer, silver plated brass backstrap and trigger guard, one-piece walnut stocks, 27 oz. 5,306 mfg. 1979-1981.

	$600	$425	$250	$200

Last MSR was $394.

1862 POCKET POLICE — .36 cal. perc., 5.5 in. round barrel, creeping loading lever, five-shot half fluted cylinder, "F" Series Colt Blue barrel and cylinder, case hardened frame, loading lever, plunger, and hammer, silver plated brass backstrap and trigger guard, one-piece walnut stocks. 3,756 mfg. 1980-81.

	$650	$475	$275	$225

Last MSR was $394.

"F" SERIES LIMITED/SPECIAL EDITIONS

WALKER COLT HERITAGE MODEL — .44 cal. perc., 9 in. round barrel, hinged loading lever, six-shot cylinder, blue barrel, cylinder, and backstrap, case hardened frame, loading lever, plunger, and hammer, brass trigger guard, one-piece walnut stocks. This model is embellished with gold etched portraits of Samuel Colt and Samuel Walker on the barrel lugs and a floral pattern banner gold etched on the barrel. Includes a French fit walnut presentation case with green velvet lining, walnut book rack, and a signed, leather bound edition of R.L. Wilson's book *The Colt Heritage* numbered to the gun. 1,853 mfg. 1980-81.

	$1,250	$750	N/A	N/A

Last MSR was $1,475.

1ST MODEL DRAGOON YORKTOWN VICTORY LIMITED EDITION — .44 cal. perc., 7.5 in. round barrel, hinged loading lever, six-shot cylinder with oval bolt cuts and roll engraved Texas Ranger and Indian scene, "F" Series Colt Blue barrel and cylinder, color case hardened frame, loading lever, plunger, and hammer, brass backstrap and square back trigger guard, one-piece walnut stocks. Includes a French fit, walnut presentation case with Tyrol red velvet interior built to house a single revolver without accessories. A brass plaque is affixed to the lid, which reads as follows: "America's Victory Celebration, Yorktown Virginia, October 19, 1981, One of One Hundred, 1781-1981, S-N." 100 mfg. 1981 only.

	$1,400	$875	N/A	N/A

3RD MODEL DRAGOON GIUSEPPE GARIBALDI LIMITED EDITION — .44 cal. perc., 7.5 in. round barrel, hinged loading lever, six-shot cylinder with rectangular bolt cuts, "F" Series Colt Blue barrel and cylinder, case hardened frame, loading lever, plunger, and hammer, brass backstrap and round trigger guard, one-piece walnut stocks. This model is embellished with gold etched portraits of Samuel Colt and Giuseppe Garibaldi on the cylinder and gold etched panels on the barrel. This set includes a French fit, walnut presentation case with a swiveling etched glass lid. The Tyrol red velvet lined interior is designed to accommodate a single Colt 3rd Model Dragoon without accessories. 106 mfg.

	$1,050	$675	N/A	N/A

Last MSR was $950.

GRADING - PPGS™	100%	98%	90%	80%

* ***3rd Model "Freak" Dragoon*** — this model was produced from a small quantity of unfinished Garibaldi Models and is within the same unique serial number range. The barrel and blank cylinder remain "in-the-white" and without any of the gold etching. Case hardened frame, loading lever, plunger, and hammer, brass backstrap and round trigger guard, one-piece walnut stocks. Also, no presentation case was furnished. 94 mfg.

	$750	$450	N/A	N/A

Last MSR was $395.

BABY DRAGOON 1 OF 500 LIMITED EDITION — .31 cal. perc., 4 in. octagon barrel without loading lever, five-shot cylinder roll engraved with Texas Ranger and Indian scene, "F" Series Colt Blue barrel and cylinder, case hardened frame and hammer, silver-plated brass backstrap and triggerguard, one-piece walnut stocks. This set includes a black painted walnut French fit presentation case with gold velvet lining, and a complete Colt Baby Dragoon accessory set (eagle style powder flask, brass two cavity bullet mold, "L" shaped nipple wrench, and cap tin) 500 mfg. 1979-80.

	$1,150	$675	N/A	N/A

1860 ARMY 1 OF 500 CASED LIMITED EDITION — .44 cal. perc., 8 in. round barrel, creeping loading lever, six-shot cylinder roll engraved with naval battle scene, "F" Series Colt Blue barrel, cylinder and backstrap, case hardened frame, loading lever, plunger, and hammer, brass trigger guard, one-piece walnut stocks. This set includes a black painted walnut French fit presentation case with gold velvet lining, gold plated 2nd edition belt buckle, complete Colt 1860 Army accessory set including "stand of flags" powder flask, two cavity blue steel bullet mold, "L" shaped nipple wrench, and cap tin. 500 mfg. 1979 only.

	$1,250	$750	N/A	N/A

1860 ARMY 150TH ANNIVERSARY ENGRAVING SAMPLER — .44 cal. perc., 8 in. round barrel, creeping loading lever, six-shot cylinder roll engraved with naval battle scene, high polish blue barrel, cylinder, and backstrap, case hardened frame, loading lever, plunger, and hammer, brass trigger guard, one-piece ivory stocks. Four different engraving styles are executed in class "B" coverage. The left grip is scrimshawed as follows: R. Henshaw 1831, L. Nimschke 1850-1900, C. Helfricht 1871-1921, Contemporary. Only 20 mfg., 10 in high polish blue, 10 in full bright nickel.

* ***1860 Army 150th Ann. Eng. Sampler w/High Polish Blue Finish***

	$3,250	$2,250	N/A	N/A

Last MSR was $1,290.

* ***1860 Army 150th Ann. Eng. Sampler w/Full Bright Nickel Finish***

	$3,500	$2,450	N/A	N/A

Last MSR was $1,484.

1860 ARMY BUTTERFIELD OVERLAND DESPATCH SPECIAL EDITION — .44 cal. perc., 5.5 in. round barrel, creeping loading lever, six-shot cylinder engraved with Butterfield Stagecoach scene, spare cylinder with engraved portrait of Col. David Butterfield, Conestoga wagon, and longhorn steer, barrel engraved with "BUTTERFIELD OVERLAND DESPATCH", surrounded by vine scroll detail on left side, "SPECIAL EDITION 1 of 500" on the right side, "F" Series Colt Blue barrel, cylinders and backstrap with cut for shoulder stock, case hardened frame, loading lever, plunger, and hammer, brass trigger guard, one-piece walnut stocks. Includes French fit book-style presentation case. 500 mfg. 1979 only.

	$1,250	$750	N/A	N/A

Last MSR was $995.

1860 ARMY ELECTROLESS NICKEL CASED WITH SHOULDER STOCK — .44 cal. perc., 8 in. round barrel, creeping loading lever, six-shot cylinder roll engraved with naval battle scene, electroless nickel finish on all steel parts, brass trigger guard, one-piece walnut stocks. Includes a walnut presentation case with French fit green velvet interior, complete set of Colt 1860 Army accessories, 3rd model shoulder stock with brass yoke and buttplate and electroless nickel finish on latch, thumbscrew, swivel, ring, and screws. This set also includes a Colt two-tone 2nd ed. belt buckle. Approx. 10-20 sets were produced.

	$3,000	$2,075	N/A	N/A

1860 FLUTED ARMY SPECIAL XFC SERIES — .44 cal. perc., similar to 1860 Fluted Army, except full bright nickel finish, and XFC serial number prefix. They were among the last 2nd gen. percussion revolvers produced by Colt. Serial number range XFC1-XFC10.

* ***1860 Fluted Army w/Ivory Stocks*** — One-piece smooth ivory stocks.

	$2,750	$1,875	N/A	N/A

* ***1860 Fluted Army w/Ebony Stocks and "C" Engraved*** — One-piece ebony stocks, and class "C" engraving coverage.

	$3,750	$2,625	N/A	N/A

GRADING - PPGS™	100%	98%	90%	80%

* ***1860 Fluted Army w/Ivory Stocks and "C" Engraved*** — One-piece smooth ivory stocks, and class "C" engraving coverage.

	$4,250	$3,000	N/A	N/A

1860 ARMY INTERSTATE COMMEMORATIVE EDITION CASED SET — .44 cal. perc., 8 in. two revolver set with creeping loading levers, six-shot cylinders roll engraved with naval battle scene and one-piece walnut stocks. Revolver #1 has a full antique gold finish. Revolver #2 has a full antique silver finish. This set includes an English fit walnut presentation case with Tyrol red interior. The case accommodates the two revolvers and a complete set of Colt 1860 Army accessories - "Stand of Flags" powder flask, two cavity blue steel bullet mold, "L" shaped nipple wrench, and Eley cap tin. Limited edition of approx. 20 sets.

	$4,000	$2,625	N/A	N/A

Last MSR was $1,495.

1860 ARMY MN SERIES (BRIGHT NICKEL) — .44 cal. perc., 8 in. round barrel, creeping loading lever, six-shot cylinder roll engraved with naval battle scene, full bright nickel finish and one-piece ivory stocks, 42 oz. 12 mfg.

	$2,500	$1,675	N/A	N/A

Last MSR was $580.

1860 ARMY U.S. CAVALRY COMMEMORATIVE CASED PAIR — .44 cal. perc., includes two Colt Model 1860 Army percussion revolvers with 8 in. round barrel, creeping loading lever, six-shot cylinder roll engraved with naval battle scene, blue barrel marked "UNITED STATES CAVALRY COMMEMORATIVE" on left side, cylinder, and backstrap, case hardened frame, loading lever, plunger, and hammer, brass trigger guard, one-piece walnut stocks, and English fit walnut presentation case with blue velvet lining. The case accommodates two revolvers and a "stand of flags" powder flask, blue two cavity bullet mold, "L" shaped nipple wrench, cap tin, and a detachable 3rd model shoulder stock. 2,945 cased sets mfg. 1977-1980.

	$1,500	$950	N/A	N/A

Last MSR was $995.

* ***1860 Army U.S. Cavalry Commemorative Cased Pair w/"C" Suffix*** — similar to 1860 Army U.S. Cavalry Commemorative Cased Pair, except these sets have a "C" stamped beneath the serial number on the frame. These sets have duplicate serial numbers therefore, the "C" was assigned to these revolvers in order for each revolver to have a unique serial number. 40 sets mfg. with "C" suffix serial no.

	$1,650	$1,050	N/A	N/A

Last MSR was $995.

* ***1860 Army U.S. Cavalry Commemorative w/Stock "C" Suffix*** — similar to 1860 Army U.S. Cavalry Commemorative Cased Pair, except single gun cased set with a matching 3rd model shoulder stock, a complete set of Colt 1860 Army accessories, and with "C" stamped beneath the ser. no. Issued from the same production quantity as the model above. 40 mfg.

	$1,400	$950	N/A	N/A

* ***1860 Army U.S. Cavalry Commemorative w/Custom Gold Inlaid*** — similar to 1860 Army U.S. Cavalry Commemorative Cased Pair, except has gold inlaid barrel band at the muzzle, gold star flush inlaid between each chamber at the rear of the cylinder, and inscription "XX of 40" engraved on the left side of each frame. 17 pair mfg.

	$3,750	$2,625	N/A	N/A

* ***1860 Army U.S. Cavalry Commemorative w/Custom Engraved and Gold Inlaid*** — similar 1860 Army U.S. Cavalry Commemorative Custom Gold Inlaid, except class "A" vine style scroll engraving on the barrels, class "B" engraving on the frames and stock mount, with wolf's head engraving on the hammers. Vine style engraving embellishes all accessories except the cap tin. 23 pair mfg.

	$6,750	$4,875	N/A	N/A

Last MSR was $4,500.

GRADING - PPGS™	100%	98%	90%	80%

1862 POCKET NAVY 1 OF 500 LIMITED EDITION — .36 cal. perc., 5.5 in. octagon barrel, hinged loading lever, five-shot cylinder with roll engraved stagecoach scene, "F" Series Colt Blue barrel and cylinder, case hardened frame, loading lever, plunger, and hammer, silver plated brass backstrap and trigger guard, one-piece walnut stocks. This set includes a black painted walnut French fit presentation case with gold velvet lining, special Colt 1st edition gold plated belt buckle with black anodized background, and a complete Colt accessory set (eagle style powder flask, two cavity blued steel bullet mold, "L" shaped nipple wrench, and cap tin). 500 mfg. 1979-80.

	$1,000	$575	N/A	N/A

1862 POCKET NAVY 150TH ANNIVERSARY ENGRAVING SAMPLER — .36 cal. perc., 5.5 in. octagon barrel, hinged loading lever, five-shot cylinder with roll engraved stagecoach scene, high polish blue barrel and cylinder, case hardened frame, loading lever, plunger, and hammer, brass backstrap and trigger guard, one-piece ivory stocks. Four different engraving styles are executed in class "B" coverage. The scrimshawed left grip reads as follows: R. Henshaw 1831, L. Nimschke 1850-1900, C. Helfricht 1871-1921, contemporary. 20 mfg., 10 in high polish blue, 10 in bright nickel.

* ***1862 Pocket Navy 150th Ann. Eng. Sampler w/High Polish Blue Finish***

	$2,400	$1,625	N/A	N/A

Last MSR was $960.

* ***1862 Pocket Navy 150th Ann. Eng. Sampler w/Full Bright Nickel Finish***

	$2,650	$1,800	N/A	N/A

Last MSR was $1,155.

1862 POCKET NAVY MN SERIES (BRIGHT NICKEL) — .36 cal. perc., 5.5 in. octagon barrel, hinged loading lever, five-shot cylinder with roll engraved stagecoach scene, full bright nickel finish and one-piece ivory stocks. 25 Mfg. 1984 only.

	$1,900	$1,250	N/A	N/A

Last MSR was $450.

1862 POCKET POLICE 1 OF 500 LIMITED EDITION — .36 cal. perc., 5.5 in. round barrel, creeping loading lever, five-shot half fluted cylinder, "F" Series Colt Blue barrel and cylinder, case hardened frame, loading lever, plunger, and hammer, silver-plated brass backstrap and trigger guard, one-piece walnut stocks. This set includes a black painted walnut French fit presentation case with gold velvet lining, special Colt 1st edition gold plated belt buckle with a black anodized background, and a complete Colt accessory set (eagle style powder flask, two cavity blued steel bullet mold, "L" shaped nipple wrench, and cap tin). 500 mfg. 1979-80.

	$1,050	$600	N/A	N/A

1862 POCKET POLICE 150TH ANNIVERSARY ENGRAVING SAMPLER — .36 cal. perc., 5.5 in. round barrel, creeping loading lever, five-shot half fluted cylinder, high polish blue barrel and cylinder, case hardened frame, loading lever, plunger, and hammer, brass backstrap and trigger guard, one-piece ivory grip. Class "B" engraving coverage is executed in four different styles. The scrimshawed left grip reads, R. Henshaw 1831, L. Nimschke 1850-1900, C. Helfricht 1871-1921, Contemporary. Four examples were produced. Another 16 were manufactured as described above but with a full bright nickel finish.

* ***1862 Pocket Police 150th Ann. Eng. Sampler w/High Polish Blue Finish***

	$4,250	$3,000	N/A	N/A

Last MSR was $960.

* ***1862 Pocket Police 150th Ann. Eng. Sampler w/Full Bright Nickel Finish***

	$2,750	$1,875	N/A	N/A

Last MSR was $1,155.

1862 POCKET POLICE MN SERIES (BRIGHT NICKEL) — .36 cal. perc., 5.5 in. round barrel, creeping loading lever, five-shot half fluted cylinder, full bright nickel finish with one-piece ivory stocks. 25 mfg. 1984 only.

	$2,150	$1,425	N/A	N/A

Last MSR was $450.

CONNECTICUT VALLEY ARMS (CVA)

Current manufacturer/distributor located in Norcross, GA. A division of Blackpowder Products, Inc. Catalog and dealer sales.

In August 1997, CVA implemented a voluntary recall of In-Line rifle models with serial numbers ending in "-95" or "-96" (sample serial # 61-13-xxxxxx-95). If you have a CVA In-Line model with such a serial number, do not allow anyone to use the rifle. Call CVA immediately at 770-449-4687 for complete details.

In May 1999, Blackpowder Products, Inc. purchased the assets of Connecticut Valley Arms, Inc.and now operates under the trade name of Connecticut Valley Arms and/or CVA. Blackpowder Products, Inc. assumed no liability for any products manufactured prior to January 1, 1998.

GRADING - PPGS™	100%	98%	90%	80%

PISTOLS: FLINTLOCK & PERCUSSION

All CVA pistols have color case hardened finishes with solid brass trim.

COLONIAL PISTOL — .45 cal. perc., 6.75 in. octagon barrel, 31 oz. Mfg. 1989-1994.

	$140	$105	$75	$55

Last MSR was $115.

HAWKEN PISTOL — .50 cal. flintlock or perc., 9.75 in. octagon barrel, 50 oz. Disc. 2004.

	$150	$135	$100	$70

Last MSR was $168.

Add 10% for flintlock.

KENTUCKY PISTOL — .45 or .50 cal. perc., 10.25 in. octagon barrel, brass blade front sight, 40 oz. Disc. 2004.

	$145	$130	$95	$65

Last MSR was $168.

MOUNTAIN PISTOL — .45 or .50 cal. perc., 9 in. octagon barrel, German silver wedge plate with pewter cap, 40 oz.

	$155	$140	$105	$75

PHILADELPHIA DERRINGER — .45 cal. perc., 3.25 in. octagon barrel, 16 oz. Disc. 1994.

	$125	$105	$75	$50

Last MSR was $90.

PROSPECTOR — .44 cal. perc., 8.5 in. tapered octagon barrel, 1:22 in. twist, fixed sights, brass rear grip strap and trigger guard, engraved steel frame, blue finish, revolver style walnut grip and forearm, 12.75 OAL, 42 oz. Mfg. 1984-1987.

	$185	$165	$125	$105

Last MSR was $89.

Was available as a kit, last MSR was $63.

SIBER PISTOL — .45 cal. perc., 10.5 in. octagon, white steel engraved barrel, lock also engraved white steel, checkered walnut grip, 38 oz. Disc. 1994.

	$425	$350	$275	$185

Last MSR was $440.

TOWER PISTOL — .45 cal. perc., 9 in. octagon barrel (tapers to round at muzzle), antique brass trigger, 36 oz.

	$150	$135	$100	$70

REVOLVERS: PERCUSSION

All revolvers have solid brass triggerguards and backstraps, and walnut grips.

WALKER MODEL — .44 cal. perc., 9 in. barrel, color case hardened frame, hammer, and loading lever, 72 oz. Disc. 1996.

	$315	$275	$215	$165

Last MSR was $280.

3RD MODEL DRAGOON — .44 cal. perc., 7.5 in. barrel, rectangular bolt cuts in cylinder, color case hardened frame, loading lever, plunger, and hammer, round trigger guard, one-piece grip, 66 oz. Disc. 1994.

	$265	$225	$175	$100

Last MSR was $220.

1849 POCKET WELLS FARGO — .31 cal. perc., 3, 4, or 5 in. octagon barrel, 5 shot, color case hardened frame, hammer, no loading lever, brass trim, 1.5 lbs. Disc. 1994.

	$165	$125	$95	$60

Last MSR was $130.

1851 NAVY — .36 (disc. 1996) or .44 cal. perc., 7.5 in. octagon barrel, brass frame, 38 oz. Disc. 2004.

	$165	$125	$95	$60

Last MSR was $144.

Add 50% for steel frame.

GRADING - PPGS™	100%	98%	90%	80%

1861 NAVY — .36 or .44 cal. perc., 7.5 in. round barrel, six-shot engraved cylinder, color case hardened frame, trigger, and loading lever, or brass frame (.44 cal. only), 44 oz. New 1986.

	$165	$125	$95	$60

Last MSR was $140.

Add 50% for color case hardened steel frame.
Add 50% for presentation grade Sheriff's Model with matching powder flask.
Add 10% for brass frame on Standard Sheriff's Model.
Add 25% for steel frame on Standard Sheriff's Model.

1851 NAVY/1851 SHERIFF'S MODEL (WAR AND PEACE) — .36 cal. perc., includes 1851 Navy and 1851 Sheriff's Models, heavily engraved in rosewood presentation case. Disc. 1994.

	$425	$375	$250	$195

Last MSR was $630.

1858 REMINGTON ARMY — .44 cal. perc., 8 in. octagon barrel, color case hardened hammer, steel or brass frame, 38 oz. Disc. 2004.

	$195	$160	$115	$75

Last MSR was $160.

Add 30% for steel frame.

1858 REMINGTON BISON — .44 cal. perc., brass frame, 10.25 in. octagon barrel, adj. sights, 3 lbs.

	$165	$125	$95	$60

Last MSR was $200.

NEW MODEL REMINGTON POCKET — .31 cal. perc., 5 shot, 4 in. octagon barrel, brass frame, 15 oz. Mfg. 1989-disc.

	$145	$115	$85	$55

Last MSR was $150.

1858 REMINGTON TARGET — .44 cal. perc., 12 in. octagon barrel, brass frame and trigger guard, adj. sights, based on 1858 Navy frame, 38 oz.

	$265	$225	$175	$100

Last MSR was $205.

1860 ARMY — .44 cal. perc., 8 in. round barrel, six-shot engraved cylinder, color case hardened frame, trigger, and loading lever, 44 oz. Disc. 1996.

	$220	$185	$115	$70

Last MSR was $195.

Subtract 25% for brass frame.

1873 COLT SINGLE ACTION — .44 cal. perc., 7 in. round barrel, brass backstrap and trigger guard, color case hardened frame and cylinder, new in 1991 (this is a ball and cap version of the 1873 Colt SAA). Disc. 1994.

	$345	$300	$225	$190

Last MSR was $350.

OFFICER AND THE GENTLEMAN — matched set .44 cal. perc., 1858 Rem. Army and .31 cal. perc. New Model Remington Pocket, heavily engraved in rosewood presentation case. Disc. 1994.

	$475	$425	$315	$260

Last MSR was $650.

POCKET POLICE — .36 cal. perc., 5.5 in. round barrel, color case hardened frame, loading lever, plunger, and hammer, round trigger guard, fluted cylinder, one-piece grip, 25 oz. Disc. 1996.

	$145	$115	$85	$55

Last MSR was $140.

Add 40% for steel frame.
Add 5% for Sheriff's Model.
Add 50% for engraved, nickel plated Sheriff's Model w/matching powder flask.

RIFLES: FLINTLOCK & PERCUSSION

BLUNDERBUSS — .69 cal. flintlock, 16 in. tapered to flared muzzle barrel, brass trim, available right or left hand, 5 lbs. 5 oz. Disc. 1994.

	$240	$195	$145	$95

Last MSR was $255.

GRADING - PPGS™	100%	98%	90%	80%

BOBCAT HUNTER RIFLE — .36, .50, or .54 (disc.) cal. perc., 26 in. octagon barrel, (1:48 in. twist) matte black finish, adj. sights, hardwood or synthetic stock. Mfg. 1995-2005.

	$65	$50	N/A	N/A

Last MSR was $70.

Add 60% for .36 cal. Disc.
Subtract 25% for fixed sights.
Add $30 for hardwood stock.

BUSHWACKER RIFLE — .50 cal. perc., 26 in. octagon barrel, color case hardened hammer, lock, and nipple, blue furniture, 7.5 lbs. Disc. 1994.

	$140	$120	$85	$55

Last MSR was $160.

EXPRESS RIFLE — .50 or .54 cal. perc., double barrel, 28 in. tapered round barrel, color case hardened plate, hammers, and trim, adj. sights. Mfg. 1986-disc.

	$575	$400	$350	$275

Last MSR was $430.

Add 40% for extra set of 12 ga. barrels.
Add 100% for presentation grade.

FRONTIER RIFLE/CARBINE — .45, .50, or .54 cal. flintlock or perc., 28 in. octagon barrel, brass trim, right or left-hand, 7.9 lbs. Disc. 1994.

	$160	$145	$95	$65

Last MSR was $190.

Add $15 for flintlock.
Add $10 for left-hand.
Add $10 for carbine model.

FRONTIER HUNTER CARBINE — .50 or .54 cal. perc., 24 in. blue octagon barrel, color case hardened hammer and lock, blue furniture, adj. rear sight, 7.5 lbs. Disc. 2002.

	$190	$165	$125	$90

Last MSR was $220.

During 1995, a laminated stock became standard on this model.

HAWKEN RIFLE/CARBINE — .50 or .54 cal. flintlock or perc., 28 in. octagon chrome bore barrel, brass trim, beavertail select walnut stock, 7 lbs. 15 oz. Disc. 1994.

	$335	$290	$235	$175

Last MSR was $440.

Add $10 for flintlock.

HAWKEN DEERSLAYER RIFLE/CARBINE — .50 cal. perc., similar to above, 7.5 lbs. Mfg. 1992 only.

	$220	$185	$135	$80

Last MSR was $250.

HUNTER HAWKEN RIFLE/CARBINE — .50 or .54 cal. perc., 24 in. (carbine) or 28 in. octagon barrel, color case hardened lock and nipple, sling swivels, adj. hunting sights. 8 lbs. Disc. 1994.

	$230	$190	$140	$85

Last MSR was $330.

Add $70 for premier grade (.50 cal. only).

KENTUCKY RIFLE/HUNTER — .45 or .50 cal. flintlock or perc., 33.5 in. octagon barrel, color case hardened hammer and plate, antique brass trigger, 7.25 lbs. Disc. 1996.

	$210	$180	$120	$75

Last MSR was $280.

Add $10 for flintlock, or adj. hunting sights.

LYNX RIFLE — .50 or .54 cal. perc., similar to Bobcat Hunter but with camo Realtree gray stock and 1:32 in. twist barrel. Disc. 1996.

	$160	$130	$100	$70

Last MSR was $180.

GRADING - PPGS™	100%	98%	90%	80%

MISSOURI HUNTER RIFLE — .50 cal. perc., 28 in. octagon barrel, adj. hunting sights, color case hardened hammer and lock, recoil pad, 9 lbs. 6 oz. Mfg.1991-94.

	$240	$190	$140	$95

Last MSR was $300.

MISSOURI RANGER — .50 cal. perc., 28 in. octagon barrel, color case hardened trim, right or left-hand, 7.5 lbs.

	$190	$155	$115	$85

MOUNTAIN RIFLE — .50 or .54 cal. flintlock or perc., 32 in. octagon barrel, German silver wedge plate and patch box, pewter or German silver nose cap, 7 lbs. 14 oz. Disc. 1994.

	$240	$190	$140	$95

Last MSR was $260.

Add 30% for premier grade (chrome bore and German silver trim).

MOUNTAIN RIFLE CLASSIC — .50 cal. perc., 32 in. brown steel barrel, 1:66 inch rifling twist, brown hardware, German silver wedge plates and blade front sight, buckhorn rear sight, American hard maple stock, 9 lbs. Modeled after the original CVA Mountain Rifle. Made in the USA. In limited quantities. Disc. 2004.

	$350	$275	$225	$170

Last MSR was $400.

MOUNTAIN RIFLE HUNTER — .50 cal. perc., 32 in. blue steel barrel, 1:48 inch rifling twist, blue hardware, blade front sight, buckhorn rear sight, hardwood stock, 9 lbs. Modeled after the original CVA Mountain Rifle. Made in the USA. Limited quantities. Mfg. 2002-05.

	$235	$185	$135	$95

Last MSR was $260.

OVER/UNDER DOUBLE BARREL CARBINE — .50 cal. perc., O/U, 26 in. octagon tapering to round barrels, color case hardened lock, hammers, and triggers, checkered walnut stock, 8.5 lbs. Disc. 1994.

	$575	$500	$375	$275

Last MSR was $800.

PANTHER CARBINE — .50 or .54 cal. perc., 24 in. octagon blue barrel, color case hardened hammer (45 degree offset) and lock, modern trigger, adj. rear sight, available in left-hand (.50 cal. only), epoxy coated hardwood stock with recoil pad, 7.5 lbs. Disc. 1994.

	$170	$145	$105	$70

Last MSR was $190.

Add 10% for left-hand.

PENNSYLVANIA LONG RIFLE — .50 cal. flintlock or perc., 40 in. octagon barrel, color case hardened hammers and plate, brass trim, 8 lbs. 3 oz. Disc. 1993.

	$395	$345	$235	$195

Last MSR was $455.

PLAINSHUNTER RIFLE — .50 cal. flintlock or perc., octagon barrel, 1:48 in. twist, color case hardened hammer and lock, brass nose cap and trigger guard. New 1995. Disc.

	$160	$130	$95	$70

Last MSR was $175.

PLAINSMAN RIFLE — .50 cal. flintlock or perc., 26 in. blue octagon barrel, color case hardened lock and nipple, select hardwood stock, 6.5 lbs. Disc. 2004.

	$150	$125	$95	$65

Last MSR was $180.

SIERRA STALKER RIFLE — .50 cal. perc., 28 in. blue octagon barrel, color case hardened hammer and lock, adj. sight (rear), 7.25 lbs. Mfg. 1993-94.

	$170	$145	$105	$70

Last MSR was $190.

GRADING - PPGS™	100%	98%	90%	80%

SQUIRREL RIFLE — .32 cal. flintlock or perc., 25 in. octagon barrel, color case hardened hammer and plate, brass trim, stainless steel nipple, 5 lbs. 12 oz. Disc. 1994.

	$235	$180	$130	$95

Last MSR was $250.

Add 5% for flintlock or left-hand.

ST. LOUIS HAWKEN — .50 or .54 cal. flintlock or perc., 28 in. blue octagon barrel, select hardwood stock, fully adjustable sights, brass trim, buttplate, patch box, 7 lbs. 13 oz. Also available in left-hand percussion model. Mfg. 1995-2005.

	$205	$165	$125	$125

Last MSR was $230.

Add $45 for left-hand percussion model. Disc. 2004.

STALKER RIFLE — .50 cal. perc., 28 in. octagon barrel, hunting style sight (click adj.) color case hardened hammer and lock, recoil pad, 7 lbs. 4 oz. Mfg. 1991-94.

	$190	$155	$115	$80

Last MSR was $220.

Add 50% for premier grade.
Add 10% for left-hand.

TRACKER CARBINE — .50 cal. perc., 21 in. blue half round/half octagon barrel, color case hardened nipple, hammer and lock, new laminated stock in 1994, 6.5 lbs. Disc. 1994.

	$195	$160	$120	$85

Last MSR was $230.

TROPHY CARBINE — .50 or .54 cal. perc., 24 in. half round/half octagon, similar to above with sling swivel mounts and dark stained Monte Carlo stock, 7.5 lbs. Disc. 1994.

	$230	$175	$130	$90

Last MSR was $260.

VARMINT RIFLE — .32 cal. perc., 24 in. octagon, blue barrel, color case hardened hammer and lock, brass trigger guard and furniture, adj. rear sight, 6.75 lbs. New 1993.

	$200	$160	$120	$85

Last MSR was $220.

WOLF SERIES RIFLES — .50 or .54 cal. perc., 26 in. matte blue barrel, color case hardened hammer and lock, adj. sights, Tuff-Lite stock, 6.5 lbs.

	$140	$115	$85	$55

Last MSR was $170.

Add 10% for Lone Wolf Rifle with better rear sight and vent. recoil pad (.50 cal. only).
Add 20% for Timber Wolf Rifle with RealTree all purpose camo stock (.50 cal. only).
Add 10% for Silver Wolf Rifle with stainless steel barrel & nickel hardware.

WOODSMAN RIFLE — .50 or .54 cal. perc., 26 in. octagon blue barrel, color case hardened hammer and lock, brass tip ramrod, adj. sights, laminated stock, 6.5 lbs.

	$170	$145	$105	$75

Last MSR was $190.

YOUTH HUNTER — .50 cal. perc., 24 in. octagon blue barrel, shortened half stock, adj. sights, select hardwood stock, designed according to input from the YMCA, Hunter Education, Boy Scouts of America, and 4-H Clubs, 5 lbs. Disc. 2004.

	$125	$105	$70	$50

Last MSR was $136.

ZOUAVE RIFLE — .58 cal. perc., 32.5 in. tapered barrel with bayonet mount, brass trim, and adj. sight, 9.75 lbs. Mfg. 1989-1994.

	$295	$220	$165	$115

Last MSR was $335.

GRADING - PPGS™	100%	98%	90%	80%

RIFLES: IN-LINE IGNITION

All Apollo models are percussion, and were discontinued in 1997. In August 1997, CVA implemented a voluntary recall of In-Line rifle models with serial numbers ending in "-95" or "-96" (sample serial # 61-13-xxxxxx-95). If you have a CVA In-Line model with such a serial number, do not allow anyone else to use the rifle. Call CVA immediately at 1-770-449-4687 for complete details.

Note: All Apex and Optima Elite break-action muzzleloading rifles with the interchangeable barrel system are classified as FIREARMS and, therefore, require form 4473 for purchase.

ACCURA 209 MAGNUM — .45 or .50 cal., #209 primer ignition, break-action, 27 in. round fluted barrel w/ bullet guiding muzzle, stainless steel or matte blue finish, 1:28 in. twist rifling, stainless steel breech plug, ambidextrous black FiberGrip or Realtree® APG™ HD® camo composite stock w/high comb PG or thumbhole, CrushZone™ recoil pad, adj. DuraSight® fiber optic sights, drilled and tapped for scope mounts, Quake Claw™ sling, extendable aluminum loading rod 14.5 in. LOP, 7.3 lbs. New 2008.

MSR $346	$315	$280	$210	$175

Add $58 for stainless steel.
Add $57 for Realtree® APG™ HD® camo stock.
Add $35 for thumbhole stock.

APEX 209 MAGNUM — .45 or .50 cal., #209 primer ignition, patent pending E-Z OpenTM break-action breeching mechanism, interchangeable barrel system, 27 in. stainless steel round fluted muzzleloading barrel, stainless steel breech plug, 1:28 in. twist rifling, ambidextrous black FiberGrip or Realtree® APG™ HD synthetic PG stock w/ rubber grip panels, CrushZone™ recoil pad, custom DuraSight® Z-2 Alloy™ rail mount, Quake Claw™ sling, extendable aluminum loading rod, 14.5 in. LOP, 42 in. OAL, 8 lbs. New 2009.

MSR $577	$520	$460	$345	$285

Add $75 for Realtree® APG™ HD® camo stock.

Requires Form 4473 for purchase.

APOLLO RIFLE — .50 or .54 cal. perc., 22 in. (carbine), 24, 25, or 27 in. round tapered barrel with chrome bore, straight pull bolt design.

* ***Apollo 90 Rifle***

	$240	$185	$135	$95

Last MSR was $260.

* ***Apollo 90 Shadow Rifle*** — with duragrip synthetic stock.

	$220	$170	$125	$90

Last MSR was $240.

* ***Apollo Brown Bear*** — with hardwood stock and Williams Hunter sight.

	$200	$160	$120	$85

Last MSR was $224.

* ***Apollo Buckmaster*** — with camo duragrip synthetic stock.

	$220	$170	$125	$90

Last MSR was $247.

* ***Apollo Carbelite*** — similar to Apollo 90 models, except has Carbelite stock.

	$295	$265	$215	$175

Last MSR was $350.

* ***Apollo Comet*** — with duragrip stock and adj. trigger.

	$250	$190	$135	$95

Last MSR was $280.

* ***Apollo Dominator*** — with Bell & Carlson synthetic stock, stainless steel barrel, and modern adj. trigger.

	$250	$190	$135	$95

Last MSR was $330.

* ***Apollo Eclipse*** — this is the standard model.

	$175	$150	$105	$75

Last MSR was $208.

GRADING - PPGS™	100%	98%	90%	80%

* ***Apollo Shadow Rifle*** — similar to Apollo 90 Shadow model.

	$220	$170	$125	$90

Last MSR was $240.

* ***Apollo Sporter*** — with standard sporter stock and 25 in. barrel.

	$200	$160	$120	$85

Last MSR was $225.

* ***Apollo Stag Horn*** — basic version of Apollo rifle with duragrip synthetic stock.

	$160	$130	$100	$70

Last MSR was $185.

* ***Apollo Starfire*** — with duragrip stock and stainless steel barrel.

	$240	$185	$135	$95

Last MSR was $270.

ACCUBOLT RIFLE — .50 cal. perc., 24 in. round barrel, synthetic standard thumbhole stock. 7.5 lbs.

	$305	$250	$190	$145

Last MSR was $340.

Accubolt Pro with Thumbhole Stock	$500	$425	$300	$205

Last MSR was $560.

BLAZER I/II RIFLE — .50 cal. perc., 28 in. octagon barrel, stainless steel nipple, brass tipped ramrod, 6.75 lbs. Disc. 1994.

	$150	$125	$95	$65

Last MSR was $210.

Subtract $10 for Blazer II.

BUCKHORN 209 MAGNUM — .50 cal., #209 primer ignition, 24 in. round MonoBlock barrel/receiver (drilled and tapped), 1:28 in. twist, bullet guiding muzzle, blue finish, adj. Illuminator (disc. 2007)DuraSight® (new 2008) fiber optic sights, black solid composite PG stock w/molded-in grip panels and sling swivel studs, CrushZone recoil pad, 42 in. OAL, 14.25 in. LOP, 6.3 lbs. New 2004.

courtesy CVA

MSR $157	$140	$125	$95	$75

ECLIPSE SERIES — .50 or .54 cal. perc., 24 in. round blue barrel, regular or black synthetic stock. 7 lbs. New 1998.

	$145	$120	$90	$65

Last MSR was $180.

Subtract $10 for black synthetic stock.

ECLIPSE 209 MAGNUM — .45 or .50 cal. perc., 24 in. round matte blue MonoBlock barrel/receiver, adjustable fiber optic sights, black synthetic, Mossy Oak Break-Up (new 2003), Timber Blue (disc. 2003), or Bigwoods Blue (disc. 2003) stock, 3-way ignition, #209 shot shell primer, musket cap, and No. 11 percussion cap, 6 lbs. Disc. 2004.

	$130	$105	$70	$50

Last MSR was $150.

Add 30% for Mossy Oak Break-Up, Bigwoods, or Timber Blue stock.

GRADING - PPGS™	100%	98%	90%	80%

ELECTRA — .50 cal., electronic ARC™ ignition, 26 in. blue or stainless steel fluted bbl. w/ bullet guiding muzzle, 1:28 in. twist rifling, adj. DuraSight® fiber optic sights and scope mount rail, ambidextrous PG semi-solid composite stock w/black FiberGrip or Realtree Hardwoods Green HD Camo finish, extendable aluminum loading rod, Quake™ Claw sling, CrushZone™ recoil pad, 14.5 LOP., 7.5 lbs. New 2007.

courtesy CVA

MSR $404	**$365**	**$325**	**$240**	**$200**

Add $116 for stainless steel barrel with Realtree Hardwoods Green HD Camo stock.
Add $57 for stainless steel barrel.

ELKHORN PRO 209 MAGNUM — .50 cal., 3-way ignition (#11, musket or 209 primer) system w/primer ejecting bolt face, bolt action, 26 in. round fluted blue bbl. w/bullet guiding muzzle, 1:28 in. twist rifling, aluminum loading rod, ergonomic PG black fleck (disc. 2007), black FiberGrip (new 2008), Realtree Advantage Timber HD camo composite stock, Quake™ Claw sling, adj. DuraBright® fiber optic sights, drilled and tapped for scope mounts, CrushZone™recoil pad, 14.25 LOP., 7 lbs. New 2005.

courtesy CVA

MSR $271	**$250**	**$220**	**$165**	**$140**

Add $52 for Realtree Timber HD Camo stock.

FIREBOLT RIFLE — .50 or .54 cal. perc., 24 in. round barrel, synthetic standard stock. 7 lbs. New 1998.

	$245	**$190**	**$135**	**$95**

Last MSR was $280.

FireBolt Stainless	**$260**	**$200**	**$145**	**$100**

Last MSR was $300.

* ***Firebolt Thumbhole*** — with steel barrel.

	$245	**$190**	**$135**	**$95**

Last MSR was $280.

FIREBOLT TEFLON RIFLES — .50 or .54 cal. perc., 24 in. round Teflon coated barrel, Teflon coating on all metal parts, synthetic standard stock. 7 lbs. New 1998.

	$260	**$200**	**$145**	**$100**

Last MSR was $300.

FIREBOLT LEFT-HAND RIFLE — .50 cal. perc., 24 in. round matte blue barrel, hardwood stock. 7.5 lbs. New 1998.

	$260	**$200**	**$145**	**$100**

Last MSR was $300.

GRADING - PPGS™	100%	98%	90%	80%

FIREBOLT 209 ULTRAMAG — .45 or .50 cal. perc., 26 in. fluted round MonoBlock barrel/receiver (drilled and tapped), bolt-action, matte blue or nickel finish, black FiberGrip synthetic, Mossy Oak Break-Up (new 2003), Bigwoods Blue (disc. 2003), or Timber Blue (disc. 2003) stock, adjustable fiber optic sights, ventilated recoil pad, 3-way ignition - #209 shot shell primer (standard 2004), musket or No. 11 percussion cap (disc. 2004), 44 in. OAL, 7 lbs. Mfg. 2001-05.

	$175	$150	$105	$75

Last MSR was $200.

Add $20 nickel barrel.
Add $40 for Mossy Oak Break-Up stock (new 2003).
Add $60 for Bigwoods Blue, or Timber Blue stock (disc. 2003).

HUNTERBOLT 209 MAGNUM RIFLES — .45 (new 2002) or .50 cal. perc., 26 in. round MonoBlock barrel/receiver (drilled and tapped), matte blue or nickel finish, adjustable fiber optic sights, black synthetic or Mossy Oak Break-Up (new 2003) stock, 3-way ignition - #209 shot shell primer (standard 2004), musket or No. 11 percussion cap (disc. 2004), 44 in. OAL, 7 lbs. Disc. 2005.

	$160	$130	$100	$70

Last MSR was $180.

Add $15 for nickel barrel.
Add $40 for Mossy Oak Break-Up (new 2003).
Add $40 for Bigwoods Blue, or Timber Blue stock (disc. 2003).

KODIAK 209 MAGNUM — .45 or .50 cal., #209 primer ignition, pivot block action, 28 in. round barrel, blue or nickel finish, 1:28 in. twist rifling, ambidextrous PG solid composite black or Mossy Oak Camo finish stock, Quake Claw® sling (new 2006), adj. Illuminator fiber optic sights, CrushZone™ recoil pad, 42 in. OAL, 7.5 lbs. Mfg. 2004-2007.

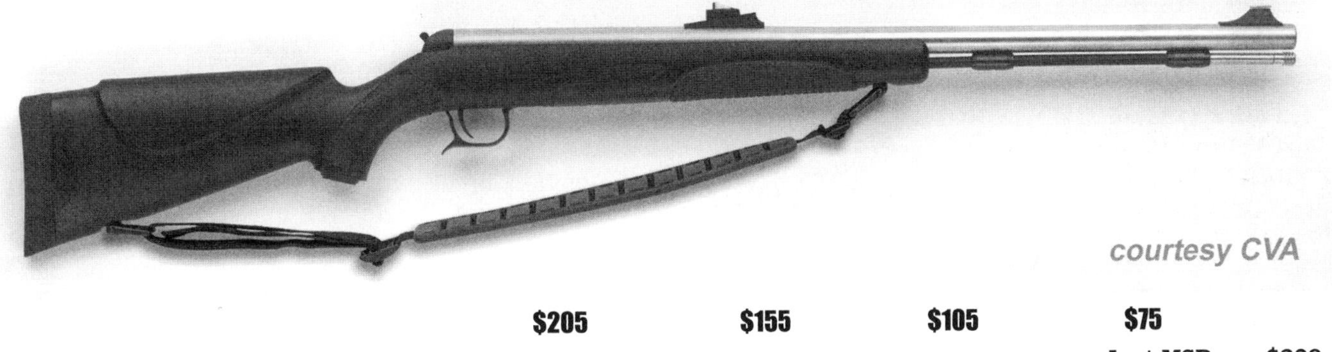
courtesy CVA

	$205	$155	$105	$75

Last MSR was $230.

Add $59 for Mossy Oak Camo stock.
Add $10 for nickle finish.

KODIAK PRO 209 MAGNUM — .45 or .50 cal., #209 primer ignition, pivot block action, 29 in. round fluted bbl. w/bullet guiding muzzle, blue, stainless steel or Realtree Hardwoods Green HD Camo bbl., 1:28 in. twist rifling, extendable aluminum loading rod, ambidextrous semi-solid black fleck (disc. 2006), black FiberGrip (new 2007) or Realtree Hardwoods Green HD camo composite or laminated (2006-2007) PG or thumbhole stock, Quake™ Claw sling, adj. DuraBright® fiber optic sights, drilled and tapped for scope mounts, CrushZone™recoil pad, 14.37 LOP., 7.5 lbs. New 2005.

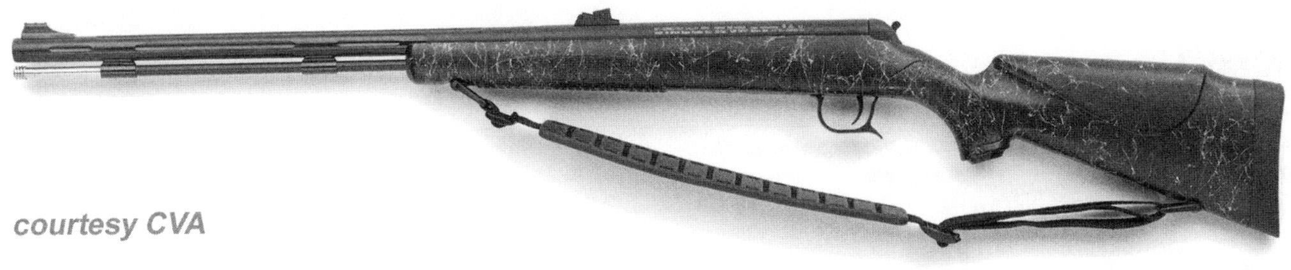
courtesy CVA

MSR $230	$205	$185	$140	$120

Add $118 for PG laminated wood stock. Disc. 2007.
Add $143 for thumbhole laminated wood stock. Disc. 2007.
Add $59 for stainless steal.
Add $12 for Realtree Hardwoods Green HD Camo.

GRADING - PPGS™	100%	98%	90%	80%

MONSTER BUCK RIFLE — .50 or .54 cal. perc., 24 in. round matte blue barrel, synthetic X-Tra Brown camo stock. 7 lbs.

	$250	$190	$135	$95

Last MSR was $290.

OPTIMA 209 MAGNUM — .45 (disc. 2006) or .50 cal., #209 primer ignition, break-action, 26 in. round barrel w/ bullet guiding muzzle, 1:28 in. twist rifling, blue or nickel finish, high comb PG or thumbhole (new 2008) ambidextrous solid composite stock w/black, Mossy Oak Break-Up (disc. 2007), Realtree® Hardwoods HD (new 2008) or Realtree® Hardwoods Green HD (new 2009) camo finish, adj. Illuminator (disc. 2007) or DuraSight® (new 2008) all metal fiber optic sights, drilled and tapped for scope mounts, Quake Claw™ sling (new 2006), ventilated or Crush-Zone (new 2008) recoil pad, 14.43 in. LOP, 41 in. OAL, 8.2 lbs. New 2003.

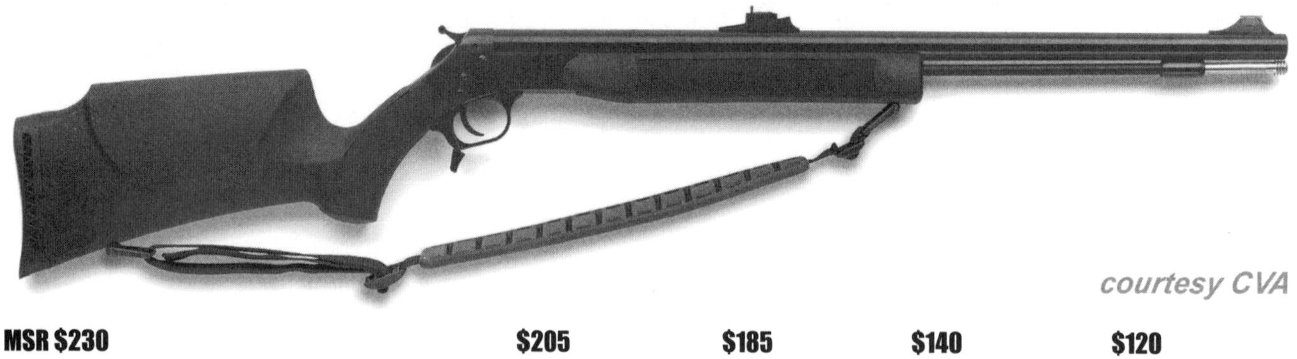

courtesy CVA

MSR $230	$205	$185	$140	$120

Add $23 for thumbhole stock.
Add $21 for nickel finish.
Add $72 for Realtree Hardwoods Green HD® stock. New 2008.
Add $57 for Mossy Oak Break-Up stock. Disc. 2007.
Add $83 for additional blue barrel. Disc. 2006.
Add $98 for additional nickel barrel. Disc. 2006.

OPTIMA ELITE 209 MAGNUM — .45 or .50 cal., #209 primer ignition, break-action, interchangeable barrel system, 28 (new 2007) or 29 (disc. 2006) in. fluted round barrel w/bullet guiding muzzle,1:28 in. twist rifling, extendable loading rod, stainless steel or blue finish, PG or thumbhole (new 2006), high comb ambidextrous laminate (2007 only) or solid composite stock w/black FiberGrip, Mossy Oak (disc. 2007), Realtree Hardwoods HD (2008 only) or Realtree Hardwoods Green HD finish, all metal adj. Dura-Bright fiber optic sights, Quake Claw™ sling, CrushZone™ recoil pad, 14.5 in. LOP, 8.8 lbs. New 2005.

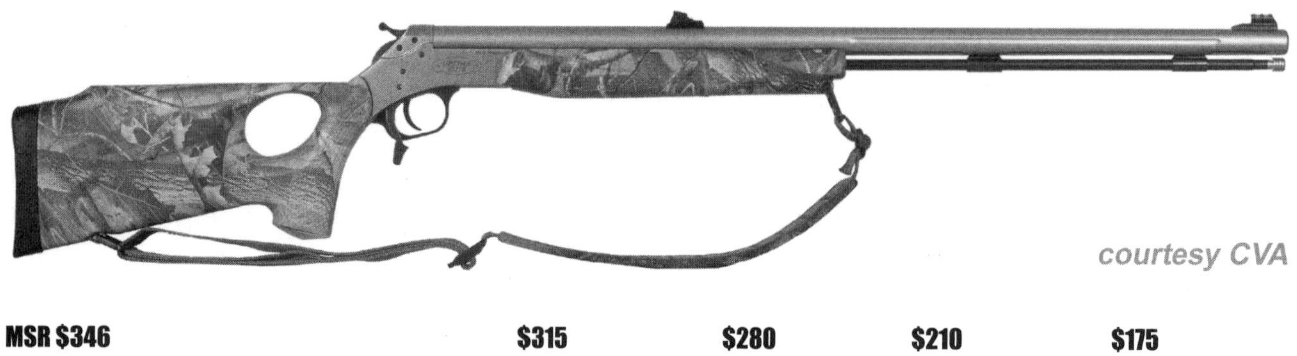

courtesy CVA

MSR $346	$315	$280	$210	$175

Add $21 to $51 for thumbhole stock.
Add $22 for Realtree Hardwoods HD or Realtree Hardwoods Green HD stock.
Add $28 for Mossy Oak Hardwoods Green HD stock.
Add $115 for laminate thumbhole stock.
Add $55 for stainless steel.

Requires Form 4473 for purchase.

OPTIMA ELITE COMPACT — .45 or .50 cal., #209 primer ignition, break-action, 24 in. round blue barrel, 1:28 in. twist rifling, ambidextrous PG solid composite black FiberGrip stock, all metal adj. Dura-Bright® fiber optic sights, Quake Claw™ sling, CrushZone™ recoil pad, 13.3 in. LOP, 6 lbs. New 2006.

MSR $311	$280	$245	$175	$145

Requires Form 4473 for purchase.

GRADING - PPGS™	100%	98%	90%	80%

OPTIMA PRO 209 MAGNUM — .45 or .50 cal., #209 primer ignition, break-action, interchangeable 28 (new 2007) or 29 (disc. 2006) in. fluted round blue or nickel finish barrel, 1:28 in. twist rifling, bullet guiding muzzle, PG or thumbhole (new 2006), laminate (new 2007) or solid composite w/black FiberGrip or Mossy Oak Break-Up finish stock, all metal adj. Dura-Bright fiber optic sights, Quake Claw™ sling, ventilated recoil pad, 44 in. OAL, 8.8 lbs. Mfg. 2003-2007.

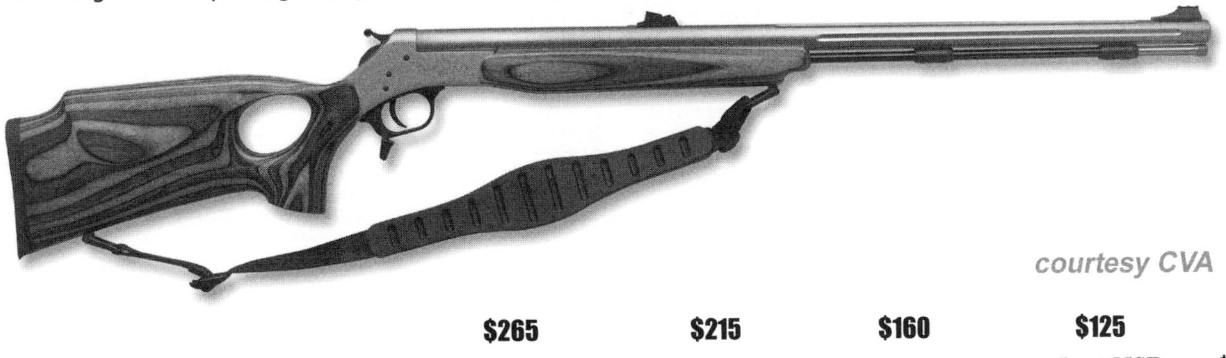

courtesy CVA

	$265	$215	$160	$125

Last MSR was $298.

Add $37 for blue barrel w/black FiberGrip Thumbhole stock (new 2006).
Add $32 for nickel barrel w/black FiberGrip PG stock.
Add $90 for nickel barrel w/Mossy Oak Break-Up PG stock.
Add $70 for nickel barrel w/black FiberGrip thumbhole stock (new 2006).
Add $127 for nickel barrel w/Mossy Oak Break-Up thumbhole stock.
Add $159 for nickel barrel w/Laminate thumbhole stock (new 2007).
Add $103 for Mossy Oak Break-Up barrel w/Mossy Oak Break-Up PG stock.
Add $139 for Mossy Oak Break-Up barrel w/ Mossy Oak Break-Up Thumbhole stock.
Add $202 for additional blue barrel.
Add $213 for additional nickel barrel.

ROCKY MOUNTAIN ELK FOUNDATION RIFLE — .54 cal. perc., Apollo action, designed to commemorate the Rocky Mountain Elk Foundation. Standard or thumbhole camo. stocks. 7.5 lbs.

	$275	$200	$145	$100

Last MSR was $330.

Add 25% for thumbhole stock.

STAG HORN SERIES — .50 or .54 cal. #209 primer ignition, 24 in. round blue barrel, synthetic stock, 42 in. OAL, 7 lbs. Disc. 2004.

	$105	$85	$55	$50

Last MSR was $122.

WOLF 209 MAGNUM — .50 cal., #209 primer ignition, break-action, 24 in. round bbl., blue or nickel (new 2007) finish, 1:28 in. twist rifling, solid composite black, Mossy Oak Break-Up (disc. 2006) or non-branded (new 2007) camo finish stock, adj. DuraSight® (new 2008) fiber optic sights, drilled and tapped for scope mounts, ventilated CrushZone™ (new 2008) recoil pad, extendable aluminum loading rod, 14.43 in. LOP, 7 lbs. New 2005.

courtesy CVA

MSR $181	$160	$145	$110	$90

Add $40 for Mossy Oak Break-Up stock (disc. 2006).
Add $51 for non-branded camo stock (new 2007).
Add $22 for nickel finish.

SHOTGUNS: PERCUSSION

BRITTANY SHOTGUN SxS — 12 ga. perc., 28 in. barrels, 7 lbs. 7 oz. Disc. 1989.

	$275	$200	$145	$100

Last MSR was $295.

GRADING - PPGS™	100%	98%	90%	80%

BRITTANY SHOTGUN II SxS — .410 bore perc., 24 in. barrels, 6 lbs. 4 oz. Disc. 1989.

	$275	$200	$145	$100

Last MSR was $210.

CLASSIC TURKEY SxS — 12 ga. perc., 28 in. round barrels, color case hardened lock, stainless steel nipple, recoil pad, 9 lbs.

	$390	$335	$245	$205

Last MSR was $460.

NWTF GOBBLER SERIES — 12 ga., 28 in. single chrome-lined blue barrel, color case hardened hammer and lock, select hardwood stock with laser engraved, full color Tom flying down from the roost, lock plate with official seal of the NWTF, 6 lbs. Limited production with a portion of all sales donated to the NWTF. Mfg. 2001-02.

	$330	$255	$195	$155

Last MSR was $368.

OPTIMA PRO 209 SHOTGUN — 12 ga, #209 primer ignition, break-action, 26 in. muzzleloading bbl. w/screw-in extra full choke, PG ambidextrous solid composite stock, Mossy Oak™ New Breakup Camo finish on stock and bbl., adj. Dura-Bright fiber optic sights w/integral scope rail, Quake Claw™ sling, CrushZone™ recoil pad, 7.5 lbs. Mfg. 2005-2007.

	$395	$350	$280	$230

Last MSR was $453.

SHOTGUN SxS — 12 ga. or .410 bore perc., 28 in. (24 in. on .410 bore) barrels, 6 lbs. 10 oz (6 lbs. 4 oz. on .410 bore). Mfg. 1987-89.

	$275	$200	$145	$100

Last MSR was $275.

Subtract $85 for .410 bore.
Add $350 for Presentation grade.

TRAPPER SHOTGUN — 12 ga., 28 in. single chrome-lined blue barrel, color case hardened hammer and lock, select hardwood stock, 6 lbs. Mfg. 1988-2004.

	$245	$185	$135	$95

Last MSR was $288.

CONTEMPORARY LONGRIFLE ASSOCIATION (CLA)

Current non-profit organization of collaborative members, who are collectors, makers, and students dedicated to the art of contemporary longrifles, accoutrements and related items made after the mid-twentieth century.

Today, as it has been for decades, the interest in contemporary muzzleloading firearms, accoutrements and related objects is sensational. Makers provide handmade contemporary muzzleloading firearms and related items that are truly works of art. These objects thrill the collector, inspire young makers, become visual aids to the student and serve the owner.

The CLA was organized as an association of contemporary muzzleloading collectors/makers. This association recognizes the scope of collecting as traditional muzzleloading rifles, pistols, fowlers, their accoutrements and related objects handmade after the mid-twentieth century.

Membership Benefits: Bulletins, Newsletters, Educational experiences, Annual show, Regional mini-shows

Membership dues are $45 annually, January through December.

Please contact the CLA directly (see contact listing in Trademark Index) with any questions. Their web site is easy to navagate and full of information.

COWEN, ERNIE E.

Current contemporary longrifle artisan located in Chambersburg, PA.

Mr. Cowen is one of the few contemporary longrifle artisan in the country that builds the British Ferguson rifle and the rather rare British fusil, the Pattern 1776 rifle.

CUMBERLAND MOUNTAIN ARMS, INC.

Previous manufacturer located in Winchester, TN. Dealer and consumer direct sales.

RIFLES: IN-LINE IGNITION

MOUNTAIN MUZZLE LOADER — .50 cal., utilizes #209 primer ignition, falling block action, 22 or 28 in. heavy round barrel, manual safety, adj. rear sights, gold front sight, walnut stock.

	$850	$695	$550	$400

Last MSR was $950.

GRADING - PPGS™	100%	98%	90%	80%

D SECTION

DAVIDE PEDERSOLI & C. Snc

Please refer to the Pedersoli listing in the P section of this text.

DALY, CHARLES

Current trademark previously imported and distributed by K.B.I., Inc., located in Harrisburg, PA, and previously distributed by Outdoor Sports Headquarters in Dayton, OH.

RIFLES: FLINTLOCK & PERCUSSION

All Charles Daly rifles feature adj. sights, investment cast brass trim, patch boxes, color case hardened hammer and locks, octagon rifle barrels, adj. double set triggers, and European hard wood stocks.

DELUXE HAWKEN RIFLE — .50 or .54 cal. perc. or flintlock, 29 in. barrel, right and left-hand. Disc. 2000.

	100%	98%	90%	80%
	$340	**$265**	**$200**	**$160**

Last MSR was $390.

Add $20 for left-hand.
Subtract $50 for percussion.

HAWKEN CARBINE — .50 cal. flintlock, 22 in. barrel. Disc. 1994.

	100%	98%	90%	80%
	$250	**$190**	**$135**	**$95**

Last MSR was $240.

HAWKEN RIFLE — .45, .50, or .54 cal. perc., 29 in. barrel, right-hand only. Disc. 2000.

	100%	98%	90%	80%
	$250	**$190**	**$135**	**$95**

Last MSR was $270.

Add $70 for Hunter Carbine Model.

DEER CREEK MFG.

Previous manufacturer located in Waldron, IN. Previously sold exclusively by Mountain States Muzzle Loading in Williamstown, WV.

For current Deer Creek Mfg. listings, refer to Mowrey Gun Works, Inc.

RIFLES: PERCUSSION

HIGHLANDER RIFLE — .50 or .54 cal. perc., 32 in. octagon brown barrel, brown furniture, hammer, lock, and patchbox, maple half stock, 7.5-7.75 lbs. Disc. 1994.

	100%	98%	90%	80%
	$200	**$160**	**$120**	**$85**

Last MSR was $280.

ROUGHRIDER RIFLE — .45, .50, or .54 cal. perc., 32 in. octagon blue barrel, pewter nosecap, German silver cap box and wedge plates, maple half stock, 7.5-7.75 lbs. Disc. 1994.

	100%	98%	90%	80%
	$200	**$160**	**$120**	**$85**

Last MSR was $280.

DIXIE GUN WORKS, INC.

Current importer and catalog house located in Union City, TN, established in 1954. Consumer direct (store or mail order) and dealer sales.

Dixie Gun Works is one of the oldest suppliers of black powder arms and kits (not listed), and offers a complete line of flintlock, percussion lock, and cap and ball revolvers manufactured by F.lli Pietta, Uberti, and Palmetto, as well as an extensive selection of longarms, bayonets, Civil War uniforms, sabers, military accouterments, holsters, presentation cases, period camping supplies, and tents.

Please contact Dixie Gun Works, Inc. directly (see Trademark Index) to receive a catalog.

Short descriptions are for models of standard configuration. Also, since 1986, many models are imported from A. Uberti (see Uberti section).

GRADING - PPGS™	100%	98%	90%	80%

PISTOLS: FLINTLOCK & PERCUSSION, SINGLE SHOT

1805 HARPERS FERRY — .58 cal. flintlock, 10 in. barrel, color case hardened hammer and lock. Mfg. by Pedersoli.

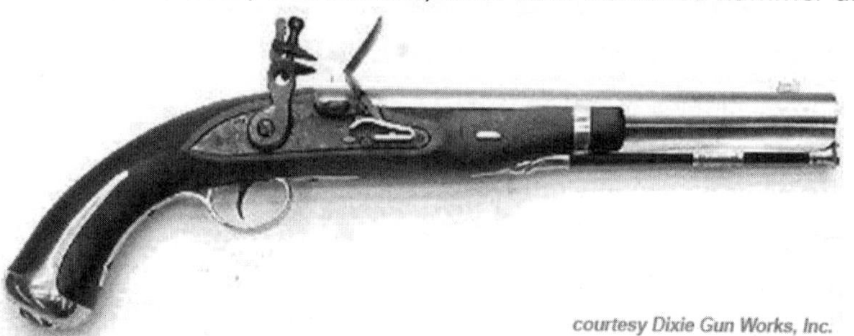

courtesy Dixie Gun Works, Inc.

MSR $495	$450	$400	$300	$250

1855 U.S. DRAGOON PISTOL W/DETACHABLE SHOULDER STOCK — .58 cal. perc., 12 in. blue round barrel, 1:72 in. twist, satin finish birch three quarter stock w/detachable shoulder stock, brass furniture, color case lockplate, blue steel swivel style ramrod w/tulip head, 18.25-29 (w/stock) in. OAL, 3.75-5.5 (w/stock) lbs. Mfg. by Palmetto. New 2008.

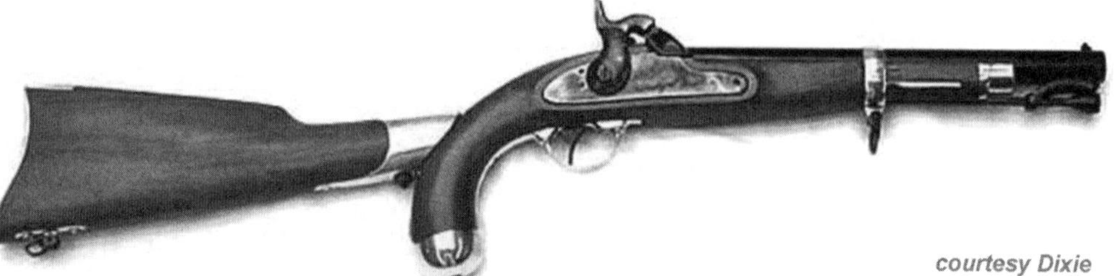

courtesy Dixie

MSR $550	$500	$440	$330	$275

ABILENE DERRINGER — .41 cal. perc., 2-3/8 in. blue finish round steel bbl., case color finish frame and hammer. Mfg. by Palmetto 2003-2008.

courtesy Dixie Gun Works, Inc.

	$135	$115	$90	$75

Last MSR was $150.

BLACK WATCH SCOTTISH PISTOL — .58 cal. flintlock, 7 in. smoothbore white steel barrel, brass frame, ram's horn grips with round ball trigger. Disc. 2004.

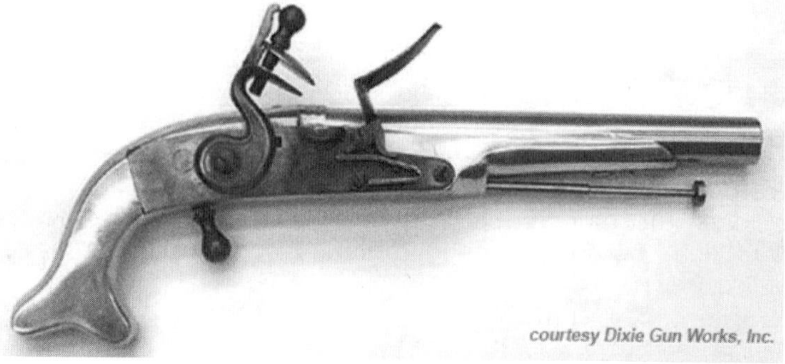

courtesy Dixie Gun Works, Inc.

	$225	$200	$175	$125

Last MSR was $250.

GRADING - PPGS™	100%	98%	90%	80%

BRASS FRAME DERRINGER — .41 cal. perc., approx. 2.25 in. round brass smoothbore bbl. marked "MISSISSIPPI" on top, brass frame, case color finish hammer, satin finish European walnut grips, 5.25 in. OAL, approx. .5 lbs. Mfg. by Palmetto. New 2008.

MSR $140	$130	$115	$85	$55

CHARLES MOORE ENGLISH DUELING PISTOL — .36 (disc. 2002), .44 (disc. 2002), or .45 cal. flintlock (.44 (disc.) or .45 cal.) or perc. (.36 (disc.) or .45 cal.), 11 in. octagon barrel, white steel hammer and lock (flintlock), color case hardened (percussion), brass furniture, adj. trigger, hand-checkered walnut stock, 2.5 lbs. Mfg. by Pedersoli.

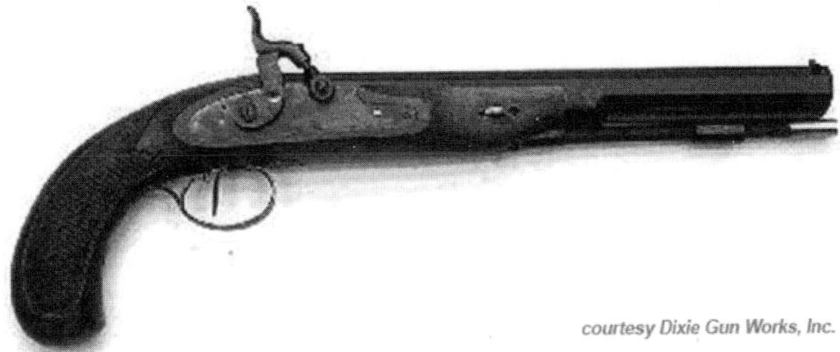
courtesy Dixie Gun Works, Inc.

MSR $595	$545	$480	$360	$295

Add $55 for flintlock model.

CHARLEVILLE PISTOL — .69 cal. flintlock, 7.5 in. white steel barrel. Disc. 1994.

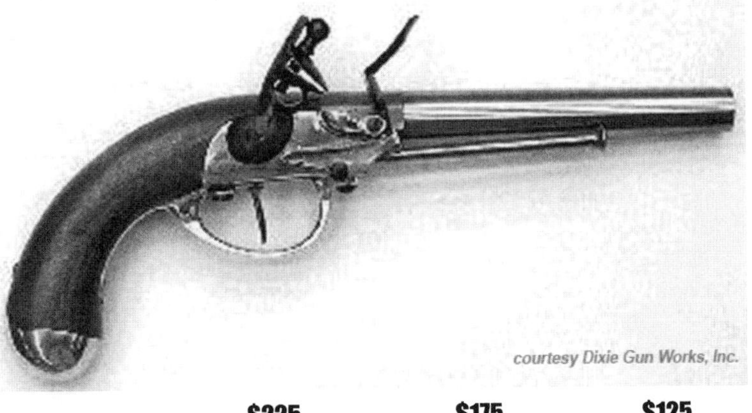
courtesy Dixie Gun Works, Inc.

	$225	$175	$125	$85

Last MSR was $195.

ENGLISH DUELING PISTOL — .45 cal. perc., 11 in. octagon barrel, silver thimble and nose cap. Mfg. by Pedersoli.

	$425	$350	$255	$220

Last MSR was $310.

HOWDAH HUNTER PISTOL — .50 cal. and/or 20 ga. perc., SxS pistol, 11.25 in. blue steel barrel, 1:18 in. twist and/or smoothbore, checkered satin finished European walnut w/three-quarter PG stock,18.25 in. OAL, 4.5-5 lbs. Mfg. by Pedersoli. New 2008.

courtesy Dixie

MSR $675	$610	$540	$405	$335

Add $25 for combination .50 cal. and 20 ga. SxS.
Subtract $25 for 20 ga. SxS.

GRADING - PPGS™	100%	98%	90%	80%

KENTUCKY-PENNSYLVANIA PISTOL — .45 cal. flintlock or perc., 10.25 in. blue barrel, color case hardened hammer and lock, brass furniture. Mfg. by Pedersoli. Disc. 2008.

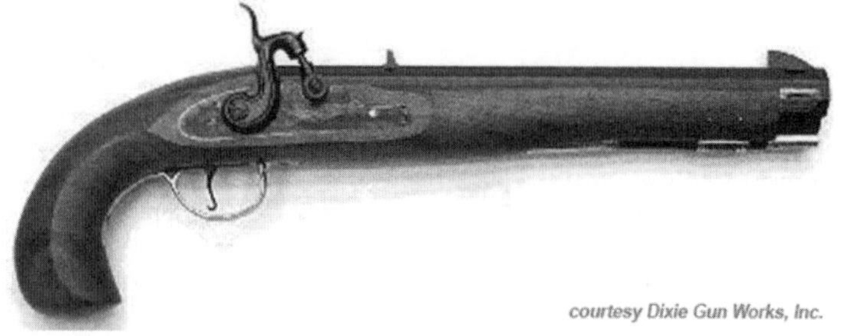

courtesy Dixie Gun Works, Inc.

	$275	$235	$175	$145

Last MSR was $295.

Add $55 for flintlock ignition.

KENTUCKY PISTOL — .45 cal. flintlock or perc., 9.75 (new 2008) 10.25 in. blue barrel, 1:18 in. twist, color case hardened hammer and lock, brass furniture, 15.5 in. OAL, 2.5 lbs. Disc. 1993. Re-introduced 2008. Mfg. by Armi Sport.

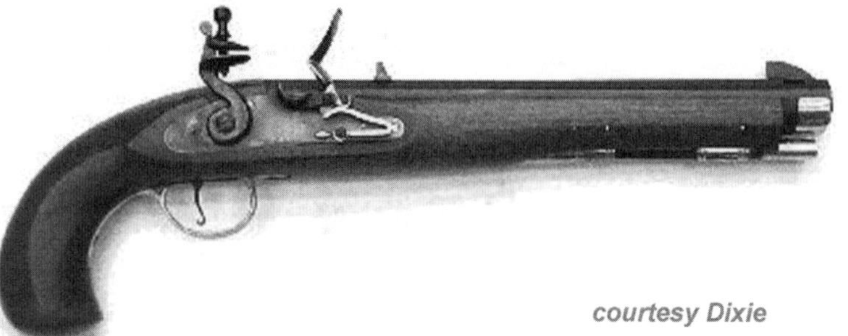

courtesy Dixie

MSR $200	$180	$155	$120	$85

Add $25 for flintlock.

LE PAGE DELUXE TARGET PISTOL — .44 cal. flintlock (International) or perc., 9.25 in. white or brown (International) steel barrel, 1:18 in. twist, satin finish and checkered European walnut halfstock, 16.25 in. OAL, 2.5 lbs. Mfg. by Pedersoli.

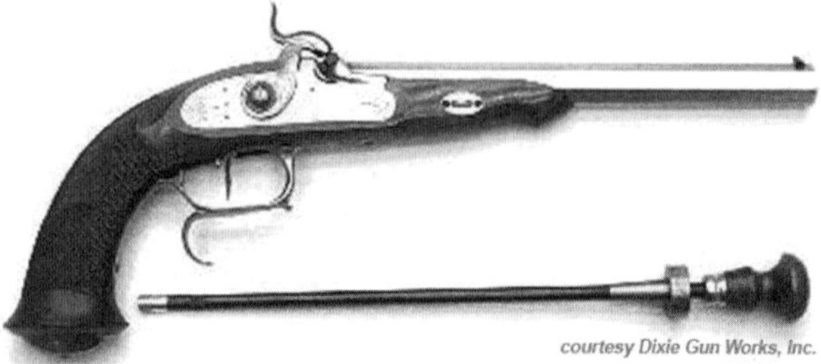

courtesy Dixie Gun Works, Inc.

MSR $750	$675	$595	$450	$375

Add $225 for Flintlock International Pistol.

LE PAGE DUELING PISTOL — .45 cal. perc., 10 in. octagonal barrel, 1:18 in. twist, fluted grip, satin finish European walnut halfstock, brass furniture silver plated, white engraved lockplate, double set and phase triggers, 15.5 in. OAL, 2.25 lbs. Mfg. by Armi Sport.

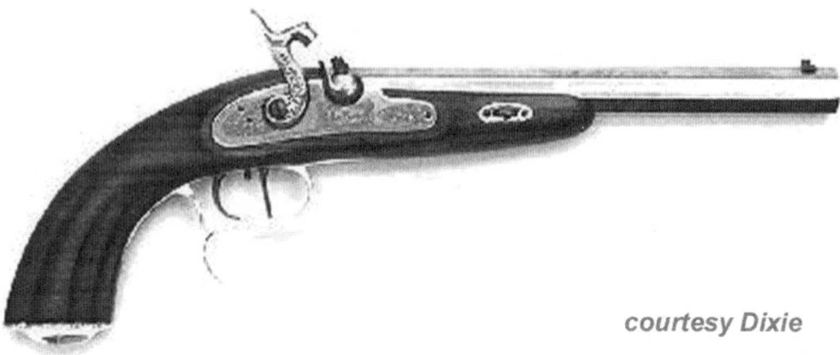

courtesy Dixie

MSR $525	$475	$420	$315	$260

GRADING - PPGS™	100%	98%	90%	80%

LINCOLN DERRINGER — .41 cal. perc., 2 in. barrel, with case. Mfg. By Palmetto. Disc., reintroduced 2000-2004.

courtesy Dixie Gun Works, Inc.

	$350	$275	$225	$175

Last MSR was $425.

MANG IN GRÄZ TARGET PISTOL — .38 cal. perc., 11.5 in. octagon brown barrel, white steel hammer and lock, color case hardened furniture, fluted grip. Mfg. by Pedersoli.

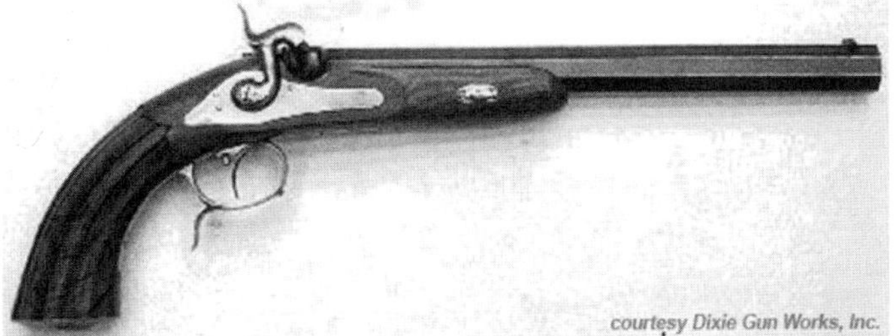
courtesy Dixie Gun Works, Inc.

MSR $1,250	$1,125	$995	$750	$625

MOORE AND PATRICK PISTOL — .45 cal. flintlock, 10 in. octagon brown barrel, white steel hammer and lock, silver plated trigger guard, checkered walnut grip.

	$310	$240	$185	$145

Last MSR was $335.

MURDOCK SCOTTISH HIGHLANDERS PISTOL — .52 cal. flintlock, 7.75 in. white steel barrel, hammer, lock, and furniture, 4 lbs. Mfg. 1989-1991, reintroduced 2003.

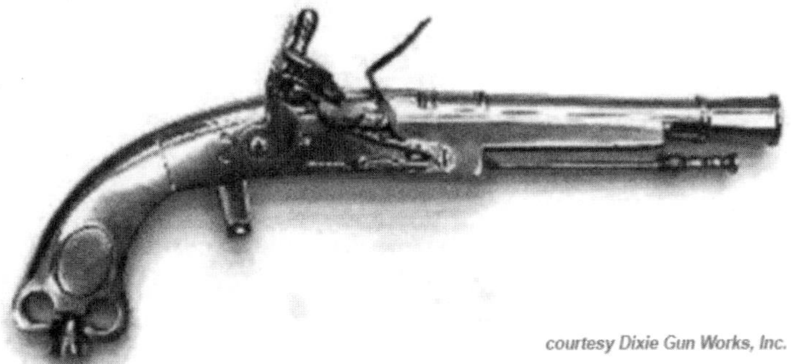
courtesy Dixie Gun Works, Inc.

MSR $370	$335	$230	$165	$110

PENNSYLVANIA PISTOL — .44 cal. flintlock or perc., 10 in. barrel, brass furniture, white steel hammer and lock. Mfg. by Pedersoli.

	$195	$160	$120	$85

Last MSR was $175.

Add $5 for flintlock.

QUEEN ANNE PISTOL — .50 cal. flintlock, 7.5 in. bronzed steel barrel. Mfg. by Pedersoli.

MSR $350	$315	$275	$215	$165

GRADING - PPGS™	100%	98%	90%	80%

SCREW BARREL DERRINGER — .44 cal. perc., 2-3/8 in. round steel barrel, .5 lb. Mfg. by Pedersoli.

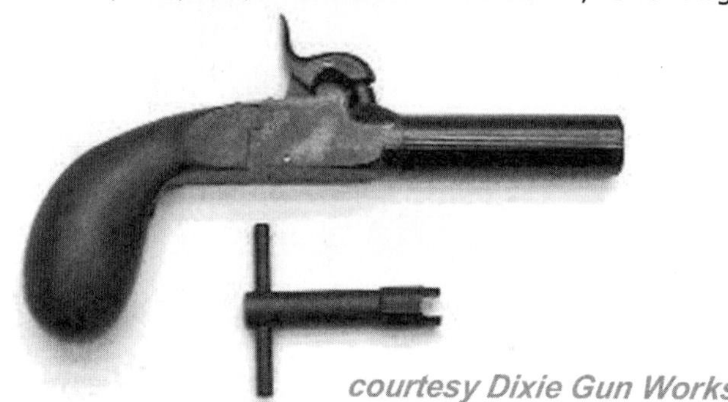

courtesy Dixie Gun Works

MSR $185	$165	$145	$115	$85

TORNADO TARGET — .44 cal. perc., 10 in. octagon barrel. Built on Remington 1860 Army frame.

	$195	$160	$120	$85

Last MSR was $215.

WILLIAM PARKER PISTOL — .45 cal. flintlock, 11 in. barrel, hand checkered half stock, 2 lbs. 8 oz.

	$270	$200	$145	$100

Last MSR was $335.

REVOLVERS: PERCUSSION

Dixie offers an extensive line of hard to find Confederate models such as the Dance, Spiller & Burr, and LeMat revolvers.

1ST MODEL DRAGOON — .44 cal. perc., 7.5 in. blue finish oct. bbl. and cylinder w/fighting dragoons scene and oval stops, 1:48 in. twist, 6 shot, color case hardened frame, hammer and loading lever, brass grip straps w/squareback trigger guard, 14 in. OAL, 4 lbs. Mfg. by Uberti.

MSR $350	$315	$275	$210	$165

2ND MODEL DRAGOON — .44 cal. perc., 7.5 in. blue finish oct. bbl. and cylinder w/fighting dragoons scene and rectangular stops, 1:48 in. twist, 6 shot, color case hardened frame, hammer and loading lever, brass grip straps w/ squareback trigger guard, 14 in. OAL, 4 lbs. Mfg. by Uberti.

MSR $350	$315	$275	$210	$165

3RD MODEL DRAGOON — .44 cal. perc., 7.5 in. blue finish oct. bbl. and cylinder w/fighting dragoons scene and rectangular stops, 1:48 in. twist, 6 shot, color case hardened frame, hammer and loading lever, brass grip straps w/ oval trigger guard, cut for shoulder stock, 14 in. OAL, 4 lbs. Mfg. by Uberti.

courtesy Dixie Gun Works

MSR $350	$265	$195	$145	$100

1848 BABY DRAGOON — .31 cal. perc., 6 in. barrel, color case hardened frame. Mfg. by Uberti.

MSR $295	$265	$255	$175	$135

GRADING - PPGS™	100%	98%	90%	80%

1849 POCKET — .31 cal. perc., with loading lever, 3, 4, 5, or 5.5 in. barrel, 5 shot, color case hardened frame, hammer, and loading lever, brass trim, 1.5 lbs. Mfg. by Uberti and Palmetto.

courtesy Dixie Gun Works

MSR $275	$250	$220	$165	$125

Add $20 for Uberti mfg.

1851 NAVY .44 — .44 cal. perc., 7.5 in. octagon barrel, antiqued finish, steel frame. Disc. 2003, re-introduced by Pietta 2008.

MSR $265	$245	$195	$155	$95

1851 NAVY (BRASS FRAME) — .36 cal. perc., 7.5 in. oct. barrel, 1:30 in. twist, brass frame, naval cylinder scene, color case hardened hammer, and loading lever, brass trigger guard and back strap, satin finish hardwood grips, 13 in. OAL, 2.75 lbs. Mfg. by Pietta.

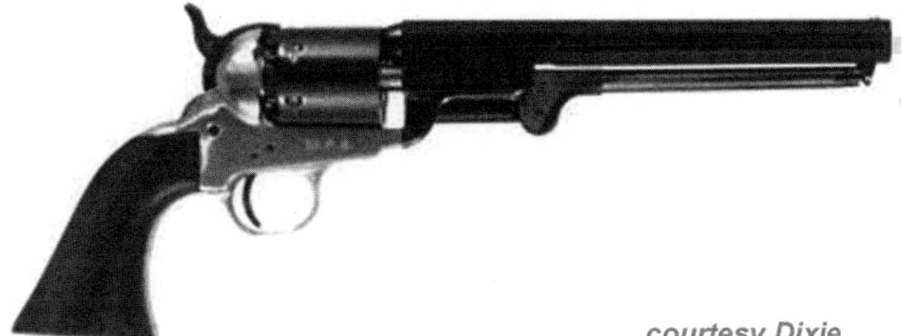
courtesy Dixie

MSR $275	$250	$200	$150	$125

1851 NAVY (STEEL FRAME) — .36 cal. perc., 7.5 in. oct. barrel, 1:30 in. twist, color case hardened steel frame, hammer and loading lever, blue triggerguard and backstrap, satin finish select hardwood grips, 13 in. OAL, 2.75 lbs. Mfg. by Pietta. New 2003.

courtesy Dixie

MSR $200	$180	$160	$120	$90

Add $50 for antique finish. Disc.

Add $170 for Navy shoulder stock.

1851 Navy shoulder stock mfg. w/select walnut, highly polished brass attachment and includes replacement hammer screw for mounting. May require some hand fitting.

GRADING - PPGS™	100%	98%	90%	80%

1851 NAVY LONDON MODEL — .36 cal. perc., 7.5 in. octagon barrel, color case hardened frame, hammer, and loading lever, blue trigger guard and backstrap. Mfg. 2003-2008.

	$225	$175	$125	$90

Last MSR was $270.

Add $50 for antique finish (mfg. by Pietta, disc.).
Add $102 for mfg. by Uberti.

Also available with antique finish (disc. 2003).

1851 NAVY "WYATT EARP" .44 REVOLVER — .44 cal. perc., 12 in. octagon barrel, brass backstrap, trigger guard, and frame. Mfg. By Pietta.

courtesy Dixie Gun Works, Inc.

MSR $180	$160	$135	$95	$60

Add $145 for detachable shoulder stock.

1851 NAVY YANK CIVILIAN — .36 cal. perc., 7.5 in. blue finish octagon barrel and cylinder w/naval scene, 1:30 in. twist, color case hardened frame, hammer, and loading lever, silver plated brass round back trigger guard and back strap, satin finish European walnut grips, 13 in. OAL, 2.75 lbs. Mfg. by Pieta. New 2008.

courtesy Dixie

MSR $225	$200	$175	$135	$105

1851 NAVY YANK LONDON MODEL — .36 cal. perc., 7.5 in. blue finish octagon barrel and cylinder w/naval scene, 1:30 in. twist, color case hardened frame, hammer, and loading lever, brass squareback trigger guard and back strap, satin finish European walnut grips, 13 in. OAL, 2.75 lbs. Mfg. by Pieta. New 2008.

MSR $225	$200	$175	$135	$105

1858 REMINGTON — .44 cal. perc., 8 in. octagon barrel, oversize frame and grips, blue or antique (disc. 2003) finish. Mfg. by Pietta. Disc. 2004.

	$215	$170	$125	$85

Last MSR was $265.

1858 REMINGTON INOX TARGET REVOLVER — .44 cal. perc., 8 in. stainless steel oct. barrel and cylinder, 1:30 in. twist, adj. rear sight, brass frame and triggerguard, color case hardened hammer, satin finish European walnut grips, 13.75 in. OAL, 2.75 lb. Mfg. by Pietta. New 2008.

MSR $375	$340	$300	$225	$175

GRADING - PPGS™	100%	98%	90%	80%

1858 REMINGTON NEW MODEL ARMY SHOOTERS REVOLVER — .44 cal. perc., 8 in. octagon barrel with progressive rifling, blued steel frame, silver plated trigger guard, blue steel backstrap.

courtesy Dixie Gun Works, Inc.

MSR $675	$610	$540	$405	$335

1858 REMINGTON TEXAS REVOLVER — .44 cal. perc., 8 in. blue finish oct. barrel and cylinder, 1:30 in. twist, brass frame and triggerguard, color case hardened hammer, satin finish European walnut grips, 13.75 in. OAL, 2.75 lb. Mfg. by Pietta. New 2008.

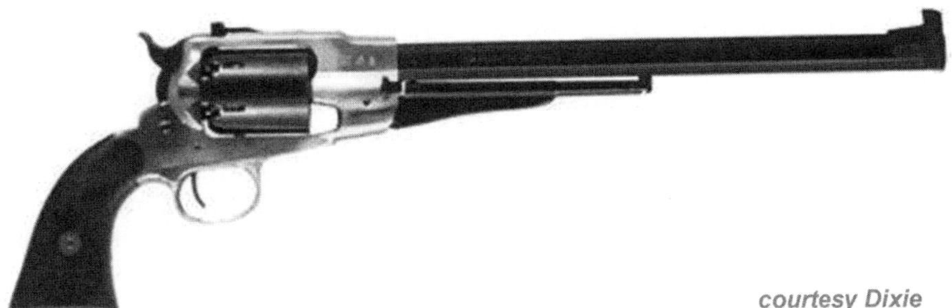

courtesy Dixie

MSR $195	$180	$155	$115	$95

1860 ARMY — .44 cal. perc., 8 in. barrel, color case hardened hammer, frame, and loading lever, antique or blue finish round or half fluted cylinder, barrel and backstrap, brass trigger guard, cut for shoulder stock, 14 in. OAL, 2.75 lbs. Mfg. by Pietta and Uberti.

MSR $225	$195	$155	$115	$85

Add $15 for half fluted cylinder.
Add $45 for antique finish.
Add $175 for detachable shoulder stock.
Add $70 for Uberti mfg.

1861 ARMY SHERIFF'S MODEL — .36 cal. perc., 5.5 in. blue finish barrel and cylinder w/naval scene, blue finish steel backstrap and round trigger guard, color case hardened frame, hammer and loading lever, satin finish European walnut grips, 11.5 in. OAL, 2.5 lbs. Mfg. Pietta. New 2008.

MSR $225	$200	$180	$135	$115

1861 NAVY — .36 cal. perc., 5 (disc. 2007) or 8 in. blue finish barrel and cylinder w/naval scene, brass (disc. 2007) or blue finish steel backstrap and round trigger guard, stainless steel (disc. 2007) or color case hardened frame, hammer, and loading lever, satin finish European walnut grips, 10.75 or 13.75 in. OAL, 2.5-2.75 lbs. Mfg. by Uberti (disc. 2007) or Pietta beginning 2008.

MSR $265	$245	$210	$155	$125

Add $15 for silver plated backstrap and trigger guard.
Add $15 for fluted military cylinder.
Add $50 for stainless steel.
Add $175 for shoulder stock.

GRADING - PPGS™	100%	98%	90%	80%

1861-62 DANCE & BROTHERS — .44 cal. perc., 7.75 in. octagon to round barrel, steel frame Confederate copy of the Colt 1851 Navy. The Dance differs from the Colt design in that it has a Dragoon-style barrel and lacks a recoil shield behind the cylinder. Mfg. By Pietta.

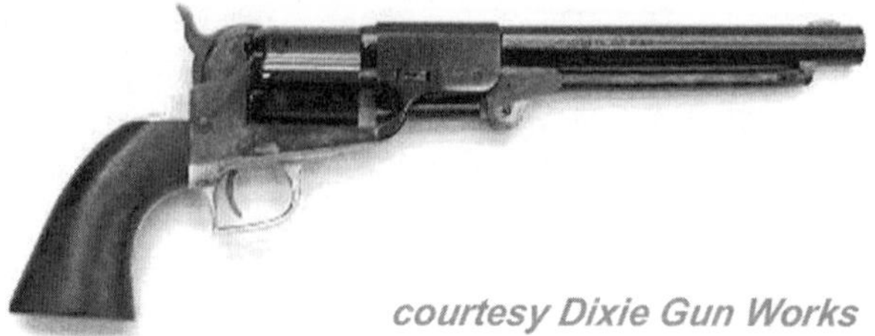
courtesy Dixie Gun Works

MSR $335	$295	$255	$195	$165

1862 POCKET NAVY — .36 cal. perc., 5.5 in. blue finish oct. bbl. and rebated engraved cylinder, 1:32 in. twist, color case hardened steel frame, loading lever and hammer, satin finish European walnut grips, 10.5 in. OAL, 1.5 lbs. Mfg. by Uberti. New 2003.

MSR $240	$200	$160	$120	$85

1862 POLICE — .36 cal. perc., 4.5, 5.5, or 6.5 in. barrel, stainless steel or color case hardened frame, hammer, and loading lever, cylinder, semi-fluted or engraved, 1.6 lbs. Mfg. by Uberti.

MSR $280	$235	$180	$130	$95

Add $15 for silver plated backstrap and trigger guard.
Add $50 for stainless steel.

1873 COLT SAA PERCUSSION REVOLVER — .44 cal. perc., 6 shot, 5.5 in. barrel, color case hardened frame. Designed by Uberti for countries where black powder is legal and cartridge-firing pistols are not, the authentic-looking Colt SAA has a black powder cylinder and an optional loading tool. Disc. 2004. Reintroduced 2007.

courtesy Dixie Gun Works

MSR $300	$270	$240	$180	$150

Add $25 for loading tool.

HOLSTER MODEL PATERSON — .36 cal. perc., 7.5 in. barrel, has hidden trigger and no loading lever. Mfg. by Uberti. Disc. 2006.

	$450	$400	$300	$225

Last MSR was $360.

LEECH and RIGDON — .36 cal. perc., 7 in. round barrel, Confederate copy of the Colt Navy, 2.75 lbs. New in 1989. Mfg. by Uberti.

courtesy Dixie Gun Works

MSR $275	$245	$195	$135	$95

GRADING - PPGS™	100%	98%	90%	80%

LEMAT ARMY, NAVY & CAVALRY — .44 cal. perc., includes 16 ga. smoothbore shotgun barrel, 6.75 in. octagon barrel, blue steel furniture, case hardened hammer and trigger, barrel marked "Col. LeMat", checkered grips, lanyard ring, round or spur (Cavalry Model) trigger guard, 3.5 lbs. Mfg. by Pietta.

courtesy Dixie Gun Works

MSR $795	$725	$640	$480	$400

REMINGTON 44 REVOLVER — .44 cal. perc., 8 in. octagon barrel, blue finish. Mfg. by Euro Arms.

	$215	$185	$135	$95

Last MSR was $250.

REMINGTON NEW MODEL ARMY/TARGET MODEL — .44 cal. perc., 8 in. oct. bbl., 1:30 in. twist, adj. rear and ramp w/blade front sights (Target Model), antique or blue finish, brass trigger guard, color case hardened hammer and trigger, satin finish European walnut grips, 13.75 in. OAL, 2.75 lbs. Mfg. by Euro Arms, Pietta and Uberti.

MSR $265	$240	$220	$165	$140

Add $30 for Uberti mfg.
Add $10 for Pietta mfg.

REMINGTON NEW MODEL ARMY STAINLESS — .44 cal. perc., 8 in. satin stainless steel oct. bbl. and frame, 1:30 in. twist, satin finish European walnut grips, 13.75 in. OAL, 2.75 lbs. Mfg. by Pietta and Uberti.

MSR $325	$295	$255	$195	$165

Add $40 for Uberti mfg.

REMINGTON NEW MODEL BELT REVOLVER — .36 cal. perc., 6.625 in. octagon barrel, 1:30 in. twist, blue finish, brass trigger gaurd, color case hardened loading lever, hammer and trigger, satin finish European walnut grips, 12.5 in. OAL, 2.75 lbs. Mfg. by Pietta. New 2008.

MSR $220	$195	$175	$135	$95

REMINGTON NEW MODEL NAVY — .36 cal. perc., 6.25 in. octagon barrel, .36 cal. variation of the 1858 Remington, 2.5 lbs. Mfg. by Pietta.

	$245	$195	$135	$95

Last MSR was $275.

REMINGTON NEW MODEL POCKET — .31 cal. perc., 3.5 in. octagon barrel, spur trigger, brass or iron (new 2008) frame, blue finish (new 2008) or nickel plated, color case hardened hammer and trigger, satin finish European walnut grips, 7.625 in. OAL, 1 lb. Mfg. by Palmetto. Disc. 2004. Reintroduced 2006.

courtesy Dixie Gun Works

MSR $200	$180	$160	$115	$95

Add $20 for nickel plated model.
Add $75 for iron frame w/blue finish.

GRADING - PPGS™	100%	98%	90%	80%

ROGERS & SPENCER — .44 cal. perc., 6 shot, 7.5 in. octagon barrel, walnut grips, 3 lbs. Mfg. by Euroarms.

courtesy Dixie Gun Works

MSR $425	$385	$340	$255	$215

SPILLER and BURR — .36 cal. perc., octagon barrel, color case hardened hammer and loading lever, brass frame and trigger guard. Mfg. by Pietta.

courtesy Dixie Gun Works, Inc.

MSR $235	$210	$185	$135	$115

STARR ARMS CO. DOUBLE ACTION AND SINGLE ACTION 1858 ARMY — .44 cal. perc., 6 in. tapered round barrel DA model, 8 in. round barrel SA model, all blue steel frame, backstrap and trigger guard. Unique Starr top break design for takedown. DA model fires double action or single action. Mfg. by Pietta. Disc. 2004. Reintroduced 2007.

courtesy Dixie Gun Works, Inc.

MSR $395	$360	$320	$240	$195

Add $30 for Single Action Model.

TEXAS PATERSON — .36 cal. perc., 9 in. barrel, has hidden trigger and no loading lever. Mfg. by Pietta.

courtesy Dixie Gun Works, Inc.

MSR $535	$485	$425	$325	$265

GRADING - PPGS™	100%	98%	90%	80%

WALKER — .44 cal. perc., 9 in. barrel, 6 shot, color case hardened frame, hammer, and loading lever, brass trim, 4.5 lbs. Mfg. by Palmetto & Uberti.

courtesy Dixie Gun Works, Inc.

MSR $350	$315	$275	$210	$165

Subtract $75 for Palmetto Walker.

RIFLES: FLINTLOCK & PERCUSSION

1766 CHARLEVILLE MUSKET — .69 cal. flintlock, 44.5 in. Armory bright tapered round barrel, all steel hammer, lock, and furniture. Lockplate marked "Charleville", 10.5 lbs. Mfg. by Pedersoli. Disc. 2004. Reintroduced 2007.

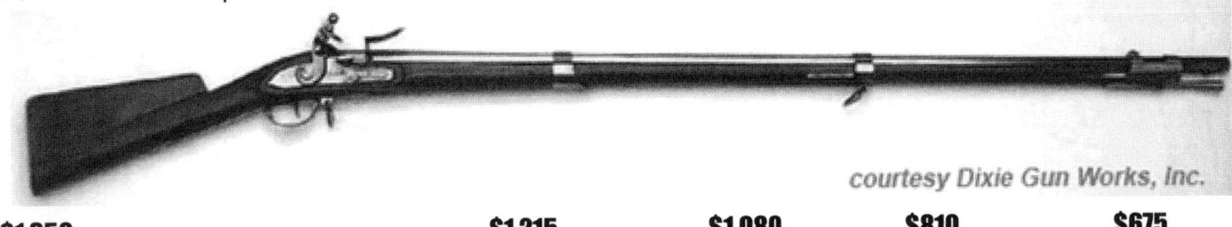
courtesy Dixie Gun Works, Inc.

MSR $1,350	$1,215	$1,080	$810	$675

Subtract $230 for earlier models mfg. by Miroku.

1777 FRENCH MODEL CHARLEVILLE — .69 cal. flintlock, 44.75 in. Armory bright tapered round barrel, all steel hammer, lock, and furniture. Lockplate marked "St. Etienne" with (84 over crown over E) proof, 10.25 lbs. Mfg. by Pedersoli.

courtesy Dixie

MSR $1,200	$1,080	$960	$720	$600

1803 HARPERS FERRY RIFLE — .54 (disc. 2003) or .58 cal. flintlock, 35.5 in. octagon to round barrel, color case hardened hammer and lock, brass trigger guard and patchbox. Mfg. by Euroarms Italia.

courtesy Dixie Gun Works

MSR $995	$915	$800	$600	$500

1816 U.S. MODEL FLINTLOCK MUSKET AND COLT STYLE CONVERSION — .69 cal. flintlock or perc., 42 in. round tapered smoothbore barrel, Armory bright steel furniture, brass pan on lock, lock marked "Harpers Ferry 1816" on tail w/American eagle over "U.S." ahead of hammer. 9.75 lbs. Available with Colt style conversion to percussion lock. Mfg. by Pedersoli.

MSR $1,200	$1,080	$960	$720	$600

GRADING - PPGS™	100%	98%	90%	80%

1842 SPRINGFIELD MUSKET — .69 cal. perc., 42 in. round tapered smoothbore barrel, white steel furniture, 9 lbs. 4 oz. Mfg. By Armi Sport.

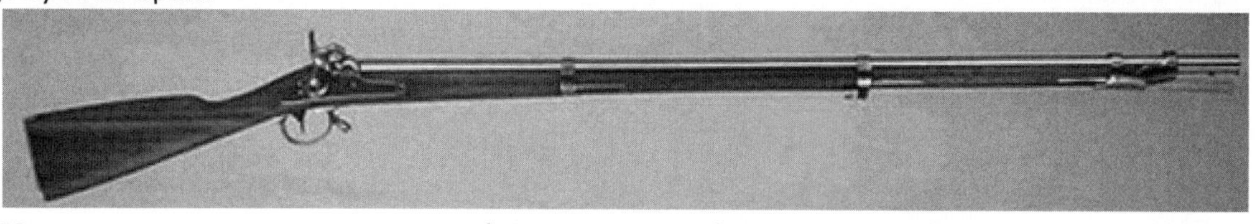

MSR $650	$585	$520	$395	$325

Add $100 for rifled barrel.

1853 3-BAND ENFIELD — .58 cal. perc., 39 in. rifled 1:56 (Armi Sport) or 1:72 (Euro Arms) or smoothbore barrel, satin finish European walnut stock, three barrel bands, 51.5 in. OAL, 10.5 lbs. Mfg. by Euro Arms (disc. 2007). Re-introduced by Armi Sport 2008 and by Euro Arms 2009.

MSR $650	$585	$520	$390	$325

Add $65 for Euro Arms mfg.
Subtract $75 for smoothbore.
Subtract $40 for Euro Arms kit.

Euro Arms introduced kit form in 2009.

1855 1st MODEL SPRINGFIELD RIFLE-MUSKET — .58 cal. perc. musket cap, 40 in. round tapered barrel, 1:48 in twist, long range rear sight, lockplate marked "U.S. Springfield" forward of non-functioning tape primer door, spread eagle on door w/"1857" on tail, satin finish European walnut, white steel furniture, 56 in. OAL, 10.5 lbs. Mfg. by Armi Sport Italia. New 2008.

MSR $700	$635	$560	$420	$350

1855 2nd MODEL SPRINGFIELD RIFLE-MUSKET — .58 cal. perc. musket cap, 40 in. round tapered barrel, 1:72 in twist, lockplate marked "U.S. Springfield" forward of non-functioning tape primer door, spread eagle on door w/"1857" on tail, satin finish European walnut, white steel furniture, 56 in. OAL, 10.5 lbs. Mfg. by EuroArms. New 2008.

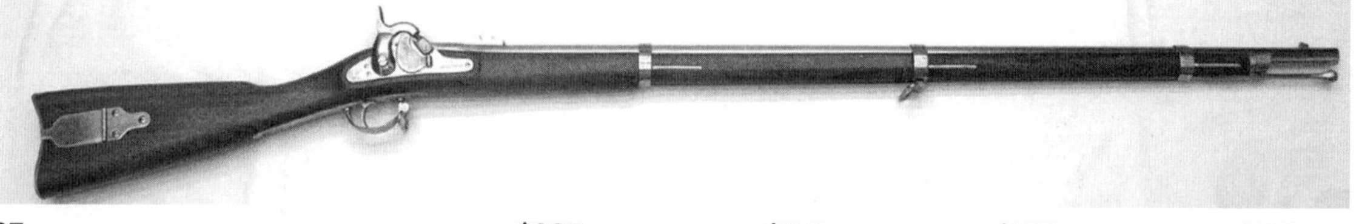

MSR $995	$895	$750	$595	$475

1855 ROOT REVOLVING RIFLE — .44 cal. perc., 31.25 in. tapered round barrel, 1:38 in. twist, blue finish, color case hardened furniture, satin finish birch wood stock, 50.5 in. OAL, 10.5 lbs. Mfg. by Palmetto. New 2008.

MSR $1,600	$1,450	$1,275	$960	$800

1857 MAUSER RIFLE — .547 cal. perc. patterned after the Mauser rifles manufactured by The Royal Wurttemburg Gun Factory in Oberndorf from 1857-1862. Full stock of European walnut, Armory bright 39-3/8 in. octagon to tapered round barrel, adjustable rear sight for elevation and windage, steel blade front sight on upper barrel band, steel furniture, color case hardened lock and barrel tang, engraved lockplate "KÖNIGI.WÜRT FABRIK." Mfg. by Pedersoli. Mfg. 2001-2004.

courtesy Dixie

	$1,000	$795	$650	$475

Last MSR was $925.

GRADING - PPGS™	100%	98%	90%	80%

1858 2-BAND ENFIELD — .58 cal. perc., two barrel bands, 9 lbs. 4 oz. Mfg. by Euro Arms and by Armi Sport beginning 2008.

courtesy Dixie Gun Works

MSR $600	$545	$480	$360	$295

Add $50 for Euro Arms mfg.

1861 SPRINGFIELD MUSKET — .58 cal. perc., 40 in. round tapered barrel, rifled or smoothbore (new 2009) white steel furniture, 10 lbs. 8 oz. Mfg. by Miroku Japan and EuroArms Italy. Disc. 2004. Reintroduced mfg. by Armi Sport Italy in 2008 and by EuroArms in 2009.

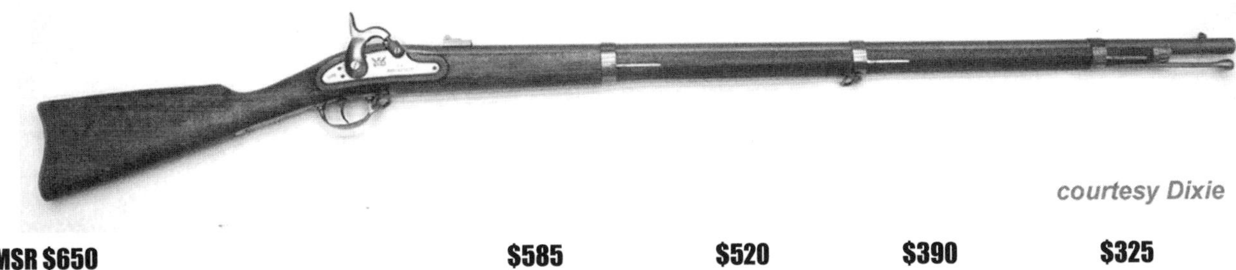

courtesy Dixie

MSR $650	$585	$520	$390	$325

Add $290 for Euro Arms mfg. Musket.
Add $245 for Euro Arms Musket kit.
Subtract $25 for Armi Sport smoothbore.

This model is available as a kit from Euro Arms.

1863 SPRINGFIELD MUSKET — .58 cal. perc., 41.5 in. barrel. Mfg. by Miroku Japan and EuroArms.

courtesy Dixie Gun Works, Inc.

MSR $700	$635	$560	$420	$350

Subtract $35 for EuroArms model.

AUSTRIAN LORENZ — .54 cal. perc., 28 in. tapered octagon barrel, full stock of select hardwood, Armory bright steel furniture, open-style adjustable rear sight, dovetailed front blade, barrel marked "Lorenz 1854 cal. 13.9 m/m." Reproduction of Austrian model (often referred to as the "Austrian Enfield") imported and used by both Federal and Confederate troops during the Civil War, 9 lbs. Mfg. by Arms-Moravia, Ltd., Czech Republic. Disc. 2004.

	$700	$565	$440	$325

Last MSR was $825.

BRISTLEN MORGES — .44 cal. perc., 29.5 in. tapered octagon barrel, color case hardened hammer and lock, European walnut halfstock, palm rest, Creedmoor-style rear sight, color case hardened furniture. 15.5 lbs. Mfg. by Pedersoli.

courtesy Dixie Gun Works

MSR $2,500	$2,250	$1,950	$1,650	$1,350

GRADING - PPGS™	100%	98%	90%	80%

BRITISH OFFICERS LIGHT INFANTRY FUSIL — .54 cal. flintlock, 37.25 in. white tapered round barrel, full stock of select American walnut with gloss finish, brass furniture, lock in the white, lockplate marked with a crown, single trigger, steel sling swivels on trigger guard and forearm. A continuation of the legendary "Officers' Model Musket" developed by the late "Curley" Gostomski, founder of North Star Gun Company. Four years in development, this latest version was produced by Bob Rathburn and Bill Wescombe, who were chosen by Gostomski to succeed him. The musket was custom manufactured to original British government specifications. 8 lbs. Manufactured by North Star West/USA. Disc. 2004. Reintroduced 2006.

MSR. $1,200	$1,000	$795	$650	$475

BROWN BESS MUSKET 2ND MODEL — .75 cal. flintlock, 42 in. tapered round barrel, one-piece European walnut stock, brass furniture, lockplate border line engraved "GRICE 1762" on tail, crown over "GR" ahead of hammer, single trigger, sling swivels, 9 lbs. The traditional British longarm for nearly a century. Mfg. by Pedersoli.

MSR $1,100	$990	$880	$630	$550

BROWN BESS TRADE MODEL — .75 cal. flintlock, 30.5 in. brown barrel, one-piece European walnut stock, brass furniture, serpentine sideplate, brown engraved lockplate, lock marked "GRICE 1762", crown over "GR" under pan, 7 lbs. 8 oz. Carbine version of the English Brown Bess Musket originally made from surplus guns bought from the British government in the early 1700s. The trade gun became a favorite of American Indians in the 1700s.

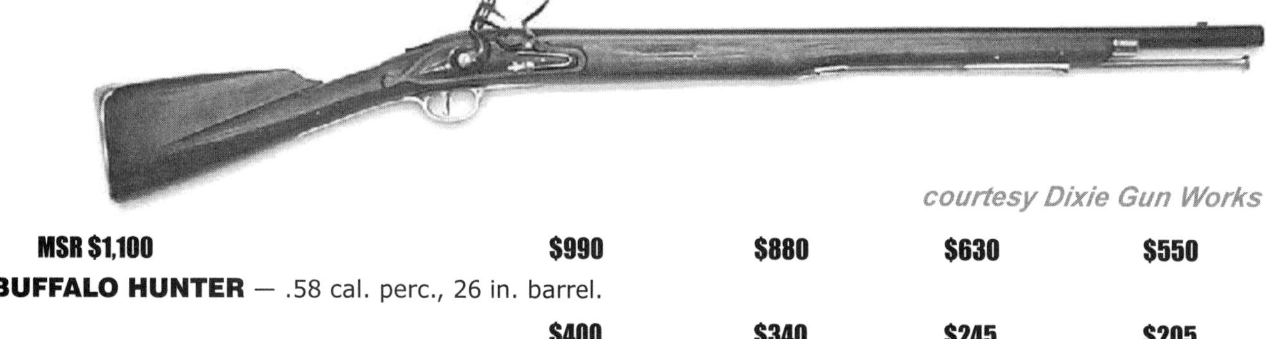

courtesy Dixie Gun Works

MSR $1,100	$990	$880	$630	$550

BUFFALO HUNTER — .58 cal. perc., 26 in. barrel.

	$400	$340	$245	$205

C.S. RICHMOND MUSKET — .58 cal. perc., 40 in. round barrel, white steel hammer and lock, brass buttplate and end cap, walnut stock, 10.5 lbs.

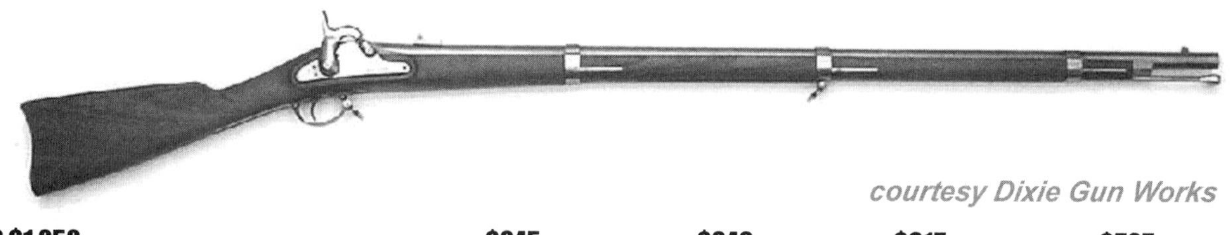

courtesy Dixie Gun Works

MSR $1,050	$945	$840	$615	$525

COOK & BROTHER CARBINE — .58 cal. perc., 24 in. barrel, adj. front sight (windage only), two barrel bands, walnut stock, 7.5 lbs. Mfg. By Euro Arms. Disc. 2007.

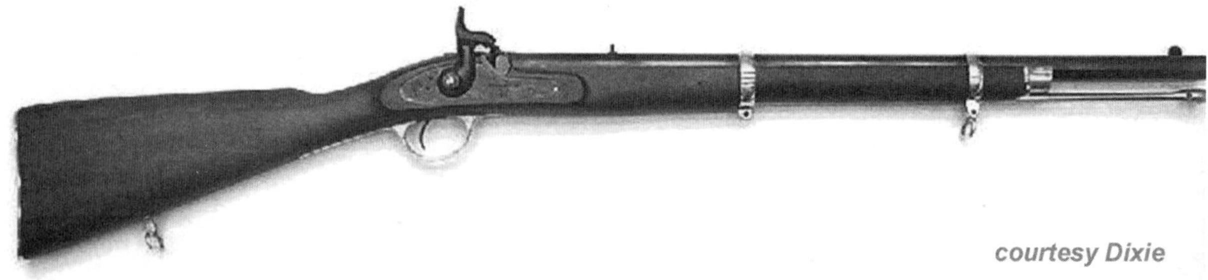

courtesy Dixie

MSR $740	$675	$600	$450	$375

DELUXE CUB RIFLE — .32 (New 2007), .36 (New 2007), .40 (Disc. 2003) and .45 cal. flintlock or perc., 28 in. octagon barrel, color case hardened hammer, plate and triggers, brass trim and patch box, double set triggers. Mfg. by Pedersoli.

MSR $675	$610	$540	$405	$335

Add $50 for flintlock models.

GRADING - PPGS™	100%	98%	90%	80%

ENFIELD MUSKETOON LONDON ARMORY — .58 cal. perc., 24 in. round barrel, color case hardened hammer and lock, brass buttplate, trigger guard, and nose cap. Mfg. by EuroArms.

MSR $650	$585	$520	$385	$325

ENGLISH MATCHLOCK — .72 cal. matchlock, 44 in. octagon to round barrel (with cannon type muzzle), all white steel, walnut stock. Disc. 2007.

	$800	$650	$515	$375

Last MSR was $895.

GIBBS RIFLE — - .40 or .451 cal. perc. #11 cap., 35.25 in. blue octagon to round barrel, 1:24 and 1:16 (.40 cal.) or 1:18 (.451 cal.) in. twist, satin finish European walnut half stock, checkered wrist and forearm, dovetailed front sight with hood, adjustable rear peep sight on wrist, 52.5 in. OAL, 12 (.40 cal.) or 11.5 (.451 cal.) lbs. Mfg. by Pedersoli beginning 2008.

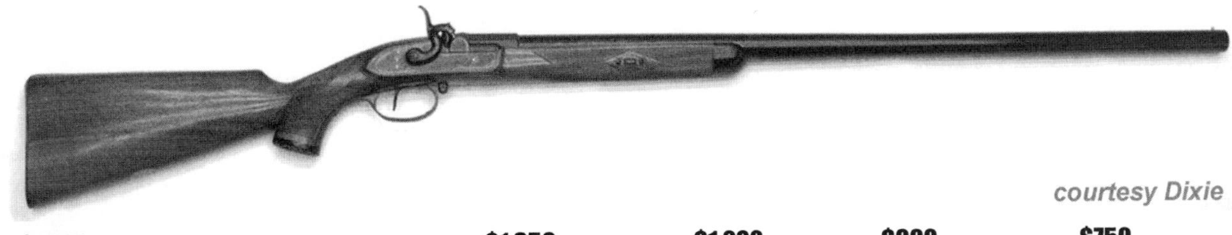

courtesy Dixie

MSR $1,500	$1,350	$1,200	$900	$750

Add $100 for .451 cal.

HAWKEN RIFLE — .45 (disc. 2008), .50, .54, or .58 (disc. 2008) cal. perc. or flintlock (.50 cal. new 2008), 28.75 in. blue bbl., 1:48 in. twist, color case hardened hammer and lock, brass patch box, satin finish European walnut half stock, 45.5 in. OAL, 8.5-9 lbs. Mfg. by Armi San Marco (disc. 2004), mfg. by Investarms new 2004.

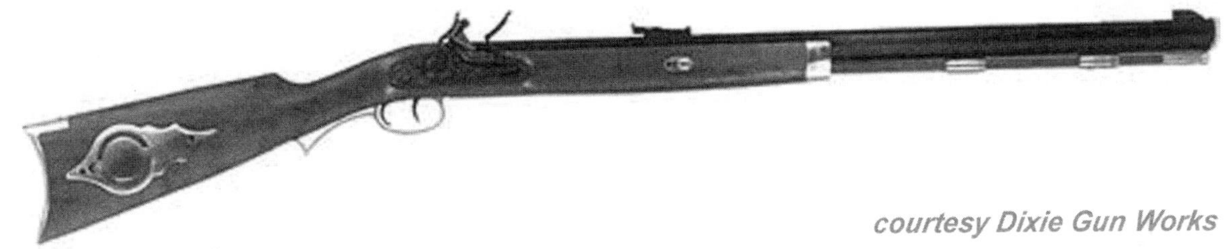

courtesy Dixie Gun Works

MSR $425	$385	$340	$255	$215

Add $70 for left or right hand flintlock.

INDIAN MODEL — similar to Brown Bess Musket, except has 31 in. barrel. Mfg. by Pedersoli. Disc. 2004.

	$635	$500	$400	$300

Last MSR was $750.

JAEGER RIFLE — .54 cal. flintlock, or perc., 27-5/8 in. matte brown octagon barrel, matte brown hammer, lock, and trigger guard, sliding wooden patchbox, double set triggers, 8.25 lbs. Mfg. by Pedersoli. Mfg. 2000-2004. Re-introduced 2008.

MSR $995	$915	$800	$600	$500

Last MSR was $750.

JAPANESE TANEGASHIMA MATCHLOCK RIFLE — .50 cal. matchlock, smoothbore barrel, all brass furniture, trigger guard, trigger and matchlock, buttstock was held against shooter's cheek, cherry stock, OAL 54.75 in., 8.5 lbs. Mfg. by Miroku.

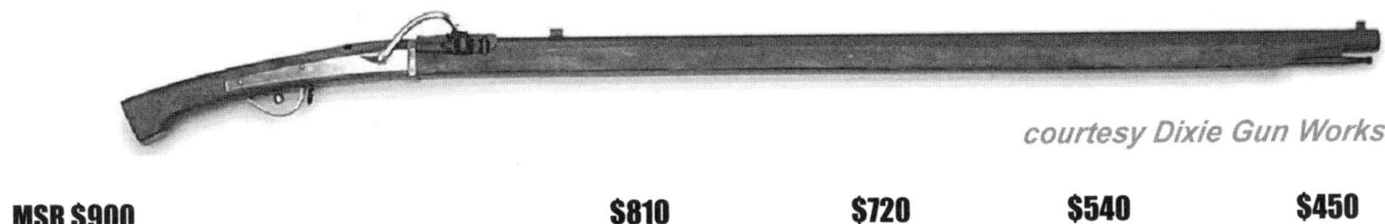

courtesy Dixie Gun Works

MSR $900	$810	$720	$540	$450

GRADING - PPGS™	100%	98%	90%	80%

J.P. MURRAY ARTILLERY CARBINE — .58 cal. perc., 23.5 in. round barrel, color case hardened hammer and lock, brass buttplate, trigger guard, and barrel bands (two), factory sling swivels. Mfg. by EuroArms.

courtesy Dixie Gun Works, Inc.

MSR $750	$675	$600	$450	$375

KENTUCKY RIFLE — .45 cal. flintlock or perc., 33.5 in. barrel, brass patch box and furniture. Disc. 1994.

	$300	$225	$165	$115

Last MSR was $270.

Add $10 for flintlock.

KENTUCKIAN RIFLE/CARBINE — .45 cal. flintlock or perc., 27.5 (carbine, disc. 1993) or 35 in. octagon barrel, color case hardened hammer and lock, brass patch box, trigger guard and furniture. Carbine disc. 1993. Mfg. by Armi Sport (disc. 2004), mfg. by Pedersoli 2005-2008.

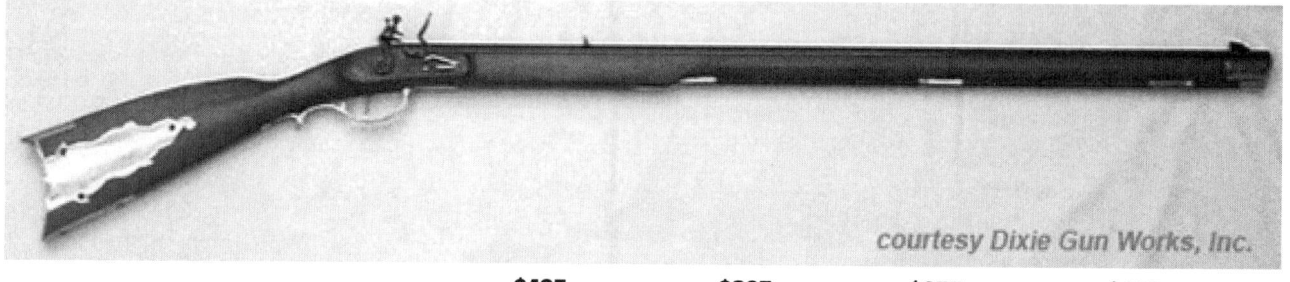

courtesy Dixie Gun Works, Inc.

	$495	$325	$255	$195

Last MSR was $525.

Add $10 for flintlock.

KODIAK DOUBLE RIFLE SxS — .50, .54, or .58 (combo barrels .50 x 12 ga. and .58 x 12 ga.) cal. perc., 28.5 in. barrels regulated at 75 yards, hand checkered walnut stock, adj. sights, approx. 10.5 lbs. Mfg. By Pedersoli.

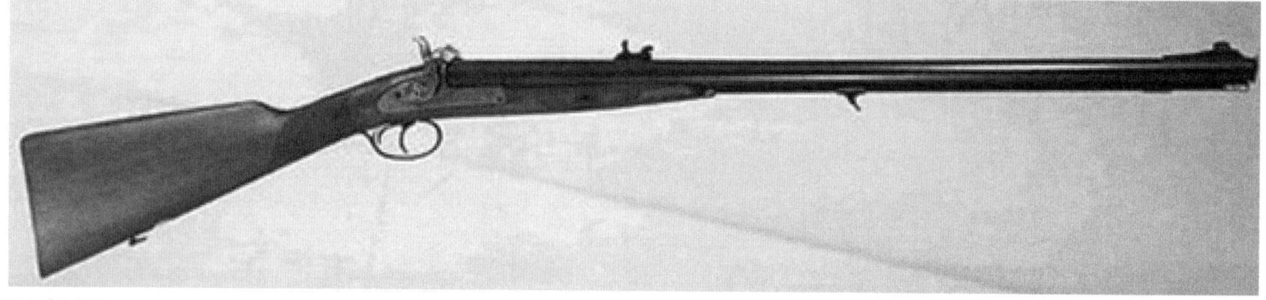

MSR $1,100	$990	$880	$630	$550

KODIAK EXPRESS DOUBLE RIFLE SxS — .72 cal. perc., 25.5 in. barrels, hand checkered walnut half stock, adj. Sights, 10.5 lbs. Mfg. By Pedersoli. Disc. 2004.

	$990	$880	$630	$550

Last MSR was $725.

KODIAK MKIII RIFLE/SHOTGUN COMBO — .50 or .58 cal. perc., similar to Kodiak Double Rifle, except has one 12 ga. barrel. Mfg. By Pedersoli. Disc. 2007.

	$990	$880	$630	$550

Last MSR was $850.

GRADING - PPGS™	100%	98%	90%	80%

LANCASTER COUNTY RIFLE — .45 cal. flintlock or perc., similar to Pennsylvania Rifle, except less ornate trigger guard and patch box.

	$300	$225	$165	$115

Add $5 for flintlock.

MISSOURI RIVER HAWKEN — .50 cal. perc. #11 cap, 30 in. brown oct. bbl., 1:24 in. twist, color case hardened furniture, hammer and lock, double set and double phase trigger, satin finish American walnut half stock, 46.5 in. OAL, 9.5 lbs. Mfg. Pedersoli beginning 2008.

MSR $895	$815	$715	$535	$450

MISSISSIPPI RIFLE — .54 or .58 (disc. 2004) cal. perc. patterned after the U.S. Rifle Model 1841, 33.5 in. barrel, color case hardened hammer and lock, solid brass furniture, similar to Zouave with nose cap replacing front barrel band, 48.5 in. OAL, 9.5 lbs. Mfg. by EuroArms Italia. Disc. 2007. Reintroduced 2009.

courtesy Dixie

MSR $825	$745	$660	$495	$410

MORTIMER RIFLE — .54 cal. flintlock, 36.25 in. octagon to round barrel, color case hardened hammer, lock and trigger guard, waterproof pan, 8.875 lbs. Mfg. by Pedersoli.

courtesy Dixie Gun Works

MSR $1,050	$945	$840	$615	$525

MORTIMER WHITWORTH RIFLE — .451 cal. perc., 32 in. blue octagonal to round barrel, European walnut half stock, checkered wrist and forearm, dovetailed front sight with hood, adjustable rear peep sight on wrist, lock marked "MORTIMER." Target version of standard Mortimer. This rifle won World Muzzleloading Championship gold medals in 1989, 1991, and 1992. Mfg. by Pedersoli.

courtesy Dixie Gun Works

MSR $1,200	$1,080	$960	$720	$600

PENNSYLVANIA RIFLE — .45 or .50 cal. flintlock or perc., 41.5 in. octagon barrel, brown hammer, lock and barrel, brass patchbox and furniture, walnut full stock, 8 lbs. Mfg. by Pedersoli.

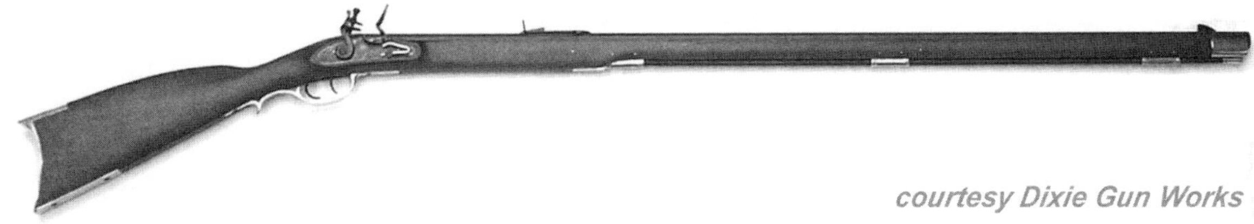

courtesy Dixie Gun Works

MSR $800	$725	$640	$480	$400

Add $50 for flintlock.

GRADING - PPGS™	100%	98%	90%	80%

REVOLVING CARBINE — .44 cal. perc., 18 in. tapered octagon barrel, brass trigger guard and buttstock. Reproduction of 1866-1879 Remington revolving carbine. Mfg. by Uberti. Disc. 2004.

	$385	$340	$255	$215

Last MSR was $375.

SANFTL SCHUETZEN TARGET RIFLE — .45 cal. perc., 29 in. barrel, adj. sights. Disc. 1991.

	$700	$565	$440	$325

Last MSR was $595.

SHARPS MILITARY CARBINE — .54 cal. perc. 22.25 in. tapered blue round barrel, 1:48 in. twist, color case hardened frame, blue or color case hardened furniture, 39.5 in. OAL, 8 lbs. N.S.S.A. approved. Mfg. by IAB/Italy. Disc. 2004. Reintroduced 2008 by IAB and Pedersoli.

MSR $775	$700	$620	$465	$385

Add $220 for Pedersoli mfg.

SHARPS MILITARY RIFLE — .54 cal. perc. 30 in. barrel with three bands, patchbox in stock. Mfg. by Pedersoli.

courtesy Dixie

MSR $1,350	$1,215	$1,075	$810	$675

SHARPS SPORTING RIFLE — .54 cal. perc. 28 or 29.25 (disc. 2004) in. oct. or 29 in. round blue barrel, 1:48 in. twist, satin finish checkered European walnut stock and forearm, color case hardened lock, frame and buttplate, single or double set and double phase triggers, 46.25-46.5 in. OAL, 8-9 lbs. Mfg. by IAB/Italy. Disc. 2004. Reintroduced 2009.

MSR $725	$650	$580	$435	$365

Add $100 for oct. barrel w/double set and double phase triggers.

SMITH CARBINE — .50 cal. perc., 21.5 in. octagon to round barrel, walnut buttstock and forearm, blue steel folding leaf rear sight with sliding elevator, blue steel furniture, color case hardened receiver and hammer. Cavalry model with saddle bar and ring on left side of receiver, Artillery model has sling swivel on buttstock and barrel band. Mfg. by Pedersoli. Disc. 2004. Reintroduced 2009.

courtesy Dixie

MSR $825	$745	$660	$495	$410

SUPER CUB RIFLE — .50 cal., flintlock or perc., 28.5 in. barrel, 7 lbs. Mfg. by Pedersoli.

courtesy Dixie Gun Works, Inc.

MSR $675	$610	$540	$405	$335

Add $50 for flintlock.

GRADING - PPGS™	100%	98%	90%	80%

TENNESSEE MOUNTAIN/SQUIRREL RIFLE — .32 (squirrel rifle) or .50 cal. perc. or flintlock, 41.5 in. brown barrel, brown furniture, cherry full stock, 8.5 or 9.5 lbs., right or left-hand. Mfg. by Miroku. Disc. 2002.

	$575	$450	$345	$275

Last MSR was $625.

TRYON CREEDMOOR RIFLE — .50 cal. perc., 32 in. octagon all black barrel, matte finish furniture and patchbox adj. Creedmoor sights, 9.5 lbs. Mfg. by Pedersoli.

MSR $1,100	$990	$880	$630	$550

TRYON RIFLE — .50 cal. perc., 32 in. octagon barrel, color case hardened furniture and patch box, chrome bore, 9.5 lbs. Mfg. by Pedersoli.

courtesy Dixie Gun Works

MSR $850	$765	$680	$510	$425

VOLUNTEER TARGET RIFLE (2 BAND AND 3 BAND) — .451 cal. perc., 33 in. round barrel with two barrel bands, 36 in barrel with three bands, color case hardened hammer and lock, brass furniture, adj. rear and hooded front sights, walnut stock, 10.5 lbs, 11.5 lbs. New 1993.

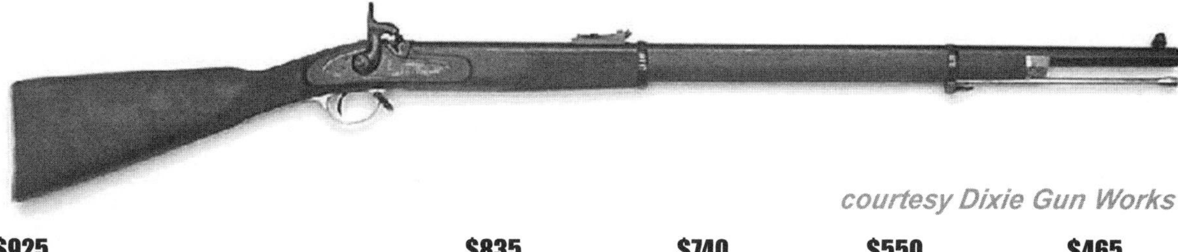
courtesy Dixie Gun Works

MSR $925	$835	$740	$550	$465

Add $30 for 3 Band model.

WAADTLANDER RIFLE — .44 cal. perc., 31 in. octagon brown barrel, color case hardened hammer, lock, trigger guard, and heavy buttplate, adj. sights, professional target model. Mfg. by Pedersoli.

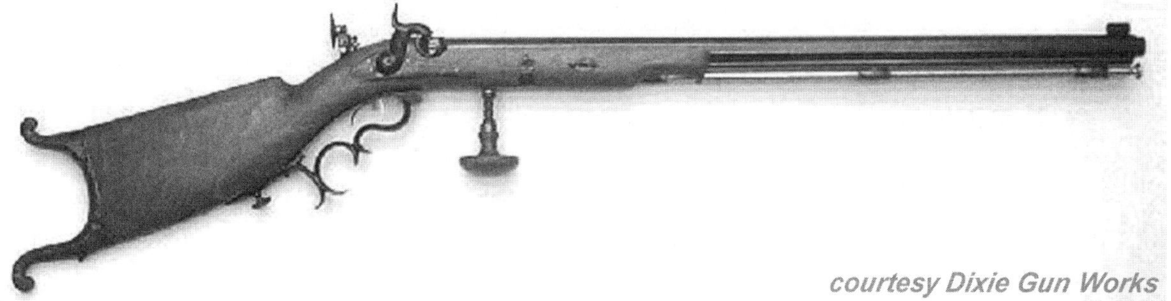
courtesy Dixie Gun Works

MSR $2,500	$2,250	$1,950	$1,650	$1,350

WESSON RIFLE — .50 cal. perc., 28 in. barrel, adj. sights. Disc. 1994. Reintroduced 2002-2003.

	$525	$415	$310	$250

Last MSR was $595.

GRADING - PPGS™	100%	98%	90%	80%

WHITWORTH MILITARY TARGET RIFLE — .451 cal. perc., 36 in. tapered round barrel, color case hardened lockplate, brass buttplate, trigger guard and nosecap, flip-up adj. blue steel rear sight. This is a reproduction of the long-range Whitworth rifle used by Confederate snipers during the Civil War, and is accurate up to 1,000 yards! Mfg. by EuroArms. Disc. 2004. Reintroduced 2009.

courtesy Dixie

MSR $1,095	$990	$880	$630	$550

YORK COUNTY RIFLE — .45 cal. flintlock or perc., 36 in. barrel. Disc. 1987.

	$275	$200	$145	$100

Last MSR was $210.

Add $15 for flintlock.

ZOUAVE RIFLE — .58 cal. perc., 33.5 in. blue barrel, color case hardened lock, hardwood stock, 9 lbs. 8 oz. Mfg. by Armi Sport and EuroArms.

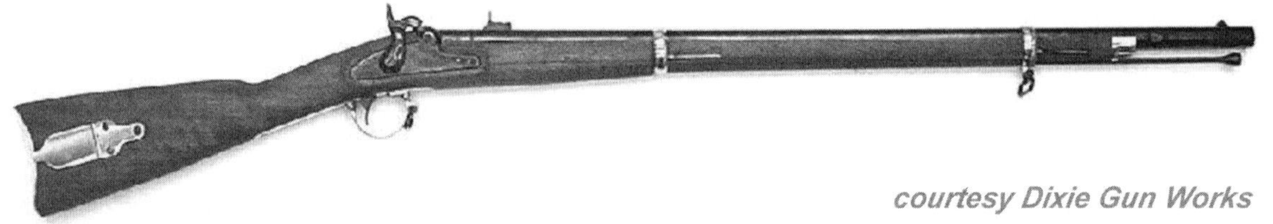

courtesy Dixie Gun Works

MSR $550	$500	$440	$330	$275

Add $90 for EuroArms version with European Walnut stock, color case hardened hammer, trigger, and lock.

RIFLES: IN-LINE

IN-LINE CARBINE — .50 or .54 cal. perc., 22 in. round barrel, three-quarter length walnut stock, adj. single trigger, open adj. rear sight, 7 lbs. Mfg. by Pedersoli. Disc. 2004.

	$325	$250	$195	$155

Last MSR was $350.

SHOTGUNS: FLINTLOCK & PERCUSSION

GIBBS SINGLE BARREL SHOTGUN — 12 ga. perc., blue 32 in. tapered oct. barrel, satin finish European PG walnut stock w/ebony forend and grip caps, color case hardened steel furniture and lock, 48.75 in. OAL, 7.75 lbs. Mfg. by Pedersoli. New 2008.

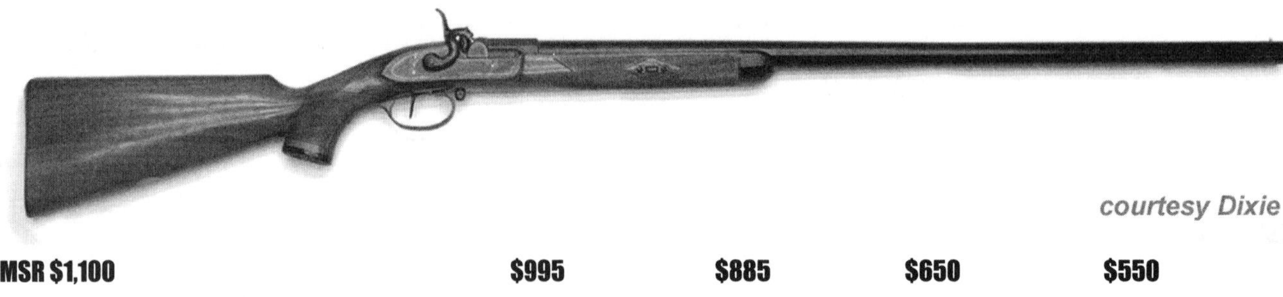

courtesy Dixie

MSR $1,100	$995	$885	$650	$550

GRADING - PPGS™	100%	98%	90%	80%

MAGNUM SxS — 10 or 12 ga. perc., 28.5 (12 ga.) or 30 (10 ga.) in. barrels, chrome bore, color case hardened hammer and lock, (engraved white steel on 10 ga.), checkered walnut stock, 45 (12 ga.) or 46.5 in. (10 ga.) OAL, 7 (12 ga.) or 7.5 (10 ga.) lbs. Mfg. by Pedersoli.

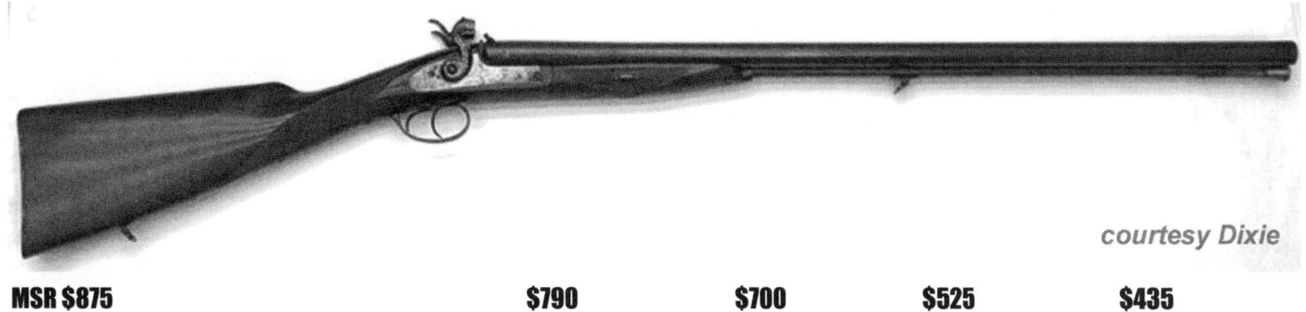
courtesy Dixie

MSR $875	$790	$700	$525	$435

Add $25 for 10 ga.

MAGNUM CAPE — 12 ga. perc., 32 in. barrel, engraved with walnut stock, 5.5 lbs. Mfg. by Armi San Paolo. Disc. 2002.

	$375	$300	$235	$190

Last MSR was $395.

MORTIMER — 12 ga. flintlock or percussion (new 2007), single shot, similar to Mortimer Rifle listed in rifle section, 9 lbs. Mfg. by Pedersoli.

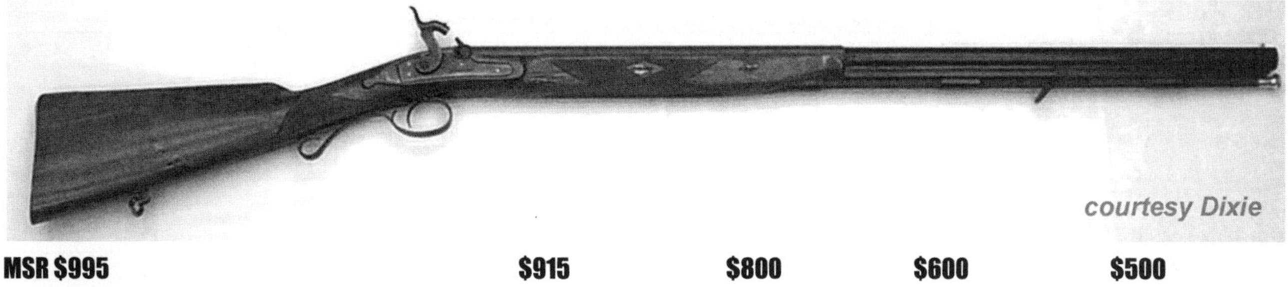
courtesy Dixie

MSR $995	$915	$800	$600	$500

Add $155 for flintlock.

NORTHWEST TRADE — 20 ga. flintlock, 36 in. octagon tapering to round barrel, brown barrel and lock assembly, 11 lbs. Mfg. 1989-1991.

	$425	$350	$255	$220

Last MSR was $495.

PEDERSOLI SxS — 20 ga. perc., brown 25 or 27.5 (disc. 2003) in. tapered round barrels, European walnut stock, color case hardened steel furniture and lock (except blue trigger guard and buttplate), engraved locks, tang, and triggerplate, double triggers, 6.75 lbs.

courtesy Dixie

MSR $875	$790	$700	$525	$435

GRADING - PPGS™	100%	98%	90%	80%

PEDERSOLI COACH GUN — 12 ga. perc., brown 20 in. tapered blue round barrels, European walnut half stock, checkered wrist, color case hardened locks, trigger guard, tang, entry thimble and wedge plates. Engraved locks and tang, 6.75 lbs. Mfg. 2001-2004. Mfg. By Pedersoli.

courtesy Dixie

	$450	$365	$265	$225

Last MSR was $500.

NOTES

GRADING - PPGS™	100%	98%	90%	80%

E SECTION

E.M.F. COMPANY INC.

Current importer and distributor located in Santa Ana, CA. Consumer direct and dealer sales.

E.M.F. is one of the oldest names in the black powder industry and has been importing and selling revolvers and longarms for more than 41 years. The majority of E.M.F. revolvers are manufactured in Italy and are frequently used in Civil War reenactments. E.M.F. is well known for its extensive line of cartridge-firing revolvers and longarms, holsters, accessories, and presentation cases. Please refer to the *Blue Book of Gun Values* by S.P. Fjestad for current information on E.M.F.'s firearms models.

PISTOLS: FLINTLOCK & PERCUSSION

1775 BLACK WATCH SCOTTISH PISTOL — .58 cal. flintlock, 7 in. smoothbore white steel barrel, brass frame, ram's horn grips with round ball trigger. Disc. 1994.

	$225	$200	$175	$125

Last MSR was $260.

CHARLES MOORE — .45 cal. flintlock, 10 in. octagon barrel, 2 lbs. Disc. 1994.

	$350	$275	$225	$170

Last MSR was $400.

1777 CHARLEVILLE PISTOL — .69 cal. flintlock, 7.5 in. white steel barrel, brass frame. Disc. 1994.

	$275	$235	$175	$145

Last MSR was $315.

CORSAIR PISTOL SxS — .36 or .44 cal. perc., color case hardened hammers and locks, brass trim. Disc. 1987.

	$325	$285	$210	$175

Last MSR was $160.

HARPERS FERRY — .58 cal. flintlock, brass mounted brown barrel. Disc. 1994.

	$415	$365	$265	$215

Last MSR was $405.

HAWKEN PISTOL — .54 cal. perc., 9 in. octagon barrel, adj. trigger, 2 lbs. 9 oz. Disc. 1994.

	$325	$285	$210	$175

Last MSR was $370.

HOWDAH HUNTER PISTOL — .50 cal. and/or 20 ga. perc., SxS pistol, 11.25 in. blue steel barrel, 1:18 in. twist and/or smoothbore, checkered satin finished European walnut w/three-quarter PG stock, 18.25 in. OAL, 4.5-5 lbs. Mfg. by Pedersoli. New 2009.

MSR $650	$585	$525	$395	$325

KENTUCKY PISTOL — .44 cal. flintlock or perc., available engraved or with brass barrel. Disc. 1994. Reintroduced 2009.

MSR $290	$265	$235	$195	$150

Add $30 for flintlock.
Add $20 for brass barrel.
Add $25 for engraved percussion.

LE PAGE PISTOL — .45 cal. perc., 9 in. octagon white steel barrel and trim, adj. sights, 2 lbs. 2 oz. Disc. 1994.

	$350	$275	$225	$175

Last MSR was $400.

REMINGTON STYLE TARGET PISTOL — .44 cal. perc., 9 in. octagon barrel, factory engraved, adj. sights (windage only), based on Rem. frame, 43 oz. Disc. 1994.

	$230	$205	$155	$125

Last MSR was $310.

GRADING - PPGS™	100%	98%	90%	80%

WM. PARKER PISTOL — .45 cal. perc., 10 in. octagon barrel, German silver lock and trim, double set triggers, 2.5 lbs. Disc. 1994.

	$415	$365	$265	$215

Last MSR was $400.

REVOLVERS: PERCUSSION

E.M.F. percussion revolvers are available in two series - the Standard and the Hartford. The Hartford Series, introduced in 1993, features a German silver plated backstrap and trigger guard, in addition to walnut grips with original type inspector's cartouche. Currently, the Hartford Series is standard for the 1851 Colt Navy, 1860 Colt Army, 1861 Colt Navy/Sheriff, and 1858 Remington.Also available in cased sets - prices range from $270-$325, depending on the model and finish. E.M.F. models are manufactured in Italy by Uberti and Pietta.

1847 WALKER — .44 cal. perc., 9 in. blue barrel, blue cylinder, color case hardened frame and loading lever, or antique finish, brass trim, 4 lbs. 8 oz.

courtesy E.M.F. Company Inc.

MSR $390	$350	$230	$180	$130

Add $70 for Antique finish.

1ST MODEL DRAGOON — .44 cal. perc., 7.5 in. barrel, color case hardened frame, brass trim, engraved cylinder, 4 lbs. 2 oz. Disc.

	$295	$220	$160	$110

Last MSR was $315.

2ND MODEL DRAGOON — .44 cal. perc., 7.5 in. blue barrel, color case hardened frame, brass trim, engraved cylinder, 4 lbs.

MSR $360	$325	$275	$215	$165

3RD MODEL DRAGOON — .44 cal. perc., 7.5 in. barrel, color case hardened frame and loading lever, brass trim, engraved cylinder, 4 lbs. 2 oz., adj. target sights. Disc.

	$295	$220	$160	$110

Last MSR was $350.

Add $25 for Buntline Model.
Add $15 for Texas Dragoon Model (Tucker and Sherrard and Co., Confederate States, Texas Star engraved on cylinder, square brass trigger guard).

1848 BABY DRAGOON — .31 cal. perc., 5 shot, 4 or 6 in. barrel, color case hardened frame and loading lever, brass trim.

MSR $285	$250	$215	$165	$125

1849 POCKET MODEL — .31 cal. perc., 5 shot, 4 in. blue barrel, color case hardened frame and loading lever.

	$200	$160	$120	$85

Last MSR was $255.

1849 WELLS FARGO — .31 cal. perc., 5 shot, 5 in. barrel, w/o loading lever. Disc.

	$200	$160	$120	$85

Last MSR was $255.

1851 NAVY — .36 or .44 cal. perc., 7.5 in. barrel, brass or steel frame, color case hardened hammer and loading lever, factory engraved cartouche in walnut grips. Standard Hartford model has brass frame.

MSR $200	$175	$150	$115	$85

Add $15 for case hardened steel frame.
Add $190 for shoulder stock.
Add $105 if engraved (disc.).

GRADING - PPGS™	100%	98%	90%	80%

1851 NAVY "BUNTLINE" BUFFALO — .44 cal. perc., similar to 1851 Navy Brass, except with 12 in. barrel.

MSR $215	$195	$175	$125	$95

Add $190 for shoulder stock.

1851 NAVY SHERIFF — .44 cal. perc., 5.5 in. barrel, brass or steel frame, color case hardened hammer and loading lever, factory engraved cartouche in walnut grips. Standard Hartford model has brass frame.

courtesy E.M.F. Company Inc.

MSR $200	$180	$160	$125	$90

Add $15 for case hardened steel frame.

1851 GRISWOLD CONFEDERATE — .36 or .44 cal. perc., 7.5 in. round barrel, brass frame, 2 lbs. 12 oz. Disc.

	$115	$100	$60	$50

Last MSR was $145.

1858 REMINGTON ARMY BRASS — .44 cal. perc., 8 in. blue finish barrel, loading lever and cylinder, brass frame, 2 lbs. 8 oz.

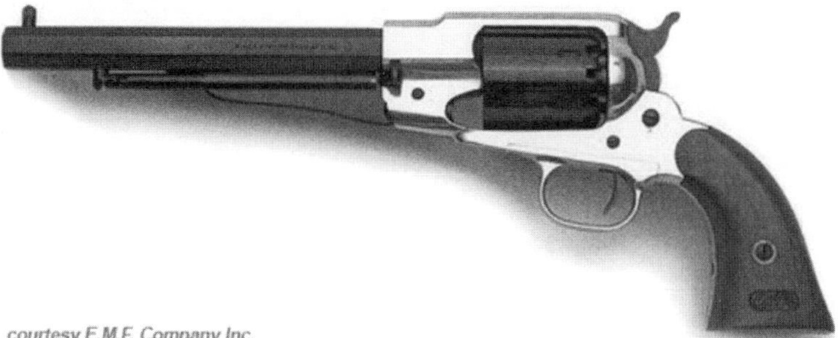

courtesy E.M.F. Company Inc.

MSR $204	$285	$255	$195	$165

1858 REMINGTON ARMY STAINLESS — .44 cal. perc., 5.5 or 8 in. stainless steel barrel, frame and loading lever, brass trigger guard, 2 lbs. 8 oz. Disc. 2007. Reintroduced 2009.

MSR $389	$350	$310	$230	$195

1858 REMINGTON ARMY STEEL — .36 or .44 cal. perc., 5.5 or 8 in. blue finish barrel, loading lever and round or fluted cylinder, blue or color case hardened finish steel frame, brass trigger guard, 2 lbs. 8 oz. Disc. 2007. Reintroduced 2009.

MSR $254	$225	$195	$135	$115

Add $96 for color case hardened frame.

1858 REMINGTON SHERIFF — .36 or .44 cal. perc., 5.5 or 6.5 in. blue finish steel barrel, loading lever, frame and round cylinder, brass trigger guard, 2 lbs. 8 oz. New 2009.

MSR $254	$225	$195	$135	$115

1860 ARMY — .44 cal. perc., 8 in. barrel, brass or steel frame, blue finish, walnut grips. Standard Hartford model has brass frame.

MSR $215	$190	$165	$125	$95

Add $25 for case hardened frame.
Add $190 for shoulder stock.

GRADING - PPGS™	100%	98%	90%	80%

1860 ARMY SHERIFF — .44 cal. perc., 5.5 in. barrel, steel frame, blue finish, walnut grips. Standard Hartford model has brass frame.

MSR $240	$215	$190	$145	$115

Add $190 for shoulder stock.

1861 NAVY — .36 cal. perc., steel frame, 7.5 in. round barrel, color case hardened frame, hammer and loading lever. Disc. Reintroduced 2003.

MSR $290	$260	$230	$175	$145

1862 POLICE — .36 cal. perc., 5 shot, 5.5 in. round barrel, color case hardened frame, hammer and loading lever, blue finish, walnut grips. Disc. 2007. Reintroduced 2008.

MSR $320	$285	$250	$195	$150

1862 POLICE BRASS — .36 cal. perc., 5 shot, brass frame, blue finish, walnut grips. Disc.

	$150	$125	$95	$65

Last MSR was $170.

1862 POCKET NAVY — .36 cal. perc., 5 shot, color case hardened frame. Disc.

	$195	$160	$115	$80

Last MSR was $200.

1862 POCKET POLICE — .36 cal. perc., 5 shot fluted cylinder, 5.5 in. round barrel, color case hardened frame, hammer and loading lever, blue finish, walnut grips.

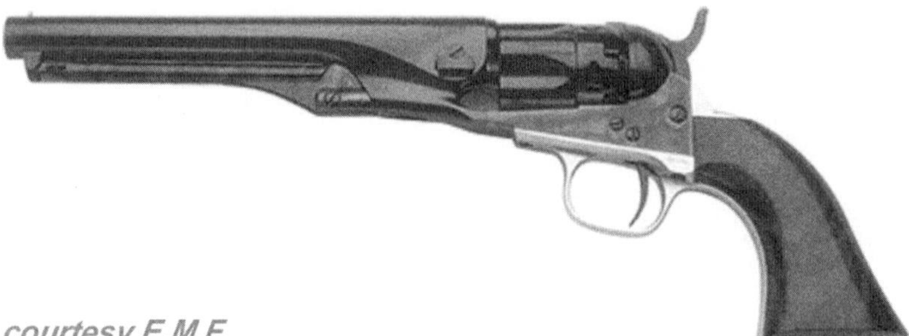

courtesy E.M.F.

MSR $300	$275	$245	$185	$155

NAVY SQUAREBACK — .36 or .44 cal. perc., 7.5 in. barrel, color case hardened frame and loading lever, Dragoon style square back trigger guard. Disc. 1994.

	$135	$110	$75	$50

Last MSR was $130.

Additional options are priced similar to the Model 1851 Navy.

1863 REMINGTON POCKET PISTOL — .31 cal. perc., 4 in. barrel, brass frame, blue barrel.

MSR $175	$150	$125	$95	$65

1862 NY MODEL POLICE — .36 cal. perc., 5 shot fluted cylinder, 5.5 in. blue finish round barrel, color case hardened frame, hammer and loading lever, brass backstrap and trigger guard, walnut grips.

MSR $300	$275	$245	$185	$155

RIFLES: FLINTLOCK & PERCUSSION

BOSTONIAN — .45 cal. perc. Mfg. 1989-disc.

	$220	$170	$125	$90

Last MSR was $285.

ALAMO COMMEMORATIVE — .45 cal. perc., embellished to commemorate the anniversary of the Alamo. Mfg. 1989-1994.

	$425	$350	$255	$220

Last MSR was $435.

GRADING - PPGS™	100%	98%	90%	80%

DELUXE BROWN BESS MUSKET — .75 cal. flintlock. Disc. 1994.

	$625	$500	$400	$300

Last MSR was $850.

Add $60 for bayonet.

HAWKEN RIFLE — .50 cal. perc., brass trim, color case hardened lock and hammer, adj. sights and stainless steel nipple. Disc. 1996.

	$235	$180	$130	$95

Last MSR was $325.

KENTUCKY RIFLE — .36, .44, or .45 cal. perc. or flintlock, factory engraved, brass trim, color case hardened lock and hammer.

	$300	$225	$160	$110

Add $10 for flintlock.
Add $30 for deluxe model.
Add $50 for deluxe engraved.

LONDON ARMORY ENFIELD — .58 cal. perc.

	$450	$365	$265	$225

Last MSR was $575.

Subtract $20 for Musketoon Model.

MINUTEMAN KENTUCKY RIFLE — .45 cal. flintlock or perc., 36 in. octagon barrel, brass blade front sight, brass trim, color case hardened lock, hammer and trigger.

	$300	$225	$160	$110

Add $15 for engraving, $15 for flintlock.

PENNSYLVANIA KENTUCKY RIFLE — .50 cal. perc., brass trim, color case hardened lock, hammer, and trigger. Disc. 1994.

	$425	$350	$255	$220

Last MSR was $440.

PLAINSMAN KENTUCKY RIFLE — .44 cal. perc., shorter forearm than Pennsylvania with more ornate finish. Disc. 1994.

	$345	$300	$225	$185

Last MSR was $450.

PURDEY DELUXE RIFLE/CARBINE — .50 cal. perc., half stock English style, select checkered walnut, color case hardened nose cap, lock, tang, buttplate and patch box, adj. sights, double set triggers.

	$350	$275	$225	$170

SAN FRANCISCO TO ST. LOUIS COMMEMORATIVE — .45 cal. perc., Kentucky rifle, highly embellished, made to commemorate the 130th Anniversary of the stage coach crossing "2,400 miles in 24 days." Mfg. 1989-1991.

	$375	$300	$235	$190

Last MSR was $395.

1863 SHARPS HARTFORD RIFLE/CARBINE — .54 cal. perc., 22 (round carbine) or 28 (octagon rifle) in. blue barrel, case hardened receiver, hammer and lever, standard falling block action, 9.5 (rifle) or 7.75 (carbine) lbs. Mfg. by Industria Armi Bresciane (IAB).

MSR $730	$665	$595	$345	$285

Add $70 for rifle with 28 in. barrel.

WESSON BERDAN RIFLE — .45 cal. perc., engraved brass frame.

	$395	$335	$245	$205

ZOUAVE RIFLE DELUXE — .58 cal. perc., brass trim, color case hardened lock and hammer, blue finish, adj. "Sniper Sight." Disc.

	$450	$365	$265	$225

Last MSR was $625.

GRADING - PPGS™	100%	98%	90%	80%

SHOTGUNS: PERCUSSION

SHOTGUN SxS — 12 ga. perc., based on early English design, brown barrel, color case hardened lock and hammer, imported from Italy. Disc. 1994.

	$425	$350	$255	$220

Last MSR was $535.

SHOTGUN O/U — 12 ga. perc. Mfg. 1989-1991.

	$475	$385	$280	$230

Last MSR was $640.

EASTERN MUZZLELOADERS SUPPLY

Previous importer/distributor located in Bear, Delaware. Dealer and catalog sales.

RIFLES

CRISTOFORO COLOMBO QUINCENTENARY MATCHLOCK — classic period matchlock styling, rear sight is a dolphin (a sign of good luck), the front sight, a stylized dolphin. The hammer is shaped like a sea monster (trigger being the tail), walnut stock, 500 scheduled to be mfg. and serial numbered CC1492-CC1992, custom mfg. by Pedersoli.

	$745	$610	$475	$350

Last MSR was $780.

FRENCH MODEL 1777 NAVY MUSKET — .69 cal. flintlock, 42.5 in. white steel barrel, brass furniture, split ring iron center barrel band, non-corrosive brass priming pan, walnut stock, 8.5 - 9.5 lbs. (similar to Charleville Musket) custom mfg. by Pedersoli.

	$625	$500	$400	$300

EUROARMS ITALIA S.r.l.

Current manufacturer located in Concesio, Italy. Armi San Paolo S.r.l. changed its name to Euroarms Italia S.r.l. in January 2002. Euroarms Italia S.r.l. (formerly Armi San Paolo) also owns Euroarms of America. Currently imported by Euroarms of America, located in Winchester, VA. Previously imported by and currently distributed by Cabela's, located in Sydney, NE, Dixie Gun Works, Inc., located in Union City, IN, and Navy Arms Co., located in Union City, NJ. Dealer and catalog sales.

PISTOLS: PERCUSSION

BOOMER "LUDWIG II" — .58 cal. perc., 7.25 in. smoothbore, brass or steel barrel.

	$275	$200	$145	$100

Last MSR was $300.

REVOLVERS: PERCUSSION

1851 NAVY SCHNEIDER & GLASSICK — .36 or .44 cal. perc., 5 or 7 in. octagon barrel, brass frame.

	$115	$100	$60	$50

Last MSR was $125.

1851 NAVY GRISWOLD & GUNNISON — .36 or .44 cal. perc., 7.5 in. octagon round barrel, brass frame. Disc. 1987.

	$115	$100	$60	$50

Last MSR was $100.

1851 NAVY — .36 or .44 cal. perc., 7.5 in. barrel, steel frame, 39-43 oz.

	$135	$110	$75	$50

Last MSR was $156.

Add $10 for square back trigger.
Add $25 for silver strap.
Subtract $24 for brass frame.

1851 NAVY POLICE — .36 cal. perc., 5 or 7.5 in. octagon barrel, steel frame, 5 shot fluted cylinder, 38-41 oz. Disc. 1994.

	$135	$110	$75	$50

Last MSR was $135.

GRADING - PPGS™	100%	98%	90%	80%

1851 NAVY SHERIFF'S MODEL — .36 or .44 cal. perc., 5 in. barrel, steel frame, 39 oz. Disc. 1994.

	$135	$110	$75	$50

Last MSR was $105.

1860 ARMY — .44 cal. perc., 5 or 8 in. barrel, brass or steel frame, 41 oz.

	$160	$130	$100	$70

Last MSR was $177.

Subtract $32 for brass frame.

1861 NAVY — .36 cal. perc., 7.5 in. barrel, steel frame, 42 oz.

	$160	$130	$100	$70

Last MSR was $245.

1862 POLICE — .36 cal. perc., 7.5 in. barrel, steel frame, 40 oz. Disc. 1987.

	$160	$130	$100	$70

Last MSR was $135.

REMINGTON 1858 ARMY — .36 or .44 cal. perc., 8 in. octagon barrel, 40 oz.

MSR $265	$235	$190	$155	$115

Last MSR was $200.

Add $75 for engraving, and $48 for stainless steel.

REMINGTON 1858 NAVY — .36 cal. perc., 6.5 in. octagon barrel, 40 oz. Disc.

	$190	$155	$115	$80

Last MSR was $200.

ROGERS & SPENCER — .44 cal. perc., 7.5 in. octagon barrel, high gloss blue finish, 47 oz. Winner of the Product Merit Award for 1977 from the National Association of Federally Licensed Firearms Dealers, the Euroarms Rogers & Spencer recreates a historic Civil War era pistol in authentic detail. Available through Dixie Gun Works and Navy Arms.

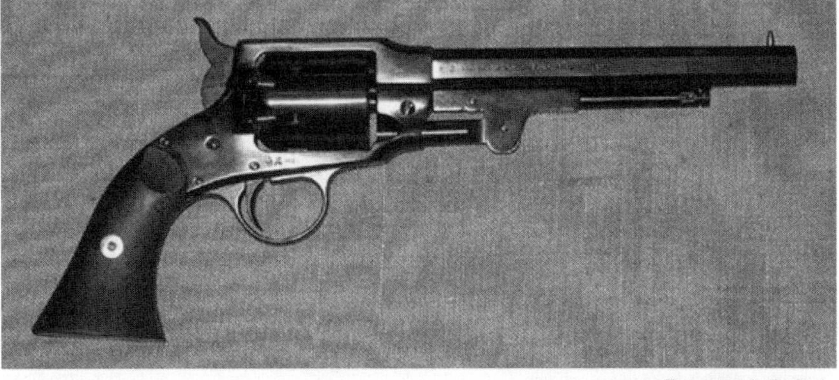

courtesy Euroarms Italia S.r.l.

MSR $425	$395	$345	$245	$195

RIFLES: FLINTLOCK & PERCUSSION

BROWN BESS MUSKET (TOWER FLINTLOCK) — .75 cal. flintlock, 41.75 in. barrel, smooth bore. Disc. 1994.

	$525	$415	$310	$250

Last MSR was $755.

BUFFALO CARBINE — .58 cal. perc., 26 in. round barrel, color case hardened hammer and lock, brass patchbox and furniture, 7.75 lbs.

	$375	$300	$235	$190

Last MSR was $440.

C.S. RICHMOND MUSKET — .58 cal. perc., 40 in. round barrel, white steel hammer and lock, brass buttplate and end cap, walnut stock, 10.5 lbs.

MSR $1,050	$950	$850	$625	$525

GRADING - PPGS™	100%	98%	90%	80%

CAPE RIFLE — .50 cal. perc., 32 in. barrel, engraved with walnut stock. Mfg. 1989-1991.

	$425	$350	$255	$220

Last MSR was $515.

CHARLEVILLE 1777 FLINTLOCK MUSKET — .69 cal. flintlock, 44.75 in. white steel barrel, smooth bore. Disc. 1994.

	$600	$465	$385	$285

Last MSR was $835.

COOK & BROTHER RIFLE/CARBINE — .58 cal. perc., 24 in. barrel, adj. front sight (windage only), two barrel bands, walnut stock, 7.5 lbs.

MSR $740	$675	$605	$475	$385

Add $33 for rifle.

1853 ENFIELD RIFLE MUSKET (PARKER-HALE) — .58 cal. perc., 39 in. barrel, adj. rear sight), three barrel bands, walnut stock, 9.5 lbs.

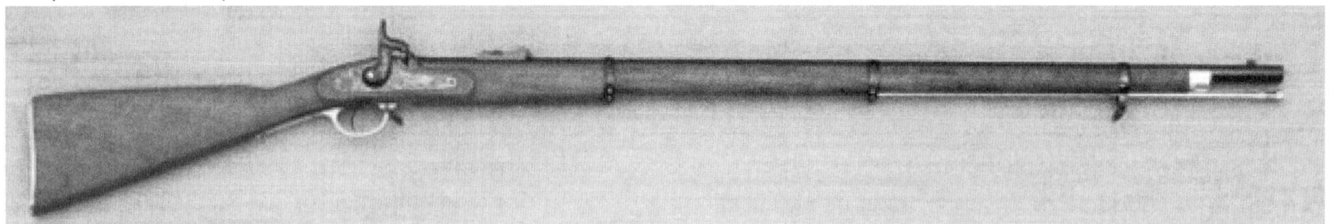

courtesy Euroarms Italia S.r.l

MSR $650	$585	$515	$385	$295

Add $40 for satin finish.

1858 ENFIELD RIFLE MUSKET (LONDON ARMORY CO.) — .58 cal. perc., 33 in. barrel, adj. rear sight, two barrel bands, walnut stock, 7.5 lbs.

MSR $650	$585	$515	$385	$295

1861 ENFIELD ARTILLERY CARBINE MUSKETOON — .58 cal. perc., 24 in. barrel, adj. rear sight, two barrel bands, walnut stock, 7.5 lbs.

MSR $650	$585	$515	$385	$295

MODEL 1803 HARPER'S FERRY FLINTLOCK — .54 or .58 cal. flintlock, 32.5 in. brown barrel, walnut stock, 9 lbs.

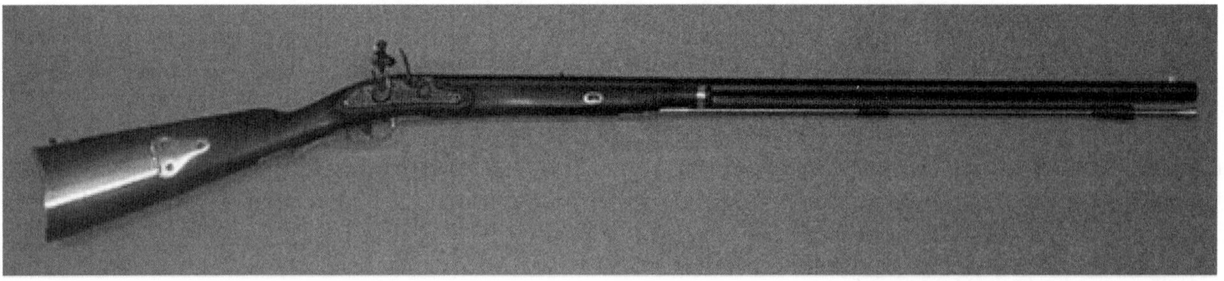

courtesy Euroarms Italia S.r.l.

MSR $995	$895	$795	$595	$495

HAWKEN RIFLE — .58 cal. perc., 28 in. oct. barrel, double set triggers, target model, 9 lbs. 6 oz. Disc. 1989.

	$265	$200	$145	$100

Last MSR was $295.

1862-1864 CONFEDERATE CARBINE (J.P. MURRAY) — .58 cal. perc., 23 in. round barrel, color case hardened hammer and lock, brass patch box and furniture, 7.75 lbs.

MSR $750	$685	$615	$485	$395

GRADING - PPGS™	100%	98%	90%	80%

MATCHLOCK SMOOTHBORE — .63 cal. perc., 42 in. barrel.

	$550	$425	$320	$260

Last MSR was $637.

MISSISSIPPI RIFLE MODEL 1841 — .54 or .58 cal. perc., 33 in. barrel, 9 lbs. 8 oz.

MSR $825	$765	$675	$495	$395

PENNSYLVANIA RIFLE — .45 or .50 cal. flintlock or perc., 36 in. barrel, adj. rear sight (windage only), walnut stock, 7 lbs. Disc. 1987.

	$330	$255	$195	$155

Last MSR was $285.

Add $30 for flintlock.

1862 REMINGTON RIFLE — .58 cal. perc., 33 in. barrel, three leaf folding rear sight, three barrel bands, beechwood stock, 9.5 lbs. Disc. 1987.

	$315	$245	$185	$145

Last MSR was $285.

1863 SPRINGFIELD RIFLE MUSKET — .58 cal. perc., 40 in. barrel with three bands.

MSR $665	$595	$525	$395	$235

U.S. MODEL 1855 RIFLE MUSKET — .58 cal. perc., 40 in. barrel.

MSR $995	$895	$795	$595	$495

VOLUNTEER TARGET RIFLE (2 BAND) — .451 cal. perc., 33 in. round barrel, color case hardened hammer and lock, two barrel bands, brass furniture, adj. rear and hooded front sights, walnut stock, 9.5 lbs. New 1993.

MSR $925	$865	$775	$595	$495

VOLUNTEER TARGET RIFLE (3 BAND) — .451 cal. perc., same as above except with 3 bbl. bands and longer barrel.

MSR $715	$645	$575	$445	$355

WHITWORTH MILITARY TARGET RIFLE (3 BAND) — .451 cal. perc., 36 in. barrel.

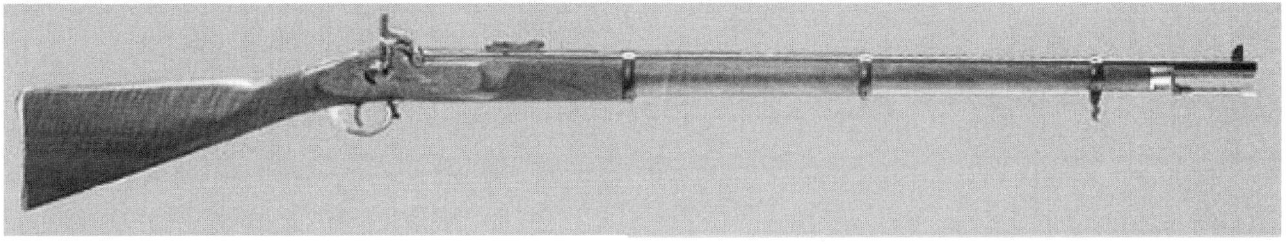

courtesy Euroarms Italia S.r.l

MSR $1,095	$995	$895	$665	$565

1863 REMINGTON ZOUAVE RIFLE — .58 cal. perc., brass trim, color case hardened lock and hammer, blue finish, adj. sniper sight.

MSR $640	$575	$505	$375	$285

Add $115 for "Range" grade Target Model.

SHOTGUNS: PERCUSSION

MAGNUM CAPE — 12 ga. perc., 32 in. barrel, engraved with walnut stock, 5.5 lbs.

	$375	$300	$235	$190

Last MSR was $395.

DUCK MODEL — 8, 10, or 12 ga. perc., 33 in. round barrel, color case hardened hammer and lock, brass patchbox and furniture, 8.5 lbs. Mfg. 1989-1992.

	$375	$300	$235	$190

Last MSR was $455.

STANDARD SxS — 12 ga. perc., 28 in. barrels, engraved with walnut stock, 6 lbs. Disc. 1994.

	$350	$275	$225	$170

Last MSR was $405.

NOTES

GRADING - PPGS™	100%	98%	90%	80%

F SECTION

FABER BROTHERS

Current distributor located in Chicago, IL. Dealer sales.

Faber Brothers is currently marketing customized C.V.A. (see Connecticut Valley Arms) and InvestArms Hawken rifles. These rifles come drilled and tapped for scope with offset hammers and chrome bores. Faber Brothers rifles may command a slight premium over similar configurations from C.V.A. & InvestArms.

FEDERAL ORDNANCE CORPORATION

Previous manufacturer/importer located in South El Monte, CA. All black powder models were discontinued during 1990.

PISTOLS: FLINTLOCK & PERCUSSION

DURS EGG SAW HANDLED PISTOL — .45 cal. flintlock or perc., 9.5 in. blue octagon barrel, unique stock, hand checkered, German silver trim, white steel hammer and lock. Disc. 1994.

	100%	98%	90%	80%
	$210	**$165**	**$125**	**$90**

Last MSR was $225.

F. ROCHATTE — .45 cal. perc., single set trigger, hand checkered stock. Disc. 1994.

	100%	98%	90%	80%
	$250	**$190**	**$135**	**$95**

Last MSR was $250.

KENTUCKY PISTOL — .45 cal. perc., 10.25 in. octagon barrel, brass blade front sight, 40 oz. Disc. 1994.

	100%	98%	90%	80%
	$200	**$160**	**$120**	**$85**

Last MSR was $110.

WILLIAM MOORE PISTOL — .45 cal. flintlock or perc., 10 in. octagon barrel, white steel hammer and lock, silver plated trim, 2 lbs. Disc. 1994.

	100%	98%	90%	80%
	$315	**$245**	**$185**	**$145**

Last MSR was $230.

Add $10 for flintlock.

NAPOLEON LE PAGE PISTOL — .45 cal. perc., 10 in. octagon white steel barrel and lock, brass trim, adj. double set triggers, fluted grip, 2 lbs. 7 oz. Disc. 1994.

	100%	98%	90%	80%
	$170	**$145**	**$105**	**$75**

Last MSR was $185.

WILLIAM PARKER PISTOL — .45 cal. flintlock or perc., 11 in. octagon brown barrel, silver plated furniture, double set triggers. Disc. 1994.

	100%	98%	90%	80%
	$275	**$200**	**$145**	**$100**

Last MSR was $200.

Add $10 for flintlock.

REVOLVERS: PERCUSSION

1858 REMINGTON — .44 cal. perc., 7.5 in. octagon barrel, 6 shot, brass frame and trigger guard, 2 lbs. 10 oz. Disc. 1994.

	100%	98%	90%	80%
	$90	**$75**	**$50**	**$40**

Last MSR was $110.

Add $30 for steel.
Add $100 for stainless steel frame.
Add $75 for target model.

1860 ARMY — .44 cal. perc., 8 in. barrel, 6 shot, color case hardened hammer, lock and loading lever, brass backstrap and trigger guard. Disc 1994.

	100%	98%	90%	80%
	$175	**$150**	**$105**	**$75**

Last MSR was $125.

Add $15 for Sheriff's Model.
Add $75 for shoulder stock.

GRADING - PPGS™	100%	98%	90%	80%

1862 POCKET NAVY — .36 cal. perc., 6.5 in. barrel, color case hardened frame, hammer and loading lever, cylinder semi-fluted or engraved. 1 lb. 9 oz. Disc. 1994.

	$160	$130	$100	$70

Last MSR was $205.

ROGERS & SPENCER — .44 cal. perc., 7.5 in. octagon barrel, blue steel, 3 lbs. Disc. 1994.

	$200	$160	$120	$85

Last MSR was $200.

RIFLES: FLINTLOCK & PERCUSSION

1853 ENFIELD (3-BAND) — .58 cal. perc., 39 in. round barrel, color case hardened hammer and lock, brass trim, blue bands, adj. rear sight, 9.5 lbs. Disc. 1994.

	$450	$365	$265	$225

Last MSR was $400.

1858 ENFIELD (2-BAND) — similar to 1853 3-Band Enfield, except has 33 in. round barrel, 10 lbs. Disc. 1994.

	$425	$350	$255	$220

Last MSR was $340.

ENFIELD MUSKETOON — .58 cal. perc., 24 in. barrel, adj. rear sight (windage only), 2 barrel bands, walnut stock, 8 lbs. Disc. 1994.

	$450	$365	$265	$225

Last MSR was $480.

HARPERS FERRY FLINTLOCK — .58 cal. flintlock, 35 in. round barrel, color case hardened hammer and lock, brass trim, 8.5 lbs. Disc. 1994.

	$575	$450	$345	$275

Last MSR was $440.

HAWKEN RIFLE — .45 or .50 cal. flintlock or perc., 28.5 in. octagon barrel, color case hardened hammer and lock, double set triggers, 7.75 lbs. Disc. 1994.

	$275	$200	$145	$100

Last MSR was $220.

KENTUCKY RIFLE — .45 cal. perc., color case hardened hammer and lock, percussion cap holder in stock, brass trim. Disc. 1994.

	$300	$220	$160	$110

Last MSR was $210.

J.P. MURRAY CARBINE — .58 cal. perc., 23.5 in. brown round barrel, color case hardened hammer and lock, brass trim and bands, 7.5 lbs. Disc. 1994.

	$395	$335	$245	$205

Last MSR was $370.

MISSISSIPPI RIFLE — .58 cal. perc., 33 in. brown round barrel, color case hardened hammer and lock, brass trim and bands, 9.5 lbs. Disc. 1994.

	$450	$365	$265	$225

Last MSR was $410.

SANFTL SCHUETZEN RIFLE — .45 cal. perc., 31 in. octagon barrel, both aperture and iron sights, Schuetzen buttplate and trigger guard, brass furniture. Disc. 1994.

	$800	$650	$515	$375

Last MSR was $590.

ZOUAVE RIFLE — .58 cal. perc., 32.5 in. round barrel, color case hardened hammer, lock and trigger, brass trim, adj. rear sight, 9 lbs. Disc. 1994.

	$295	$220	$160	$110

Last MSR was $360.

GRADING - PPGS™	100%	98%	90%	80%

FEINWERKBAU

Current manufacturer established circa 1951, and located in Oberndorf, Germany. Currently imported beginning 2005 by Brenzovich Firearms & Training Center located in Ft. Hancock, TX. Previously Feinwerkbau firearms had limited importation until 2004 by Nygord Precision, located in Prescott, AZ and by Beeman Precision Airguns, located in Huntington Beach, CA.

Feinwerkbau manufactures world championship winning a black powder pistol. Feinwerkbau also manufactures some of the world's finest quality target rifles and pistols (.22 LR rimfire and airgun). Target rifles and pistols have had limited importation into the U.S. For more information and current pricing on both new and used Feinwerkbau airguns, please refer to the *Blue Book of Airguns* by Dr. Robert Beeman & John Allen (also online). For more information and current pricing on both new and used Feinwerkbau firearms, please refer to the *Blue Book Gun Values* by Dr. S.P. Fjestad (also online).

PISTOLS: SINGLE SHOT

HISTORY NO 1 (BILLINGHURST MODEL) — .36 cal., perc., under hammer, high polish blue, walnut grips, 10.1 in. barrel, adj. sight, 2.4 lbs. Limited U.S. importation beginning 2002.

courtesy Feinwerkbau

MSR $1,230	$1,150	$1,035	$825	$665

REVOLVERS

HISTORY NO 2 (ROGERS & SPENCER) — .44 cal. perc., 6 shot, 7.5 octagon barrel, high polish blue, walnut grips, 3 lbs. New 2004.

courtesy Feinwerkbau

MSR $1,840	$1,675	$1,485	$1,125	$950

FORT WORTH FIREARMS

Previous manufacturer located in Fort Worth, TX 1995-2000.

RIFLES: PERCUSSION

PECOS RIFLE — .50 cal. perc., 22 in. tapered round stainless steel barrel, adj. sights and trigger, trigger safety, checkered black composite stock with recoil pad, 6.5 lbs.

	$450	$365	$265	$225

Last MSR was $500.

Add $35 for black stainless steel.
Add $50 for camo stock.

RIO GRANDE RIFLE — .50 cal. perc., 22 or 24 in. tapered round stainless steel barrel, adj. sights and trigger, checkered black composite stock with recoil pad, 6.5 lbs.

	$450	$365	$265	$225

Last MSR was $500.

Add $35 for black stainless steel.
Add $50 for thumbhole or camo stock.

GRADING - PPGS™	100%	98%	90%	80%

BRAZOS — .50 cal. perc., in-line ignition, 22 in. tapered round stainless steel barrel, adj. sights, checkered black composite stock with recoil pad, 6.5 lbs.

	$275	$200	$145	$100

Last MSR was $300.

SABINE RIFLE — .22 cal. perc., in-line ignition, 16.25 round blue barrel, safety, Monte Carlo walnut finish stock, 3.5 lbs.

	$175	$150	$105	$75

Last MSR was $190.

FREEDOM ARMS INC.

Current manufacturer located in Freedom, WY. Dealer sales.

REVOLVERS

STAINLESS MINI-REVOLVER — .22 cal. perc., 5 shot, 1, 1.75, or 3 in. barrel, stainless steel. Disc. 1994.

	$250	$190	$135	$95

Last MSR was $205.

Add $15 for 3 in. barrel.
Add $40 for brass buckle.

NOTES

GRADING - PPGS™	100%	98%	90%	80%

G SECTION

GIBBS RIFLE COMPANY

Current manufacturer, importer, and distributor located in Martinsburg, WV since 1991. A division of Forgett Militaria L.L.C.

Founded in 1991, the Gibbs Rifle Company has purchased the rights to manufacture the Parker-Hale Enfield black powder replicas from Parker-Hale located in Birmingham, England. Navy Arms remains the only distributor of Parker-Hale black powder replicas. Beginning in 1996, Parker-Hale Enfield rifles are being manufactured by EuroArms Italia S.r.l. (formally Armi San Paolo) under license.

GONIC ARMS

Previous manufacturer located in Gonic, NH until 2006. Dealer and consumer direct sales.

Gonic Arms designed a true hunter's Magnum rifle. Equipped with an ambidextrous safety, it eliminates the noisy "click" often associated with bringing a hammer back from half cock or setting the first of double set triggers. A specially designed firing pin and housing allow spent caps to blow out the bottom of the rifle, thus eliminating the need to "dig out" the spent cap from the breech. This, combined with its modern appearance and loading system designed, made it a true hunters rifle without the problems associated with most black powder arms. Gonic also produced black powder Magnum barrels to fit the Thompson Contender frame, easily converting the T.C. single shot pistol into a black powder model with in-line ignition, and an optional Contender shoulder stock can be included.

PISTOLS: BARREL ASSEMBLIES

MODEL 90 MAGNUM PISTOL BARREL — .45 or .50 cal. perc., #11 percussion cap or #209 primer ignition, 16 or 24 in. blue or stainless steel barrel, 1:22 (.45 cal.) or 1:24 in. twist, designed to fit into a Thompson Contender frame, standard Thompson forearm must also be replaced. Disc. 2006.

	100%	98%	90%	80%
	$245	**$215**	**$180**	**$145**

Last MSR was $276.

Add $28 for 24 in. barrel.
Add $32 for stainless steel barrel.

Additional features are available, call for pricing.

RIFLES: IN-LINE IGNITION

MODEL 87 RIFLE/CARBINE — .308 Spitfire, .38, .44, .458 Express, .50 cal., (rifle only), .54, and 20 ga., 26 in. round barrel, (24 in. carbine custom shop only) single stage trigger with left or right safety, cap is placed in breech, 6 lbs. Disc. 1987.

	100%	98%	90%	80%
	$500	**$400**	**$295**	**$240**

Last MSR was $570.

Add $25 for sights.
Add $20 for Deluxe.
Add $70 for laminated stock.
Add $250 for 1-1,000 limited edition.

MODEL 87 MAGNUM — .45 or .50 cal. perc., similar to Model 87, Deluxe Model, American walnut stock, checkered with 1 in. recoil pad.

	100%	98%	90%	80%
	$675	**$545**	**$425**	**$315**

Last MSR was $800.

Add $25 for open sights.
Add $40 for aperture sights.

MODEL 90 CARBINE — .45 or .50 cal. perc., #11 percussion cap or #209 primer in-line ignition, 24 in. blue or stainless steel barrel, 1:22 (.45 cal.) or 1:24 in. twist, walnut, black, or grey laminated wood stock and forearm, recoil pad. Mfg. 2003-06.

	100%	98%	90%	80%
	$875	**$785**	**$650**	**$475**

Last MSR was $982.

Add $26 for grey laminated stock.
Add $42 for stainless steel barrel.

Additional features are available, call for pricing.

GRADING - PPGS™	100%	98%	90%	80%

MODEL 93 MAGNUM — .45 (new 2003) or .50 cal. perc., 24 or 26 (new 2003) in. barrel, 1:22 (.45 cal.) or 1:24 in. twist, adj. trigger, drilled and tapped for scope, adj. fiber optic sights, hardwood stock, recoil pad, sling swivel studs, approx. 6.5-7 lbs. Disc. 2006.

	$650	$575	$465	$335

Last MSR was $720.

Add $62 for stainless steel barrel (new 1994).

Additional features are available, call for pricing.

MODEL 93 MAGNUM DELUXE — .45 (new 2003) or .50 cal. perc., similar to Model 93 Magnum. Disc. 2006.

	$850	$765	$615	$440

Last MSR was $950.

Add $62 for stainless steel barrel.

Additional features are available, call for pricing.

MODEL 93 MAGNUM SAFARI — .50 cal. perc., in-line action, similar to Model 93 Magnum Standard, except is available with any or all options (built to the purchasers specifications). Disc.

	$1,300	$1,100	$880	$725

Last MSR was $1,560.

MODEL 93 MAGNUM SAFARI CLASSIC — .50 cal., in-line action, similar to Model 93 Magnum Safari, except has classic cheek piece, walnut stock with hand checkering, available with all options (built to the purchaser's specifications). Disc.

	$1,450	$1,225	$900	$775

Last MSR was $1,612.

MODEL 93 MAGNUM MOUNTAIN CLASSIC RIFLE — .50 cal, in-line ignition, custom version of Model 93 Magnum Standard, available with any or all options (built to purchaser's specifications). Available with thumbhole stock at no additional charge. Disc.

	$1,775	$1,400	$1,000	$795

Last MSR was $2,132.

MODEL 93 THUMBHOLE RIFLE — .45 (new 2003) or .50 cal. perc., custom version of Model 93 Magnum Standard, available with any or all options (built to purchaser's specifications). Mfg. 2003-06.

	$2,350	$2,075	$1,700	$1,350

Last MSR was $2,600.

MODEL SS-01 — .50 cal. perc., inline ignition, 26 in. satin stainless steel barrel, 1:24 in. twist, adj. sights and detacable scope bases, adj. trigger, grey laminated stock, 1 in. Pachmayer Decelerator recoil pad, sling swivel studs, approx. 7-8 lbs. Mfg. 2003-06.

	$950	$850	$675	$495

Last MSR was $1,050.

Additional features are available, call for pricing.

MODEL SS-01-T — .50 cal. perc., inline ignition, similar to Model SS-01, except includes the best of all available features. Mfg. 2003-06.

	$2,450	$2,175	$1,775	$1,350

Last MSR was $2,700.

GUN WORKS MUZZLELOADING EMPORIUM INC.

Current distributor and maker of custom muzzleloading pistols and rifles located in Springfield, OR.

The Gun Works Muzzleloading Emporium Inc. specializes in English pistols, English sporting rifles, Hawken rifles, North West Trade guns, Pennsylvania rifles, and American Fowlers.

GRADING - PPGS™	100%	98%	90%	80%

PISTOLS: FLINTLOCK & PERCUSSION

ENGLISH FLINTLOCK AND PERCUSSION PISTOLS — .32, .36, .40, .45, or .50 cal. flintlock or perc., single set trigger, walnut or maple stock, iron furniture, 2 lb. 10 oz. Left-hand versions available.

courtesy Gun Works Muzzleloading Emporium Inc.

MSR $550	$495	$405	$365	$300

Add $25 for Flintlock.

SAW HANDLE PISTOL — .32, .36, .40, .45, or .50 cal. flintlock, 10.75 in. brown barrel, 1:20 in. twist, single set trigger, checkered select walnut or maple stock w/ebony butt and nose caps, approx. 3 lbs. New 2008.

courtesy Gun Works

MSR $895	$815	$725	$550	$475

RIFLES: PERCUSSION

AMERICAN FOWLER RIFLE #2 — .50 or .54, cal, flintlock or perc., 38 in. Oregon Barrel Co. tapered octagon barrels, 1:56 twist, single trigger, silver lock, select maple or walnut stock.

courtesy Gun Works Muzzleloading Emporium Inc.

MSR $1,750	$1,500	$1,375	$1,200	$1,030

Add $100 for ENGLISH SPORTING RIFLE #3. New 2009.

ENGLISH SPORTING RIFLE #2 — .45, .50, .54, .58, .62, or .69 cal perc., 28 in. to 36 in. Oregon Barrel Co. tapered octagon barrels, single trigger, brown lock, hammer, furniture and trigger guard, walnut or maple stock.

courtesy Gun Works Muzzleloading Emporium

MSR $1,750	$1,500	$1,375	$1,200	$1,030

Add $100 for ENGLISH SPORTING RIFLE #3. New 2009.

GRADING - PPGS™	100%	98%	90%	80%

ENGLISH SPORTING RIFLE ULTIMATE — 4 or 8 bore cal. perc., 31 (4 bore) or 31.5 (8 bore) in. Oregon Barrel Co. tapered octagon barrel, 1:104 (4 bore) or 1:144 (8 bore) in. twist, single trigger, brown lock, hammer, furnitur, and trigger guard, checkered walnut or maple stock w/ebony nose and pistol grip cap. New 2009.

courtesy Gun Works

MSR $4,750	$4,500	$3,950	$3,250	$2,500

HAWKEN RIFLE #2 — .50 or .54 cal. perc., 34 in. octagon barrel, 1:66 in. twist, L&R lock, double set triggers, fixed rear sight, maple stock.

courtesy Gun Works Muzzleloading Emporium

MSR $1,750	$1,500	$1,375	$1,200	$1,030

Add $300 for HAWKEN RIFLE #3. New 2009.

PENNSYLVANIA RIFLE #2 — .32, .36, .40, .45, .50, or .54 cal. perc. or flintlock, 38 in. swamped barrel, double set triggers, iron or brass furniture, optional patchbox.

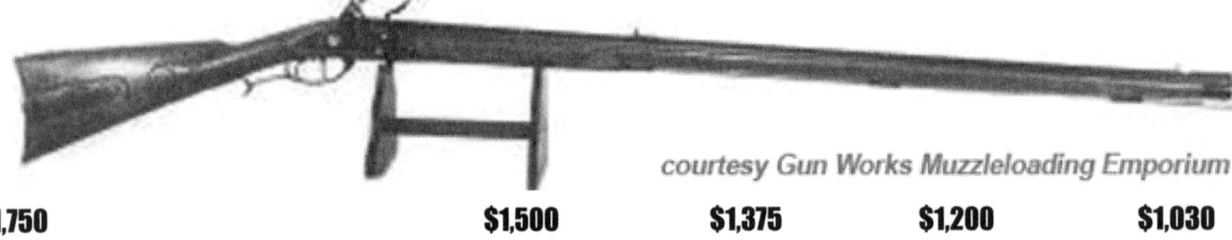
courtesy Gun Works Muzzleloading Emporium

MSR $1,750	$1,500	$1,375	$1,200	$1,030

Add $300 for PENNSYLVANIA RIFLE #3. New 2009.

SHOTGUNS: FLINTLOCK & PERCUSSION

AMERICAN FOWLER #2 — 20, 24, or 28 ga. flintlock or perc., smoothbore or rifled, 38 in. barrel, maple or walnut stock.

MSR $1,675	$1,500	$1,265	$1,125	$945

Add $100 for AMERICAN FOWLER #3. New 2009.

NORTH WEST TRADE GUN — 20, 24, or 28 ga. perc., smoothbore, 42 in. barrel, maple stock.

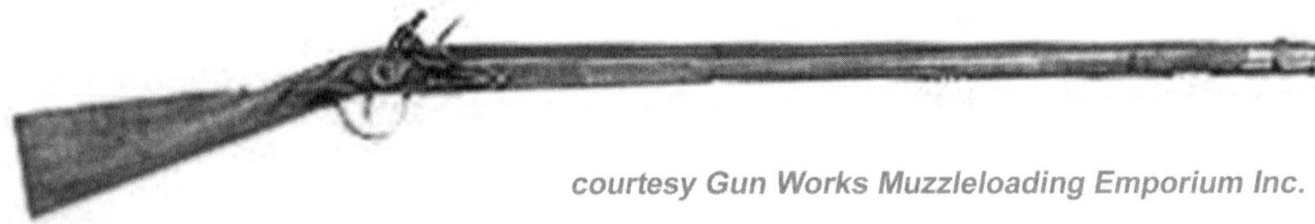
courtesy Gun Works Muzzleloading Emporium Inc.

MSR $1,050	$855	$725	$580	$415

GRADING - PPGS™	100%	98%	90%	80%

H SECTION

HATFIELD

Previous trademark manufactured by Mountain River Rifle Works, and by Hatfield Gun Co. Inc. until 1996.

RIFLES: FLINTLOCK & PERCUSSION

MOUNTAIN RIFLE — .50 or .54 cal. perc., 32 in. octagon barrel, brown furniture, half stock, 9 lbs.

	100%	98%	90%	80%
	$575	$450	$345	$275

Last MSR was $665.

During 1992-93, extensive work was done to all internal working parts to insure greater longevity for target or field use. All internal parts were U.S. made.

SQUIRREL RIFLE — .32, .36, .45, or .50 cal. flintlock or perc., 39 in. barrel, adj. sights, double set triggers, brass trim, 7.5 lbs.

	100%	98%	90%	80%
	$525	$415	$310	$250

Last MSR was $600.

Add $20 for flintlock.
Add $65 for extra fancy maple Grade II.
Add $175 for hand selected fancy Grade III.

Custom models could run 200% over standard.

HAWKEN SHOP

Current manufacturer of original Hawken rifles and kits, located in Oak Harbor, WA. Dealer or consumer direct sales.

The Hawken Shop (owned by the Dayton Traister Company) has purchased the rights and machinery to manufacture the original Hawken Rifle from Arthur Ressel. Mr. Ressel had previously purchased the rights to manufacture these rifles from the heirs of John Gemmer, who purchased S. Hawken Manufacturing directly from Samuel Hawken in 1860. Because of the continual lineage of ownership, these models are considered original Hawken rifles.

Standard Hawken rifle kits start at $1,100. Rifles in new condition (100%) are selling for $2,000+, with the Hawken Commemorative Plains Rifle (1 of 50) selling in excess of $4,000.

The Hawken Shop is a distributor for Lyman, CVA and others. Contact them directly (see Trademark Index) for information.

HEGE

Currently manufactured by Hege Jagd und Sporthandels GmbH, located in Überlingen, Germany. No current importation.

Contact HEGE directly (see Trademark Index) for current availability.

PISTOLS: PERCUSSION

HEGE-SIBER PISTOL — .33 or .44 cal. perc., 10 in. blue octagon barrel, exceptional finish, color case hardened hammer and lock. Importation disc. 1994.

	100%	98%	90%	80%
	$1,055	$835	$700	$500

Last MSR was $1,000.

FRENCH STYLE HEGE-SIBER PISTOL — .33 or .44 cal. perc., 10 in. blue octagon barrel, exceptional finish, London grey finish, 24Kt. gold inlays, blue trigger guard. Importation disc. 1994.

	100%	98%	90%	80%
	$1,850	$1,575	$1,260	$995

Last MSR was $1,795.

* ***French Style Hege-Siber Pistol (Matched Set)*** — same serial numbers. Importation disc. 1994.

	100%	98%	90%	80%
	$3,700	$3,140	$2,510	$1,450

Last MSR was $2,995.

RIFLES: FLINTLOCK

HEGE-MANTON — .44 cal. flintlock, 6 lbs. Importation disc. 1994.

	100%	98%	90%	80%
	$1,800	$1,525	$1,225	$995

Last MSR was $1,695.

Add $100 for engraving.

GRADING - PPGS™	100%	98%	90%	80%

HIGH STANDARD

Previous manufacturer located in New Haven, Hamden, and East Hartford, CT. High Standard Mfg. Co was founded in 1926. They purchased Hartford Arms and Equipment Co. in 1932. The original plant was located in New Haven, CT. During WWII, High Standard operated plants in Hew Haven and Hamden. After the war the operations were consolidated in Hamden. In 1968 the company was sold to the Leisure Group, Inc. The Leisure group sold High Standard to High Standard Inc. in January 1978. A final move was made to East Hartford, CT in 1977 where they remained until the doors closed in late 1984.

The author and publisher wish to thank Mr. John J. Stimson, Jr. for the following information in this edition of *Blue Book of Modern Black Powder Arms*.

LIMITED/SPECIAL EDITIONS

These guns were a series of .36 caliber cap and ball revolvers which began production in 1974 and ran through 1976. These are reproductions of the Confederate copies of the Colt Model 1851 Navy Revolver. Note that most Confederate copies of the Colt had round barrels, not the octagonal barrel found on the Colt. The frames were made by High Standard and the balance of the parts by Uberti. The guns were assembled and finished by High Standard.

GRISWOLD & GUNNISON — .36 cal., perc., SA, six-shot copy of Confederate Revolver, 7.5 in. barrel, blue finish w/brass frame. Commemorative gun in a pine presentation case w/brass belt plate depicting the Georgia State seal. Catalog no. 9333 Commemorative (S/N 00001-00500), Catalog no. 9331 (S/N 00501-02600). Mfg. 1974 only.

	100%	98%	90%	80%
	$450	$275	$225	$175

Last MSR was $145.

Add 30% for case and accessories.

LEECH & RIGDON — .36 cal., perc., SA, six shot, blue finish with steel frame. Commemorative gun cased with reproduction of a Civil War belt buckle. Catalog no. 9334 Commemorative (S/N 00001-00500), Catalog no. 9332 (S/N 00501-01199). Mfg. 1974 only.

	100%	98%	90%	80%
	$450	$275	$225	$175

Last MSR was $145.

Add 30% for case and accessories.

SCHNEIDER & GLASSICK — .36 cal. perc., SA, six shot, blued finish w/steel frame, cased w/Confederate "D guard" Bowie knife. Catalog no. 9335 (S/N 0-1000). Mfg. 1975 only.

	100%	98%	90%	80%
	$500	$365	$265	$225

Last MSR was $325.

BICENTENNIAL BLACK POWDER — .36 cal. perc., SA, six shot, 1776-1976 Bicentennial Edition, two versions, pine case marked High Standard and the trigger logo on the lid with a powder flask and silver dollar sized medallion inside, or brown leatherette covered case with American Bicentennial 1776-1976 and contains a pewter Bicentennial belt buckle. Catalog no. 9336 (S/N A 0000-A 2028).

	100%	98%	90%	80%
	$450	$275	$225	$175

H&R 1871, LLC

Current manufacturer and holding company located in Madison, NC since 2008. Previously located in Gardner, MA since 1991.

In late 2007, Remington Arms Company, Inc. announced it had entered into a definitive agreement to acquire Marlin Firearms Company, Inc. The agreement includes Marlin, H&R 1871, LLC, New England Firearms and LC Smith. The transaction closed in early 2008 and was followed by a strategic manufacturing consolidation move that resulted in the closure of its Gardner, Massachusetts plant.

During 2000, Marlin Firearms Co. purchased the assets of H&R 1871, Inc., and the name was changed to H&R 1871, LLC. H & R 1871 LLC utilizes the original brand names of Harrington & Richardson and New England Firearms, and does not accept warranty work for older (pre-1986 mfg.) Harrington & Richardson, Inc. firearms. See New England Firearms for information on available models and pricing.

HANKLA, MEL

Current contemporary longrifle artisan gunmaker located in Jamestown, KY.

Mr. Hankla began building longrifles in 1982 under the direction of Dr. Terry Leeper at Western Kentucky University. He continues to build on a part-time basis. Mel's trademark is his initials, M and H within a circle and M. Hankla in script on top of the barrell or block letter engraving on the lock plate. Please contact Mr. Hankla directly (see contact listing in Trademark Index) regarding availability.

GRADING - PPGS™	100%	98%	90%	80%

I SECTION

I.A.B. srl

Current manufacturer (Industria Armi Bresciane) of modern firearms, black powder replicas, and historical Sharps rifles located in Gardone, Valtrompia, Brescia, Italy. Currently imported by Kiesler's, located in Jeffersonville, IN, E.M.F. & Co., located in Santa Ana, CA, Dixie GunWorks, located in Union City, TN, Tristar Sporting Arms, located in Kansas City, MO.

Please refer to individual importer/distributor listing in this text for model information and pricing.

IAR, INC.

Current importer and distributor since 1995 located in San Juan Capistrano, CA.

IAR, Inc. imports and distributes a wide variety of firearms, including revolvers (MSR $395 for .45 LC cal., $380 for .22 LR cal.), derringers, rolling block pistols (MSR $400-$490), rifle reproductions (MSR $490), and exposed hammer shotguns (MSR $470). IAR, Inc. also imports black powder reproduction and replica revolvers (MSR $115-$650), derringers (MSR $85), Civil War Muskets (MSR $550-$570), plus a complete lineup of blank firing arms, including pistols, revolvers, and rifles. Please contact them directly regarding their current product lineup and consumer pricing (see Trademark Index).

IVER JOHNSON

Previous manufacturer located in Jackson, AR.

RIFLES: PERCUSSION, O/U

MODEL BP50HB — .50 cal. perc., double hammers and triggers, color case hardened hammers and furniture.

	100%	98%	90%	80%
	$395	**$335**	**$245**	**$205**

NOTES

GRADING - PPGS™	100%	98%	90%	80%

J SECTION

JIM CHAMBERS FLINTLOCKS, LTD.

Current maker of flintlock pistol and rifle kits located in Candler, NC.

Jim Chambers Flintlocks, Ltd. pistol and rifle kits use barrels from Rice Barrel Co., Long Hammock Barrels, and W. E. Rayl, Inc. supplied by Buckeye Barrels, LLC. In 1993 Chambers Flintlocks purchased Siler Lock Company to produce locks for their kits. Their pre-carved stocks are produced by L & G Woodcarving. Please contact the maker directly (see Trademark Index) for additional information.

J.P. GUN STOCK, INC.

Previous manufacturer located in Las Vegas, NV. Previously distributed by Mountain States Muzzleloading Supplies, Inc. located in Williamstown, WV.

RIFLES: FLINTLOCK & PERCUSSION

J.P. BECK RIFLE — .50 cal. flintlock, 42 in. oct. barrel. Pennsylvania long rifle style, brass furniture, 9 lbs.

	100%	98%	90%	80%
	$795	**$715**	**$650**	**$475**

Last MSR was $795.

J.P. HENRY TRADE RIFLE — .54 cal. flintlock, 35 in. oct. brown barrel, brass trigger guard, buttplate and patchbox, curly maple stock, 10 lbs.

	100%	98%	90%	80%
	$795	**$715**	**$650**	**$475**

Last MSR was $795.

J.P. MCCOY SQUIRREL RIFLE — .32 or .45 cal. flintlock or perc., 42 in. brown barrel, brown hammer and lock, brass buttplate and trigger guard, full length select curly maple stock, 7.5 lbs.

	100%	98%	90%	80%
	$690	**$600**	**$480**	**$350**

Last MSR was $700.

Add $20 for flintlock.

NOTES

GRADING - PPGS™	100%	98%	90%	80%

K SECTION

K.B.I., INC.

Current importer/distributor located in Harrisburg, PA. K.B.I. discontinued all black powder arms during late 1994, and are currently importing firearms only.

For more information and current pricing on both new and used K.B.I. firearms, please refer to the *Blue Book of Gun Values* by S.P. Fjestad (now online also).

REVOLVERS: PERCUSSION

1851 NAVY — .44 cal. perc., 7.5 in. barrel, brass frame, 39-43 oz. Disc. 1994.

	100%	98%	90%	80%
	$115	$100	$60	$50

Last MSR was $150.

Add $30 for engraving, or for Pony Express Sheriff Model.

1858 REMINGTON ARMY — .36 or .44 cal. perc., 6.5 or 8 in. oct. barrel, 40 oz. Disc. 1994.

	100%	98%	90%	80%
	$135	$110	$75	$50

Last MSR was $170.

Add $25 for steel frame.
Add $140 for stainless steel.
Add $20 for 12 in. Buffalo Model.

1860 ARMY — .44 cal. perc., 5 or 8 in. barrel, steel frame, 41 oz. Disc. 1994.

	100%	98%	90%	80%
	$170	$145	$105	$75

Last MSR was $240.

RIFLES: FLINTLOCK & PERCUSSION

HAWKEN RIFLE — .45, .50, .54, or .58 cal. flintlock or perc., 28 in. oct. barrel, color case hardened hammer and lock, 9 lbs. Disc. 1994.

	100%	98%	90%	80%
	$265	$200	$145	$100

Last MSR was $300.

Add $30 for flintlock.
Add $10 for left-hand.
Subtract $45 for Field Grade.

KENTUCKY RIFLE — .50 cal. perc., 35 in. oct. barrel, color case hardened hammer and lock, brass furniture and trigger guard, 7 lbs. Disc. 1994.

	100%	98%	90%	80%
	$300	$225	$160	$110

Last MSR was $420.

KAHNKE GUN WORKS

Previous manufacturer located in Redwood Falls, MN. Previously the Kahnke/Denali Gun Works trademark was manufactured by Mid-Western Outdoor Specialties, Inc. located in Joplin, MO.

Kahnke developed a lightweight contemporary style .50 cal. rifle and a companion .54 cal. single-shot model. Both featured in-line ignition and resemble the Thompson Contender in appearance. The first version was introduced in 1982.

PISTOLS: IN-LINE IGNITION

KAHNKE .54 CAL. MODEL — .54 cal. perc., single-shot hunting pistol, adj. sights, unusual combination of both old and new technologies, walnut grips. 3.5 lbs. Mfg. 1988-disc.

	100%	98%	90%	80%
	$350	$275	$225	$170

Last MSR was $295.

MODEL 82 — .36, .45, .50, or .54 cal. perc., hammer block safety, 10.5, 12, or 14 in. quick change barrel, drilled and tapped for scope mounts, Millett adj. sights, Herrett's walnut grips. Disc. 2007.

	100%	98%	90%	80%
	$350	$310	$250	$220

Last MSR was $389.

Add $40 for stainless steel.

GRADING - PPGS™	100%	98%	90%	80%

RIFLES: IN-LINE IGNITION

MODEL 94 — .45 (new 2006), .50, or .54 (new 2006) cal. perc., 24 or 30 (new 2006) in. blue or stainless steel barrel, 1:26 in. twist, adj. sights, walnut or laminated (new 2006) stock and forearm, 38 in. OAL, 6 lbs. Disc. 2007.

	$475	$425	$345	$275

Last MSR was $529.

Add $20 for stainless steel.

KNIGHT RIFLES

Current manufacturer and distributor located in Centerville, IA. Previously located in Lancaster, MO. Available through dealers, catalog houses, or consumer direct.

The Knight MK Series is the forerunner of the modern black powder rifle designed as a true hunting/sporting rifle. These black powder rifles feature a straight through Posi-Fire ignition system, double safety, in-line bolt assembly, and Timney deluxe trigger system. Beginning 1997, Knight Rifles used the Knight Disc #209 primer ignition system, which holds the primer in an easily managed plastic disc. Knight's "Full Plastic Jacket" (new 2002) ignition system completely seals the #209 primer against moisture, and beginning 2004, the #209 primer (FPJ) ignition system was incorporated into every muzzleloader Knight Rifles produces. All Knight Rifles feature Green Mountain barrels. Knight Rifles is a division of Modern Muzzleloading, Inc., a subsidiary of EBSCO Industries, Inc.

PISTOLS: IN-LINE IGNITION

HAWKEYE — .50 cal. perc., 12 in. round barrel, adj. trigger, drilled and tapped for scope, synthetic stock, also available in stainless, 3.25 lbs. Mfg. 1993-98.

	$350	$275	$225	$170

Last MSR was $400.

Subtract $25 for black composite stock.
Add $40 for stainless steel.

RK-88 HAWK — .45, .50 or .54 cal. perc., same action as MK rifles, modern (swept back) black composite stock. Mfg. 1991-92 only. Disc. 1994.

	$375	$300	$225	$190

Last MSR was $430.

RIFLES: IN-LINE IGNITION

AMERICAN KNIGHT — .50 cal. perc., #209 primer (FPJ) ignition system (new 2003), 22 in. round barrel, 1:28 in. twist, blue finish, adj. Fiber-Lite rear and fiber optic front sights, drilled and tapped for scope, double safety, black solid composite stock w/sling swivel studs, 41 in. OAL, 6.5 lbs. Disc. 2004.

	$190	$155	$115	$80

Last MSR was $200.

BLACK LEGEND/BLACK LEGEND PLUS — .50 cal. perc., 22 in. round blue barrel (24 in. on Black Legend Plus), double safety, fiber-tuff, walnut stained hardwood, or black Prolight stock, 6.25 lbs. Disc. 1994.

	$260	$195	$140	$100

Last MSR was $290.

Add $45 for stained hardwood stock or Black Legend Plus Model with 24 in. barrel.

BH-99 BIGHORN — .50 cal. perc., 22 in. or 26 in. blue or stainless round barrel, double safety, black, camo, or black thumbhole composite stock, right or left-hand versions, 7 lbs. Disc. 2001.

	$315	$245	$185	$145

Last MSR was $350.

Add $50 for camo stock.
Add $30 for thumbhole stock.
Add $60 for stainless steel barrel.
Add $20 for 26 in. barrel.

BK-89 SQUIRREL — .36 cal. perc., 24 in. barrel, Monte Carlo stock, double safety, 5.5 lbs. Disc. 1992.

	$450	$365	$265	$225

Last MSR was $500.

GRADING - PPGS™	100%	98%	90%	80%

BK-92 BLACK KNIGHT — .50 or .54 cal. perc., 24 in. blue barrel, wood, epoxy coated wood, or composite Monte Carlo stock (standard 1995-96), double safety, under 7 lbs. Mfg. 1991-96.

	$350	$275	$225	$170

Last MSR was $400.

Subtract $40 for standard wood stock.

DELUXE RIFLE WITH DISC SYSTEM — .50 cal. perc., 22 in. round barrel, disc system allows the shooter the choice of a #11 percussion cap or a standard #209 primer, either can be pre-loaded into a disc for fast loading and higher grain loads, double safety, adj. trigger and sights, black composite stock. Designed to use the disc system in conjunction with Pyrodex pellets. Disc. 1997.

	$350	$275	$225	$170

Last MSR was $400.

Add $45 for camo stock.
Add $60 for stainless steel.
Add $40 for deluxe.

DISC ELITE — .45 or .50 cal. perc., #209 primer (FPJ) ignition system, bolt-action, 26 in. fully contoured blue or stainless steel barrel, 1:30 (.45 cal.) or 1:28 in. twist, drilled and tapped for scope, black, Mossy Oak Break-Up, or HD Hardwoods Green composite stock with recoil pad and sling swivel studs, adj. trigger, 45 in. OAL, approx. 7.4 lbs. Mfg. 2003-05.

	$450	$365	$265	$225

Last MSR was $510.

Add $70 for stainless steel.
Add $40 for Mossy Oak Break-Up or HD Hardwoods Green stock.

DISC EXTREME — .45 or .50,cal. perc., #209 primer (FPJ) ignition system, bolt-action, 26 in. fluted (.45 cal.) or smooth barrel, blue or stainless steel finish, 1:30 (.45 cal.) or 1:28 in. twist, adj. metallic fiber optic sights, drilled and tapped for scope, walnut, black composite with or without thumbhole, laminated hardwood, Mossy Oak Break-Up (new 2003), or HD Hardwoods Green (new 2003) stock with recoil pad and sling swivel studs, adj. trigger, 45 in. OAL, approx. 7.8 lbs. New 2002.

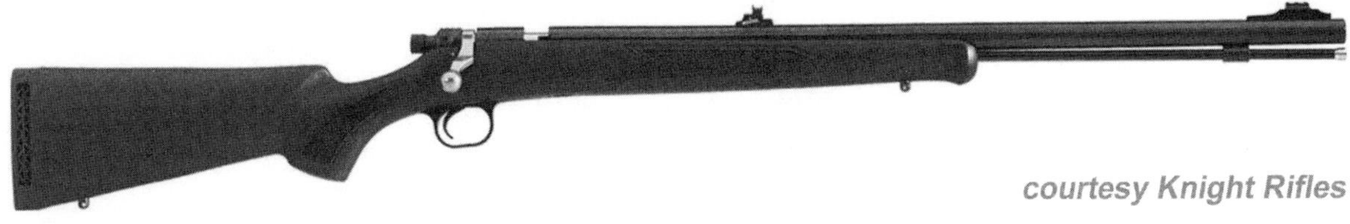

courtesy Knight Rifles

MSR $460	$415	$365	$265	$215

Add $70 for .45 cal.
Add $70 for stainless steel.
Add $30 for black composite thumbhole stock avail. w/blue or stainless.
Add $100 for walnut stock avail. w/blue.
Add $100 for laminated stock avail. w/stainless.
Add $30 for Mossy Oak Break-Up stock avail. w/blue.
Add $50 for HD Hardwoods Green stock avail. w/stainless.

* ***Disc Extreme Master Hunter*** — .45 or .50 cal. perc., #209 primer (FPJ) ignition system, similar to Disc Extreme, except Cryogenically accurized 26 in. fluted stainless steel barrel, black composite and laminated hardwood thumbhole stock (comes with both), 45 in. OAL, 7.5 lbs. Mfg. 2002-2007.

	$900	$725	$580	$415

Last MSR was $1,000.

* ***.52 Disc Extreme*** — .52 cal. perc., #209 primer (FPJ) ignition system w/Power Stem breech plug, bolt-action, 26 in. stainless steel barrel,1:26 in. twist, adj. Metallic fiber optic sights, drilled and tapped for scope, thumbhole HD Hardwoods Green stock with recoil pad and sling swivel studs, adj. trigger, 45 in. OAL, approx. 7.3 lbs. Mfg. 2003-2007.

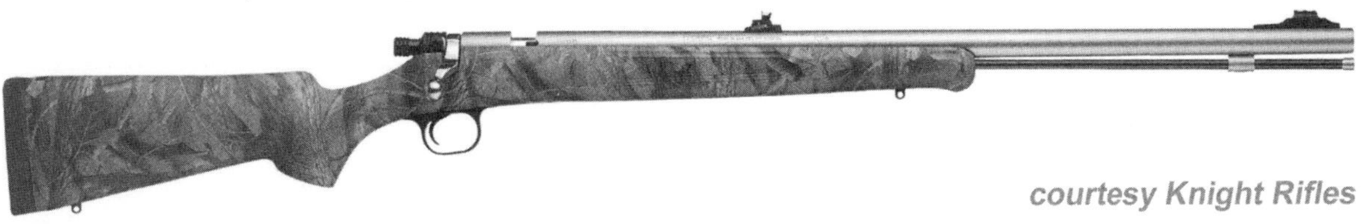

courtesy Knight Rifles

	$550	$425	$320	$260

Last MSR was $620.

GRADING - PPGS™	100%	98%	90%	80%

DISC (ORIGINAL) — .45 and .50 cal. perc., #209 primer (Original Disc) ignition system, 24 or 26 in. blue or stainless steel barrel, 1:30 (.45 cal.) or 1:28 in. twist, adj. Metallic fiber optic sights, drilled and tapped for scope, adj. trigger, black composite stock with recoil pad and sling swivel studs, 7.8 lbs. Mfg. 1998-2004.

	100%	98%	90%	80%
	$395	$335	$245	$205

Last MSR was $440.

Add $55 for Mossy Oak Break-Up or Advantage Timber HD stock.
Add $22 for 26 in. barrel.
Add $110 for .45 cal.
Add $90 for stainless steel.

* ***Disc (Original) Master Hunter*** — .45 or .50 cal. perc., 26 in. fluted stainless steel barrel, bolt-action, black composite thumbhole and laminated hardwood stock, (comes with both stocks) 7.44 lbs. Mfg. 2000-02.

	100%	98%	90%	80%
	$900	$725	$580	$415

Last MSR was $1,000.

GRAND AMERICAN — .50 or .54 cal. perc., hand selected deluxe model of MK-85 Hunter, with thumbhole stock and gold inlaid barrel. Special order only. Disc. 2000.

	100%	98%	90%	80%
	$1,170	$995	$750	$595

Last MSR was $1,300.

KNIGHT BIGHORN — .50 or .52 (new 2006) cal. #209 primer (FPJ) ignition system, 26 in. blue or stainless round barrel, 1:28 in. twist, double safety, composite black, Mossy Oak Break-Up, or Realtree Hardwoods Green camo, PG or thumbhole stock, right or left-hand versions, 45 in. OAL, 7.8 lbs. New 2005.

courtesy Knight Rifles

MSR	100%	98%	90%	80%
MSR $415	$370	$325	$265	$195

Add $40 for Mossy Oak Break-Up camo stock with blue barrel.
Add $40 for Black stock with stainless steel barrel.
Add $105 for Black thumbhole stock with .52 cal. stainless steel barrel.
Add $80 for Realtree Hardwoods Green camo stock with stainless steel barrel.

KNIGHT REVOLUTION — .50 or .52 (new 2005) cal. perc., #209 primer (FPJ) ignition system, Quick Detachable pivoting breech action, 27 in. smoothbarrel, blue or stainless steel finish, 1:28 in. twist, adj. metallic fiber optic sights, drilled and tapped for scope, black composite, Mossy Oak Break-Up, HD Hardwoods Green, laminated hardwood, or walnut stock and forearm, recoil pad and sling swivel studs, adj. trigger, 43.25 in. OAL, approx. 7.8 lbs. New 2004.

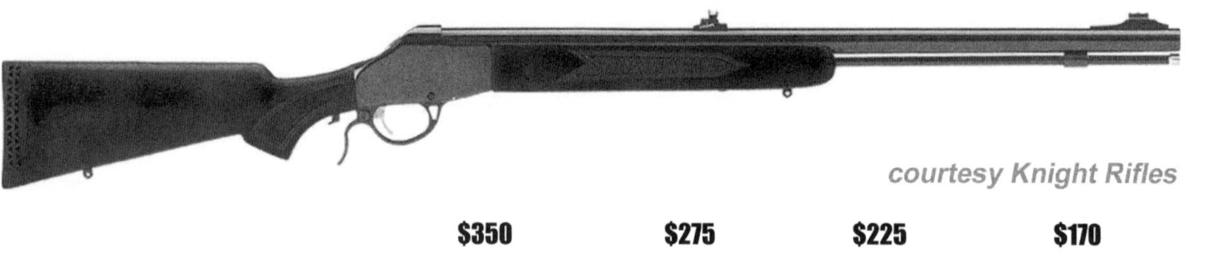

courtesy Knight Rifles

	100%	98%	90%	80%
	$350	$275	$225	$170

Last MSR was $420.

Add $70 for stainless steel.
Add $100 for walnut stock and forearm.
Add $95 for laminated stock and forearm.
Add $50 for Mossy Oak Break-Up stock and forearm.
Add $45 for HD Hardwoods Green stock avail. w/stainless.

GRADING - PPGS™	100%	98%	90%	80%

KNIGHT REVOLUTION II — .50 or .52 cal. perc., #209 primer (FPJ) ignition system, Quick Detachable pivoting breech action, 27 in. smoothbarrel, blue or stainless steel or Next Gen-1 green camo finish, 1:28 in. twist, adj. metallic fiber optic sights, drilled and tapped for scope, black, Next Gen-1 green camo or laminated hardwood stock, recoil pad and sling swivel studs, 43.25 in. OAL, approx. 8.2 lbs. Mfg. 2006-2008.

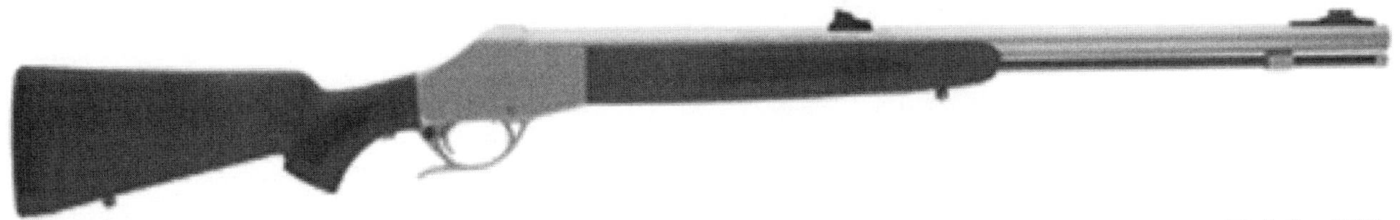

courtesy Knight Rifles

	$375	$325	$245	$195

Last MSR was $410.

Add $27 for stainless steel.
Add $95 for laminated stock and forearm.
Add $63 for camo stock and forearm.

Knight Revolution 20th Anniversary Collector's Edition — .50 cal. perc., #209 primer (FPJ) ignition system, Quick Detachable pivoting breech action, 27 in. fluted stainless steel finish, 1:28 in. twist, adj. metallic fiber optic sights, drilled and tapped for scope, checkered laminated Black/Rose thumbhole stock and forearm, recoil pad and sling swivel studs, adj. trigger, 43.25 in. OAL, approx. 7.8 lbs. Mfg. 2005-2008.

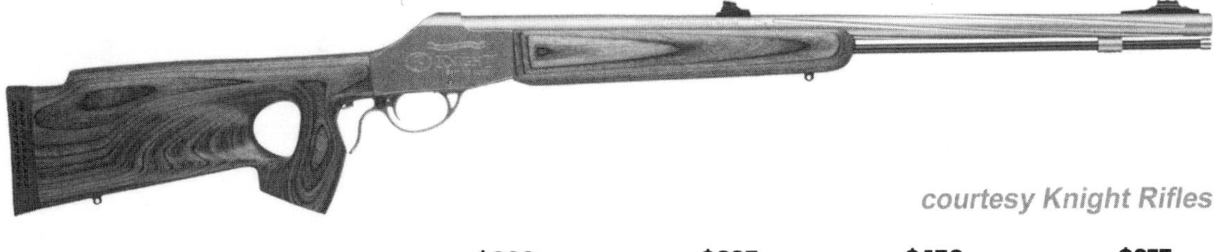

courtesy Knight Rifles

	$800	$625	$450	$275

Last MSR was $800.

KNIGHT ROLLING BLOCK — .50 or .52 (new 2008) cal. #209 primer ignition, rolling block action, 27 in., blue, stainless steel or Next Gen-1 camo finish barrel, 1:28 in. twist, adj. metallic fiber optic sights, drilled and tapped for scope, black or Next Gen-1 camo finish composite stock and forearm, recoil pad and sling swivel studs, adj. removable trigger, 43.25 in. OAL, approx. 7.8 lbs. New 2007.

courtesy Knight Rifles

MSR $330	$295	$255	$185	$150

Add $74 for stainless steel barrel.
Add $116 for Next Gen-1 camo stock and forearm w/stainless steel barrel.
Add $116 for full coverage Next Gen-1 camo stock, forearm, and barrel.

KNIGHT SHADOW — .50 cal. perc., #209 bare primer ignition system, top button hammer break-open action, 26 in. blue or stainless steel barrel, 1:28 in. twist, adj. metallic fiber optic sights, drilled and tapped for scope, adj. trigger, black composite stock and forearm, recoil pad and sling swivel studs, 43.5 in. OAL, approx. 8 lbs. New 2008.

courtesy Knight Rifles

MSR $290	$265	$225	$165	$135

Add $40 for stainless steel barrel.

GRADING - PPGS™	100%	98%	90%	80%

KNIGHT VISION — .50 cal. perc., #209 primer (FPJ) and bare primer ignition system, under lever, hammerless break-open action w/polymer butt stock overmolding, Quick Detachable trigger, 26 in. blue, stainless steel finish, Mossy Oak Break-Up, or HD Hardwoods Green barrel, 1:28 in. twist, adj. metallic fiber optic sights, drilled and tapped for scope, checkered black, Mossy Oak Break-Up, or HD Hardwoods Green composite stock, recoil pad and sling swivel studs, 43.25 in. OAL, approx. 7.8 lbs. Mfg. 2006-2008.

courtesy Knight Rifles

	$365	$285	$235	$175

Last MSR was $420.

Add $51 for stainless steel barrel.
Add $20 for Mossy Oak Break-Up or HD Hardwoods Green full camo finish.

KNIGHT WOLVERINE 209 — .45 (2003 only) or .50 cal. perc., #209 primer (FPJ) ignition system, 22 or 26 (new 2003) in. blue or stainless round barrel, double safety, adj. metallic fiber optic sight, drilled and tapped for scope, adj. trigger, black with or without thumbhole, Mossy Oak Break-Up, Hardwoods Green HD (new 2003), or Advantage Timber HD (disc. 2002) composite stock with recoil pad and sling swivel studs, 41-45 in. OAL, 7-7.3 lbs. Left-hand model available. Mfg. 2002-2008.

	$255	$215	$145	$95

Last MSR was $290.

Add $40 for Mossy Oak Break-Up stock.
Add $40 for stainless steel.
Add $25 for thumbhole stock.
Add $40 for Advantage Timber HD or Realtree Hardwoods Green Rocky Mountain Elk Foundation model.
Subtract $20 for 22 in. barrel.

KP1 MAGNUM — .50 cal. perc., #209 primer (FPJ) and bare primer ignition system, top button hammer break-open action, 28 in. blue or stainless steel barrel,1:28 in. twist, adj. metallic fiber optic sights, drilled and tapped for scope, removable and adj. trigger, black or Next G-1 camo composite or laminate wood stock, and forearm recoil pad and sling swivel studs, 43.5 in. OAL, approx. 8 lbs. New 2007.

courtesy Knight Rifles

MSR $580	$525	$475	$365	$285

Add $100 for stainless steel.
Add $60 for Next G-1 camo stock and forearm.
Add $210 for brown sandstone laminate stock and forearm.

LKII WOLVERINE II — .50 or .54 cal. perc., 22 in. blue or stainless round barrel, double safety, full length composite stock in black, camo, or with thumbhole, 6.69 lbs. Disc. 2001.

	$235	$180	$130	$95

Last MSR was $270.

Add $40 for camo stock.
Add $40 for thumbhole stock.
Add $60 for stainless steel barrel.

GRADING - PPGS™	100%	98%	90%	80%

LONG RANGE HUNTER — .50 or .52 cal. perc., #209 primer (FPJ) ignition system, 27 in. spiral fluted, free-floating, stainless steel barrel, .52/1:26 in. and .50/1:28 in. twist, fully adj. trigger, checkered and vented laminate forest green or sand stone hardwood, PG or thumbhole (new 2007) Cas-off stock, beaver tail forend, recoil pad, sling swivel studs, 46 in. OAL, 7.5 lbs. New 2006.

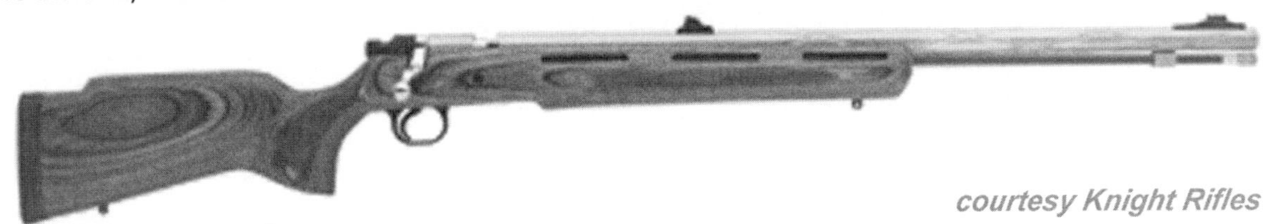

courtesy Knight Rifles

MSR $770	$695	$615	$465	$375

Add $15 for thumbhole stock.

MK-85 BACK COUNTRY CARBINE — .45, .50, or .54 cal. perc., 20 in. round barrel, Monte Carlo stock, double safety, 6.63 lbs. Disc. 1992.

	$430	$365	$255	$170

Last MSR was $520.

Add $60 for stainless steel.

MK-85 GRIZZLY (PLB) — .54 cal. perc., brown laminate stock, double safety. Mfg. 1991-92.

	$475	$385	$280	$230

Last MSR was $650.

Add $100 for stainless steel.

MK-85 HUNTER — .45, .50, or .54 cal. perc., 24 in. round barrel drilled and tapped for scope, walnut stock, double safety system, under 7 lbs. Disc. 2001.

	$395	$335	$245	$205

Last MSR was $550.

MK-85 KNIGHT HAWK — .50 or .54 cal. perc., 24 in. blue barrel, blue steel, synthetic thumbhole stock, tapped for scope, double safety system (6.75 lbs. stainless), 7.25 lbs. Disc. 2001.

	$575	$450	$345	$275

Last MSR was $770.

Add $70 for stainless.

MK-85 LIGHT KNIGHT — .50 or .54 cal. perc., 20 in. round barrel, walnut or black composite stock, lightweight version of MK-85 Hunter. Disc. 1993.

	$450	$365	$265	$225

Last MSR was $500.

Add $20 for composite stock.

MK-85 PREDATOR — .50 or .54 cal. perc., 20 or 24 in. round barrel, black synthetic stock, double safety system, under 7 lbs. Disc 2001.

	$575	$450	$345	$275

Last MSR was $650.

Add $40 for camo composite stock.
Add $25 for forest green or shadow black laminate.

MK-85 STALKER — .45, .50, or .54 cal. perc., 22 or 24 in. round barrel, Monte Carlo stock, double safety system, under 7 lbs. Disc. 2001.

	$475	$385	$280	$230

Last MSR was $570.

Add $40 for camo composite stock.
Add $25 for forest green or shadow black laminate.

MK-86 MBS (MULTI-BARREL SYSTEM) — .50 cal., .54 cal., or 12 ga. perc., 22 in. round rifle or shotgun barrel, double safety, adj. trigger, black composite stock, 7.75 lbs. (6.75 shotgun). Disc. 2000.

	$500	$400	$295	$240

Last MSR was $600.

Add $150 for combo, .50, .54, or 12 ga. barrel.

GRADING - PPGS™	100%	98%	90%	80%

MK-93 WOLVERINE — .50 or .54 cal. perc., 22 in. blue or stainless round barrel, double safety, composite stock in black, camo, or with thumbhole, 6 lbs. Disc. 1999.

courtesy Knight Rifles

	$210	$165	$125	$85

Last MSR was $270.

Add $50 for camo stock.
Add $70 for stainless steel barrel.

MK-95 MAGNUM ELITE — .50 or .54 cal. perc., unique new posi-fire system which uses a Magnum rifle primer, 24 in. round stainless steel barrel, all parts stainless steel, black composite or Realtree camo stock, 6.75 lbs. Mfg. 1994-98.

	$650	$520	$415	$310

Last MSR was $740.

Add $60 for Realtree camo stock.

T-5 WOODSMAN — .50 or .54 cal. perc., 20 in. round barrel, hardwood stock, double safety, adj. sights, approx. 7 lbs. Mfg. 1991-92.

	$210	$165	$125	$85

Last MSR was $230.

T-BOLT RIFLE — .50 cal. perc., 22 or 26 in. blue or stainless round barrel, double safety, composite stock in black or camo, 7.88 lbs. Disc. 2000.

	$350	$275	$225	$170

Last MSR was $400.

Add $50 for camo stock.
Add $70 for stainless steel barrel.
Add $20 for 26 in. barrel.

SHOTGUNS: IN-LINE IGNITION

TK 2000MC — 12 ga., #209 primer (FPJ) ignition system (new 2003), 26 in. blue (disc. 2004), Advantage Timber HD (disc. 2004) or Realtree Hardwoods Green (new 2004) barrel, adj. metallic fiber optic sight, adj. trigger, black (disc. 2004), Advantage Timber HD (disc. 2004) or Realtree Hardwoods Green (new 2004) composite stock with recoil pad and sling swivel studs, 45 in. OAL, 7.5 lbs. Mfg. 2000-2008.

courtesy Knight Rifles

	$350	$275	$225	$170

Last MSR was $400.

Add $44 for Advantage Timber HD disc. 2004.
Add $20 for thumbhole stock.

GRADING - PPGS™	100%	98%	90%	80%

L SECTION

LOVEN-PIERSON, INC.

Previous trademark of the Appalachia Arsenal located in Appalachia, NY.

RIFLES: PERCUSSION

All rifles have rotating over and under set of barrels to facilate a fast 2nd shot.

MODEL 10 — .45 cal. perc., swivel breech, 22 (carbine) or 28 in. (rifle) octagon or half round barrel, blue furniture, maple stock, 7.75-8.5 lbs. Disc. 1994.

	$300	$220	$160	$110

Last MSR was $330.

MODEL 13 — .45, .50, or .54 cal. perc., similar to Model 10, except brass furniture and walnut stock. Disc. 1994.

	$400	$335	$245	$205

Last MSR was $440.

MODEL 16 — .45, .50, or .54 cal. perc., similar to Model 10, except has color case hardened lock and furniture, brown barrels and curly or birds eye maple or figured walnut stock. Disc. 1994.

	$600	$465	$385	$285

Last MSR was $880.

LYMAN PRODUCTS CORP.

Current manufacturer located in Middletown, CT. Lyman Products Corp. also carries a complete line of black powder accessories. Dealer and consumer direct sales.

PISTOLS: PERCUSSION

1851 NAVY — .36 cal. perc. Disc.

	$115	$100	$60	$50

Last MSR was $165.

1858 REMINGTON .36 NAVY — .36 cal. perc., 6 shot, 5.5 in. barrel. Disc.

	$125	$105	$70	$50

Last MSR was $170.

1858 REMINGTON .44 ARMY — .44 cal. perc., 6 shot. Disc.

	$125	$105	$70	$50

Last MSR was $170.

1860 ARMY — .44 cal. perc. Disc.

	$160	$130	$100	$70

Last MSR was $170.

PLAINS PISTOL — .50 or .54 cal. perc., color case hardened hammer and lock, brass trigger guard, blue octagonal barrel, walnut stock, 3.1 lbs.

courtesy Lyman

MSR $350	$315	$275	$185	$125

GRADING - PPGS™	100%	98%	90%	80%

RIFLES: FLINTLOCK & PERCUSSION

DEERSTALKER — .50 or .54 cal. flintlock or perc., 24 in. octagon barrel, color case hardened hammer and lock, sling swivels, adj. sights, available right or left-hand action and in stainless steel, 10.1 lbs.

courtesy Lyman

MSR $388	$350	$305	$225	$185

Add $54 for flintlock model.
Add $100 for stainless steel percussion model with stainless steel barrel, lock, trigger guard, escutcheons and wedge.
Add $15 for left-hand.

GREAT PLAINS HUNTER — .50 or .54 cal. flintlock or perc., color case hardened hammer and lock, blackened steel furniture, 32 in. octagon barrel, 1:32 in. twist, right or left-hand action, 11.38 lbs. New 2008.

MSR $655	$595	$525	$375	$285

Add $45 for flintlock.
Add $15 for left hand.

GREAT PLAINS RIFLE — .50 or .54 cal. flintlock or perc., color case hardened hammer and lock, blackened steel furniture, 32 in. octagon barrel, 1:60 in. twist, right or left-hand action, 11.38 lbs.

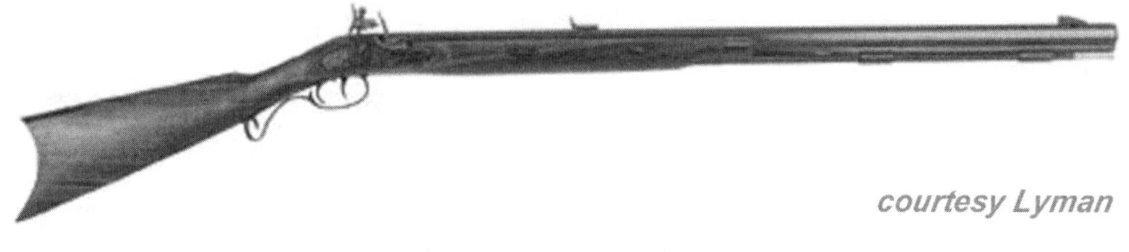

courtesy Lyman

MSR $655	$595	$525	$375	$285

Add $45 for flintlock.
Add $15 for left hand.

TRADE RIFLE — .50 or .54 cal. perc. or flintlock, 28 in. octagon barrel, color case hardened hammer and lock, right or left-hand action, 10.8 lbs.

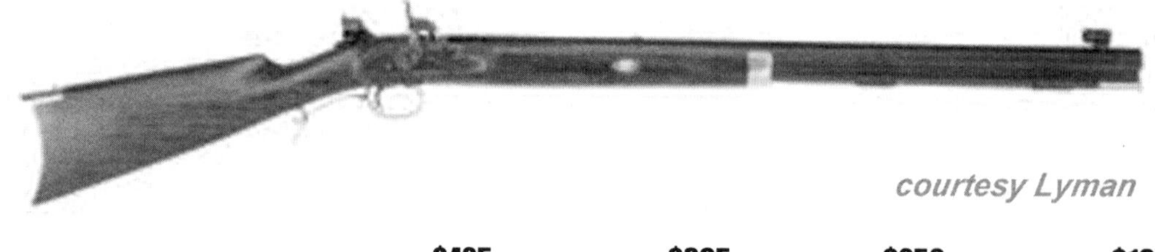

courtesy Lyman

MSR $475	$425	$365	$250	$195

Add $30 for flintlock.

RIFLES: IN-LINE IGNITION

COUGAR RIFLE — .50 or .54 cal. perc., 22 in. blue barrel, dual safety, rubber recoil pad, walnut stock with swivels, 7.25 lbs. New 1996.

	$250	$190	$135	$95

Last MSR was $300.

MUSTANG BREAKAWAY 209 MAGNUM — .50 cal. #209 primer ignition, top lever break open hammerless action, 26 in. blue barrel, adj. fiber optic sights, drilled and tapped for weaver style scope bases, premium grade "Ultra Grade" wood finished stock and forearm w/recoil pad and sling swivel studs, 11 lbs. New 2006.

MSR $500	$450	$395	$295	$245

GRADING - PPGS™	100%	98%	90%	80%

M SECTION

MANDALL SHOOTING SUPPLIES, INC.

Current retailer and dealer located in Scottsdale, AZ. Dealer or consumer direct sales.

MARKESBERY MUZZLE LOADERS, INC.

Current manufacturer located in Florence, KY. Dealer and consumer direct sales.

These in-line ignition rifles with a modular design allow for custom tailoring with a wide selection of stocks from traditional one-piece and two-piece designs to Monte Carlo, thumbhole pistol grip versions, black laminate, and camo finishes. All models feature a crossbolt safety system, "Spit-Fire" nipple threaded into the rear of the breech plug at a 45 degree angle for positive ignition, stainless steel trigger, interchangeable, precision rifled Green Mountain barrels, and investment cast receiver.

PISTOLS: IN-LINE IGNITION

MARKESBERY MODEL KM82 — .36 (10.5 in. barrel only), .45, .50 & .54 cal. perc., 10.5, 12, or 14 in. blue or stainless steel barrel. Mfg. 1994-98.

	100%	98%	90%	80%
	$450	$365	$265	$225

Last MSR was $539.

Add $30 for stainless steel.
Add $30 for Goncalo Alves grip.
Add $10 for Lamo Gamo grips.

RIFLES: IN-LINE IGNITION

MARKESBERY MODEL KM94 — .45, .50, or .54 cal. perc., 24 in. blue or stainless steel barrel, straight or pistol grip stock, rifle version of Model KM82. Many styles, 6.5 lbs.

	100%	98%	90%	80%
	$500	$400	$295	$240

Last MSR was $525.

KM BLACK BEAR — .36, .45, .50, or .54 cal. perc., 24 in. 1:26 in. twist barrel, blue or matte stainless steel finish, adj. sights, black composite or walnut Monte Carlo two-piece stock w/PG, 6.5 lbs.

courtesy Markesbery Muzzle Loaders, Inc.

	100%	98%	90%	80%
MSR $537	$480	$410	$330	$260

Add $16 for stainless steel.
Add $4 for black or green laminate stock.
Add $20 for camo stock.
Subtract $4 for black composite stock.

Markesbery will donate $10 to the NRA Foundation for every Black Bear NRA Foundation Commemorative Rifle w/ NRA Foundation, Inc. logo on frame, new 2003.

GRADING - PPGS™	100%	98%	90%	80%

KM BROWN BEAR — .36, .45, .50, or .54 cal. perc., similar to KM Black Bear, except one-piece black or crotch walnut composite thumbhole stock, 6.75 lbs.

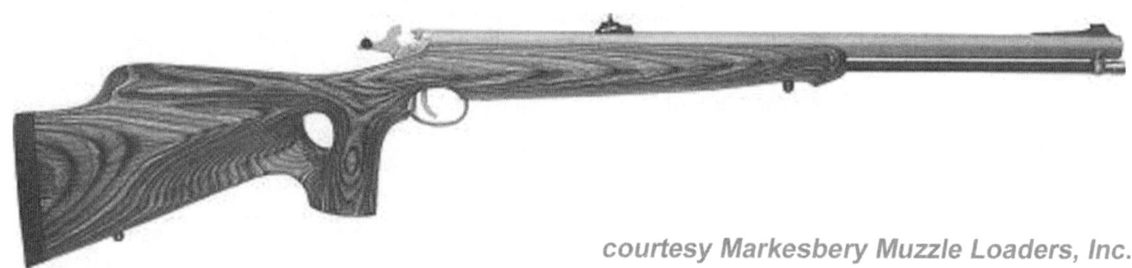

courtesy Markesbery Muzzle Loaders, Inc.

MSR $659	$600	$510	$410	$310

Add $16 for stainless steel.
Add $4 for black or green laminate stock.
Add $25 for camo stock.

KM GRIZZLY BEAR — .36, .45, .50, or .54 cal. perc., similar to KM Black Bear, except two-piece black or crotch walnut composite thumbhole stock, 6.5 lbs.

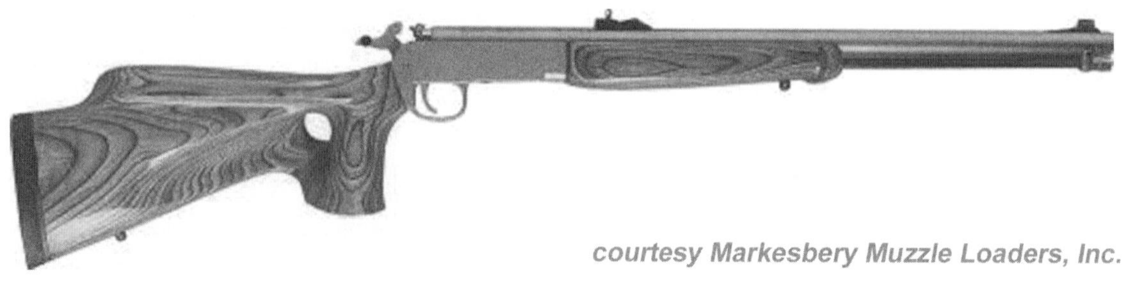

courtesy Markesbery Muzzle Loaders, Inc.

MSR $643	$578	$490	$395	$300

Add $16 for stainless steel.
Add $4 for black or green laminate stock.
Add $25 for camo stock.

KM POLAR BEAR — .36, .45, .50, or .54 cal. perc., similar to KM Brown Bear, except one-piece black composite or walnut Monte Carlo pistol grip stock, 6.75 lbs.

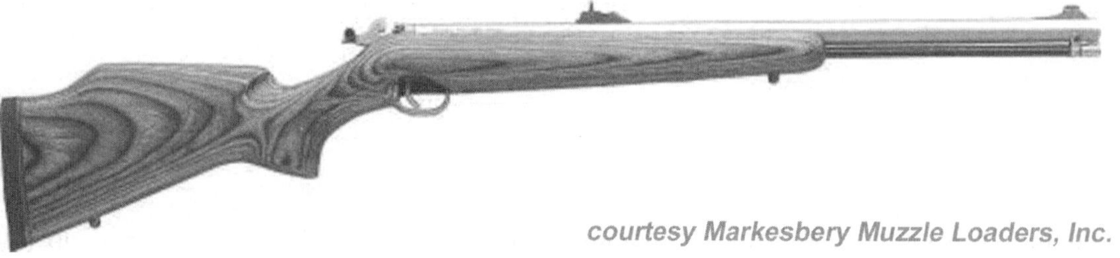

courtesy Markesbery Muzzle Loaders, Inc.

MSR $539	$485	$412	$330	$260

Add $16 for stainless steel.
Add $4 for black or green laminate stock.
Add $25 for camo stock.

KM COLORADO ROCKY MOUNTAIN — .36, .45, .50, or .54 cal. perc. 24 in. blue or stainless steel barrel, straight grip traditional walnut carbine stock with two bands, hammer action spur, 6.5 lbs.

courtesy Markesbery Muzzleloaders, Inc.

MSR $545	$490	$415	$330	$260

Add $16 for stainless steel.
Add $4 for black or green laminate stock.

GRADING - PPGS™	100%	98%	90%	80%

MARLIN FIREARMS

Current manufacturer established in 1870, and located in North Haven, CT. Distributor sales only.

In late 2007, Remington Arms Company, Inc. announced it had entered into a definitive agreement to acquire Marlin Firearms Company, Inc. The agreement includes Marlin, H&R 1871, LLC, New England Firearms and LC Smith. The transaction closed in early 2008 and was followed by a strategic manufacturing consolidation move that resulted in the closure of its Gardner, Massachusetts plant.

On Nov. 10th, 2000, Marlin Firearms Company purchased H&R 1871, Inc. This includes the brand names Harrington & Richardson, New England Firearms, and Wesson & Harrington (please refer to individual sections in this text). For more information and current pricing on Marlin Firearms firearms, please refer to the *Blue Book of Gun Values* by S.P. Fjestad (now online also).

RIFLES: IN-LINE IGNITION

MLS-50 — .50 cal. perc., 22 in. round stainless steel barrel, unique reversible cocking handle for right or left-hand shooters, adj. rear sights, composite stock, auto safety, 6.5 lbs. Disc. 1999.

	100%	98%	90%	80%
	$350	**$275**	**$225**	**$170**

Last MSR was $411.

MLS-54 — .54 cal. perc., 22 in. round stainless steel barrel, unique reversible cocking handle for right or left-hand shooters, adj. rear sights, composite stock, auto safety, 6.5 lbs. Disc. 1999.

	100%	98%	90%	80%
	$350	**$275**	**$225**	**$170**

Last MSR was $411.

MARTIN, ALLEN

Current contemporary longrifle artisan located in Swengel, PA.

Allen Martin began building flintlock rifles in Lancaster County, PA circa 1989 and moved to Union County, PA in 1993. Mr. Martin built rifles part time from 1989 to 1999 and full time ever since. Please contact Mr. Martin directly (see contact listing in Trademark Index) regarding his expertise and availability.

courtesy Allen Martin

MICHIGAN ARMS CORPORATION

Previous manufacturer located in Troy, MI.

Michigan Arms designed an extremely accurate and reliable ignition system, and was the first company to utilize a #209 shotgun primer as a source of ignition. It is not known how many of this variation were actually produced, and as a result, secondary marketplace pricing could be unpredictable.

RIFLES: IN-LINE IGNITION

WOLVERINE RIFLE — .45, .50 or .54 cal., #209 primer ignition, 25.25 in. octagon barrel, adj. sights, Dayton Traister rifle trigger with adj. pull, 8 lbs. Disc. 1994.

	100%	98%	90%	80%
	$425	**$350**	**$255**	**$220**

Last MSR was $400.

FRIENDSHIP SPECIAL MATCH — .45, .50 or .54 cal., #209 primer ignition, 25.25 in. octagon barrel, fully adj. target sights with custom maple stock, Dayton Traister rifle trigger with adj. pull, 8 lbs. Disc. 1994.

	100%	98%	90%	80%
	$495	**$400**	**$295**	**$240**

Last MSR was $600.

SILVERWOLF — similar to Wolverine, except only available in stainless steel. Disc. 1994.

	100%	98%	90%	80%
	$525	**$415**	**$310**	**$250**

Last MSR was $600.

GRADING - PPGS™	100%	98%	90%	80%

MID-WESTERN OUTDOOR SPECIALTIES, INC.

Previous manufacturer and distributor located in Joplin, MO.

RIFLES: IN-LINE IGNITION

The manufacture, exporting and importing of these inline #209 primer ignition muzzle loading rifles was picked up by Pedersoli during 2008.

DENALI SUPER MAG — .45, .50, or .54 cal. perc., #209 primer ignition, closed breech hinged frame w/trigger guard release, 26 in. matte blue (Grade I) or matte stainless steel (Grade II) round barrel, 1:28 in. twist, adj. Williams Fire Sights fiber optic sights, drilled and tapped for scope, matte blue (Grade I) or matte stainless steel (Grade II) frame, carbon fiber (Grade I) or Mossy Oak Break-Up (Grade II) finish composite stock and forearm, recoil pad, sling swivel studs, 7 lbs. Mfg. 2003-06.

* ***Denali Super Mag Grade I*** — matte blue finish and carbon fiber finish composite stock and forearm.

	100%	98%	90%	80%
	$350	**$295**	**$250**	**$220**

Last MSR was $400.

* ***Denali Super Mag Grade II*** — matte stainless steel finish and Mossy Oak Break-Up composite stock and forearm.

	100%	98%	90%	80%
	$385	**$345**	**$280**	**$230**

Last MSR was $430.

MILLENNIUM DESIGNED MUZZLELOADERS, LTD.

Current manufacturer and distributor of custom built in-line percussion rifles, located in Maidstone, VT. Previously located in Limington, ME.

Millennium Designed Muzzleloaders (MDM), manufactures a complete line of custom-built in-line rifles under the names M2K and Buckwacka. Designed for magnum loads (three 50gr. Pyrodex Pellets), the .50 caliber M2K rifles are bedded in a similar fashion as that of high powered rifles, utilizing two attachment points of stock to receiver. All barrels and receivers are precision machined from ordnance grade 400 series stainless steel. Barrels are rifled with a 1 in 24 in. right hand twist. All barrels feature a recessed crown for muzzle protection. The M2K's receiver qualifies the rifle as an open breech design, while still allowing maximum protection to the ignition system in harsh, wet, realistic hunting conditions.

All models feature an interlocking safety design, and a fully adj. trigger. M2K models were built for either left or right-hand shooters at no additional charge. Choice of two ignition systems, standard Spitfire nipple for #11 percussion caps, or Spitfire magnum musket nipple which accepts today's hot musket caps. The Buckwacka is a closed breech, break-open-action design offering a choice of calibers or a 12 ga. shotgun system. An ambidextrous design, Buckwacka lends itself to either right or left-handed shooters. Features include a multi-safety system with a primary transfer bar safety, and "Incinerating Ignition System" designed to use a #209 shotgun primer, musket caps, or #11 percussion caps.

PISTOLS: IN-LINE IGNITION

MINI-WACKA — .50 cal. #209 Incinerating-Ignition-System, 11 (new 2007), 15 (disc. 2002), or 16 (new 2007) in. blue or stainless steel (new 2007) barrel, scope base, rubber grips and black forearm (disc. 2002) or Royal Jack laminated stocks. Disc. 2002. Reintroduced 2007-2008.

	100%	98%	90%	80%
	$365	**$280**	**$215**	**$150**

Last MSR was $400.

Add $70 for BuckTracka Red Dot Scope.

GRADING - PPGS™	100%	98%	90%	80%

RIFLES: IN-LINE IGNITION, PERCUSSION

BUCKWACKA — .45 cal. Nitro Magnum or .50 cal., #209 MDM Incinerating Ignition system, break-open-action, 25 in. blue or stainless steel barrel, 1:24 (.50 cal.) or 1:20 (.45 cal.) in. twist, adj. sights, matte black (disc. 2006), walnut, Mossy Oak Break-Up, New Mossy Oak Break-Up (new 2007), Trebark Superflauge (disc. 2006), or Skyline Excel (disc. 2006) finished stock and forearm, recoil pad and sling swivel studs, 40.5 in OAL, 6.5 lbs.

courtesy Millennium Design

MSR $370	$335	$295	$215	$165

Add $50 for Mossy Oak Break-Up, Skyline Excel, or TreBark Superflauge stock and forearm.
Add $30 for stainless steel.
Add $150 for Sportsman Package includes 24 in. 12 ga. barrel (disc. 2006).

BUCKWACKA YOUTH-LADIES — .50 cal., #209 MDM Incinerating Ignition system, break-open-action, 23 in. blue or stainless steel barrel, 1:24 in. twist, adj. sights, walnut finished stock and forearm, recoil pad and sling swivel studs, 38.5 in. OAL, 6 lbs.

courtesy Millennium Design

MSR $370	$335	$295	$215	$165

Add $30 for stainless steel.

COMPETITOR — .45 cal. or .50 cal., #209 primer Magnum Nitro Ignition system, bolt action, 24 in. blue barrel, 1:28 (.50 cal.) or 1:20 in. twist, adj. sights, matte black or Mossy Oak Break-Up finished stock w/recoil pad and sling swivel studs, 43 in. OAL, 7 lbs. Mfg. 2003-04.

	$175	$150	$105	$75

Last MSR was $199.

Add $40 for Mossy Oak Break-Up stock.

M2K — .50 cal. perc., 24 in. stainless steel barrel, Shadow Black laminate stock or walnut stock, 7.75 lbs. Right or left-hand models. Disc. 2002.

	$475	$385	$280	$230

Last MSR was $529.

M2K CARBINE — .50 cal., 21 in. stainless steel barrel, Shadow Black laminate stock or walnut stock, 7-7.5 lbs. Right or left-hand models. Disc. 2002.

	$475	$385	$280	$230

Last MSR was $529.

M2K DELUXE/DELUXE CARBINE — .50 cal., 21 (carbine) or 24 in. stainless steel barrel, Deluxe Shadow Black laminate stock, 7.75 lbs. Right or left-hand models. Disc. 2002.

	$495	$400	$295	$240

Last MSR was $549.

GRADING - PPGS™	100%	98%	90%	80%

M2K LADIES/YOUTH MODEL — .50 cal., 21 or 24 in. stainless steel barrel, Shadow Black laminate stock, 7-7.5 lbs. Right or left-hand models. Disc. 2002.

	$495	$400	$295	$240

Last MSR was $549.

M2K SPORTER RIFLE/CARBINE — .50 cal., 21 (carbine) or 24 in. stainless steel barrel, Nylon composite stock, 7.5 lbs. Right or left-hand models. Disc. 2002.

	$495	$400	$295	$240

Last MSR was $549.

QUICSHOOTER MAGNUM — .50 cal., #209 MDM Incinerating Ignition system, break-open-action, 26 in. blue or stainless steel barrel, 1:24 in. twist, adj. sights, black texture, walnut pistol grip or Skyline Excel finished stock and forearm, recoil pad and sling swivel studs, 42 in OAL, 7.5 lbs.

courtesy Millennium Design

MSR $280	$265	$235	$185	$145

Add $60 for Skyline Excel or walnut pistol grip stock and forearm.
Add $20 for stainless steel.

SHOTGUNS: IN-LINE, PERCUSSION

BUCKWACKA SHOTGUN — 12 ga. perc., 28 in. barrel, walnut finish or black finish stock, 6 lbs. Disc. 2002.

	$330	$255	$195	$155

Last MSR was $359.

Add $130 for camo finish stock and barrel.

QUICSHOOTER TOMWACKA — 12 ga. perc. #209 MDM Incinerating Ignition system, break-open-action, 24 in. blue or Mossy Oak Break-Up barrel with screw-in choke system, ivory bead sight, walnut or Mossy Oak Break-Up stock with recoil pad and sling swivel studs, 5 lbs. New 2003.

MSR $290	$265	$235	$165	$135

Add $100 for Mossy Oak Break-Up.

MITCHELL ARMS

Current importer located in Fountain Valley, CA. Distributor and dealer sales only.

In 1993, Mitchell Arms discontinued the importation of black powder arms. All revolvers were imported from Pietta. Please refer to the Pietta section for pricing guidelines on similar models/configurations.

MODERN MUZZLELOADING, INC.

Please refer to Knight Rifles in the K section of this text for more information.

MOUNTAIN STATE MANUFACTURING

Current importer/distributor/manufacturer located in Williamstown, WV.

Mountain State Muzzleloading Supplies, Inc. changed its name to Mountain State Manufacturing during 2002, and continues to primarily market accessories for black powder shooters, repair parts, period clothing, holsters, leather goods, bullets and bullet molds. Also previously marketed a modest line of pistols and pistol kits, available from manufacturers such as CVA. Dealer and consumer direct sales.

GRADING - PPGS™	100%	98%	90%	80%

MOUNTAIN STATE MUZZLELOADING SUPPLIES, INC.

Previous importer/distributor/manufacturer located in Williamstown, WV. Mountain State Muzzleloading Supplies, Inc. changed its name to Mountain State Manufacturing during 2002. Dealer and consumer direct sales.

Mountain State also marketed an exclusive line of high quality American-made flint and percussion rifles manufactured by Mowrey Gun Works, Inc. under the trade name All American Golden Classic and All American Silver Classic. These were traditional antique-style muzzle loading rifles reminiscent of early 1800s Leman-Lancaster rifles manufactured in Pennsylvania. They featured fancy curly maple full stocks, hand finished in traditional satin reddish brown, a high cheekpiece, polished brass or nickel silver buttplate and trigger guard, antiqued rust brown barrel and lock, and double set triggers.

RIFLES: FLINTLOCK & PERCUSSION

GOLDEN CLASSIC — .50 cal. perc. or flintlock, 35 in. octagon barrel, authentic sand cast brass finish or nickel-silver furniture, 1:66 in. twist rifling, 7.5 lbs. Disc. 2000.

	100%	98%	90%	80%
	$675	**$545**	**$425**	**$315**

Last MSR was $750.

SILVER CLASSIC — .50 cal. perc. or flintlock, 42 in. octagon barrel, nickel-silver (white bronze) furniture, 1:66 in. twist rifling, fancy side plates, chevron nose cap, 8 lbs. Built to commemorate Mountain State Muzzleloading's 25th anniversary in 1997. Disc. 2000.

	100%	98%	90%	80%
	$895	**$725**	**$580**	**$415**

Last MSR was $995.

MOWREY GUN WORKS, INC.

Previous manufacturer and distributor located in Waldren, IN until 2006. Previously manufactured in Saginaw, TX. Previously distributed exclusively by Mountain State Muzzle Loaders Supplies, Inc. in Williamstown, WV. Dealer and consumer direct sales.

Mowrey Gun Works recreated the guns designed by Ethan Allen and marketed under the name Allen and Thurber in the early and mid 1800s. The models themselves are beautifully hand crafted with "cut rifled" brown barrels (each groove cut individually using as many as 20 passes) and actions using only five moving parts creating exceptional accuracy and reliability. The 1:30 in. twist rifling was designed specifically to stabilize conical bullets. Each specimen was available with a number of features and options (listed below).

Mowrey Gun Works standard rifle features included: curly maple stocks and forearms, front blade-buckhorn rear sights, hand rubbed finish, and brass or brown steel receivers. Options included: premium curly maple, cherry or walnut stock and forearm, custom barrel lengths from 22-40 in., primitive fixed sight, target sights, and Scheutzen style buttplate. Beginning 1994, Mowrey Gun Works also began making reproductions of Hopkins & Allen underhammer rifles.

RIFLES: FLINTLOCK

Add $30 for Fancy Grade Curly Maple.

Add $25 for fancy brass or steel Scheutzen buttplate, or shotgun buttplate.

CLASSIC — .50 cal. flintlock or perc., copy of early Leman-Lancaster rifle, 35 in. brown octagon barrel, high relief checkered on beautiful curly maple full stock, brass furniture, brown hammer and lock, brass buttplate and trigger guard. Disc. 2006.

* ***Golden Classic*** —

	100%	98%	90%	80%
	$695	**$600**	**$500**	**$365**

Last MSR was $750.

* ***Silver Classic*** — with nickel silver furniture. Disc. 2006.

	100%	98%	90%	80%
	$795	**$650**	**$475**	**$350**

Last MSR was $995.

RIFLES: PERCUSSION

Add $30 for Fancy Grade Curly Maple.

Add $25 for fancy brass or steel Scheutzen buttplate, or shotgun buttplate.

1:30 TWIST CONICAL RIFLE — .45, .50 or .54 cal. perc., 28 in. octagon barrel, brass furniture, special 1:30 in. twist rifling for conical bullets, 8 lbs. Disc. 1998.

	100%	98%	90%	80%
	$325	**$255**	**$195**	**$155**

Last MSR was $360.

GRADING - PPGS™	100%	98%	90%	80%

PLAINS RIFLE — .50 or .54 cal. perc., 28 or 32 in. full octagon barrel, brass furniture, 10 lbs. Only available in kit form. Disc. 2006.

	$300	$250	$170	$145

Last MSR was $345.

ROCKY MOUNTAIN HUNTER — .50 or .54 cal. perc., 28 in. full octagon barrel, all brown steel furniture, 8 lbs. Available only in kit form. Disc. 2006.

	$300	$250	$170	$145

Last MSR was $345.

SILHOUETTE RIFLE — .40 cal. perc., 28 or 32 in. octagon barrel, brass furniture. Available only in kit form. Disc. 2006.

	$300	$250	$170	$145

Last MSR was $345.

SQUIRREL RIFLE — .32, .36, or .45 cal. perc., 28 in. full octagon barrel, brass furniture, 7 lbs. Available only in kit form. Disc. 2006.

	$300	$250	$170	$145

Last MSR was $345.

RIFLES: PERCUSSION, HOPKINS & ALLEN DESIGN

Add $30 for Fancy Grade Curly Maple.
Add $25 for fancy brass or steel Scheutzen buttplate, or shotgun buttplate.

HERITAGE RIFLE — .36, .45, or .50 cal. perc., 32 in. octagon barrel, all metal is brown, dark stained maple stock, unique underhammer design. Available only in kit form. Disc. 2006.

	$215	$180	$145	$100

Last MSR was $239.

BUGGY RIFLE — .36, .45, or .50 cal. perc., 26 in. octagon barrel, all metal is brown, dark stained maple, unique underhammer design, approx. 6 lbs. Available only in kit form. Disc. 2006.

	$215	$180	$145	$100

Last MSR was $239.

SHOTGUNS: PERCUSSION, SINGLE SHOT

Add $30 for Fancy Grade Curly Maple.
Add $25 for fancy brass or steel Scheutzen buttplate, or shotgun buttplate.

12 GAUGE — 12 ga. perc., 32 in. full octagon barrel, brass or steel furniture, 7.5 lbs. Disc. 1998.

	$325	$250	$195	$155

Last MSR was $360.

28 GAUGE — 28 ga. perc., 28 in. full octagon barrel, brass or steel furniture, built on squirrel frame, 7.5 lbs. Disc. 1994.

	$325	$250	$195	$155

Last MSR was $350.

MUZZLELOADING TECHNOLOGIES, INC.

Previous trademark of manufacturer located in Roosevelt, UT 1997-2000. During 2000 Split Fire Sporting Goods, LLC located in Orem, UT acquired Muzzeleloading Technologies, Inc. During 2001 Split Fire Sporting Goods, LLC changed its name to White Rifles, LLC. For current information and model availability refer to these trademarks.

MTI offered two series of in-line muzzleloading rifles: Model 97 Whitetail Hunter, and Model 98 Elite Hunter. Both feature Doc White's new "MultiSystem Technology." Whitetail Hunter and Elite Hunter are constructed of ordnance-grade stainless steel, and feature a side-cocking action, large recoil absorption block and a two-point stock engagement system to increase accuracy and reduce felt recoil with heavy loads. These rifles are handcrafted and come with either checkered black composite or smooth black laminate stocks with straight comb, slender pistol grip, and English-styled butt stock.

GRADING - PPGS™	100%	98%	90%	80%

RIFLES: IN-LINE IGNITION

MODEL 97 WHITETAIL HUNTER — .41, .45, or .50 cal. perc., 22 in. straight tapered barrel, 1:16 in. twist (.41 cal.), 1:20 in. twist (.45 cal.), 1: 24 in. twist (.50 cal.), fully adj. hunting sights, aluminum ramrod with integral bullet puller. 6.5 lbs. Mfg. 1998-2000.

	100%	98%	90%	80%
	$475	$385	$280	$230

Last MSR was $550.

Add $30 for black laminate stock.

MODEL 98 ELITE HUNTER — .41, .45, or .50 cal. perc., 24 in. straight tapered barrel with two ramrod guides, 1:16 in. twist (.41 cal.), 1:20 in. twist (.45 cal.), 1:24 in. twist (.50 cal.), custom fiber optic high visibility fully adj. hunting sights, aluminum ramrod with integral bullet puller. Mfg. 1998-2000.

	100%	98%	90%	80%
	$600	$465	$385	$285

Last MSR was $700.

Add $30 for black laminate stock.

MUZZLE LOADERS, INC.

Previous importer/distributor located in Burke, VA.

PISTOLS: FLINTLOCK & PERCUSSION

DELUXE KENTUCKY PISTOL — .44 cal. perc. or flintlock, 10.25 in. octagon barrel, brass blade front sight, 2.5 lbs.

	100%	98%	90%	80%
	$200	$160	$120	$85

Add $15 for flintlock mfg. by Armi San Paolo.

REVOLVERS: PERCUSSION

1847 WALKER — .44 cal. perc., charcoal finish, color case hardened frame, hammer, and loading lever, brass trim, engraved cylinder, 4.4 lbs. Mfg. by Uberti.

	100%	98%	90%	80%
	$275	$200	$145	$100

1848 1ST MODEL DRAGOON — .44 cal. perc., 6 shot, brass grip straps, color case hardened frame, hammer, and loading lever, brass trim, 3.9 lbs. Mfg. by Uberti.

	100%	98%	90%	80%
	$275	$200	$145	$100

1850 2ND MODEL DRAGOON — .44 cal. perc., 6 shot, brass grip straps, color case hardened frame, hammer, and loading lever, brass trim, 3.9 lbs. Mfg. by Uberti.

	100%	98%	90%	80%
	$275	$200	$145	$100

1851 3RD MODEL DRAGOON — .44 cal. perc., 6 shot, brass grip straps, color case hardened frame, hammer, and loading lever, brass trim, 3.9 lbs.

	100%	98%	90%	80%
	$275	$200	$145	$100

Add $15 for silver plated straps, or cut for stock.
Add $35 for Military Model (mfg. by Uberti).

1851 NAVY — .36 or .44 cal. perc., 7.5 in. octagon barrel, engraved (roll) cylinder, color case hardened frame and loading lever, silver plated brass backstrap and square back trigger guard. Sheriff's Model has 5 in. barrel, brass trigger guard and backstrap.

	100%	98%	90%	80%
	$135	$110	$75	$50

Subtract $10 for Sheriff Model.
Subtract $20 for brass backstrap and trigger guard.
Subtract $25 for brass frame (mfg. by Armi San Paolo).

1860 ARMY — .44 cal. perc., 8 in. round barrel, color case hardened frame, hammer and loading lever, 2.56 lbs. Mfg. by Armi San Paolo.

	100%	98%	90%	80%
	$175	$150	$105	$75

Subtract $50 for brass frame.

1862 POLICE — .36 cal. perc., 5.5 in. round barrel, color case hardened frame, loading lever, plunger, and hammer, round trigger guard, fluted cylinder, one-piece stock, 1.56 lbs. Mfg. by Armi San Paolo.

	100%	98%	90%	80%
	$160	$130	$100	$70

GRADING - PPGS™	100%	98%	90%	80%

1858 REMINGTON — .36 or .44 cal. perc., blue or brass frame, brass trigger guard, steel backstrap, 6 shot, 2.44 lbs.

	$190	$155	$115	$80

Add $30 for stainless.
Subtract $50 for brass frame (mfg. by Armi San Paolo).

ROGERS & SPENCER — .44 cal. perc., 7.5 in. octagon barrel, 2.94 lbs. Mfg. by Armi San Marco.

	$200	$160	$120	$85

Add $15 for target sights, and $25 for engraved London grey finish.

RIFLES: FLINTLOCK & PERCUSSION

1858 2-BAND ENFIELD — .58 cal. perc., 33 in. barrel, 2 barrel bands. Mfg. by Armi San Paolo.

	$450	$365	$265	$225

DELUXE HAWKEN RIFLE — .45 or .50 cal. perc. or flintlock, color case hardened hammer and lock, percussion cap holder in stock, chrome lined barrels. Mfg. by Uberti.

	$395	$335	$245	$205

DELUXE KENTUCKY RIFLE — .45 or .50 cal. perc. or flintlock, color case hardened hammer and lock, percussion cap holder in stock, chrome lined barrels, brass trim.

	$350	$275	$225	$170

Add $15 for flintlock (mfg. by Pedersoli).

ST. LOUIS HAWKENS — .50 cal. perc., color case hardened hammer and lock, 28 in. octagon barrel, brass trim, 7.94 lbs. Mfg. by CVA.

	$200	$160	$120	$85

ZOUAVE RIFLE — .58 cal. perc., brass trim, color case hardened hammer and lock, blue finish. Mfg. by Armi San Paolo.

	$295	$220	$160	$110

GRADING - PPGS™	100%	98%	90%	80%

N SECTION

NAVY ARMS CO.

Current manufacturer/importer/distributor established in 1958, and located in Martinsburg, WV beginning late 2003. Previously located in Union City, NJ.

Navy Arms is one of the oldest black powder importers and distributors in the United States. In addition to black powder pistols and longarms, Navy Arms also sells black powder cartridge conversions of Colt pistols, western cartridge-firing pistols, rifles and shotguns, edged weapons, muzzle loading accessories, Civil War leather accessories, accouterments, and presentation cases. Navy Arms black powder pistols are principally manufactured by A. Uberti & Co., and by F.lli Pietta. Dealer, catalog, and consumer direct sales.

The late Val Forgett, Sr., former president of Navy Arms Co. is given credit for starting the Italian black powder reproduction and replica business. When in Italy on a gun tour during 1959, he placed the first American order for a quantity of Colt 1851 Navy reproductions. These black powder reproductions and replicas are marked "Navy Arms Co." on the top of the barrel, "Made In Italy" on the right side of the barrel, and "NAVY ARMS CO." on the frame.

He also ordered and purchased Uberti's first gun, a Colt 1860 Navy, which was entered into the Uberti factory log book on Oct. 14, 1959. Forgett was also the first supplier of components for Colt Industries and produced the earliest examples of the 2nd Generation Colt 1851 Navy models.

For more information and current pricing on both new and used Navy Arms Co. firearms, please refer to the *Blue Book of Gun Values* by S.P. Fjestad (now online also).

PISTOLS: FLINTLOCK & PERCUSSION

1775 BLACK WATCH SCOTTISH PISTOL — .58 cal. flintlock, 7 in. smooth bore white steel barrel, brass frame, ram's horn grip with round ball trigger. Disc. 1994.

	$180	$155	$110	$75

Last MSR was $200.

BRITISH DRAGOON PISTOL — .614 cal. flintlock, white steel with brass trim, first 240 production pistols were used in Governor's palace restoration, Colonial Williamsburg. Disc. 1994.

	$360	$280	$225	$175

Last MSR was $395.

Add $100 for official Williamsburg crest.

1777 CHARLEVILLE PISTOL — .69 cal. flintlock, 7.5 in. white steel smooth bore barrel, brass furniture, belt hook, walnut stock, 2.75 lbs. Disc. 1994.

	$190	$155	$115	$80

Last MSR was $225.

DURS EGG SAW HANDLED PISTOL — .45 cal. flintlock, 9.5 in. blue octagon barrel, unique stock, hand checkered, German silver trim, white steel hammer and lock. Disc. 1994.

	$210	$165	$125	$85

Last MSR was $235.

1805 HARPERS FERRY PISTOL — .58 cal. flintlock, 10 in. browned barrel, color case hardened lock and hammer, brass trim, 2.6 lbs. New 2002.

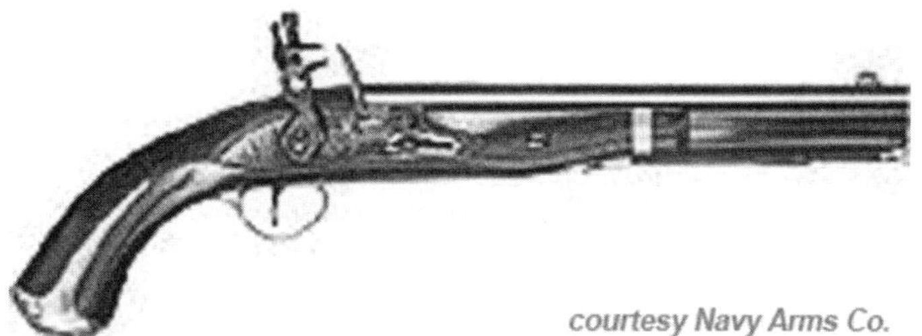

courtesy Navy Arms Co.

MSR $455	$435	$350	$285	$200

1806 HARPERS FERRY PISTOL — .58 cal. flintlock, 11.75 in. barrel, color case hardened lock and hammer, brass trim, 3 lbs. 14 oz. Mfg. by Pedersoli. Disc. 2002.

	$300	$225	$165	$115

Last MSR was $345.

GRADING - PPGS™	100%	98%	90%	80%

J.S. HAWKINS PISTOL — .50 or .54 cal. perc., 9 in. octagon barrel, German silver trim, blue barrel, adj. trigger, 2 lbs. 9 oz. Disc. 1994.

	$235	$180	$130	$95

Last MSR was $200.

KENTUCKY PISTOL — .44 cal. flintlock or perc., 10.13 in. barrel, color case hardened lock and hammer, brass trim, 2 lbs. Mfg. by Pedersoli.

	$265	$225	$170	$130

Last MSR was $235.

Add $15 for brass barrel.
Subtract $10 for percussion.

* ***Kentucky Pistol Cased***

	$350	$295	$215	$165

Last MSR was $355.

* ***Kentucky Pistol Double Cased Set***

	$545	$465	$350	$285

Last MSR was $600.

LE PAGE PISTOL — .45 cal. flintlock or perc., 9 in. octagon white steel barrel and trim, adj. sights, engraved spur type trigger guard, 2 lbs. 2 oz. Disc. 1996.

	$625	$550	$425	$320

Last MSR was $625.

Subtract $100 for percussion.
Add $200 for percussion cased pair.

Values also apply to smooth bore model (flintlock only).

* ***Le Page Pistol Cased***

	$875	$735	$595	$435

Last MSR was $905.

* ***Le Page Pistol Cased Pair***

	$1,475	$1,235	$835	$675

Last MSR was $1,575.

* ***Le Page Pistol 1985 Cased Set*** — custom order only, gold trim, consecutive serial number. Disc. 1994.

	$1,895	$1,275	$875	$695

Last MSR was $1,975.

JOHN MANTON MATCH PISTOL — .45 cal. perc., 10 in. white steel barrel and lock, brass trim, 2 lbs. 4 oz. Disc. 1994.

	$215	$170	$125	$85

Last MSR was $225.

MOORE AND PATRICK PISTOL — .45 cal. flintlock or perc., 10 in. octagon barrel, white steel hammer and lock, German silver trim, 2 lbs. Disc. 1987.

	$315	$245	$185	$145

Last MSR was $295.

MOUNTAIN PISTOL — .50 cal. flintlock or perc., 10 in. octagon barrel, color case hardened hammer and lock, brass furniture, 2 lbs. 4 oz. Disc. 1994.

	$225	$170	$125	$90

Last MSR was $215.

Add $10 for flintlock.

NAPOLEON LE PAGE PISTOL — .45 cal. perc., 10 in. octagon white steel barrel and lock, brass trim, adj. double set triggers, fluted grip, 2 lbs. 7 oz. Disc. 1994.

	$175	$150	$105	$75

Last MSR was $175.

GRADING - PPGS™	100%	98%	90%	80%

W. PARKER PISTOL — .45 cal. perc., 10 in. blue octagon barrel, German silver lock and trim, adj. double set triggers, 2 lbs. 8 oz. Disc. 1994.

	$275	$200	$145	$100

Last MSR was $250.

QUEEN ANNE PISTOL — .50 cal. flintlock, 7.5 in. smooth bore, unique cannon style bronzed steel barrel, 2 lbs. 4 oz.

	$180	$155	$120	$80

Last MSR was $200.

F. ROCHATTE PISTOL — .45 cal. perc., 10 in. round barrel with flat top, white steel lock and trim, adj. double set triggers, 2 lbs. 8 oz. Disc. 1994.

	$250	$190	$135	$95

Last MSR was $250.

ELGIN CUTLASS KNIFE PISTOL — .44 cal. perc., combination knife pistol, white steel hammer and barrel, brass trim, 2 lbs. Disc. 1994.

	$75	$60	$55	$50

Last MSR was $80.

PHILADELPHIA DERRINGER — .45 cal. perc., 3 in. barrel, color case hardened lock and hammer, German silver trim, checkered stock, .75 lb. Disc. 1994.

	$125	$105	$70	$50

Last MSR was $130.

ENGRAVED (SNAKE EYES) DERRINGER — .36 cal. perc., 2.63 in. brass double barrel, double hammers, 1.5 lbs. Disc. 1994.

	$125	$105	$70	$50

Subtract $75 if not engraved.

REVOLVERS: PERCUSSION

COLT PATERSON — .36 cal. perc., 7.5 or 9 in. octagon barrel, standard design, blue steel hardware, no loading lever, 2 lbs. 9 oz. Mfg. by Pietta. Disc. 2003.

	$315	$245	$185	$145

Last MSR was $340.

Add $160 for hand engraved Paterson model.

1836 PATERSON — .36 cal. perc., 9 in. octagon barrel, standard design, blue steel hardware, no loading lever, 2.75 lbs. New 2003.

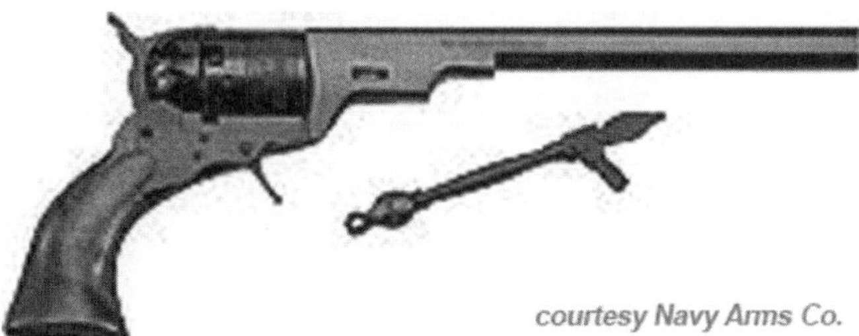

courtesy Navy Arms Co.

MSR $449	$395	$345	$245	$195

Add $165 for hand engraved Paterson model (disc.).

1847 WALKER DRAGOON — .44 cal. perc., 9 in. round barrel, color case hardened hammer, frame, and loading lever, brass trim, engraved barrel and cylinder, 4 lbs. 11 oz. Mfg. by Uberti.

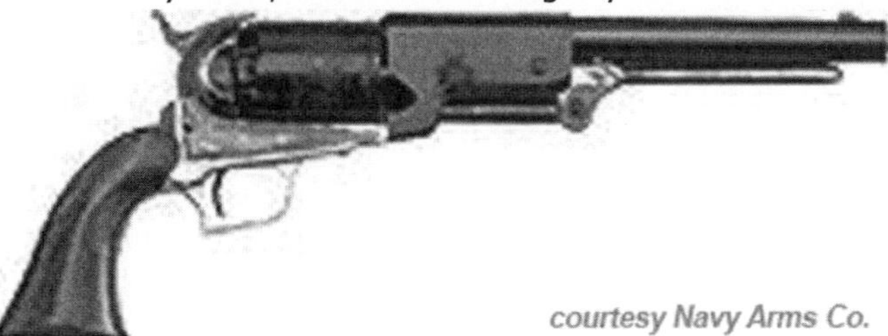

courtesy Navy Arms Co.

MSR $355	$295	$245	$200	$165

Add $130 for cased set (disc.).
Add $265 for deluxe cased set (disc.).

GRADING - PPGS™	100%	98%	90%	80%

1ST MODEL DRAGOON — .44 cal. perc., 7.5 in. barrel, color case hardened frame, brass trim, engraved cylinder, 4 lbs. 2 oz. Disc.

	$250	$190	$135	$95

Last MSR was $275.

3RD MODEL DRAGOON — .44 cal. perc., 7.5 in. barrel, color case hardened frame and loading lever, brass trim, engraved cylinder, adj. target sights, 4 lbs. 2 oz. Disc.

	$250	$190	$135	$95

Last MSR was $275.

Add $25 for Buntline model.

Add $10 for Texas Dragoon Model (Tucker and Sherrard and Co., Confederate States, Texas Star engraved on cylinder, square brass trigger guard).

1851 NAVY (YANK) — .36 or .44 cal. perc., 7.5 in. octagon barrel, color case hardened hammer, frame, and loading lever, brass trim. Mfg. by Pietta.

courtesy Navy Arms Co.

MSR $255	$235	$190	$145	$90

* ***1851 Navy (Yank) Cased Set***

	$250	$190	$135	$95

Last MSR was $290.

* ***1851 Navy (Yank) Double Cased Set***

	$410	$345	$275	$215

Last MSR was $470.

AUGUSTA CONFEDERATE — .36 cal. perc., 5 or 7.5 in. barrel, brass frame (Confederate copy of 1851 Navy), walnut grips. Disc. 1994.

	$115	$100	$60	$50

Last MSR was $200.

1860 ARMY — .44 cal. perc., 8 in. round barrel, color case hardened hammer, frame, and loading lever, roll engraved or fluted cylinder, 2 lbs. 12 oz. Mfg. by Pietta.

courtesy Navy Arms Co.

MSR $278	$245	$180	$145	$90

Add $100 for shoulder stock.

* ***1860 Army Cased Set***

	$270	$200	$145	$100

Last MSR was $310.

* ***1860 Army Double Cased Set***

	$440	$350	$260	$225

Last MSR was $505.

GRADING - PPGS™	100%	98%	90%	80%

1860 REB MODEL GRISWOLD & GUNNISON — .36 or .44 cal. perc., 5 in. (Sheriff Model) or 7.5 in. round barrel, brass frame, color case hardened hammer and loading lever, 2 lbs. 12 oz. Mfg. by Pietta. Disc. 2008.

	$115	$100	$60	$50

Last MSR was $132.

Due to overstock, several 1860 Reb revolvers were factory deactivated and cannot be reactivated. These revolvers can be used only as props - values currently are in the $55 range.

* ***1860 Reb Model Griswold & Gunnison Cased Set***

	$295	$245	$200	$165

Last MSR was $245.

* ***1860 Reb Model Griswold & Gunnison Double Cased Set***

	$395	$345	$245	$195

Last MSR was $380.

1861 NAVY — .36 cal. perc., 5.5 (Sheriff's Model) or 7.5 in. round barrel, cylinder engraved with navy scene, color case hardened hammer, frame, and loading lever, brass trim, 2.75 lbs. Disc. 1994.

	$145	$125	$95	$65

Last MSR was $140.

Add $60 for shoulder stock.

* ***1861 Navy Cased Set*** — disc. 1994.

	$300	$225	$165	$115

Last MSR was $230.

* ***1861 Navy Double Cased Set*** — disc. 1994.

	$440	$350	$260	$225

Last MSR was $385.

1862 (NEW MODEL) POLICE — .36 cal. perc., 5.5 in. round to octagon barrel, color case hardened hammer, frame, and loading lever, brass trim, 1 lb. 10 oz. Also available with nickel finish (new 2003). Mfg. by Uberti.

MSR $278	$245	$180	$130	$95

Add $125 for cased Law and Order set (book style presentation case with accessories, disc.).

LEECH & RIGDON — .36 cal. perc., 7.5 in. barrel, color case hardened hammer, frame, and loading lever, brass trim, 2 lbs. 10 oz. Disc. 1994.

* ***Leech & Rigdon Non-Uberti Mfg.***

	$125	$105	$70	$50

* ***Leech & Rigdon Uberti Mfg.***

	$210	$165	$125	$85

STARR DOUBLE/SINGLE ACTION — .44 cal. perc., 6 in. round barrel, 6-shot, two-piece blue steel frame. Available in original double action version, and later 1863 single action model with 8 in. barrel. Disc. 2001.

	$300	$225	$165	$115

Last MSR was $355.

GRADING - PPGS™	100%	98%	90%	80%

LE MAT REVOLVERS — .44 cal. perc., 9 shot cylinder, .65 cal. center barrel, 7.63 in. octagon barrel, white steel frame, 3 lbs. 7 oz. Mfg. for Navy Arms by F.lli Pietta. Available in Cavalry (with spur trigger guard and lanyard ring), Navy (spur barrel selector), or Army version (cross-pin barrel selector).

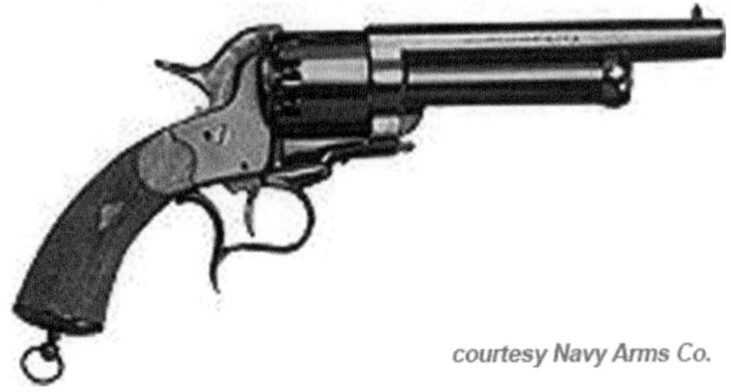

courtesy Navy Arms Co.

MSR $748	$650	$520	$415	$310

Add $405 for engraved Beauregard Model (disc.).
Add $200 for 18th Georgia engraved model (disc.)
Add $100 for single case (disc.)
Add $125 for double case (not including revolver, disc.).

1858 REMINGTON NEW ARMY — .44 cal. perc., 6.5 (disc.), 7.75 (brass frame only), or 8 in. barrel, brass trigger guard, 2.5 lbs. Mfg. by Pietta.

courtesy Navy Arms Co.

MSR $278	$245	$170	$125	$90

* ***1858 Remington New Model Army (Stainless)*** — .44 cal. perc., 8 in. barrel, stainless steel, brass trigger guard, 2.5 lbs.

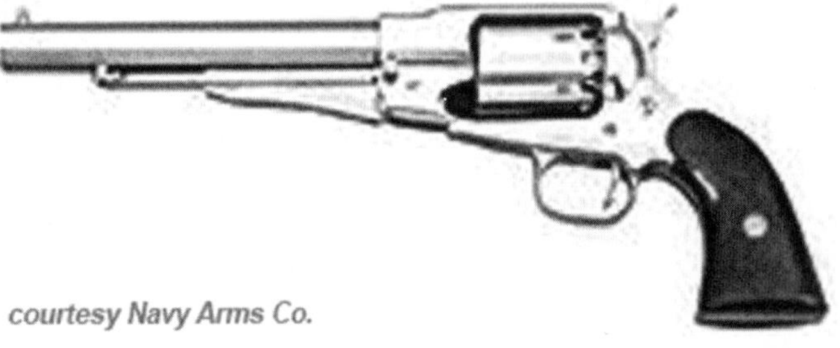

courtesy Navy Arms Co.

MSR $369	$345	$245	$170	$125

* ***1858 Remington New Model Army (Brass)*** — .44 cal. perc., 7.75 in. barrel, brass frame and trigger guard, 2.5 lbs.

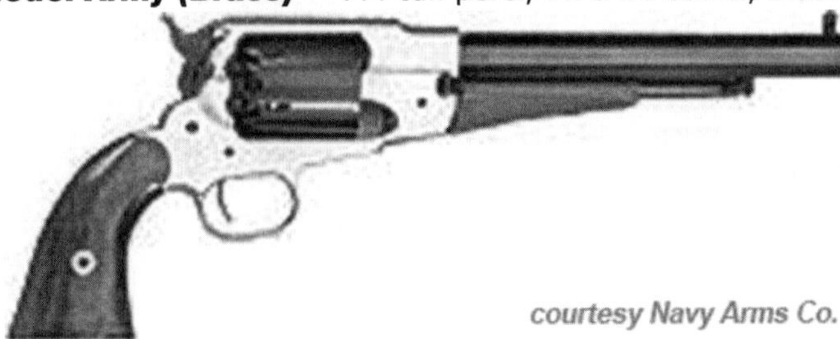

courtesy Navy Arms Co.

MSR $183	$170	$145	$95	$55

GRADING - PPGS™	100%	98%	90%	80%
*** 1858 Remington New Army Cased Set**				
	$260	$195	$135	$95
				Last MSR was $300.
*** 1858 Remington New Army Cased Double Cased Set**				
	$430	$365	$265	$225
				Last MSR was $495.

ROGERS & SPENCER — .44 cal. perc., 7.5 in. octagon barrel, all steel construction with bluing, smooth walnut grips, 3 lbs.

courtesy Navy Arms Co.

	100%	98%	90%	80%
MSR $363	$285	$210	$150	$100

SPILLER & BURR — .36 cal. perc., 7 in. barrel, brass frame, color case hardened hammer and loading lever, 2 lbs. 8 oz. Mfg. by Pietta.

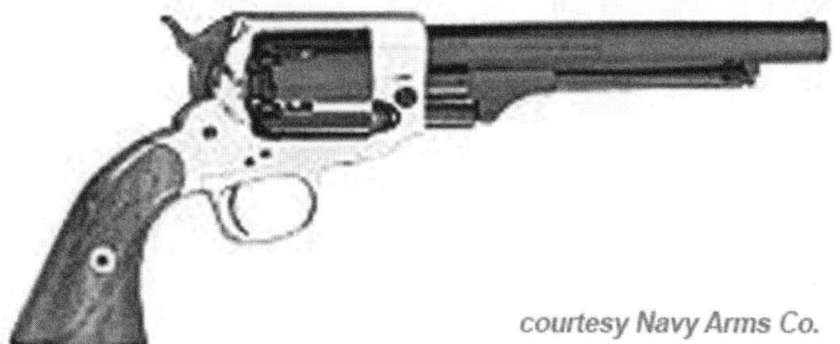

courtesy Navy Arms Co.

	100%	98%	90%	80%
MSR $196	$160	$130	$100	$70
*** Spiller & Burr Cased Set**				
	$295	$245	$200	$165
				Last MSR was $270.
*** Spiller & Burr Double Cased Set**				
	$395	$345	$245	$195
				Last MSR was $430.

1851 NAVY FRONTIERSMAN — .36 cal. perc., 5 in. octagon barrel, charcoal blue finish, color case hardened hammer, frame, and loading lever, brass trim w/silver plated backstrap. Mfg. 2007-current.

courtesy Navy Arms Co.

	100%	98%	90%	80%
MSR $306	$295	$235	$190	$145

GRADING - PPGS™	100%	98%	90%	80%

REVOLVERS: CARTRIDGE CONVERSIONS & OPEN TOP

Since these are cartridge firing revolvers converted from black powder reproduction pistols, and require an FFL to transfer, these listings have been moved to the *Blue Book of Gun Values* by S.P. Fjestad (now online also).

RIFLES: FLINTLOCK & PERCUSSION

BROWN BESS MUSKET — .75 cal. flintlock, 42 in. white steel barrel, hammer, and lock, brass trim, 9.5 lbs.

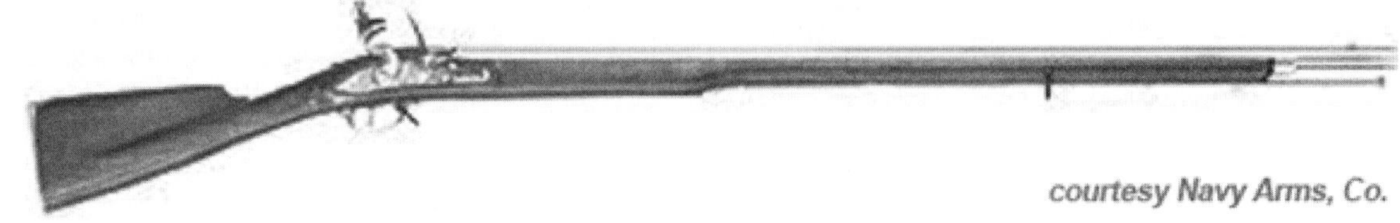

courtesy Navy Arms, Co.

MSR $1,133	$975	$770	$595	$400

Add $100 for Colonial Williamsburg seal.

BROWN BESS CARBINE — similar to Brown Bess Musket, except has 30 in. barrel, 7 lbs., 11 oz.

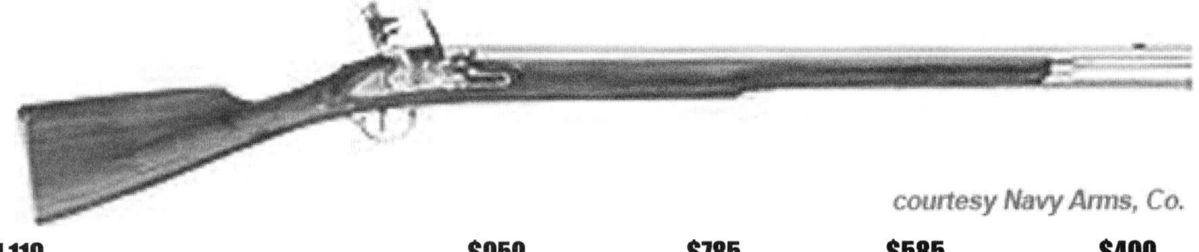

courtesy Navy Arms, Co.

MSR $1,119	$950	$785	$585	$400

1763 CHARLEVILLE MUSKET — .69 cal. flintlock, 44.63 in. white steel barrel, hammer, and lock, brass trim, 8.75 lbs. Mfg. by Pedersoli.

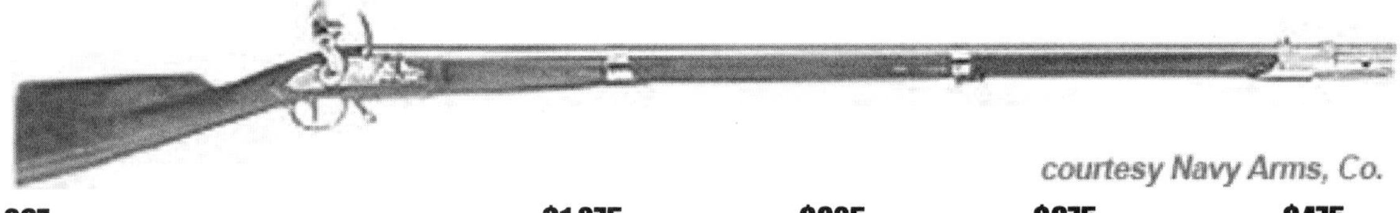

courtesy Navy Arms, Co.

MSR $1,267	$1,075	$825	$675	$475

Used prices are equal for 1777 Model, or 1816 Mt. Wickman Model with steel ramrod and brass flash pan.

BUFFALO HUNTER — .58 cal. perc., 26 in. round barrel, color case hardened hammer and lock, brass trim, 8 lbs. Disc. Reintroduced 2003.

MSR $691	$650	$475	$350	$295

COUNTRY BOY — .32, .36, .45, or .50 cal. perc., 26 in. octagon barrel, matte black metal finish on all parts, based on mule ear percussion lock, adj. sights, 6 lbs. Disc. 1994.

	$235	$180	$130	$95

Last MSR was $165.

Add $60 for extra barrel.

CUB RIFLE — .36 cal. perc., 26 in. octagon barrel, adj. sights, color case hardened lock, walnut stock, 5.75 lbs. Disc. 1994.

	$250	$190	$135	$95

Last MSR was $185.

Add $60 for extra barrel.
Add $115 for Deluxe Pedersoli Model.

1853 ENFIELD 3 BAND (PARKER-HALE) — .58 cal. perc., 39 in. round barrel, color case hardened hammer and lock, brass trim, blue bands, adj. rear sight, 9.5 lbs.

MSR $848	$791	$675	$535	$425

1858 ENFIELD 2 BAND (PARKER-HALE) — .58 cal. perc., 33 in. round barrel, color case hardened hammer and lock, brass trim, blue bands, adj. rear sight, 8.5 lbs.

MSR $819	$775	$575	$450	$345

GRADING - PPGS™	100%	98%	90%	80%

1861 ENFIELD MUSKETOON (PARKER-HALE) — .58 cal. perc., 24 in. round barrel, color case hardened hammer and lock, brass trim, two blue bands, adj. rear sight, 7 lbs.

MSR $734	$675	$595	$465	$385

1803 HARPERS FERRY RIFLE — .54 cal. flintlock, 35 in. round barrel, color case hardened hammer and lock, brass trim, 8.5 lbs. Disc. 2004.

	$625	$500	$400	$300

Last MSR was $695.

* ***1803 Lewis & Clark Edition Harpers Ferry Rifle*** — .54 cal. flintlock, similar to 1803 Harpers Ferry Rifle, except authentic brown finish barrel, upgrade walnut finished stock, patchbox engraved "Lewis and Clark Journey of Discovery 1803-1806," and German Pewter replica Friendship Medalion attached to the trigger guard by a ribbon. New 2003.

MSR $999	$950	$775	$630	$495

HAWKEN RIFLE — .50, .54, or .58 cal. flintlock or perc., 28 in. octagon barrel, double set triggers, brass trim, 8.5 lbs.

	$200	$160	$120	$85

Last MSR was $220.

Subtract $15 for percussion.

HAWKEN MARK 1 RIFLE — .50 or .54 cal. flintlock or perc. 26 in. octagon barrel, adj. double set triggers and sights, brass trim, 9 lbs. Disc. 1994.

	$220	$170	$125	$90

Last MSR was $260.

Add $15 for flintlock.
Add $140 for commemorative model.

HAWKEN HUNTER RIFLE/CARBINE — .50, .54, or .58 cal. perc., 28.5 in. octagon barrel, (22.5 in. carbine), color case hardened hammer and lock, double set triggers, 7 lbs. 12 oz. (6 lbs. 12 oz. carbine).

	$220	$170	$125	$85

Last MSR was $240.

ITHACA-NAVY HAWKEN — .50 or .54 cal. flintlock or perc., 26 in. octagon barrel, adj. double set triggers and sights, brass trim, 9 lbs. Disc. 1994, left-hand version disc. 1987.

	$400	$340	$250	$205

Last MSR was $445.

Add $65 for flintlock.

J.P. MURRAY ARTILLERY CARBINE — .58 cal. perc., 23.5 in. brown round barrel, color case hardened hammer and lock, brass trim and bands, 7.5 lbs.

MSR $748	$675	$595	$450	$375

KENTUCKY RIFLE — .45 or .50 cal. perc. or flintlock, 35 in. barrel, color case hardened hammer and lock, brass trim, adj. brass rear sight (windage only), 6 lbs. 14 oz.

	$395	$335	$245	$205

Last MSR was $425.

Add $10 for flintlock or .50 cal.
Add $125 for .45 cal. deluxe.

KODIAK DOUBLE RIFLE — .50, .54, or .58 cal. perc., 28 in. double barrel, white steel furniture. Mfg. 1989-98.

	$695	$565	$440	$325

Last MSR was $775.

GRADING - PPGS™	100%	98%	90%	80%

1841 MISSISSIPPI RIFLE — .54 or .58 cal. perc., 33 in. brown round barrel, color case hardened hammer and lock, brass trim and bands, 9.5 lbs.

courtesy Navy Arms, Co.

MSR $791	$675	$545	$425	$315

MORSE RIFLE — .50 cal. perc., 26 in. octagon barrel, brass trim and action, blue barrel and hammer, adj. rear sight, (windage only), 6 lbs. Disc. 1987.

	$275	$200	$145	$100

MORTIMER RIFLE — .54 cal. flintlock, 36 in. brown barrel, color case hardened furniture, waterproof flash pan, chrome lined bore, 9 lbs. Disc. 1998.

	$700	$565	$440	$325

Last MSR was $780.

Add $300 for extra 12 ga. barrel.
Add $100 for flintlock match rifle.

MULE EAR MOUNTAIN MAN SQUIRREL RIFLE — .32, .36, or .45 cal. perc., 26 in. octagon barrel, brass trim, blue barrel, hammer, lock, and trigger, 5.5 lbs. Disc. 1994.

	$235	$180	$130	$95

Last MSR was $185.

PARKER HALE VOLUNTEER RIFLE — .451 cal. perc., 32 in. barrel, target model featuring Alexander Henry rifling, brass trim, blue band, color case hardened hammer and lock, adj. sights, hand checkered walnut stock, 9.5 lbs.

MSR $1,133	$1,075	$925	$740	$595

PARKER HALE WHITWORTH RIFLE — .451 cal. perc., 36 in. barrel with Whitworth hexagonal bore rifling system, brass trim, blue barrel and bands, color case hardened hammer and lock, adj. sights, detented lock hammer, long range accuracy app. 1,000 yds., comes with accessories, approx. 9.5 lbs.

MSR $1,175	$985	$775	$625	$450

PENNSYLVANIA HALF STOCK HUNTER — .50 cal. perc., 30 in. octagon barrel, white steel hammer and lock, brass patchbox and trim, walnut stock, 6 lbs. 4 oz. Disc. 1994.

	$225	$175	$125	$85

Last MSR was $220.

PENNSYLVANIA LONG RIFLE — .32 or .45 cal. flintlock or perc., 40.5 in. brown octagon barrel, adj. buckhorn rear sight, double set triggers, color case hardened hammer and lock, brass patch box and trim, walnut stock, 7 lbs. 8 oz.

	$450	$365	$265	$225

Last MSR was $490.

Add $15 for flintlock.

PIONEER RIFLE — .45 or .50 cal. flintlock, 30 in. octagon barrel, color case hardened hammer and lock, walnut stock, 6 lbs. 4 oz. Disc. 1994.

	$225	$175	$125	$85

Last MSR was $200.

1859 SHARPS RIFLE (BERDAN) MODEL — .54 cal. perc., 30 in. round blue barrel, color case hardened hammer, lock, patch box, trigger guard, and furniture, 3 barrel bands, double set triggers, walnut stock, 8 lbs. 8 oz. New 1994.

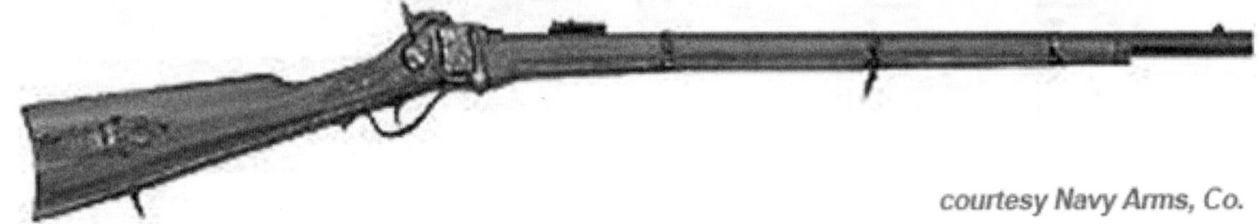

courtesy Navy Arms, Co.

MSR $1,347	$1,195	$950	$725	$550

GRADING - PPGS™	100%	98%	90%	80%

1859 SHARPS RIFLE/CARBINE — .45 (disc. 2003) or .54 cal. perc., 22, 28, 30 or 32 in. octagon or round barrel, color case hardened hammer, frame and buttplate.

* ***1859 Sharps Rifle*** — - 30 in. barrel, three barrel bands, 8.5 lbs.

MSR $1,432	**$1,375**	**$1,195**	**$825**	**$575**

* ***1859 Sharps Carbine*** — 22 in. barrel with one barrel band, and saddle bar with ring, 7.75 lbs.

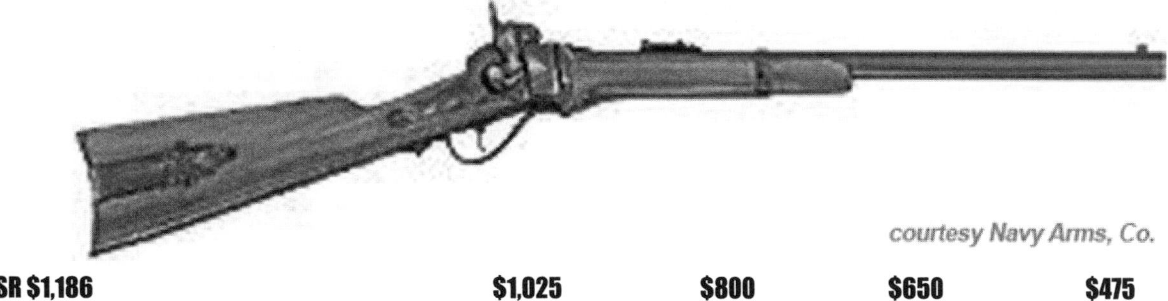

courtesy Navy Arms, Co.

MSR $1,186	**$1,025**	**$800**	**$650**	**$475**

1861 SPRINGFIELD — .58 cal. 1858 Maynard priming perc., 40 in. barrel, all white steel, 3 barrel bands, 10.25 lbs.

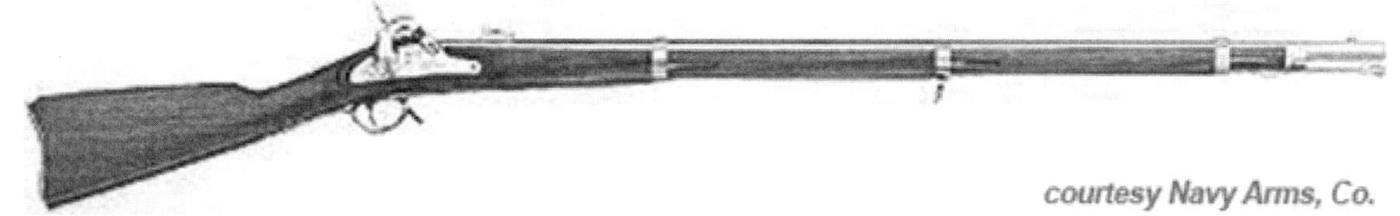

courtesy Navy Arms, Co.

MSR $976	**$875**	**$715**	**$545**	**$395**

1863 C.S. RICHMOND RIFLE — .58 cal. perc., 40 in. barrel, all white steel, 3 barrel bands, 10.25 lbs.

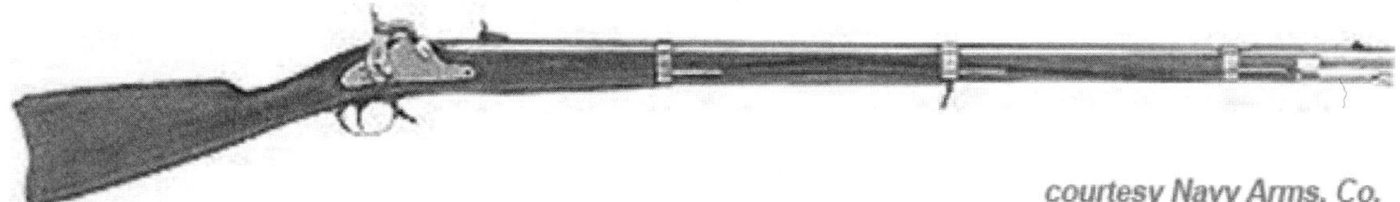

courtesy Navy Arms, Co.

MSR $976	**$860**	**$725**	**$575**	**$450**

1863 SPRINGFIELD — .58 cal. perc., 40 in. barrel, all white steel, 3 barrel bands, 10.1 lbs.

MSR $976	**$875**	**$715**	**$545**	**$395**

SMITH ARTILLERY/CAVALRY CARBINE — .50 (Cavalry) or .54 (Artillery) cal. perc., 21.5 in. octagon tapering to round barrel, color case hardened hammer and receiver, 7.75 lbs. New 1989. Mfg. by Pietta.

MSR $790	**$675**	**$545**	**$425**	**$315**

This model is also available in a Skirmisher variation at no extra charge.

SWISS FEDERAL TARGET RIFLE — .45 cal. perc., 32 in. octagon barrel, color case hardened hammer, lock, and trim, double set triggers, classic Bristlen and Morges design, adj. sights, 13.25 lbs. Imported from West Germany by Neumann Co. Disc. 1994.

	$1,510	**$1,310**	**$975**	**$800**

Last MSR was $1,200.

Add $35 for palm rest.

TRYON RIFLE — .451 cal. perc., 34 in. octagon barrel, white steel hammer and engraved lock and patchbox, double set triggers, walnut stock, 9 lbs. 12 oz. Disc. 1996.

	$425	**$350**	**$255**	**$220**

Last MSR was $455.

Add $35 for target sights.

GRADING - PPGS™	100%	98%	90%	80%

TRYON CREEDMOOR RIFLE — .451 cal. perc., Creedmoor target version of above. Disc. 1996.

	$700	$565	$440	$325

Last MSR was $780.

ZOUAVE RIFLE — .58 cal. perc., 33 in. round barrel, color case hardened hammer, lock, and trigger, brass trim, adj. rear sight, 9 lbs. Mfg. by Armi Sport and EuroArms.

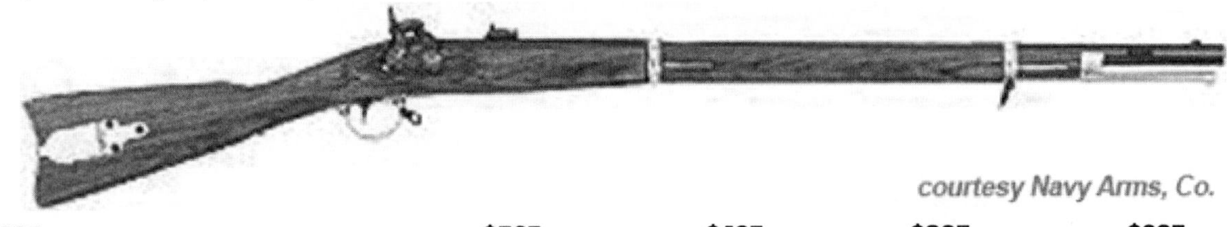

courtesy Navy Arms, Co.

MSR $634	$585	$495	$395	$295

Add $115 for deluxe Range Model (mfg. by EuroSport).

RIFLES: IN-LINE IGNITION

COUNTRY BOY — .50 cal. perc., 24 in. round barrel, hard chrome breech plug, nipple and bolt, chrome lined barrel, Williams aperture sight, synthetic stock with storage compartment, 8 lbs. Disc. 1998.

	$150	$125	$95	$65

Last MSR was $165.

Add $10 for all chrome.

M98 IN-LINE — .50 cal. perc., 22 in. round barrel, hard chrome breech plug, nipple and bolt, chrome lined barrel, checkered synthetic stock, Williams aperture sight, modeled after the "M-98 Mauser," 8 lbs. Disc. 1998.

	$350	$275	$225	$170

Last MSR was $390.

Add $10 for all chrome.

SHOTGUNS: FLINTLOCK & PERCUSSION

MORSE MODEL — 12 ga. perc., 26 in. barrel, brass receiver and trim, blue hammer and buttplate, 5.75 lbs. Disc. 1987.

	$300	$225	$165	$115

Last MSR was $165.

MORTIMER MODEL — 12 ga. flintlock or perc., 36 in. brown barrel, color case hardened furniture, walnut stock, waterproof pan and chrome bore. New in 1989. Disc. 1998.

	$650	$525	$415	$310

Last MSR was $735.

STEEL SHOT MAGNUM SxS — 10 ga. perc., 28 in. barrels, engraved polished lock plates, chrome lined bores, checkered walnut stock, 7 lbs. 9oz.

	$525	$415	$310	$250

Last MSR was $605.

COUNTRY BOY IN-LINE MUZZLE LOADER — 12 ga. perc., 25 in. round smooth bore barrel with adj. rotary choke, bead front sight, hard chrome breech plug, nipple and bolt, chrome lined barrel, synthetic stock, 7 lbs. Disc. 1998.

	$150	$125	$95	$65

Last MSR was $165.

TURKEY AND TRAP (T&T) SxS — 12 ga. perc., 28 in. blue barrels bored F/F, color case hardened locks and furniture, walnut stock. Mfg. by Pedersoli.

	$525	$415	$310	$250

Last MSR was $580.

UPLAND MODEL SxS — 12 ga. perc., 28 in. blue barrels bored cyl./mod.

	$525	$415	$310	$250

Last MSR was $580.

GRADING - PPGS™	100%	98%	90%	80%

NEW ENGLAND FIREARMS

Current trademark located in Madison, NC beginning 2008. New England Firearms was established during 1987 and was previously located in Gardner, MA until 2007.

In late 2007, Remington Arms Company, Inc. announced it had entered into a definitive agreement to acquire Marlin Firearms Company, Inc. The agreement includes Marlin, H&R 1871, LLC, New England Firearms and LC Smith. The transaction closed in early 2008 and was followed by a strategic manufacturing consolidation move that resulted in the closure of its Gardner, Massachusetts plant.

During 2000, Marlin Firearms Co. purchased the assets of H&R 1871, Inc., and the name was changed to H&R 1871, LLC. Brand names include Harrington & Richardson, New England Firearms, and Wesson & Harrington. Production will remain at the Gardner, MA plant.

All NEF firearms utilize a transfer bar safety system and have a $10 service plan which guarantees lifetime warranty.

New England Firearms should not be confused with New England Arms Corp. For more information and current pricing on New England Firearms firearms, please refer to the *Blue Book of Gun Values* by S.P. Fjestad (now online also).

RIFLES: IN-LINE IGNITION

HUNTSMAN MODEL SMO-050/SMO-056 — .50 cal. (#209 shotshell primer w/patented reusable carrier) perc., 24 SMO-050 (disc. 2004) or 26 SMO-056 (new 2005) in. 1:28 in. twist blue barrel, color case hardened finish break-open side lever release action, American hardwood full PG stock and forearm w/ventilated recoil pad, telescoping ramrod (new 2005), adj. fiber-optic sights, tapped for scope base, 40 or 42 in. OAL, 6.5 lbs. Disc. 2008.

	$180	$155	$135	$115

Last MSR was $207.

Since a modern center fire rifle or shotgun barrel can be fitted to this muzzleloader, the BATF has classified the Huntsman as a "firearm" making it subject to all federal firearms regulations.

HUNTSMAN MODEL SMS-050 — .50 cal. (#209 shotshell primer) perc., 24 in. stainless steel barrel, 1:28 in. twist, matte nickel finish break-open side lever release action, matte black polymer full PG stock and forearm w/ventilated recoil pad, adj. fiber-optic sights, tapped for scope base, 40 in. OAL, 6.5 lbs. Mfg. 2003-2008.

	$245	$185	$135	$90

Last MSR was $281.

The BATF has classified the Huntsman as a "firearm," making it subject to all federal firearms regulations.

SIDEKICK MODEL SPO-050/SPO-056 — .50 cal. (#209 shotshell primer) perc., 24 (Model SPO-050) or 26 (Model SPO-056) in. 1:28 in. twist blue barrel, color case-hardened finish break-open side lever release action, American hardwood full PG stock and forearm w/ventilated recoil pad, adj. fiber-optic sights, tapped for scope base, 40-42 in. OAL, 6.5 lbs. Mfg. 2004-2008.

	$170	$145	$105	$75

Last MSR was $195.

Add $6 for Model SPO-056 with 26 in. barrel.

SIDEKICK MODEL SPS-050/SPS-056 — .50 cal. (#209 shotshell primer) perc., 24 (Model SPS-050) or 26 (SPS-056) in. stainless steel barrel, 1:28 in. twist, matte nickel finish break-open side lever release action, matte black polymer full PG stock and forearm w/ventilated recoil pad, adj. fiber-optic sights, tapped for scope base, 40-46 in. OAL, 6.5 lbs. Mfg. 2004-2008.

	$245	$185	$135	$90

Last MSR was $285.

Add $7 for Model SPS-056 with 26 in. barrel.

NEW ULTRA LIGHT ARMS LLC

Current manufacturer located in Granville, WV, previously located in Morgantown, WV. Dealer and consumer direct sales.

For more information and current pricing on both new and used New Ultra Light Arms, LLC firearms, please refer to the *Blue Book of Gun Values* by S.P. Fjestad (now online also).

GRADING - PPGS™	100%	98%	90%	80%

RIFLES: IN-LINE IGNITION

MODEL 90 — .45 or .50 cal., 28 in. button rifled barrel, adj. Timney trigger, Kevlar/graphite stock with colors optional, Williams rear sight, 6 lbs., includes hard case. Disc. 1999.

	$875	$710	$565	$410

Last MSR was $950.

MODEL 209 — .45 or .50 cal. perc., #209 primer ignition, 24 in. button rifled barrel, 1:32 in. twist, adj. Timney trigger, Kevlar/graphite stock with optional colors, ULA scope mounts, under 5 lbs., includes hard case. New 2004.

MSR $1,300	$1,195	$875	$710	$565

NORTH AMERICAN ARMS, INC.

Current manufacturer located in Provo, UT. Dealer and consumer direct sales.

For more information and current pricing on both new and used North American Arms, Inc. firearms, please refer to the *Blue Book of Gun Values* by S.P. Fjestad (now online also).

REVOLVERS: PERCUSSION

COMPANION MODEL NAA-22LR-CB — .22 cal. perc., 5 shot cylinder, 1.63 in. barrel, all stainless steel construction, 5.25 in. OAL, .4 lbs.

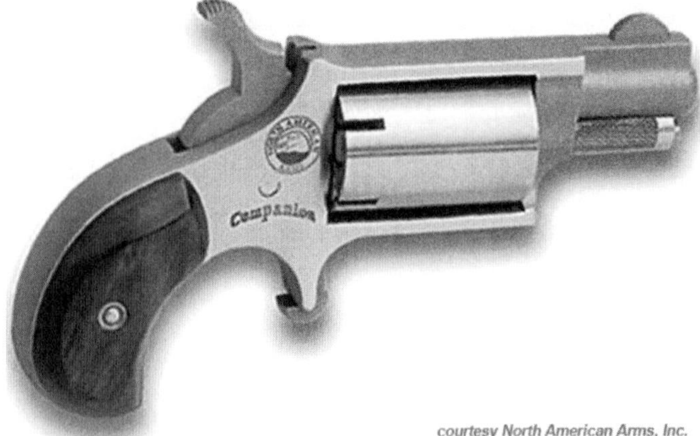

courtesy North American Arms, Inc.

	$195	$175	$125	$105

Last MSR was $215.

Add $44 for Companion Model Kit w/2 cylinders, bullet bag, flap holster and 250 bullets.

SUPER COMPANION MODEL NAA-22M-CB — .22 cal. perc., 5 shot cylinder, 1.13 in. barrel, all stainless steel construction, 4 in. OAL, 3 lbs.

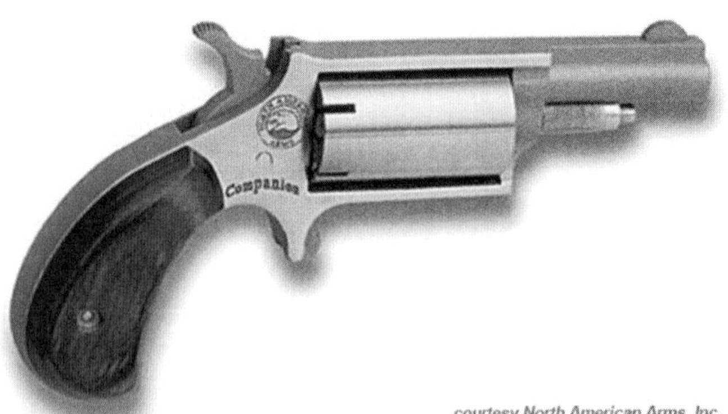

courtesy North American Arms, Inc.

MSR $230	$205	$180	$135	$115

Add $43 for Super Companion Model Kit w/2 cylinders, bullet bag, flap holster and 250 bullets.

NORTH STAR WEST, INC.

Current manufacturer currently located in Frenchtown, MT, previously located in Glencoe, CA. Dealer and consumer direct sales.

GRADING - PPGS™	100%	98%	90%	80%

PISTOLS: FLINTLOCK

TRADE PISTOL — 28, 24, or 20 ga. flintlock, 10 in. browned octagon to round barrel, steel trigger guard, serpent sideplate, walnut stock, 2.6 lbs. New 2002.

MSR $715	$650	$575	$425	$350

RIFLES: FLINTLOCK

OFFICER'S MODEL MUSKET — .66 cal., flintlock, 37.5 in. octagon to round barrel, brass furniture, steel trigger guard, serpent sideplate, walnut stock, 8 lbs.

MSR $1,365	$1,225	$995	$675	$585

SHOTGUNS: FLINTLOCK

BLANKET GUN — 24 or 20 ga., flintlock, 18 in. octagon to round barrel, brass furniture, steel trigger guard, steel lock and sideplate, walnut stock cut 4 in. past trigger guard.

MSR $945	$845	$745	$545	$445

BUFFALO RUNNER — 24 or 20 ga., flintlock, 12 in. octagon to round barrel, brass furniture, steel trigger guard, serpent sideplate, walnut stock cut at the end of the trigger guard.

MSR $945	$845	$745	$545	$445

CANOE GUN — 24 or 20 ga., flintlock, 18 in. octagon to round barrel, brass furniture, steel trigger guard, serpent sideplate, walnut stock 12 in. LOP. New 1994.

MSR $918	$830	$765	$585	$495

CHIEF'S GRADE — 28, 24, or 20 ga., flintlock, 30, 36, or 41 in. octagon to round barrel, brass furniture, steel trigger, brass trigger guard, serpent sideplate, full length walnut stock.

MSR $1,265	$1,145	$995	$750	$625

Add $71 for left-hand.

EARLY ENGLISH — 28, 24, or 20 ga., flintlock, 30, 36, or 41 in. octagon to round barrel, brass furniture, steel trigger, cast steel trigger guard, serpent sideplate, full length walnut stock.

MSR $1,250	$1,130	$975	$735	$600

Add $25 for left-hand.

NORTHWEST TRADE MODEL — 20 ga., flintlock, 36 in. octagon to round barrel, brass furniture, steel trigger guard, serpent sideplate, walnut stock, 6 lbs.

MSR $1,190	$1,075	$965	$725	$595

Add $44 for left-hand.

NOTES

GRADING - PPGS™	100%	98%	90%	80%

O SECTION

OCTOBER COUNTRY MUZZLELOADING, INC.

Current manufacturer/distributor specializing in the manufacturing of large bore muzzleloaders, and located in Hayden, ID.

October Country Muzzleloading, Inc. changed ownership in October, 2005. All models are handmade and custom finished, utilizing maple, walnut, or English walnut stocks. October Country Muzzleloading, Inc. also manufactures custom bullet molds, patches, and wads for large bore rifles.

RIFLES: PERCUSSION

GREAT AMERICAN SPORTING RIFLE — 12, 14, 16, or 20 bore perc., 28 in. octagon to round barrel, rifled 1 turn in 8 feet, 8 in., adj. rear sight, steel furniture, pewter nosecap, patented two piece breech, 10 lbs. Disc. 2006.

	$1,525	$1,350	$1,100	$825

Last MSR was $1,695.

This model's design is based on theories of Lt. James Forsyth from his book *The Sporting Rifle and its Projectiles.*

LIGHT AMERICAN SPORTING RIFLE — .62 cal. perc., 28 in. barrel, fixed buckhorn rear sight, blue iron furniture, two piece breech, single trigger, iron trigger guard, walnut pistol grip stock, 8 lbs. Disc. 2006.

	$1,425	$1,275	$1,050	$825

Last MSR was $1,595.

EIGHT BORE DOUBLE (SxS) HEAVY RIFLE — .85 cal. perc., 30 in. tapered round barrels, patented two-piece breech, steel furniture, bead front sight, 3 blade express rear sight, English walnut shotgun style stock, 14 lbs. 8 oz. Disc. 2006.

	$4,495	$3,995	$2,995	$2,500

Last MSR was $4,995.

HEAVY RIFLE — .85 or 1.00 cal. perc., 30 in. tapered octagon barrel, patented two piece breech, steel furniture, 3 blade express rear sight, steel bead front sight, English walnut pistol grip stock, checkered at the forestock and pistol grip, 18 lbs. Disc. 2006.

	$2,695	$2,195	$1,650	$995

Last MSR was $2,995.

OCTOBER COUNTRY EXTREME — 12, 14, 16, or 20 bore perc., 36 in. Moody Metal Works tapered octagon barrel, rifled 1:104 in. twist, English style fixed "V" rear and blade front sights, L & R English Bar lock, iron mounted, cold brown finish, curly maple stock 14.5 in. LOP, patented two piece breech, 45 in. OAL, 11 lbs.

	$2,295	$1,825	$1,450	$1,100

Last MSR was $2,295.

Many options available, contact October Country for listing and prices.

OCTOBER COUNTRY 4 BORE SPORTING RIFLE — 8 bore perc., 32 in. tapered octagon barrel, rifled 1:144 in. twist, English express two blade rear and blade front sights, iron mounted, cold brown finish, curly maple stock, pachmayr recoil pad w/2 lbs mercury recoil reducer in butt stock, 11 lbs. New 2008.

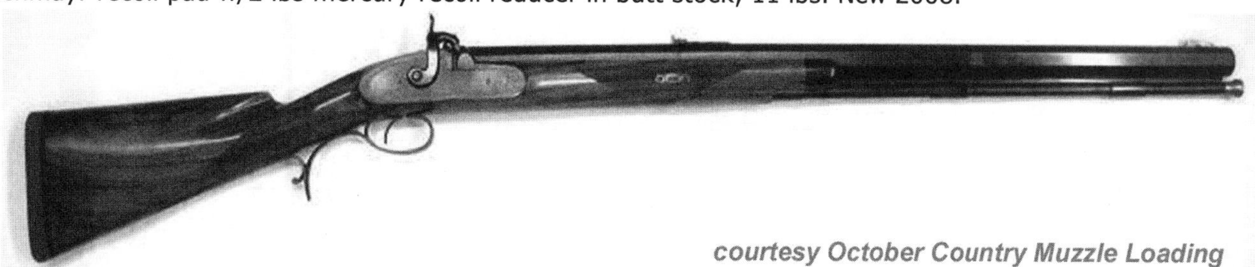

courtesy October Country Muzzle Loading

MSR $4,750	$4,250	$3,725	$2,950	$2,500

Many options available, contact October Country for listing and prices.

GRADING - PPGS™	100%	98%	90%	80%

OCTOBER COUNTRY .69 CALIBER SPORTING RIFLE — .69 cal. perc., 28 in. tapered octagon barrel, rifled 1:144 in. twist, English express two blade rear and blade front sights, iron mounted, cold brown finish, curly maple stock, pachmayr recoil pad w/2 lbs. mercury recoil reducer in butt stock, 45 in. OAL, 12 lbs. New 2008.

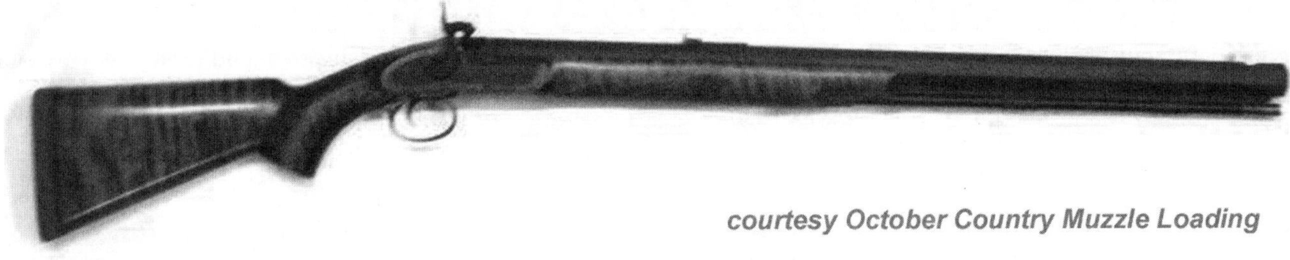

courtesy October Country Muzzle Loading

MSR $2,300	$2,050	$1,825	$1,450	$1,195

Many options available, contact October Country for listing and prices.

OLD DOMINION ARMS

Current custom rifle maker located in Ruther Glen, VA.

Al Edge is a master gunsmith offering recreations of early American rifles. Mr. Edge's specialty is Virginia rifles with prices starting in the $3,000 range, and restoration of contemporary arms. Please contact the maker directly (see Trademark Index) for additional information.

courtesy Old Dominion Arms

OLD-WEST GUN CO.

Previous importer and distributor that took over the inventory of Allen Firearms after they went out of business in early 1987. Old-West Gun Co. became Cimarron F.A. Co. in 1987.

Older variations marked Old-West have approx. the same values as those of Cimarron Arms Co. (Please refer to the Cimarron heading in this text.)

GRADING - PPGS™	100%	98%	90%	80%

P SECTION

PACIFIC RIFLE COMPANY

Current manufacturer located in Lake Oswego, OR. Pacific Rifle Company specializes in underhammer rifles utilizing the James Forsyth rifling technique developed in the 19th Century. Consumer direct sales.

Christened "The Zephyr" by gunmaker Roger Renner of Pacific Rifle Co., this unique long rifle utilizes an advanced underhammer mechanism providing the fewest number of moving parts in any percussion rifle. The trigger guard serves as the mainspring. The Zephyr uses the Forsyth rifling technique for superior long range accuracy. Each rifle is hand crafted to order.

RIFLES: PERCUSSION, UNDERHAMMER

1837 ZEPHYR MODEL — 12 or 20 bore perc., underhammer lock, 30 in. tapered octagon barrel, color case hardened (disc.) or slow-rust browned finish, fire-blue hammer, trigger and screws, oil finish black walnut stock and forend, semi-buckhorn rear and german silver blade front sight, 7.75 lbs.

courtesy Pacific Rifle Company

MSR $1,500	**$1,500**	**$1,250**	**$995**	**$795**

Add $100 for Peephorn rear sight.
Add $100 for upgrade walnut.
Add $100 for Damascus Bronze receiver and buttplate.

AFRICAN ZEPHYR 12 BORE — .72 cal. perc., underhammer lock, dual cap ignition, 26 in. tapered octagon barrel, cast steel, color case hardened receiver with "B" engraving, nitrite-blue hammer, trigger, screws and mainspring, English walnut stock and forend, smooth shotgun color case hardened plate on buttstock, short caterpillar of .090 in. diameter at the front of integral full-length sighting rib, U notched rear blade sight, rust brown finish on barrel, 9 lbs. Disc. 2001.

	$2,000	**$1,500**	**$1,100**	**$895**

Last MSR was $2,000.

AFRICAN ZEPHYR 8 BORE — .82 cal. perc., underhammer lock, dual cap ignition, 26 in. tapered octagon barrel, cast steel, color case hardened receiver with "B" engraving, nitrite-blue hammer, trigger, screws and mainspring, English walnut stock and forend, smooth shotgun color case hardened plate on buttstock, short caterpillar of .090 in. diameter at the front of integral full-length sighting rib, U notched rear blade sight, rust brown finish on barrel, 12 lbs.

courtesy Pacific Rifle Company

MSR $2,750	**$2,500**	**$1,750**	**$1,350**	**$995**

ALASKAN ZEPHYR — .72 cal. perc., underhammer lock, dual cap ignition, 26 in. tapered octagon barrel, 1:104 in. twist, cast steel, rust brown finish receiver, hammer, trigger, screws and mainspring, English walnut stock and forend, smooth shotgun color case hardened plate on buttstock, semi-buckhorn rear and German silver front blade sight, rust brown finish on barrel, 43 in. OAL, 11 lbs. New 2006.

MSR $2,000	**$2,000**	**$1,500**	**$1,100**	**$895**

GRADING - PPGS™	100%	98%	90%	80%

PALMETTO ARMS CO.

Previous manufacturer located in Brescia, Italy. Previously imported by Caliber, Inc., located in Middlefield, CT.

For more information and current pricing on used Palmetto Arms Co. firearms, please refer to the *Blue Book of Gun Values* by S.P. Fjestad (now online also).

PEDERSOLI, DAVIDE & C. Snc.

Current manufacturer located in Gardone, Italy. Currently imported by Cabela's, located in Sidney, NE, Cimarron F.A., located in Fredricksburg, TX, E.M.F., located in Santa Ana, CA, Navy Arms located in Union City, WV and Taylor's Company, Inc. located in Winchester, VA. Previously imported by Jeff's Outfitters, located in Cape Girardeau, MO, Flintlocks, Etc. located in Richmond, MA. Current full line distributors include Cherry's Fine Guns, located in Greensboro, NC, Dixie Gun Works, located in Union City, TN, and Flintlocks, Etc. located in Richmond, MA.

Davide Pedersoli & C. is a family company, founded in 1957 by Davide Pedersoli (1924-1996). In 1960, it started production of muzzle loading guns, and from 1970-73, several models of O/U shotguns were produced. Flasks became the first accessory in 1973, starting a wide range of accessories for muzzle loading shooting.

In 1975, Davide's son, Dr. Pierangelo Pedersoli directs and manages the company together with his brother-in-law, production manager Giovanni Gottardi. Today, the company keeps its family character, by education and training of the younger family members (Stefano Pedersoli, son of Dr. Pierangelo Pedersoli) who will become the third generation of the Pedersoli family to control and operate the company.

Currently the company has 40 people on staff, divided into three departments. Since 1982, the production of stocks, barrels, and small parts has been "in-house," as well as final assembly. Since 1990, the company has undergone a constant technology change, replacing much of the older equipment with modern CNC technology and designs utilizing CAD-CAM systems.

Pedersoli actively sponsors important shooting competitions for muzzle loading, Western target shooting, as well as long distance target shooting competitions with metallic cartridge rifles. Pedersoli's wide range of muzzle loading reproductions and replicas have won all the major international shooting competitions, and continue to capture many gold, silver, and bronze medals annually.

For more information and current pricing on currently available Pedersoli models see the Full Line distibutors listings.

For more information and current pricing on both new and used Pedersoli firearms, please refer to the *Blue Book of Gun Values* by S.P. Fjestad (now online also).

Black Powder Reproductions & Replicas by Dennis Adler is also an invaluable source for most black powder reproductions and replicas, and includes hundreds of color images on most popular makes/models, provides manufacturer/trademark histories, and up-to-date information on related items/accessories for black powder shooting - www.bluebookinc.com

PISTOLS: FLINTLOCK & PERCUSSION

1806 HARPERS FERRY — .58 cal. flintlock, 10 in. barrel, color case hardened lock, brass furniture, and inlaid buttcap, 2.5 lbs.

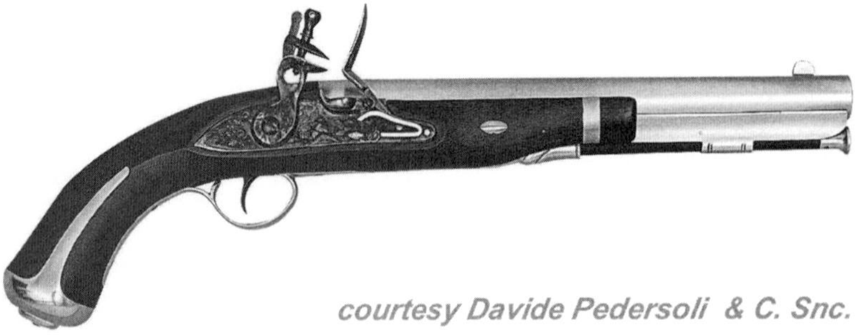

courtesy Davide Pedersoli & C. Snc.

MSR $456	$415	$365	$265	$215

Add $165 for commemorative model with silver plated hardware and white steel barrel stamped "U.S. Army Commemorative."

GRADING - PPGS™	100%	98%	90%	80%

CARLESTON UNDERHAMMER PISTOL — .36 cal. perc., 8.5 in. octagon to round brown barrel, metal fittings are color case hardened, walnut stock, 2 lbs.

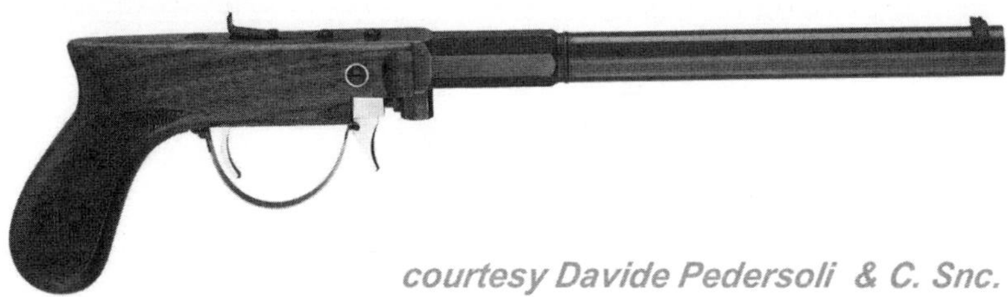

courtesy Davide Pedersoli & C. Snc.

MSR $753	$675	$600	$450	$375

CHARLES MOORE PISTOL — .36, .44 smoth bore, or .45 cal., flintlock (.44 or .45 cal.) or perc. (.36 or .45 cal.), 11 in. blue octagon barrel, color case hardened hammer and lock, brass furniture, adj. trigger, hand checkered walnut stock, 2.5 lbs.

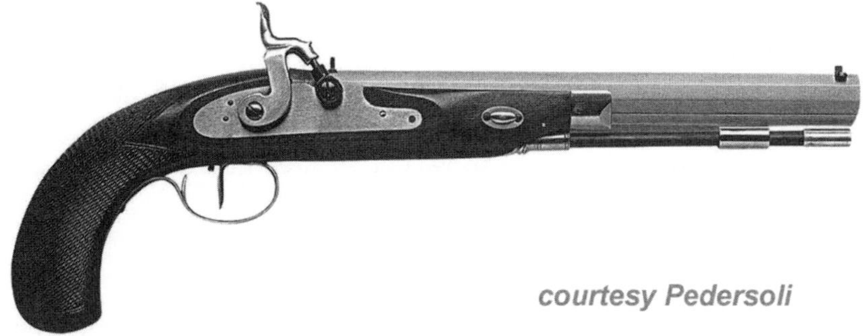

courtesy Pedersoli

	$545	$480	$360	$295

Last MSR was $594.

Add $75 for flintlock.

* ***Charles Moore Target Pistol*** — .36, .44, or .45 cal., similar to Charles Moore Pistol, except polished steel German silver color barrel and all parts.

MSR $594	$545	$480	$360	$295

Add $45 for flintlock.

CONTINENTAL DUELING PISTOL — .45 cal. flintlock or perc., 11 in. blue octagon barrel, color case hardened hammer and lock, checkered walnut stock, 16.3 in. OAL, 2.4 lbs. New 2008.

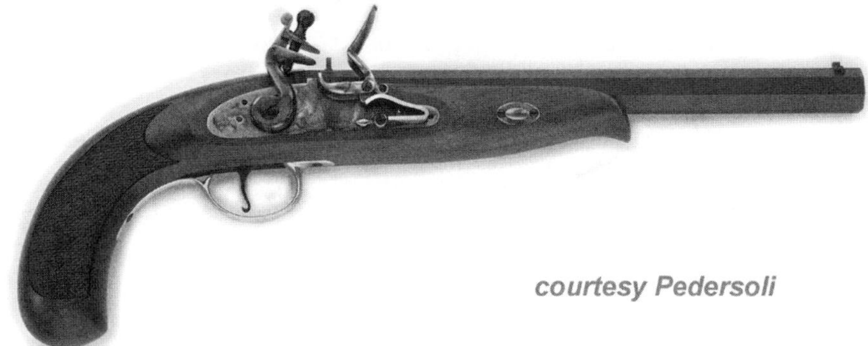

courtesy Pedersoli

MSR $385	$350	$310	$225	$195

Add $63 for flintlock model.

ENGLISH DUELING PISTOL — .45 cal. perc., 11 in. octagon barrel, silver thimble and endcap.

	$240	$210	$165	$115

GRADING - PPGS™	100%	98%	90%	80%

FRENCH AN IX MILITARY PISTOL — .69 cal. flintlock, 8.25 in. bright finish barrel and lock, brass furniture and buttcap, 14 in. OAL, 3 lbs. New 2008.

courtesy Pedersoli

MSR $614	$555	$495	$365	$305

FRENCH AN XIII MILITARY PISTOL — .69 cal. flintlock, 8.25 in. bright finish barrel and lock, brass furniture and buttcap, 14 in. OAL, 3 lbs. New 2008.

MSR $599	$545	$485	$355	$295

HOWDAH HUNTER PISTOL — .50 cal. and/or 20 ga. perc., SxS pistol, 11.25 in. blue steel barrel, 1:18 in. twist and/or smoothbore, checkered satin finished European walnut w/three-quarter PG stock,18.25 in. OAL, 4.5-5 lbs. Mfg. by Pedersoli. New 2008.

courtesy Pedersoli

MSR $698	$635	$5650	$425	$355

Add $25 for combination .50 cal. and 20 ga. SxS.
Subtract $25 for 20 ga. SxS.

KENTUCKY PISTOL — .45, .50 & .54 cal. flintlock or perc., 10.25 octagon barrel (steel or brass), walnut stock, brass furniture and trigger guard, 2.25 lbs. Available in deluxe versions and Silver Star model.

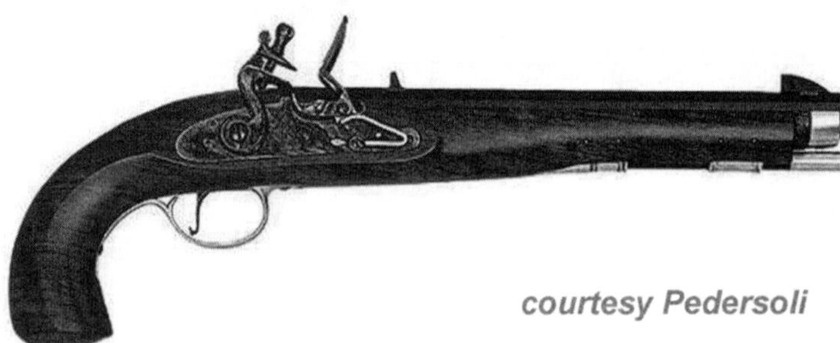

courtesy Pedersoli

MSR $331	$295	$255	$195	$155

Add $23 for .50 and .54 cal. "Big Bore" Models.
Add $143 for maple stock.
Add $130 for deluxe model.
Add $215 for Silver Star flintlock model with engraved white steel hammer and lock, German silver furniture, inlaid stock (star on forearm), and brown barrel.
Add $26 for flintlock.

GRADING - PPGS™	100%	98%	90%	80%

* ***Kentucky Bounty*** — .44 or .50 cal. flintlock or perc., 16.5 in. octagon barrel, white steel hammer and lock, brass furniture and trigger guard, walnut stock, 3 lbs.

courtesy Pedersoli

MSR $361	$325	$285	$210	$175

Add $27 for flintlock.

KUCHENREUTER — .38, .40, or .44 cal., 11.25 in. octagon brown barrel, color case hardened, hammer lock, trigger guard, and furniture, walnut stock, 2 lbs. 10 oz. New 1994.

courtesy Davide Pedersoli & C. Snc.

MSR $1,460	$1,325	$1,155	$860	$725

Add $1,025 for deluxe engraved and cased model. Special Order only.

LE PAGE INTERNATIONAL PISTOL — .31 (disc.), .36, .38, and .44 cal. flintlock or perc., 10.5 in. brown or white octagon barrel, white steel or color case hardened hammer and lock, adj. triggers, 2 lbs. (cased set, gold trim, consecutive serial number).

courtesy Davide Pedersoli & C. Snc

MSR $753	$675	$600	$450	$375

Add $252 for flintlock model.
Add $211 for deluxe maple stock.
Add $1,020 for engraved Target International model with presentation case.
Add $1,220 for engraved Target International flintlock with wood case.
Subtract $50 for white barrel.

GRADING - PPGS™	100%	98%	90%	80%

LIEGE DERRINGER/LIEGE POCKET DERRINGER — .36 (Pocket) or .44 cal. perc., 2.37 or 4 in. round barrel, color case hardened frame, screw-on barrel, folding trigger, .5 lb.

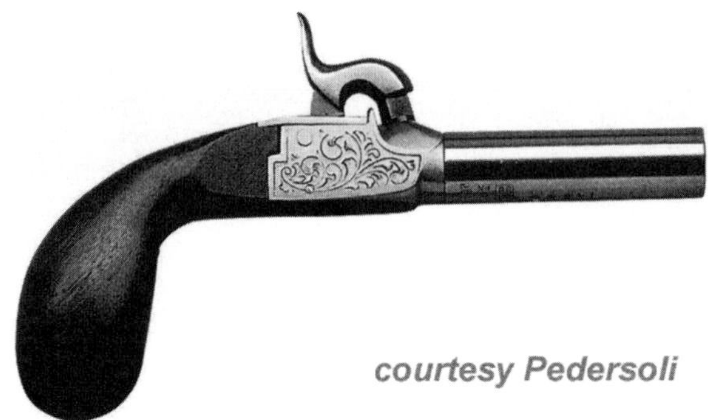

courtesy Pedersoli

MSR $171	$150	$130	$95	$80

Add $15 for .36 cal. Pocket Model new 2003.
Add $35 for gold finish w/simulated ivory grip new 2003.
Add $45 for engraved white steel.

MANG IN GRÄZ PISTOL — .38 or .44 cal. perc., 11.5 in. octagon brown barrel, color case hardened or white hammer and lock, fluted walnut stock, 2.5 lbs.

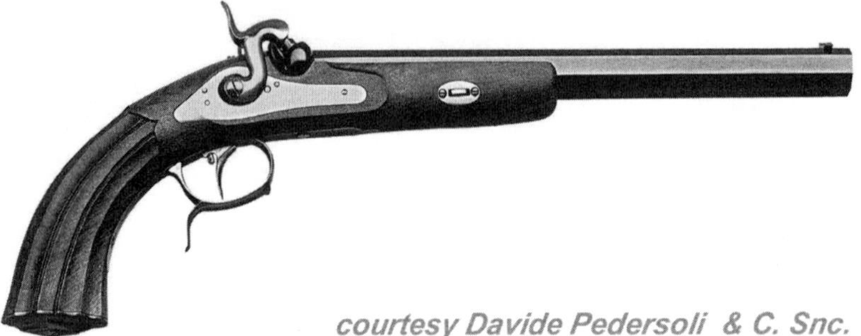

courtesy Davide Pedersoli & C. Snc.

MSR $1,375	$1,250	$1,085	$815	$675

Add $2,980 for deluxe engraved model with presentation case.

MORTIMER "SAW HANDLE" PISTOL — .36, .44 (smooth bore), or .45 (new 2003) cal. flintlock or perc., brown 10.07 in. octagon barrel, color case hardened hammer and lock, hand checkered walnut "saw grip." Authentic reproduction of the historic Mortimer target pistol. New 2001.

courtesy Davide Pedersoli & C. Snc.

MSR $886	$795	$720	$535	$445

Add $60 for flintlock model.
Add $55 for flintlock "Match" pistol. Imported 2002 only.
Add $30 for percussion "Match" pistol. Imported 2002 only.
Add $755 for Deluxe engraved, silver plated, flintlock model with gold barrel inlays by master engraver Renato Sanzogni.
Add $700 for percussion model. Imported 2002 only.

MOUNTAIN KENTUCKY PISTOL — .44 or .50 cal. flintlock or perc., 14.5 in. octagon barrel, color case hardened hammer and lock, brass furniture and trigger guard, hand checkered walnut stock, 2.25 lbs.

	$225	$190	$140	$100

Last MSR was $255.

Add $10 for flintlock.

GRADING - PPGS™	100%	98%	90%	80%

NAVY MOLL PISTOL — .45 cal. flintlock or perc., 10.25 octagon barrel (steel or brass), walnut stock, brass furniture and trigger guard, 15 in. OAL, 2.5 lbs.

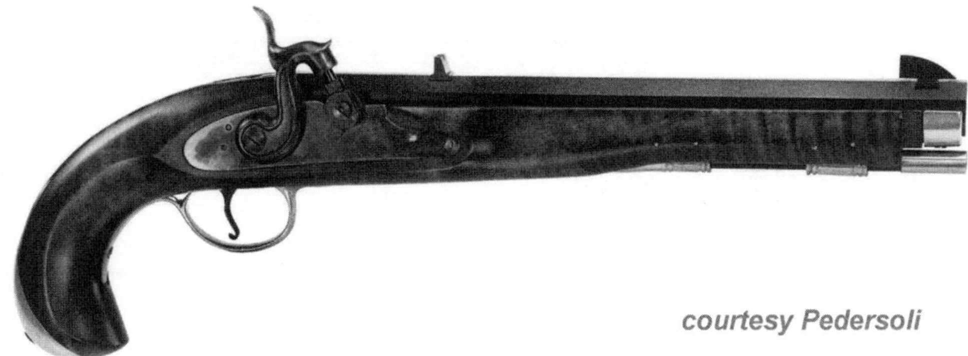

courtesy Pedersoli

MSR $461	$415	$355	$265	$215

Add $39 for flintlock.

PENNSYLVANIA PISTOL — .44 cal. flintlock or perc., 10 in. octagon barrel, brass furniture, locks left in white.

	$150	$130	$95	$65

QUEEN ANNE PISTOL — .50 cal. flintlock, 7.5 in. cannon shaped brass or white steel barrel (smooth bore), white steel hammer and lock, grotesque mask under buttstock, 2.25 lbs.

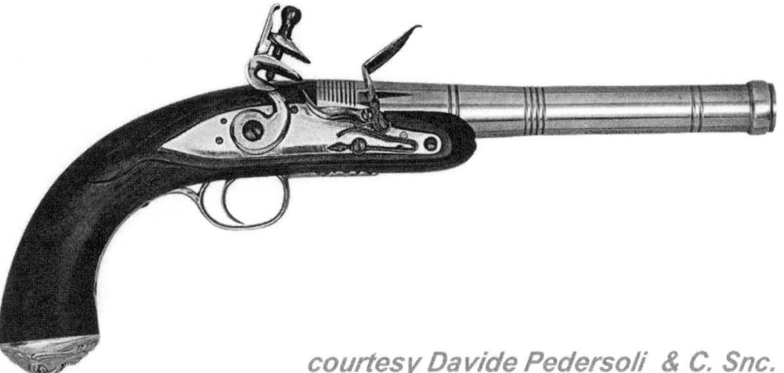

courtesy Davide Pedersoli & C. Snc.

MSR $361	$325	$290	$215	$180

Add $70 for silver plated or deluxe model.

Add $45 for Queen Anne "Gold" w/brass barrel, simulated ivory grip, and silver color lock new 2003.

RIDER DERRINGER — 4.3mm (.17) cal., perc., 2 .07 in. round barrel, reproduction of the Remington Rider single shot "Parlor Pistol", fires a 4.3mm (.17) cal. ball using a No. 11 percussion cap for propellant (no powder), white or color case hardened finish. Imported 2002 only. Reintroduced 2008.

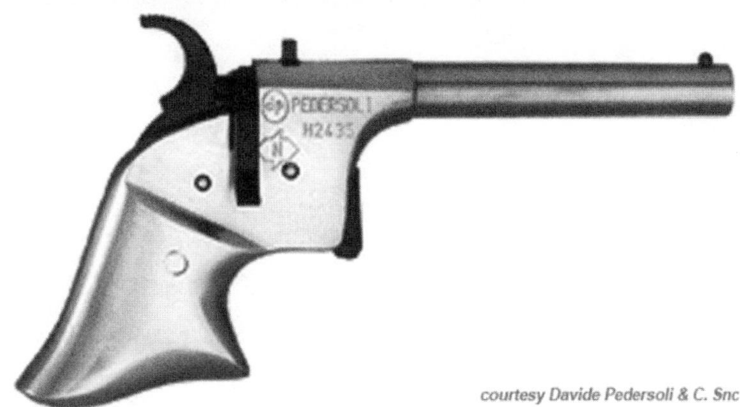

courtesy Davide Pedersoli & C. Snc

MSR $166	$145	$125	$95	$80

GRADING - PPGS™	100%	98%	90%	80%

SALOON PISTOL — .36 cal. perc., straight through ignition, 8 in. rounded barrel, color case hardened hammer and frame, walnut stock, 1.75 lbs.

courtesy Pedersoli

MSR $256	$230	$205	$155	$125

ZIMMER PISTOL — .36 cal. perc., 8 in. octagon blue barrel, white steel hammer and frame, fluted walnut stock.

courtesy Davide Pedersoli & C. Snc.

MSR $371	$340	$295	$225	$180

Add $45 for deluxe model.

REVOLVERS: PERCUSSION

Add approximately 25% for engraving, and 200% for extra luxury engraving.

PATERSON — .36 cal. perc., 5 shot, 9 in. octagon barrel, no loading lever, walnut stock, 2.5 lbs. Mfg. for Pedersoli. Disc. 1997.

	$300	$260	$200	$160

Last MSR was $310.

REMINGTON PATTERN — .44 cal. perc. 8 in. barrel, blue finish, brass triggerguard, 13.75 in. OAL, 2.75 lbs.

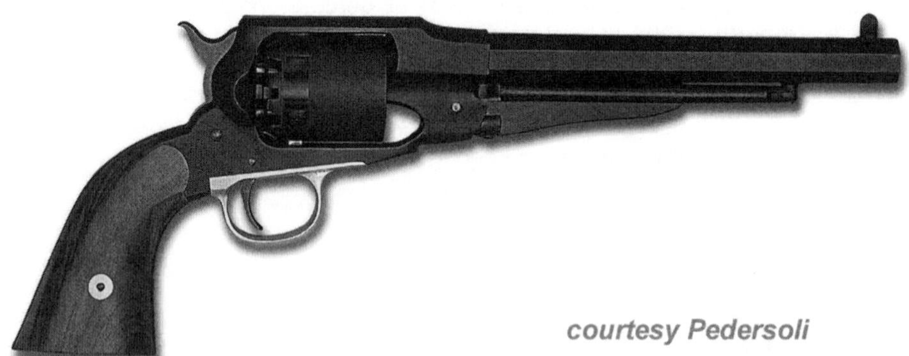

courtesy Pedersoli

MSR $788	$715	$640	$490	$405

ROGERS & SPENCER (FEINWERKBAU MFG.) — .44 cal. perc., 6 shot, 7.5 in. octagon barrel, walnut grips, 3 lbs. Disc. 1997.

	$1,600	$1,380	$1,100	$850

Last MSR was $1,850.

Manufactured by Feinwerkbau using the latest technology, molybdenum chrome steel frame, etc. Weight balanced for accurate firing.

GRADING - PPGS™	100%	98%	90%	80%

ROGERS & SPENCER — similar to the model above. Mfg. by Pedersoli.

courtesy Davide Pedersoli & C. Snc.

MSR $1,128	$1,075	$920	$650	$575

RIFLES: FLINTLOCK & PERCUSSION

1766 CHARLEVILLE MUSKET — .69 cal. flintlock or perc., 44.62 in. white steel barrel, hammer, lock, and trim, 9.75 lbs. New 2003.

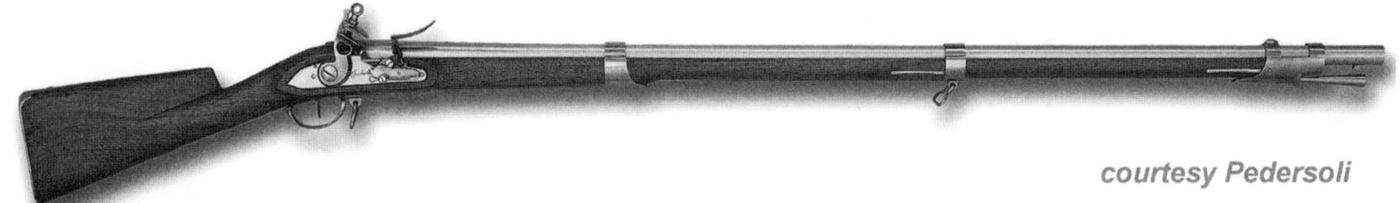

courtesy Pedersoli

MSR $1,350	$1,215	$1,085	$795	$675

1777 CHARLEVILLE MUSKET — .69 cal. flintlock or perc., 44.62 in. white steel barrel, hammer, lock, and trim, 9.75 lbs. Imported 1989-2002.

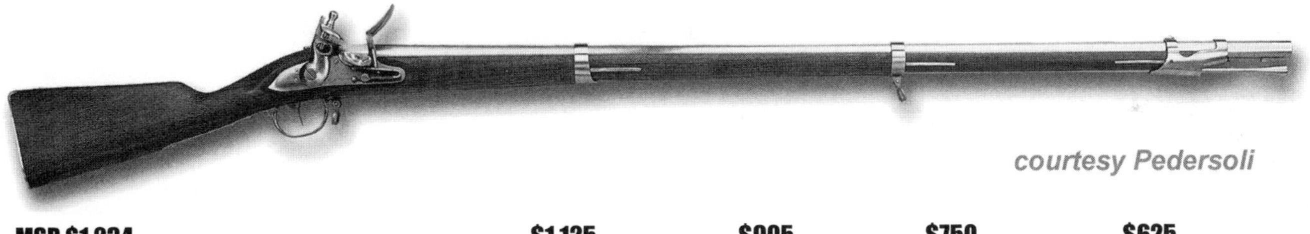

courtesy Pedersoli

MSR $1,234	$1,125	$995	$750	$625

Last MSR was $970.

1777 REVOLUTIONNAIRE — .69 cal. flintlock, 44 7/8 in. white steel barrel, hammer, lock, and trim. Predecessor of the 1777 Corrigé An IX. Issue arm of the infantry during the French Revolution., 9.69 lbs.

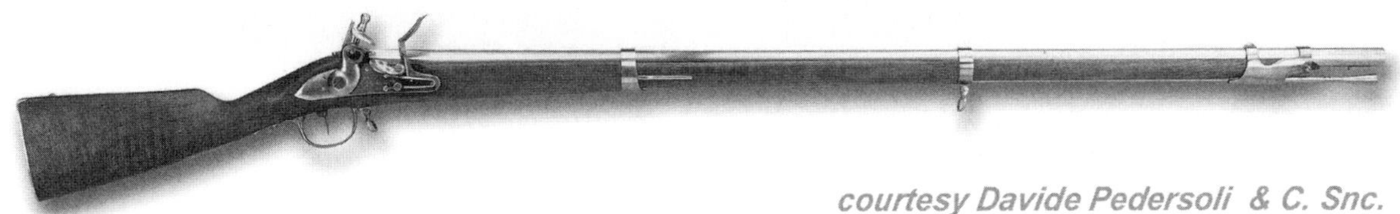

courtesy Davide Pedersoli & C. Snc.

MSR $1,234	$1,125	$995	$750	$625

1777 CORRIGÉ ANNO IX MUSKET — .69 cal. flintlock., 44 7/8 in. white steel barrel, hammer, lock, and trim. Exact copy of the 1777 Corrigé employed during the ninth year of the French Revolution, 9.69 lbs.

MSR $1,234	$1,125	$995	$750	$625

1777 CORRIGÉ ANNO IX DRAGOONS MUSKET — .69 cal. flintlock., 40.5 in. white steel barrel, hammer, lock, and trim., 9.47 lbs.

MSR $1,234	$1,125	$995	$750	$625

GRADING - PPGS™	100%	98%	90%	80%

1786 USSARO LIGHT CAVALRY MUSKET — .69 cal. flintlock, 27.6 in. blue steel barrel, bright hammer and lock, brass trim, 42 in. OAL, 7 lbs.

courtesy Pedersoli

MSR $1,006	$895	$750	$625	$500

1795 SPRINGFIELD — .69 cal. flintlock, 44.75 in. white steel round barrel, all white steel hardware, sling swivels, walnut stock 60 IN. oal, 10 lbs.

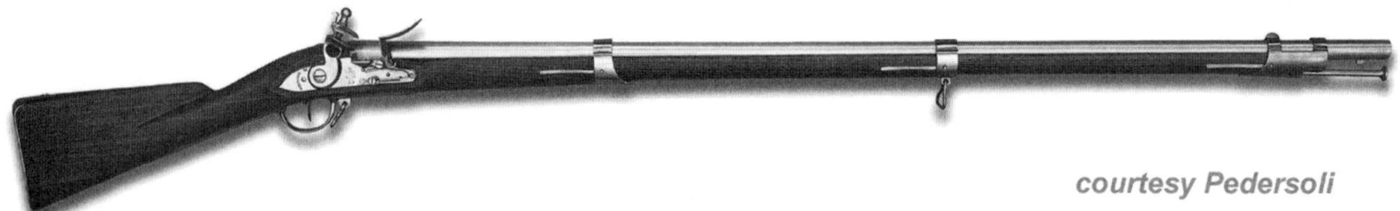

courtesy Pedersoli

MSR $1,274	$1,155	$1,035	$795	$675

1798 AUSTRIAN INFANTRY MUSKET — .69 cal. flintlock., 44 5/16 in. white steel barrel, hammer, lock, and trim. Exact copy of the 1798 based on the French 1777 French Corrigé but incorporating characteristics of Austrian design, 10 lbs.

MSR $1,274	$1,165	$1,045	$795	$655

1809 PRUSSIAN — .75 cal. flintlock, 41 1/8 in. round white steel barrel, white steel hammer and lock, brass furniture, walnut stock, lock marked "Potsdam", 9.25 lbs.

MSR $1,234	$1,125	$995	$750	$625

1816 MT. WICKHAM RIFLE — similar to 1777 Charleville musket, except has shorter barrel. Disc. 1997.

	$625	$550	$455	$335

Last MSR was $840.

1816 SPRINGFIELD/HARPERS FERRY — .69 cal. flintlock, 40 in. white steel round barrel, all white steel hardware, sling swivels, walnut stock, 9.75 lbs.

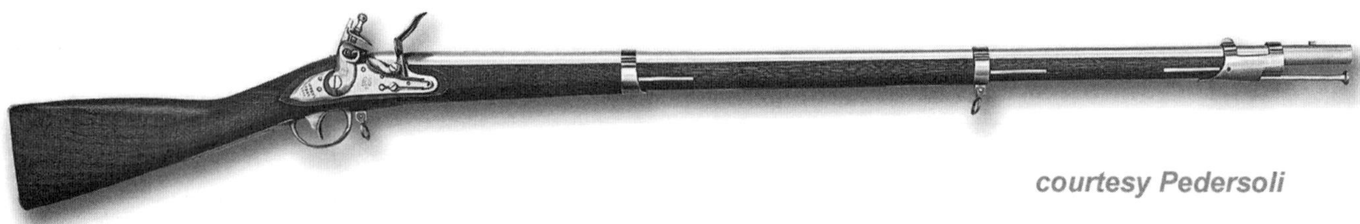

courtesy Pedersoli

MSR $1,234	$1,125	$995	$750	$625

1848 SPRINGFIELD — .69 cal. perc., 40 in. white steel barrel, white steel or color case hardened hammer and lock, white steel furniture, walnut full stock, lock stamped "U.S. Springfield." Accurate reproduction of the "Colt conversion style" from flintlock to percussion lock done by Harper's Ferry and Springfield arsenals between 1848-1860, 9.75 lbs.

MSR $1,234	$1,125	$995	$750	$625

1857 WÜRTTEMBERGISCHEN MAUSER — .54 cal. perc., 38.37 in. white steel barrel, adj. sights, color case hardened hammer and lock, walnut full stock, 9.47 lbs. New 2003.

MSR $1,350	$1,215	$1,085	$795	$675

GRADING - PPGS™	100%	98%	90%	80%

1859 SHARPS — .54 cal. perc., 22, 28, or 30 in. round barrel, color case hardened hammer, frame and buttplate, 7.75 lbs. average. Base price for Cavalry Carbine.

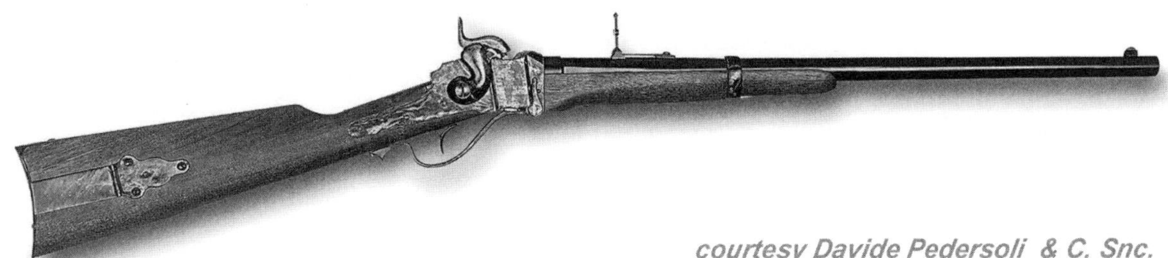

courtesy Davide Pedersoli & C. Snc.

MSR $995	$875	$750	$585	$420

Add $165 for 1859 Infantry model with single trigger, 30 in. barrel.
Add $240 for 1859 Infantry model with set triggers, 30 in. barrel.

1861 SPRINGFIELD RIFLE — .58 cal. perc., 40 in. white steel barrel, white steel or color case hardened hammer and lock, white steel furniture, walnut full stock, lock stamped "U.S. Springfield", 9.75 lbs. Disc. 1997.

MSR $1,200	$1,105	$975	$720	$605

Last MSR was $870.

1863 SHARPS SPORTING RIFLE — .45 or .54 cal. perc., 32 in. octagon barrel, color case hardened hammer, frame and buttplate, 10.15 lbs.

	$975	$850	$700	$565

Add $1,125 for engraved Sporting Rifle.
Add $1,700 for engraved and gold inlay Sporting Rifle.
Add $175 for Sporting Rifle with patch box.

ALAMO — .32, .45., or .50 cal. perc. or flintlock, 36 in. octagon barrel with double set triggers, white steel hammer and lock, brass furniture, patchbox engraved with scenes of the period, walnut stock, 6.5 lbs.

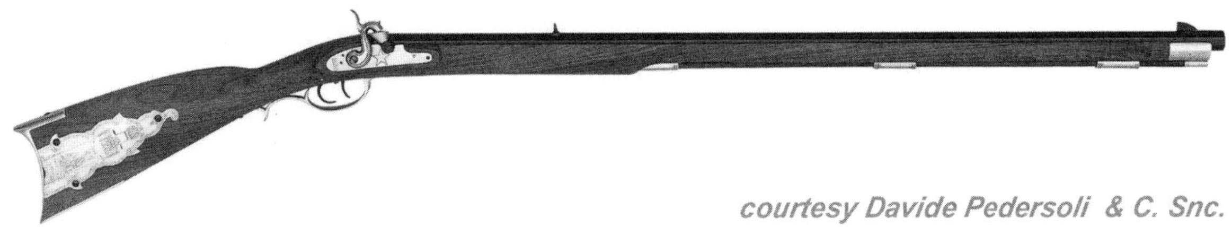

courtesy Davide Pedersoli & C. Snc.

MSR $665	$610	$535	$395	$325

Add $15 for flintlock.

BRISTLEN MORGES — .44 cal. perc., 29.5 in. octagon barrel, color case hardened hammer and lock, walnut half stock, palm rest professional target rifle, 16.75 lbs.

courtesy Pedersoli

MSR $2,491	$2,250	$1,995	$1,750	$1,500

Add $910 for deluxe version with engraved white steel hammer and lock.

GRADING - PPGS™	100%	98%	90%	80%

BROWN BESS MUSKET/CARBINE — .75 cal. flintlock, 31.5 (carbine) or 42 (musket) in. smooth bore barrel, white steel hammer and lock, brass furniture, three quarter stock (walnut), 8.75 lbs. (7.75 lbs. carbine).

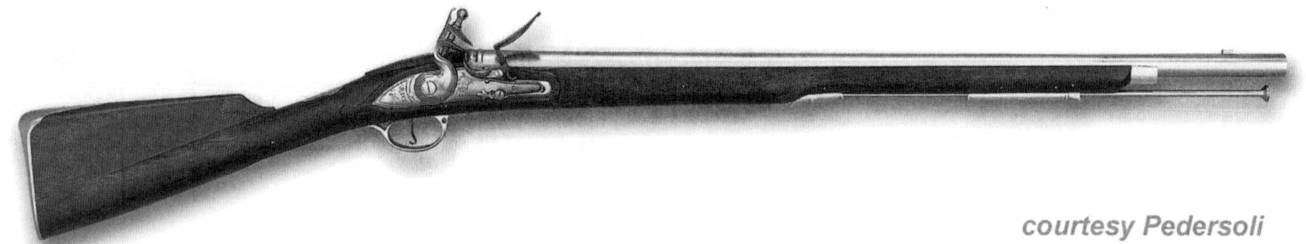

courtesy Pedersoli

MSR $1,105	$995	$850	$650	$550

Add $30 for Musket Model.

COUNTRY BOY — .32, .36, .45, or .50 cal. perc., 26 in. octagon barrel, color case hardened hammer and lock, unique mule ear hammer, blue furniture, adj. sights, walnut half stock, 5.5 lbs. Disc. 1994.

	$230	$200	$165	$115

Last MSR was $240.

COUNTRY HUNTER — .36, .45, and .50 cal. flintlock or perc., 28.25 in. octagon barrel, blue hardware, color case hardened hammer and lock, walnut half stock, 6 lbs.

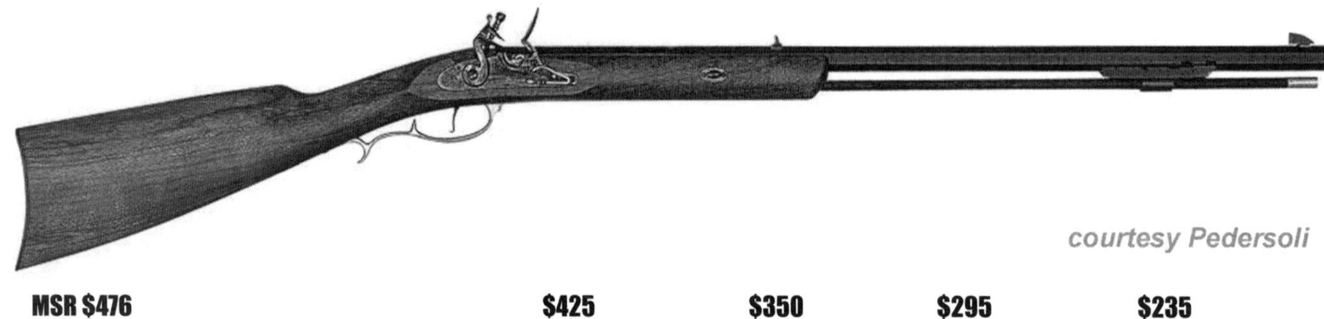

courtesy Pedersoli

MSR $476	$425	$350	$295	$235

Add $25 for flintlock.

DELUXE CUB RIFLE — .40 cal. flintlock or perc., 28 in. octagon barrel, color case hardened hammer, plate and triggers, brass trim and patch box, double set triggers.

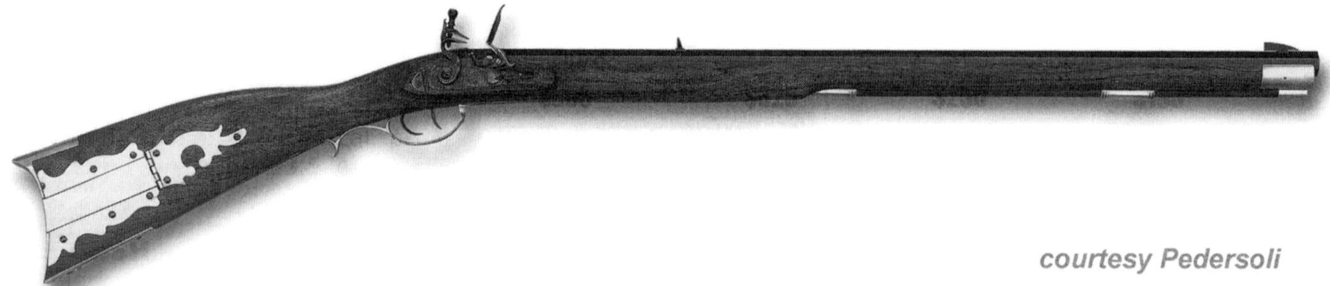

courtesy Pedersoli

	$345	$300	$240	$205

Last MSR was $385.

FREDERICKSBURG MUSKET — .75 cal. flintlock. Disc.

	$610	$555	$470	$350

FRONTIER RIFLE/CARBINE — .32, .36, .45, .50, or .54 cal. flintlock (.54 cal. carbine only) perc., 39 in. octagon brown barrel, color case hardened hammer and lock, brass furniture, walnut or bird's eye maple full stock, 7.75 lbs. (7.25 lbs. .45 and .50 cal.).

MSR $619	$545	$485	$425	$365

Add $15 for flintlock.
Subtract $35 for Carbine Model.
Add $450 for Grade 5 maple.
Add $575 for Grade 7 with bird's-eye maple stock and patchbox.

This model is also sold as the Blue Ridge Rifle by Cabela's with walnut stock.

GRADING - PPGS™	100%	98%	90%	80%

GIBBS RIFLE WITH TARGET SIGHTS — .451 .cal. perc. 35.25 in. octagonal to round barrel, color case hardened hammer and lock, European walnut stock with fine hand checkering on the wrist and forend, Creedmoor sight, adjustable spirit level tunnel front sight with 18 interchangable inserts. Reproduction of the 1865 target model produced by English gunsmith George Gibbs. Designed for 100 meter target shooting, 10.79 lbs. Imported 2002 only.

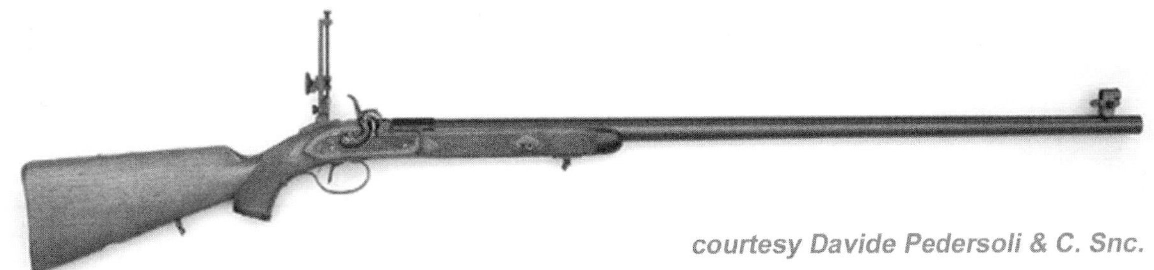

courtesy Davide Pedersoli & C. Snc.

MSR $1,575	$1,425	$1,275	$950	$775

Last MSR was $1,125.

HAWKEN RIFLE — .54 cal. perc., 32.25 in. octagon brown barrel, color case hardened hammer, lock, and furniture, double set triggers, walnut or bird's eye maple half stock, 8.75 lbs. Disc. 1994.

	$425	$350	$255	$220

Last MSR was $450.

Add $115 for bird's-eye maple stock.

JAGER HUNTER/TARGET RIFLE — .54 cal. flintlock or perc., 27.65 in. octagon brown barrel, color case hardened hammer, lock and trigger guard, waterproof pan, double set/phase triggers, 43.75 in. OAL, 8.25 lbs.

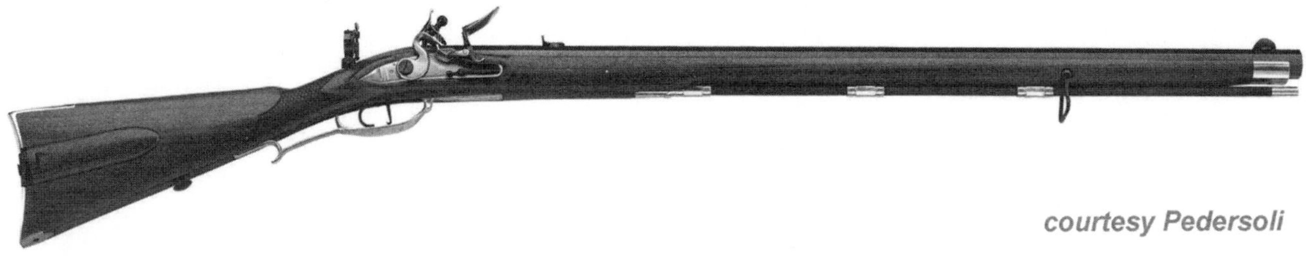

courtesy Pedersoli

MSR $1,085	$950	$850	$650	$525

Add $51 for flintlock.
Add $219 for .Target Model.

JAPANESE RIFLE — .492 cal., matchlock, 41.5 in. octagon brown barrel, brass matchlock and furniture, authentic reproduction of 16th century Tomonobu rifle.

	$1,040	$850	$695	$500

Last MSR was $1,155.

KENTUCKY — .32, .45, or .50 cal. perc. or flintlock, 35 in. barrel, color case hardened hammer and lock, brass furniture and patchbox, walnut full stock, 6.5 lbs.

courtesy Davide Pedersoli & C. Snc.

MSR $561	$495	$445	$350	$295

Add $20 for flintlock.
Add $425 for Silver Star model with engraved silver plated hammer, lock, trigger guard and patchbox, also has silver stars inlaid in stock.

GRADING - PPGS™	100%	98%	90%	80%

KODIAK EXPRESS SxS DOUBLE RIFLE — .50, .54, .58 .72 (new 2003) cal. or 12 ga. (slug) perc., 25.62 (.72 cal. or 12 ga.) or 28 in. SxS blue barrels, adj. sights, blue or silver finish hammers and locks, pistol or straight grip walnut stock, 9.25-10.79 lbs.

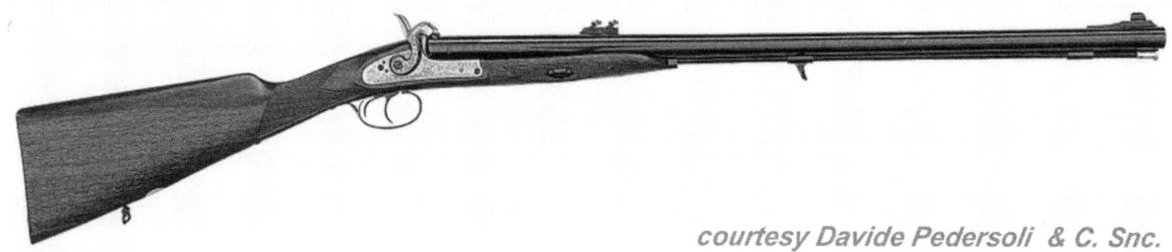

courtesy Davide Pedersoli & C. Snc.

MSR $1,115	$995	$885	$645	$550

Add $33 for .72 cal. New 2003.
Add $495-$574 for interchangeable shotgun barrels.

MORTIMER STANDARD/TARGET/VETTERLI/WHITWORTH RIFLE — .45, .541 or .54 (new 2003) cal. flintlock or perc., 36.25 in. octagon to round brown barrel, color case hardened hammer, lock and trigger guard, waterproof pan, 8.87 lbs.

courtesy Pedersoli

MSR $1,184	$1,025	$895	$695	$575

Add $50 for .54 cal. flintlock model.
Add $200 for .54 cal. flintlock Target Model.
Add $2,050 for deluxe engraved .54 cal. flintlock Target Model.
Add $1,850 for .45 cal. engraved "Vetterli" Model.
Add $100 for .451 cal. Whitworth Model (disc. 1994) reintroduced 2003.
Add $1,875 for engraved .451 cal. Mortimer Whitworth.

PENNSYLVANIA CHAMBERSBURG/DIXIE RIFLE — .32 or .45 cal. flintlock or perc., 41.5 in. barrel, brass trim, color case hardened or white steel lock, hammer, and double set trigger, walnut full stock, 8.25 lbs. New 1989.

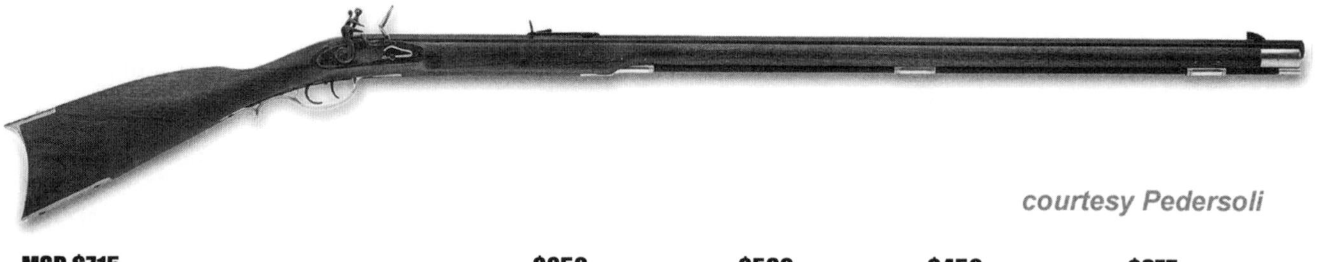

courtesy Pedersoli

MSR $715	$650	$580	$450	$375

Add $39 for flintlock.
Add $205 for Chambersburg Pennsylvania Rifle.
Add $129 for Pennsylvania Dixie Rifle.

CUB RIFLE — .32 or .45 cal. flintlock or perc., 41.5 in. barrel, brass trim, color case hardened or white steel lock, hammer, and double set trigger, walnut full stock, 8.25 lbs. New 1989.

MSR $720	$650	$575	$425	$350

Add $36 for flintlock.

PLAINSMAN RIFLE — .38, .45, or .50 cal. flintlock or perc., 37 in. octagon barrel, white steel hammer and lock, brass furniture and patch box, adj. sights and double set triggers, 6.5 lbs. Disc. 1994.

	$400	$340	$245	$205

Last MSR was $435.

Add $20 for flintlock.
Add $65 for engraved model.

GRADING - PPGS™	100%	98%	90%	80%

ROLLING BLOCK MUZZLELOADER RIFLE/CARBINE — .50 or .54 cal. perc., 22.25 (carbine) or 26.25 in. octagon barrel color case hardened hammer, block & buttplate, brass trigger guard. Based on Remington rolling block frame, adj. sights, 8.5 lbs. (7.75 lbs carbine).

	$350	$275	$225	$170

Last MSR was $300.

SANFTL — .45 cal. perc., 32.25 in. octagon white steel barrel, white steel hammer and lock, brass trigger guard and buttplate (copy of Tyrolese Target Rifle), walnut stock, 10 lbs. Mfg. 1994-2008.

	$1,495	$1,195	$850	$600

SCOUT RIFLE — .32, .45, or .50 cal. flintlock or perc., carbine version of Pennsylvania rifle listed above with 28.25 in. barrel, 6 lbs.

MSR $598	$525	$475	$325	$275

Add $36 for flintlock.

SWISS MATCH RIFLE — .45 cal. flintlock., 31 in. octagon brown barrel, 1:47 in. twist, target sights, hook buttplate, 48.5 in. OAL, 1.31 lbs.

MSR $2,559	$2,295	$2,075	$1,625	$1,395

SWIVEL BARREL RIFLE/SHOTGUN/COMBINATION O/U — 20 ga.x 20 ga. or 20 ga. x 50 cal., .50 x .50 cal., .54 x .54 cal. perc., 23.62 in. double (O/U) octagon barrel, blue barrel, hammer, lock and furniture (after 1st shot barrel simply needs to be rotated 180 degrees for second shot), checkered walnut stock, 9.5 lbs. (9.75 lbs. on .54 cal.). New 1994.

	$450	$365	$265	$225

Last MSR was $495.

TRYON RIFLE — .45, .50, or .54 cal. perc., 32.25 in. octagon barrel, color case hardened hammer, lock, patchbox, and furniture, double set triggers, walnut half stock, 9.5 lbs.

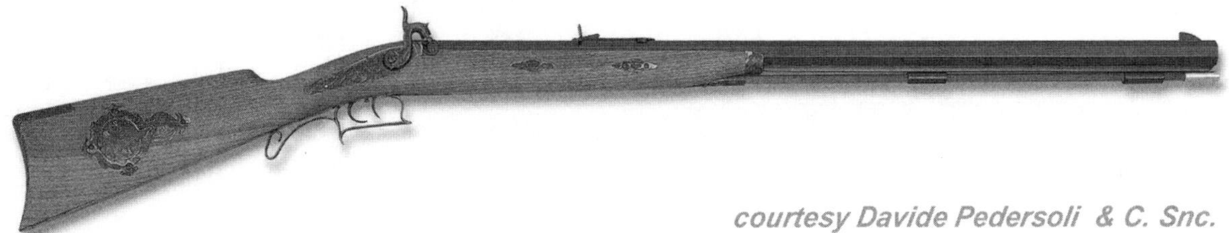

courtesy Davide Pedersoli & C. Snc.

MSR $869	$785	$695	$515	$425

Add $385 for maple stock.
Add $200 for engraved model.

TRYON CREEDMOOR — .451 cal. perc., 32.75 in. oct. barrel, all blue hardware, target version of the Tryon Rifle, double set triggers, walnut half stock, 9.5 lbs.

MSR $1,200	$1,085	$965	$725	$635

Add $79 for Tryon Creedmoor Match.

WAADTLANDER RIFLE — .45 cal. perc., 31 in. octagon brown barrel, target sights, 14.37 lbs. Target version of Bristlen Morges Model.

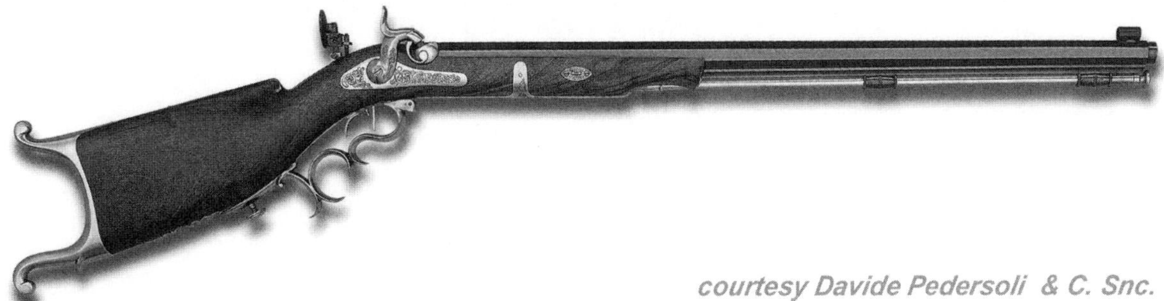

courtesy Davide Pedersoli & C. Snc.

MSR $2,509	$2,250	$1,995	$1,550	$1,350

Add $985 for deluxe engraved model with white steel hardware and silver inlays.

GRADING - PPGS™	100%	98%	90%	80%

RIFLES: IN-LINE IGNITION

BRUTUS MODEL 94 — .50 cal. perc. #209 primer ignition, 28 in. magnum chamber, matte finish round barrel, 1:24 in. twist, stainless steel breach plug, adj. fiber optic sights, automatic safety, black or Mossy Oak PG synthetic stock and forearm, sling swivel studs, recoil pad, fiber ramrod with brass starter jag, 44.5 in. OAL, 7.7 lbs. New 2007.

MSR $439	$395	$335	$265	$195

BRUTUS OVATION — .50 cal. perc. #209 primer ignition, 28 in. magnum chamber matte finish round barrel, 1:24 in. twist, stainless steel breach plug, adj. fiber optic sights, automatic safety, black, Mothwing or Mossy Oak molded synthetic stock and trigger guard, sling swivel studs, recoil pad, 44.5 in. OAL, 7.5 lbs. New 2007.

MSR $359	$325	$285	$215	$185

DENALI SUPER MAG — .50 cal. perc., #209 primer ignition, closed breech hinged frame w/fast opening trigger guard release, 28 in. matte blue round barrel, adj. Williams Fire Sights fiber optic sights, drilled and tapped for scope, color case hardened frame, blue or Mossy Oak Break-Up composite stock and forearm, recoil pad, sling swivel studs, fiber ramrod with brass starter jag and detachable handle, 14.5 in. OAL, 8.59 lbs.

MSR $555	$495	$445	$355	$275

GAMMA 901 — .50 or .54 cal. perc., 28 in. round barrel, all salt blue except bolt (hammer), automatic safety, walnut stock, 6.5 lbs. (.54 cal.) or 7.25 lbs. (.50 cal.).

	$335	$260	$200	$155

Last MSR was $370.

GAMMA 900 — similar to Gamma 901, except with sight upgrade, recoil pad, blue aluminum ramrod and better wood.

	$395	$335	$265	$205

Last MSR was $440.

GAMMA 9000 — similar to Gamma 900, except 32 in. barrel, sight upgrade, and checkered walnut stock.

	$475	$385	$280	$230

Last MSR was $530.

SHOTGUNS: PERCUSSION

CLASSIC TURKEY SxS — 12 ga., perc., 28 in. round double barrels, color case hardened lock, stainless steel nipple, recoil pad, 9 lbs.

	$425	$350	$255	$220

KODIAK SxS SHOTGUN/EXPRESS/COMBO — 12 ga. x .50, or .58 cal., or .50 x .50, .54 x .54, and .58 x .58 cal. perc., 28 in. double barrels, engraved white steel hammer and lock, blue furniture, checkered walnut .5 stock, 9 lbs.

MSR $1,115	$995	$875	$725	$595

Add $574 for rifle or comb. barrels (extra set).

SxS MODEL — 10, 12, or 20 ga., perc., 28 in. barrels, chrome bore, color case hardened hammer and lock, (engraved white steel on 10 ga.), checkered walnut stock, double triggers, 7.5 lbs. Deluxe hand engraved models available on special order.

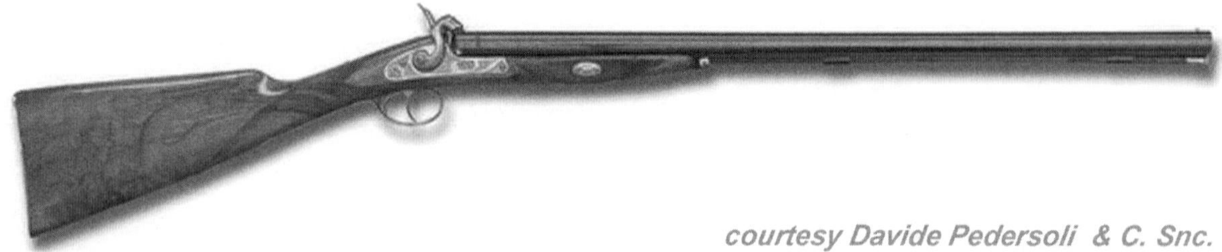

courtesy Davide Pedersoli & C. Snc.

MSR $809	$725	$650	$495	$415

Add $70 for 10 ga.
Add $265 for extra 12 ga. barrels, and $290 for extra 10 ga. barrels.
Add $1,070 for engraved model.
Add $2,500 for extra deluxe engraved model with gold inlays.
Add $4,570 for super deluxe engraved model with gold inlays.

GRADING - PPGS™	100%	98%	90%	80%

MORTIMER SHOTGUN — 12 ga., flintlock or perc., version of Mortimer Rifle.

MSR $1,034	$935	$835	$650	$550

Add $60 for flintlock.
Add $1,795 for deluxe engraving with gold inlays.

INDIAN TRADE MUSKET — 12 ga. flintlock, 36.25 in. octagonal to round barrel, large trigger guard and trigger (for gloved hand). A faithful reproduction of the late 18th century fowler used by well known trade companies such as Hudson Bay Co., and American Fur Co., and produced with period fit and finish, including engraved brass snake decoration on the left side of the stock, 6.60 lbs. Imported 2002 only.

MSR $876	$795	$715	$550	$465

PEIFER RIFLE CO.

Previous manufacturer located in Nokomis, IL. Consumer direct sales.

RIFLES: PERCUSSION

TS-93 RIFLE — .45 or .50 cal. perc., uses #209 primer instead of percussion cap for ignition, 24 in. blue chrom-moly or stainless steel barrel, cocking action provided by moving trigger guard to right or left, primer holder rotates 90 degrees for added safety, tang safety, synthetic stock with recoil pad, 7 lbs. Disc. 2006.

	$625	$500	$400	$300

Last MSR was $730.

Add $50 for wood look synthetic stock.
Add $50 for stainless steel.

PIETTA, F.LLI

Current manufacturer established in 1960, and located in Brescia, Italy. Distributor sales only.

Fratelli Pietta is one of Italy's premier black powder makers utilizing modern, high-tech facilities. Quality ranges from very good to excellent, depending upon the model. Pietta is the only manufacturer of the LeMat, Starr, and John Henry Dance & Bros. percussion revolvers, all of which have exceptional construction, fit, and finish. Pietta models can be special ordered with period engraving (Young, Nimschke, Helfricht-style scrollwork) handcrafted in Gardone and Brescia Italy, through Navy Arms, Taylor's & Co, Dixie Gun Works, Cabela's, Traditions Inc., & E.M.F., Inc.

Well-known and appreciated in international circles for the quality and the reliability of their products, the arms factory F.lli Pietta plays an important part in the world production of replicas. The company history began in 1960 with the production of hunting guns. During 1964, following a large increase in demand for American Civil War arms reproductions, the company began making muzzleloading revolvers. The first model, the Colt 1851 Navy, enjoyed immediate success, and was followed by some other popular variations. Other models quickly followed, including the Colt 1860 Army, the 1858 Remington New Model Army, the Spiller & Burr, the LeMat, which was awarded the prestigious prize in 1985 as "the best gun of the year" by the American National Association of Federally Licensed Firearms Dealers, and finally the Starr.

Each piece is produced with exacting quality control standards in order to guarantee parts interchangeability. Skilled and highly specialized personnel perform fitting, polishing, and assembly by hand. As a result, Pietta has achieved both success and industry respect worldwide.

Please refer to *Colt Blackpowder Reproductions & Replicas - A Collector's & Shooter's Guide*for color pictures of the Pietta makes and models listed below. Pietta revolvers can be found on pages 43-44, 46-50, 69-70, and 102.

Note that MSR prices are generally not shown for revolvers that have been in production for many years, as their prices vary with different distributors. F.lli Pietta arms are sold by Navy Arms, Taylor's & Co., Dixie Gun Works, Cabela's, Traditions Inc., and E.M.F., Inc., as well as in retail gun stores. Please refer to individual listings for the latest retail pricing.

REVOLVERS: PERCUSSION

1851 NAVY — .36 or .44 cal. perc., 7.5 in. octagon barrel, many styles, 6 shot engraved cylinder, 2 lbs. 12 oz.

	$150	$125	$95	$65

Add $30 for steel frame.

Prices are similar for Sheriff's Model & Confederate Model with round barrel.

1860 ARMY — .44 cal. perc., 7.5 in. barrel, 6 shot rebated cylinder, color case hardened or brass frame, hammer and loading lever, steel backstrap and brass trigger guard, 2 lbs. 9 oz.

	$200	$160	$120	$85

GRADING - PPGS™	100%	98%	90%	80%

1861 NAVY — .36 or .44 (disc.) cal. perc., 7.5 in. barrel, brass backstrap and trigger guard, color case hardened frame, hammer, and loading lever, 2 lbs. 8 oz.

	$150	$125	$95	$65

1862 POLICE — .36 cal. perc., 5.5 in. round to octagon barrel, color case hardened hammer, frame, and loading lever, brass trim, 1 lb. 10 oz.

	$165	$135	$100	$70

COLT PATERSON — .36 cal. perc., 7.5 in. octagon barrel, standard "hidden trigger" design, blue steel hardware, no loading lever, 2 lbs. 9 oz.

	$350	$275	$225	$170

Add $160 for engraved version.

LEMAT REVOLVER — .44 cal. perc., 9 shot cylinder plus 1 shot center barrel (maximum fire power for its day), 7.62 in. octagon barrel, blue steel frame, 3 lbs. 7 oz.

	$650	$520	$415	$310

Add $375 for engraved Beauregard model.
Add $175 for 18th Georgia engraved model.
Add $1,145 for fully engraved models in the white or blue. Special order only.

1858 REMINGTON (BRASS FRAME) — .36 or .44 cal. perc., 8 or 12 (Buffalo Model) in. octagon barrel, 6 shot, brass frame and trigger guard.

	$115	$100	$60	$50

Add $20 for Buffalo Model with 12 in. barrel.

1858 REMINGTON (STEEL FRAME) — similar to 1858 Remington, except has steel frame with brass backstrap and trigger guard.

	$135	$110	$75	$50

Add $70 for stainless steel.
Add $30 for Target Model.
Add $125 for stainless steel Buffalo model with 12 in. barrel.

SPILLER & BURR — .36 cal. perc., 7.5 in. barrel, brass frame, color case hardened hammer and loading lever, 2 lbs. 8 oz.

	$150	$125	$95	$65

STARR DOUBLE/SINGLE ACTION — .44 cal. perc., 6 in. round barrel, 6-shot, two-piece blue steel frame. Available in original double action version, and later single action model with 8 in. barrel. Available through Taylor's & Co., Traditions, Cabela's, and Navy Arms. Available in nickel finish 2002.

	$300	$225	$160	$110

1861 J.H. DANCE NAVY — .36 cal. perc., 7.5 in. round barrel, 6 shot smooth cylinder, color case hardened frame without recoil shield, brass backstrap and squareback trigger guard, 2 lbs. 12 oz.

	$210	$165	$125	$90

This model is available through Dixie Gun Works.

RIFLES: PERCUSSION

SMITH ARTILLERY/CAVALRY CARBINE — .54 cal. perc., 20.5 in. octagon tapering to round barrel, color case hardened hammer and receiver.

	$550	$425	$320	$260

SHOTGUNS: PERCUSSION

FOWLER SxS — 10 or 12 ga., 28 in. barrels, color case hardened hammer and lock, 7 lbs. 6 oz.

	$450	$365	$265	$225

Add $25 for 10 ga.

PRAIRIE RIVER ARMS

Previous manufacturer located in Princeton, IL. Consumer direct and dealer sales.

Prairie River Arms has developed a new percussion ignition system that contains the firing mechanism entirely within the stock. Advantages include more weather resistance, protection from percussion cap fragmentation, and better balance.

GRADING - PPGS™	100%	98%	90%	80%

RIFLES: PERCUSSION

BULLPUP — .50 or .54 cal. perc., 28 in round barrel (alloy or stainless steel), unique Bullpup design, hardwood or synthetic all weather thumbhole stock, 7.5 lbs.

	$340	$275	$225	$170

Last MSR was $375.

Add $50 for stainless steel.
Add $50 for carry handle and rear sight assembly.
Add $15 for all weather synthetic stock.

CLASSIC — .50 or .54 cal. perc., 28 in. round barrel (alloy or stainless), hardwood or synthetic all weather stock.

	$350	$275	$225	$170

Last MSR was $375.

Add $15 for all weather stock.
Add $50 for stainless steel.

NOTES

GRADING - PPGS™	100%	98%	90%	80%

R SECTION

REMINGTON ARMS CO., INC.

Current manufacturer and trademark established in 1816, with factories currently located in Ilion, NY, and Mayfield, KY.

Founded by E. Remington II and originally located in Litchfield, Herkimer County, NY, circa 1816-1828. Remington moved to Ilion, NY, in 1828, where they continue to manufacture a wide variety of products. Corporate offices were moved to Madison, NC, in 1996. Distributor and dealer sales.

For more information and current pricing on both new and used Remington Arms Co., Inc. firearms, please refer to the *Blue Book of Gun Values* by S.P. Fjestad (now online also).

RIFLES: FLINTLOCK

1816 COMMEMORATIVE FLINTLOCK RIFLE — .50 cal. Ketland-style flintlock, 39 in. oct. blue barrel, 1:66 in. twist, extra fancy curly maple stock, polished brass buttplate, toe and nose cap, and hand engraved patch box, manufactured by an outside custom gunsmith for Remington, special ordered through the Remington Custom Shop, 56 in. OAL, and approx. 8 lbs. Mfg. circa 1995.

	100%	98%	90%	80%
	$1,795	$1,250	N/A	N/A

Last MSR was $1,899.

RIFLES: IN-LINE IGNITION

GENESIS ML — .50 cal., #209 primer ignition, Xylan coated (new 2007) TorchCam rotating action, ambidextrous hammer spur, crossbolt safety, 28 in. blue bbl. w/bullet guiding muzzle 1:28 in. twist, adj. Williams fiber optic sights, drilled and tapped, black synthetic PG stock w/recoil pad, sling swivel studs, 43 in. OAL, 7.8 lbs. New 2006.

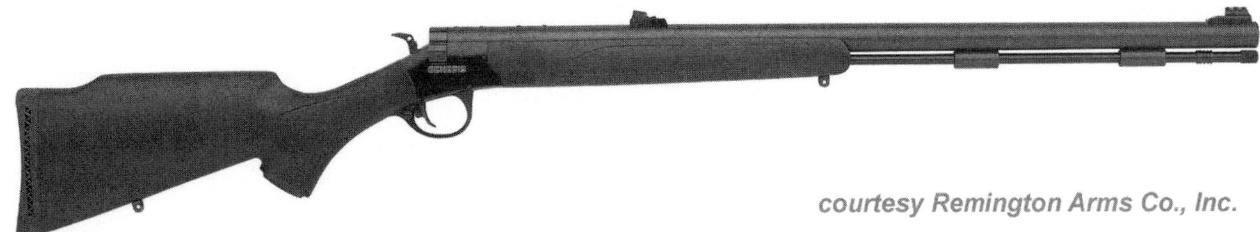

courtesy Remington Arms Co., Inc.

MSR	100%	98%	90%	80%
MSR $237	$210	$160	$130	$95

GENESIS ML CAMO — .50 cal., #209 primer ignition, Xylan coated (new 2007) TorchCam rotating action, ambidextrous hammer spur, crossbolt safety, 28 in. blue bbl. w/bullet guiding muzzle, 1:28 in. twist, adj. Williams fiber optic sights, drilled and tapped, Mossy Oak New Break-Up camo, stock w/recoil pad, sling swivel studs, 43 in. OAL, 7.8 lbs. New 2006.

courtesy Remington Arms Co., Inc.

MSR	100%	98%	90%	80%
MSR $349	$335	$255	$205	$155

GENESIS ML FULL CAMO — .50 cal., #209 primer ignition, Xylan coated (new 2007) TorchCam rotating action, ambidextrous hammer spur, crossbolt safety, 28 in. Mossy Oak New Break-Up camo bbl. w/bullet guiding muzzle, 1:28 in. twist, adj. Williams fiber optic sights, drilled and tapped, Mossy Oak New Break-Up camo, stock w/recoil pad, sling swivel studs, 43 in. OAL, 7.8 lbs. New 2006.

courtesy Remington Arms Co., Inc.

MSR	100%	98%	90%	80%
MSR $405	$370	$335	$255	$205

GRADING - PPGS™	100%	98%	90%	80%

GENESIS MLS CAMO — .50 cal., #209 primer ignition, TorchCam rotating action, ambidextrous hammer spur, crossbolt safety, 28 in. stainless bbl. w/bullet guiding muzzle, 1:28 in. twist, adj. Williams fiber optic sights, drilled and tapped, Mossy Oak New Break-Up camo, stock w/recoil pad, sling swivel studs, 43 in. OAL, 7.8 lbs. Mfg. 2006 only.

courtesy Remington Arms Co., Inc.

MSR $342	$335	$255	$205	$155

Last MSR was $391.

GENESIS ML SF BUCKMASTERS EDITION — .50 cal., #209 primer ignition, Xylan coated TorchCam rotating action, ambidextrous hammer spur, crossbolt safety, 28 in. stainless fluted bbl. w/bullet guiding muzzle, 1:28 in. twist, adj. Williams fiber optic sights, drilled and tapped, synthetic Realtree Hardwoods HD camo stock w/recoil pad and laser-engraved Buckmasters Logo on left-hand receiver panel, sling swivel studs, 43 in. OAL, 7.8 lbs. New 2007.

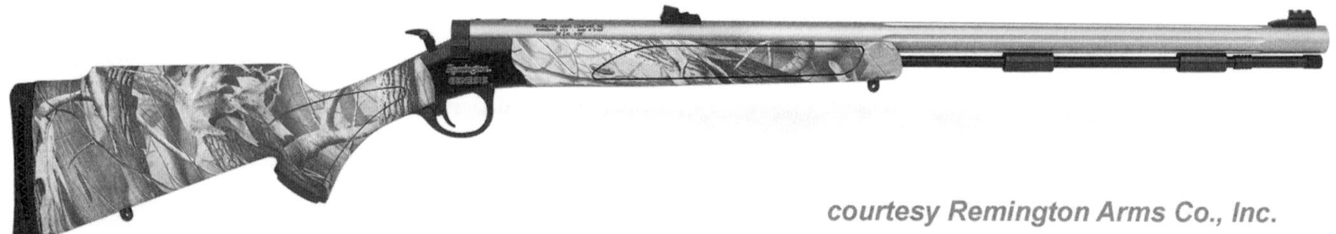

courtesy Remington Arms Co., Inc.

MSR $363	$345	$315	$245	$165

GENESIS ML SF CAMO THUMBHOLE — .50 cal., #209 primer ignition, Xylan coated (new 2007) TorchCam rotating action, ambidextrous hammer spur, crossbolt safety, 28 in. stainless bbl. w/bullet guiding muzzle and fluted, 1:28 in. twist, adj. Williams fiber optic sights, drilled and tapped, Mossy Oak New Break-Up camo thumbhole stock w/recoil pad, sling swivel studs, 43 in. OAL, 7.5 lbs. New 2006.

MSR $405	$370	$335	$255	$205

GENESIS ML SF LAMINATE THUMBHOLE — .50 cal., #209 primer ignition, Xylan coated (new 2007) TorchCam rotating action, ambidextrous hammer spur, crossbolt safety, 28 in. stainless fluted bbl. w/bullet guiding muzzle and fluted, 1:28 in. twist, adj. Williams fiber optic sights, drilled and tapped, grey laminate thumbhole stock w/recoil pad, sling swivel studs, 43 in. OAL, 8 lbs. New 2006.

MSR $538	$460	$415	$365	$285

GENESIS ML SF SYNTHETIC THUMBHOLE — .50 cal., #209 primer ignition, Xylan coated (new 2007) TorchCam rotating action, ambidextrous hammer spur, crossbolt safety, 28 in. stainless bbl. w/bullet guiding muzzle and fluted, 1:28 in. twist, adj. Williams fiber optic sights, drilled and tapped, synthetic black thumbhole stock w/recoil pad, sling swivel studs, 43 in. OAL, 7.5 lbs. New 2006.

courtesy Remington Arms Co., Inc.

MSR $349	$335	$255	$205	$155

GENESIS MLS OVERMOLD — .50 cal., #209 primer ignition, Xylan coated (new 2007) TorchCam rotating action, ambidextrous hammer spur, crossbolt safety, 28 in. stainless bbl. w/ bullet guiding muzzle, 1:28 in. twist, adj. Williams fiber optic sights, drilled and tapped, synthetic black Overmold PG stock w/recoil pad, sling swivel studs, 43 in. OAL, 7.8 lbs. New 2006.

MSR $307	$265	$235	$165	$135

GRADING - PPGS™	100%	98%	90%	80%

MODEL 700 ML — .50 or .54 (disc. 2001) cal. perc., 3-way ignition system for #209 primer, musket or No. 11 percussion caps (new 2002) ignition, short throw bolt action, 24 in. carbon steel barrel, satin blue finish, black or Mossy Oak Break-Up camo (1999-2002) synthetic stock with recoil pad, 42.5 in. OAL, 7.75 lbs. Mfg. 1996-2004.

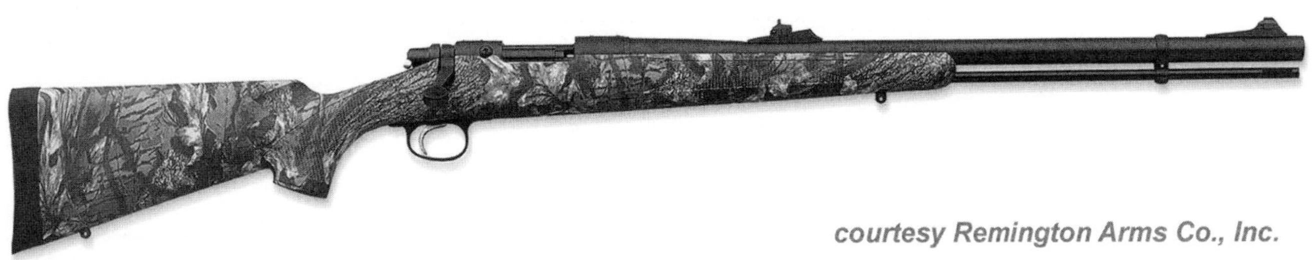

courtesy Remington Arms Co., Inc.

	$375	$300	$235	$190

Last MSR was $415.

Add 15% for camo finish stock.

MODEL 700 MLS MAGNUM — .45 or .50 cal. perc. 3-way ignition system for #209 primer, musket or No. 11 percussion caps ignition, short throw bolt action, 26 in. stainless steel barrel, satin finish, black or Mossy Oak Break-Up camo synthetic stock with recoil pad, 44.5 in. OAL, 7.75 lbs. Mfg. 2002-04.

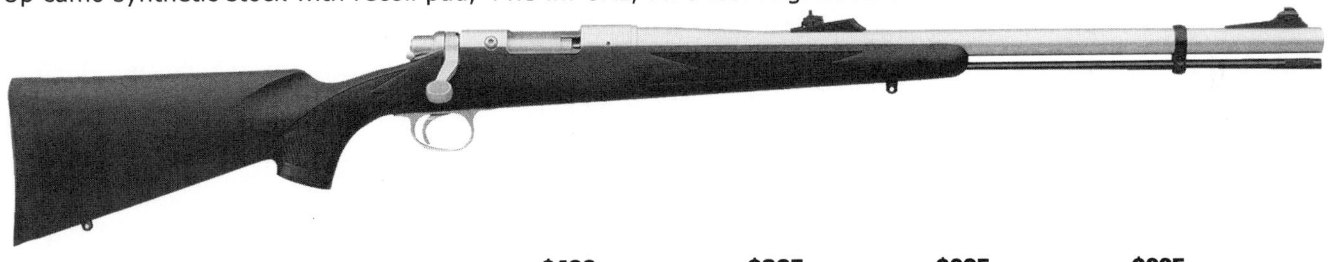

	$469	$365	$265	$225

Last MSR was $533.

Add $36 for Mossy Oak Break-Up camo stock.

MODEL 700 ML/MLS CUSTOM — .50 cal. perc., similar to 700 ML/MLS, except has grey laminated thumbhole stock. Mfg. 2000-01.

* ***Model 700 ML Custom***

	$700	$565	$440	$325

Last MSR was $799.

* ***Model 700 MLS Custom***

	$775	$630	$495	$365

Last MSR was $896.

RESTORATION FIREARMS

Current manufacturer of custom Hawken rifles and percussion pistols located in Folsom, CA.

PISTOLS: PERCUSSION

PLAINS PERCUSSION PISTOL — .50 or .54 cal. perc., plains pistol, draw filed, polished and rust blued octagon barrel, lathe turned brass ramrod, steel machine screws, hand rubbed oil finished stock with brass endcap.

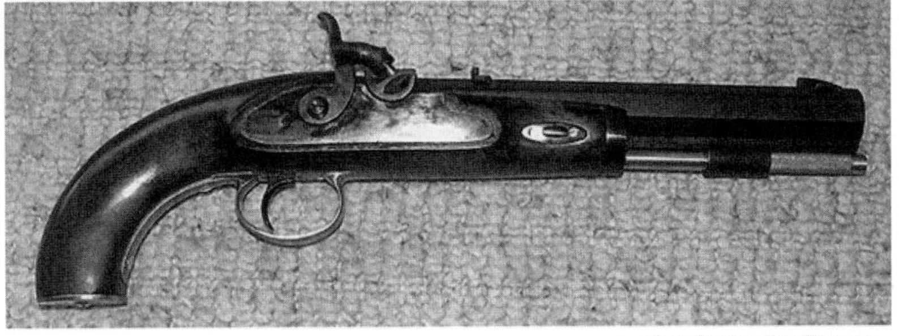

courtesy Restoration Firearms

MSR $395	$395	$325	$250	$175

GRADING - PPGS™	100%	98%	90%	80%

RIFLES: PERCUSSION

BLACK BEAUTY — .50 or .54 cal., 32 in. rust blued oct. barrel, 1:48 in. twist, tang mounted peep sight, Carbona heat blued lock and hammer, hardware, brushed brass furniture, hand rubbed and oil finished high grade European walnut stock, solid brass .375 in. lathe turned ramrod.

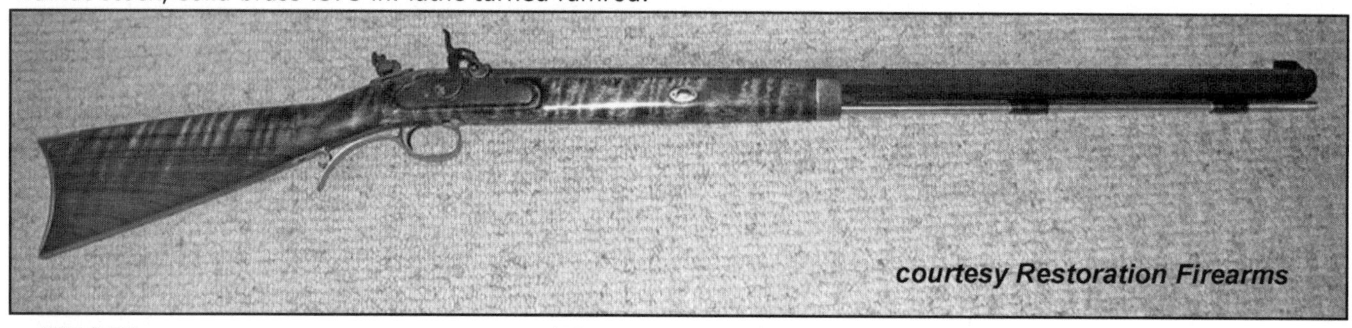
courtesy Restoration Firearms

MSR $795	$795	$650	$450	$250

This is a hybrid model that uses the Lyman Trade rifle as a basis for a custom gun.

CUSTOM HAWKEN RIFLE — .45 .50 .54 or .58 cal., 1 in. x 36 in. octagon Green Mountain rust blued barrel, 1:70 in. twist, Carbona heat blued hardware, L & R lock, double set triggers, AAA grade walnut or maple stock.

MSR $1,795	$1,795	$1,495	$1,250	$950

CUSTOM LYMAN GREAT PLAINS RIFLE — .50 or .54 cal., 1 in. x 32 in. draw filed, polished and rust blued oct. barrel, 1:60 in. twist, Carbona heat blued hardware, L & R lock, double set triggers, hand rubbed oil finished high grade French red or dark walnut or stock.

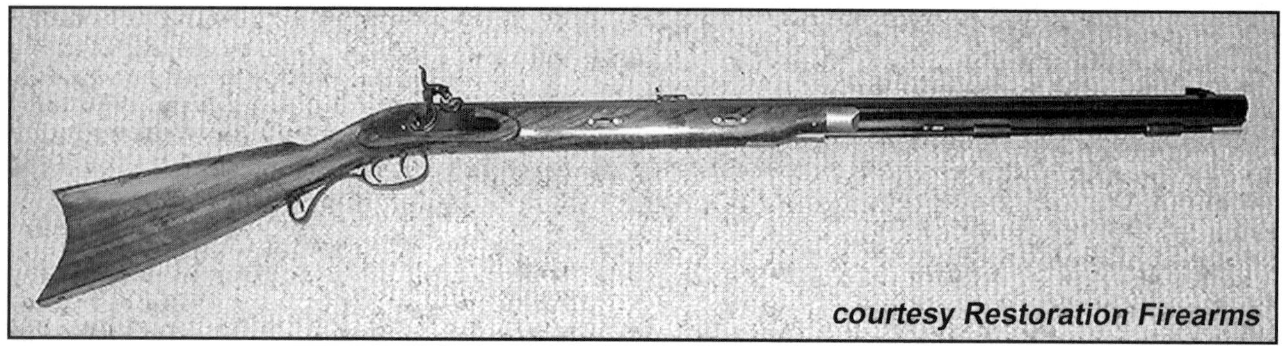
courtesy Restoration Firearms

MSR $795	$795	$650	$450	$250

This is a hybrid model that uses the Lyman Great Plains rifle as a basis for a custom gun.

CUSTOM THOMPSON-CENTER HAWKEN — .50 cal., 28 in. T/C QLA system blued oct. barrel, 1:48 in. twist, adj. rear and bead front sights, blued lock and hammer, brushed brass furniture, hand rubbed and oil finished walnut stock, solid brass .375 in. lathe turned ramrod, 45.25 OAL, approx. 8.5 lbs.

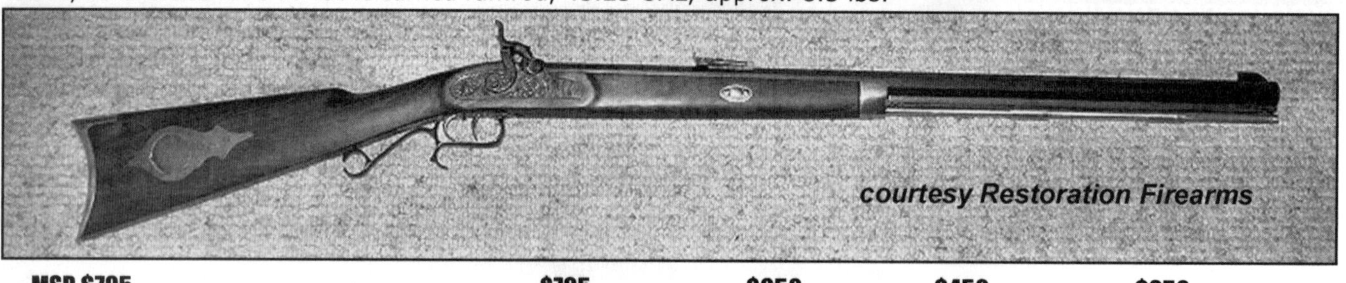
courtesy Restoration Firearms

MSR $795	$795	$650	$450	$250

This is a custom made Hawken hybrid model that uses the Thompson/Center rifle as a basis for a custom gun.

GRADING - PPGS™	100%	98%	90%	80%

CUSTOM THOMPSON-CENTER RENEGADE BIG BORE 58 — .58 cal., 28 in. T/C QLA system blued oct. barrel, 1:48 in. twist, adj. rear and bead front sights, blued lock and hammer, double set triggers, brushed brass furniture, hand rubbed and oil finished walnut stock, solid brass .375 in. lathe turned ramrod, 45.25 OAL, approx. 8.5 lbs.

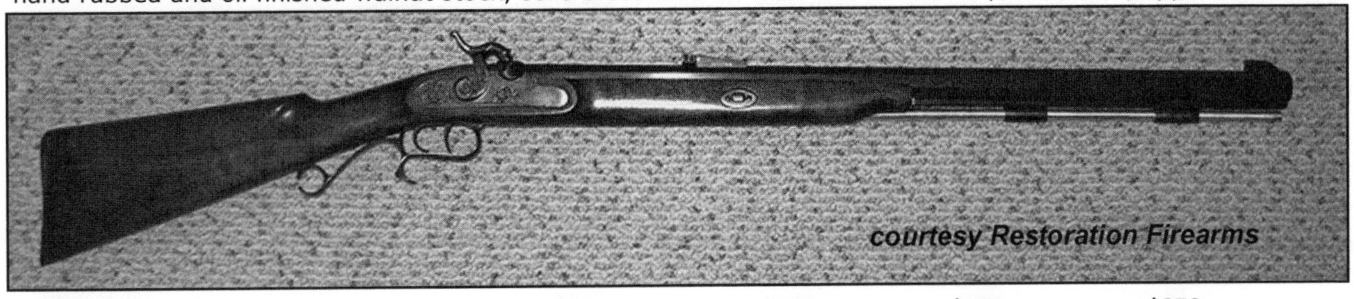
courtesy Restoration Firearms

MSR $795	$795	$650	$450	$250

This is a custom made Hawken hybrid model that uses the Thompson/Center rifle as a basis for a custom gun.

HIGH SIERRA — .50 or .54 cal., 1 in. x 32 in. draw filed, polished and rust blued oct. barrel, 1:60 in. twist, Carbona heat blued hardware, L & R lock, double set triggers, hand rubbed oil finished high grade French red or dark walnut or stock.

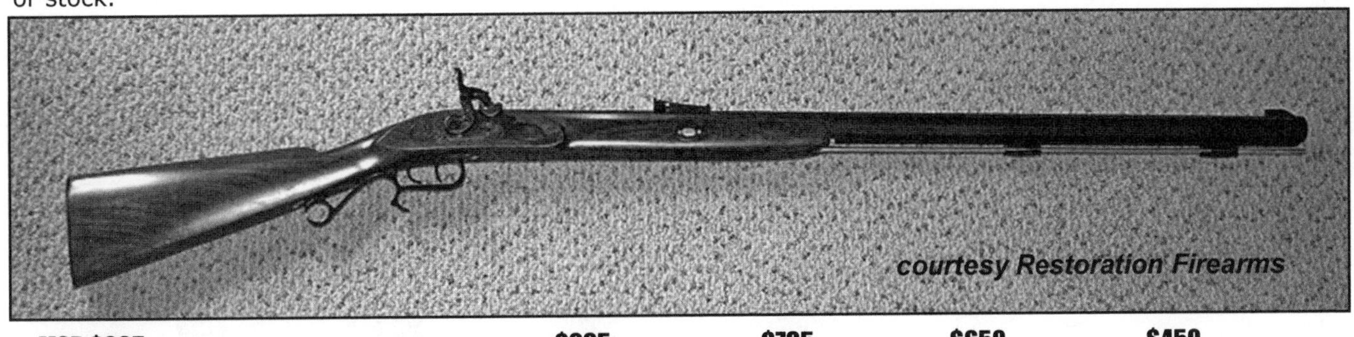
courtesy Restoration Firearms

MSR $995	$995	$795	$650	$450

This rifle features Thompson-Center lock and triggers.

RICHLAND ARMS

Previous importer/distributor located in Blissfield, MI.

PISTOLS: PERCUSSION

ANDREW TARGET — .32, .36 or .45 cal. perc., 10 in. octagon barrel, white steel hammer, barrel, frame, and sights, brass trigger guard, adj. trigger and sights, blue and engraved, 2 lbs. 10 oz. Disc. 1994.

	$200	$160	$120	$85

Last MSR was $150.

Add $55 for deluxe grade.

REVOLVERS: PERCUSSION

WALKER — .44 cal. perc., 9 in. round barrel, color case hardened hammer, frame, trigger and loading lever, engraved cylinder, brass trigger guard, 73 oz. Disc. 1994.

	$275	$200	$145	$100

Last MSR was $185.

3rd MODEL DRAGOON — .44 cal. perc., 7.5 in. barrel, color case hardened hammer, frame, trigger and loading lever, engraved cylinder, 66 oz. Disc. 1994.

	$275	$200	$145	$100

Last MSR was $165.

1851 NAVY — .36 cal. perc., 7.5 in. octagon barrel, color case hardened loading lever and hammer, brass or steel frame and trigger guard, 44 oz. Disc. 1994.

	$115	$100	$60	$50

Last MSR was $100.

Add $25 for steel frame.

GRADING - PPGS™	100%	98%	90%	80%

1860 ARMY — .44 cal. perc., 8 in. barrel, color case hardened hammer, steel or brass frame and trigger, loading lever, engraved cylinder. Disc. 1994.

	$175	$150	$105	$75

Last MSR was $160.

Subtract $35 for brass frame.

1858 REMINGTON ARMY — .44 cal. perc., 8 in. octagon barrel, brass frame and trigger guard, 44 oz. Disc. 1994.

	$135	$110	$75	$50

Last MSR was $125.

Add $35 for steel frame.

1858 REMINGTON NAVY BUFFALO TARGET — .44 cal. perc., 12 in. octagon barrel, brass frame and trigger guard, adj. sights, based on 1858 Navy frame, 38 oz. Disc. 1994.

	$200	$160	$120	$85

Last MSR was $150.

RIFLES: PERCUSSION

BRISTOL HUNTER — .50 or .54 cal. perc., 28 in. octagon barrel, color case hardened hammer and lock, rubber recoil pad, adj. rear sights, chrome plated bore, double set triggers. Disc. 1994.

	$225	$170	$125	$90

Last MSR was $240.

HAWKEN RIFLE — .50 cal. perc., 28 in. octagon barrel, color case hardened hammer and lock, brass trim, adj. sights, double set triggers. Disc. 1994.

	$190	$155	$115	$80

Last MSR was $225.

KODIAK SxS RIFLE — .50 or .58 cal. perc., 28 in. octagon barrels. Disc. 1994.

	$650	$520	$415	$310

Last MSR was $560.

Add $280 for extra 12 ga. shotgun barrels.

SHOTGUNS: PERCUSSION

MUZZLE LOADING MODEL — 10 or 12 ga., perc. Disc. 1994.

	$315	$245	$185	$145

Last MSR was $320.

Add $20 for 10 ga.

RIFLE SHOPPE INC.

Current maker of custom muzzle loading arms and parts located in Jones, OK.

The authentic replacement parts for older weapons are cast or hand made to exact specifications of originals. Please contact the Rifle Shoppe directly (see Trademark Index) for current availability and price.

RIGHTNOUR MANUFACTURING, CO., INC. (RMC SPORTS)

Current manufacturer located in Mingoville, PA.

RIFLES: FLINTLOCK

ACCUSPORTER — .32 or .50 cal. flintlock, L & R lock, 24 or 28 in. Green Mountain barrel, 1:28 or 1:48 in. twist, adj. fiber optic sights, Rosewood, black, brown, green, or dark Rosewood laminated wood stock, hard case. Mfg. 2005-06.

	$425	$350	$255	$220

Last MSR was $500.

ACCUSPORTER LTD — .32 or .50 cal. flintlock, L & R lock, 24 or 28 in. Green Mountain barrel, 1:28 or 1:48 in. twist, removable breech plug, EC Load System (relieved muzzle bore), all metal adj. fiber optic sights, Rosewood, black, brown, green, or dark Rosewood laminated wood stock, threaded wedge pin, hard case. New 2006.

MSR $625	$575	$475	$395	$325

GRADING - PPGS™	100%	98%	90%	80%

ACCUSPORTER LTD PRO — .32 or .50 cal. flintlock, L & R lock, 24 or 28 in. Green Mountain barrel, 1:28 or 1:48 in. twist, removable breech plug, double set trigger, EC Load System (relieved muzzle bore), all metal adj. fiber optic sights, Rosewood, black, brown, green, or dark Rosewood laminated wood stock, threaded wedge pin, hard case. New 2007.

	$550	$475	$375	$295

Last MSR was $599.

ROSSI

Current trademark manufactured by Amadeo Rossi, S.A. located in Sao Leopoldo, Brazil. Currently imported exclusively by BrazTech, International located in Miami, FL.

For more information and current pricing on both new and used Rossi firearms, please refer to the *Blue Book of Gun Values* by S.P. Fjestad (now online also).

RIFLES: IN-LINE IGNITION

MODEL S50BM — .50 cal. perc., #209 primer ignition, top button break open action, 23 in. barrel, matte blue finish, adj. Tru-Glo sights, drilled and tapped for scope base, wood stock and forearm, ventilated recoil pad, 38 in. OAL, 6.3 lbs. New 2003.

courtesy Rossi

MSR $180	$160	$130	$100	$70

* ***Model S45YBM*** — .45 cal. perc., #209 primer ignition, top button break open action, 20 in. barrel, matte blue finish, adj. Tru-Glo sights, drilled and tapped for scope base, wood stock and forearm, ventilated recoil pad, 34 in. OAL, 5 lbs. Mfg. 2004-06.

courtesy Rossi

	$170	$145	$105	$75

Last MSR was $196.

* ***Model S50YBM*** — .50 cal. perc., #209 primer ignition, top button break open action, 20 in. barrel, matte blue finish, adj. Tru-Glo sights, drilled and tapped for scope base, wood stock and forearm, ventilated recoil pad, 34 in. OAL, 5 lbs. Mfg. 2004-05.

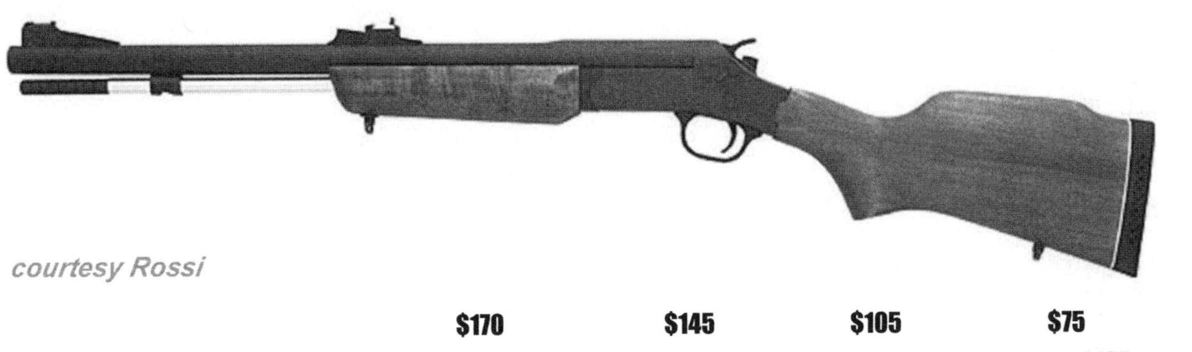

courtesy Rossi

	$170	$145	$105	$75

Last MSR was $196.

GRADING - PPGS™	100%	98%	90%	80%

MODEL S50SM — .50 cal. perc., #209 primer ignition, top button break open action, 23 in. barrel, matte stainless steel finish, adj. Tru-Glo sights, drilled and tapped for scope base, wood stock and forearm, ventilated recoil pad, 38 in. OAL, 6.3 lbs. Mfg. 2003-05.

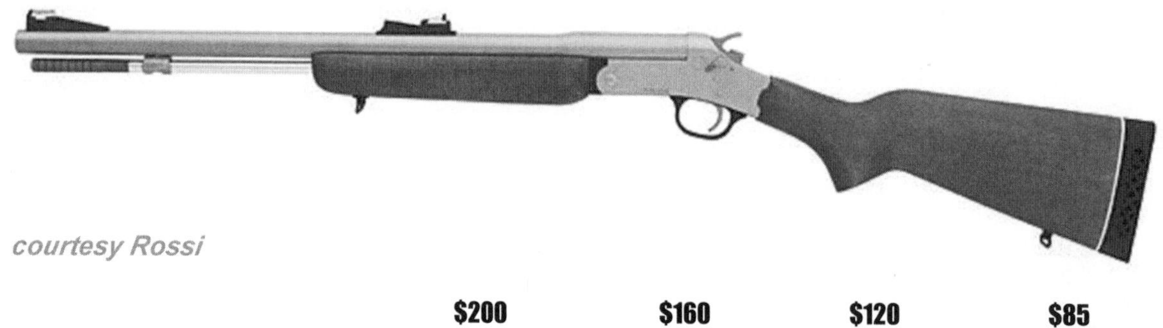

courtesy Rossi

	$200	$160	$120	$85

Last MSR was $230.

* ***Model S45YSM*** — .45 cal. perc., #209 primer ignition, top button break open action, 20 in. barrel, matte stainless steel finish, adj. Tru-Glo sights, drilled and tapped for scope base, wood stock and forearm, ventilated recoil pad, 34 in. OAL, 5 lbs. Mfg. 2004-06.

courtesy Rossi

	$210	$165	$125	$85

Last MSR was $243.

* ***Model S50YSM*** — .50 cal. perc., #209 primer ignition, top button break open action, 20 in. barrel, matte stainless steel finish, adj. Tru-Glo sights, drilled and tapped for scope base, wood stock and forearm, ventilated recoil pad, 34 in. OAL, 5 lbs. New 2004.

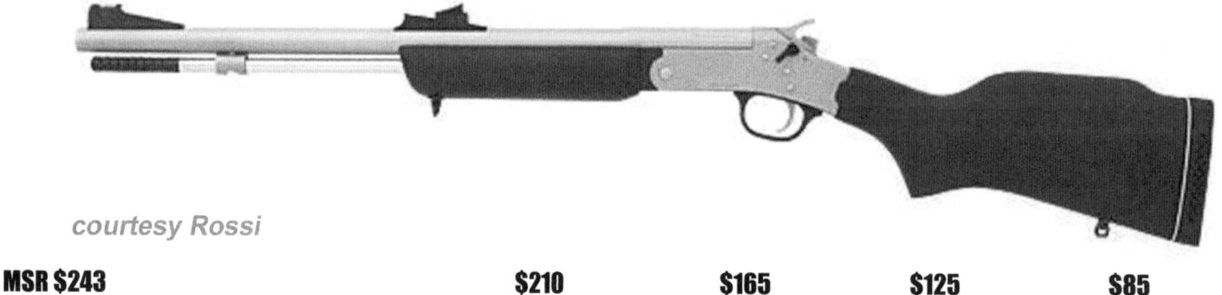

courtesy Rossi

MSR $243	$210	$165	$125	$85

MODEL S50BMS — .50 cal. perc., #209 primer ignition, top button break open action, 23 in. barrel, matte blue finish, adj. Tru-Glo sights, drilled and tapped for scope base, black synthetic stock and forearm, ventilated recoil pad, 38 in. OAL, 6.3 lbs. New 2009.

MSR $209	$195	$160	$130	$100

MODEL S50YNM — .50 cal. perc., #209 primer ignition, top button break open action, 20 in. barrel, matte nickel finish, adj. Tru-Glo sights, drilled and tapped for scope base, black synthetic stock and forearm, ventilated recoil pad, 38 in. OAL, 6.3 lbs. New 2009.

MSR $269	$245	$195	$160	$130

GRADING - PPGS™	100%	98%	90%	80%

S SECTION

SAVAGE ARMS, INC.

Current manufacturer located in Westfield, MA.

Originally established in 1895 in Utica, NY. In addition to cartridge rifles, Savage now produces a line of bolt-action, in-line muzzleloaders, first introduced in 2001.

For more information and current pricing on both new and used Savage Arms, Inc. firearms, please refer to the *Blue Book of Gun Values* by S.P. Fjestad (now online also).

RIFLES: IN-LINE IGNITION

Savage Arms, Inc. indicates the Model 10ML-II (Model 10ML) can be loaded using your choice of propellant including smokeless powder, black powder, Pyrodex, or other black powder substitutes. Beginning 2004 the Model 10ML-II features Savage's AccuTrigger.

MODEL 10ML-II (MODEL 10ML) — .50 cal. perc., #209 primer ignition, bolt action, 24 in. barrel, blue or stainless finish, black or Realtree Hardwoods camo synthetic, brown laminate stock, recoil pad, 44 in. OAL, 7.75-9.25 lbs.

* ***Model 10ML-II Blue Steel (Model 10ML Blue Steel)*** — black synthetic stock. New 2001.

courtesy Savage Arms, Inc.

MSR $660	$595	$535	$395	$325

* ***Model 10ML-II Blue Steel Camo*** — Realtree Hardwoods camouflage synthetic stock, blue steel barrel. New 2002.

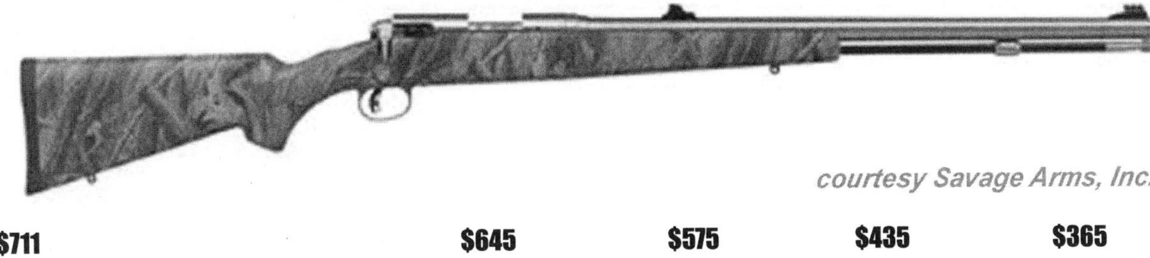

courtesy Savage Arms, Inc.

MSR $711	$645	$575	$435	$365

* ***Model 10MLSS-II Stainless (Model 10MLSS Stainless)*** — black synthetic stock. New 2001.

MSR $738	$675	$595	$455	$385

* ***Model 10MLSS-II Stainless Camo*** — Realtree Hardwoods camouflage synthetic stock. New 2002.

courtesy Savage Arms, Inc.

MSR $787	$705	$625	$485	$415

GRADING - PPGS™	100%	98%	90%	80%

* ***Model 10MLBSS-II (Stainless)*** — brown laminate stock, stainless steel barrel, adjustable fiber optic hunting sights. New 2002.

courtesy Savage Arms, Inc.

MSR $839	$765	$675	$535	$445

* ***Model 10ML-IIXP*** — similar to Model 10ML-II, except 3-9x40mm matte finish scope mounted and bore sighted. Available with blue or stainless barrel. Black synthetic stock w/nylon sling and swivel studs. Mfg. 2002-2008.

	$595	$535	$395	$335

Last MSR was $667.

* ***Model 10MLSS-IIXP*** — similar to Model 10ML-II, except 3-9x40mm matte finish scope mounted and bore sighted. Available with stainless barrel. Black synthetic stock w/nylon sling and swivel studs. Mfg. 2002-2008.

	$675	$595	$445	$375

Last MSR was $744.

* ***Model 10MLBTSS-II (Stainless)*** — brown laminate thumbhole stock, stainless steel barrel, adjustable fiber optic hunting sights. New 2007.

MSR $888	$805	$625	$475	$395

SHILOH RIFLE MFG. CO.

Current manufacturer located in Big Timber, MT since 1983.

RIFLES: PERCUSSION

SHARPS MODEL 1863 CARBINE — .50 or .54 cal. perc., 22 in. round blue barrel, color case hardened receiver and hammer, single trigger, adj. sights, walnut stock and forearm, barrel band, steel military buttplate, approx. 7.5 lbs.

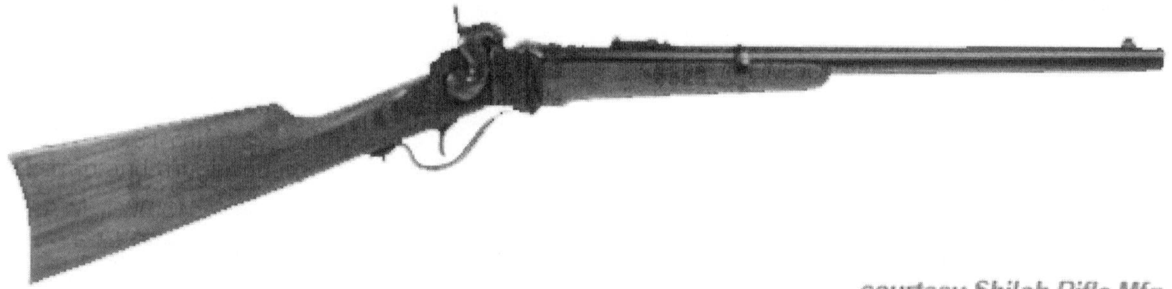

courtesy Shiloh Rifle Mfg.

MSR $1,800	$1,645	$1,475	$1,125	$950

SHARPS MODEL 1863 MILITARY RIFLE — .50 or .54 cal. perc., 30 in. round blue barrel, color case hardened receiver and hammer, single trigger, adj. sights, walnut stock and long forearm w/cap, three barrel bands, military buttplate, sling swivels.

courtesy Shiloh Rilfe Mfg.

MSR $2,092	$1,995	$1,795	$1,395	$1,150

GRADING - PPGS™	100%	98%	90%	80%

SHARPS MODEL 1863 SPORTING RIFLE — .50 or .54 cal. perc., 30 in. octagon blue barrel, color case hardened receiver and hammer, double triggers, adj. sights, walnut stock and forearm, steel military buttplate.

courtesy Shiloh Rilfe Mfg.

MSR $1,800	$1,645	$1,475	$1,125	$950

SILE DISTRIBUTORS

Previous importer and distributor of Invest Arms brand and D. Pedersoli brand, located in New York, NY until 1999.

REVOLVERS: PERCUSSION

1858 REMINGTON ARMY — .44 cal. perc., 8 in. white octagon barrel, white steel frame, brass trigger guard, 2 lbs. 9 oz. Disc.

	$135	$110	$75	$50

Add $70 for stainless steel.
Add $30 for Target Model.

1860 COLT ARMY — .44 cal. perc., 8 in. blue round barrel, brass or color case hardened steel frame, brass trigger guard and backstrap, color case hardened hammer, trigger and loading lever, 2 lbs. 11 oz. Disc.

	$100	$85	$55	$50

Add $35 for steel frame.

RIFLES: FLINTLOCK & PERCUSSION

BROWN BESS MUSKET — .75 cal. flintlock, 41.75 in. smooth bore barrel, brass furniture, white steel barrel, hammer and lock, engraved lock, 9 lbs. Disc. 1994.

	$475	$385	$280	$230

Last MSR was $565.

HAWKEN RIFLE — .45, .50, or .54 cal. flintlock or perc. (.50 cal. only in flintlock), 29 in. octagon barrel, solid brass furniture, color case hardened engraved lock, coil spring mechanism with adj. set triggers, stainless steel nipple, chrome bore, brass patch box, adj. sights, 8 lbs. 10 oz. Disc. 1994.

	$200	$160	$120	$85

Last MSR was $230.

Add $35 for flintlock.

HAWKEN RIFLE CARBINE — .45, .50, or .54 cal. flintlock or perc. (.50 cal. only in flintlock), 22 in. octagon barrel, solid brass furniture, color case hardened engraved lock, coil spring mechanism with adj. set triggers, stainless steel nipple, chrome bore, brass patch box, adj. sights, 7 lbs. Disc. 1994.

	$190	$155	$115	$80

Last MSR was $250.

Add $10 for flintlock.

HAWKEN HUNTER CARBINE — .45, .50, or .54 cal. flintlock or perc. (.50 cal. only in flintlock), 22 in. octagon barrel, solid brass furniture, color case hardened engraved lock, coil spring mechanism with adj. set triggers, stainless steel nipple, chrome bore, brass patch box, adj. sights, 7 lbs. Disc. 1994.

	$190	$155	$115	$80

Last MSR was $225.

Add $10 for flintlock.

KENTUCKY RIFLE — .45 or .50 cal. flintlock or perc., 32 in. blue octagon barrel, solid brass furniture, color case hardened hammer and engraved lock, brass patch box, adj. rear sight, 7 lbs. 2 oz. Disc. 1994.

	$300	$225	$160	$110

Add $10 for flintlock.

PENNSYLVANIAN SQUIRREL RIFLE — .32 cal. flintlock, 40.5 in. brown octagon barrel, adj. double set triggers, polished white steel hammer and lock, 9 lbs. Disc.

	$415	$340	$250	$220

GRADING - PPGS™	100%	98%	90%	80%

SHOTGUNS: PERCUSSION

SxS MODEL — 10 or 12 ga., perc., 28 in. blue barrels, engraved furniture, color case hardened hammer and engraved lock, chrome lined bores, 7 lbs. 12 oz. (8 lbs. 12 oz. for 10 ga.). Disc.

	$425	$350	$255	$220

Add $20 for 10 ga.

SOUTHWEST MUZZLE LOADERS SUPPLY

Previous importer/distributor located in Angleton, TX until 1994.

Southwest Muzzle Loaders Supply imported many Uberti models.

REVOLVERS: PERCUSSION

DANCE MODEL — .36 or .44 cal., exact reproduction of the original J.H. Dance and Brothers revolver manufactured in Columbia, Texas, advertising listed 500 as total production, less than 50 were actually assembled and delivered. Mfg. by Aldo Uberti and Co. from Gardone, Italy, cased. Mfg. 1985-1994. Scarce.

	$800	$650	$515	$375

Last MSR was $1,500.

SPLIT FIRE SPORTING GOODS, LLC

Previous distributor of White Rifles, located in Orem, UT. During 2001 the name was changed to White Rifles, LLC. Split Fire was the exclusive distributor for all White models manufactured by Muzzleloading Technologies, Inc.

For current information refer to White Rifles, LLC, and for White models produced through 1997, refer to the White Muzzleloading Systems section.

STONE MOUNTAIN ARMS, INC.

Previous manufacturer located in Norcross, GA. Previously marketed exclusively by Connecticut Valley Arms. Colt and Remington reproductions are imported from Italy. Dealer and consumer direct sales.

REVOLVERS: PERCUSSION

1848 BABY DRAGOON — .31 cal. perc., 5 shot, 4 in. octagon barrel, color case hardened steel frame, 1.4 lbs.

	$200	$160	$120	$85

Last MSR was $240.

3RD MODEL DRAGOON — .44 cal. perc., 6 shot, 7.5 in. barrel, roll engraved cylinder, color case hardened steel frame, 3.9 lbs.

	$220	$170	$125	$90

Last MSR was $250.

1851 NAVY — .36 cal. perc., 6 shot, 7.5 in. barrel, (5.5 in. on Sheriff's model), color case hardened steel frame, brass backstrap and trigger guard, 2.8 lbs.

	$135	$110	$75	$50

Last MSR was $180.

1858 REMINGTON — .31 (Pocket Model) or .44 cal. perc., 6 shot, 8 in. barrel, adj. rear sight, fixed sights with color case hardened frame.

	$140	$115	$85	$55

Last MSR was $243.

Subtract $15 for .31 cal. Pocket Model.

ROGERS & SPENCER — .44 cal. perc., 6 shot, 7.5 in. octagon barrel, 3 lbs.

	$200	$160	$120	$85

Last MSR was $290.

RIFLES: FLINTLOCK & PERCUSSION

1803 HARPERS FERRY — .54 cal. flintlock, 32.5 in. brown barrel, brass furniture, walnut stock, 9 lbs.

	$575	$450	$345	$275

Last MSR was $730.

GRADING - PPGS™	100%	98%	90%	80%

1841 MISSISSIPPI RIFLE — .54 cal. perc., 33.5 in. barrel, brass furniture, walnut stock, 9.5 lbs.

	$450	$365	$265	$225

Last MSR was $575.

1853 ENFIELD (3 BAND) — .58 cal. perc., 39 in. barrel, color case hardened hammer and lock, blue barrel bands, brass furniture, walnut stock, 9.5 lbs.

	$450	$365	$265	$225

Last MSR was $550.

SILVER EAGLE RIFLE/HUNTER — .50 cal. perc., 26 in. octagon barrel, matte Weatherguard nickel finish, synthetic stock.

	$125	$105	$70	$50

Last MSR was $140.

Add $20 for Hunter model w/adj. hunting sights and sling swivels.

1861 SPRINGFIELD — .58 cal. perc., 40 in. barrel, all white steel, walnut stock.

	$475	$385	$280	$230

Last MSR was $600.

RIFLES: IN-LINE IGNITION

PRO I — .50 cal. perc., 24 in. round barrel with Weatherguard nickel finish, std. trigger, blade front sight, duragrip synthetic stock, chrome plated bolt, 6.5 lbs.

	$175	$150	$105	$75

Last MSR was $200.

PRO II RIFLE — .50 cal. perc., similar to Pro I, except adj. sights and trigger, and stainless steel bolt, 6.5 lbs.

	$175	$150	$105	$75

Last MSR was $220.

STURM, RUGER, AND COMPANY, INC.

Current manufacturer located in Newport, NH and Prescott, AZ. Distributor and dealer sales.

The first series of Ruger Old Army revolvers were blue and had adj. sights. Current models are available in blue, stainless steel, and polished stainless steel finishes. Based on the 1858 Remington New Army design, the Ruger Old Army incorporates significant advances in design and operation. Old Army revolvers are constructed using the latest investment casting and precision CNC machining techniques.

For more information and current pricing on both new and used Sturm, Ruger, And Co., Inc. firearms, please refer to the *Blue Book of Gun Values* by S.P. Fjestad (now online also).

Please refer to *Colt Blackpowder Reproductions & Replicas - A Collector's & Shooter's Guide* for color pictures of all Ruger Old Army models listed below. Ruger Old Army pistols can be found on pages 52 through 57.

REVOLVERS: PERCUSSION

Current models offer both fixed and adj. sights, blue alloy, satin, or gloss stainless steel finishes.

OLD ARMY — .45 cal. perc., 6 shot, 5.5 (new 2003) or 7.5 in. barrel, fixed or adj. rear (7.5 in. barrel only) sight, blue finish, Rosewood or simulated Ivory grips. 2.5 (5.5 in. barrel) lbs. Disc. 2008.

courtesy Sturm, Ruger, and Company, Inc.

	$550	$445	$350	$250

Last MSR was $595.

Add $40 for simulated ivory grips avail. 1997-2004.

GRADING - PPGS™	100%	98%	90%	80%

STAINLESS OLD ARMY — .44 cal. perc., stainless steel variation of current Old Army Model, satin or high gloss finish with fixed or adj. (7.5 in. barrel) rear sight, Rosewood or simulated Ivory grips. 2.87 (7.5 in. barrel) lbs. Disc. 2008.

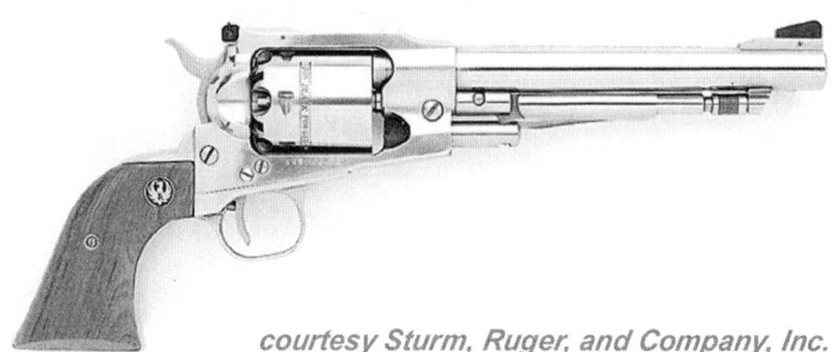

courtesy Sturm, Ruger, and Company, Inc.

	$575	$465	$360	$265

Last MSR was $635.

Add $50 for simulated ivory grips (new 1997).

NATIONAL MUZZLE LOADING RIFLE ASSOCIATION SPECIAL EDITION — serial no. range 140-14000 to 140-14100. Identified by N.M.L.R.A. logo on the grip panel.

	$825	$675	$530	$400

RUGER COLLECTORS ASSOCIATION FIRST SERIES — serial no. range 1500-1599, "RCA" marked on the top strap and a star motif preceding the serial number.

	$825	$675	$530	$400

RUGER COLLECTORS ASSOCIATION SECOND SERIES 1976 — serial no. range 145-01401 through 145-01600. Total of 201. Engraved RCA logo and intertwined RCA monogram on top strap, eagle marked before serial number. Last Rugers with barrel inscription "MADE IN THE 200th YEAR OF AMERICAN LIBERTY."

	$825	$675	$530	$400

RUGER COLLECTORS ASSOCIATION THIRD SERIES 1997 — commemorates the 25th anniversary of the Ruger Old Army. Limited to 2000 pistols serial numbered 1-2000. Floral engraving on top strap and frame, bottom of trigger guard with RCA logo, Ruger Collectors Association bordered with scrollwork along both sides of the barrel, 24Kt. gold plated cylinder with engraved Ruger emblem and scrollwork, 24Kt. gold plated front sight, white Micarta grips with RCA logo.

	$600	$465	$385	$285

Last MSR was $700.

This model was sold through Sportsman's Guide.

RIFLES: IN-LINE IGNITION

MODEL 77/50RS SPORTER MODEL — .50 cal. perc., No. 11 or musket cap ignition, bolt-action, 22 in. barrel with one band, blue finish, 1:28 in. twist, folding adj. rear sight, 3 position safety, hardwood stock, black rubber recoil pad, sling swivel studs, 41.5 in. OAL,7 lbs. Mfg. 1997-2004.

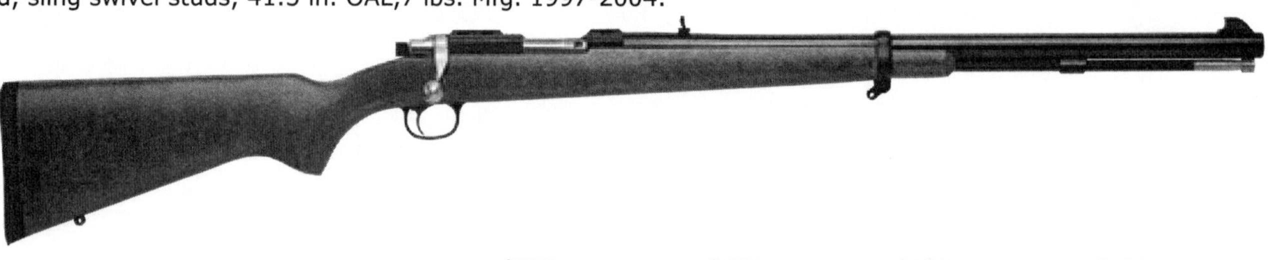

	$550	$425	$320	$260

Last MSR was $616.

GRADING - PPGS™	100%	98%	90%	80%

* ***Model 77/50RSO Officers Model*** — .50 cal. perc., No. 11 or musket cap ignition, bolt-action, 22 in. barrel with one band, blue finish, 1:28 in. twist, folding adj. rear sight, 3 position safety,checkered black walnut stock, black rubber recoil pad, sling swivel studs, 41.5 in. OAL, 6.5 lbs. Mfg. 1998-2004.

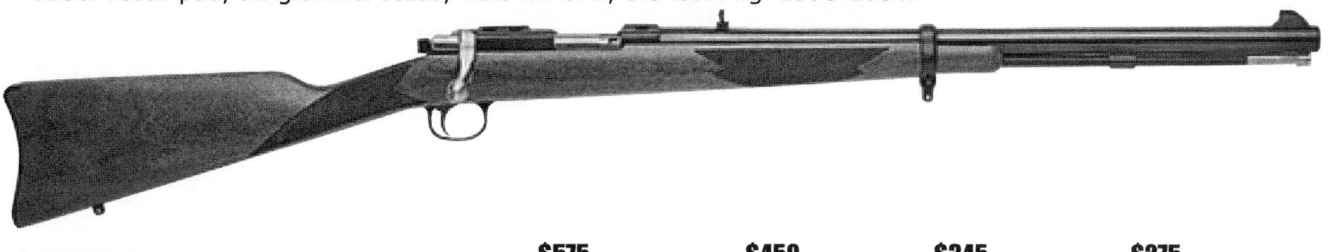

	$575	$450	$345	$275

Last MSR was $662.

* ***Model 77/50RSP*** — .50 cal. perc., No. 11 or musket cap ignition, bolt-action, 22 in. barrel with one band, blue finish, 1:28 in. twist, folding adj. rear sight, 3 position safety, synthetic stock, black rubber recoil pad, sling swivel studs, 42 in. OAL, 6.5 lbs. Mfg. 1999-2004.

	$500	$400	$295	$240

Last MSR was $562.

MODEL K77/50RS — .50 cal. perc., bolt-action, 22 in. barrel with one band, stainless finish, folding adj. rear sight, 3 position safety, synthetic stock, black rubber recoil pad, sling swivel studs, 42 in. OAL, 6.5 lbs. Mfg. 1999-2004.

	$525	$415	$310	$250

Last MSR was $604.

MODEL K77/50RSBBZ — .50 cal. perc., bolt-action, 22 in. barrel with one band, stainless finish, folding adj. rear sight, 3 position safety, black laminated stock, black rubber recoil pad, sling swivel studs, 41.5 in. OAL, 7 lbs. Mfg. 1998-2004.

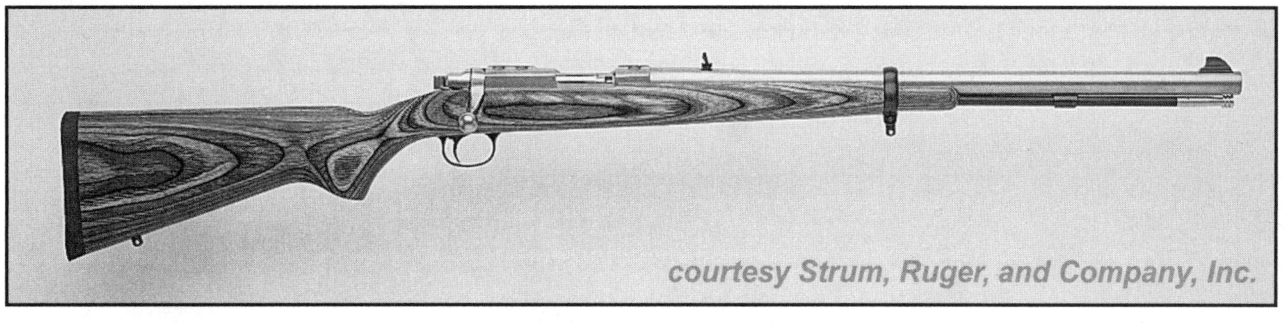

courtesy Strum, Ruger, and Company, Inc.

	$600	$465	$385	$285

Last MSR was $674.

NOTES

T SECTION

TAYLOR'S & CO., INC.

Current importer/distributor located in Winchester, VA. Taylor's imports black powder pistols and longarms produced by Armi Sport, Pietta, and Uberti. Dealer or consumer direct sales.

For more information and current pricing on Taylor's & Co., Inc. Firearms, please refer to the *Blue Book of Gun Values* by S.P. Fjestad (now online also).

Black Powder Reproductions & Replicas by Dennis Adler is also an invaluable source for most black powder reproductions and replicas, and includes hundreds of color images on most popular makes/models, provides manufacturer/trademark histories, and up-to-date information on related items/accessories for black powder shooting - www.bluebookinc.com

PISTOLS: PERCUSSION

F. ROCHATTE DUELING PISTOL — .45 cal. perc., 10 in. round barrel with flattop, white steel lock and trim, adj. double set triggers, 2.5 lbs. Disc. 1994.

	100%	98%	90%	80%
	$250	**$190**	**$135**	**$95**

Last MSR was $395.

KENTUCKY PISTOL — .45 cal. flintlock or perc., 10 in. octagon barrel, brass blade front sight, brass nose cap, color case hardened sidelock, one piece stock with bird's head grip, 2.5 lbs. Mfg. by Armi Sport.

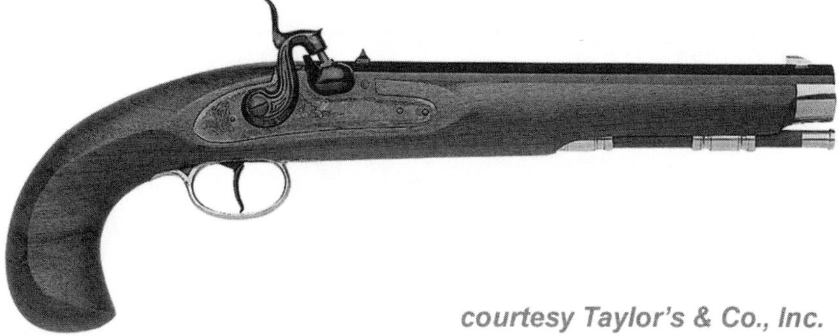

courtesy Taylor's & Co., Inc.

	100%	98%	90%	80%
MSR $410	**$375**	**$325**	**$245**	**$195**

Add $25 for flintlock model.

NAPOLEON LE PAGE PISTOL — .45 cal. perc., 10 in. barrel, white steel barrel and lock, fixed sights with single barrel wedge, fluted grip, silver plated butt cap and trigger guard with spur, double set triggers, 2 lbs. 7 oz. Disc. 2009.

	100%	98%	90%	80%
	$415	**$300**	**$225**	**$165**

Last MSR was $460.

REVOLVERS: PERCUSSION

1847 WALKER — .44 cal. perc., 9 in. blue barrel, color case hardened frame, hammer, and loading lever, brass trigger guard and steel backstrap, 4 lbs. 6 oz. Mfg. by Uberti.

courtesy Taylor's & Co., Inc.

	100%	98%	90%	80%
MSR $380	**$350**	**$315**	**$250**	**$215**

GRADING - PPGS™	100%	98%	90%	80%

1848 BABY DRAGOON — .31 cal. perc., 4 in. octagon barrel, 5 shot, color case hardened frame, hammer, no loading lever, roll engraved cylinder, brass backstrap and trigger guard, also available in white steel, 1.4 lbs. Mfg. by Uberti. Disc. 2004.

	$175	$150	$105	$75

Last MSR was $205.

Add $32 for model in the white.

1849 POCKET — .31 cal. perc., 4 in. octagon barrel, 5 shot, color case hardened frame, hammer, with or w/o (Wells Fargo) loading lever, roll engraved cylinder, brass backstrap and round trigger guard, 1.4 lbs. Mfg. by Uberti.

courtesy Taylor's & Co., Inc.

MSR $303	$275	$245	$185	$145

1849 WELLS FARGO MODEL — .31 cal. perc., 4 in. octagon barrel, 5 shot, color case hardened frame, hammer, w/o loading lever, roll engraved cylinder, brass backstrap and round trigger guard, 1.4 lbs. Mfg. by Uberti.

courtesy Taylor's & Co., Inc.

MSR $296	$265	$235	$175	$135

1851 NAVY (STEEL FRAME) — .36 or cal. perc., 7.5 in. octagon blue barrel, rolled cylinder scene, color case hardened frame, hammer, and loading lever, brass backstrap and trigger guard oval or squareback (1st Model). Mfg. by Uberti & Pietta.

courtesy Taylor's & Co., Inc.

MSR $255	$225	$195	$145	$115

Add $33 for Uberti Mfg.

Add $33 for 1st Model w/squareback trigger guard.

GRADING - PPGS™	100%	98%	90%	80%

1851 NAVY (BRASS FRAME) — .36 or .44 (new 2003) cal. perc., 7.5 in. octagon blue finish barrel and cylinder w/ rolled scene, brass frame, backstrap and trigger guard. Referred to as a Confederate version of the Colt 1851 Navy. Mfg. by Uberti (disc. 2003) & Pietta.

courtesy Taylor's & Co., Inc.

MSR $226	$205	$185	$145	$105

Add $34 for engraved barrel and frame.

1851 NAVY LONDON MODEL — .36 cal. perc., 7.5 in. octagon barrel, blue finish steel backstrap and trigger guard, rolled cylinder scene, color case hardened frame, hammer, and loading lever. Mfg. by Uberti. New 2006.

courtesy Taylor's & Co., Inc.

MSR $315	$285	$250	$195	$165

1851 NAVY SHERIFF'S MODEL — .36 (disc.) or .44 cal. perc., 5.5 in. octagon barrel, rolled cylinder scene, brass (.36 cal.) or steel (.44 cal.) frame, color case hardened frame (.36 cal.), hammer, and loading lever, brass backstrap and trigger guard. Mfg. by Uberti (disc. 2003) & Pietta.

MSR $255	$230	$205	$150	$125

1858 REMINGTON ARMY — .44 cal. perc., 8 in. octagon barrel, blue or old silver finish, color case hardened hammer, steel frame, backstrap, and trigger guard, 3 lbs. Mfg. by Uberti & Pietta.

courtesy Taylor's & Co., Inc.

MSR $295	$265	$235	$175	$145

Add $225 for "Old Silver" silver plated frame.

* ***1858 Remington Army (Short Model)*** — .44 cal. perc., 5.5 in. octagon barrel, steel frame, blue, white or color case hardened finish, brass backstrap, and trigger guard, 2.75-3 lbs. Mfg. by Uberti & Pietta.

MSR $305	$275	$245	$185	$155

Add $45 for white finish.
Add $82 for stainless steel.

GRADING - PPGS™	100%	98%	90%	80%

1858 REMINGTON BRASS — .44 cal. perc., 8 in. octagon barrel, color case hardened hammer, brass frame, backstrap and trigger guard, blue finish, 2 lbs. 6 oz. Mfg. by Uberti & Pietta.

courtesy Taylor's & Co., Inc.

MSR $250	$225	$195	$145	$115

1858 REMINGTON NAVY — .36 cal. perc., 7.37 in. octagon barrel, color case hardened hammer, steel frame and back strap, brass trigger guard, 2 lbs. 6 oz. Mfg. by Uberti & Pietta.

courtesy Taylor's & Co., Inc.

MSR $295	$265	$235	$175	$145

Add $10 for Uberti Mfg.

1858 REMINGTON NEW ARMY — .44 cal. perc., 8 in. octagon barrel, blue or antique, color case hardened hammer, forged steel frame (new 2007), brass backstrap and trigger guard, 3 lbs. Mfg. by Uberti & Pietta.

courtesy Taylor's & Co., Inc.

MSR $305	$275	$245	$185	$155

Add $36 for color case hardened frame.
Add $110 for antique finish.

GRADING - PPGS™	100%	98%	90%	80%

1858 REMINGTON STAINLESS STEEL — .44 cal. perc., 5.5 (new 2004) or 8 in. octagon barrel, stainless steel hammer and frame, groove or adj. (Target Model) rear sight, walnut grips. Mfg. by Uberti.

courtesy Taylor's & Co., Inc.

MSR $387	$345	$305	$225	$185

Add $50 for adj. rear sight (Target Model).

1858 STARR ARMY SINGLE/DOUBLE ACTION — .44 cal. perc., 6 in. tapered round barrel, all blue steel frame, backstrap and trigger guard. Mfg. by Pietta.

	$340	$265	$200	$160

Last MSR was $400.

Add $12 for Double Action Model.

1860 ARMY — .44 cal. perc., 8 in. round barrel, brass (disc.) or steel frame and backstrap, brass trigger guard, rebated cylinder, color case hardened frame, hammer and loading lever, blue or charcoal blue finish, 2.75 lbs. Mfg. by Pietta & Uberti.

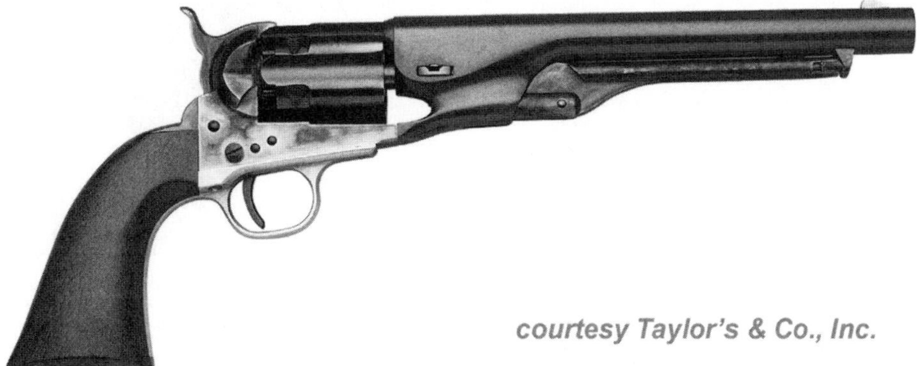

courtesy Taylor's & Co., Inc.

MSR $290	$265	$235	$175	$145

Add $12 for Uberti Mfg.

Add $75 for charcoal blue finish.

1860 ARMY SHERIFF'S MODEL — .44 cal. perc., 5.5 in. round barrel, rebated w/rolled scene or fluted (Civilian Model) cylinder, color case hardened frame, hammer and loading lever, steel backstrap, brass trigger guard, walnut grips. Mfg. by Pietta.

courtesy Taylor's & Co., Inc.

MSR $290	$265	$235	$175	$145

Add $15 for Civilian Model w/fluted cylinder.

GRADING - PPGS™	100%	98%	90%	80%

1861 NAVY — .36 cal. perc., 7.5 in. barrel, brass (Civilian Model) or steel backstrap and trigger guard, color case hardened frame, hammer and loading lever, 2.5 lbs. Mfg. by Uberti and Pietta.

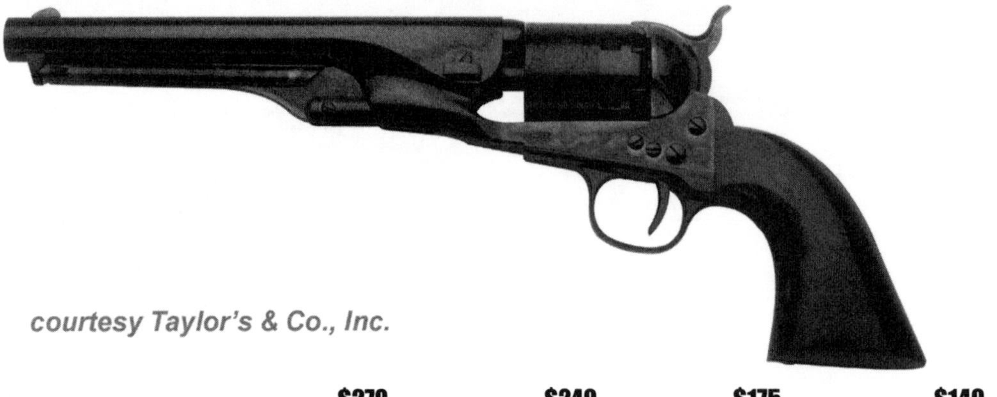

courtesy Taylor's & Co., Inc.

MSR $305	$270	$240	$175	$140

Add $15 for steel backstrap and trigger guard.

1862 POCKET NAVY — .36 cal. perc., 5.5 in. barrel, half fluted cylinder, brass backstrap and trigger guard, color case hardened frame, hammer and loading lever. Mfg. by Uberti.

courtesy Taylor's & Co., Inc.

MSR $312	$285	$255	$195	$165

1862 POLICE — .36 cal. perc., 5.5 (new 2003) or 6.5 in. barrel, brass backstrap and trigger guard, color case hardened frame, hammer and loading lever. Mfg. by Uberti and Pietta.

courtesy Taylor's & Co., Inc.

MSR $317	$285	$250	$190	$155

GRADING - PPGS™	100%	98%	90%	80%

1863 REMINGTON POCKET — .31 cal. perc., 3.5 in. 5 shot, octagon barrel, brass or steel frame, walnut grips. Mfg. by Armi San Marco (disc.) and Pietta.

courtesy Taylor's & Co., Inc.

MSR $285	$255	$225	$165	$135

Add $15 for nickel finish or steel frame.

1873 CATTLEMAN SINGLE ACTION REVOLVER — .44 cal. perc., 4.75, 5.5, or 7.5 in. blue barrel, color case hardened hammer and frame, blue backstrap and trigger guard, walnut grips. New 2003.

	$350	$275	$225	$170

Last MSR was $395.

FIRST MODEL DRAGOON — .44 cal. perc., 7.5 in. barrel, roll engraved cylinder, brass backstrap, square back trigger guard. Mfg. by Uberti.

courtesy Taylor's & Co., Inc.

MSR $350	$315	$280	$210	$185

SECOND MODEL DRAGOON — .44 cal. perc., 7.5 in. barrel, roll engraved cylinder, brass backstrap, square back trigger guard. Mfg. by Uberti.

courtesy Taylor's & Co., Inc.

MSR $350	$315	$280	$210	$185

GRADING - PPGS™	100%	98%	90%	80%

THIRD MODEL DRAGOON — .44 cal. perc., 7.5 in. barrel, roll engraved cylinder, brass backstrap, round trigger guard. Mfg. by Uberti.

courtesy Taylor's & Co., Inc.

MSR $358	$320	$285	$210	$185

LEMAT CAVALRY REVOLVER — .44 cal. perc., 9 shot cylinder, w/20 ga. smoothbore center single shot shotgun barrel, 8 in. octagon barrel, blue steel finish, case hardened hammer and trigger, checkered walnut grips, lanyard ring, spur trigger guard, 5 lbs. New 2007.

courtesy Taylor's & Co., Inc.

MSR $980	$895	$795	$595	$495

RIFLES: FLINTLOCK & PERCUSSION

1777 CHARLEVILLE MUSKET — .69 cal. flintlock, 44.75 in. smooth bore barrel, white steel lockplate, hammer and ramrod, brass barrel bands, trigger guard and buttplate, walnut stock. Disc. 1993.

	$500	$400	$300	$245

Last MSR was $595.

1842 SPRINGFIELD U.S. MUSKET — .69 cal. perc., 42 in. round smooth or rifled bore white steel barrel, hammer, lock trigger guard and trigger, marked "SPRING-FIELD" in two lines behind the hammer, lock and tang dated 1847, barrel stamped with the correct style V.P. and eagle head proof marks on the breech, one-piece American walnut stock, 9.75 lbs. Mfg. by Armi Sport. N.S.S.A. approved.

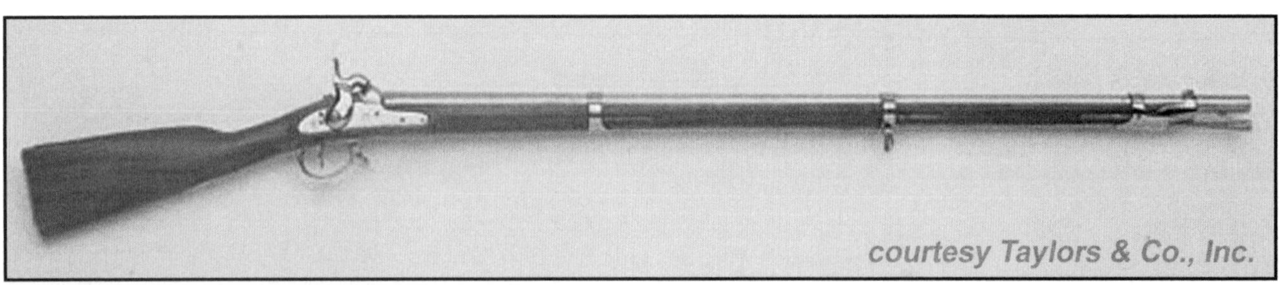
courtesy Taylors & Co., Inc.

MSR $760	$685	$615	$465	$385

Add $85 for 1842 Musket with rifled barrel and adj. rear sight. N.S.S.A. approved.

GRADING - PPGS™	100%	98%	90%	80%

1842 U.S. SHORT RIFLED MUSKET — .69 cal. perc., 33 in. round rifled bore white steel barrel, hammer, lock trigger guard and trigger, marked "SPRING-FIELD" in two lines behind the hammer, lock and tang dated 1847, barrel stamped with the correct style V.P. and eagle head proof marks on the breech, one-piece American walnut stock, 49 in. OAL, 9.75 lbs. Mfg. by Armi Sport. N.S.S.A. approved. New 2008.

MSR $815	**$745**	**$665**	**$495**	**$425**

1853 ENFIELD 1853 (3 BAND) — .58 cal. perc., 39 in. round barrel, color case hardened hammer and lock, brass furniture, blue barrel bands, 9.5 lbs. Mfg. by Armi Sport.

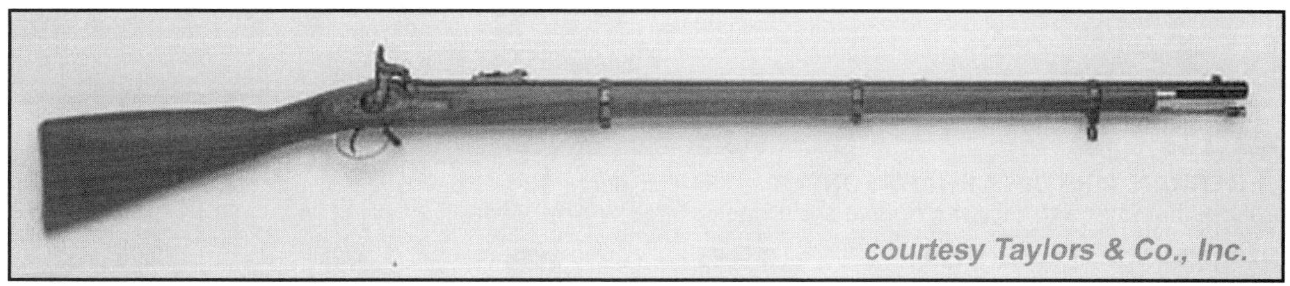
courtesy Taylors & Co., Inc.

MSR $665	**$595**	**$535**	**$415**	**$350**

1855 U.S. MUSKET (2ND MODEL) — .58 cal. perc., 40 in. round barrel, white steel barrel, hammer, lock, trigger and trim, one-piece American walnut stock, white satin furniture, brass endcap. 9.75 lbs. New 1998. Mfg. by Armi Sport.

courtesy Taylors & Co., Inc.

MSR $895	**$815**	**$735**	**$550**	**$475**

1858 ENFIELD (2 BAND) — .58 cal. perc., 33 in. round barrel, color case hardened hammer and lock, brass furniture, blue barrel bands, adj. rear sight, 9.5 lbs. Mfg. by Armi Sport.

courtesy Taylors & Co., Inc.

MSR $645	**$585**	**$525**	**$395**	**$335**

1858 REMINGTON REVOLVING CARBINE — .44 cal. perc., 18 in. octagon barrel, color case hardened hammer, steel frame, brass trigger guard, blue finish, adj. rear sight, walnut stock w/brass buttplate. Mfg. by Uberti. New 2003.

courtesy Taylor's & Co., Inc.

MSR $510	**$465**	**$415**	**$325**	**$265**

GRADING - PPGS™	100%	98%	90%	80%

1859 INFANTRY SHARPS RIFLE — .54 cal. perc., 30 in. round barrel, 3 metal band stock, color case hardened hammer and receiver. Mfg. by Armi Sport.

courtesy Taylors & Co., Inc.

MSR $1,140	$1,025	$925	$725	$625

1859 BERDAN MILITARY SHARPS RIFLE — .54 cal. perc., 30 in. round barrel, 3 metal band stock, color case hardened hammer and receiver, double set triggers. Mfg. by Armi Sport.

MSR $1,185	$1,065	$945	$705	$595

1859 CAVALRY SHARPS CARBINE — .54 cal. perc., 22 in. round barrel, 1 metal band, color case hardened hammer and receiver, includes patchbox. Mfg. by Armi Sport.

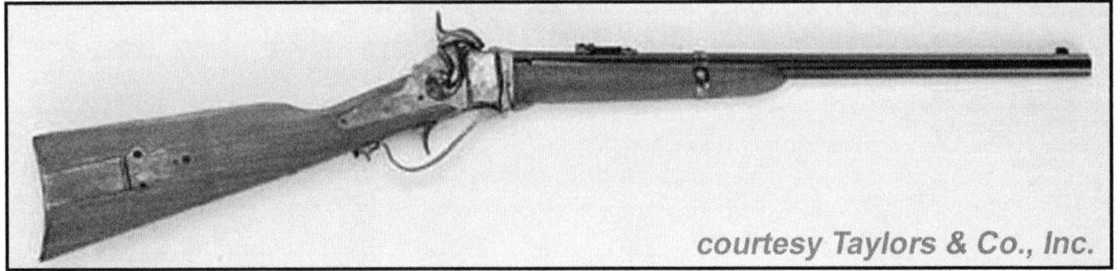

courtesy Taylors & Co., Inc.

MSR $990	$895	$795	$595	$495

1861 SPRINGFIELD MUSKET — .58 cal. perc., 40 in. round barrel, white steel barrel, hammer, lock, trigger and trim, 10.25 lbs. Mfg. by Armi Sport.

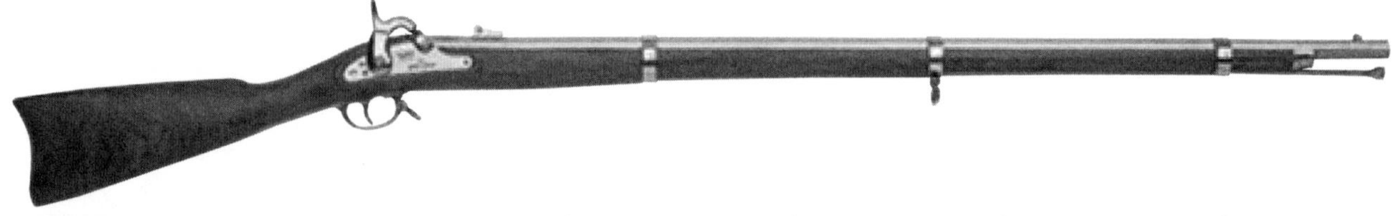

MSR $700	$625	$550	$395	$315

1862 C.S. RICHMOND MUSKET — .58 cal. perc., 40 in. barrel, white satin finish, brass nosecap, similar to 1861 Springfield, 9 lbs. Mfg. by Armi Sport.

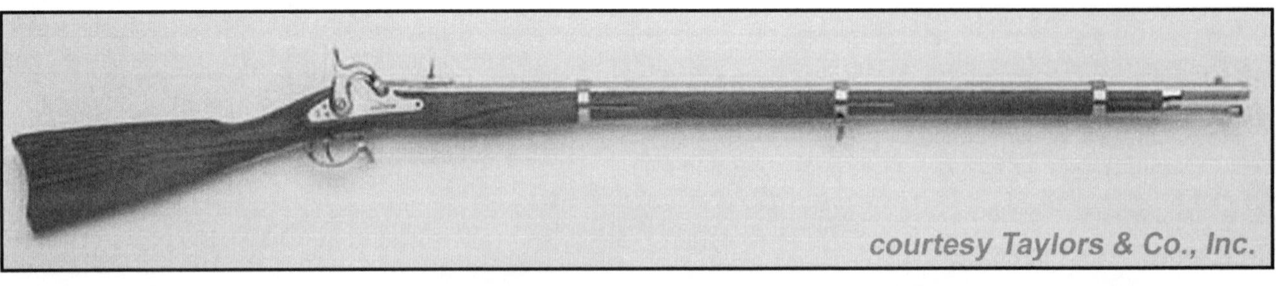

courtesy Taylors & Co., Inc.

MSR $725	$650	$575	$425	$350

GRADING - PPGS™	100%	98%	90%	80%

1863 CAVALRY SHARPS CARBINE — .54 cal. perc., 22 in. round barrel 1 metal band, color case hardened hammer and receiver. Mfg. by Armi Sport.

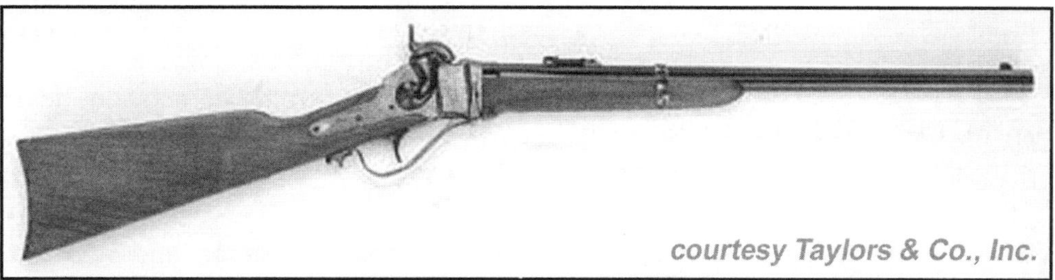

courtesy Taylors & Co., Inc.

MSR $965	$875	$785	$595	$495

1863 SHARPS SPORTING RIFLE — .54 cal. perc., 30 or 32 in. octagon barrel, color case hardened hammer and receiver, single or double set triggers, adj. rear sight, walnut stock and forearm. New 2003.

	$775	$630	$495	$365

Last MSR was $885.

Add $35 for double set triggers.

1863 ZOUAVE RIFLE — .58 cal. perc., 32.5 in. round barrel, color case hardened hammer, lock and trigger, brass patchbox, trigger guard and barrel bands, 9 lbs. Mfg. by Armi Sport.

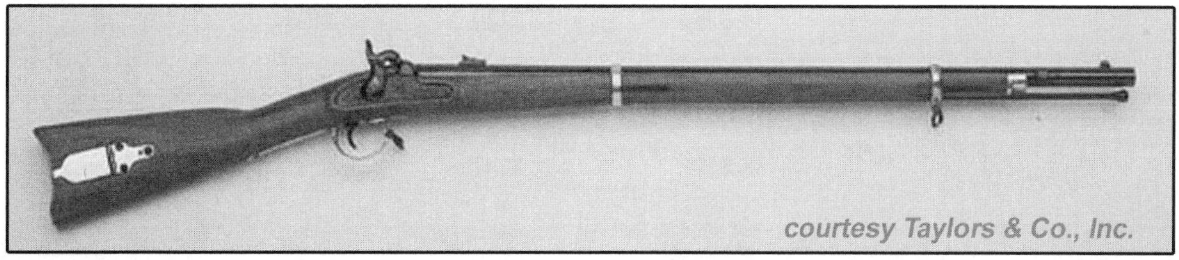

courtesy Taylors & Co., Inc.

MSR $700	$635	$575	$425	$350

BROWN BESS MUSKET — .75 cal. flintlock, 31.5 in. or 42 in. smooth bore barrel, white steel barrel, hammer, lock and furniture, 8.5 lbs. Disc. 1993. Reintroduced 2008.

MSR $1,265	$1,125	$995	$765	$645

DELUXE HAWKEN RIFLE — .50 cal. perc., 30 in. octagon chrome lined barrel, brass patchbox, target sights, double set triggers, 8 lbs. Mfg. by Invest Arms.

	$200	$160	$120	$85

Last MSR was $260.

Subtract $40 for Trailsman Model.

HAWKEN HUNTER CARBINE — .50 cal. perc., 24 in. octagon chrome lined barrel, rubber recoil pad, sling swivels, double set triggers. Mfg. by Invest Arms.

	$190	$155	$115	$80

Last MSR was $285.

KENTUCKY RIFLE — .32, .45 or .50 cal. perc. or flintlock, 35 in. octagon barrel, color case hardened lock, brass buttplate, trigger guard, patchbox, sideplates, thimbles and nosecap, walnut stock with large or small patchbox, rifle weighs 7.5 lbs., carbine is 6 lbs. Mfg. by Armi Sport.

courtesy Taylor's & Co., Inc.

MSR $625	$565	$495	$375	$315

Add $40 for flintlock version.

GRADING - PPGS™	100%	98%	90%	80%

* ***Kentucky Carbine Model*** — .50 cal. perc., chrome lined barrel. Disc. 1993.

	$255	$220	$180	N/A

Last MSR was $325.

Add $10 for large patch box.

MORTIMER HUNTER RIFLE — .50 or .54 cal. perc., 25 in. blue (matte finish) half octagon, half round barrel, adj. sights (rear), 8-7/8 lbs. Disc. 1993. Mfg. by Pedersoli.

	$450	$365	$285	$225

Last MSR was $485.

PENNSYLVANIA RIFLE — .45 cal. perc., octagon barrel, color case hardened hammer and lock, small brass patchbox, approx. 7 lbs.

	$200	$160	$120	$85

Last MSR was $215.

Add $185 for new Pedersoli model.

ROCKY MOUNTAIN HAWKEN — .54 cal. perc., 32.375 in. rust brown octagon barrel, color case hardened steel furniture, double set triggers, maple half stock, 48.75 in. OAL, approx. 9.7 lbs. New 2009.

MSR $1,245	$1,050	$950	$735	$595

ST. LOUIS HAWKEN RIFLE — .50 cal. perc., 30 in. octagon barrel, all black steel furniture, adj. rear sight, double set triggers, approx. 8 lbs. Disc. 1994.

	$250	$190	$135	$95

Last MSR was $260.

TRYON RIFLE — .50 or .54 cal. perc., 32.25 in. octagon barrel, all white steel, engraved lock and hammer, 9.5 lbs. Disc. 1994.

	$415	$340	$265	$225

Last MSR was $595.

RIFLES: IN-LINE IGNITION

SPIRIT OVERTOP MUZZLELOADER — .50 cal., #209 primer ignition, hammerless break open action, 28 in. round barrel, adj. Williams fiber optic sights, case hardened frame and blue barrel finish, fiber ram rod w/brass tip, high quality PG walnut stock and forearm, recoil pad and sling swivels, 33 in. OAL, 7 lbs. New 2006.

MSR $749	$695	$625	$500	$350

THOMPSON/CENTER ARMS CO., INC.

Current manufacturer located in Rochester, NH. Distributor and dealer sales.

For more information and current pricing on both new and used Thompson/Center Arms Co., Inc. firearms, please refer to the *Blue Book of Gun Values* by S.P. Fjestad (now online also).

PISTOLS: PERCUSSION

PATRIOT — .36 or .45 cal. perc., 9 in. barrel, double set triggers, target stock, walnut, color case hardened hammer and lock. Disc. 1987.

	$240	$185	$135	$95

Last MSR was $235.

PISTOLS: IN-LINE IGNITION

SCOUT PISTOL — .45, .50, or .54 cal. perc., 12 in. barrel, walnut grips, 4 lbs. 6 oz. Disc.

	$325	$275	$200	$145

Last MSR was $350.

Add $125 for extra barrel.

This model is similar in design to the old style single shot Remington Target Model.

ENCORE 209X50 MODEL — .50 cal. perc., #209 primer ignition, closed breech break open design, 15 in. blue barrel, adj. rear and ramp front sights, walnut grip and forend, 20.5 in. OAL, approx. 4 lbs. Disc. 2004.

	$565	$525	$415	$310

Last MSR was $611.

GRADING - PPGS™	100%	98%	90%	80%

RIFLES: FLINTLOCK & PERCUSSION

BLACK MOUNTAIN MAGNUM — .50 or .54 cal. perc., musket cap ignition, cap lock, 26 in. round barrel, blue finish, composite stock. Disc. 2002.

	$315	$245	$185	$145

Last MSR was $353.

Add $34 for walnut stock.

Add $34 for .54 cal. Westerner model with walnut stock.

BIG BOAR — .58 cal. perc., 26 in. octagon barrel, color case hardened hammer and lock, single hunting style trigger, American walnut stock, recoil pad and swivels, 7 lbs. 12 oz. Disc.

	$300	$220	$160	$110

Last MSR was $355.

CHEROKEE — .32, .36, or .45 cal. perc., 24 in. octagon barrel, double set triggers, color case hardened hammer and lock, brass trim, American walnut. Disc. 1994.

	$300	$220	$160	$110

Last MSR was $320.

Add $105 for extra barrel.

FIRESTORM (FLINTLOCK) — .50 cal. flintlock, 26 in. round barrel, blue or stainless steel finish, 1:48 in. twist, composite stock, fiber optic sights, 41.75 in. OAL, 7 lbs. New 2000.

courtesy Thompson/Center Arms Co., Inc.

MSR $528	$485	$385	$285	$195

Add $55 for stainless steel.

FIRESTORM (PERCUSSION) — .50 cal. perc., percussion lock, #209 primer ignition, 26 in. round barrel, blue finish, composite stock, fiber optic sights. Mfg. 2000-02.

	$365	$265	$165	$95

Last MSR was $391.

GREY HAWK — .50 cal. perc., 24 in. round barrel, all stainless steel construction, Rynite stock, 7 lbs. Mfg. 1993-disc.

	$260	$195	$135	$95

Last MSR was $330.

HAWKEN — .50 or .54 (disc. 2004) cal. perc. or flintlock, 28 in. octagon barrel, color case hardened hammer and lock, double set triggers, American walnut stock with brass trim, 45.25 in. OAL, 8.5 lbs.

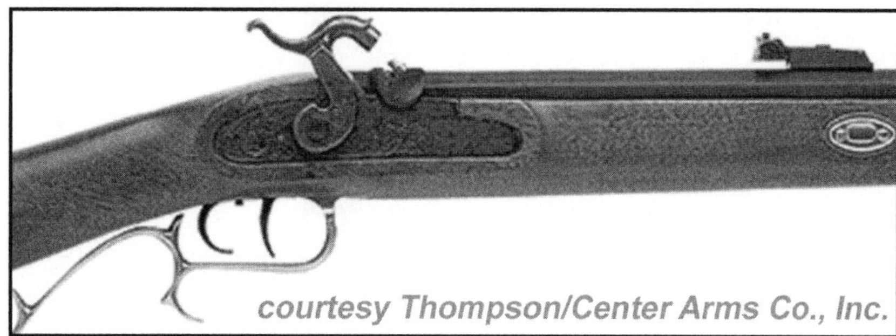

courtesy Thompson/Center Arms Co., Inc.

MSR $763	$715	$650	$535	$435

Add $31 for flintlock model.

GRADING - PPGS™	100%	98%	90%	80%

HAWKEN SILVER ELITE — .50 cal. perc., 28 in. stainless steel octagon barrel and lock, double set triggers, semi fancy wood stock.

	$475	$385	$280	$230

Last MSR was $535.

HAWKEN COUGAR — .45 or .50 cal. perc., stainless steel version of Hawken, select hardwood stock.

	$360	$295	$225	$170

HIGH PLAINS SPORTER — .50 cal. perc., 24 in. round blue barrel, blue furniture, sling swivels, walnut stock w/ recoil pad, 7 lbs. Mfg. 1992-94.

	$315	$245	$185	$145

Last MSR was $340.

NEW ENGLANDER RIFLE — .50 or .54 cal. perc., 24 and 28 in. barrel, brass furniture, walnut or Rynite (new 1991) stock, 5 lbs. 2 oz. Disc. 2002.

	$300	$225	$160	$110

Last MSR was $335.

Add $105 for extra .50 cal. barrel, and $15 for left-hand.
Subtract $15 for Rynite stock.

PENNSYLVANIA HUNTER RIFLE/CARBINE — .50 cal. flintlock, 21 (carbine) or 31 (rifle) in. octagon to round barrel, color case hardened hammer and lock, 7 lbs. 9 oz. Disc. 2002.

	$395	$335	$245	$205

Last MSR was $438.

Add $15 for left-hand.
Add $135 for 21 in. extra carbine barrel.
Add $20 for Match Rifle (Percussion Model Disc.).

RENEGADE — .50, .54, or .56 (smooth bore) cal. perc. or flintlock, 26 in. octagon barrel, color case hardened hammer and lock, double set triggers, 8 lbs. Disc.

	$295	$220	$160	$110

Last MSR was $360.

Add $10 for flintlock.
Add $105 for 12 ga. barrel.
Add $10 for left-hand.
Subtract $25 for single trigger Hunter Model (new 1987) and smooth bore model.

RENEGADE HUNTER — .50 cal. perc. 26 in. octagon blue barrel, 1:48 in. twist, color case hardened hammer and lock, adj. rear sight, walnut stock w/recoil pad, 42.5 in. OAL, 8 lbs. Mfg. 2003-05.

	$425	$350	$255	$220

Last MSR was $469.

SENECA — .36 or .45 cal. perc., 27 in. octagon barrel, color case hardened hammer and lock, double set triggers, American walnut, 6 lbs. Disc. 1987.

	$300	$225	$175	$115

Last MSR was $300.

TREE HAWK CARBINE — .50 cal. perc., 21 in. round camo barrel, camo furniture, Rynite camo stock, with swivels and sling, 6.75 lbs. Mfg. 1992-94.

	$295	$220	$160	$115

Last MSR was $340.

Add $135 for extra 12 ga. barrel.

WHITE MOUNTAIN CARBINE — .50 cal. flintlock or perc., 21 in. octagon tapering to round barrel, color case hardened furniture, single hunting trigger, walnut stock, 6.5 lbs. Mfg. 1989-disc.

	$295	$220	$165	$120

Last MSR was $350.

Add $20 for flintlock.

GRADING - PPGS™	100%	98%	90%	80%

RIFLES: IN-LINE IGNITION

BLACK DIAMOND — .50 cal. perc., #11 or musket percussion cap, or #209 primer Flame Thrower ignition system, 22.5 in. round blue or stainless steel barrel, 1:28 in. twist, adj. Tru-Glo fiber optic sights, drilled and tapped for scope mounts, Rynite stock, 41.5 in. OAL, 6 lbs., 9 oz. New 1998.

	$285	$215	$150	$100

Last MSR was $317.

Add $49 for stainless steel.

BLACK DIAMOND XR — .50 cal. perc., #11 or musket percussion cap, or #209 primer Flame Thrower ignition system, 26 in. round blue or stainless steel barrel, 1:28 in. twist, adj. Tru-Glo fiber optic sights, drilled and tapped for scope mounts, black composite, Realtree Hardwoods Camo composite, or walnut stock, recoil pad, 46 in. OAL, 6.75 lbs. New 2003.

	$300	$235	$160	$115

Last MSR was $337.

Add $44 for stainless steel.
Add $75 for walnut stock.
Add $59 for Realtree Hardwoods Camo stock.

BLACK DIAMOND SUPER 45 XR — .45 cal., similar to Black Diamond XR, except Super .45 cal. and black composite stock only, 7.25 lbs. Mfg. 2003.

	$315	$245	$185	$145

Last MSR was $348.

Add $47 for stainless steel.

ENCORE 209X50 ENDEAVOR — .50 cal. perc., #209 primer ignition, closed breech break-open action w/ peed Breech XT™ and E-Z Tip Extractor™, 28 in. fluted round stainless steel barrel w/QLA muzzle system, 1:28 in. twist, adj. fiber optic sights, drilled and tapped for scope mounts, black or Realtree AP Camo composite FlexTech™ w/ Energy Burners™ stock and forend, Powder Rod®, 42.5 in. OAL, approx. 7 lbs. New 2008.

courtesy Thompson/Center Arms Co., Inc.

MSR $1,040	$950	$850	$650	$550

Add $70 for Realtree AP Camo stock and forend.

ENCORE 209X50 KATAHDIN CARBINE — .50 cal. perc., #209 primer ignition, closed breech break-open action, 20 in. round blue barrel (ported) w/built in Muzzle Tamer, 1:28 in. twist, adj. rear peep and Tru-Glo fiber optic front sights, drilled and tapped for scope mounts, Realtree Hardwoods HD composite stock and forend, 34 in. OAL, approx. 6.75 lbs. New 2004.

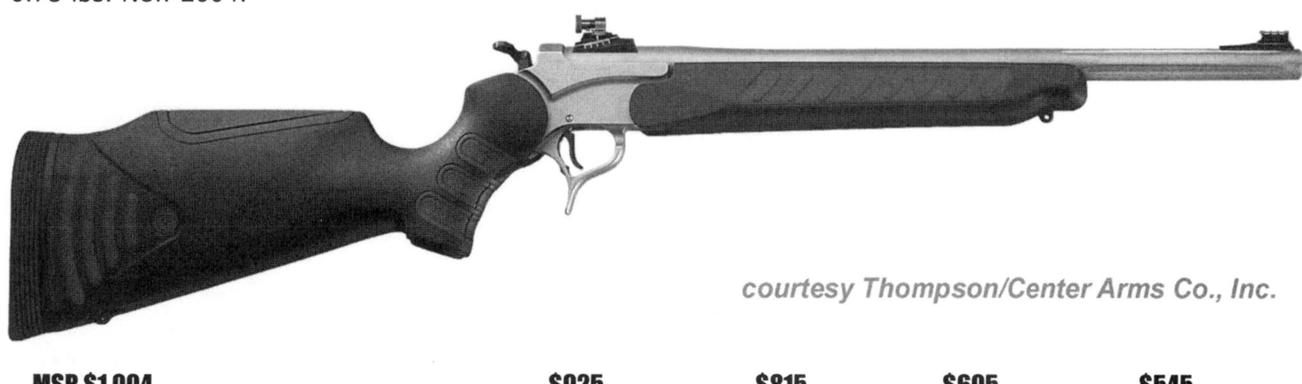

courtesy Thompson/Center Arms Co., Inc.

MSR $1,004	$925	$815	$695	$545

GRADING - PPGS™	100%	98%	90%	80%

ENCORE 209X50 MAGNUM — .50 cal. perc., #209 primer ignition, closed breech break-open action, 26 in. round blue, Realtree Hardwoods HD (new 2004), or stainless steel barrel, 1:28 in. twist, adj. Tru-Glo fiber optic sights, drilled and tapped for scope mounts, black composite, Realtree Hardwoods HD composite, or walnut PG or thumbhole (new 2008) stock and forend, 40.5 in. OAL, approx. 7 lbs.

courtesy Thompson Center Arms Co., Inc.

MSR $798	$715	$625	$450	$365

Add $45 for walnut stock and forend.
Add $90 for stainless steel.
Add $65 for Realtree Hardwoods HD stock.
Add $30 for Realtree Hardwoods HD barrel.
Add $15 for thumbhole stock.

ENCORE 209X50 PRO HUNTER™ — .50 cal. perc., #209 primer ignition, closed breech break-open action w/Speed Breech XT™ and E-Z Tip Extractor™, 28 in. fluted round blue or stainless steel barrel w/QLA muzzel system, 1:28 in. twist, adj. fiber optic sights, drilled and tapped for scope mounts, black or Realtree Hardwoods HD® composite FlexTech™ w/Energy Burners™ PG or thumbhole stock and forend, Powder Rod®, 42.5 in. OAL, approx. 7 lbs. New 2008.

MSR $920	$825	$725	$525	$435

Add $60 for Realtree Hardwoods HD® camo stock and forend.
Add $105 for stainless steel.

ENCORE 209X45 SUPER MAGNUM — .45 cal. perc., #209 primer ignition, closed breech break-open action, 26 in. round blue barrel w/walnut stock and forend or stainless steel barrel w/black composite stock and forend, 1:28 in. twist, adj. Tru-Glo fiber optic sights, drilled and tapped for scope mounts, 40.5 in. OAL, approx. 7 lbs. Mfg. 2003-05.

	$600	$465	$385	$285

Last MSR was $680.

Add $41 for stainless steel barrel w/black composite stock and forend.

FIRE HAWK — .50 or .54 cal. perc., 24 in. round blue steel barrel, walnut stock.

	$345	$270	$220	$165

Last MSR was $384.

Add $50 for stainless steel barrel assembly.
Add $40 for composite stock and stainless steel barrel assembly.

FIRE HAWK DELUXE — .50 or .54 cal. perc., 24 in. round blue steel barrel, deluxe checkered walnut stock.

	$475	$385	$280	$230

Last MSR was $520.

Add $52 for stainless steel barrel assembly.

FIRE HAWK THUMBHOLE STOCK MODEL — .50 or .54 cal. perc., 24 in. round blue steel barrel, composite thumbhole stock.

	$365	$300	$235	$180

Last MSR was $404.

Add $50 for stainless steel barrel assembly.

FIRE HAWK BANTAM — .50 cal. perc., 21 in. round blue steel barrel, 13.25 in. LOP walnut stock.

	$345	$275	$225	$165

Last MSR was $383.

FIRE HAWK ADVANTAGE CAMO — .50 or .54 cal. perc., 24 in. round blue steel barrel, camouflage composite stock.

	$375	$300	$235	$190

Last MSR was $415.

G2 CONTENDER 209X45 — .45 cal. perc., #209 primer ignition, closed breech break-open action, 24 in. round blue barrel, 1:28 in. twist, walnut stock and forend, adj. Tru-Glo fiber optic sights, drilled and tapped for scope mounts, 37.75 in. OAL, approx. 5.5 lbs. Mfg. 2003-2005.

	$575	$450	$345	$275

Last MSR was $636.

GRADING - PPGS™	100%	98%	90%	80%

G2 CONTENDER 209X50 — .50 cal. perc., #209 primer ignition, closed breech break-open action, 24 in. round blue barrel W/ Quick Load Accurizer Muzzle System, 1:28 in. twist, walnut stock and forend, adj. Tru-Glo fiber optic sights, drilled and tapped for scope mounts, 37.75 IN. oal, approx. 5.5 lbs. Mfg. 2006-2008.

courtesy Thompson Center Arms Co., Inc.

	$675	$550	$445	$375

Last MSR was $706.

OMEGA — .45 (2003-2007) or .50 cal., perc., #209 primer ignition, sealed pivoting breech under lever action, Speed Breech 90 degree removable breech plug (new 2006), round or fluted X7 (2006-2007) receiver, 28 in. round or fluted (new 2004) stainless steel barrel w/Quick Load Accurizer Muzzle System (new 2005), 1:28 in. twist, adj. Tru-Glo fiber optic sights, drilled and tapped for scope mounts, Realtree Hardwoods HD Camo composite, or gray laminated wood stock with or w/o thumbhole (new 2004), recoil pad, 42 in. OAL, approx. 7 lbs. New 2002.

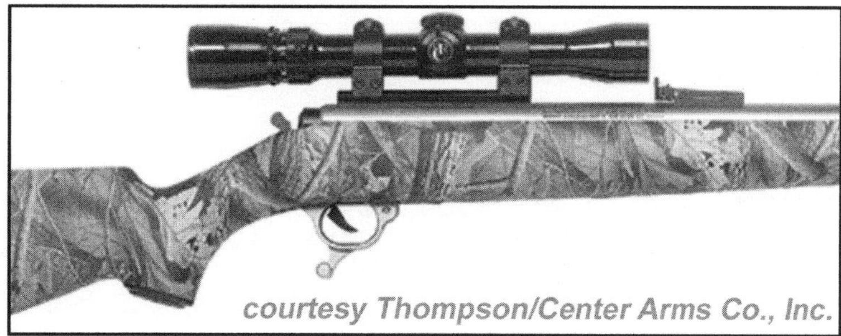

courtesy Thompson/Center Arms Co., Inc.

MSR $536	$475	$395	$285	$295

Add $81 for gray laminated wood stock.
Add $72 for Realtree Hardwoods HD Camo stock.
Add $14 for .45 cal.
Add $160 for Omega X7 fluted receiver barrel thumbhole stock.

OMEGA Z5 — .50 cal., perc., #209 primer ignition, sealed pivoting breech under lever action, Speed Breech 90 degree removable breech plug (new 2006), 28 in. round blue or Weather Shield™ w/Quick Load Accurizer Muzzle System, 1:28 in. twist, adj. Tru-Glo fiber optic sights, drilled and tapped for scope mounts, black or Realtree Hardwoods HD Camo composite stock, recoil pad, 42 in. OAL, approx. 7 lbs. New 2007.

MSR $384	$350	$305	$235	$195

Add $70 for Realtree Hardwoods HD Camo stock.
Add $43 for gray Weather Shield barrel.

SCOUT RIFLE/CARBINE — .50 and .54 cal. perc., 21 (carbine) or 24 in. round barrel, 7 lbs. 4 oz.

	$350	$275	$225	$170

Last MSR was $435.

Add $135 per extra barrels.
Subtract $90 for Rynite stock model (new 1993).

SYSTEM 1 — .32, .50, .54, or .58 cal., 12 ga., perc., 26 in. interchangeable round blue steel barrel, walnut stock.

	$350	$275	$225	$170

Last MSR was $389.

Add $40 for composite stock.
Add $75 for camo composite stock.
Add $170 for .32 or .58 cal. blue steel barrel.
Add $170 for 12 ga. blue steel barrel with screw-in full choke.
Add $220 for .50 cal. or .54 cal. stainless steel barrel.

GRADING - PPGS™	100%	98%	90%	80%

THUNDER HAWK SHADOW — .50 cal. perc., 24 in. round blue steel barrel, composite stock.

	$250	$190	$135	$95

Last MSR was $289.

Add $51 for stainless steel barrel assembly.

THUNDER HAWK SHADOW CAMO — .50 cal. perc., 24 in. round blue steel barrel, camouflage composite stock.

	$285	$220	$160	$90

Last MSR was $320.

TRIUMPH — .50 cal. perc., #209 primer ignition, closed breech break-open action, Speed Breech XT 90 degree removable breech plug, 28 in. round blue, Realtree AP HD (new 2009) or Weather Shield barrel w/Quick Load Accurizer Muzzle System, 1:28 in. twist, adj. Tru-Glo fiber optic sights, drilled and tapped for scope mounts, black or Realtree AP HD composite stock and forend, 40.5 in. OAL, approx. 7 lbs. New 2007.

courtesy Thompson Center Arms Co., Inc.

MSR $473	$435	$365	$235	$195

Add $62 for Weather Shield barrel.
Add $83 for Realtree AP HD stock.
Add $15 for Realtree AP HD barrel.

TRIUMPH BONE COLLECTOR™ — .50 cal. perc., #209 primer ignition, closed breech break-open action, Speed Breech XT 90 degree removable breech plug, 28 in. round fluted Realtree AP HD or Weather Shield barrel w/Quick Load Accurizer Muzzle System, 1:28 in. twist, adj. Tru-Glo fiber optic sights, drilled and tapped for scope mounts, black or Realtree AP HD composite stock w/Flex Tech™ and Energy Burners, 42.5 in. OAL, approx. 7 lbs. New 2009.

MSR $664	$595	$525	$395	$335

Add $44 for Realtree AP HD camo.

SHOTGUNS: PERCUSSION & IN-LINE IGNITION

BLACK MOUNTAIN MAGNUM — 12 ga., Turkey cap lock, 27 in. round barrel with special Turkey Choke Tube, blue finish, composite stock. Disc. 2002.

	$350	$275	$225	$175

Last MSR was $387.

ENCORE MUZZLELOADING TURKEY GUN — 12 ga., perc., #209 primer In-Line ignition, closed breech break-open action, 24 in. smoothbore barrel w/screw-in Turkey choke tube, blue or Realtree Hardwoods Camo (new 2004) frame, adj. fiber optic sights, Realtree Hardwoods Camo finish barrel, Realtree Hardwoods Camo composite stock and forend, Thompson Contender styling. New 2003.

courtesy Thompson Center Arms Co., Inc.

MSR $907	$805	$705	$565	$475

NEW ENGLANDER — 12 ga., perc., 26 or 28 in. barrel, brass furniture, 5 lbs. 2 oz.

	$275	$200	$145	$100

Last MSR was $330.

Add $105 for extra .50 cal. barrel.
Add $15 for left-hand.
Add $20 for full choke.
Subtract $15 for Rynite stock.

GRADING - PPGS™	100%	98%	90%	80%

TREE HAWK — 12 ga., similar to New Englander. Mfg. 1994-disc.

	$275	$200	$145	$100

Last MSR was $345.

TRADITIONS PERFORMANCE FIREARMS

Current importer located in Old Saybrook, CT. Distributor and dealer sales.

Traditions Performance Firearms imports Italian made black powder cap & ball pistols, revolvers, and longrifles, manufactured by Uberti, Pietta, and Pedersoli along with Spanish made in-line muzzle loaders manufactured by Ardesa.

For more information and current pricing on both new and used Traditions firearms, please refer to the *Blue Book of Gun Values* by S.P. Fjestad (now online also).

Black Powder Reproductions & Replicas by Dennis Adler is also an invaluable source for most black powder reproductions and replicas, and includes hundreds of color images on most popular makes/models, provides manufacturer/trademark histories, and up-to-date information on related items/accessories for black powder shooting - www.bluebookinc.com

CANNONS: MINIATURE

MINI NAPOLEON III — .50 cal., 7.25 in. smoothbore, fuse ignition, nickel finish, wheel diameter 6 in., OAL 14.5 in., 2 lbs. 6 oz.

MSR $265	$245	$215	$155	$115

MINI OLD IRONSIDES — .50 cal., 9 in. smoothbore, fuse ignition, nickel finish, wheel diameter 2-1/8 in., OAL 11.5 in., 3 lbs. 14 oz.

MSR $231	$195	$175	$125	$100

MINI YORKTOWN — .50 cal., 7-3/8 in. smoothbore, fuse ignition, nickel finish, wheel diameter 4.5 in., OAL 13 in., 2 lbs. 6 oz.

MSR $258	$230	$205	$155	$130

NAPOLEON III - GOLD — .69 cal., 14.5 in. smoothbore, fuse ignition, gold finish, wheel diameter 11.5 in., OAL 27.5 in., 15 lbs.

MSR $760	$685	$605	$450	$355

NAPOLEON III - NICKEL — .69 cal., 14.5 in. smoothbore, fuse ignition, nickel finish, wheel diameter 11.5 in., OAL 27.5 in., 15 lbs.

MSR $705	$635	$560	$425	$350

OLD IRONSIDES — .69 cal., 12.5 in. smoothbore, fuse ignition, black finish, wheel diameter 2-1/8 in., OAL 14 in., 9 lbs. 3 oz.

MSR $293	$265	$225	$170	$135

PISTOLS: IN-LINE IGNITION

BUCKHUNTER PRO — .45 (new 2002) or .50 cal. perc., 9.5 or 12.5 in. round, or 14.75 in. fluted barrel with muzzle brake, 1:28 or 1:20 in. (.45 cal.) twist, blue or nickel finish, adj. sights, walnut or all weather finish hardwood grip and forearm, 14.75-20 in. OAL, 3 lbs. 1 oz. to 3 lbs. 11 oz. Disc. 2009.

courtesy Traditions Performance Firearms

	$295	$260	$195	$165

Last MSR was $324.

Add $15 for 12.5 in. barrel or nickel finish w/AW finish wood on 9.5 in. barrel.
Add $30 for 14.75 in. fluted barrel with muzzle brake.

GRADING - PPGS™	100%	98%	90%	80%

PISTOLS: PERCUSSION

BUCKSKINNER PISTOL — .50 cal. perc., 10 in. octagon blue barrel, color case hardened hammer and lock, black furniture, beech or laminated stock, 2.5 lbs. Mfg. 1993-disc.

	$135	$110	$75	$50

Last MSR was $146.

Add $15 for laminated stock.

CROCKETT PISTOL — .32 cal. perc., 10 in. octagon blue barrel, fixed tang, single trigger, select hardwood stock, 2 lbs. 4 oz. New 2000.

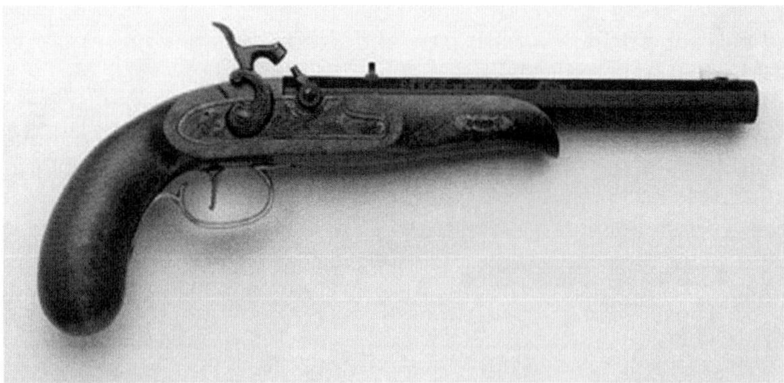

courtesy Traditions Performance Firearms

MSR $214	$190	$165	$115	$95

KENTUCKY PISTOL — .50 cal. perc., 9.75 in. octagon barrel, 1:20 in. twist, color case hardened hammer and lock, brass trigger guard and endcap, select hardwood stock, 15 in. OAL, 2.5 lbs.

courtesy Traditions Performance Firearms

MSR $209	$185	$165	$125	$100

PIONEER PISTOL — .45 or .50 cal. perc., 9-5/8 in. octagon barrel, German silver furniture, blackened hardware, select hardwood stock, 2 lbs. 4 oz. New 1991.

courtesy Traditions Performance Firearms

MSR $197	$185	$165	$115	$85

PIRATE PISTOL — - .50 cal. flintlock, 10 in. polished round barrel, 1:20 in. twist, ST, blade front sight, polished lock, 15 in. OAL, 2.75 lbs. New 2009.

MSR $337	$310	$275	$195	$165

GRADING - PPGS™	100%	98%	90%	80%

TRAPPER PISTOL — .45 or .50 cal. flintlock or perc., 9.75 in. octagon barrel, hooked breech, double set triggers, adj. sights, brass trim, 3 lbs. 4 oz.

courtesy Traditions Performance Firearms

MSR $286	$260	$225	$165	$135

Add $19 for black laminate stock and nickel finish (new 2007).
Add $26 for flintlock.

VEST POCKET DERRINGER — .31 cal. perc., 2.25 in. brass barrel, spur trigger, simulated ivory grips.

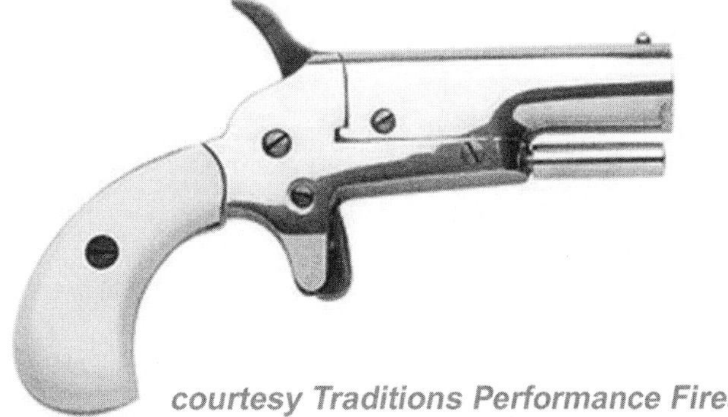
courtesy Traditions Performance Firearms

MSR $165	$145	$130	$95	$85

WILLIAM PARKER PISTOL — .50 cal. perc., 10-3/8 in. octagon polished steel barrel, hooked breech, double set triggers, checkered walnut stock, 2 lbs. 8 oz.

courtesy Traditions Performance Firearms

MSR $381	$345	$305	$235	$195

REVOLVERS: PERCUSSION

1847 COLT WALKER — .44 cal. perc., 9 in. barrel, color case hardened hammer, frame and loading lever, brass trigger guard, 3.9 lbs. Disc. 2001.

	$260	$195	$140	$100

Last MSR was $293.

GRADING - PPGS™	100%	98%	90%	80%

1851 COLT NAVY — .36 (new 2003) or .44 cal. perc., 7.5 in. octagon barrel, color case hardened hammer and loading lever, steel or brass frame, cylinder has roll engraving.

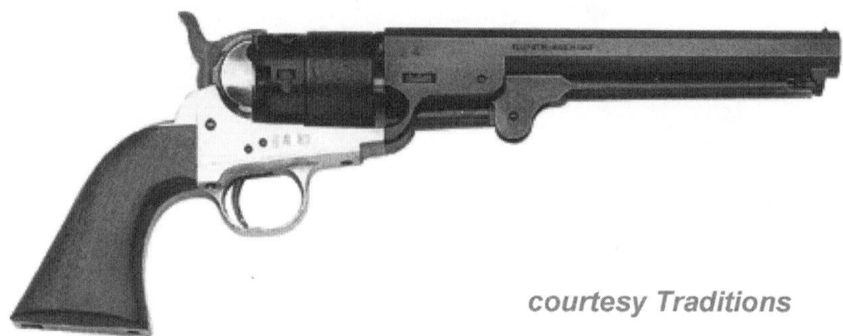

courtesy Traditions

MSR $219	$195	$175	$135	$100

Add $30 for steel frame model.

* ***1851 Colt Navy Antiqued*** — .44 cal. perc., 7.375 in. octagon barrel, steel color case hardened frame, hammer and loading lever, brass trigger guard, roll engraved cylinder, 13.5 in. OAL, 2.75 lbs. New 2008.

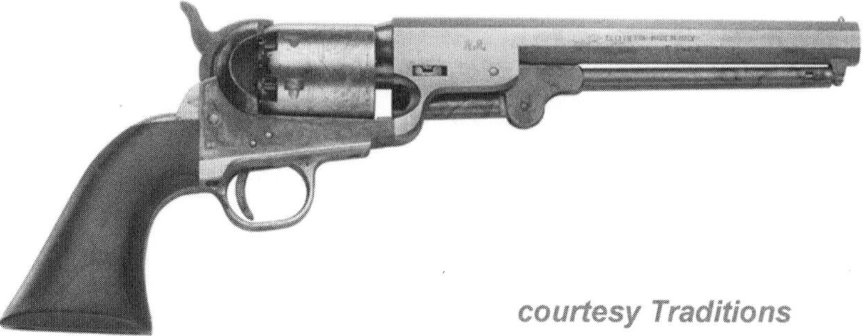

courtesy Traditions

MSR $378	$340	$300	$225	$190

* ***1851 Navy Old Silver/Sheriff Model*** — .44 cal. perc., 5.5 (Sheriff Model engraved) or 7.5 in. octagon barrel, old silver finish, steel frame, cylinder has roll engraving.

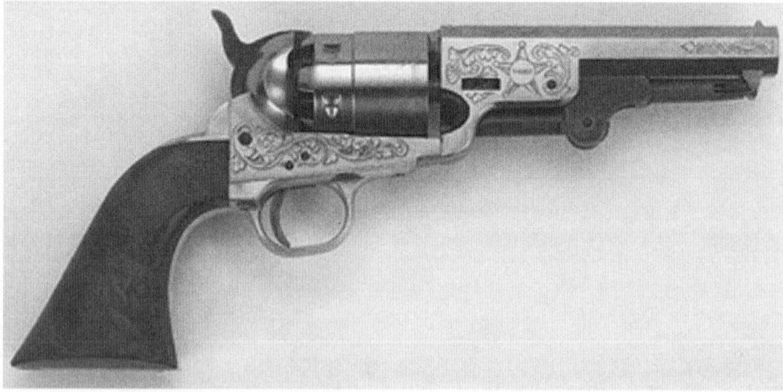

courtesy Traditions Performance Firearms

MSR $315	$285	$255	$185	$155

Add $52 for Sheriff Model.

GRADING - PPGS™	100%	98%	90%	80%

1858 REMINGTON BISON — .44 cal. perc., 12 in. octagon barrel, brass frame and nickel trigger guard.

courtesy Traditions Performance Firearms

MSR $290	$260	$230	$170	$140

1858 REMINGTON NEW ARMY — .44 cal. perc., 6.5 in. octagon barrel, brass or steel frame and brass trigger guard, adjustable target sights.

courtesy Traditions Performance Firearms

MSR $250	$225	$200	$150	$125

Add $58 for steel frame.

* ***1858 New Army Short Barrel*** — - .44 cal. perc., 5.5 in. octagon barrel, blue finish, old silver trigger guard, 11.5 in. OAL, 2.5 lbs. New 2009.

MSR $352	$315	$280	$210	$175

1858 REMINGTON NEW ARMY W/TARGET SIGHTS — .44 cal. perc., 6.5 in. octagon barrel, stainless steel, adj. rear target sight.

MSR $514	$465	$410	$310	$255

1860 COLT ARMY — .44 cal. perc., 8 in. round barrel, color case hardened steel or brass frame, brass trigger guard.

courtesy Traditions Performance Firearms

MSR $236	$215	$185	$145	$115

Add $51 for color case hardened steel frame.
Add $106 for nickel finish and simulated ivory grips.
Add $119 for steel frame and simulated ivory grips.

GRADING - PPGS™	100%	98%	90%	80%

* ***1860 Colt Army Antiqued*** — .44 cal. perc., 8 in. round barrel, antique finish, color case hardened steel frame, brass trigger guard, 13.75 in. OAL, 2.75 lbs. New 2008.

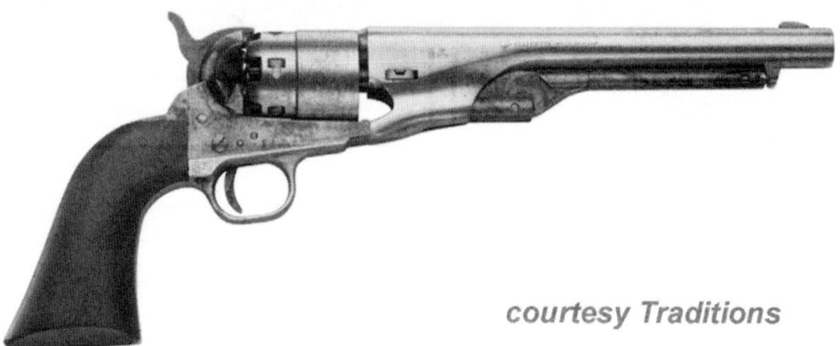

courtesy Traditions

MSR $417	$375	$340	$245	$105

1863 POCKET REMINGTON — .31 cal. perc., 3.5 in. octagon blue barrel, brass frame w/spur trigger, fixed sights, walnut grips, approx. 1 lb. New 2003.

MSR $219	$195	$160	$120	$85

1873 COLT PEACEMAKER — .44 cal. perc., 4.75 in. or 7.5 in. barrel, color case hardened steel frame, brass grip straps and trigger guard, walnut grips. Colt SAA style revolver fitted with cap and ball cylinder.

courtesy Traditions Performance Firearms

MSR $411	$365	$325	$250	$195

ACES AND EIGHTS — .44 cal. perc., 7.375 in. octagon barrel, laser engraved barrel and grips, old silver finish, simulated Ivory grips, 13.5 in. OAL, 2.75 lbs. New 2009.

MSR $523	$475	$425	$315	$255

GOLD RUSH — .44 cal. perc., 3.25 in. octagon barrel, laser engraved barrel and grips, old silver finish, simulated Ivory grips, 7.25 in. OAL, 1.5 lbs. New 2009.

MSR $543	$485	$430	$320	$265

JESSIE JAMES — .44 cal. perc., 7.375 in. octagon barrel, laser engraved barrel and grips, old silver finish, simulated Ivory grips, 13.5 in. OAL, 2.75 lbs. New 2009.

MSR $470	$425	$375	$280	$225

GRADING - PPGS™	100%	98%	90%	80%

J.H. DANCE — .44 cal. perc., 8 in. round blue barrel, color case hardened steel frame, brass trigger guard, 13.5 in. OAL, 2.75 lbs. New 2008.

courtesy Traditions

MSR $377	$340	$300	$225	$185

JOSEY WALES NAVY REVOLVER — .36 cal. perc., 7.5 in. round barrel, antique finish, brass trigger guard, 13.75 in. OAL, 2.75 lbs. New 2008.

courtesy Traditions

MSR $455	$405	$360	$265	$225

POCKET REMINGTON — .31 cal. perc., 3.5 in. octagon barrel, brass frame, walnut grips. Disc. 2001.

	$150	$125	$95	$65

Last MSR was $168.

REB CONFEDERATE — .44 cal. perc., 7.375 in. round blue barrel and cylinder, brass frame, brass trigger guard,13.5 in. OAL, 2.75 lbs. New 2008.

courtesy Traditions

MSR $225	$200	$180	$135	$115

REMINGTON BEALS NAVY NEW MODEL — .36 cal. perc., 6.5 in. octagon barrel, steel frame, blue finish, brass trigger guard, walnut grips, fixed sights, approx. 2.75 lbs. New 2003.

MSR $305	$275	$245	$185	$145

GRADING - PPGS™	100%	98%	90%	80%

SPILLER & BURR — .36 cal. perc., 6.5 in. octagon barrel, brass frame and brass trigger guard, 12.5 in. OAL, 2.75 lbs. New 2008.

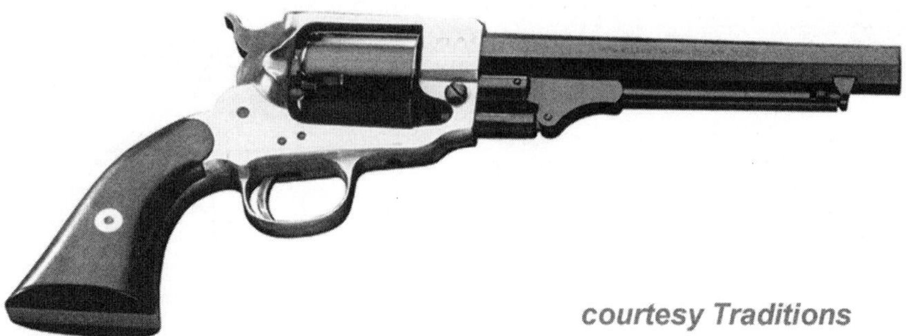

courtesy Traditions

MSR $277	$250	$220	$165	$140

WELLS FARGO — . 31 cal. perc., 4 in. octagon barrel, 5 shot, brass frame, backstrap and trigger guard, no loading lever, 1.5 lbs. Disc. 2001.

	$125	$105	$70	$55

Last MSR was $140.

WILD BILL — .44 cal. perc., 7.375 in. octagon barrel, laser engraved barrel and grips, old silver finish, simulated Ivory grips, 13.5 in. OAL, 2.75 lbs. New 2009.

MSR $551	$500	$440	$330	$275

RIFLES: FLINTLOCK & PERCUSSION

BUCKSKINNER FLINTLOCK CARBINE — .50 cal. flintlock, 21 in. octagon to round barrel w/blue finish or full octagon w/nickel (new 2004), 1:48 in. twist, blackened hardware, select hardwood Monte Carlo stock with pistol grip, adj. TruGlo fiber optic sights (new 2000), recoil pad, 37.5 in. OAL, 6 lbs. Disc. 2008.

courtesy Traditions Performance Firearms

	$285	$245	$185	$125

Last MSR was $322.

Add $74 for black laminated stock.
Add $104 for black laminated stock and nickel barrel (new 2004).

CREEDMOOR MATCH RIFLE — .451 cal. perc., 32 in. octagon to round blue barrel, color case hardened hammer, lock, and trigger guard, hooded front and adj. spindle diopter rear sight, checkered walnut stock, 8.5 lbs. Mfg. 1994-disc.

	$975	$775	$625	$455

Last MSR was $1,150.

CROCKETT SMALL GAME RIFLE — .32 cal. perc., 32 in. octagon barrel, 1:48 in. twist, fixed rear and blade front sights, color case hardened hammer and lock, brass buttplate, trigger guard, double set triggers, 49 in. OAL, 6 lbs. 7 oz. New 2000.

MSR $434	$395	$350	$260	$220

DEERHUNTER RIFLE — .32, .50, or .54 cal. flintlock or perc., 24 in. octagon barrel, blue or nickel finish, 1:48 in. twist, adj. Lite optic sights, color case hardened or nickel hammer and lock, single trigger, hardwood, Mossy Oak Break-Up, or black AW synthetic stock, 40 in. OAL, approx. 6 lbs.

GRADING - PPGS™	100%	98%	90%	80%

* ***Deerhunter Rifle (Hardwood Blue)*** — .32 or .50 cal. flintlock or perc., blue finish with hardwood stock.

courtesy Tradition Performance Firearms

MSR $264	**$240**	**$205**	**$140**	**$120**

Add $51 for flintlock.
Add $11 for .32 cal. perc.
Add $22 for left-hand.

* ***Deerhunter Rifle (All Weather Synthetic Blue)*** — .50 or .54 cal. flintlock or perc., blue finish with black AW synthetic stock.

courtesy Tradition Performance Firearms

MSR $224	**$200**	**$175**	**$135**	**$110**

Add $32 for flintlock.

* ***Deerhunter Rifle (All Weather Synthetic Nickel)*** — .50 or .54 cal. flintlock or perc., Nickel finish with black, Mossy Oak Treestand (new 2009) or Mossy Oak Break-Up AW synthetic stock.

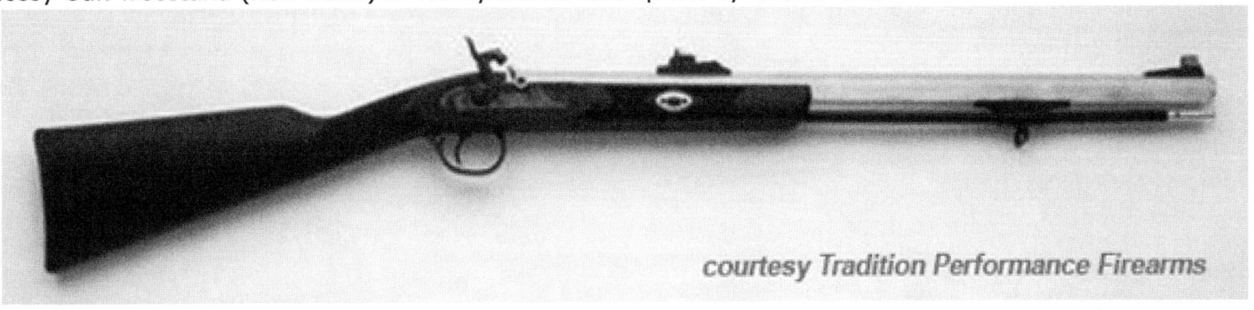

courtesy Tradition Performance Firearms

MSR $228	**$205**	**$185**	**$140**	**$105**

Add $50 for flintlock.
Add $91 for Mossy Oak Break-Up stock.
Add $66 for Mossy Oak Treestrand stock.

1853 ENFIELD (3 BAND) — .58 cal. perc., 39 in. round barrel, 3 barrel bands, color case hardened hammer, lock and barrel bands, brass buttplate, trigger guard and nosecap, full length walnut stock, 10 lbs.

	$435	**$350**	**$260**	**$225**

Last MSR was $484.

GRADING - PPGS™	100%	98%	90%	80%

FRONTIER RIFLE/CARBINE — .45 or .50 cal. perc. or flintlock, 24 (carbine) or 28 in. octagon barrel, double set triggers, adj. sights, brass trim, 6 lbs. 14 oz (6 lbs. 8 oz. carbine). Disc. 1993.

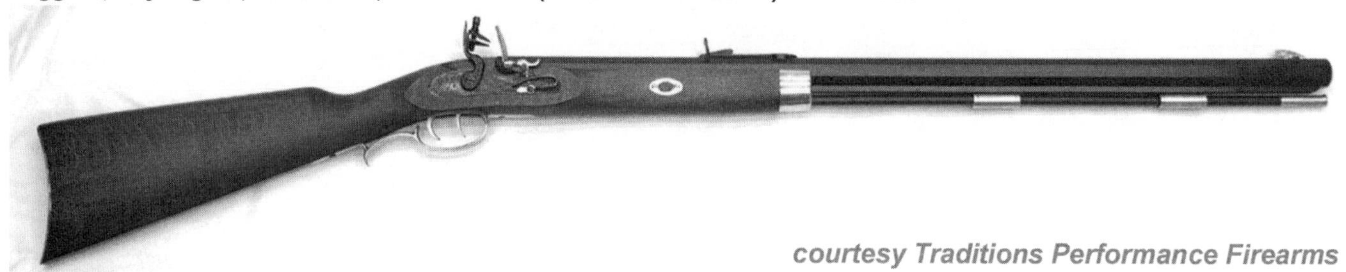

courtesy Traditions Performance Firearms

	$195	$160	$120	$80

Last MSR was $255.

Add $15 for flintlock (.50 cal. only).

* ***Frontier Rifle*** — .50 cal. perc. or flintlock, 28 in. octagon barrel, 1:48 in. twist, double set triggers, adj. sights, brass trim, synthetic ramrod, 44.5 in. OAL, 7.875 lbs. New 2008.

MSR $337	$305	$270	$200	$165

Add $44 for flintlock.

FRONTIER SCOUT RIFLE — .36, .45, or .50 cal. flintlock or perc., 26 in. octagon barrel, double set triggers, adj. sights, brass trim, 5 lbs. 8 oz., lock has adj. sear.

	$160	$130	$100	$70

Last MSR was $215.

Add $10 for flintlock.
Add $15 for carbine.

HAWKEN RIFLE — .50, .54, or .58 cal. perc. or flintlock, 32.25 in. octagon barrel, double set triggers, adj. sights, brass trim, 8 lbs. 2 oz. Disc. 1993.

	$300	$235	$165	$110

Last MSR was $415.

Add $10 for flintlock (.50 and .54 cal. only).

A fiberglass ramrod and deluxe rear sight were introduced in 1989.

HAWKEN MATCH RIFLE — .451 cal. perc., 32 in. octagon blue barrel, engraved brass patchbox, color case hardened hammer and lock, brass trigger guard, buttplate, and furniture, checkered walnut stock, 10 lbs.

	$450	$365	$265	$225

Last MSR was $605.

HAWKEN WOODSMAN RIFLE — .50 or .54 cal. perc. or flintlock, 28 in. octagon blue barrel, 1:48 in. twist, adj. rear blade front sights, color case hardened hammer and lock, double set trigger, hardwood stock, brass furniture and patchbox, 44.5 in. OAL, 7.5 lbs.

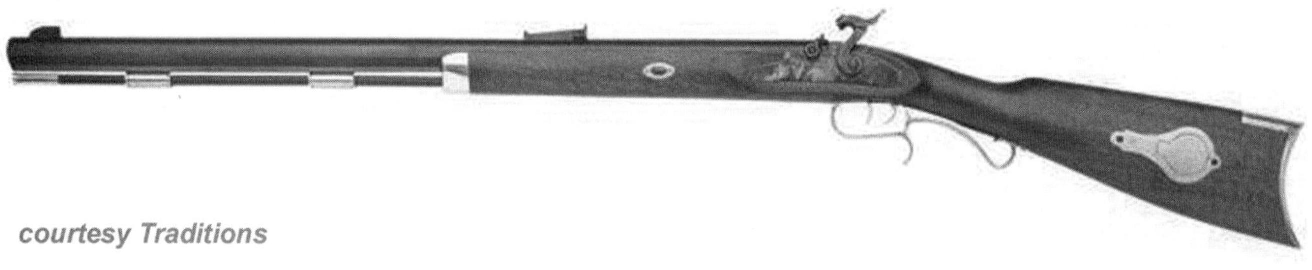

courtesy Traditions

MSR $396	$360	$320	$240	$200

Add $19 for left-hand.
Add $38 for flintlock.
Add $38 for Black Laminate wood stock. New 2007.

HAWKEN MAGNUM RIFLE — .50 cal. perc., musket cap ignition, 28 in. octagon barrel, color case hardened hammer and lock, dual wedges, fiber optic sights, double set trigger, brass furniture and patchbox, select hardwood stock. Designed for use with Pyrodex Pellets. Disc. 2001.

	$325	$255	$195	$150

Last MSR was $259.

GRADING - PPGS™	100%	98%	90%	80%

HENRY TARGET RIFLE — .451 cal. perc., 32 in. octagon blue barrel, color case hardened hammer and lock, hooded front and spindle diopter rear sight, blue steel trim, checkered walnut stock, 11 lbs.

	$1,000	$795	$650	$475

Last MSR was $1,325.

HUNTER RIFLE — .50 or .54 cal. perc., 28 in. octagon barrel, double set triggers, adj. sights, black chrome brass trim with German silver wedge plates, lock has adj. sear, walnut stock, 8 lbs., 10 oz. Disc. 1994.

	$300	$235	$165	$110

Last MSR was $425.

A fiberglass ramrod and deluxe rear sight were introduced in 1989.

KENTUCKY RIFLE (PERCUSSION) — 50 cal. perc., 33.5 in. octagon barrel, 1:66 in. twist, blue finish, color case hardened hammer and lock, fixed rear and blade front sights, full length hardwood stock, brass buttplate, 49 in. OAL, 7 lbs. 4 oz.

MSR $364	$330	$290	$215	$180

KENTUCKY RIFLE — 50 cal. flintlock, 33.5 in. octagon barrel, 1:66 in. twist, blue finish, color case hardened hammer and lock, fixed rear and blade front sights, full length hardwood stock, brass buttplate, 49 in. OAL, 7.25 lbs. New 2002.

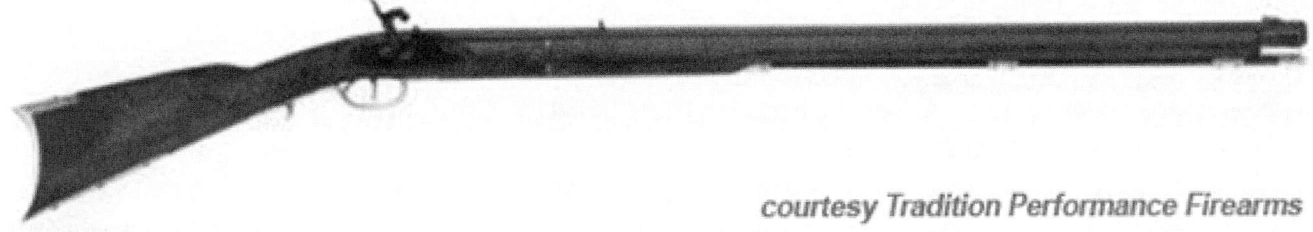

courtesy Tradition Performance Firearms

MSR $408	$365	$325	$245	$205

KENTUCKY SCOUT RIFLE — .45 or .50 cal. perc. or 26 in. octagon barrel, double set triggers, adj. sights, brass trim, full length stock, lock has adj. sear, 5 lbs. 8 oz. Disc. 1989.

	$185	$155	$115	$80

Last MSR was $135.

Add $10 for flintlock.

MOUNTAIN RIFLE — .50 cal. flintlock or perc., 32 in. octagon matte blue finish barrel, hammer, buttplate, furniture and lock, 1:48 in. twist, double set triggers, traditional sights, select hardwood half stock, 49 in. OAL, 7.875 lbs. New 2009.

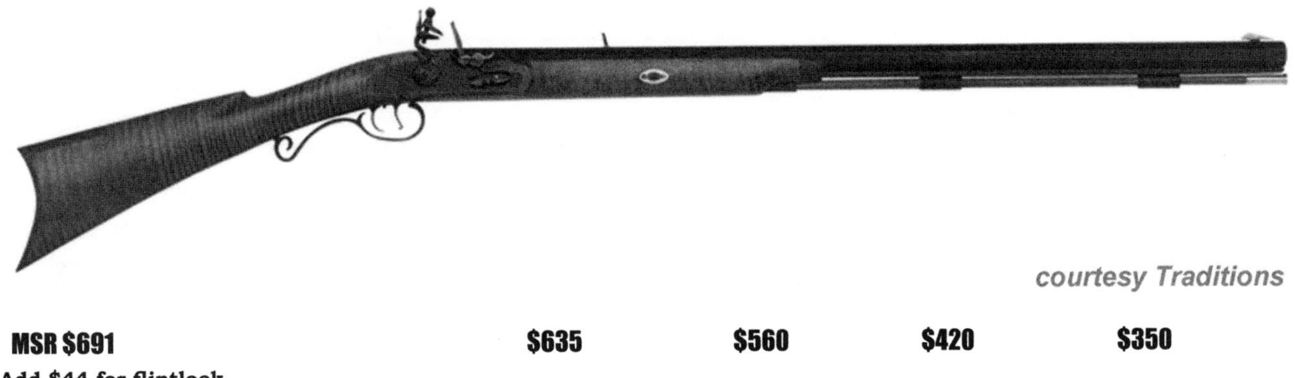

courtesy Traditions

MSR $691	$635	$560	$420	$350

Add $44 for flintlock.

GRADING - PPGS™	100%	98%	90%	80%

PA PELLET FLINTLOCK — .50 cal. flintlock, 26 in. blue, nickel, Hardwoods HD or Mossy Oak Treestand (new 2009) finish octagon barrel, 1:48 in. twist, adj. Tru-Glo or Williams Metal (new 2009) fiber optic sights, heavy-duty lock and deep priming pan, removable breech plug, Hardwoods HD, Mossy Oak Break-Up, Mossy Oak Treestand (new 2009) or black AW synthetic stock, 45 in. OAL, 7 lbs. New 2002.

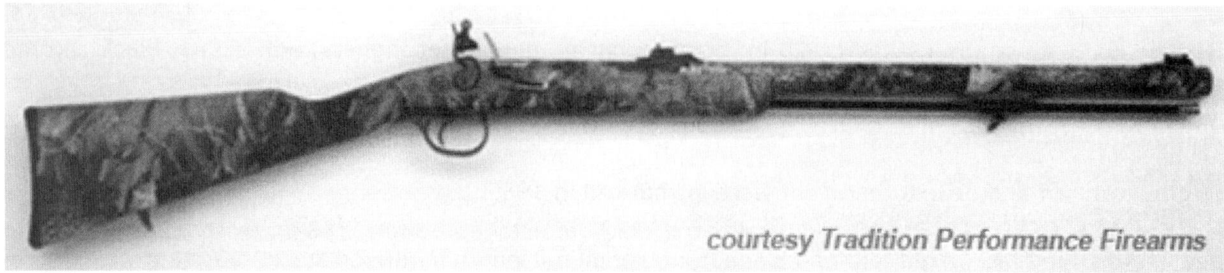
courtesy Tradition Performance Firearms

MSR $337	$310	$275	$205	$165

Add $22 for left-hand model.
Add $27 for nickel barrel.
Add $37 for hardwood stock.
Add $66 for Mossy Oak Break-Up stock.
Add $52 for Double Triggers. New 2007.
Add $56 for Mossy Oak Treestand stock.
Add $103 for Laminate stock.
Add $20 for Mossy Oak Break-Up barrel.
Add $20 for Mossy Oak Treestand barrel.

PANTHER RIFLE — .50 or .54 (new 2002) cal. perc., 24 in. blue octagon barrel, 1:48 in. twist, fixed rear sight, black AW synthetic stock, 40 in. OAL, approx. 6 lbs.

	$115	$95	$65	$50

Last MSR was $129.

PENNSYLVANIA RIFLE (FLINTLOCK) — .50 cal. flintlock, 40.25 in. blue octagon barrel, 1:66 in. twist, double set triggers, adj. sights, full length walnut stock, brass buttplate, brass trim, 57 in. OAL, 8 lbs. 8 oz.

courtesy Tradition Performance Firearms

MSR $720	$650	$575	$435	$365

PENNSYLVANIA RIFLE (PERCUSSION) — .50 cal. perc., 40.25 in. blue octagon barrel, 1:66 in. twist, double set triggers, adj. sights, full length walnut stock, brass buttplate, brass trim, 57 in. OAL, 8 lbs. 8 oz.

MSR $664	$595	$535	$405	$335

PIONEER CARBINE/RIFLE — .50 or .54 cal. perc., 24 (carbine) or 27.25 in., octagon barrel, color case hardened hammer, lock and furniture, German silver blade front sight, recoil pad, carbine style stock.

	$175	$150	$105	$75

Last MSR was $214.

SHENANDOAH RIFLE — .36 (new 2002) or .50 cal. flintlock or perc., 33.5 in. octagon blue barrel, 1:48 in. twist (.36 cal.) or 1:66 in. twist (.50 cal.), color case hardened hammer and lock, double set triggers, adj. sights, full length hardwood stock, brass buttplate, brass furniture, 49.5 in. OAL, 7.2 lbs.

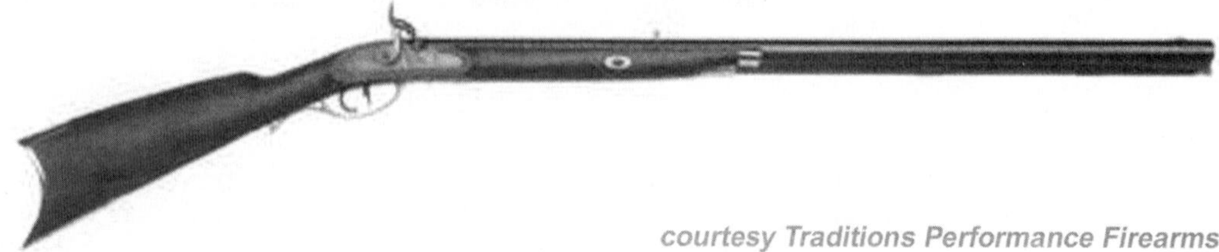
courtesy Traditions Performance Firearms

MSR $551	$500	$440	$330	$275

Add $37 for flintlock model.
Add $7 for .36 cal. (new 2002).

GRADING - PPGS™	100%	98%	90%	80%

1861 SPRINGFIELD — .58 cal. perc., 40 in. round barrel, 3 barrel bands, full length walnut stock, all white steel. 10.25 lbs. Disc.

	$475	$385	$280	$230

Last MSR was $513.

TENNESSEE RIFLE — .50 cal. flintlock or perc., 24 in. octagon blue barrel, 1:66 in. twist, color case hardened hammer and lock, brass buttplate, trigger guard and nosecap, fixed sights, double set triggers, full length hardwood stock, 40.4 in. OAL, 6 lbs.

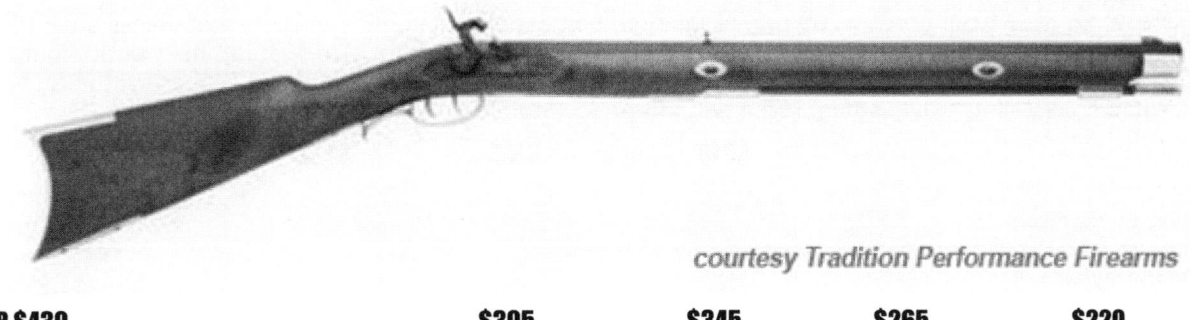

courtesy Tradition Performance Firearms

MSR $439	$395	$345	$265	$220

Add $45 for flintlock.

THUNDER MAGNUM RIFLE — .50 cal. perc., musket cap ignition, 24 in. round barrel, blackened furniture, fiber optic sights, removable breech plug, single trigger, select hardwood stock. Designed for use with Pyrodex Pellets. Disc. 2001.

	$315	$245	$185	$145

Last MSR was $349.

Add $10 for all-weather model with nickel finish.

TRAPPER RIFLE — .36, .45, or .50 cal. perc., 25 in. octagon barrel, color case hardened hammer and lock, brass trim, 5 lbs. Disc. 1989.

	$200	$160	$120	$80

Last MSR was $200.

TROPHY RIFLE — .50 or .54 cal. perc., 27.5 in. octagon tapering to round barrel, adj. trigger, fiberglass ramrod, carbine style walnut stock, 7 lbs. Disc. 1994.

	$350	$275	$225	$170

Last MSR was $425.

WHITETAIL CARBINE/RIFLE — .50 or .54 cal. flintlock or perc., 21 (carbine) or 26 in. octagon to round barrel, color case hardened hammer and lock, single trigger, adj. sights, 5.75 lbs. New 1993.

	$175	$150	$105	$75

Last MSR was $240.

Add $10 for flintlock.
Add $60 for synthetic stock and stainless steel barrel.

RIFLES: IN-LINE IGNITION

BUCKHUNTER/BUCKHUNTER PRO — .50 or .54 cal. perc., 24 in. tapered round blue barrel, three way safety, adj. fiber optic sights, Buckhunter Pro Model was available with all-weather camo stock and nickel finish, 7 lbs. 4 oz. Disc. 2001.

	$135	$110	$75	$60

Last MSR was $149.

Add $10 for nickel finish.
Add $40 for Buckhunter Pro models.
Add $70 for Buckhunter Pro w/camo stock with nickel finish.

BUCKSTALKER — .50 cal. perc., #209 primer ignition, LT-1 alloy break open action, 24 in. blue or nickel barrel, 1:28 in. twist, PAS system, Tru-Glo adj. fiber optic sights, drilled and tapped for scope, all-weather black or G-1 Vista synthetic Monte Carlo style stock and forearm, sling swivel studs, recoil pad, 40 in. OAL, 6 lbs. New 2009.

MSR $181	$165	$150	$105	$85

Add $38 for nickel barrel.
Add $30 for G-1 Vista stock.

GRADING - PPGS™	100%	98%	90%	80%

E-BOLT 209 BOLT-ACTION — .45 and .50 cal. perc., #209 primer ignition, 22 in. blue or nickel barrel, fully adj. fiber optic sights, all-weather black synthetic, AW (all-weather) synthetic Break-Up, and AW (all-weather) Advantage Timber stock, 6 lbs. 5 oz. Mfg. 2002 only.

	$150	$125	$95	$65

Last MSR was $169.

Add $10 for nickel barrel.
Add $50 for Mossy Oak Break-Up stock.
Add $60 for High Definition Advantage Timber stock.

EVOLUTION — .50 or .54 cal. perc., #209 primer ignition, bolt action, 24 in. blue, nickel, or stainless steel (fluted w/ screw-on muzzle brake) round tapered barrel, 1:28 or 1:48 (.54 cal.) in. twist, Tru-Glo adj. fiber optic sights, drilled and tapped for scope, all-weather black, Mossy Oak Break-Up, High Definition Advantage Timber synthetic, beech, or walnut X-Wood stock, sling swivel studs, recoil pad, 43 or 45 (stainless w/MB) in. OAL, 6.75-7.5 lbs. New 2003.

	$210	$165	$125	$85

Last MSR was $239.

Add $10 for nickel barrel.
Add $70 for stainlees steel fluted barrel w/screw-on muzzle brake.
Add $50 for beech stock.
Add $60 for walnut X-Wood stock (beech stock dipped in walnut finishing film).
Add $40 for High Definition Advantage Timber stock.
Add $20-$40 for Mossy Oak Break-Up stock.

* ***Evolution LD*** — .45 or .50 cal. perc., #209 primer ignition, bolt action, 26 in. blue or nickel fluted round tapered barrel with or without porting, 1:28 or 1:20 (.45 cal.) in. twist, Tru-Glo adj. fiber optic sights, drilled and tapped for scope, all-weather black, Mossy Oak Break-Up, Hardwoods HD (new 2008) or High Definition Advantage Timber synthetic stock, sling swivel studs, recoil pad, 45 in. OAL, 7 lbs. New 2003.

courtesy Traditions Performance Firearms

MSR $293	$265	$235	$165	$130

Add $10 for ported barrel.
Add $21 for nickel barrel with porting.
Add $44 for High Definition Advantage Timber stock.
Add $30 for Mossy Oak Break-Up stock.
Add $56 for Hardwoods HD stock.

* ***Evolution Premier*** — .50 cal. perc., #209 primer ignition, bolt action, 26 in. blue or stainless steel round fluted and ported barrel, 1:28 in. twist, Williams steel adj. fiber optic sights, drilled and tapped for scope, all-weather black or High Definition Advantage Timber synthetic, walnut X-Wood, or brown laminated stock, sling swivel studs, recoil pad, 45 in. OAL, 7-7.75 lbs. Mfg. 2003-2007.

courtesy Traditions Performance Firearms

	$325	$280	$215	$155

Last MSR was $ 349.

Add $70 for walnut X-Wood stock (beech stock dipped in walnut finishing film).
Add $90 for (HD) High Definition Advantage Timber stock.
Add $190 for brown laminated stock.

GRADING - PPGS™	100%	98%	90%	80%

EXPRESS DOUBLE — .50 cal. perc., #209 primer ignition, steel break open O/U action, DT, 24 in. blue or nickel barrel, Projectile Alignment System (PAS), 1:28 in. twist, adj. fiber optic sights, drilled and tapped for scope, walnut or all-weather camo synthetic stock and forearm, sling swivel studs, recoil pad, 41.5 in. OAL, 11.5 lbs. New 2006.

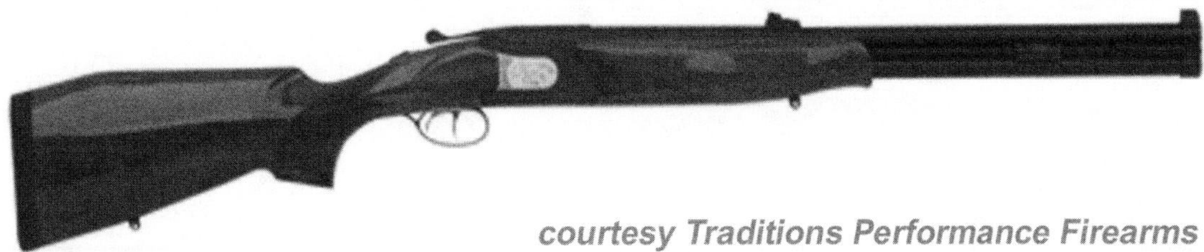

courtesy Traditions Performance Firearms

MSR $1,599	$1,440	$1,280	$960	$800

Add $167 for nickel and camo stock and forearm.
Add $167 for high gloss blue barrel and high gloss stock finish.

LIGHTNING BOLT — .50 or .54 cal. perc., #209 primer ignition, 24 in. round barrel, fully adj. fiber optic sights, stainless steel breech plug, bolt-action, composite stock, blue, nickel, or stainless steel fluted barrel with muzzle brake (new 2000), camo finish stock, 6 lbs. 8 oz. to 7 lbs. 12 oz. Mfg. 1997-2002.

	$180	$150	$105	$75

Last MSR was $199.

Add $130 for fluted stainless steel barrel with muzzle brake.
Add $40 for all-weather walnut stock. New 2002.
Add $30 for blue barrel with muzzle brake.
Add $160 for all-weather synthetic/Break-up with fluted stainless steel barrel and muzzle brake.
Add $80 for stainless steel barrel.
Add $20 for nickel barrel.

LIGHTNING LD BOLT-ACTION — .45 and .50 (new 2002) cal. perc., #209 primer ignition, 26 in. blue or nickel fluted barrel, fully adj. fiber optic sights, all-weather synthetic stock, all-weather synthetic Break-Up (New 2002), and High Definition Advantage Timber stock, 7 lbs. Disc. 2002.

	$215	$170	$125	$90

Last MSR was $239.

Add $10 for nickel barrel.
Add $40 for Mossy Oak Break-Up stock.
Add $60 for High Definition Advantage Timber stock.

LIGHTNING LIGHTWEIGHT BOLT-ACTION — .50 cal. perc., #209 primer ignition, 21 in. blue or nickel fluted barrel, fully adj. fiber optic sights, all-weather Spider Web pattern composite stock, or Mossy Oak Break-Up stock, 6 lbs. 5 oz. Mfg. 2000-02.

	$195	$155	$115	$85

Last MSR was $219.

Add $10 for nickel barrel.
Add $40 for Mossy Oak Break-Up stock.

PURSUIT — .50 cal. perc., #209 primer ignition, steel break open action, interchangeable 26 in. blue, nickel, or Mossy Oak Break-Up round barrel, 1:28 in. twist, Tru-Glo adj. fiber optic sights, drilled and tapped for scope, all-weather black or Mossy Oak Break-Up synthetic stock and forearm, sling swivel studs, recoil pad, 42 in. OAL, 8 lbs. Mfg. 2004-2007.

	$250	$190	$135	$95

Last MSR was $279.

Add $30 for nickel barrel.
Add $50 for Hardwoods Green HD stock and forearm.

GRADING - PPGS™	100%	98%	90%	80%

* **Pursuit LT** — .50 cal. perc., #209 primer ignition, alloy break open action, interchangeable 26 in. blue, nickel, or Mossy Oak Break-Up round barrel, 1:28 in. twist, Tru-Glo adj. fiber optic sights, drilled and tapped for scope, all-weather black or Mossy Oak Break-Up synthetic stock and forearm, sling swivel studs, recoil pad, 42 in. OAL, 6.75 lbs. Mfg. 2004-2008.

courtesy Tradition Performance Firearms

	$225	$195	$145	$115

Last MSR was $249.

Add $40 for nickel barrel.
Add $40 for Mossy Oak Break-Up stock.
Add $90 for Snow Camo stock. New 2007.

»**Pursuit LT West — .50 cal. perc., #11 cap ignition, alloy break open action, 26 in. nickel barrel, 1:28 in. twist, Tru-Glo** adj. fiber optic sights, drilled and tapped for scope, all-weather black synthetic stock and forearm, sling swivel studs, recoil pad, 42 in. OAL, 6.75 lbs. Mfg. 2008 only.

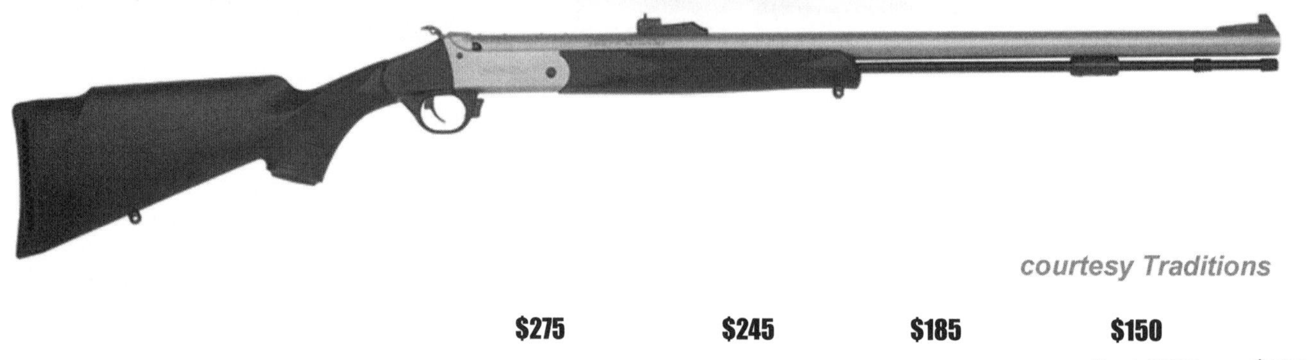

courtesy Traditions

	$275	$245	$185	$150

Last MSR was $308.

* **Pursuit Pro** — .45 or .50 cal. perc., #209 primer ignition, steel break open action, interchangeable 28 in. fluted blue or nickel round barrel, 1:20 (.45 cal.) or 1:28 in. twist, Tru-Glo adj. fiber optic sights, drilled and tapped for scope, all-weather black or Hardwoods Green HD synthetic stock and forearm, sling swivel studs, recoil pad, 44 in. OAL, 8.25 lbs. Mfg. 2004-2008.

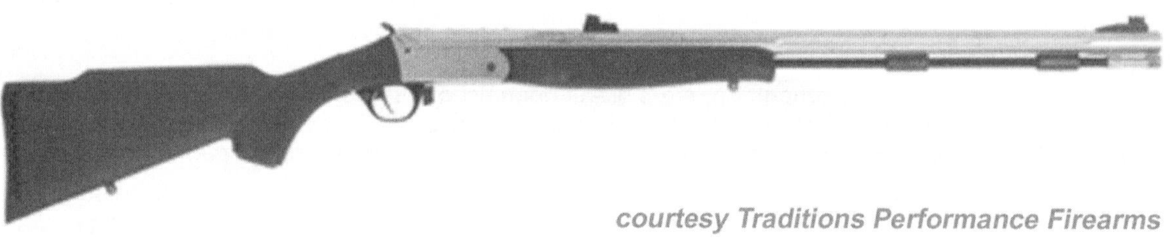

courtesy Traditions Performance Firearms

	$295	$265	$195	$165

Last MSR was $333.

Add $20 for nickel barrel.
Add $50 for Hardwoods Green HD stock and forearm.

GRADING - PPGS™	100%	98%	90%	80%

* ***Pursuit XLT*** — .50 cal. perc., #209 primer ignition, alloy break open action, interchangeable 28 in. fluted and ported nickel round barrel, 1:28 in. twist, Tru-Glo adj. fiber optic sights, drilled and tapped for scope, thumbhole all-weather black synthetic or black laminate stock and forearm, sling swivel studs, recoil pad, 44 in. OAL, 8.25 lbs. Mfg. 2006-2008.

courtesy Tradition Performance Firearms

	$295	$255	$195	$145

Last MSR was $322.

Add $20 for nickel barrel.
Add $50 for black laminate stock and forearm.

* ***Pursuit XLT Extreme*** — .50 cal. perc., #209 primer ignition, alloy break open action, interchangeable 28 in. fluted and ported nickel round barrel, Projectile Alignment System (PAS), 1:28 in. twist, Tru-Glo adj. fiber optic sights, drilled and tapped for scope, Ultra-Sure Grip all-weather black synthetic or Hardwoods HD camo stock and forearm, sling swivel studs, Quick Relief recoil pad, 44 in. OAL, 8.25 lbs. Mfg. 2007 only.

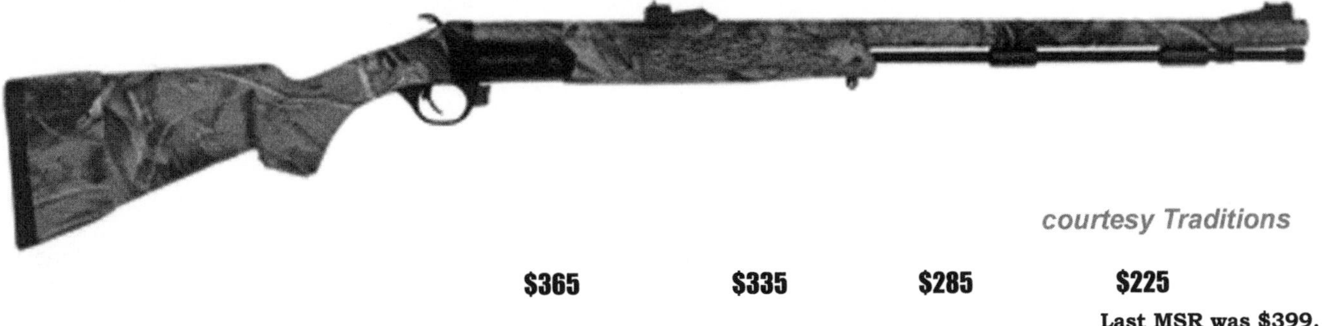

courtesy Traditions

	$365	$335	$285	$225

Last MSR was $399.

Add $80 for nickel barrel.
Add $20 for Harwoods HD stock and forearm.

PURSUIT II XLT — .50 cal. perc., #209 primer ignition w/accelerator breech plug, alloy break open action, 24 or 28 in. fluted and ported round barrel w/blue, nickel or Mossy Oak Treestand finish and PAS, 1:28 in. twist, Tru-Glo adj. fiber optic sights, drilled and tapped for scope, Monte Carlo style or thumbhole all-weather select hardwood, black or Mossy Oak Treestand synthetic Soft-Touch stock and forearm, sling swivel studs, Quick Relief recoil pad, 40 or 44 in. OAL, 7.5 lbs. Mfg. 2008 only.

courtesy Traditions

	$295	$255	$195	$145

Last MSR was $322.

Add $157 for Mossy Oak Treestand stock and forearm.
Add $145 for select hardwood stock and forearm.
Add $23 for thumbhole stock.
Add $20 for nickel barrel.
Add $29 for Mossy Oak Treestand barrel.

GRADING - PPGS™	100%	98%	90%	80%

PURSUIT II XLT EXTREME — .50 cal. perc., #209 primer ignition w/accelerator breech plug, LT-1 alloy break open action, 28 in. fluted and ported round barrel w/blue, nickel or Hardwoods HD finish and PAS, 1:28 in. twist, Tru-Glo adj. fiber optic sights, drilled and tapped for scope, Monte Carlo style all-weather black, Hardwoods HD or Mossy Oak Treestand Soft-Touch synthetic stock and forearm w/Knox Stock recoil system, sling swivel studs, pad, 44 in. OAL, 7.5 lbs. New 2008.

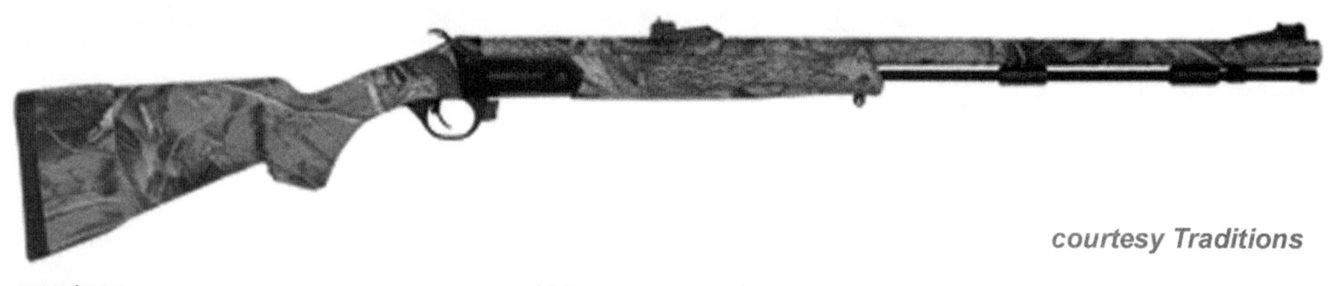

courtesy Traditions

MSR $399	$360	$320	$240	$195

Add $127 for Mossy Oak Treestand stock/forearm and nickel barrel.
Add $100 for Hardwoods HD stock, forearm and barrel.
Add $127 for Hardwoods HD stock/forearm and nickel barrel.

PURSUIT LT ACCELERATOR — .50 cal. perc., #209 primer ignition w/Accelerator breech plug, LT-1 alloy break open action, 26 in. round barrel w/PAS and blue, nickel, Hardwood HD or Mossy Oak Treestand finish, 1:28 in. twist, Tru-Glo adj. fiber optic sights, drilled and tapped for scope, black, Hardwood HD or Mossy Oak Treestand synthetic Monte Carlo or thumbhole style Soft Touch stock and forearm, sling swivel studs, Quick Relief recoil pad, 42 in. OAL, 6.75 lbs. New 2009.

MSR $278	$250	$225	$165	$140

Add $20 for nickel barrel.
Add $22 for thumbhole stock.
Add $67 for Hardwoods HD stock and forearm.
Add $67 for Mossy Oak Treestand stock and forearm.

PURSUIT LT NORTHWEST — .50 cal. perc., #11 cap ignition, alloy break open action, 26 in. blue or nickel barrel, 1:28 in. twist, Tru-Glo adj. fiber optic sights, drilled and tapped for scope, all-weather black or Mossy Oak Treestand Monte Carlo style synthetic stock and forearm, sling swivel studs, Quick Relief recoil pad, 42 in. OAL, 6.75 lbs. New 2009.

MSR $290	$260	$230	$165	$140

Add $22 for nickel.
Add $71 for Mossy Oak Treestand.

PURSUIT XLT ACCELERATOR — .50 cal. perc., #209 primer ignition w/Accelerator breech plug, alloy break open action, 24 or 28 in. fluted and ported round barrel w/PAS and blue, nickel or Mossy Oak Treestand finish, 1:28 in. twist, Tru-Glo adj. fiber optic sights, drilled and tapped for scope, select hardwood, black or Mossy Oak Treestand synthetic Monte Carlo or thumbhole style Soft Touch stock and forearm, sling swivel studs, Quick Relief recoil pad, 40 or 44 in. OAL, 7.5 lbs. New 2009.

MSR $322	$295	$255	$195	$145

Add $20 for nickel barrel.
Add $23 for thumbhole stock.
Add $59 for select hardwood stock and forearm.
Add $56 for Mossy Oak Treestand stock and forearm.
Add $106 for Mossy Oak Treestand stock, forearm and barrel.

T93 CARBINE/RIFLE — .50 cal. perc., 21 (carbine) or 28 in. round barrel, adj. sights, black furniture, modern hunting rifle style, approx. 8 lbs. Disc. 1993.

	$250	$190	$135	$95

Last MSR was $430.

Subtract $160 for Sporter Model.

GRADING - PPGS™	100%	98%	90%	80%

THUNDER BOLT — .45 or .50 cal. perc., #209 primer ignition, bolt action, 24 in. blue or nickel cylindrical barrel, 1:20 (.45 cal.) or 1:28 in. twist, adj. Lite optic sights, drilled and tapped for scope, all-weather black, Mossy Oak Break-up (new 2008) or Advantage Timber synthetic stock, sling swivel studs, recoil pad, 43 in. OAL, 6.75 lbs. Mfg 2003-2008.

courtesy Traditions

	$205	$185	$145	$95

Last MSR was $234.

Add $20 for nickel barrel.
Add $44 for Advantage Timber stock.

* ***Thunder Bolt (Youth Model)*** — .50 cal. perc., #209 primer ignition, bolt action, 21 in. blue cylindrical barrel, 1:28 in. twist, adj. Lite optic sights, drilled and tapped for scope, all-weather black synthetic stock, sling swivel studs, recoil pad, 40 in. OAL, 6. lbs. New 2003.

	$155	$125	$100	$65

Last MSR was $179.

TRACKER 209 — .45 (new 2002) and .50 cal. perc., #209 primer ignition, 22 (.45 cal.) or 24 (new 2003) in. blue or nickel barrel, 1:20 (.45 cal.) or 1:28 in. twist, fully adj. fiber optic sights, all-weather black synthetic, Mossy Oak Break-Up (new 2008), G-1 Vista (new 2009) or all-weather Advantage Timber stock, 41 (.45 cal.) or 43 in. OAL, 6.5 lbs. New 2001.

courtesy Tradition Performance Firearms

MSR $172	$155	$135	$105	$80

Add $21 for nickel barrel.
Add $44 for Advantage Timber stock.
Add $54 for Mossy Oak Break-Up stock.
Add $56 for G-1 Vista stock.

VORTEK — .50 cal. perc., #209 primer ignition w/Accelerator breech plug, alloy break open action, 28 in. fluted and ported round barrel w/PAS and blue, stainless, 1:28 in. twist, Williams adj. fiber optic sights, drilled and tapped for scope, black or Mossy Oak Treestand synthetic Monte Carlo or thumbhole style Soft Touch or Overmolding stock and forearm, sling swivel studs, Quick Relief recoil pad, 44 in. OAL, 12.5 lbs. New 2009.

MSR $390	$350	$315	$225	$195

Add $20 for stainless barrel.
Add $21 for thumbhole stock.
Add $56 for Mossy Oak Treestand stock and forearm.

GRADING - PPGS™	100%	98%	90%	80%

YUKON — .50 cal. perc., #209 primer ignition, drop breech action, or 24 in. blue or nickel barrel, 1:28 in. twist, fully adj. fiber optic sights, all-weather black or Mossy Oak Break-Up synthetic stock, 39 in. OAL, 6.5 lbs. New 2006.

courtesy Traditions

MSR $190	$175	$155	$115	$95

Add $21 for nickel barrel.
Add $56 for Mossy Oak Break-Up stock.
Add $51 for 3-9x32 scope kit.

SHOTGUNS: IN-LINE IGNITION

BUCKHUNTER MODEL — 12 ga. perc., 24 in. round barrel, bead sight, blackened furniture, composite black or camo stock, 6.25 lbs. Disc.

	$275	$200	$145	$100

Last MSR was $313.

Add $40 for Treestand or Advantage camo stock.

BUCKHUNTER PRO — 12 ga. perc., 24 in. tapered round blue barrel with full choke, three way safety, bead sight, 6 lbs. 6 oz. Disc.

	$225	$175	$120	$90

Last MSR was $248.

Add $44 for Comp/Advantage model.

PURSUIT PRO — 12 ga. perc., #209 primer ignition, break open action, 28 in. matte blue (disc. 2009), Hardwoods HD (new 2008) or Hardwoods Green HD smooth bore barrel, screw-in full choke tube, bead front sight, all-weather black (disc. 2009), Hardwoods HD (new 2008) or Hardwoods Green HD PG or thumbhole stock and forearm, sling swivel studs, 44 in. OAL, 8.25 lbs. New 2004.

courtesy Tradition Performance Firearms

MSR $515	$465	$415	$315	$250

Add $70 for Hardwoods Green HD or Hardwoods HD finish.
Add $30 for thumbhole stock.

TURKEY PRO — 12 ga. perc., #209 primer ignition, 24 in. matte blue or Mossy Oak Break-Up (new 2003) barrel, full choke, bead front sight, all-weather black, Advantage, or Mossy Oak Break-Up (new 2003) stock, 6 lbs. 6 oz. Mfg. 2001-04.

	$195	$155	$115	$80

Last MSR was $219.

Add $30 for Advantage stock.
Add $110 for Mossy Oak Break-Up barrel and stock.

GRADING - PPGS™	100%	98%	90%	80%

SHOTGUNS: PERCUSSION

FOWLER SHOTGUN — 12 ga., perc., 32 in. octagon to round blue barrel, color case hardened hammer and lock, German silver furniture, checkered walnut stock, 5.5 lbs. Disc.

	100%	98%	90%	80%
	$375	$300	$235	$185

Last MSR was $430.

SINGLE BARREL — 12 ga. perc., 32 in. octagon tapering to round barrel, German silver wedge plate, blue furniture, scroll engraving, and polished steel furniture on deluxe version, 4 lbs. Disc. 1994.

	100%	98%	90%	80%
	$260	$195	$140	$95

Last MSR was $315.

Add $85 for deluxe model.

TRAIL GUNS ARMORY

Previous importer/distributor located in Conroe, TX. All reproductions and replicas are manufactured by D. Pedersoli Co. Italy. Please refer to the Pedersoli section for current pricing and model information.

NOTES

GRADING - PPGS™	100%	98%	90%	80%

U SECTION

UBERTI, A. S.r.l.

Current firearms, black powder, and accessories manufacturer established in 1959, and currently located in Serezzo, Italy. In late 1999, Beretta purchased Aldo Uberti & Co. S.r.l., and the company name was changed to A. Uberti S.r.l. Currently imported and distributed (beginning 2003) by Stoegers Industries located in Accokeek, MD, Navy Arms, located in Martinsburg, WV, Cimarron F.A. & Co, located in Fredricksburg, TX, Taylor's & Co, located in Winchester, VA, Dixie Gun Works, located in Union City, TN, E.M.F., located in Santa Ana, CA, Cabela's, located in Sidney, NE, and Tristar Sporting Arms, located in N. Kansas City, MO. Previously imported until Dec. 2002 by Uberti USA, located in Lakeville, CT.

In 1958, company founder Aldo Uberti became the first Italian black powder manufacturer to build a reproduction Colt black powder pistol. At the time, he was an employee of Beretta, and his wife Gepi (still living), is directly related to the Beretta family. Inspection of the factory records reveals that the first black powder reproduction (1851 Navy) was returned from the proof house on Oct. 14, 1959. Mr. Uberti, who passed away in 1998, began manufacturing reproductions and replicas in quantity for Val Forgett of Navy Arms in 1959, and throughout his career produced all of the original Colt black powder designs. Please refer to *Colt Blackpowder Reproductions & Replicas - A Collector's & Shooter's Guide* (ISBN: 1-886768-11-0) for color pictures of Uberti makes and models listed below. Uberti pistols can be found on pages 61 through 67, and pages 71, 79, and 96.

For more information and current pricing on both new and used A. Uberti S.r.l. firearms, please refer to the *Blue Book of Gun Values* by S.P. Fjestad (now online also).

Black Powder Reproductions & Replicas by Dennis Adler is also an invaluable source for most black powder reproductions and replicas, and includes hundreds of color images on most popular makes/models, provides manufacturer/trademark histories, and up-to-date information on related items/accessories for black powder shooting - www.bluebookinc.com.

REVOLVERS: PERCUSSION

Add $85 for antique finish on select models below.
Add $50 for stainless steel on select models below.

1836-39 PATERSON MODELS — .36 cal. perc., 7.5 in. octagon barrel, 5 shot, one piece smooth walnut grips, all blue finish, hidden trigger design, case colored hammer and frame, No. 5 Holster model with or w/o loading lever, 2 lbs. 9 oz. Mfg. 1998-2008.

	100%	98%	90%	80%
	$355	**$285**	**$230**	**$185**

Last MSR was $400.

Add $25 for model with loading lever.

1847 WALKER — .44 cal. perc., 9 in. barrel, 6 shot, charcoal finish, color case hardened frame, hammer, and loading lever, one piece smooth walnut grips, brass trigger guard, engraved cylinder with Texas Ranger/Indian fight scene, 4.4 lbs.

courtesy Uberti

	100%	98%	90%	80%
MSR $429	**$395**	**$350**	**$250**	**$195**

GRADING - PPGS™	100%	98%	90%	80%

1848 BABY DRAGOON — .31 cal. perc., 3 (disc. 2003), 4, or 5 (disc. 2003) in. barrel, 5 shot, color case hardened frame, hammer, no loading lever, brass backstrap and trigger guard, one piece walnut grips, engraved cylinder, 1.4 lbs. Disc. 2008.

courtesy Uberti

	$275	$225	$175	$135

Last MSR was $300.

Add $40 for silver backstrap and trigger guard.

1848 WHITNEYVILLE HARTFORD DRAGOON AND 1ST, 2ND, 3RD MODELS — .44 cal. perc., 7.5 in. barrel, 6 shot, steel (Whitneyville model only) or brass backstrap and trigger guard (square design on Whitneyville, 1st and 2nd models, round design on 3rd model), color case hardened frame, hammer, and loading lever, cylinder engraved with Texas Ranger/Indian battle scene, 3.9 lbs.

courtesy Uberti

MSR $409	$365	$325	$245	$195

Add $20 for Whitneyville Dragoon.

1849 POCKET — .31 cal. perc., with or w/o loading lever, 4 in. barrel, 5 shot, color case hardened frame, hammer, brass backstrap and trigger guard, cylinder engraved with stagecoach holdup scene, 1.5 lbs.

courtesy Uberti

MSR $339	$295	$265	$195	$150

Add $30 for silver backstrap and trigger guard.

GRADING - PPGS™	100%	98%	90%	80%

1849 WELLS FARGO — .31 cal. perc., 4 in. octagon barrel, 5 shot, color case hardened frame and hammer, no loading lever, brass backstrap and trigger guard, 1.5 lbs.

courtesy Uberti

MSR $339	$295	$265	$195	$150

Add $30 for silver backstrap and trigger guard.

1851 NAVY — .36 cal. perc., 7.5 in. barrel, loading lever, 6 shot, brass or steel backstrap and trigger guard, cylinder engraved with Texas Navy battle with Mexico, available with square trigger guard or round trigger guard, and in Leech & Rigdon Confederate version, 2.6 lbs.

courtesy Uberti

MSR $329	$280	$250	$175	$145

Add $250 for detachable shoulder stock (disc. 2004).
Add $30 for silver plated backstrap and trigger guard (disc. 2004).
Add $20 for "London" Model w/steel backstrap and trigger guard or if cut for stock (3rd Model Navy) (disc. 2004). Reintroduced 2008.
Add $10 for Leech & Rigdon (round barrel) Confederate Navy (disc. 2004). Reintroduced 2008.

1860 ARMY — .44 cal. perc., 8 in. barrel, 6 shot, round engraved (Texas Navy scene) or fluted cylinder, color case hardened frame, hammer, and loading lever, brass (new 2008) or steel backstrap, brass trigger guard, 2.6 lbs.

courtesy Uberti

MSR $339	$295	$265	$195	$150

Add $250 for detachable shoulder stock (disc. 2004).
Add $30 for silver plated backstrap and trigger guard (disc. 2004).
Add $10 for fluted cylinder.

GRADING - PPGS™	100%	98%	90%	80%

1861 NAVY — .36 cal. perc., 7.5 in. barrel, 6 shot, engraved (Texas Navy battle with Mexico) round or fluted cylinder, color case hardened frame, hammer, and loading lever, brass or steel backstrap and trigger guard, 2.5 lbs.

courtesy Uberti

MSR $329	$280	$250	$175	$145

Add $20 for steel backstrap and trigger guard.
Add $30 for silver plated strap and trigger guard (disc. 2004).
Add $250 for detachable shoulder stock (disc. 2004).

1862 POCKET NAVY — .36 cal. perc., 5.5 or 6.5 in. octagon barrel, 5 shot, color case hardened frame, hammer, and loading lever, brass backstrap and trigger guard, roll engraved cylinder with stagecoach scene, 1 lb. 6 oz.

courtesy Uberti

MSR $349	$315	$275	$205	$160

Add $30 for silver plated backstrap and trigger guard (disc. 2004).

1862 POLICE — .36 cal. perc., 5.5 or 6.5 in. round barrel, 5 shot, color case hardened frame, hammer, and loading lever, semi fluted cylinder, brass backstrap and trigger guard, 1 lb. 6 oz.

courtesy Uberti

MSR $349	$315	$275	$205	$160

Add $30 for silver plated straps and trigger guard.

AUGUSTA CONFEDERATE — .36 cal. perc., 7.5 in. octagon barrel, color case hardened hammer and trigger, all brass frame, engraved cylinder, 2.5-2.75 lbs. Disc.

	$215	$165	$125	$85

Last MSR was $210.

GRADING - PPGS™	100%	98%	90%	80%

GRISWOLD AND GUNNISON — .36 or .44 cal. perc., 5.5 or 7.5 in. barrel, similar to Augusta Confederate model, except has round barrel forward of lug, does not have engraved cylinder. Disc. 1994.

	$210	$165	$125	$90

Last MSR was $220.

TEXAS CONFEDERATE DRAGOON — .44 cal. perc., 7.5 in. round barrel, color case hardened frame, hammer, and loading lever, brass trim, "Tucker, Sherrard, and Co.," 4 lbs. Disc. 1994.

	$275	$200	$145	$100

Last MSR was $235.

Add $35 for stainless steel.

1858 REMINGTON NEW ARMY — .44 cal. perc., 8 in. octagon barrel with ejector rod housing, 6 shot, blue steel, brass trigger guard, two piece walnut grips, 2.7 lbs.

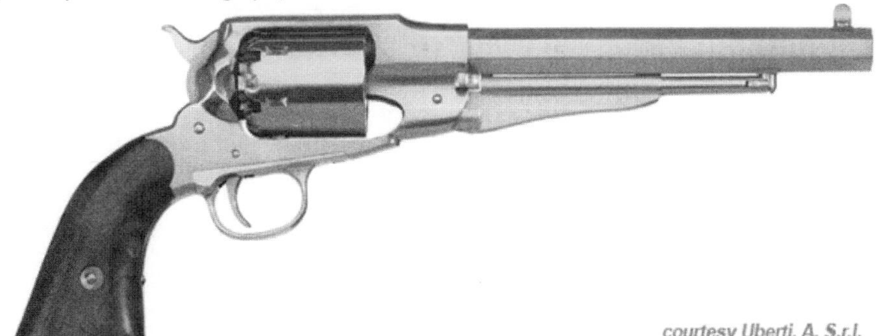

courtesy Uberti, A. S.r.l.

MSR $349	$315	$275	$205	$160

Add $35 for adj. sights (disc. 2004).
Add $35 for color case hardened frame (disc. 2004).
Add $80 for stainless steel model.
Add $130 for target model in stainless steel (disc. 2004).

1858 REMINGTON NEW ARMY "MILLENNIUM FINISH" — .44 cal. perc., 8 in. barrel, 6 shot, matte black fiish, 2.6 lbs. Disc. 2002.

	$175	$150	$105	$75

Last MSR was $195.

1858 REMINGTON NEW NAVY — .36 cal. perc., 7.38 in. octagon barrel, 6 shot, blue frame, 2.5 lbs. Disc. 2002.

	$225	$175	$125	$85

Last MSR was $260.

1873 COLT SINGLE ACTION ARMY — .44 cal. perc., 3.5, 4.75, 5.5, or 7.5 in. barrel, color case hardened frame, walnut grips. A special black powder percussion version of the famous Colt Peacemaker, with a custom-made cylinder designed to use percussion caps. Available in three variations: with brass backstrap and trigger guard; steel backstrap and trigger guard; and Bisley quick draw model with steel backstrap and trigger guard. Optional loading tool and spare cylinder. New 1998. Bisley Model new 2001. All disc. 2002.

	$250	$190	$135	$95

Last MSR was $275.

Add $20 for loading tool.
Add $55 for spare cylinder (requires fitting).
Add $25 for steel backstrap and trigger guard.
Add $40 for 3.5 in. model with bird's head grip.
Add $115 for Bisley Model.

REVOLVERS: CARTRIDGE CONVERSIONS

Since these are cartridge firing revolvers converted from black powder reproduction pistols, and require a FFL to transfer, these listings have been moved to the *Blue Book of Gun Values* by S.P. Fjestad (now online also).

RIFLES: FLINTLOCK & PERCUSSION

HAWKEN RIFLE — .50 or .54 cal. perc., 32 in. octagon barrel, double set triggers, approx. 9 lbs. Disc. 1994.

	$400	$340	$245	$205

Last MSR was $535.

GRADING - PPGS™	100%	98%	90%	80%

1858 REMINGTON REVOLVING CARBINE — .44 cal. perc., 18 in. tapered octagon barrel, 6 shot, blue steel, enlarged brass trigger guard with finger rest, adj. rear sight, blue finish, 4.4 lbs.

MSR $549	$495	$445	$335	$285

1866 REVOLVING CARBINE — .44 cal. perc., 18 in. barrel, 6 shot, blue steel, brass trigger guard, walnut stock, 4.6 lbs.

	$350	$275	$225	$170

Last MSR was $420.

SANTA FE HAWKEN — .50 or .54 cal. perc., single shot, 32 in. octagon barrel, damascened finish, double set triggers, 9.5 lbs., walnut stock.

	$395	$335	$245	$205

Last MSR was $445.

ST. LOUIS RIFLE — .45, .50, .54, or .58 cal. flintlock or perc., color case hardened hammer, lock, and trigger guard, octagon barrel. Disc. 1994.

	$350	$275	$225	$170

Last MSR was $265.

Add $25 for .54 and .58 cal. percussion.
Add $15 for flintlock.
Add $30 for 54 cal. flintlock.

SQUIRREL RIFLE — .32 cal. perc. or flintlock, color case hardened hammer and lock, brass trigger guard, 28 in. octagon barrel.

	$275	$200	$145	$100

Add $15 for flintlock.

UFDA INC.

Previous manufacturer located in Scottsdale, AZ.

RIFLES: PERCUSSION

TETON RIFLE — .45, .50 cal., 12 ga. or 12 bore (.72 cal.) perc., blue chromemoly steel or stainless steel barrel, straight through ignition, Remington style heavy target action, interchangeable barrels, black or brown laminated stock. Walnut or maple upgrade available, recoil pad.

	$700	$565	$440	$325

Last MSR was $834.

Add $100 for walnut or maple stock.
Add $150 for extra barrel.

TETON BLACKSTONE — .50 cal. perc., 26 in. barrel. Same as above but in matte finish stainless steel with black epoxy coated wood stock.

	$400	$335	$245	$205

Last MSR was $534.

GRAND TETON — .45 or .50 cal. perc., similar to Teton Blackstone, but with 30 in. octagon barrel.

	$800	$650	$515	$375

Last MSR was $995.

ULTIMATE FIREARMS INC.

Current manufacturer located in Howell, MI. Dealer and consumer direct sales.

Ultimate Firearms, Inc. began manufacturing the BP Xpress, a .45 or .50 caliber inline muzzleloader circa 2001.

RIFLES: IN-LINE IGNITION

BP XPRESS HUNTER — .50 cal., magnum rifle primer ignition (primer seated in .45 magnum case), Howa bolt action, drilled and tapped for scope, stainless steel, custom trigger, laminate thumbhole stock.

MSR $1,800	$1,800	$1,650	$1,350	$1,150

BP XPRESS INFINITY — .50 cal., magnum rifle primer ignition (primer seated in .45 magnum case), Howa bolt action, custom trigger, drilled and tapped for scope, stainless steel, laminate thumbhole stock, aluminum chassis, Sims Limbsaver recoil pad.

MSR $2,100	$2,100	$1,900	$1,500	$1,300

GRADING - PPGS™	100%	98%	90%	80%

BP XPRESS ULTRA — .50 cal., magnum rifle primer ignition (primer seated in .45 magnum case), Remington 40X bolt action, custon trigger, in. barrel, drilled and tapped for scope, stainless steel, presentaion grade walnut sporter stock, aluminum chassis, Sims Limbsaver recoil pad.

MSR $2,800	$2,800	$2,500	$2,000	$1,650

BP XPRESS CARBON STEALTH — .50 cal., magnum rifle primer ignition (primer seated in .45 magnum case), Howa or Remington 40X bolt action, custom trigger, carbon wrapped barrel, drilled and tapped for scope, stainless steel, synthetic sporter stock, aluminum chassis, Sims Limbsaver recoil pad.

MSR $3,750	$3,750	$3,250	$2,750	$2,150

UNITED STATES FIREARMS MANUFACTURING COMPANY, INC.

Current manufacturer established during 1995 and located in Hartford, CT. Previously located at Colt's original armory in Hartford, CT. Company name changed during 1997 from United States Patent Firearms Manufacturing Company.

USFA manufactured reproduction Colt black powder revolvers circa 1995-2000.

REVOLVERS: PERCUSSION

All guns have color case hardened (bone) frames, hammers & loading levers, dome blue barrels and cylinders, silver plated backstraps and trigger guards, exceptions will be noted.

1847 WALKER — .44 cal., perc., 9 in. barrel. Bright finish brass trigger guard, dome blue backstrap, 4.4 lbs.

$430	$375	$285	$235

Last MSR was $445.

DRAGOON (1ST, 2ND, OR 3RD MODEL) — .44 cal.perc., 6 shot, 7-½ in. barrel, 3.9 lbs.

$430	$375	$285	$235

Last MSR was $435.

Add $200 for carbine stock attachment.

1848 BABY DRAGOON — .31 cal. perc., 5 shot, 4 in. octagonal barrel, 1.4 lbs.

$285	$250	$195	$150

Last MSR was $315.

1849 POCKET — .31 cal. perc., 5 shot, 4 in. octagonal barrel, 1.5 lbs.

$270	$240	$180	$150

Last MSR was $300.

1851 NAVY — .36 cal. perc., 6 shot 7½ in. barrel, many styles including Squareback, London & Oval, 2.8 lbs.

$345	$305	$230	$195

Last MSR was $385.

Add $10 for steel backstrap.
Add $180 for carbine breech attachment.
Add $60 for London Navy with steel backstrap.

1860 ARMY — .44 cal. perc., 6 shot, 8 in. barrel, 2.6 lbs. Available with fluted or rebated cylinder.

$355	$315	$235	$195

Last MSR was $395.

Add $180 for carbine stock attachment.

1861 NAVY — .36 cal. perc., 6 shot, 7½ in. barrel.

$345	$305	$230	$195

Last MSR was $385.

Add $180 for carbine stock attachment.

1862 POCKET NAVY — . 36 cal. perc., 4½, 5½ & 6½ in. barrel, 1.6 lbs.

$305	$275	$205	$170

Last MSR was $335.

1862 POCKET POLICE — .36 cal. perc., 4½, 5½ & 6½ in. barrel, 1.6 lbs.

$305	$275	$205	$170

Last MSR was $335.

U.S. HISTORICAL SOCIETY

Previous organization which marketed historically significant firearms and black powder reproductions until April 1994. Located in Richmond, VA. Most firearms were manufactured by the Williamsburg Firearms Manufactory and the Virginia Firearms Manufactory.

On April 1, 1994, the Antique Arms Divison of the U.S. Historical Society was acquired by America Remembers located in Mechanicsville, VA. America Remembers affiliates include the Armed Forces Commemorative Society, American Heroes & Legends, and the United States Society of Arms and Armor. Issues that were not fully subscribed are now available through America Remembers (please refer to listing in A section).

Please refer to *Colt Blackpowder Reproductions & Replicas - A Collector's & Shooter's Guide* for color pictures of the U.S. Historical Society pistols described below. U.S. Historical Society Colt commemoratives can be found on pages 74, 89, 92, 103, 104, 105, and 106.

The information listed below represents current information up to the date that America Remembers acquired the Antique Arms Division of the U.S. Historical Society.

PISTOLS: LIMITED/SPECIAL EDITIONS

ANDREW JACKSON –

* ***Andrew Jackson Silver Edition*** – 2,500 mfg.

  Last issue price was $2,100.

* ***Andrew Jackson Gold Edition*** – 100 mfg.

  Last issue price was $5,500.

GEORGE WASHINGTON – includes pair of flintlocks, cased, 975 mfg. 1976.

Original issue price was $3,000.
Last issue price was $3,500.

HAMILTON - BURR DUELING PISTOLS – 1,200 mfg. in 1981.

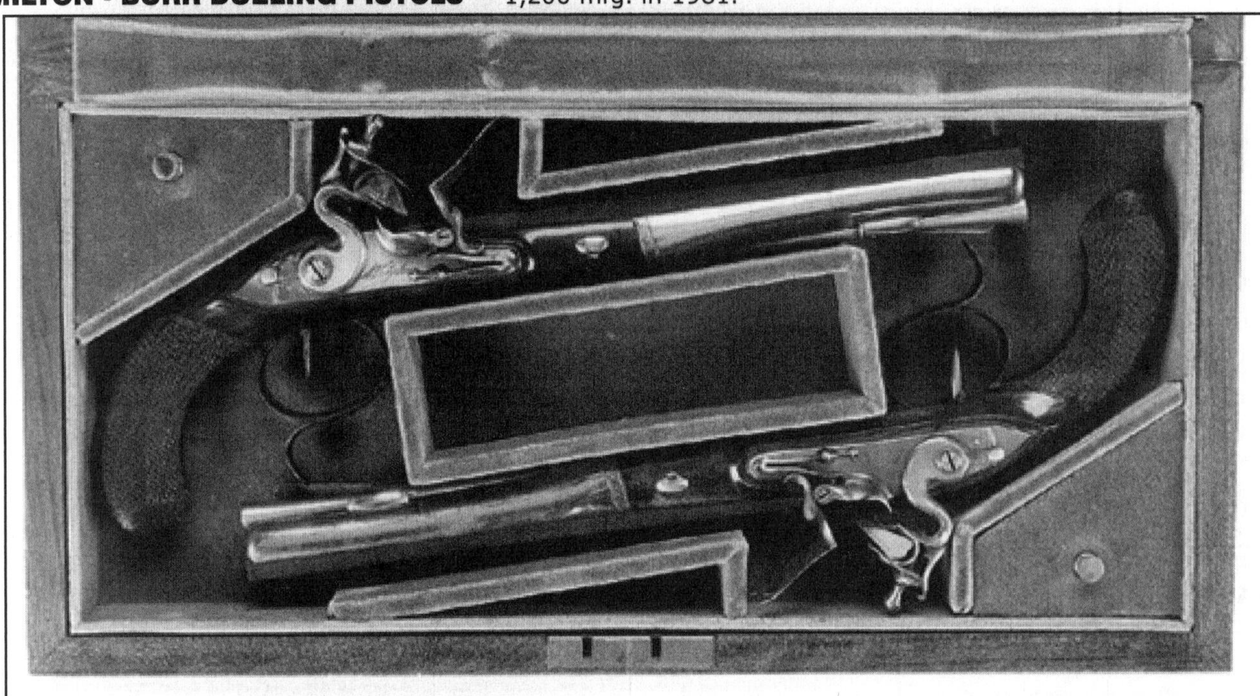

courtesy U.S. Historical Society

Last issue price was $2,995.

HENRY DERINGER PISTOL SET – .41 cal. perc., reproduction of Deringer pistol, available with sterling silver mounts (1,000 pair mfg.), 14Kt. gold mounted (100 pair mfg.), precious gem stone mounted (5 pair mfg.). Mfg. 1978.

* ***Henry Deringer Pistol Silver Mounted Pair***

  Last issue price was $1,900.

* ***Henry Deringer Pistol 14Kt. Gold Mounted Pair***

  Last issue price $2,700.

* ***Henry Deringer Pistol 18Kt. Jewel Mounted Pair***

Last issue price was $25,000.

MAJOR JOHN PITCAIRN — .60 cal. flintlock Scottish pistol, 7.5 in. round bbl., all metal pistol w/silver finish and silver grips, covered w/Celtic style fine engraving, lock plate engraved "10 MUIDOCH", medallion engraved w/serpent and swords on right grip, 900 mfg.

Last issue price was $2,950.

THOMAS JEFFERSON — 1,000 mfg.

Last issue price was $1,900.

WASHINGTON AND LEE FLINTLOCK PISTOLS — .69 cal., flintlock pistols with 9-15/16 in. barrels, burl walnut stocks with sterling silver fittings, engraved silver plated lock plates, trigger guard, and sideplate, firing capability, cased with accessories, limited issue of 1,000 in 1989.

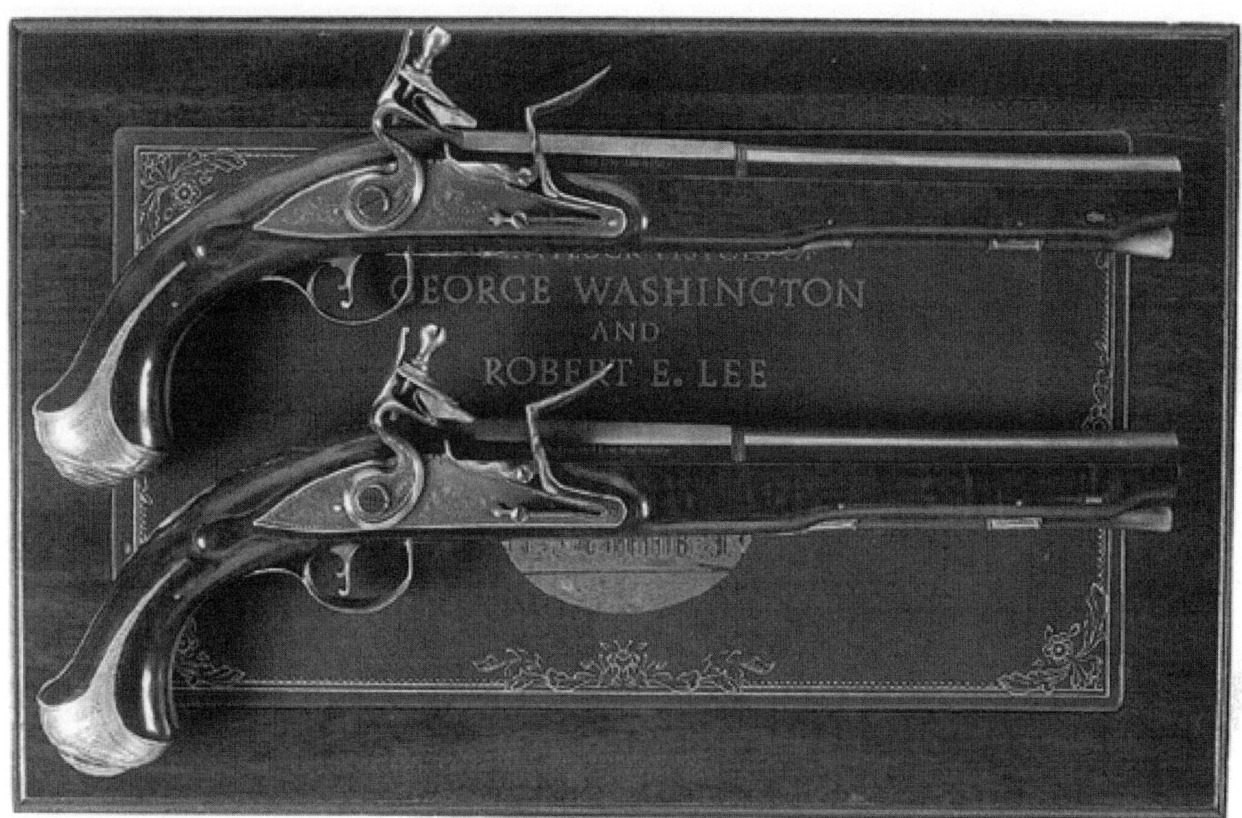

courtesy U.S. Historical Society

Last issue price was $2,700.

REVOLVERS: LIMITED/SPECIAL EDITIONS

BAT MASTERSON MODEL 1860 ARMY — .44 cal., original roll engraved pattern on cylinder, walnut grips, blue barrel decorated in 24Kt. gold. 2,500 mfg. beginning 1991.

Last issue price was $1,250.

BUFFALO BILL CENTENNIAL MODEL 1860 ARMY — .44 cal., reproduction of the Colt Model 1860, bonded ivory stocks, extensive gold etchings portraying various wild west scenes, bonded ivory powder flask, brass accessories, cased. 2,500 mfg. 1983.

Last issue price was $1,950.

FREDERIC REMINGTON MODEL 1860 ARMY REVOLVER — .44 cal., issued to commemorate Frederic Remington's 100th anniversary as an associate of the National Academy of Design, features gold etched barrel, cylinder (with 5 panels), trigger, frame, and gripstraps, cased with accessories, 42 oz. 1,000 mfg. in 1990 only.

Last issue price was $1,500.

GETTYSBURG 1860 ARMY — .44 cal., blue steel with gold plated cylinder scene, backstraps, and other small parts, walnut grips, cased with belt buckle. 1,863 mfg. beginning 1994.

Add $145 for case.

Last issue price was $1,270.

JEFFERSON DAVIS 1851 NAVY REVOLVER — .36 cal., extensive Nimschke style engraving on barrel, loading lever, frame and trigger, case hardened frame with silver plated brass backstrap and trigger guard, includes engraved, silver plated detachable shoulder stock, cased with accessories, 41 oz. 1,000 mfg. in 1990 only.

Last issue price was $2,750.

MERRILL LINDSAY WHITNEYVILLE HARTFORD DRAGOON — .44 cal. Dragoon with gold leaf highlights on the roll engraved cylinder scene, and the legend "1915 MERRILL LINDSAY 1985" along the barrel commemorating the great author and historian, who wrote the book *One Hundred Great Guns*. Color case hardened frame, backstrap, hammer and loading lever, gold plated trigger guard. Edition of 500 cased revolvers produced in 1987.

Original and last issue prices N/A.

MONITOR AND VIRGINIA MODEL 1851 NAVY REVOLVER — .44 cal., issued to commemorate the Civil War naval battle between the USS Monitor and Confederate Virginia, features gold etchings on barrel, frame, and Monitor/ Virginia battle scene on cylinder, cased, 41 oz. 1,000 mfg. in 1991.

Last issue price was $1,250.

PONY EXPRESS REVOLVER MODEL 1851 — .36 cal., features gold plated cylinder scene, other scroll work and barrel address, walnut grips, cased. 1,000 mfg. beginning 1992.

Last issue price was $1,650.

ROBERT E. LEE MODEL 1851 NAVY — .36 cal. only, reproduction of the 1851 Navy Colt, extensive gold etching, cylinder scene portrays historical Civil War events, walnut stocks with Robert E. Lee medallion, cased with accessories, 41 oz. 2,500 mfg. during 1984.

Last issue price was $2,100.

SAM HOUSTON WALKER — .44 cal., reproduction of the Colt Walker, 9 in. barrel, extensive gold etching on highly polished blue surface, smooth walnut stocks with S. Houston medallions, cased with accessories. 2,500 mfg.

Last issue price was $2,300.

SECRET SERVICE MUSEUM EDITION — fully checkered ivory grips, silver plate, gold plate, and royal blue finish, fully engraved, includes walnut presentation case, silver plated powder flask, screwdriver, Secret Service badge and key. 500 mfg. beginning 1988.

Last issue price was $1,250.

STONEWALL JACKSON MODEL 1851 REVOLVER — .36 cal., reproduction of Colt's Model 1851 Navy, elaborate gold etching on frame and barrel, walnut grip with medallion, cased with sterling medallion and silver plated powder flask. 1988 release. 2,500 total mfg.

Last issue price was $2,100.

TEXAS PATERSON EDITION — reproduction of the famous Colt folding trigger model mfg. in Paterson, NJ. This hand engraved example with genuine mother-of-pearl stocks and silver bands around the barrel muzzle, cylinder and recoil shield, was a reproduction of an original Paterson, serial No. 755. Delivered in a two-drawer display case with a copy of "Paterson Colt Pistol Variations" by Philip R. Phillips and R.L. Wilson. Edition limited to 1,000 examples starting in 1988.

Last issue price was $2,500.

TEXAS RANGER DRAGOON — .44 cal., features silver plated cylinder, trigger guard and gripstraps, color case hardened frame and loading lever, multiple 24Kt. etchings on barrel and frame front, cased with accessories, 66 oz. 1,000 mfg. in 1990 only.

Last issue price was $1,585.

TOWER OF LONDON COL. SAM COLT DRAGOON — .44 cal., exact reproduction of the Second Model Dragoon, 7.5 in. barrel, hand engraved, Texas Ranger cylinder scene, one-piece adj. walnut grip with inscribed sterling silver plaque, case hardened frame, hammer, loading lever and rammer, cased with accessories, limited issue of 1,000 in 1989.

Last issue price was $2,450.

U.S. CAVALRY MODEL 1860 ARMY — .44 cal., reproduction of the Colt Model 1860, stag grips, gold etched cylinder scene, cased with brass buckle. 975 manufactured 1988.

Last issue price was $1,450.

U.S. NAVY REVOLVER MODEL 1851 — .36 cal., 7.5 in. octagon barrel, features gold etched cylinder and other embellishments, brass trigger guard and backstrap plated with 24Kt. gold, 41 oz. 1,000 mfg. in 1988 only.

Last issue price was $1,250.

REVOLVERS: MINIATURE, LIMITED/SPECIAL EDITIONS

1847 WALKER PRESIDENTIAL EDITION — miniature reproduction of 1847 Colt Walker, color case hardened receiver, all parts operational, sterling silver grips, full coverage engraving, cased. 1,500 mfg. starting 1990.

Last issue price was $1,575.

* ***1847 Walker Classic Edition*** — similar to Presidential Edition, except has walnut grips and frame is not engraved, cased. 1,500 mfg. starting 1990.

Last issue price was $625.

1851 NAVY PRESIDENTIAL EDITION — miniature reproduction of 1851 Navy Colt, color case hardened receiver, all parts operational, mother-of-pearl grips, full coverage engraving, cased. 1,500 mfg. starting 1988.

Last issue price was $1,575.

* ***1851 Classic Edition*** — similar to Presidential Edition, except has walnut grips and cylinder is roll engraved, cased. 3,500 mfg. starting 1986.

Last issue price was $525.

1860 ARMY PRESIDENTIAL EDITION — miniature reproduction of 1860 Army Colt, color case hardened engraved receiver and barrel, roll engraved cylinder scene, all parts operational, ivory grips, cherry cased. 1,500 mfg. starting 1988.

Last issue price was $1,575.

* ***1860 Classic Edition*** — similar to Presidential Edition without engraving, except has rosewood grips, cased. 3,500 mfg. starting 1988.

Last issue price was $525.

1861 NAVY PRESIDENTIAL EDITION — miniature reproduction of 1861 Navy Colt, color case hardened engraved receiver and barrel, roll engraved cylinder scene, all parts operational, includes detachable shoulder stock, cased. 1,500 mfg. starting 1990.

Last issue price was $1,500.

* ***1861 Navy Classic Edition*** — similar to Presidential Edition without engraving, cased. 1,500 mfg. starting 1990.

Last issue price was $750.

RIFLES: LIMITED/SPECIAL EDITIONS

CONFEDERATE COMMEMORATIVE RIFLE — replicates Cook & Brother original 1861 Model Carbine, 1,500 mfg. during 1986, includes wood wall mount and velvet sleeved bag, 24Kt. gold plating and accenting.

Last issue price was $1,900.

NOTES

GRADING - PPGS™	100%	98%	90%	80%

W SECTION

WATSON, WAYNE P.

Current contemporary longrifle master gunmaker located in Ocala, FL.

Master Longrifle maker Wayne Watson builds exact reproductions of existing masterpieces of the eighteenth century. He will make exact copies of particular rifles if he finds them pleasing overall, or he will take several rifles by the same maker and incorporate the best features from each.

In 1992, Mr. Watson's work came to the attention of Twentieth Century Fox Studios and Michael Mann, producer/director of the movie, "The Last of the Mohicans". He was hired to produce historically-accurate war clubs, tomahawks and the legendary "kill-deer" rifle carried by Daniel Day-Lewis, the star of the movie.

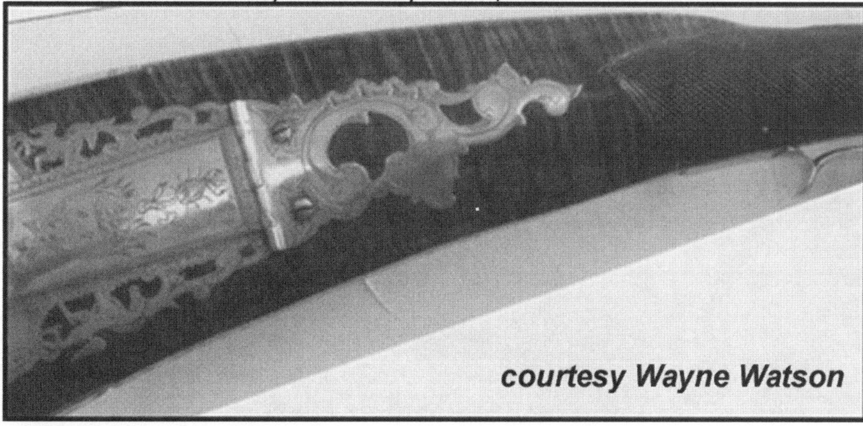

courtesy Wayne Watson

WHITE MUZZLELOADING SYSTEMS

Previous manufacturer located in Roosevelt, Utah until 1997.

All White Muzzleloading Systems models were discontinued during 1997. Manufacture and distribution was changed to Muzzleloading Technologies, Inc. until 2000 when Split Fire Sporting Goods, LLC picked up distribution. During 2001 Split Fire Sporting Goods, LLC changed its name to White Rifles, LLC. For current information refer to White Rifles, LLC.

PISTOLS: IN-LINE IGNITION

CHAMPION — .41, .45, or .50 cal. perc., stainless steel barrel, SC Series lock, composite stock.

	100%	98%	90%	80%
	$285	$235	$175	$125

Last MSR was $300.

JAVELINA — .45 or .50 cal. perc., G series "Insta-Fire" in-line ignition, 14 in. barrel, double safeties, match grade trigger, adj. sights, unique two handed black composite stock.

	100%	98%	90%	80%
	$445	$390	$300	$255

Last MSR was $500.

RIFLES: IN-LINE IGNITION

BISON — .50 or .54 cal. perc., G Series "Insta-Fire" in-line ignition action, 22 in. slightly tapered non-glare blue bull barrel, fully adj. open hunting sights, drilled and tapped for scope, hardwood stock, 6.5 lbs. New 1993.

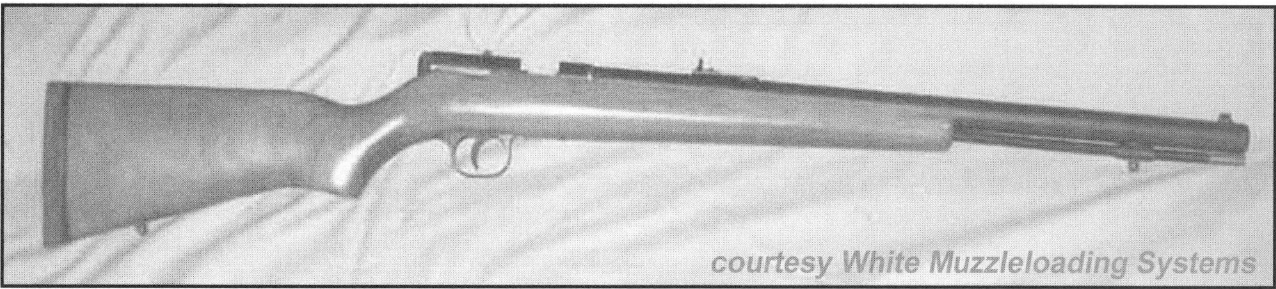

courtesy White Muzzleloading Systems

	100%	98%	90%	80%
	$315	$245	$185	$145

Last MSR was $400.

Add $50 for older model with black composite stock.

GRADING - PPGS™	100%	98%	90%	80%

GRAND ALASKAN/GRAND ALASKAN II — .54 cal. perc., W Series "Insta Fire" in-line ignition, 24 in. stainless steel bull barrel, stainless steel hardened nipple, green laminate stock, 7.75 lbs.

	$640	$495	$410	$295

Last MSR was $700.

ORIGINAL 68 — .45 or .50 cal. perc., W Series in-line ignition action, 24 in. round tapered blue barrel, fully adj. hunting sights, drilled and tapped for scope, black composite stock, 7.75 lbs. Mfg. 1993 only, very limited production. Disc. 1994.

	$615	$475	$400	$290

Last MSR was $600.

This model may have more value as a collectible due to its limited production.

PRO HUNTER STAINLESS STEEL — .41, .45, or .50 cal. perc., stainless steel tapered barrel, bolt action styling, black composite or laminated stock.

	$595	$465	$355	$280

Last MSR was $660.

Add $20 for black laminated stock.

SPORTING RIFLE — .41, .45 (.451), or .50 (.504) cal. perc., super nipple "Insta-Fire" ignition, 26 in. straight tapered barrel, GR (Green River) Series sidelock with half-cock, Manton style hooked breech, checkered crotchwood English styled composite stock, non-glare hunter's blue, 8.75 lbs. Mfg. 1994-97.

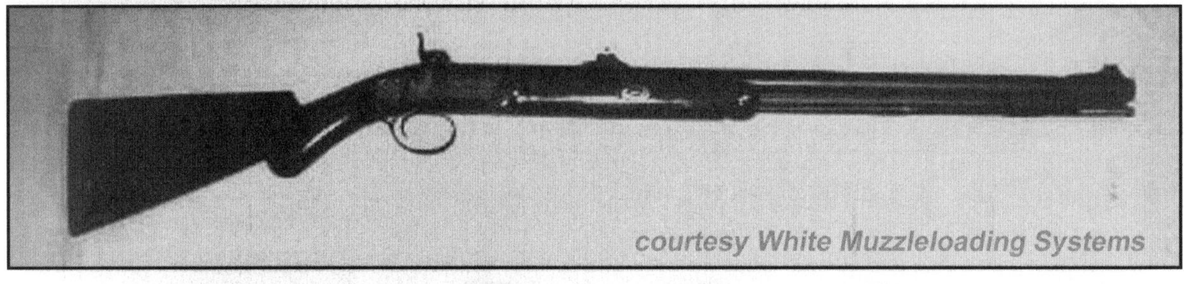

courtesy White Muzzleloading Systems

	$525	$425	$310	$250

Last MSR was $600.

SUPER 91 — .410, .451 and .504 cal. perc., W Series in-line ignition, "Insta-Fire" stainless steel hardened nipple, 24 in. barrel, blue steel or #416 stainless steel throughout, cleans with soap and water, walnut or composite stock, approx. 7.75 lbs.

	$500	$400	$295	$240

Last MSR was $600.

Add $50 for stainless steel, and $70 for stainless steel with black laminate stock.

* ***Super 91 w/Side Swing Safety*** — limited mfg. Disc. Oct. 1993.

	$750	$595	$425	$340

Last MSR was $700.

This model may have more value as a collectible due to its limited production.

SUPER SAFARI/SUPER SAFARI II — .41, .45 (.451), or .50 (.504) cal. perc., W Series straight-line "Insta-Fire" ignition, 24 in. Magnum tapered barrel, straight pull cocking handle, double safety system, drilled and tapped for scope or receiver sight, full length Mannlicher style black composite stock, non-glare #416 stainless, 7.75 lbs.

courtesy White Muzzleloading Systems

	$640	$495	$410	$295

Last MSR was $800.

GRADING - PPGS™	100%	98%	90%	80%

WHITE LIGHTNING — .50 cal. perc., "Insta Fire" in-line ignition, 22 in. tapered stainless steel barrel, recoil pad, adj. sights, black hardwood stock.

	$285	$220	$160	$115

Last MSR was $300.

WHITETAIL RIFLE — .410, .451, .504, or .54 cal. perc., "Insta-Fire" in-line ignition, 22 in. bull barrel (blue) tapered (stainless), new G series action, beech stock (blue), composite stock (stainless), 6.5 lbs. Mfg. 1992-97.

courtesy White Muzzleloading Systems

	$335	$260	$195	$150

Last MSR was $400.

Add $70 for stainless steel.
Add $100 for stainless steel with black laminate stock.
Add $160 for 1 of 1,000 Roger Ragun Signature Series with super sights and super sling factory installed.

The Whitetail Bull Barrel was disc. 1992.

SHOTGUNS: IN-LINE IGNITION

TOMINATOR — 12 ga. perc., "Insta-fire" in-line ignition, 26 in. blue barrel w/vent rib, new BG series action (larger version of G series), interchangeable chokes. Part of the "Ray Eye" signature series - black laminate stock.

	$425	$350	$255	$220

Last MSR was $500.

WHITE THUNDER — 12 ga. perc., "Insta-fire" in-line-ignition, 26 in. blue barrel w/vent rib. New BG series action (larger version of G Series), interchangeable chokes, black hardwood stock.

	$325	$250	$195	$155

Last MSR was $400.

WHITE RIFLES, LLC

Current manufacturer located back in Orem, UT during 2008. Previously located in Lindon, UT 2003-2008 and in Orem, UT 2001-03.

All White Rifles, LLC products are being sold via the web site (see listing in Trademark Index). During 2001, Split Fire Sporting Goods, LLC changed its name to White Rifles, LLC. Split Fire was the exclusive distributor for all White models manufactured by Muzzleloading Technologies, Inc. For information on White Rifles models produced prior to 1997, refer to the White Muzzleloading Systems section.

RIFLES: IN-LINE IGNITION

BLACKTAIL HUNTER — .504 cal. perc., standard or magnum #11 percussion caps in-line ignition, 22 in. straight tapered black Teflon coated stainless steel barrel, 1:24 in. twist, black laminate laser engraved deer scene or elk scene stock, silent double safety system, adj. White/Marble/Tru-Glo Fiber Optic steel hunting sights, recoil pad, sling swivel studs, 7.7 lbs.

courtesy White Rifles, LLC

	$500	$400	$295	$250

Last MSR was $500.

GRADING - PPGS™	100%	98%	90%	80%

ELITE HUNTER (MODEL 98) — .451 or .504 cal. perc., standard or magnum #11 percussion caps in-line ignition, 24 in. straight tapered stainless steel barrel, 1:24 (.451 cal.) or 1:24 in. twist, black composite or laminate stock, silent rotary double safety system, adj. White/Marble/Tru-Glo Fiber Optic steel hunting sights, recoil pad, sling swivel studs, 8.6 lbs.

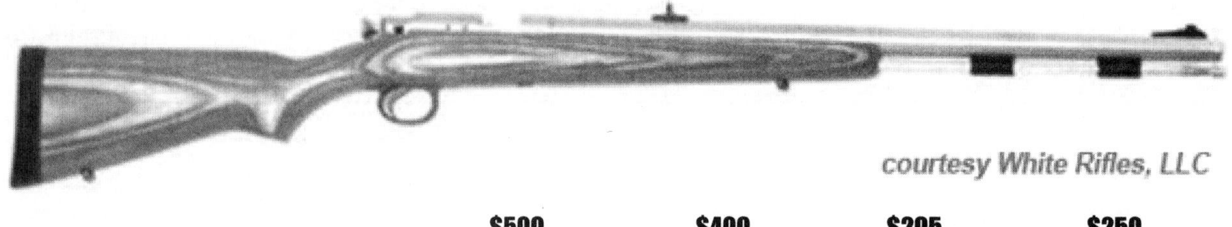

courtesy White Rifles, LLC

	$500	$400	$295	$250

Last MSR was $500.

SUPER 91 COLLECTOR'S EDITION — .504 cal. perc., standard or magnum #11 percussion caps in-line ignition, FlashFire one piece nipple/breachplug, 24 in. smooth tapered blue barrel, black composite or laminate stock, adj. Bold trigger, adj. Williams steel hunting sights, drilled and tapped, recoil pad, sling swivel studs, 7.6 lbs. New 2006.

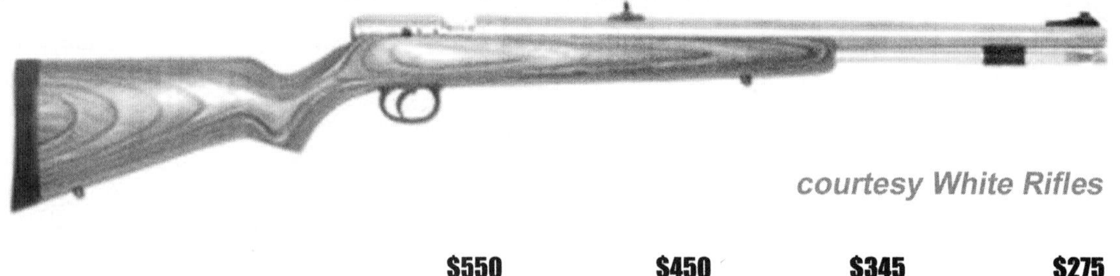

courtesy White Rifles

	$550	$450	$345	$275

Last MSR was $550.

THUNDER BOLT — .451 or .504 cal. perc., #209 primer in-line ignition, bolt-action, 26 in. straight tapered stainless steel barrel, 1:24 (.451 cal.) or 1:24 in. twist, black composite or laminate stock, silent rotary double safety system, adj. White/Marble/Tru-Glo Fiber Optic steel hunting sights, recoil pad, sling swivel studs, 9.3 lbs. New 2002.

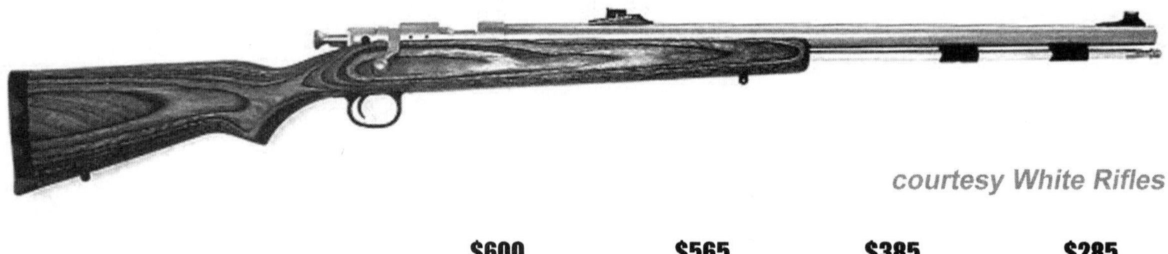

courtesy White Rifles

	$600	$565	$385	$285

Last MSR was $600.

ULTRA-MAG — .504 cal. perc., standard or magnum #11 percussion caps and #209 primer in-line ignition, 26 in. straight tapered black Teflon coated stainless steel barrel, 1:24 in. twist, black composite or laminate stock, silent double safety system, adj. White/Marble/Tru-Glo FiberOptic steel hunting sights, recoil pad, sling swivel studs, 8.3 lbs. Mfg. 2003.

	$350	$275	$225	$175

Last MSR was $399.

Was available exclusively through Sportsman's Warehouse.

WHITETAIL ADVENTURER — .451 or .504 cal. perc., standard or magnum #11 percussion caps and #209 primer in-line ignition, 26 in. straight tapered stainless steel barrel, 1:24 (.451 cal.) or 1:24 in. twist, black laminate thumbhole stock, silent rotary double safety system, adj. White/Marble/Tru-Glo Fiber Optic steel hunting sights, recoil pad, sling swivel studs, 8.3 lbs. New 2003.

	$700	$565	$450	$325

Last MSR was $700.

GRADING - PPGS™	100%	98%	90%	80%

WHITETAIL HUNTER (MODEL 97) — .451 or .504 cal. perc., standard or magnum #11 percussion caps in-line ignition, 22 in. straight tapered stainless steel barrel, 1:24 (.451 cal.) or 1:24 in. twist, black composite or laminate stock, silent double safety system, adj. White/Marble/Tru-Glo Fiber Optic steel hunting sights, recoil pad, sling swivel studs, 7.7 lbs.

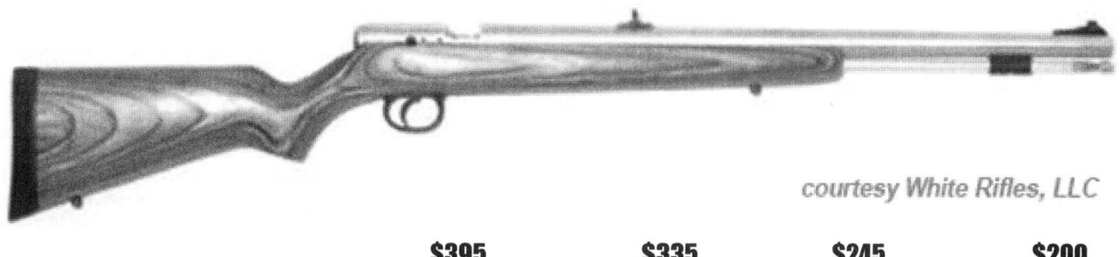

courtesy White Rifles, LLC

	$395	$335	$245	$200

Last MSR was $430.

WHITETAIL ODYSSEY — .451 (new 2003) or .504 cal. perc., standard or magnum #11 percussion caps and #209 primer (new 2003) in-line ignition, 24 in. straight tapered Christiansen Arms carbon fiber wrapped stainless steel barrel, 1:24 (.451 cal.) or 1:24 in. twist, glass bedded action, black laminate laser engraved Whitetail deer or Elk scene thumbhole stock, silent double safety system, drilled and tapped for scope or peep sight mounting, recoil pad, sling swivel studs, 6.7 lbs.

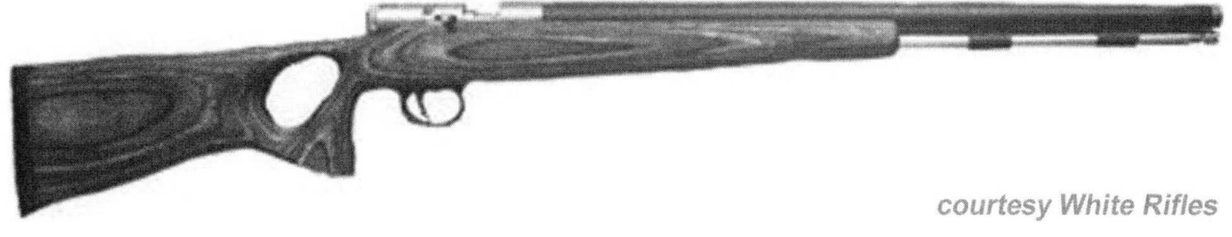

courtesy White Rifles

	$1,300	$950	$795	$650

Last MSR was $1,300.

SHOTGUNS: IN-LINE IGNITION

WHITE'S ORIGINAL SHOTGUN — 12 ga. perc., 25 in. straight tapered stainless steel barrel, interchangeable choke tubes, custom vent rib with high visibility front bead sight, in-line ignition, black laminate or black wood stock with recoil pad and sling swivel studs, double safety system, fully-adjustable custom trigger, 5.75 lbs. Disc. 2002.

	$315	$280	$255	$220

Last MSR was $350.

TOMINATOR SHOTGUN — 12 ga. perc., standard or magnum #11 percussion caps in-line ignition, 25 in. straight tapered blue barrel, interchangeable choke tubes, custom vent rib with high visibility front bead sight, black laminate stock with recoil pad and sling swivel studs, double safety system, 6 lbs. New 2002.

courtesy Winchester

	$315	$245	$185	$145

Last MSR was $350.

WILDERNESS RIFLE WORKS/LEMAN RIFLES

Previous manufacturer of flintlock and percussion rifles located in Waldron, IN. Previously distributed by Mountain State Muzzle Loading Supplies Inc., Williamstown, WV.

RIFLES: FLINTLOCK & PERCUSSION

CLASSIC — .50 cal. flintlock or perc., copy of early Leman-Lancaster rifle, 35 in. brown octagon barrel, high relief checkering on beautiful curly maple full stock, brass furniture, brown hammer and lock, brass buttplate and trigger guard.

GRADING - PPGS™	100%	98%	90%	80%
* ***Golden Classic***				
	$695	$565	$440	$325
				Last MSR was $750.
* ***Silver Classic*** — with nickel silver furniture.				
	$795	$650	$475	$350
				Last MSR was $995.

CUMBERLAND RIFLE — .32, .36, .40, .45, or .50 cal. flintlock or perc. 39.5 in. octagon brown barrel, brown hammer and lock, brass buttplate and trigger guard, 7.25 lbs. Mfg. 1994-disc.

	100%	98%	90%	80%
	$450	$325	$245	$195
				Last MSR was $495.

Add $20 for flintlock. Mfg. 1994.

ELKHUNTER RIFLE — .50 or .54 cal. perc., 32 in. octagon brown barrel, brown furniture, hammer and lock, curly maple stock, double set triggers, adj. buckhorn rear sight, 9 lbs.

	100%	98%	90%	80%
	$445	$365	$265	$225
				Last MSR was $475.

MOUNTAINEER RIFLE — .36, .40, .45, or .50 cal. flintlock or perc., 39 in. octagon brown barrel, brass or brown furniture, hammer and lock, curly maple full stock, double set triggers, adj. buckhorn rear sight, 7.25 to 8 lbs.

	100%	98%	90%	80%
	$375	$295	$235	$180
				Last MSR was $425.

Add $20 for flintlock.

PLAINS RIFLE — .50 or .54 cal. perc., 32 in. octagon barrel, fancy maple stock, furniture is brass or brown steel, single set double action trigger, 9 lbs. Disc. 1993.

	100%	98%	90%	80%
	$375	$295	$235	$180
				Last MSR was $495.

PRAIRIE RIFLE — .36, .40, .45, or .50 cal. perc., 32 in. barrel, brass or brown steel furniture, double set triggers, fancy figure maple stock, 8 lbs.

	100%	98%	90%	80%
	$395	$315	$245	$195
				Last MSR was $425.

SUMMIT RIFLE — .50 or .54 cal. perc., 30 in. octagon barrel, brass or brown steel furniture, single set double action trigger, fancy figure maple stock, 9 lbs. Disc. 1993.

	100%	98%	90%	80%
	$375	$295	$235	$180

WINCHESTER MUZZLELOADING

Previous licensed brand of Blackpowder Products, Inc., an importer and distributor located in Norcross, GA. Mfg. 2002-06.

The Winchester name was licensed to Winchester Muzzleloading, a division of Blackpowder Products, Inc. Circa 2002-06. Current Winchester trademark established in 1886 in New Haven, CT. Currently manufactured by Miroku of Japan since circa 1992, and in Herstal, Belgium (O/U shotguns). Previously manufactured in New Haven, CT, 1866-2006, and by U.S. Repeating Arms from 1981-2006 through a licensing agreement from Olin Corp. to manufacture shotguns and rifles domestically using the Winchester Trademark. Corporate offices are located in Morgan, UT. Olin Corp. previously manufactured shotguns and rifles bearing the Winchester Hallmark at the Olin Kodensha Plant (closed 1989) located in Tochigi, Japan and also in European countries. In 1992, U.S. Repeating Arms was acquired by GIAT located in France. In late 1997, the Walloon region of Belgium acquired controlling interest of both Browning and U.S. Repeating Arms.

For more information and current pricing on both new and used Winchester firearms, please refer to the*Blue Book of Gun Values* by S.P. Fjestad (now online also).

GRADING - PPGS™	100%	98%	90%	80%

RIFLES: IN-LINE IGNITION

APEX MAGNUM 209 RIFLE — .45 or.50 cal. # 209 primer perc., swing action breech, external hammer, in-line ignition, 28 (new 2004) or 30 (disc. 2004) in. blue, Mossy Oak (new 2004), or stainless steel monoblock fluted barrel, 1:28 in. twist, solid composite black fleck, or Mossy Oak Break-Up finish stock, sling swivel studs and Winchester Muzzleloading sling, ventilated recoil pad, adj. metallic fiber optic sights, 44-46 in. OAL, 7.75-8.4 lbs. Mfg. 2003-06.

courtesy Winchester

	$225	$180	$145	$115

Last MSR was $250.

Add 25% for Mossy Oak Break-Up finish stock. Last MSR was $350.
Add 25% for stainless steel barrel. Last MSR was $300 - $350.
Add 40% for full Mossy Oak camo finish (barrel and stock). Last MSR was $350.

X-150 MAGNUM 209 RIFLE — .45 or .50 cal. # 209 primer perc., bolt-action, in-line ignition, 26 in. blue or stainless steel monoblock fluted barrel, 1:28 in. twist, stainless steel bolt, solid composite gray or black fleck, HD Advantage Timber or Hardwoods, or Mossy Oak Break-up (new 2003) finish stock, sling swivel studs and Winchester Muzzleloading sling, ventilated recoil pad, adj. metallic fiber optic sights, 46 in. OAL, 8.2 lbs. Mfg. 2002-05.

courtesy Winchester

	$210	$165	$125	$85

Last MSR was $230.

Add 22% for Advantage HD Timber, Hardwoods, or Mossy Oak Break-Up finish stock. Last MSR was $280 - $350.
Add 25% for stainless steel barrel. Last MSR was $350.

NOTES

COLT BLACKPOWDER 2ND GENERATION MODEL SPECIFICATIONS

.44 cal. Model 1847 Walker, Revolver, with Hinged Loading Lever, 6 Shot, 9½-inch Half Round, Half Octagonal Barrel, Steel Backstrap, Brass Square Back Trigger Guard, US 1847 stamped above wedge screw, N.Y. Address. Produced 1980-1982.

.44 cal. Model 1847 Walker Heritage, Revolver, with Hinged Loading Lever, 6 Shot, 9½-inch Half Round, Half Octagonal Barrel, Steel Backstrap, Brass Square Back Trigger Guard, US 1847 stamped above wedge screw, Gold Engraved Portraits of Capt. Walker and Samuel Colt on Left Side, Heritage Banner on Right, N.Y. Address. In Presentation Case With *The Colt Heritage* book by R.L. Wilson. Produced 1980-1981.

.44 cal. 1st Model Dragoon, Revolver, with Hinged and Latched Loading Lever, 6 Shot, 7½-inch Half Round, Half Octagonal Barrel, Oval Cylinder Stop Slots, Brass Backstrap and Square Back Trigger Guard, N.Y. Address. Produced 1980-1982.

.44 cal. 2nd Model Dragoon, Revolver, with Hinged and Latched Loading Lever, 6 Shot, 7½-inch Half Round, Half Octagonal Barrel, Rectangular Cylinder Stop Slots, Brass Backstrap and Square Back Trigger Guard, N.Y. Address. Produced 1980-1982.

.44 cal. 3rd Model Dragoon, Revolver, with Hinged and Latched Loading Lever, 6 Shot, 7½-inch Half Round, Half Octagonal Barrel, Rectangular Cylinder Stop Slots, Brass Backstrap and Round Trigger Guard, N.Y. Address. Produced 1980-1982

.31 cal. Model 1848 Baby Dragoon, Revolver, Pocket Pistol, no Loading Lever, 5 Shot, 4-inch Octagonal Barrel, Silver-Plated Backstrap and Square Back Trigger Guard, Two line New York address. Produced 1981.

.36 cal. Model 1851 Navy, Revolver, with Hinged and Latched Loading Lever, 6 Shot, 7½-inch Octagonal Barrel, Silver-Plated Backstrap and Square Back Trigger Guard, N.Y. Address. [Also Made with Brass Backstrap and Square Back Trigger Guard, or with Stainless Steel Finish.] Produced 1971-1978.

.36 cal. Model 1851 Navy U.S. Grant Commemorative, Revolver, with Hinged and Latched Loading Lever, 6 Shot, 7½-inch Octagonal Barrel, Silver-Plated Backstrap and Square Back Trigger Guard, N.Y. Address, Barrel Engraved, Ulysses S. Grant Commemorative Nineteen Seventy One. In Blue Satin and Felt Lined Presentation Case with Pewter Powder Flask and tools. Produced 1971.

.36 cal. Model 1851 Navy Robert E. Lee Commemorative, Revolver, with Hinged and Latched Loading Lever, 6 Shot, 7½-inch Octagonal Barrel, Silver-Plated Backstrap and Round Trigger Guard, N.Y. Address, Barrel Engraved, Robert E. Lee Commemorative Nineteen Seventy One. In Grey Satin and Felt Lined Presentation Case with Pewter Powder Flask and tools. Produced 1971.

.44 cal. Model 1860 Army, Revolver, with Creeping-Style Loading Lever, 6 Shot Rebated Cylinder, 8-inch Round Barrel, Steel Backstrap and Brass Trigger Guard, N.Y. U.S. America Address. [Also produced with Stainless Steel Finish.] Produced 1978-1982

.44 cal. Model 1860 Army, Revolver, with Creeping-Style Loading Lever, 6 Shot Fluted Cylinder, 8-inch Round Barrel, Steel Backstrap and Brass Trigger Guard, N.Y. U.S. America Address. Produced 1980-1981.

.36 cal. Model 1861 Navy, Revolver, with Creeping-Style Loading Lever, 6 Shot, 7½-inch Round Barrel, Silver-Plated Backstrap and Trigger Guard, N.Y. U.S. America Address. Produced 1980-1981.

.36 cal. Model 1862 Pocket Navy, Revolver, with Hinged and Latched Loading Lever, 5 Shot Rebated Cylinder, 5½-inch Octagonal Barrel, Silver-Plated Backstrap and Square Back Trigger Guard, N.Y. U.S. America Address. Produced 1979-1981 and 1984.

.36 cal. Model 1862 Pocket Police, Revolver, with Creeping-Style Loading Lever, 5 Shot Semi-Fluted Cylinder, 5½-inch Round Barrel, Silver-Plated Backstrap and Round Trigger Guard, N.Y. U.S. America Address. Produced 1979-1981 and 1984.

COLT BLACKPOWDER 3RD GENERATION MODEL SPECIFICATIONS

.36 cal. Model 1842 Paterson, Revolver, No. 5 Holster Model with Hinged Loading Lever, 5 Shot, 7½-inch Octagonal Barrel, Steel Backstrap, Period-Style Scrollwork with Punch-Dot Background on both sides of Barrel Lug, Frame and Standing Breech, Loading Lever Rod Tip, Hammer and Backstrap. Two 18 Kt. Gold Bands inlaid at the Muzzle, encircling the Cylinder and one Gold Band around the circumference of the front of the Standing. Royal Blue mirror finish, premium Walnut Stocks, authentic "- Patent Arms Mg.Co. Paterson, NJ - Colt's PL -" barrel address. Introduced in 1998.

.44 cal. Model 1847 Walker, Revolver, with Hinged Loading Lever, 6 Shot, 9½-inch Half Round, Half Octagonal Barrel, Steel Backstrap, Brass Square Back Trigger Guard, US 1847 stamped above wedge screw, N.Y. Address. Introduced in 1994.

.44 cal. Model 1847 Walker, 150th Anniversary Edition, Revolver, with Hinged Loading Lever, 6 Shot, 9½-inch Half Round, Half Octagonal Barrel, Steel Backstrap, Brass Square Back Trigger Guard, US 1847 stamped above wedge screw, A COMPANY No.1 Engraved on Left Side of Barrel, Frame, and on Cylinder, N.Y. Address. Series Begins With Serial Number 221. Introduced in 1997.

.44 cal. Model 1848 Whitneyville-Hartford Dragoon, Revolver, with Hinged and Latched Loading Lever, 6 Shot, 7½-inch Half Round, Half Octagonal Barrel, Oval Cylinder Stop Slots, Silver-Plated Backstrap and Square Back Trigger Guard, N.Y. Address, Sam Colt Signature engraved on Backstrap. Introduced in 1996.

.44 cal. Model 1848 Whitneyville-Hartford Commemorative "Marine" Dragoon, Revolver, with Hinged and Latched Loading Lever, 6 Shot, 7½-inch Half Round, Half Octagonal

Barrel, Oval Cylinder Stop Slots, Silver-Plated with 24 Kt. Gold-Plated Cylinder, Backstrap and Square Back Trigger Guard, N.Y. Address, Semper Fidelis engraved on Backstrap. Introduced in 1997.

.31 **cal. Model 1848 Baby Dragoon,** Revolver, 5 Shot, 4-inch Octagonal Barrel, Silver Plated Backstrap and Square Back Trigger Guard, N.Y. Address, Sam Colt Signature engraved on Backstrap. Introduced in 1998.

.44 **cal. Model 1848 1st Model Dragoon,** Revolver, with Hinged and Latched Loading Lever, 6 Shot, 7½-inch Half Round, Half Octagonal Barrel, Oval Cylinder Stop Slots, Brass Backstrap and Square Back Trigger Guard, N.Y. Address, Sam Colt Signature engraved on Backstrap. Introduced in 1998.

.44 **cal. Model 1850 2nd Model Dragoon,** Revolver, with Hinged and Latched Loading Lever, 6 Shot, 7½-inch Half Round, Half Octagonal Barrel, rectangular Cylinder Stop Slots, Brass Backstrap and Square Back Trigger Guard, N.Y. Address, Sam Colt Signature engraved on Backstrap. Introduced in 1998.

.44 **cal. 3rd Model Dragoon,** Revolver, with Hinged and Latched Loading Lever, 6 Shot, 7½-inch Half Round, Half Octagonal Barrel, Rectangular Cylinder Stop Slots, Brass Backstrap Civilian Model with Round Trigger Guard, N.Y. Address, Sam Colt Signature engraved on Backstrap. Introduced in 1996.

.44 **cal. 3rd Model Dragoon,** Revolver, with Hinged and Latched Loading Lever, 6 Shot, 7½-inch Half Round, Half Octagonal Barrel, Rectangular Cylinder Stop Slots, Steel Backstrap Military Model with Brass Round Trigger Guard, N.Y. Address, Sam Colt Signature engraved in Gold on Backstrap. Introduced in 1996.

.44 **cal. 3rd Model Dragoon,** Revolver, with Hinged and Latched Loading Lever, 6 Shot, 7½-inch Half Round, Half Octagonal Barrel, Fluted Cylinder, Rectangular Cylinder Stop Slots, Silver-Plated Backstrap and Round Trigger Guard, N.Y. Address, Sam Colt Signature engraved on Backstrap. Introduced in 1996.

.44 **cal. Model 1851 3rd Model Dragoon,** Cochise Edition, Revolver, with Hinged and Latched Loading Lever, 6 Shot, 7½-inch Half Round, Half Octagonal Barrel, Gold Engraved Cylinder, Gold Backstrap and Trigger Guard, N.Y. Address, Sam Colt Signature engraved on Backstrap. Gold Plated Pony Scene on Left Side of Barrel, Cochise legend on Octagonal Portion of Barrel along with Peace Pipe and Tomahawk, Gold-Plated Buffalo on Lower Corner of Frame, Blackhorn stocks with Cochise Portrait on Left Side. Introduced in 1997.

.31 **cal. Model 1849 Pocket,** Revolver, with Hinged and Latched Loading Lever, 5 Shot, 4-inch Octagonal Barrel, Silver-Plated Backstrap and Trigger Guard, N.Y. Address, Sam Colt Signature engraved on Backstrap. Introduced in 1994.

.36 **cal. Model 1851 Navy,** Revolver, with Hinged and Latched Loading Lever, 6 Shot, 7½-inch Octagonal Barrel, Silver-Plated Backstrap and Square Back Trigger Guard, N.Y. Address, Sam Colt Signature engraved on Backstrap. Also available in London Navy Model. Introduced in 1994, London Navy in 1997.

.44 **cal. Model 1860 Army,** Revolver, with Creeping-Style Loading Lever, 6 Shot Rebated Cylinder, 8-inch Round Barrel, Steel Backstrap and Brass Trigger Guard, N.Y. U.S. America Address, Sam Colt Signature engraved in Gold on Backstrap. [Also issued in nickel finish, and Officer's Model with Fluted Cylinder and Embellished with Crossed Sabers and the legend US 1860, Engraved in Gold on Right Side of Barrel.] Introduced in 1994, Officer's Model in 1995, Nickel in 1997.

.44 **cal. Model 1860 Army Gold U.S. Cavalry,** Revolver, with Creeping-Style Loading Lever, 6 Shot Gold-Plated Rebated Cylinder Engraved on Both Sides with Crossed Sabers and the legend US 1860, 8-inch Round Barrel with Double Gold Bands around the Muzzle, Gold Backstrap and Trigger Guard, N.Y. U.S. America Address, Sam Colt Signature engraved on Backstrap. Introduced in 1996.

.44 **cal. Model 1860 Army, Revolver,** with Creeping-Style Loading Lever, 6 Shot Fluted Cylinder, 8-inch Round Barrel, Steel Backstrap and Brass Trigger Guard, N.Y. U.S. America Address, Sam Colt Signature engraved in Gold on Backstrap. Introduced in 1995.

.44 **cal. Model 1860 Army Tiffany Revolver,** with Creeping-Style Loading Lever, 6 Shot Rebated Cylinder, 8-inch Round Barrel, Fully Covered with L.D. Nimschke Style Scrollwork, Silver and 24 Kt. Gold-Plated, N.Y. U.S. America Address, Deluxe Tiffany-Style Grips plated in Pure Silver. Introduced in 1998.

.36 **cal. Model 1861 Navy,** General Custer Edition, Revolver, with Creeping-Style Loading Lever, 6 Shot Non-Rebated Cylinder, 7½-inch Round Barrel, Steel Backstrap and Trigger Guard, N.Y. Address, Sam Colt Signature Engraved on Backstrap. Antiqued Silver Finish, Nimschke-Style Engraving on Barrel, Loading Lever, Cylinder, Frame, Hammer, Trigger Guard, and Backstrap. Walnut Stocks with Eagle and Shield on Left, Checkered on Right. Introduced in 1996.

.36 **cal. Model 1861 Navy,** Revolver, with Creeping-Style Loading Lever, 6 Shot Non-Rebated Cylinder, 7½-inch Round Barrel, Steel Backstrap and Trigger Guard, N.Y. Address, Sam Colt Signature Engraved in Gold on Backstrap. Introduced in 1995.

.36 **cal. Model 1862 Pocket Navy,** Revolver, with Hinged Loading Lever, 5 Shot Rebated Cylinder, 5½-inch Octagonal Barrel, Silver-Plated Backstrap and Square Back Trigger Guard, N.Y. Address, Sam Colt Signature Engraved on Backstrap. Introduced in 1996.

.36 **cal. Model 1862 Pocket Police,** Revolver, with Creeping-Style Loading Lever, 5 Shot Semi-Fluted Cylinder, 5½-inch Round Barrel, Silver-Plated Backstrap and Square Back Trigger Guard, N.Y. Address, Sam Colt Signature Engraved on Backstrap. Introduced in 1997.

.36 **cal. Model 1862 Trapper,** Revolver, No Loading Lever, 5-Shot Semi-Fluted Cylinder, 3½-inch Round Barrel, Silver-Plated Backstrap and Trigger Guard, N.Y. Address, Sam Colt Signature Engraved on Backstrap. Comes with Brass Ramrod. Introduced in 1995.

IDENTIFYING POPULAR MODERN BLACK POWDER Revolvers

After Sam Colt patented the Paterson in 1836, (distinguished by its folding trigger and absence of a trigger guard), his fortunes faded, and by 1842 his Paterson, New Jersey manufacturing company was out of business. Undaunted, he soldiered back, quite literally, with the most powerful military revolver of the early 19th century, the 1847 Walker. This massive and unmistakable .44 caliber pistol played a significant role in the War with Mexico. Sam Colt and Captain Samuel Walker, who convinced the U.S. government to place its initial order for the mighty sidearm, worked together on the gun's design. Tragically, Walker was killed in action, but is remembered more than 150 years later by the guns that bear his name.

The Walker was a handful, and Sam Colt returned to his Paterson roots briefly by following the big .44 with two small pocket pistols, the .31 caliber 1848 Baby Dragoon and the 1849 Pocket Dragoon, which is differentiated by having a loading lever. Both resemble a small version of the 1st Model Dragoon.

The need for a lighter weight but still potent revolver led to the 1st, 2nd, and 3rd Model Dragoons in the late 1840s, which were a slightly smaller .44 caliber evolution of the Walker, and one of the most successful of the Colt percussion era.

Both the U.S. military and civilian market were clamoring for an even lighter but sufficiently powerful revolver by the end of the 1840s, and in 1851 Sam Colt brought out the most famous gun of his career, the 1851 Navy, chambered in .36 caliber. This distinctive firearm is recognized by its smaller frame and elegant octagon barrel. Two basic versions were offered, one with a square back trigger guard, and another with a round trigger guard.

The 1860 Army chambered in .44 caliber came next and is often considered the best looking gun ever built. A great departure from the squared lines of the Dragoons and Navy models, the Army had a slender round barrel and new loading lever design, and either a rebated or fluted cylinder. A slightly scaled down version, the 1861 Navy, fitted with the 1851 Navy's rebated cylinder, followed in .36 caliber.

Colt's again returned to its pocket pistols around 1862 with the addition of the compact .36 caliber Police model, resembling a scaled down 1861 Navy with a half rebated, half fluted cylinder. The Pocket model of Navy size caliber followed in 1865, also chambered in .36 caliber, and resembling a compact 1851 Navy. This marked the end of new percussion models for Colt's.

The Colt's patent for the revolving cylinder had prevented other American gun manufacturers from producing revolvers until 1858, whereupon Remington introduced the .44 caliber Army model and .36 caliber Navy. Both can be distinguished by their use of a top strap design and fixed barrel.

Another popular model from the 1850s that has been reproduced in Italy is the Starr single and double action revolver. A distinctive design, the Starr has a break open frame secured by a screw. The guns have an easily recognizable profile.

The most elegant pistol design of the percussion era was the LeMat, set apart by its sheer size, large nine-shot .44 caliber cylinder, and 20-gauge shotgun barrel! Once you've seen a LeMat, you'll never forget it.

There are other Civil War reproductions built today, such as the Dance, which resembles an 1851 Navy without a recoil shield, and the Rogers & Spencer, which is similar in appearance to the 1858 Remington Army. The identification guide presented, however, should help in recognizing the majority of models currently available for black powder shooters. ■

IDENTIFYING POPULAR
MODERN BLACK POWDER Revolvers

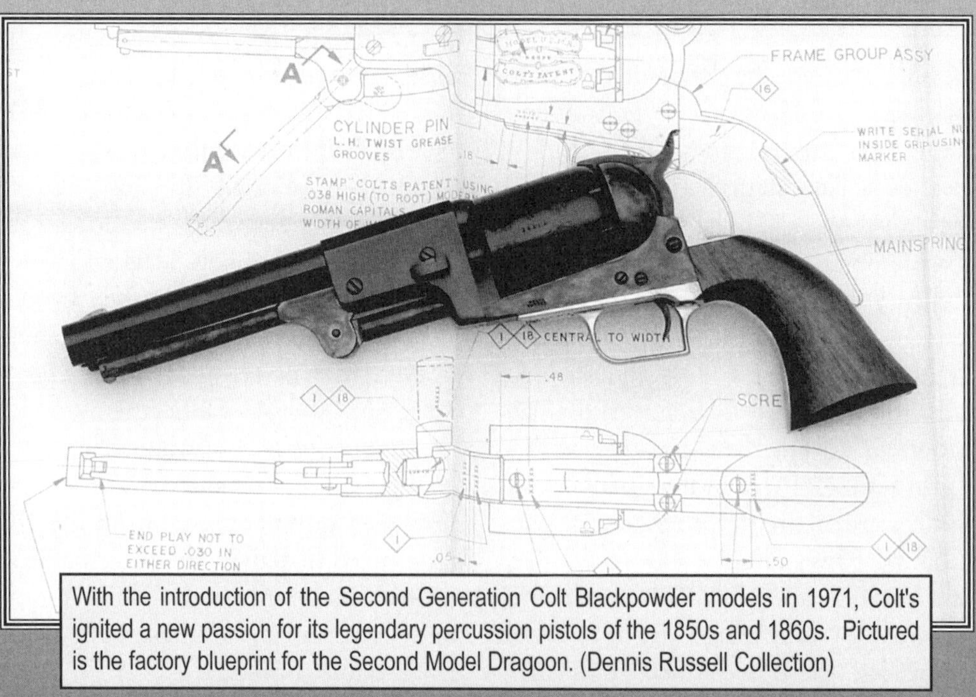

With the introduction of the Second Generation Colt Blackpowder models in 1971, Colt's ignited a new passion for its legendary percussion pistols of the 1850s and 1860s. Pictured is the factory blueprint for the Second Model Dragoon. (Dennis Russell Collection)

The 2nd Generation Colt line encompassed a total of 11 standard models recreating the most famous percussion revolvers of the 19th century. (Author's collection)

IDENTIFYING POPULAR MODERN BLACK POWDER Revolvers

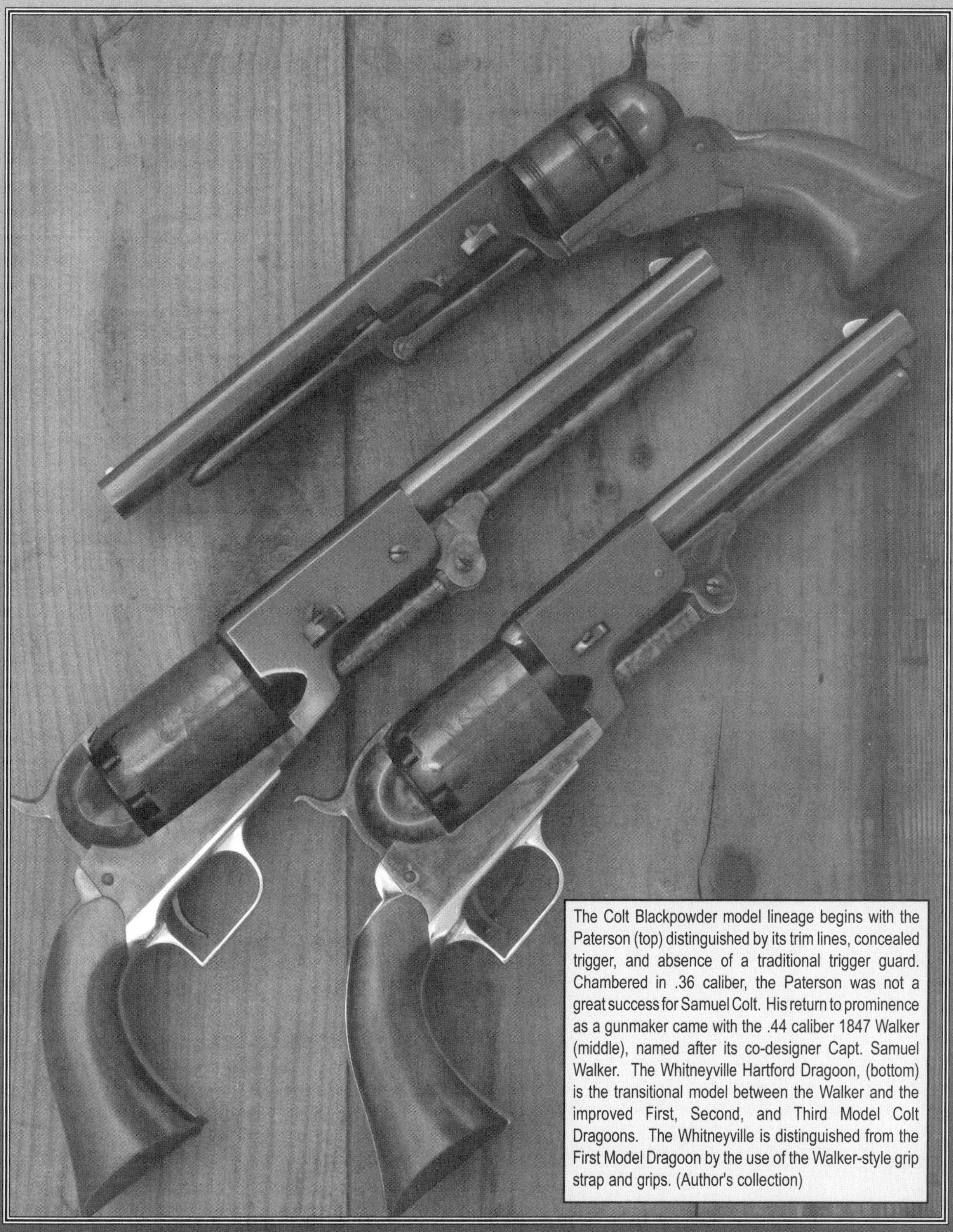

The Colt Blackpowder model lineage begins with the Paterson (top) distinguished by its trim lines, concealed trigger, and absence of a traditional trigger guard. Chambered in .36 caliber, the Paterson was not a great success for Samuel Colt. His return to prominence as a gunmaker came with the .44 caliber 1847 Walker (middle), named after its co-designer Capt. Samuel Walker. The Whitneyville Hartford Dragoon, (bottom) is the transitional model between the Walker and the improved First, Second, and Third Model Colt Dragoons. The Whitneyville is distinguished from the First Model Dragoon by the use of the Walker-style grip strap and grips. (Author's collection)

IDENTIFYING POPULAR MODERN BLACK POWDER Revolvers

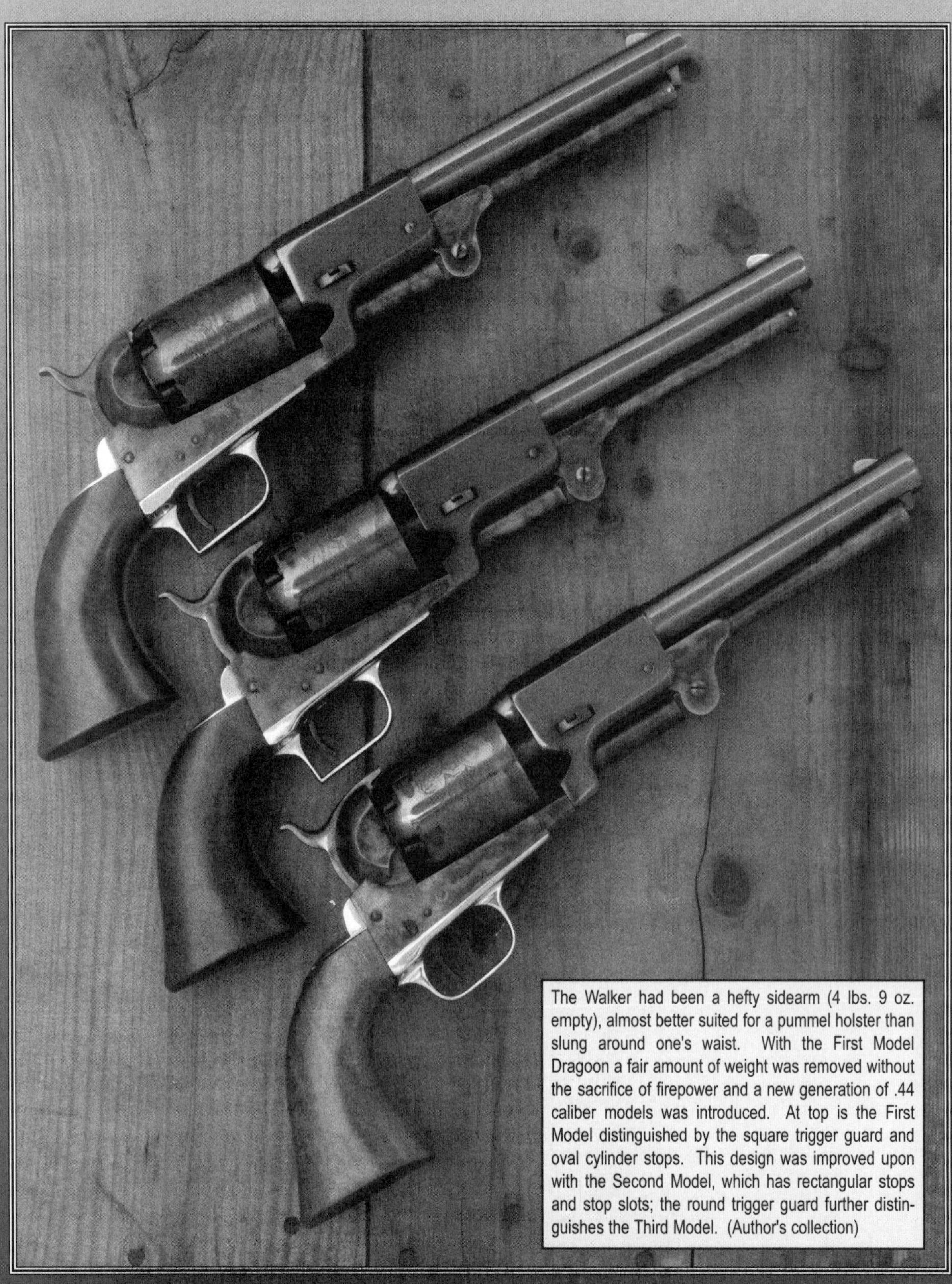

The Walker had been a hefty sidearm (4 lbs. 9 oz. empty), almost better suited for a pummel holster than slung around one's waist. With the First Model Dragoon a fair amount of weight was removed without the sacrifice of firepower and a new generation of .44 caliber models was introduced. At top is the First Model distinguished by the square trigger guard and oval cylinder stops. This design was improved upon with the Second Model, which has rectangular stops and stop slots; the round trigger guard further distinguishes the Third Model. (Author's collection)

IDENTIFYING POPULAR MODERN BLACK POWDER Revolvers

Colt's introduced the .36 caliber Navy Model in 1851. This has become one of the most recognized and popular Colt models ever produced. Used extensively throughout the Civil War by both sides, two versions of the 1851 Navy are easily recognized by their square back or rounded trigger guards. (Author's collection)

IDENTIFYING POPULAR MODERN BLACK POWDER Revolvers

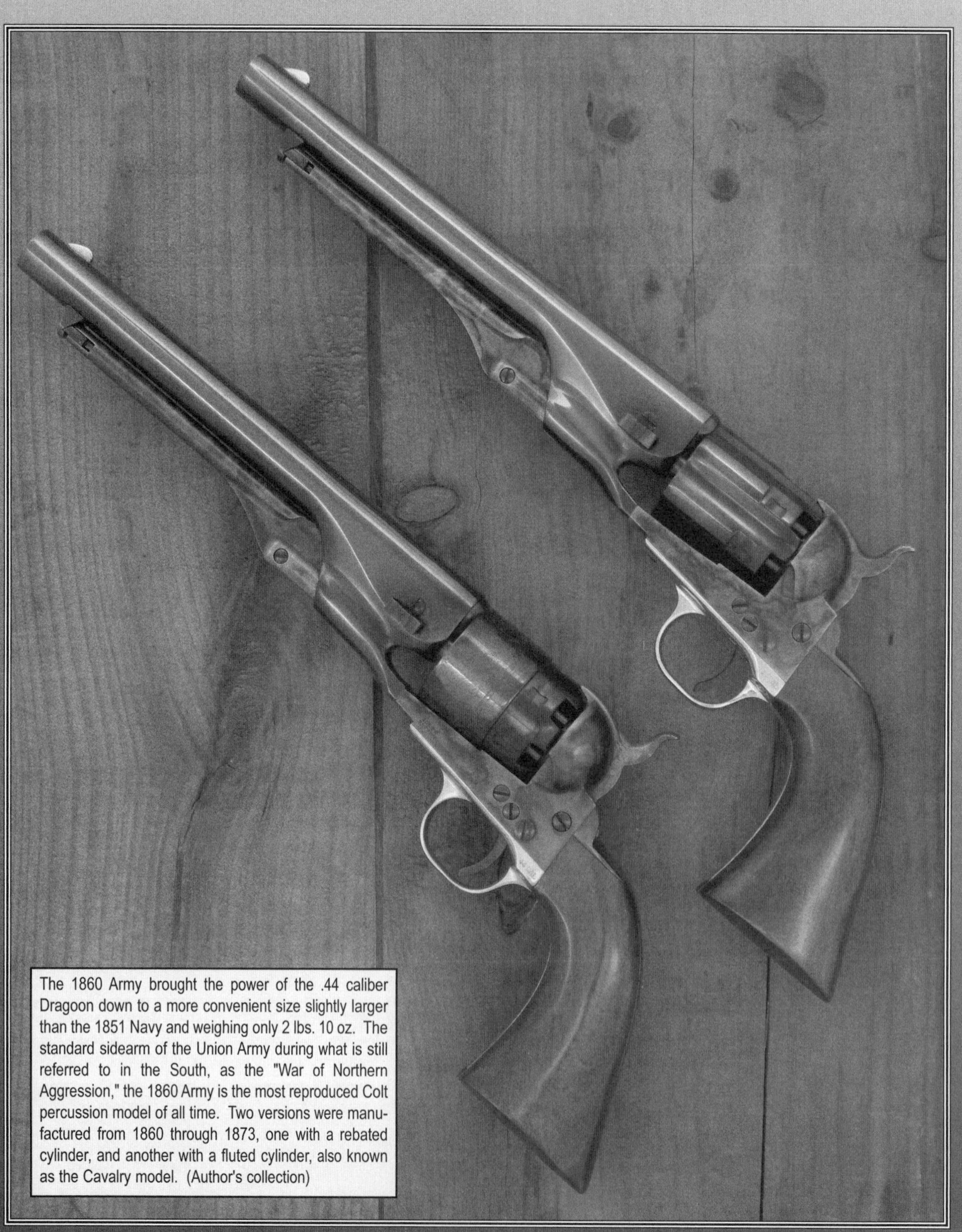

The 1860 Army brought the power of the .44 caliber Dragoon down to a more convenient size slightly larger than the 1851 Navy and weighing only 2 lbs. 10 oz. The standard sidearm of the Union Army during what is still referred to in the South, as the "War of Northern Aggression," the 1860 Army is the most reproduced Colt percussion model of all time. Two versions were manufactured from 1860 through 1873, one with a rebated cylinder, and another with a fluted cylinder, also known as the Cavalry model. (Author's collection)

Identifying Popular Modern Black Powder Revolvers

Shortly after the introduction of the gracefully designed Colt 1860 Army, Colt's emulated the styling with a slightly smaller and lighter weight .36 caliber model designated as the 1861 Navy (top). Another, even smaller .36 caliber pistol, reminiscent of the 1851 Navy, was introduced around 1862-65 and described as a Pocket Model of Navy Caliber. (Author's collection)

Identifying Popular Modern Black Powder Revolvers

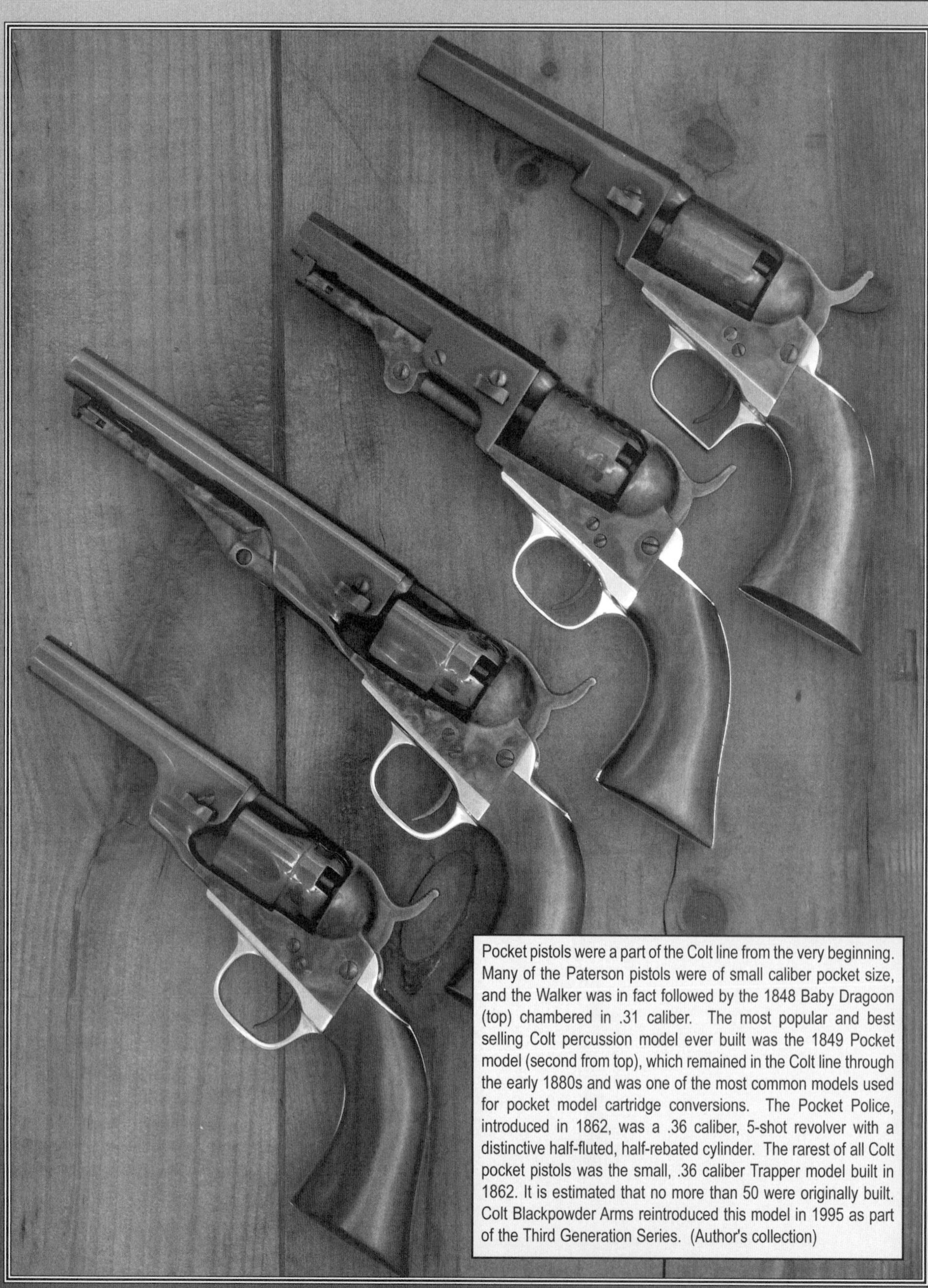

Pocket pistols were a part of the Colt line from the very beginning. Many of the Paterson pistols were of small caliber pocket size, and the Walker was in fact followed by the 1848 Baby Dragoon (top) chambered in .31 caliber. The most popular and best selling Colt percussion model ever built was the 1849 Pocket model (second from top), which remained in the Colt line through the early 1880s and was one of the most common models used for pocket model cartridge conversions. The Pocket Police, introduced in 1862, was a .36 caliber, 5-shot revolver with a distinctive half-fluted, half-rebated cylinder. The rarest of all Colt pocket pistols was the small, .36 caliber Trapper model built in 1862. It is estimated that no more than 50 were originally built. Colt Blackpowder Arms reintroduced this model in 1995 as part of the Third Generation Series. (Author's collection)

IDENTIFYING POPULAR MODERN BLACK POWDER Revolvers

Not every great percussion revolver of the 1850s and 1860s wore the Colt signature. Among the more innovative and advanced designs of the mid 19th century was the Starr single and double action revolvers (top two) and the Remington Army, which featured a solid frame with top strap and threaded barrel. Due to its superior design, the Remington was the easiest revolver to either reload or for which to exchange cylinders. (Author's collection)

Colt Blackpowder 2nd Generation Serialization

Model No.	Serial # Range	Total Prod.	Prod. Began	Prod. Ended
MODEL 1851 NAVY				
C-1121	4201 - 25100	20,900	1971	1978
C-1122	As above but at higher range of numbers	–	–	1978
MODEL 1851 NAVY, R. E. LEE				
C-9001	251REL - 5000REL	4,750	–	1971
MODEL 1851 NAVY, U. S. GRANT				
C-9002	251USG - 5000USG	4,750	–	1971
MODEL 1851 GRANT-LEE PAIR				
C-9003	01GLP - 250GLP	250	–	1971
3rd MODEL DRAGOON				
C-1770	20801 - 208 *Prototype*	25	1974	1978
	20901 - 24501	3,601		
C-1770MN	S/N's As Above	20	1984	1984
MODEL 1851 NAVY				
F-1100	24900 - 29150	4,250	5/80	10/81
F-1101	S/N's As Above *W/Blank Cylinders*	300	10/81	11/81
F-1110	29151S - 29640S *Stainless Steel*	489	6/82	10/82
MODEL 1860 ARMY				
F-1200	201000 - 212835 *Rebated Cylinder*	7,593	11/78	11/82
F-1200EBO	S/N's As Above *Butterfield*	500	1979	1979
F-1200LNK	S/N's As Above *Electroless Nickel*	–	–	–
F-1200MN	S/N's As Above *Nickel/Ivory*	12	1984	1984
F-1202	S/N's As Above *Limited Edition*	500	1979	1979
F-1203	207330 - 211250 *Fluted Cylinder*	2,670	7/80	10/81
F-1210	211263S - 212540S *Stainless Steel*	1,278	1/82	4/82
1861 NAVY				
F-1300	40000 - 43165	3,166	9/80	10/81

Model No.	Serial # Range	Total Prod.	Prod. Began	Prod. Ended
1862 POCKET NAVY				
F-1400	48000 - 58850 and skip odd no's.	5,765	12/79	11/81
F-1400MN	S/N's As Above *Nickel/Ivory*	25	1984	1984
F-1401	S/N's As Above *Limited Edition*	500	1979	1980
1862 POCKET POLICE				
F-1500	49000 - 57300 and skip even no's.	4,801	1/80	9/81
F-1500MN	S/N's As Above *Nickel/Ivory*	25	1984	1984
F-1501	S/N's As Above *Limited Edition*	500	1979	1980
1847 WALKER				
F-1600	1200 - 4120	2,573	6/80	4/82
	32256 - 32500	245	5/81	9/81
1st MODEL DRAGOON				
F-1700	25100 - 34500	3,878	1/80	2/82
2nd MODEL DRAGOON				
F-172	S/N's As Above and Mix at Random for 1st, 2nd, & 3rd	2,676	1/80	2/82
3rd MODEL DRAGOON				
F-140	S/N's As Above and Mix at Random for 1st, 2nd & 3rd	2,856	1/80	2/82
	31401 - 31450	50	10/81	11/81
F-1740EGA	Unkown *(Garabaldi Model – "GCA" prefix)*	200	1982	1982
BABY DRAGOON				
F-1760	16000 - 17851	1,852	2/81	4/81
F-1761	S/N's As Above *Limited Edition*	500	1979	1980
1860 ARMY				
F-9005	US 001/001 US to US 3025/3025 US *Cavalry Commemorative (Two Gun Set)*	3,025	9/77	1/80
HERITAGE WALKER				
F-9006	01 - 1853	1,853	6/80	6/81

PIETTA SERIALIZATION

Paterson

Year	Ser. Start	Ser. End
1984	1527	1920
1985	1921	1925
1986	1926	1991
1987	1992	2456
1988	2457	2766
1989	2767	3086
1990	2087	3336
1991	3337	3366
1992	3367	3486
1993	3487	3494
1994	3495	3569
1995	none	
1996	3570	3634
1997	3635	4051

1851 Colt Navy

Year	Ser. Start	Ser. End
1986	261770	270638
1987	270639	276146
1988	276147	281728
1989	281729	289217
1990	289218	295460
1991	295461	306404
1992	306405	320700
1993	320701	334122
1994	334123	353229
1995	353230	380047
1996	380048	396921
1997	396922	410579
1998	410579	424560
1999	424561	439794

1851 Navy Deluxe

Year	Ser. Start	Ser. End
1994	000001	001199
1995	001200	001999

1858 Remington New Model Army

Year	Ser. Start	Ser. End
1986	093517	101045
1987	101046	106063
1988	106064	110724
1989	110725	116814
1990	116815	125821
1991	125822	135274
1992	135275	149530
1993	149531	164614
1994	164615	184656
1995	184657	210677
1996	210678	235809
1997	235810	252133
1998	252134	260849
1999	R260850	R273377

Remington Target Model

Year	Ser. Start	Ser. End
1984	A0001	A0021
1985	A0022	A0255
1986	A0256	A0581
1987	A0582	A1254
1988	A1255	A1552
1989	A1553	A1816
1990	A1817	A2308
1991	A2309	A2608
1992	A2609	A2887
1993	A2888	A3093
1994	A3094	A3318
1995	A3319	A3418
1996	A3419	A3724
1997	A3725	A3893
1998	A3894	A4235

Remington Pocket Revolver

Year	Ser. Start	Ser. End
1997	H00001	H00005
1998	H00006	H001064

1860 Colt Army

Year	Ser. Start	Ser. End
1986	11745	14432
1987	14433	15913
1988	15914	17301
1989	17302	18511
1990	18512	20425
1991	20426	23307
1992	23308	26528
1993	26529	29923
1994	29924	35349
1995	35350	43464
1996	43465	50816
1997	50817	53135
1998	P53136	P57436
1999	P57437	P61353

LeMat

Year	Ser. Start	Ser. End
1985	1	131
1986	132	565
1987	566	1395
1988	1396	2109
	10001	10042
1989	2110	2488
	10043	10094
1990	2489	2719
	10095	10116
1991	10117	10146
1992	10147	10220
1993	10221	10352
1994	10353	10438
1995	10439	11208
1996	none	
1997	11209	12331
1998	L12332	L12764
1999	L12765	L12922

Spiller & Burr

Year	Ser. Start	Ser. End
1987	B0001	B0450
1988	B0451	B0912
1989	none	
1990	B0913	B1547
1991	B1548	B2188
1992	B2189	B2988
1993	B2989	B3288
1994	B3289	B3538
1995	B3539	B4048
1996	B4049	B4258
1997	B4259	B4795
1998	B4796	B4995
1999	B4996	B5195

Dance

Year	Ser. Start	Ser. End
1996	C00001	C00127
1997	C00128	C00233
1999	C00234	C00437

Starr

Year	Ser. Start	Ser. End
1999	G00001	G01508

ITALIAN YEAR OF MFG. DATE CODES

Code	Year	Code	Year	Code	Year	Code	Year	Code	Year	Code	Year	Code	Year
I=	1945	XI =	1955	XXI =	1965	AA =	1975	AN =	1985	BF =	1995	BZ=	2005
II=	1946	XII =	1956	XXII =	1966	AB =	1976	AP =	1986	BH =	1996	CA=	2006
III=	1947	XIII =	1957	XXIII =	1967	AC =	1977	AS =	1987	BI =	1997	CB=	2007
IV=	1948	XIV =	1958	XXIV =	1968	AD =	1978	AT =	1988	BL =	1998	CC=	2008
V=	1949	XV =	1959	XXV =	1969	AE =	1979	AU =	1989	BM =	1999	CD=	2009
VI=	1950	XVI =	1960	XXVI =	1970	AF =	1980	AZ =	1990	BN =	2000		
VII=	1951	XVII =	1961	XXVII =	1971	AH =	1981	BA =	1991	BP =	2001		
VIII=	1952	XVIII =	1962	XXVIII =	1972	AI =	1982	BB =	1992	BS =	2002		
IX=	1953	XIX =	1963	XXIX =	1973	AL =	1983	BC =	1993	BT=	2003		
X =	1954	XX =	1964	XXX =	1974	AM =	1984	BD =	1994	BU=	2004		

Colt 1851 Navy

Schematic with Parts Listing

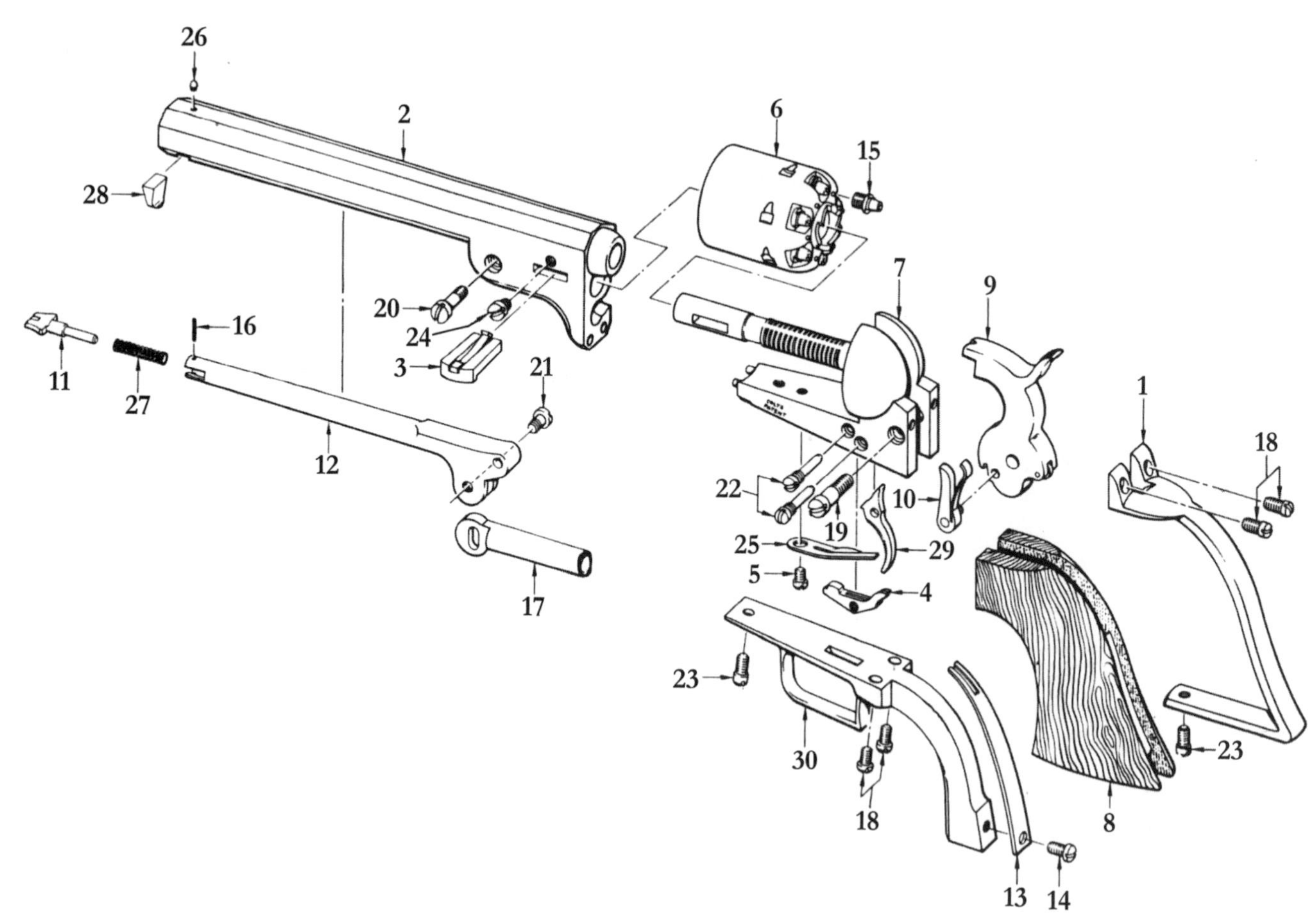

1. Backstrap
2. Barrel
3. Barrel Wedge Assembly
4. Bolt
5. Bolt Spring Screw
6. Cylinder Assembly
7. Frame
8. Grip
9. Hammer
10. Hand & Spring Assembly
11. Latch, Loading Lever
12. Lever, Loading
13. Mainspring
14. Mainspring Screw
15. Nipple
16. Pin, Latch Retaining
17. Plunger, Loading
18. Screw, Backstrap and Guard
19. Screw, Hammer
20. Screw, Loading Lever
21. Screw, Plunger
22. Screw, Trigger (Bolt & Trigger)
23. Screw, Trigger Guard & Butt
24. Screw, Wedge
25. Sear and Bolt Spring
26. Sight, Front
27. Spring, Latch
28. Stud, Barrel
29. Trigger
30. Trigger Guard

Remington Model 1858

Schematic with Parts Listing

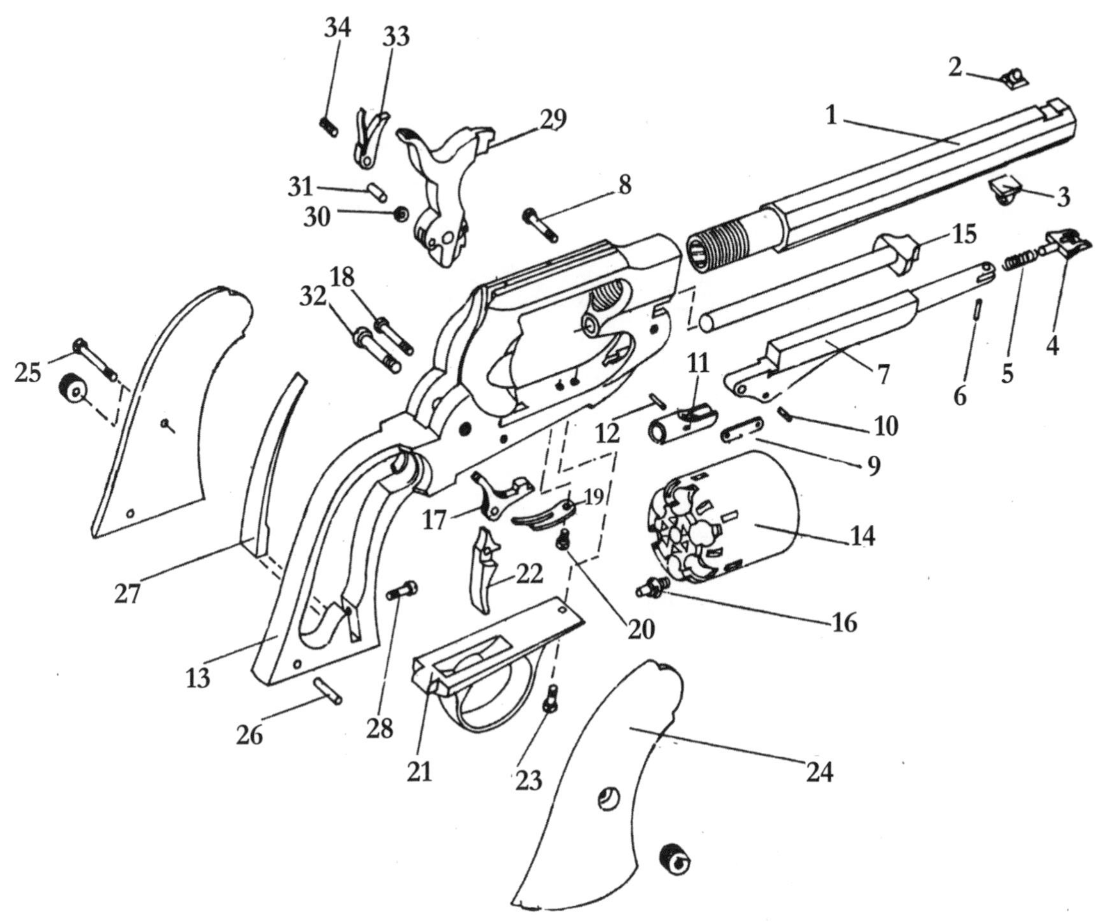

1.	Barrel	18.	Trigger & Stop Screw
2.	Front Sight	19.	Trigger & Stop Spring
3.	Loading Lever Catch	20.	Trigger & Stop Spring Screw
4.	Loading Lever Latch	21.	Trigger Guard
5.	Catch Spring	22.	Trigger
6.	Catch Pin	23.	Trigger Guard Screw
7.	Loading Lever	24.	Grips
8.	Loading Lever Screw	25.	Grip Screw
9.	Link	26.	Grip Pin
10.	Link Pin	27.	Mainspring
11.	Plunger	28.	Mainspring Screw
12.	Plunger Pin	29.	Hammer
13.	Frame	30.	Hammer Roller
14.	Cylinder	31.	Hammer Roller Pin
15.	Cylinder Pin	32.	Hammer Screw
16.	Nipple	33.	Hand & Spring
17.	Cylinder Stop	34.	Hand Screw

RIFLES ACTION/IGNITION TYPES

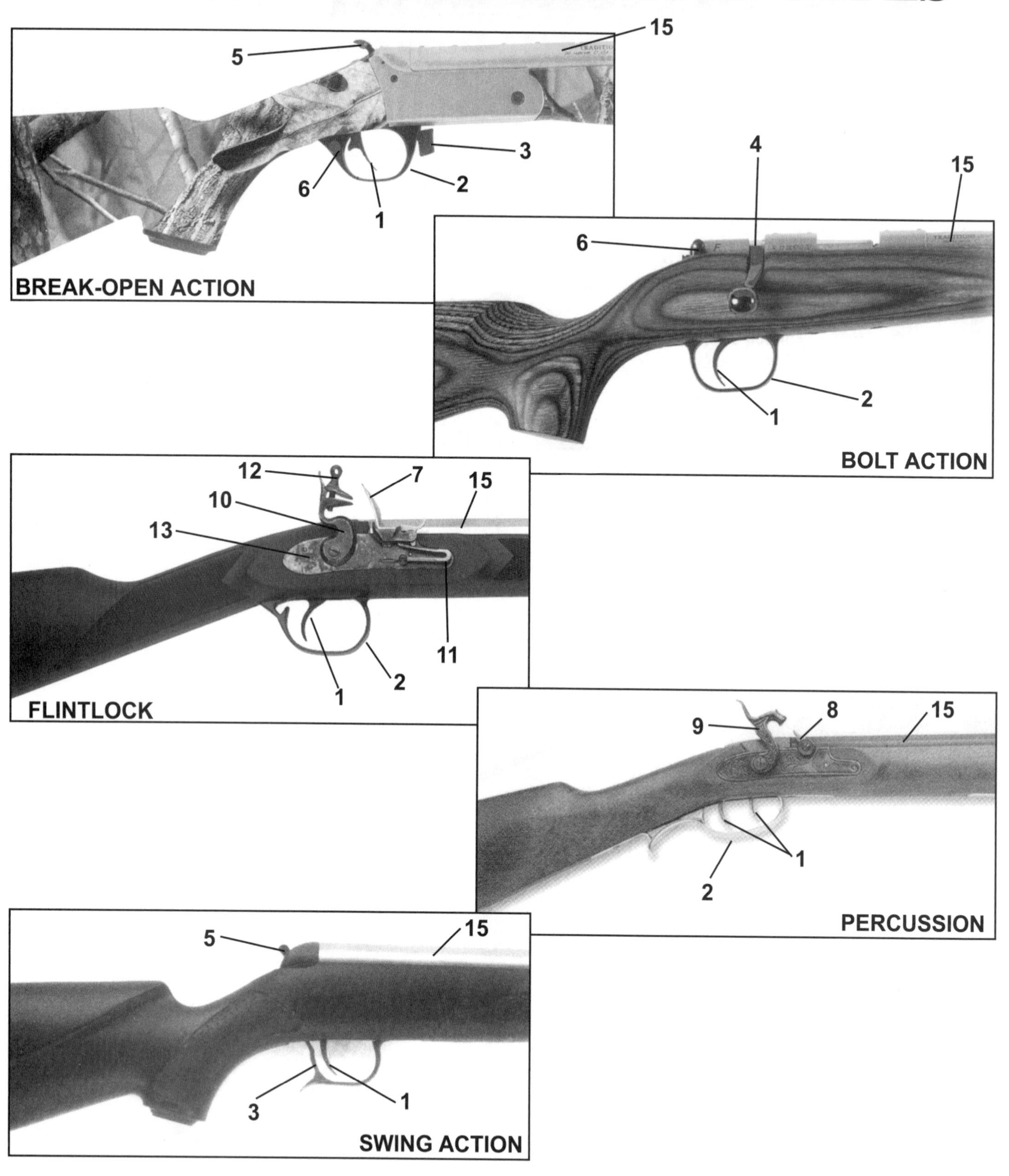

1. Trigger/Triggers
2. Trigger Guard
3. Action Release
4. Bolt
5. Hammer
6. Safety
7. Frizzen
8. Percussion Nipple
9. Percussion Hammer
10. Flintlock Hammer
11. Mainspring
12. Top Jaw & Top Jaw Screw
13. Lockplate, Flint
14. Lockplate, Percussion
15. Barrel

GLOSSARY

ACTION
The heart of a black powder arm where the barrel, trigger, and ignition system come together.

ALLOY
The combination of two or more metals, usually when in liquid form, that results in a metal with different properties than both.

AMPCO NIPPLE
Ampco is an alloy with a high tensile strength that can improve longevity of the nipple used on muzzleloader rifles to convey the spark from a percussion cap to the powder charge.

BACKSTRAP
Either brass or steel construction, the backstrap is the grip support used to attach the grips frame.

BARREL
Usually of steel construction, the barrel may vary in length and is usually either of octagonal or round design.

BARREL WEDGE
A flat metal piece which goes through the frame, barrel lug (the side of the barrel below the rifled barrel), and center pin to secure the barrel to the frame of a revolver.

BIRD'S HEAD GRIP
The bird's head grip has a curve from the backstrap, through the butt, and to the lower portion of the front strap of the grip.

BLACK POWDER
The type of propellant used in front loading arms. A superfine mix of potassium nitrate, sulphur, and charcoal. Black powder is extremely corrosive to metal surfaces and guns should be cleaned as soon after firing as possible.

BLUING
The chemical process of artificial oxidation (rusting) applied to metal to attain a dark blue or nearly black appearance.

BLUNDERBUSS
A short barreled musket with large bore and bell-shaped muzzle, used during the 17th-19th centuries because it scattered projectiles at short range.

BOLSTER
Component of a muzzleloader that attaches to the breach end of the barrel and accepts a percussion nipple. The bolster is hollow, and transmits the flame from the ignited percussion cap to the powder charge in the breech.

BOLT ACTION
A type of action that utilizes a cylindrical bolt with a handle to rotate the bolt body 45 to 90 degrees in order for it to unlock from the breech and be manually opened and closed providing access to the breech plug and primmer.

BREAK ACTION
Term used to describe any type of firearm that utilizes a hinged frame.

BREECH PLUG
On muzzleloading firearms a plug (some times removable) at the rear of barrels bore used to seal the breech against escaping gases.

BROWN BESS
A smoothbore flintlock, .75 caliber, muzzleloading musket officially adopted by the British Army in 1690 and used during the American Revolution.

BULLET MOLD
Usually of brass or steel construction, the bullet mold is used to cast round or conical lead bullets. Melted lead is poured into the mold and after the bullets are formed the mold can be opened and the rounds extracted.

BUTTPAD
Usually a soft rubber or other material attached to the back of the stock to protect the shooters shoulder from recoil (recoil pad).

BUTTPLATE
Usually a metal plate attached to the back of stock for protection of the stock.

GLOSSARY

BUTTSTOCK
The portion of stock that contacts the shooters shoulder when shooting.

CAMO (CAMOUFLAGE)
A patterned treatment using a variety of colors and patterns to blend into the environment.

CAPPER
Tool used to carry and fit the percussion cap to the nipple.

CASE HARDENING
A method used to strengthen metal parts by heating them up and then plunging the pieces into water. This hardens the outer metal shell.

COLOR CASE HARDENING
A method used to strengthen and apply a finish to metal parts by heating them up in a mixture of charcoal and bone meal and then plunging the pieces into water or other liquid. This hardens the metal and also produces the colorful, mottled finish seen on frames, loading levers, hammers and triggers.

COMBINATION TOOL
A tool with a screw driver on one end and a nipple wrench on the other.

CYLINDER
A rotating holder of the primer, propellant and bullet on a revolver.

CYLINDER PIN
The center pin is screwed into the recoil shield and serves as both the threaded shaft upon which the cylinder rotates, and the anchor for the wedge pin securing the barrel.

DISC
A primer holding device patented by Tony Knight of Knights Rifles. The Disc provides a better ignition seal, and therefore helps eliminate both dirt and moisture.

DOUBLE ACTION
On a revolver, the ability to cock and fire the action with a single pull of the trigger.

FALSE MUZZLE
A muzzleloading accessory used to properly load a projectile into the barrel and prevent damage to the sharp muzzle edge.

FLASH PAN
The small dish found on a flintlock that holds a small amount of powder used to ignite the main powder charge in the barrel. Also called a 'touch pan'.

FLASH PAN COVER
A metal lid protecting the priming charge of a flintlock from spilling, moisture or accidental discharge. When the hammer is released, the cover moves forward to reveal the charge.

FLASK
A carrying container for shot pellets or gun powder, carried by shooters of muzzleloading firearms.

FLINTLOCK
A piece of flint stone held in the hammer, when released hits a striking surface called a frizzen and the sparks ignite a small powder charge in the flash pan, which ignites the main powder charge in the bore via a small opening called a touchhole.

FLUTED CYLINDER
A cylinder with concave indentations or grooves between the chambers. The fluted and semi-fluted cylinder is still the basic design for revolver cylinder manufactured in the world today.

FOREARM
A separate piece (usually made of the same material as the buttstock) forward of the action under the barrel of a two piece stock.

FOREND
The forward portion of a one-piece stock.

FRAME
The main structure around which all other components mount. The frame is usually steel but can be of brass construction as well. The frame houses the hammer and trigger mechanisms, cylinder, and on Colt revolvers the center pin through which the cylinder and barrel are attached.

GLOSSARY

FRIZZEN
A vertical plate found with its flat side facing the hammer and flint of a flintlock that when the hammer is released, the flint strikes hard against the frizzen's surface, creating the spark which ignites the powder charge in the flash pan. The surface of a frizzen is normally found to be smooth on US and British firearms, though others around the world utilized a ribbed surface for better spark creation.

FRONT SIGHT
Either a bead or blade mounted at the front of the barrel used to pinpoint the target.

GRIP
May be referred to as stock, the portion of a hand arm held on to. Typically made of wood or other material.

HAMMER
The mechanism used to cock the pistol. The hammer may also served as the rear sight on some revolvers when fully cocked, using a "V" notch in the spur that lined up with the front sight. Pulling the trigger released the hammer which came down with the force of the mainspring to strike the percussion cap and ignite the powder charge.

HINGED LOADING LEVER
Original loading lever design which was hinged to the barrel lug. The loading lever pressed the plunger into each cylinder chamber to seat the powder charge and lead ball.

IGNITION
What happens when the propellant is ignited by the priming system.

IN-LINE IGNITION
A recent technical innovation that allows a #209 primer or percussion cap to be placed in-line with the powder and projectile (in most cases, a jacketed sabot) – hence the name. This ignition system enables improved accuracy, easier cleaning, and better lock times.

LAMINATED
The process of gluing layers of wood together.

LOADING LEVER LATCH
The release pin used to retain the loading lever under the barrel when not in use.

LOADING PLUNGER
The back half of the loading lever that usually has a concave face to seat lead balls in the individual chambers.

MAINSPRING
A strip of steel to produce tension against the hammer mechanism. The mainspring is what produces the downward force for the hammer when the trigger is pulled.

MUZZLELOADER
Any type of firearm that is made ready to fire by placing a powder charge and bullet in through the muzzle.

NIPPLE
Used to hold the percussion cap, the nipple is a removable (replaceable) threaded tube mounted to the back of each chamber and through which the percussion cap charge is directed into the chamber to ignite the powder.

NIPPLE WRENCH
A tool used to replace worn or broken nipples on a percussion lock firearm.

PERCUSSION CAP
An early form of self-contained priming mechanism that was the fore-runner of today's primer. The general type consisted of a small metal cup that contained a priming charge.

PRIMER
Small detonating cap that when struck ignites the propellant.

PYRODEX
A propellant designed by the Hodgdon Powder Company for use in muzzle loading and black powder cartridge arms found by a competent gunsmith to be in good shootable condition. Pyrodex has many advantages over black powder – more shots per pound, a much cleaner burn which alleviates fouling and the need to clean between shots, and more consistent pressures and velocities. When loaded as recommended, performance is

GLOSSARY

comparable to black powder. Available in three loose grades – RS (Rifle/Shotgun) – 2F equivalent, P (Pistol) – 3F equivalent, and Select – premium 2F, in addition to three different sized pellets (30, 50, and 60 grain equivalent), in 3 calibers (.44, .50, and .54). Not recommended for flintlocks.

REBATED CYLINDER

A modified cylinder which has been increased in dimension half way forward to provide for a larger caliber round, i.e., increasing from .36 caliber to .44 caliber.

RECOIL SHIELD

The upper rounded half of the frame which supports the cylinder pin and houses the hammer and the hand. The recoil shield serves to prevent powder flashback and secure the percussion caps.

RIFLING

Spirally cut grooves cut in the bore of a barrel that stabilizes a bullet in flight.

SABOT

A plastic/synthetic sleeve or cup that surrounds and protects the bullet and barrel when fired. Upon leaving the barrel, it drops off, and lets the bullet continue accurately to its target. Saboted bullets typically allow for a higher rate of twist in the barrel.

SAFETY

A mechanism(s) which prevents ignition of the propellant.

SINGLE ACTION

On a revolver, requires the action to be cocked before it can be fired by a single pull of the trigger.

TRIGGER

The release mechanism to drop the hammer. Also secures the hammer in the half-cock position for loading.

TRIGGER (ADJUSTABLE)

A trigger w/characteristics that can be adjusted for pull weight, overtravel, sear engagement, and creep through a change in positions of springs, screws, pins, or the like.

TRIGGER GUARD

Either brass or steel construction, the trigger guard is the lower support of the frame, the anchor for the mainspring, and serves to protect the trigger.

WEDGE SCREW

The screw used to retain the barrel wedge. The wedge must be pulled all the way through the barrel, center pin and barrel lug in order to remove the barrel and cylinder for cleaning. The screw ensures that the wedge does not come completely out.

ABBREVIATIONS

Adj.	adjustable
Approx.	approximately
B	blue
BA	bolt action
bbl.	barrel
BMG	Bullet Guiding Muzzle
Br.A	Break Action
cal.	caliber
camo	camouflage
CC	case colors
comp.	composite or compensated
DA	double action
DISC.	Discontinued
DST	double set triggers
DT	double triggers
Extend.	Extendable
F	full choke
FA	forearm
FE	forend
FFL	Federal Firearms License
FTPOS	For that piece of s...?
Ga.	gauge
HD	high definition
IBS	interlock bedding system
in.	inch
Kt.	Karat
lam.	laminated
lbs.	pounds
LOP	length of pull
mag.	magnum
Mfg.	manufactured
Mod.	Modified choke
MSR	Manufacturers Suggested Retail
N/A	Not Applicable
no.	number
OAL	over all length
Oct.	octagon
oz.	ounce
O/U	over and under
PAS	projectile alignment system
PEBF	primer ejecting bolt face
perc.	Percussion
PG	pistol grip
QD	quick detachable
QLA	quick load accurizor
S/N	Serial Number
SA	single action
ser.	serial
SG	straight grip
SS	stainless steel
SxS	Side by Side
TH	thumbhole
Twist	Rate of rifling turn in a barrel, measured by the inch
w/	with
w/o	without

GUIDE TO BLACK POWDER RESOURCES

We all know how valuable good information is, but how much do we pass by without realizing it was there. Important tips to remember when visiting web sites, don't rush, take time to read and explore areas like FAQ's (Frequently Asked Questions), Forums, and Links. Many times the new products and important information that can make life easier (i.e., cleaning your muzzleloader) is right in front of your face waiting for you to consume.
Many of these web sites offer products for sale, but just as importantly they offer useful information. Check them out. Like Steve says "Good Information Never Sleeps," and for me it's never too late to learn.

American Firearms Page
http://home.comcast.net/~americanfirearmpage
There is a reason this is the first listing, do not miss this site. Do not miss the Black Powder link.

ATF (Bureau of Alcohol, Tobacco, Firearms and Explosives)
www.atf.treas.gov
If you have a question, they should have an answer.

Auction Arms
www.auctionarms.com
Online (buy and sell) auction site.

Barnes Bullets, Inc.
www.barnesbullets.com
Bullet Talk, so what makes a good bullet?

Birchwood Casey
www.birchwoodcasey.com
Cleaning and finishing supplies, targets, How to Guides in PDF format.

Black Powder Revolvers
www.angelfire.com/ny5/shenandoah/Black_Powder.html
The address is long, but worth the energy to enter.

Cabela's
www.cabelas.com
Too much to list, just cruise.

Contemporary Longrifle Association
www.longrifle.ws
This site is dedicated to the art of contemporary longrifles, accoutrements and related items made after the mid-twentieth century. Look and learn.

Dixie Gun Works Inc.
www.dixiegun.com
Check out the FAQs.

FirearmsLocator.com
www.firearmslocator.com
A Network of Alliances Serving the Firearms Industry.

GunBroker.com
www.gunbroker.com
Online (buy and sell) auction site.

The Gun Guy
www.webcom.com/gun_guy
Links to the shooting industry and more.

GunsAmerica
www.gunsamerica.com
Online buy and sell auction and listing site for hunters, sport shooters, gun collectors, etc.

Harvester Muzzleloading
www.harvesterbullets.com
Crush rib sabot and belted bullets.

Hodgdon Powder Co.
www.hodgdon.com
Something about Triple Seven and clean up.

Hornady Manufacturing Co.
www.Hornady.com
Safety, something we all can look at again, and Links on their home page are a must.

MMP Sabots
www.mmpsabots.com
More choices.

National Muzzle Loading Rifle Association
www.nmlra.org
More than just interesting.

North American Muzzleloader Hunting Web Magazine
www.hpmuzzleloading.com
New and growing.

PowerBelt Bullets
www.powerbeltbullets.com
This could take a day.

Replica Percussion Revolver Collector's Association
htt://rprca.tripod.com/Home.html
This site will educate many.

Schuetzen Powder LLC
www.schuetzenpowder.com
Options.

Shooters. com
www.shooters.com
This is a web site containing industry links from A-Z. If you can't find it here, good luck.

Shooting-Hunting
www.shooting-hunting.com
An endless online shooting and hunting directory.

TRADEMARK INDEX

The listings below represent the most up-to-date information we have regarding black powder manufacturers (both domestic and international), trademarks, importers, and distributors (when applicable) to assist you in obtaining additional information from these sources. Even more so than last year, you will note the addition of website and email listings whenever possible—this may be your best way of obtaining up-to-date model and pricing information directly from the manufacturers, importers, and/or distributors. More and more companies are offering online information about their products and it pays to surf the net!

As this edition goes to press, we feel confident that the information listed below is the most up-to-date and accurate listing possible. Please note all the new email and website addresses. Remember, things change every day in this industry, and a phone/fax number that is current today could have a new area code or be gone tomorrow. International fax/phone numbers may require additional overseas and country/city coding. If you should require additional assistance in "tracking" any of the current black powder manufacturers, distributors, or importers listed in this publication, please contact us and we will try to help you regarding these specific requests.

AMERICA REMEMBERS
10226 Timber Ridge Drive
Ashland, VA 23005
www.americaremembers.com
america.remembers@comcast.net
Phone: (804) 550-9616
Phone: (800) 682-2291
Fax: (804) 550-9603

AMERICAN HISTORICAL FOUNDATION, THE
10195 Maple Leaf Court
Ashland, Virginia 23005
www.ahfrichmond.com
ahfrichmond@aol.com
Phone: (804) 550-7851
Phone: (800) 368-8080
Fax: (804) 550-0923

ARDESA S.A.
Importer – please refer to Traditions Performance Firearms
Camino de Talleri s/n
Zamudio, (Vizcaya) 48170
SPAIN
www.ardesa.com
ardesa@ardesa.es
Phone: 34-944-520-152
Fax: 34-944-521-372

ARMI SPORT
Importer – Chiappa Firearms Ltd.
P.O. Box 26178
Dayton, OH 45426-0178
www.chiappafirearms.com
info@chiappafirearms.com
Phone: 937-854-1040
Factory – Armi Chiappa
5020 Azzano Mella
via Milano 2, (BS) ITALY
www.chiappafirearms.com
info@armisport.com
Phone: 011-39-030-9749065
Fax: 011-39-030-9749232

ARMSPORT LLC
P.O. Box 1308
Platteville, CO 80651
www.armsportllc.net
RLMillington@armsportllc.net
Phone: 303-810-6411

ARTAX S.r.l.
via Industriale Trav. 1 n. 13
Cellatica, (BS) 25060 ITALY
www.artax.net
info@artax.net
Phone: 39-30-3733314
Fax: 39-030-3733314

AWA USA INC.
2280 West 80th Street, Suite 2
Hialeah, FL 33016
www.awaguns.com
info@awaguns.com
Phone: 305-828-1982
Fax: 305-828-1066

BERETTA
Importer - Beretta U.S.A. Corp.
17601 Beretta Drive
Accokeek, MD 20607
www.berettausa.com
Phone: 301-283-2191
Fax: 301-283-0435
Factory- Fabbrica d'Armi Pietro Beretta S.p.A.
via Pietro Beretta 18
I-25063 Gardone Val Trompia, Brescia ITALY
www.beretta.it
Fax: 011-39-030-8341421

BLACK HART LONG ARMS
227 Westford Rd.
Eastford, CT 06242
www.blackhartlongarms.com
EdParry@BlackHartLongArms.com
Phone: 860-974-3739

BRENNAN, JUDSON
Contemporary Longrifle Artisan Gunmaker
P.O. Box 1165
Delta Junction, AK 99737
Phone: 907-895-5153

BROOKS, JACK
Contemporary Longrifle Artisan Gunmaker
800 W. Oxford Ave.
Englewood, CO 80110
Phone: 303-789-4029

BROWNING
One Browning Place
Morgan, UT 84050
www.browning.com
Phone: 801-876-2711
Phone: 800-333-3288
Fax: 801-876-3331

Browning Parts and Service
3005 Arnold Tenbrook Rd.
Arnold, MO 63010
www.browning.com
Phone: 800-322-4626
Fax: 636-287-9751

BRUMFIELD, GARY
Contemporary Longrifle Master Gunmaker
209 Buford Road
Williamsburg, VA 23188
www.flintriflesmith.com

CABELA'S INC.
One Cabela Drive
Sidney, NB 69160
www.cabelas.com
Phone: 800-237-4444
Fax: 800-496-6329

CASTEEL, KEITH
Contemporary Longrifle Artisan Gunmaker
RR 1, Box 38
Bruceton Mills, WV 26525-9708
Phone: 304-379-8309

CIMARRON F.A. CO.
P.O. Box 906
105 Winding Oak Road
Fredericksburg, TX 78624
www.cimarron-firearms.com
tech@cimarron-firearms.com
Phone: 830-997-9090
Fax: 830-997-0802

COLLECTOR'S ARMOURY, LTD.
P.O. Box 1050
Lorton, VA 22199-1050
www.collectorsarmoury.com
sales@collectorsarmoury.com
Phone: 877-ARMOURY (276-6879)
Phone: 703-493-9120
Fax: 703-493-9424

COLT'S MANUFACTURING COMPANY, INC.
Corporate Office
P.O. Box 1868
Hartford, CT 06144-1868
www.coltsmfg.com
Phone: 860-236-6311
Fax: 860-244-1442
Customer Service Department
P.O. Box 1868
Hartford, CT 06144-1868
www.coltsmfg.com
Phone: 800-962-COLT
Fax: 860-244-1449

CONNECTICUT VALLEY ARMS (CVA)
5988 Peachtree Corners East
Norcross, GA 30071
www.CVA.com
info@cva.com
Phone: 770-449-4687
Fax: 770-242-8546

CONTEMPORARY LONGRIFLE ASSOCIATION (CLA)
P.O. Box 2097
Staunton, VA 24402
www.longrifle.ws
cla@longrifle.ws
Phone: 540-886-6189

DALY, CHARLES
P.O. Box 6625
Harrisburg, PA 17112-0625
www.charlesdaly.com
Phone: 866-325-9486
Fax: 717-540-8567

DIXIE GUN WORKS, INC.
P.O. Box 130
Union City, TN 38281
www.dixiegunworks.com
Phone: 800-238-6785
Phone: 731-885-0700
Fax: 731-885-0440

E.M.F. COMPANY INC.
1900 E. Warner Ave., Suite 1-D
Santa Ana, CA 92705
www.emf-company.com
Phone: 949-261-6611
Fax: 949-756-0133

EUROARMS ITALIA S.r.l.
Importer – Euroarms of America
208 East Piccadily Street
Winchester, VA 22604
www.euroarms.net
mail@euroarms.net
Phone: 540-662-1863
Fax: 540-662-4464
Factory
Via Europa 174/C
Concesio, Brescia 25062 ITALY
www.euroarms.net
Info@euroarms.net
Phone: 39-030-275-1725
Fax: 39-030-218-0365

FABER BROTHERS
4141 S. Pulaski Road
Chicago, IL 60632
Phone: 773-376-9300
Fax: 773-376-0732

FEINWERKBAU
Importer – Brenzovich Firearms & Training Center
22301 Texas 20
Fort Hancock, TX 79839
www.brenzovich.com
bftcgoods@aol.com
Phone/Fax: 877-585-3775
Factory – Westinger & Altenburger GmbH
Neckarstraße 43
Oberndorf, Neckar 78727
GERMANY
www.feinwerkbau.de
info@feinwerkbau.de
Phone: 49-7423-8140
Fax: 49-7423-814200

FREEDOM ARMS INC.
314 Highway 239
Freedom, WY 83120
www.freedomarms.com
freedom@freedomarms.com.
Phone: 307-883-2468

GIBBS RIFLE COMPANY
219 Lawn St.
Martinsburg, WV 25405
www.gibbsrifle.com
support@gibbsrifle.com
Phone: 304-262-1651
Fax: 304-262-1658

GUN WORKS MUZZLELOADING EMPORIUM INC.
247 South 2nd Street
Springfield, OR 97477
www.thegunworks.com
office@thegunworks.com
Phone: 541-741-4118
Fax: 541-988-1097

HAWKEN SHOP
P.O. Box 593
Oak Harbor, WA 98277
www.thehawkenshop.com
greg@thehawkenshop.com
Phone: 800-450-7111
Phone: 360-679-4657
Fax: 360-675-1114

HEGE
Factory – Hege Jagd & Sport
Mengener Str. 38
Messkirch, D-88605 GERMANY
www.waffen-hege.de
Phone: 49-7575-2872
Fax: 49-7575-2872

H&R 1871, LLC
PO Box 1871
Madison, NC 27025
www.hr1871.com
Phone: 336-548-7801
Fax: 866-776-9292

HANKLA, MEL
P.O. Box 156
Jamestown, KY 42629
www.americanhistoricservices.com
Phone: 270-566-3370

I.A.B. srl
via Matteotti, 311
V.T. (BS) 25063 ITALY
www.iabarms.com
info@iabarms.com
Phone: 39-030-8912366

IAR, INC.
33171 Camino Capistrano
San Juan Capistrano, CA 92675
www.iar-arms.com
sales@iar-arms.com
Phone: 877-722-1873
Phone: 949-443-3647

JIM CHAMBERS FLINTLOCKS, LTD.
116 Sam's Branch Road
Candler, NC 28715
www.flintlocks.com
chambers@flintlocks.com
Phone: 828-667-8361
Fax: 828-665-0852

K.B.I., INC.
P.O. Box 6625
Harrisburg, PA 17112
www.charlesdaly.com
Phone: 866-325-9782
Fax: 717-540-8567

KNIGHT RIFLES
Office
715B Summit Dr.
Decatur, AL 35601
www.knightrifles.com
customer_service@knightrifles.
com
Phone: 256-260-8950
Factory
21852 Highway J46 Road
Centerville, IA 52544
Phone: 641-856-2626
Fax: 641-856-2628

LYMAN PRODUCTS CORP.
475 Smith Street
Middletown, CT 06457
www.lymanproducts.com
Phone: 800-225-9626
Fax: 860-632-1699

MANDALL SHOOTING SUPPLIES, INC.
3616 N Scottsdale Rd
Scottsdale, AZ 85251-5612
Phone: (480) 945-2553

MARKESBERY MUZZLE LOADERS, INC.
7065 Production Court
Florence, KY 41042
www.markesbery.com
Sales@Markesbery.com
Phone: 859-534-5630

MARLIN FIREARMS
PO Box 248
100 Kenna Drive
North Haven, CT 06473-0905
www.marlinfirearms.com
Phone: 800-544-8892
Phone: 203-239-5621

MARTIN, ALLEN
1510 Orchard Rd.
Swengel, PA 17880
Phone: 570-922-4281

MILLENNIUM DESIGNED MUZZLELOADERS, LTD.
RR1, Box 405
Maidstone, VT 05905
www.mdm-muzzleloaders.com
mdm-muzzleloaders@outdrs.net
Phone: 802-676-3311
Fax: 802-676-3322

MITCHELL ARMS
P.O. Box 9295
Fountain Valley, CA 92728
www.mauser.org
Phone: 714-596-1013
Fax: 714-848-7208

MOUNTAIN STATE MANUFACTURING
Rt 2 Box 154-1
Williamstown, WV 26187
www.msmfg.com
msm1@msmfg.com
Phone: 304-375-2680
Fax: 304-375-7842

NAVY ARMS CO.
219 Lawn Street
Martinsburg, WV 25401
www.navyarms.com
info@navyarms.com
Phone: 304-262-9870
Fax: 304-262-1658

NEW ENGLAND FIREARMS
Office - H&R 1871, LLC
PO Box 1871
Madison, NC 27025
www.hr1871.com
Phone: 866-776-9292
Fax: 336-548-7801
Repair – single shot rifles
14 Hoefler Ave
Ilion, NY 13357
Phone: 978-630-8220
Repair – semi-auto and slide action shotguns
Please refer to Marlin listing.

NEW ULTRA LIGHT ARMS LLC
P.O. Box 340
214 Price Street
Granville, WV 26534
www.newultralight.com
Phone: 304-292-0600
Fax: 304-292-9662

NORTH AMERICAN ARMS, INC.
2150 South 950 East
Provo, UT 84606
www.naaminis.com
Phone: 800-821-5783
Phone: 801-374-9990
Fax: 801-374-9998

NORTH STAR WEST, INC.
P.O. Box 487
57 Terrace Court
Superior, MT 59872
www.northstarwest.com
Laffindog@msn.com
Phone: 406-822-8778

OCTOBER COUNTRY MUZZLELOADING, INC.
P.O. Box 969
Hayden, ID 83835
www.octobercountry.com
Phone: 800-735-6348
Phone: 208-762-4903
Fax: 208-772-9230

OLD DOMINION ARMS
2270 Horseshoe Bend Rd.
Ruther Glen, VA 22546
www.aledge.com
Phone: 804-448-1119

PACIFIC RIFLE COMPANY
PO Box 841
Carlton, OR 97111
www.pacificrifle.com
info@pacificrifle.com
Phone: 503-476-4609

PEDERSOLI, DAVIDE & C. Snc.
Distributor –
Cherry's Fine Guns
3408-N West Wendover Ave.
Greensboro, NC 27407
www.cherrys.com
Phone: 336-854-4182
Fax: 336-854-4184
Flintlocks, Etc.
PO Box 181
Richmond, MA 01254
Phone: 413-698-3822
Fax: 413-698-3866
www.flintlocksetc.com
Also refer to *Dixie Gun Works, Inc.* listing.
Importer and Distributor –
Refer to *Cabela's* listing.
Refer to *Cimarron, FA Co.* listing.
Refer to *E.M.F. Co. Inc.* listing.
Refer to *Navy Arms* listing.
Factory
via Artigiani 57
1-25063 Gardone V.T. (BS)
ITALY
www.davide-pedersoli.com
Fax: 011-39-030-891-1019

PIETTA, F.LLI
Importers and Distributors –
Refer to *Cabela's* listing.
Refer to *Dixie Gun Works, Inc.* listing.
Refer to *E.M.F. Co. Inc.* listing.
Refer to *Navy Arms* listing.
Refer to *Taylor's & Co,* listing.
Refer to *Traditions Inc.* listing.
Factory - F.A.P. F.lli Pietta di G. & C. S.n.c.
via Mandolossa, 102 - 25064
Gussago, (Brescia) ITALY
www.pietta.it
info@pietta.it
Phone: 39-030-3737098
Fax: 39-030-3737100

REMINGTON ARMS CO., INC.
870 Remington Drive
Madison, NC 27025-0700
www.remington.com
Phone: 800-243-9700
Fax: 336-548-7801
Custom Shop
14 Hoefler Avenue
Ilion, NY 13357
Phone: 315-895-3200

RESTORATION FIREARMS
6610 Folsum Auburn Rd., Ste. 5
Folsom, CA 95630
www.restorationfirearms.com
info@RestorationFirearms.com
Phone: 916-791-0596

RIFLE SHOPPE INC.
18420 E. Hefner Road
Jones, OK 73049
www.therifleshoppe.com
Phone: 405-396-2583
Fax: 405-396-8450

RIGHTNOUR MANUFACTURING, CO., INC. (RMC SPORTS)
Box 168
259 Hecla Rd.
Mingoville, PA 16856
www.rmcsports.com
rmc@zion.gotmc.net
Phone: 814-383-4079
Fax: 814-383-4509

ROSSI
Importer - Braztech International, L.C.
16175 NW 49 Ave.
Miami, FL 33014
www.rossiusa.com
Phone: 305-474-0401
Fax: 305-623-7506
Factory – Amadeo Rossi, S.A.
Rua Amadeo Rossi, 143
Sao Leopoldo, RS B-93030-220
BRAZIL
rossi.firearms@pnet.com.br

SAVAGE ARMS, INC.
100 Springdale Road
Westfield, MA 01085
www.savagearms.com
Phone: 413-568-7001
Fax: 413-568-8386

SHILOH RIFLE MFG. CO.
PO Box 279
201 Centennial Drive
Big Timber, MT 59011
www.shilohrifle.com
info@shilohrifle.com
Phone: 406-932-4266
Fax: 406-932-5627

STONE MOUNTAIN ARMS, INC.
5988 Peachtree Corners East
Norcross, GA 30071
Phone: 770-449-4687
Fax: 770-242-8546

STURM, RUGER, & COMPANY, INC.
Headquarters
1 Lacey Place
Southport, CT 06490
www.ruger-firearms.com
Service Center for Revolvers, Long Guns & Ruger Date of Manufacture
411 Sunapee Street
Newport, NH 03773
Phone: 603-865-2442
Fax: 603-863-6165
Service Center for Pistols & Carbines
200 Ruger Road
Prescott, AZ 86301
Phone: 928-778-6555
Fax: 928-778-6633

TAYLOR'S & CO., INC.
304 Lenoir Drive
Winchester, VA 22603
www.taylorsfirearms.com
info@taylorsfirearms.com
Phone: 540-722-2017
Fax: 540-722-2018

THOMPSON/CENTER ARMS CO., INC.
400 North Main St.
Rochester, NH 03867
www.tcarms.com
tca_customerservice@tcarms.com
Phone: 603-330-5659
Fax: 603-332-5133

TRADITIONS PERFORMANCE FIREARMS
1375 Boston Post Road
P.O. Box 776
Old Saybrook, CT 06475
www.traditionsfirearms.com
info@traditionsfirearms.com
Phone: 860-388-4656
Fax: 860-388-4657

UBERTI, A. S.r.l.
Importer - Stoeger Industries Corporation
17603 Indian Head Highway, Suite 200
Accokeek, MD 20607-2501
www.uberti.com
Phone: 301-283-6300
Factory – A. Uberti & C., S.r.l.
Via Artigiani 1
I-25063 Gardone, VT (BS)
ITALY
www.ubertireplicas.it
info@ubertireplicas.it
Fax: 39-030-834-1801

ULTIMATE FIREARMS, INC.
3851 Argentine Rd.
Howell, MI 48855
www.ultimatefirearms.com
randy@ultimatefirearms.com
Phone: 517-349-2976
Fax: 517-349-4857

UNITED STATES FIREARMS MANUFACTURING COMPANY, INC. (USFA)
445 Ledyard St.
Hartford, CT 06114-3211
www.usfirearms.com
usfa@usfirearms.com
Phone: 860-296-7441
Fax: 860-296-7688

WATSON, WAYNE P.
Contemporary Longrifle Master Gunmaker
12405 NW 83rd Lane
Ocala, FL 34476
www.waynepwatson.com
Phone: 352-629-4341

WHITE RIFLES, LLC
PO Box 1044
Orem, UT 84059-1044
www.whiterifles.com
whiterifles@gmail.com

WINCHESTER MUZZLELOADING
275 Winchester Ave.
Morgan, UT 84050
www.winchesterguns.com
Phone: 800-333-3288
Phone: 801-876-2711

INDEX

O

P

R

S

T

U

W